Rosemary Rossi

*"If only the Gideons were putting
free copies of this book in every nightstand drawer
of every motel room in the world!"*

Stacy Hellen/CLEAN SHEETS

Get A Grip!

BIRTH ANNOUNCEMENT

We are very pleased to announce that the Guide has a baby sister.
Or brother. Or whatever.

Guide To Great Dates

It's got a bunch of neat ideas for dates,
from going to the opera to skinnydipping.
Some people are calling it awesome. We're calling it fun.
Whether it's your first time together or your first decade together,
it's a really nice resource for when you're saying to yourself
"Oh no, where do we go?"

see it and get a free date idea at
www.goofyfootpress.com

Guide To Getting It On!

The Universe's Coolest and Most Informative
Book about Sex

for adults of all ages

author
Paul Joannides

illustrator
Dærick Gröss Sr.

Goofy Foot Press
Oregon, U.S.A.

Guide To Getting It On!
Third Edition
version 3.69-date 3/5/2001

Publisher's Cataloging-In-Publication
Joannides, Paul N.
Guide to getting it on! / Paul Joannides, author;
Daerick Gross, illustrator.-- 3rd ed.
p. cm.
Includes bibliographical references and index.
ISBN: 1-885535-10-4
1. Sex instruction. 2. Sex. 3. Man-woman
relationships. 1. Gross,Daerick. 11. Title.

HQ31.J63 2000   613.9'6

Goofy Foot Press
P.O. Box 1719
Waldport, OR 97394-1719
www.goofyfootpress.com

printed in
Saline, Michigan
McNaughton & Gunn

Fair Use

BeD of
CoNTeNTS

DiSTRibUTioN
AMERiCAN EDiTioN

U.S. & Canada by
Publishers Group West
Berkeley, California
(800) 788-3123

Down Under by Tower Books
Brookvale, Australia
612 9975 5566

Elsewhere in the Federation by Goofy Foot Press (541) 563-7550
www.goofyfootpress.com

TRANSLATioNS &
FOReiGN EDiTioNS

Croatian Edition by
Minerva
Zagreb, Croatia

Italian Edition by
Nuova Pratiche Editrice
Milano, Italy

Czech Edition by
Alpress
Prague, Czech Republic

Polish Edition by
Swiat Ksiazki
Warszawa, Poland

German Edition by
Goldmann (Bertelsmann)
Munich, Germany

Russian Edition by
Eksmo
Moscow, Russia

Hebrew Edition by
Babel Publishing House
Tel Aviv, Israel

Slovenian Edition by
Pontios
Ljubljana, Slovenia

The Queen's Edition!
South Africa & the United Kingdom
Vermilion (Random House U.K.)
London, England

Warning/Disclaimer
ReAD iT AND weeP!

Hard as we tried, this guide isn't perfect, nor was it intended as a final authority on sex. There will be times when it is better to consult your beautician, bartender, or best friend. You might also speak to a physician or licensed sex therapist. Ultimately, it is your body and your sexuality — venture beyond the bounds of common sense at your own peril. Also, this book talks about sex acts which are illegal in some states, particularly North Carolina. Know your state's laws about sex; break them at your own risk.

No one involved with the writing or publishing of this book is a physician or licensed sex therapist, although members of these professions have been consulted on thorny issues. The people who have contributed ideas to this book are mostly psychologists, psychoanalysts, social workers, lawyers, teachers, writers, a couple of surfers, and even a prostitute and a priest. The actual writing was done by a mental health professional. Just because some of these people have college degrees doesn't mean they know any more about sex or sexual relationships than you do. They all struggle at times. Still, their perspective might be helpful and even refreshing.

While the techniques mentioned in this book work well for some people, they might not be good for you. Check with a physician or licensed sex therapist before attempting any sexual act that you are unfamiliar with, or do so at your own risk and with the understanding that bad things might happen. Consult with a physician if you have any condition which precludes strenuous exercise or sexually exciting activity.

All readers, except those who are trying to get pregnant, are encouraged to use birth control and to adopt a medically sound strategy for avoiding sexually transmitted diseases. However, no form of birth control is foolproof, and diseases have been known to break through (or climb around) even the finest of barriers. These are normal consequences of having sex and are not the fault of this book.

This book was written to help expand the consciousness of its readers. Neither the Goofy Foot Press nor any of its minions shall be liable or responsible to any person or entity for any loss, damage, injury or ailment caused, or alleged to be caused, directly or indirectly, by the information or lack of information contained in this book.

If you do not wish to be bound by the above, you may return this book to the publisher for a full refund.

Operating System: Mac OS 9.04
Software: Adobe InDesign 1.5.2
Text: The Serif/Font Shop International
Headers: Triplex/Emigre Graphics
Icons: Most by P22 Type Foundry
Funky drop caps: DaddyOJunkie/P22 Type Foundry
Other funky font: Gallard (Mike & Hard)
Chapter headers: Advert/Font Shop International
Birth announcement: Pompeia & Giddyup/Adobe

Goofy foot: When a surfer leads with the right foot instead of the left. Results in a different orientation toward the wave.

This book is dedicated to Sisyphus.

The Alpha Chapter
Chapter 1

Sometimes I think life is just a rodeo,
The trick is to ride, and make it to the bell
But there is a place,
Sweet as you will ever know
In music and love
And things you never tell

Rock and Roll Girls by J.C. Fogerty, Wenaha Music Co.

kay, so this guide isn't like other books on sex. It doesn't have pictures of male or female private parts that look like they were taken from a cadaver, and it doesn't hide behind a wall of fancy sex terms or read as though it were written by Mr. Rogers.

This guide encourages you to explore dimensions of sexuality that people in our country usually aren't told about—from the emotional part of getting naked together to why a guy who takes his penis too seriously might have trouble pleasing his sweetheart. It covers subjects like hand jobs and heart throbs, kisses above and below the waist, vibrators, friendship and even sex on the interstate.

But most important of all is the Goofy Foot Philosophy, which says that it doesn't matter what you've got in your pants if there's nothing in your brain to connect it to.

Do with It What You Want

Since this is a book about sex, it might be a good idea to include a definition of what sex is. But trying to define sex is a lot like trying to insert a diaphragm. Just when you think you've got it in, the thing turns ninja on you. For instance, here are only five of several issues that need to be answered if you are trying to define the term "sex":

People think of intercourse as the ultimate sex act, the real thing–*ipsum fuctum*. If intercourse is the ultimate act, then how come making out or holding hands is sometimes sweeter and more meaningful?

🐎 Almost all sex acts can be painful, obnoxious or boring unless you do them with someone who turns you on. Does this mean that the mental part of sex is more important than the physical part?

🐎 Why does one couple find a particular sex act to be highly erotic while another couple finds the same act to be downright disgusting?

🐎 A person has sex and an orgasm, but doesn't feel particularly sexual. The next afternoon he or she catches the brief but intense stare of a total stranger and nearly implodes from sexual intrigue. How can a brief look make someone feel more sexual than an orgasm?

🐎 How can a song, car or piece of clothing be sexy?

Needless to say, we have given up on trying to pin a tail of definition on the big donkey of sex. It seems that any definition of sex needs to fit who you are as an individual as well as your particular situation. Instead of pretending to know what that might be, consider the following:

Learning about sex and intimacy is a lifelong task. Even with years of experience, we still blow it on occasion. The best we can do in the pages that follow is to tell you what we wish we had known about sex twenty years ago. Do with it what you want.

Morality & What's in Your Pants

In much of America we still try to equate morality with whether or not you keep your pants on. We also associate morality with religion. But the truth is, there are Christians, atheists and Jews who are moral people and Christians, atheists and Jews who are immoral people. The same is true for people who are sexually active and those who aren't. Morality, from this guide's perspective, is your ability to respect and care for your fellow human beings. It has little to do with the way you enjoy your sexuality, unless what you do breaks a special trust or violates the rights of others.

Birth Control & Gnarly Sex Germs

This book's chapter on birth control and sex germs talks about everything from scruffy sex rodents to things you can do to make a rubber feel right. Hopefully, its perspective on sexuality will help you avoid things like unwanted pregnancies and an early funeral. In the meantime, it might be helpful to remember that just about anything in this world that's worth doing will kill you if you're stupid about it. Having sex can be far less risky than driving on the freeway or even driving across town. It just depends on how smart you are about sex and how badly you drive.

How It Fits In...

There are many different reasons why people have sex, some having to do with love, others not. For instance, many of us have sex because it can be a great deal of fun, especially with someone whom you care deeply about. It's also an activity that couples do when they have a primal urge to get physical or need to relieve erotic tension (aka horniness). Some individuals offer sex to please or placate a partner, and some use it as a way of gaining security or status. In addition, people have sex when they want to have a baby. That kind of sex has an added dimension which can bring partners incredibly close.

An important aspect of sex is how it can mean different things at different times. For instance, you might find yourself in one relationship where the sex helps to enhance and deepen your love for each other. In another relationship the sex leaves you feeling anxious and empty. Early in a long-term relationship, the sex might excite you and rev you up; at another point it might provide you with comfort and calmness. In most long-term relationships, there will be stretches where the sex begins to bore you. That's when you need to work on making it better.

For those of you who are younger, people sometimes refer to matters of the younger heart as puppy love and treat it with disrespect. That's silly. The most powerful feelings in life are often puppy love. Cherish them. As for having sex with your puppy love, far be it from this guide to say yes or no. It might be wonderful, but then again, maybe not. Just be aware that there's usually more to a good carnal experience than the simple hydraulics of sticking hard into wet. For some people, what separates the good sexual memories from the bad are intangibles like fun, friendship, love, and caring.

It might also be helpful to remember that as you get older, your expectations about sex may change. For instance, if you just turned seventeen, getting laid in and of itself can be a huge thing. But by the time you turn thirty-four, you'll have more experience under your belt. By then, you might want your sex life to take you someplace different than when you were younger. Perhaps you will be searching for different qualities in a partner than you did when you were seventeen. Hopefully, you will want sex to be special no matter what your age.

A Red Flag—Matters of the Heart

On an emotional level, sex can be as powerful as you want to make it. But good luck if you are trying to have sex without it becoming emotional.

The emotions that accompany sexual relationships can be magical, enchanting and wonderful. Then again, they can be really awful. For instance, a once-cherished relationship can fizzle and go flat, leaving you hollow and unhappy. Or it can crash and burn, causing you so much heartache that you might wish you were dead. The tears can pour from a place so deep inside of you that you'll wonder if they will ever stop.

Lovemaking can also be a sacred ground for working through all sorts of fears and crises, as well as a place for growth, forgiveness, fun and friendship.

No Assumptions Here

Most of us make assumptions about the sex lives of other people. For example, consider Mark, a quiet, college-aged computer geek, and Jake, a well-liked twenty-seven-year-old shortstop on his company's baseball team. Mark is biceps-challenged while Jake looks like he just leapt from the pages of *GQ*. Yet Mark has a wonderfully creative and fulfilling sex life with his girlfriend, Elvira, while Jake lives in fear that someone will discover the closest he's come to having sex with a real live woman is when he masturbates to X-rated videos.

This book is just as much for Mark and Elvira as it is for Jake and Rosie. It doesn't matter if you've been around the block more times than a supercomputer can count, or if you haven't hit the ball out of the infield. This guide makes no assumptions except that you are curious about sex and might want to enjoy it even more.

The other thing to keep in mind is that no matter how old you are, there is still time left for you to have a rewarding sex life. Even if you're nearly senile, get yourself a magnifying glass and give the *Guide* a gander.

Charts, Graphs & Sex Surveys

This book has no charts or graphs. If you are the type who's bamboozled by such things, consider the following: how do you graph the value of a loving glance or heartfelt hug? Yet try to enjoy sex in a long-term relationship without such things. Rather than assuming which graph is best for you, this guide tries to accommodate a full range of sexual tastes and beliefs, be they conservative, eclectic or kinky. Are any of us just one or the other?

In addition to charts and graphs are sex surveys. These are published every couple of weeks, each claiming to be the ultimate sex census. But think about it for a moment; big as it is, the federal government has trouble doing an accurate census of its own citizens, and the only two questions it needs to ask is if a person's heart is still beating and what their address is. Imagine a team of five or ten researchers trying to document the sexuality of 250 million people! Even if all you do is masturbate, your sexuality is probably too complex to be summarized by charts, graphs or surveys.

Readers' Comments

To solicit readers' comments for this book, we sent out more than seven hundred questionnaires to men and women who ordered prior editions of the *Guide*.

We received far more completed questionnaires from women than men. The women's responses were a hoot to read. The men's responses were, for the most part, boring and uncreative. Are these the same guys who brag about their sexual prowess? Even the women in the office who helped read and tabulate the responses snored through most of the men's answers, while thoroughly enjoying the sexual creativity of their own gender.

Since there was nothing scientific about the design or distribution of our questionnaires, it is impossible to jump or even crawl to conclusions. But in case you wonder why there are more comments from women readers than men, it's because they were far more interesting, instructive and downright sexy.

Final Alpha Note

Most people would probably agree that sex is best when it's honest, caring and fun. The same should be true for books on sex. Hopefully, you'll never find a more honest assessment of love and sex than in the pages that follow, or a publication that has more respect for its readers than this one does for you.

A Brief History of Sex

Chapter 2

This chapter describes a brief history of sex in modern America from the 1950s to the time of the millennium. Don't worry, it's nothing like George Washington crossing the icy Delaware, although people have been known to do things just as drastic when they haven't had sex in a really long time.

Some writers give the impression that there was no sex in the 1950s and that sex wasn't even invented until the 1960s, when humanity supposedly started making love instead of war. This is not true. There was plenty of sex in the 1950s. It's just that couples often waited until they were married before having intercourse. Also, couples usually dated for a longer time before getting sexual. Since a woman's virginity was more of a commodity then, it's possible that unmarried couples shared more hand jobs and oral sex than intercourse.

Sexual expression was sometimes a challenge for single women in the 1950s, since they were often expected to put out enough to keep a man interested, but not so much as to gain a bad reputation. Have things changed all that much? Some women used this double standard to their advantage, while others found it oppressive.

The Rolling Stone Orgasm, Circa 1966-1977

For young people in the late 1960s and 1970s, there were at least three different types of sexual experience.

The first type of sexual experience was getting yourself off by hand. This provided a really intense jolt of sensation that left you feeling relaxed and settled. It required little social skill or effort. (Some of us who went to religious school would try giving up masturbation for Lent, which is how Palm Sunday got its name.)

The second kind of experience was better. Much better. The second kind of sexual experience was what happened when you were lucky enough to have a sweetheart. It happened when your eyes met, when you held hands, when your lips touched, and when you talked on the phone. The second kind of sexual experience sent a herd of butterflies somersaulting through your stomach and made you feel happy just to be alive. It tugged at the edges of your heart and nearly tossed you off your still-clumsy feet.

The third type of sexual experience is what happened when the second type of experience started to include intercourse. It's what happened when you went "all the way."

Did the third type of sexual experience rate as being the best of times? Not always. Sometimes it was over before it had barely started, and it usually wasn't as much fun as playing football in the mud or breaking local laws and ordinances. It never quite gave you that simple calming comfort of a summer night with your head in a close friend's lap, gazing at her moonlit face outlined by a billion stars from the sky above. But sex was progress, and it helped us put tracks on our innocence—as if that wasn't going to happen soon enough all on its own.

In the '60s and '70s, sex before marriage became acceptable. For many people, it was the best of times. With the introduction of the birth control pill they had more freedom to do what came naturally. Other factors that helped change the sexual climate included the invasion of rock'n'roll bands from Britain, the use of LSD and other psychedelic drugs, the media, marijuana, the miniskirt, the women's movement and the anti-war movement.

The Clitoris, 1966 A.D.

Aside from landing an astronaut on the moon during the 1960s, science also introduced men and women to the word "clitoris." While the clitoris was by no means an invention of the 1960s, few people had ever known what to call it, and many men as well as some women were ignorant of its function.

An unfortunate aspect of this new discovery is that people started to describe the clitoris as a mini-penis. As a result, men who were earnestly trying to please their partners began rubbing

Sex in the 1950s

the clitoris with the kind of intensity that they wished women would use when rubbing their not-so-mini male penises. Of course, rubbing a clitoris in this way can result in extreme discomfort for a woman. Who knew?

Despite the great clitoris stampede that continues to this day, one should be wary of excessive clitoral fawning. Far more important is the ability to make a lover feel wanted, safe and silly.

If men had learned only one lesson during the 1960s, it should have been to ask a lover what feels best. Instead, we often thought to ourselves "I gotta find her clitoris" and went for it like militant Moslems on a mission for Allah. Still, with the discovery of the clitoris there was simply no turning back, or so we thought.

Sex in the 1980s & 1990s — Love Takes a Backseat to Cash Flow

Much can be learned about sex during the 1980s and 1990s by considering the plight of a conservative and popular United States president who held office during that time. During the 1980s, this president spent millions of taxpayers' dollars to establish an executive office of celibacy, a governmental agency whose job it was to sell the American people on virginity. However, during the 1990s, this same president's flesh-and-blood daughter could be found posing buck naked, legs spread, in a popular men's jerk-off magazine. Go figure.

Not to be outdone, a more recent U.S. president who was trying to boost his own moral image fired the surgeon general for expressing an opinion about masturbation. This same president signed into law bills that allocated millions of dollars for abstinence-only sex education—but who would know better than he, since one of the bigger legacies of his second term was to introduce the words "oral sex" into the vocabulary of nearly every first-grade child throughout the land.

And that's how sex has been here in America during the past decade or two, a kind of Siamese twin with one head being puritanical and the other hedonistic. Or maybe that's how sex has always been, but TV and the media are now highlighting it in a way that is harder to ignore. Whatever the case, it is now a sad truth that people who hear the word "sex" are just as likely to think of disease as fun or healing, and the 1960s notion of sexual freedom has given way to warnings about sexual abuse and harassment. And while younger teenagers who haven't even started to grow pubic hair are now having intercourse, college students on some campuses in the Midwest are proving to be more conservative than their grandparents were in the 1950s.

Who knows how to summarize what's going on in this country sexually, except to say that there are many different people with many different points of view.

If ever there was a time when we needed to be tolerant of each other's sexual tendencies, whether they involve total celibacy or the occasional weekend threesome, now seems to be it.·

Learning from the Past

Learning from history is often important, but it seldom happens when the subject is sex. For instance, can you imagine a grandmother telling her sixteen-year-old granddaughter or grandson: "I didn't start having multiple orgasms until I was forty-five, after your grandfather brought home that vibrating Swedish scalp massager..." or "If you masturbate right before a date, it might help take the edge off the evening," or "It wasn't particularly easy being pregnant at seventeen; I wouldn't recommend it."

If this guide were limited to one page of advice about sex, it wouldn't be concerned with how much, what way or even when. It would, however, try to express the following:

There isn't a feeling in the entire universe that you and your sweetheart don't have stored somewhere in your bodies, feelings that are waiting to be touched, shared and released. Yet the extent of your current lovemaking is to stick your tongues down each other's throats, tweak each other's nipples a perfunctory number of times, lick each other's genitals because that's what the sex books say you should do, and then thrust away until one of you goes 'Ooo-ahh, Ooo-ahh,' and the other goes squirt, squirt, squirt. For a lot of people, sex is still an extension of grabbing for the cookie jar, which is fine as long as your expectations aren't very high.

Fortunately, there are a lot of wonderful dimensions to sex besides just huffing and puffing while the bedsprings squeak. Sharing sex with a partner allows you to discover where the different emotions are stored in each other's bodies, where your hopes and dreams are hidden, where the laughter and pain reside, and what it takes to free the fun, passion and hidden kink. To achieve that level of sharing you have to take the time to know someone, to feel what they are feeling, to see the world through their eyes, and to let a partner discover who you are in ways that might leave you feeling vulnerable. This can be scary.

Granted, there will be plenty of times when all you want from sex is a quick jolt of sensation, but if that's all you ever expect from sex, then you might be coming up a bit short.

The Next Chapters

One of the problems with adult sexuality is that few of us started with a philosophy or overview. The next couple of chapters attempt to remedy that. Please be aware that the Goofy Foot Press has about as much passion for philosophy as for rattlesnakes and flat cola. As a result, we worked hard to create chapters that are fun, interesting and hopefully relevant.

We used this stair-stepped symbol to end this chapter in the new British edition of the Guide. It's one of the symbols used in the London Underground. Can you guess what it means? Do you know what the upper symbol was used for here in the US? For those of us who grew up under the shadow of the CD symbol, it's a little amazing to think that the second largest publisher in the former Soviet Union has just made an offer to do a Russian translation of the Guide. WOWSKI! Maybe they'll finally have their own Summer of Love.

The Dirty Word Chapter
Chapter 3

You might be wondering why a chapter on dirty words would be stuck so close to the front of an otherwise fine and upstanding book. Perhaps there is more to this chapter than just dirty words.

Whether you agree with this guide's observations about dirty words is not the point. This chapter, like all of the others in this book, was written to encourage you to think.

Hans, Sven & Yellow Snow

We at the Goofy Foot Press probably use the word "fuck" more times each day than the pope says amen. The sad thing is, we mainly use our fucks to express anger or frustration. Seldom do we use them in the fun way. This is often the case with sexual slang here in America, where swear words and sex words are often one and the same.

In Sweden, a culture that is more sex-friendly than our own, sexual slang is not usually used to express anger or frustration. If Sven or Hans are really annoyed, they are more likely to yell something about yellow snow than sex. Even our own Pueblo Indians had no history of using sexual slang for hurling insults. If a Pueblo Indian was really bent out of shape, he or she might have implied that the offending party was a lousy farmer or kept a sloppy wigwam. But then again, the Pueblos had a less repressive attitude about sex than our Pilgrim forefathers.

Calling People by the Female Genitals

Back when he was a kid, the worst thing your author knew to call another person was a "cunt." He never could bring himself to use the word, but then again, he had yet to work with anyone in the entertainment industry.

Another slang word that kids often use is "pussy." While pussy is a term that refers to the female genitals, it is also an expression that boys use to taunt other boys who are being wimps or cowards.

Why does our culture associate cowardice with being a woman or having a woman's genitals? And why would we want to discredit the very female genitals that so many of us craved (and still crave) to touch and know more about? What kind of number is our culture doing on us, anyway?

Mother-Fucking, Titty-Sucking, Blue-Balled What?

A researcher by the name of Warren Johnson studied how normal eight-year-old boys and girls use slang. According to Johnson, the children's favorite expression when out of parental earshot was "mother-fucking, titty-sucking, blue-balled bitch." Johnson hadn't expected to find America's eight-year-old children capable of outswearing his former marine troop.

Of particular interest is Johnson's observation of an eight-year-old girl yelling "Suck my dick!" to another child who was annoying her. As long as she needed to use sexual slang for swearing, why didn't the little girl yell the more anatomically correct "Eat my pussy!" instead of "Suck my dick!"? Perhaps even an eight-year-old child knows that the way to insult someone in our society is by telling them to take the woman's place when she is having sex, with terms such as "You cocksucker!" "Screw you!" and "Get fucked!" being a crude way of saying, "You're the woman in sex, you piece of garbage!"[1]

It is difficult to understand how something as sweet and delicious as sex could be linked to anger or frustration. It is equally difficult to understand why being the woman in sex is a put-down. Yet these are the premises about sex that we Norte del Americanos grow up with.

---

[1] It could be argued that the implied insult behind terms like "fuck you" or "suck my dick" is that the receiver of the insult is homosexual. But wouldn't that be just as true for the hurler of the insult, who seems to be inviting the act? If someone wants to imply that the offending party is gay, there are plenty of expressions that do just that and few people hesitate to use them.

When Eight Turns Eighteen

What's going to happen when the little girl who was just mentioned wants to share sex with a boy? How is she supposed to enjoy performing the very insults that our society has taught her to hurl at others? Is she going to require the young man to swear undying love and adoration before she "sucks his dick"? Will she extract a measure of revenge by making him deliver on various goods or promises? Will she use sex as a commodity, weapon or way of achieving security? Will she learn to hide her sexuality, or perhaps become numb to it? Will she turn men into sex objects? Equally disconcerting is what this attitude does to boys. The message is that you either screw or get screwed, the former being associated with winning, the latter with losing. This turns sex into a performance or competition.

Sluts, Whores, Virginity & Sewers

Western religions have never done too well with the notion of women and sexuality. For instance, early Christians taught that a virgin daughter occupied a higher place in heaven than her mother, since the mother must have had sex for the daughter to have been born. And around 400 A.D., Christianity's St. Jerome wrote, "Though God can do all things, He cannot raise a virgin after she has fallen" (Epistles 22). Not even God can help you when you lose your virginity, if you are a woman. It's never been a problem for us men, but then again, we're the ones who wrote the scriptures. (You don't have to be religious to know that when a boy has intercourse for the first time, he becomes a man. Yet a girl who has intercourse loses her virginity and is no longer pure as the driven snow, assuming she was in the first place.)

Rigid as St. Jerome may have been about women's virginity, he was quite the feminist when compared to some of his Christian and Jewish predecessors. For instance, one early church father described woman as "a temple built over a sewer," with sewer referring to her genitals. Men who made statements like these were later declared saints.

This kind of negative imagery requires women to deny their own sexual desires lest they end up singing the afterlife blues. Perhaps it's no coincidence that many adult women who are unable to have orgasms were raised in households where the temple/sewer notion still holds sway.

To this day people still equate a woman's personal reputation with her appetite for sex: if her sex drive is too low, she is cold or frigid; too high and the sewer floods the temple, in which case she is called easy or a slut, whore, ho or nympho. In Britain, the term is "slag." While young men are free to strut their sexuality, young women learn to carefully regulate theirs. Otherwise, they risk being called dirty words.

Note: Contrary to what makes sense, women are often the first to accuse other women of being sluts or whores. Men may have been the Bozos who wrote the anti-woman theology, but women can be its cruelest enforcers. Also, it is well known that Jesus of Nazareth was loving and respectful toward women. Why did the church fathers who followed him have so many problems in this area? And if the human body was made in the image and likeness of God, as scripture says, why were church leaders so rejecting of women's genitals and sexuality? Had God been drinking the day He crafted the clitoris and vagina?

Dicks, Pricks & Morons

Why do we refer to a person who is being a total jerk as a "dick" or "prick"? A dick should be someone who brings pleasure, but that's not what our culture teaches us.

For instance, adults will praise a young boy for showing his latest drawing or for making it to the toilet on time, but if he proudly displays his pint-sized boner, throats get cleared. Boys in our society are encouraged to spend eons learning how to make a baseline jump shot or to hit an A-minor flat nine on a guitar, yet they are taught to ignore their own sexuality in hopes that it will simply go away until they get older. Maybe that's why many of us grow up having more sensitivity for what happens in music, art or sports than for what happens in bed.

Power-Booting & Name-Calling at Dartmouth

While our culture encourages its straight men to strut their sexuality, this doesn't mean we always do. For instance, the following story tells of how the term "faggot" is used by straight guys to deride other straight guys for preferring women to beer. It's from Regina Barreca's fine book *They Used to Call Me Snow White but Then I Drifted* (New York: Viking/Penguin, 1991):

> When I started my first year as a student at Dartmouth College, there were four men for every woman. I thought I had it made. Dartmouth had only recently admitted women, and the administration thought it best to get the alumni accustomed to the idea by sneaking us in a few at a time. With such terrific odds in my favor socially, how could I lose? I'd dated in high school and although I wasn't exactly Miss Budweiser, I figured I'd have no problem getting a date every Saturday night. But I noticed an unnerving pattern. I'd meet a cute guy at a party and talk for a while. We would then be interrupted by some buddy of his who would drag him off to another room to watch a friend of theirs "power-boot" (the local vernacular for "projectile vomiting"), and I realized that the social situation was not what I had expected.
>
> Then somebody explained to me that on the Dartmouth campus they think you're a faggot if you like women more than beer. This statement indicated by its very vocabulary the advanced nature of the sentiment behind it. If a guy said he wanted to spend the weekend with his girlfriend, for example, he'd be taunted by his pals, who would yell in beery bass voices "Whatsa matter with you, Skip? We're gonna get plowed, absolutely blind this weekend, then we're all gonna power-boot. And you wanna see that broad again? Whaddayou, a faggot or something?"

While many boys who end up at colleges like Dartmouth have intercourse by the age of sixteen, a fair number remain crude in their ability to value friendship with sexual partners. While they may be coordinated enough to guide a penis into a vagina, on an emotional level some still belong in the arms of their drinking buddies. Equally puzzling are the young women who agree to have sex with these emotional giants.

Sexuality here in America remains a confusing entity. A "just say no" mentality thrives in a culture that uses sex to advertise and sell everything from soap to beer. As a result, there are times when we flaunt our sexuality, and other times when we deny it completely.

Origin of the Bimbo & the Stud

"Bimbo" and "stud" aren't dirty words per se. But they achieve dirty-word status when you consider the following observation made by a female friend who was sitting on the beach:

> A father was standing a few feet into the surf with a young boy on his right side and a young girl on the left. The children were the same size. Whenever a wave came in the father would keep his right arm rigid. This helped the boy brave the oncoming splash. At the same time, the father would lift his left arm, pulling the girl into the air so she could avoid the splash altogether. The little boy was being taught how to face the wave; the little girl was being taught to expect a man to rescue her.

Bimbo training starts early in our country. All too often, the first step is getting little girls to believe that they are more fragile than boys. Then, ads in women's magazines spawn the belief that there is something unsexy about the female body unless it's plugged with a scented tampon and accessorized with perfume and high heels.

Seldom does our society encourage boys and girls to value and respect each other. More often, boys are taught to protect girls because the latter are supposed to be weak and dainty, and many girls are still taught that their worth is determined by the desirability of the boys they date.

Blow Jobs & Bounced Checks

Consider the following statement by a modern American wife of five years:

My husband's going to be furious when he finds out about the check I bounced, so I better give him a really good blow job tonight.

As you will discover in the chapters that follow, this book has no problem with really good blow jobs, but not when they are motivated by fear, lack of power, or crass manipulation. Yuck. This sort of thing gives blow jobs a bad name.

Counterpoint: Female readers might claim that trading blow jobs for money is one of the few ways that women have had throughout the ages to even the score economically. They might argue that trading sex for money brings far more joy into the world and is less destructive than the ways that many men earn their paychecks. They might also take this guide to task for ignoring the possibility that the above-mentioned housewife finds the situation to be a sexual turn-on and might totally enjoy giving the payback blow job!

Rearranging the Bed Sheets on the Titanic With the New Word "Foreplay"

The term "foreplay" was invented by people who write books on sex. Foreplay is what you are supposed to do to get a woman wet enough so the two of you can have intercourse. It may seem strange that this book considers foreplay to be a dirty word, since caring guys are usually encouraged to embrace the concept. Yet there is nothing caring about the underlying premise of foreplay: that women are somehow a little retarded and need to be warmed up before they want to become sexual. Shoot, you have to warm up the old Ford on cold days, so why not the woman you love?

Most sex books forget to mention that a woman who is masturbating can get herself off just as fast or slow as a man. Perhaps the problem isn't that women have a slower warm-up time, as the notion of foreplay seems to imply. Perhaps the real problem is our culture's concept of sexuality, where being a woman (e.g. getting fucked) is a common insult, where "scoring" makes a boy feel like a man, and where respect, friendship and caring are not necessary conditions for sex.

Unfortunately, the concept of foreplay implies that tenderness is little more than a tollbooth on the big highway to intercourse. Nonsense. Tender kisses and caresses do not need to be trailed by intercourse to justify their importance or necessity. They are just as important as intercourse, if not more so.

If you can't get past the notion of foreplay, try to think of it as everything that's happened between you and your partner since the last time you had sex. How you treat each other with your clothes on has far more impact on what happens in bed than carefully planted kisses right before intercourse. This is just as true for the way that women treat men as for how men treat women.

Why Even Care?

Studs, bimbos, bounced check—why even care? How can you not care? These are the myths about each other that we take to bed with us. It's what gets in the way.

Chapter Notes: Regarding the wigwam comment at the start of the chapter, just seeing if you were on your feet. Pueblo Indians live either in adobe/stone pueblos or caves. Unfortunately, life on the reservation has not been good to the sexual habits of the Pueblo, and incidents of rape are now being reported. 👁 In unnatural settings like prisons and expensive private boys schools, heterosexual males sometimes coerce other males into having sex as a sign of power or superiority. Or sometimes they simply do it because it's intimate and it feels good. Once men are returned to the mainstream of society, the object of their desire becomes women and the sex is referred to as "making love." 👁 Did the little girl mentioned earlier in this chapter actually understand the premise of the slang phrase "suck my dick" or was she simply mimicking the correct social usage? Does it matter? Is there any difference in the long run? 👁 Expressions like "Fuckin' great" are examples of how sexual slang is used in a positive sense. They tend to be role neutral and refer to the act of intercourse itself. The creation of foreplay was actually an improvement over what had come before, or so it is said.

Special thanks to the writings of Ira Reiss, Paul Evdokimov, David Schnarch, Regina Barreca, Carol Tavris, the late Bob Stoller and many others for inspiring concepts used in this chapter. Thanks also to Paul Kroskrity, anthro professor at UCLA, for the information about the Pueblos. And finally, thanks to the famous sex researchers who originally suggested that people think of foreplay as everything that happened since the last time you had sex.

For a list of the latest resources on sex and Paul's weekly
column *The Naked Truth*, please visit our web site at
www.goofyfootpress.com

Romance
Chapter 4

Dear Paul,

This romance thing is making me crazy. I'm dating a wonderful girl named Valerie and last night I took her to a romantic night out at an expensive restaurant. I spent more than $100 for the two of us. She seemed to be having a good time. I figured that before the night was over my Little Willy would be seeing some serious action. But when I took her home all I got was a thirty-second good-night kiss. At this rate, I'll have to spend at least $2,000 on a weekend in Acapulco just to get a hand job. Do you have any suggestions?

Randy from Norfolk

Dear Randy,

You might be confusing romance with prostitution. This is a bad mistake, unless the woman you are romancing also enjoys turning tricks on the side. If what you are looking for is sex, you shouldn't have any trouble finding a woman who will give you more than a hand job for $100. If what you are looking for is romance, then sex should not be the goal. That's because romance has its own special universe that resides somewhere between Platonic love and carnal lust. Sure, romance can evolve into sex, but it's just as possible to have a perfectly romantic evening and still end up in bed alone, lathering up Little Willy with his favorite brand of hand lotion and romancing him that way.

In case you find this answer confusing, please keep reading. You'll get the concept by the end of the chapter.

How the Free Market Has Given Romance a Bad Name

Dear Paul,

Romance is that mushy stuff that fills Harlequin novels. It is an entirely feminine construct. Men only become romantic when sheer raw sex is assured. Every time I see those pathetic diamond commercials, I nearly throw up on my television. What I want to *know is if any guy has ever been romantic without the possibility of sex hanging in the balance?*

Lennie from Leadville

Dear Lennie,

Do you realize there is not a single solitary woman in the entire universe who would date you if she knew you submitted this question? Were you abused as a child? Does your own penis cringe with fear whenever it sees your cynical hand approaching? And for another thing, research done in Atlanta shows that women who read romance novels have sex twice as often as women who thumb their noses at the bodice-ripping genre (*Archives of Sexual Behavior:* June 1984; 13(3):187-209).

In your defense, you make the same mistake that many men and women do: you associate romance with capital outlay—the proffering of diamonds and stuff. Although you probably consider yourself to be a free thinker and quite the amazing philosopher, when it comes to romance you appear to be a witless puppet of the mass media.

TV and magazine ads constantly distort the notion of romance, given how we hardly see it portrayed without some credit card being hyped in the process. The fact is, none of the huge corporations (or small ones for that matter) make a single dime when you do something simple but thoughtful for your partner. They don't want you to know that the possibility even exists.

Contrary to what your television is telling you, romance does not need to cost a thing. Romance has a lot more to do with thoughtfulness, kindness and fun than spending tons of money. It has to do with special gestures, like taking the time to help your partner do taxes, or scouring the tile in her skanky-looking shower, or getting him a bottle of his favorite imported beer, or taking a whole day to help her organize a troublesome closet or garage. Maybe it's washing her car and getting its oil changed, or just leaving a note on the refrigerator or car seat saying "I love you." Maybe it's telling him how much you appreciate how hard he works.

Romance in Action
Dating at the Goofy Foot Press

Of course, there's no reason to trust the Goofy Foot Press. Consider instead what some of our guy readers have to say about the subject of romance:

"Romance is being kind, gentle and thoughtful. Sometimes intense as when making love, sometimes only on pilot light, but never off." *male age 70*

"Romance is when we go rollerblading together at the beach." *male age 32*

"Romance is kissing at every red light while on a date, or feeling tingly when you see each other again after being apart for hours or days." *male age 38*

"Romance is when she and I can absolutely forget that the rest of the world exists. Just today we both had a million things to do to prepare for the coming workweek but I turned on the CD player and played a great Spanish song about a bull that falls in love with the moon. Soon we had dropped our work and were spinning each other around

Romance in Action
Commuting to work at the Goofy Foot Press

the living room like two people who had no idea how to dance flamenco..." *male age 25*

"Romance is being naked in the sun." *male age 42*

There's not a single thing these guys mention that will require the folks at MasterCard to increase your credit limit. Of course, maybe they are deluding themselves, thinking they can be romantic without seriously increasing the national debt. So let's check with what our women readers have to say.

Women Readers on Romance

"What is romance? Stroking my hair, holding my hand, helping me with the housework, cooking, talking, sharing the day with me." *female age 43*

"Romance is waking up in my partner's arms and being told that he loves me." *female age 27*

"Romance is sitting on a hammock together reading our books." *female age 26*

"Romance is talking to each other when we are frustrated or upset and then making love." *female age 27*

**Romance in Action
Lunch at the Goofy Foot Press**

"It's bringing home a single rose or a little something to say I was thinking of you today." *female age 34*

"Doing things that show he values me as a life partner and not just a bed partner." *female age 45*

"Being a friend AND a lover!" *female age 37*

"For romance, I enjoy a great bubble bath together with candles and wine, lots of great smelling scents whether it's perfume, incense or just the smell of my man."
female age 36

"If he brings you flowers or jewelry and he's not there in any other way, it's not romance." *female age 45*

Romance in Long-Term Relationships: Getting the Mix Right

When it comes to long-term relationships, all the romantic gestures in the world are meaningless if you aren't trustworthy and don't help maintain the mutual nest. Cooking a special dinner or sending an unexpected card won't get you far if you didn't do any of the chores that your partner was counting on you to do.

**Romance in Action
Dinner at the Goofy Foot Press**

For romance to work in a long-term relationship, it needs to be based on a foundation of reliability and trustworthiness. Then, the kind and thoughtful gestures have a footing on which to stand. They help take your relationship beyond the functional and into the sublime.

On the other hand, when you hear people who have been together for a long time say that the sparkle is gone in their relationship, they have sometimes worked so hard on being reliable that they forgot about the little gestures that help make a relationship fun.

Dear Paul,

My husband of fifteen years is the most trustworthy and hard-working man on the face of the earth. He's a great father to our kids and I love him dearly, but the romance in our relationship is gone. I can't remember the last time I received flowers from him that weren't for Mother's Day. The big trouble is, I've been noticing the pool man a lot more than I should. He compliments me on what I am wearing, asks me about the projects I am working on,

Romance in Action
Weekends at the Goofy Foot Press

and makes me laugh. By the time he leaves every Wednesday, I find myself wetter than the pool deck! It's not that he's some sort of physical ten or that we've had sexual contact, it's just his wonderful attitude and the way he takes the time to notice me. How do I get my husband to do the same?

Waiting in the Sun

Dear Waiting,

I'll be hand-delivering this reply next Wednesday afternoon, right after Mr. Chlorine pulls out of your driveway... Here are some things to consider: It's quite possible that in your husband's mind, his way of being romantic is by working his rear off for you and the kids. Worse things have happened. Be sure that at least a couple of times a week you tell him how much you appreciate how hard he works. Do this from now until the end of time. Next, think back over the past fifteen years and come up with a couple of things that both you and he have enjoyed doing together—without the kids. Hopefully, it will have nothing to do with his work or yours. Maybe it's river rafting, maybe it's shopping for antiques or going to a carnival. Whatever it is, plan it for just you and him. Don't expect much from the first five or ten excursions; rusty wheels take a long time to loosen. At the end of each of your special outings, give him the best blow job he's ever had. It might help to pretend you are doing the pool guy. When you're done, tell him something like "When you work so hard for us, it makes me love you deeply. And when you spend time with me like you did today, it makes me want you to fuck me. I'd really love to do this again next week." Come up with your own variation of this theme, but do something that will help thaw the glacier that your relationship has become. Of course, if you and he are locked into some kind of unconscious struggle where you are acting out stuff from your respective childhoods, best to get marital or individual counseling.

Some of you might say that in this example, sex is being used to get romance. Perhaps, but what better reinforcement for reconnecting emotionally.

Kissing—Lip-Smacking Good
Chapter 5

This chapter is about kissing on the upper body as opposed to kissing on the genitals, although one often leads to the other, and a lot of couples mix the two together—a little peck, a little suck, a little peck, a little suck...

Sometimes kissing is used as a starter, to help stir up various body fluids. Sometimes kissing is all there is. Whatever the case, it doesn't matter if your lips are so experienced they could dock space shuttles for NASA, you might find some helpful reminders in the pages that follow.

The Power of Talking in Tongues

It's funny how kissing a partner on the lips usually makes more of an emotional statement than kissing him or her on the genitals, even if the latter sometimes feels better. For instance, one woman who makes her living by having sex with different men reports that she won't let anyone other than her husband kiss her on the lips. And when a relationship starts to go sour, couples usually stop kissing on the lips long before they stop having intercourse.

There are reasons why lip-locking is sometimes more intimate than getting into a partner's pants. From the moment we are born, most of us are kissed constantly by moms, dads, aunts, uncles, grandparents, and anyone else whose approaching lips we can't successfully dodge. At the same time, our genitals were virtually unkissed or unsucked, in most families anyway, until we could get old enough to talk a friend or partner into doing it.

Another reason for the added power of kissing is because so many of the major senses have their outlets on the human face. There is vision, smell, hearing and taste, and the lips and skin are exquisitely sensitive to touch. There is so much sensory apparatus located on or near the human face that we have terms such as "You're in my face" or "Get out of my face" to express annoyance or social discomfort.

Interestingly, the ability to have an orgasm is not considered one of the basic senses, although it totally overwhelms the other senses when it actually happens.

When Kissing Is the Main Course

Kissing is often a prelude to other things, but there are plenty of times when kissing is all you get. Like when you are sixteen and necking all night long. Or when you are older but want to feel like you are sixteen. But don't for a moment think that extended kissing sessions are kids stuff. Some people experience make-out sessions as hotter than a lot of the intercourse they've had.

If all you plan on doing is making out, be sure to put your gum in a safe place where you can find it afterward. It will help take the edge off until you can go home and masturbate.

Readers' Smooch Advice: The Basics

"Please don't eat my mouth. A good kiss can make me wet with desire, with only the softest touch." *female age 23*

"Kissing is not just a preliminary to fucking. Gently explore with your tongue, lightly suck on her lips and tongue. If she is into it as much as you, kiss with good suction, not lazily." *female age 45*

"When you're kissing, be gentle; don't swallow a woman's entire face into your mouth or dig your teeth into her cheeks." *female age 36*

"Start really light. Barely brush your lips against hers. Be very aware of her response. Increase the pressure ever so slightly when she begins to meet your lips. Eventually, touch the tip of your tongue to her lips. If she opens her mouth, you can let your tongue enter just the smallest bit, but try not to force her mouth open." *male age 25 [Our truly excellent copyeditor left the following message in red ink beside this quote: "I want to meet this guy!"]*

French Kissing

French kissing is the oral version of spelunking. The reason it is called "French kissing" is because it is the only way the French could find to make each other stop talking.

French kissing is not a tongue-to-tonsils regatta. Try swallowing first and don't go shoving your tongue down your partner's throat. Pretend your tongue is Baryshnikov instead of Rambo and you will do just fine. There is always time for tonsil sucking later.

When you are French kissing, keep in mind that mouths, like numerous other body parts, enjoy variety. Don't cling to your partner's mouth like it's a New York City parking space. Bring your tongue out for air and change the pace with a little lip-to-lip or lip-to-neck action before re-probing the deep.

"Take it slow and easy, but not too easy." *female age 26*

"Don't jam your tongue down someone's throat until she invites you in." *female age 38*

"Getting deep throated for fifteen minutes at a whack is no fun." *female age 48*

Breathe or Die

When you are new to kissing, you might find yourself holding your breath. Sometimes there are good reasons for this, but usually it's a bad idea. When you are kissing, your mouth is often very busy, while your nose is mostly in the way. Breathing through your nose gives it a purpose and keeps your partner from feeling like you are attempting mouth-to-mouth resuscitation.

El Nino You Are Not

People who are new at kissing sometimes ask what to do with their noses when they smooch, and whether they should kiss with their eyes open or closed. We don't know. As for the issue of serious salivary action, take these comments to heart:

"Turn off the water works! There is nothing worse than a big slobbery wet kiss." *female age 27*

"Try not to slobber!" *female age 25*

"An overly wet mouth is a turn-off." *female age 32*

"Girls love slobber. At least that's what they tell me. Maybe that's 'cause I slobber, though. Hey, wait a second!"

male age 22

Lip-Sucking Good

Keep in mind that eyelids, ears, noses, cheeks and foreheads are sometimes excellent areas to kiss. And for heaven's sake, don't forget the neck. We're not talking vampire action, but something this side of raising a hickey might help create a welcome reception in body parts further to the south.

What about Hickeys?

Hickeys are what happen when a lover sucks on your neck or other body parts with enough force to cause internal bleeding. The hickey is the resulting bruise. Some people are proud of their hickeys and display them the way bikers do tattoos. Other people feel mortified when they discover a brownish or bluish blotch that wasn't there the day before. They even wear turtlenecks in the middle of summer to cover the things up.

Most drugstores and supermarkets have cosmetics sections with different shades of makeup that can help hide hickeys. If you buy one of these concoctions, make sure it matches your natural skin tone. Otherwise it will look like a big smudge.

Keep in mind that people with certain skin types hickey-up worse than others. As for hickeys between the legs, who much cares unless you are going to the beach or having an extramarital affair?

One woman who called a local radio talk show said that her boyfriend had given her a hickey in the middle of her forehead. How do you explain that one at work, unless maybe it's Ash Wednesday?

Great Kissing Advice

"The best thing you can do during a good kissing session is to ask your partner to kiss you the way he or she likes to be kissed. It really works. Just sit back and let him or her take over; you'll learn all kinds of things." *male age 26*

Flossing, Brushing & Garlic

It is raunchy to kiss with pieces of food stuck in your teeth. Flossing and brushing can make you far more attractive to a partner than wearing expensive cologne or sucking on a fistful of breath mints. If you are concerned about bad breath, check with your dentist. Dentists know all about bad breath, as many of them seem to have it. Ask if you should scrape the back of your tongue once a day with the flat edge of a spoon.

If you are eating food with garlic or onions, make sure the person you plan to smooch shares a couple of large bites. Flossing and brushing won't put a dent in breath that's laced with garlic. Your only defense is to share the offense.

If You're Wearing Braces...

For people who have braces with rubber bands, consider taking the rubber bands out ahead of time. One reader barely escaped mid-smooch tragedy when a rubber band on his sweetheart's braces came unhooked and nearly shot him in the uvula. A direct hit would have triggered the same reflex that causes projectile vomiting.

Also, be aware that a tongue entering from the outside might get scratched or caught on metal edges that don't pose a problem for you. You might even tell your partner that you are concerned about this and would feel much better if he or she slowly and thoroughly explored the inside of your mouth with his or her tongue. WOW!

Kissing on the Edge of Town...

In nearly every community where people have lips, there tend to be special places where the locals go to make out.

In the town where your author grew up there were two favorite places where people went to kiss and grope—well, three if you count the local drive-in, but that was more like an extra bedroom. One of the favorite places was at the river east of town. Another was in the orange groves. Each had its own hazard, which merely added to its allure. The road to the river twisted along a steep mountainside, which sometimes posed a problem if you were either low on gas or high on beer. As for the orange groves, a busted ditch or recent watering could result in hidden mud traps. Tires could spin aimlessly until your best friend's father arrived to tow you out.

Eskimo Pies & Eskimo Kisses: Kissing in Other Cultures

You may have heard that Eskimos don't kiss like we do. Instead of kissing on the lips they allegedly rub noses. What's closer to the truth is that Eskimos put their noses in close proximity to inhale the breath of a loved one. Perhaps they do this to keep their lips from freezing together. They may want to avoid oral-genital contact for the same reason.

Eskimos find that inhaling the breath of a lover is erotic; those of us from more temperate climates prefer exchanging wads of saliva. People raised in different cultures don't always agree on what's sexy.

The Real Estate Between Your Neck & Knees

This guide places way too much emphasis on the standard Blue Chip kissing zones—lips, nipples and genitals. Lovers who really enjoy each other sexually will often go from head to toe, discovering and rediscovering where a partner loves to be kissed. Here are a few areas to consider when kissing your partner:

🐸 **Skin Folds** The places on the body where the skin folds or creases tend to be very sensitive and love to be kissed. These include the backs of knees, the fronts of elbows, the nape of the neck, under breasts, on eyelids, armpits, crotches, between fingers and toes, and behind ears.

🐸 **Bellies & Navels** Think of the navel as a little vulva rather than a mere collecting point for lint. Some people love to have their navels licked and caressed. Others become seriously annoyed. Also, try kissing the landing strip between the navel and the genitals, and don't forget the hip bones.

🐸 **Long Licks** Don't hesitate to get your tongue really wet and take a long lick up your partner's body, from hip to armpit or tailbone to neck.

🐸 **Lower Back & Buns** The lower back and rear end can be exquisite places to kiss and kiss again.

Human Serving Tray Fruits, dessert foods, and certain liquors can be served on various parts of the body with pleasing results.

Love Bites Teeth on skin can feel really nice or really ugly. If this is what you would like to try, lube your lover's skin with oil or saliva so your teeth glide along the surface. Then raise your lips up like Dracula and gently run your teeth back and forth. You might try a little biting action on large muscle groups such as the shoulders or buns. Be sure to get lots of feedback from the bitee, and for heaven's sake, stop short of violating federal statutes.

Be Sure to Ask

Kissing is such a powerful thing, yet we seldom take the time to ask a partner how he or she likes to be kissed. Maybe he or she is turned on more by delicate little butterfly kisses than by some overly dramatic lip-lock that you saw at the movies. You'll never really know unless you ask, and it's a shame not to ask.

The Importance of Getting Naked
Chapter 6

In human relationships, there are different kinds of nakedness. For instance, in one-night stands, getting naked means exposing skin. Lots of skin. While this kind of sex can be exciting, a steady diet of it may leave you feeling a bit trashy and wanting a partnership with more depth. That's when you might start seeking a lover with whom you can get emotionally naked as well as physically naked, or maybe that has been your goal from the start. Whatever the case, this chapter talks about taking your clothes off, and suggests a kind of nakedness that has emotional as well as physical grit.

Getting Naked—An Overview

For some people, getting naked in front of a lover is as easy and natural as drinking a glass of water, but for others, getting naked can cause distress or embarrassment. There are even people who engineer things so they can get it on without taking their clothes off in front of the other person. Perhaps this gives you an idea of how powerful getting naked can be, and how vulnerable we feel about our bodies here in America.

As a culture, we are so upset about nakedness that we don't have street-corner fountains with fat marble cherubs peeing into large pools of water or public paintings of naked Botticelli babes. The mere mention of a Norman Rockwell frontal nude is enough to make most people squirm, and a bare crotch on network television is about as common as a snowstorm in Siam. At the same time, we are clearly interested in nakedness, given how so many ads and images in our society drip with prurient fury. Perhaps we have learned to cope with our society's mixed messages by becoming more aroused by near-naked images than by actual nakedness. For instance, with its suggestion of impending nakedness, the picture on the next page may have more intrigue than if the couple were buck naked.

Getting Naked—Hidden Possibilities

If you and your sweetheart are in the process of becoming more physical, you might consider some of the hidden possibilities that getting naked has to offer. A lot of honesty and trust can be generated when you are naked together, something that rarely develops if the sole purpose of taking your clothes off is to have intercourse. It's how you can learn to relate physically with more than just your crotches. It's how a guy can learn to have his penis resting on a woman's soft warm skin without feeling like he has to perform with it.

Naked Logistics

If it feels like your relationship is ready, you might consider planning a time and place where the two of you can work on getting naked. Some couples enjoy undressing each other, while others make a game out of taking their clothes off—from playing strip poker to lighthearted wrestling. Sometimes getting naked just happens naturally if you go skinny-dipping or hot-tubbing, and some couples enjoy undressing each other while dancing, slow or fast. If you try this, be sure to have birth control handy in case you get swept away and suddenly find yourselves doing the polka. There are also occasions where one partner blindfolds the other before undressing him or her.

Occasionally, people find it helpful to tell each other some of the things that they do and don't like about their bodies. Some women worry that their butts are too big or their breasts are too small or big. Some guys worry that they aren't hung well enough, or that they might be hung too well. Just getting your fears out in the open will usually help you feel more comfortable. If it doesn't, then maybe the relationship you are in isn't such a good one.

For couples who are particularly self-conscious, writer Jay Wiseman suggests getting naked in total darkness. Each partner then takes turns examining the body of the other with a small flashlight—one of those little penlight things that excites just enough photons to light up an area the size of your thumbnail. This can be a fun game that taps into all sorts of fantasies as well as helping to decrease the anxiety of being seen naked all at once.

Another way for the shy at heart to start sharing their nakedness is by getting a sexy and fun top or T-shirt to wear, with nothing on underneath. Or maybe you'd like to try a pair of silk boxers.

Guys Worry: Wood Good, Wood Bad?

When it comes to getting naked, men sometimes worry about whether they should or shouldn't have a hard-on. It doesn't matter. It's fine if you have one, it's fine if you don't. The whole point, if there needs to be one, is learning to associate nakedness with something other than just sex or taking a shower. With a little work, you might discover that being naked helps create the kind of space where you and your partner can talk about important things.

Some people don't have the slightest hesitation to get naked for sex, but if it's getting naked just to talk or hold each other, good luck. They sometimes become fidgety and fire off a rapidly dismissive "Sure, we'll have to try that sometime..." Perhaps that kind of nakedness feels too intimate.

Naked & Getting Off

While getting naked together doesn't need to include orgasms, some couples find it uplifting to have one or two somewhere along the way. So plan your naked time to include lots of holding and touching, an attempt at an orgasm or two, and then even more holding and touching afterward. (One reader comments,"Good luck on this one. I've spent a lot of lonely time while my partner sleeps immediately after orgasm.")

Coming is usually the last thing that couples do when they are having sex. Yet it might be nice to spend extra time holding and touching each other after you have orgasms, rather than simply rolling over and falling asleep or running off to work. That's because coming clears the senses in a way that allows many of us to share a special kind of warmth and tenderness.

Sex Tips with a Cranky Marxist Edge

Sometimes a half-peeled banana is more exciting than one with no peel at all, or so we've been led to believe. This type of philosophy has helped fuel the multimillion-dollar lingerie business, which for years has made a handsome profit selling flimsy wisps of underwear to women under the name of lingerie. And now, manufacturers are gouging men with similar intent. They embroider the name of some fancy clothes designer or tennis-shoe manufacturer into the spandex band of men's briefs and suddenly charge $10.00 to $20.00 for a pair that you could otherwise buy at Kmart for $2.50.

Anyway, if you find underwear to be erotic, here are a couple of possibilities:

🕺 Women who wear nylons and garters might consider putting their panties on over the garter belt instead of under, so their panties can come off while leaving the stockings and garters intact. Fine tips such as these can be found in Cynthia Heimel's wonderful book, *Sex Tips for Girls*. Her lingerie chapter offers insight about women's underwear that no male writer short of a transvestite would ever get right.

A common garter faux pas, according to Los Angeles' Trashy Lingerie store, is wearing the rear garter all the way back instead of to the side. On the right leg, the front garter should be worn at dead center (12:00) and the rear garter should attach to the nylon at 3:30-4:00 as opposed to 6:00. On the left leg the front garter attaches at 12:00 and the rear garter at 7:30 or 8:00. This helps keep the seams straight. The "Western Woman" pictured in the chapter "What's Feminine, Masculine & Erotic" almost has it right, although her rear garter is closer to 5:00 than 3:30-4:00.

🎇 Another Trashy Lingerie tip: if you are wearing a push-up bra, put it on and then reach across your chest with your right hand. Grab your left breast from under your armpit, lifting it up and dropping it into the bra cup. Do the same thing with your left hand and right breast. Another bra misdemeanor: incorrectly adjusting the straps so the bra rides up too high or droops down too low.

🎇 When out on a date, a woman should never hesitate to let a man know that she is not wearing any underwear, or reach into her purse and pull out a pair of panties while saying, "Oops, guess I forgot to put these on!" As for men doing the same thing—not around here, but maybe in your neighborhood.

🎇 When sitting down to lunch or even for a long plane flight, some women briefly hike up their dress and intentionally adjust a garter in view of a man whose salivary glands they hope to make flow. The art of doing this, of course, is in the ability to disguise the purposefulness of the act. Reaching for something in the overhead compartment can achieve similar results if you are wearing a dress or skirt that's short enough.

🎇 One oral sex variation is to go down on your partner while she or he is still wearing underwear. You can reach under the material with your tongue, push it to one side for proper access, or pull it off with your teeth. You'll probably need a fingertip assist, but the gesture is what counts!

🎇 If you're having a quickie, you might keep your underwear on and try working your way around it. Also, some couples enjoy having oral sex and intercourse while one or both partners is wearing crotchless underwear.

Dry humping with only your underwear on can be fun, as well as taking a shower or bath while still wearing your underwear. Plenty of dry humping gets done at the beach when people are wearing swimsuits, assuming they aren't sporting a nasty sunburn.

Women shouldn't hesitate to take their lovers with them when shopping for lingerie. Shopping for a new bra or skivvies might seem mundane to a woman, but it could be a fun treat for a man. It will also help give him ideas for when he wants to get you a special gift. If it's possible, ask him to accompany you into the dressing room, but don't try on every bra in the store. His tolerance for that sort of thing might not be as great as yours.

For guys, the next time you are in a big department store with your sweetheart, nudge her into the men's underwear department and ask her what style and colors she thinks might look best on you. This can make for added pleasure the next time she reaches down and pops the buttons on your blue jeans.

Dear Paul,

I get seriously turned on when my girlfriend is wearing pantyhose. There's something about the feel of them on her legs that makes Mr. Winky pop straight in the air. Any advice about this?

Seamless in Seattle

Dear Seamless,

Given how most of our mothers wore nylons or pantyhose, and considering how often our toddler selves stood next to them with arms wrapped around their legs, it's a wonder more guys aren't stirred into action by the feel of a woman in pantyhose.

Assuming your girlfriend is understanding and willing, ask her to cut out the cotton crotch on a pair of pantyhose. Thanks to the new ventilation system, you'll be able to go down on her as well as have intercourse while she is wearing her customized pantyhose. Make sure she cuts out the crotch on the inside of the seam so they don't unravel. Also, consider helping her to arrive orally first, because it isn't likely that you'll be lasting for long once the intercourse begins. If she isn't handy with scissors, she can purchase crotchless pantyhose in some stores, but probably not Target or Sears.

P.S. You're going to love the illustration in the "Kink" chapter!!! Also, it appears as though your girlfriend wrote in asking if you might have a fetish. I go to bat for you at the end of that chapter.

Men's Underwear

Men have a choice of wearing briefs, boxers, nothing, or even women's underwear if they're of that ilk. Most of us end up wearing whatever our mothers bought for us as kids, usually briefs or boxers. Each provides a different kind of feeling that a man gets used to, thus casting him for life as either a briefs guy or a boxer guy, although there are probably some men who are switch-hitters. While a briefs guy might experiment with boxers for a couple of months or even years, there's probably a tendency to go back to what he started with. Same with a boxer guy. A woman shouldn't push the issue one way or the other, unless the man doesn't care or is the type who tells her when to wear a bra.

Cramped Penis Alert

A guy's penis usually hangs downward when it's soft, but as it stiffens it needs extra head room to accommodate the expansion. Yet if a man is wearing jeans, the expanding penis often gets trapped in a downward position (ouch!) or is stuck in a horizontal pickle. So if you are fooling around with your clothes on, the penis will usually need a quick assist to rise above it all. While it might be a bit presumptuous for a woman to lend a helping hand if you are making out on a first date, this can be a really nice gesture in a longer-term relationship. When the bulge starts to grow, just reach inside his pants and pull the penis up so its head is pointing toward the man's chest!

Jocks & Cups

Some men like to wear athletic supporters for erotic purposes. Perhaps one reason is because the athletic supporter, by the nature of its design, emphasizes a man's rear end by keeping it naked while highlighting his genitals by keeping them covered. While this might be more prominent in the gay community, some straight women get turned on by seeing a lover in an athletic supporter, as long as he isn't wringing wet from playing four hours of rugby.

Special Lingerie Supplement—Learning from Lady Lawyers

During the 1970s and 1980s, there suddenly arose a large number of lady lawyers in this country who began to penetrate the traditional male lair. Being confused about how to be taken seriously, most of these women started wearing boring wool suits with blouses that had floppy bows (the lady lawyer uniform). The intent was to look as nonsexual and unalluring as humanly possible, as femininity was considered to be some sort of liability when arguing matters of law. Short of wearing a body bag to court, most of the women succeeded handily. Interestingly, some of these lady lawyers made it a point to wear steamy lingerie under their boring suits. It was a way of saying to themselves, "At least some part of me is still feminine."

In our society, wearing lingerie has been an important way for women to feel feminine. In fact, some women feel sexier wearing lingerie than they do being naked. Some women feel better masturbating while wearing lingerie or underpants.

As for guys feeling more masculine while wearing boxers, briefs, or jockstraps, nobody around here felt overwhelmed by the idea—although men sometimes feel sexy in their underwear. What feels best of all is when a lover pulls off a man's briefs or boxers.

At Work

At Home

On the Penis & the Man behind It
Chapter 7

This chapter was written for women readers, although the men who have seen it claim to be amused. The topic is boys and their toys. Hopefully the following pages provide some insight into the love and sometimes hate relationship between a man and his weenie.

Toys, Pain & Pleasure

As a woman, the first thing you will find out about penises and testicles is that most guys take them way too seriously. There are reasons for this:

The penis is the only childhood toy that a guy gets to keep and play with throughout his entire life. It is the only toy he will ever own that feels good when he tugs on it, that constantly changes size and shape, and is activated by the realm of the senses. Try to find that at Toys"R"Us.

One of the first things a man does when he wakes up in the morning and the last thing he does at night is to touch his penis and testicles. It's a male ritual of self-affirmation that has little to do with sexual stimulation. A daytime extension of this practice is known as pocket pool.

The average male pees between five and seven times a day. Each time he pees he has a specific ritual, from the way he pulls his penis out and holds it, to the way he wags it when he's done. When he is peeing alone a guy will often invent imaginary targets in the toilet to gun for. An especially fine time is had when a cigarette butt has been left in the commode. Floating cigarette butts are the male urinary equivalent of the clay pigeon. While this may be a difficult concept for a woman to fully grasp, it does make for a certain amount of familiarity, friendship and even self-bonding between a man and his penis.

You wouldn't believe how often the human male experiences a jolt of pain in his testicles. It is a discomfort that gives a guy the kind of extra-personal relationship with his reproductive equipment that menstruating women have with theirs. The source of agony can be anything from an elbow during a game of basketball to simply bending over and having your pants crimp the very life force out of you. One of the great culprits in male testicular angst is the horizontal bar on the bicycle frame. Why is it that girls' bicycle frames are V-shaped when it is guys who need the V? Not only did this confusion among bicycle makers result in our younger selves not getting to look up girls' dresses when they were mounting their bikes, but many of us still have the word Schwinn® engraved on the underside of our testicles from each time a foot slipped off the pedal.

📖 This may be difficult to fully appreciate, but there is the matter of the unwanted hard-on. The unwanted hard-on usually strikes with predictable ferociousness first thing in the morning. Not only does it interfere with the ability to relieve a full bladder, but it provides logistical problems for a guy who has to traverse shared hallways to get to the bathroom. The unwanted hard-on can be particularly excruciating and even painful for its most frequent victim, the adolescent male. The unwanted hard-on is much less of a problem after a man turns 30, and by the time he's 40 it is an event accompanied by a sigh of relief and a moment of thanks.

📖 When guys are naked together we sometimes glance down to check each other out. Do women make similar comparisons regarding their breasts? Since we males do it among ourselves, we figure that women check us out in the same way. This can make us extra conscious about what we've got between our legs.

📖 When life is full of despair, the one thing that a guy can usually count on for a good feeling is his penis, unless matters are totally out of hand, in which case he needs to consider something stronger like tequila or prayer.

📖 Our society teaches us that sexual pleasure between a man and a woman depends on the man's ability to get hard and stay hard. What a demented view of sex. This puts a lot of pressure on guys to be consummate cocksmen. It makes us more dick-oriented than necessary, at the expense of everyone.

These items aside, the most important thing for a woman to know about a penis is how it figures into a man's concept of his own manliness. Ridiculous, but important.

Manliness—A Goofy Definition

Masculinity and femininity are inventions of culture that have little foundation in science or nature, yet they remain powerful forces in the way we view ourselves and each other. In our society, everyone has an idea of what a real man is, but few people know how to define it. This guide suggests that there are at least two influences which help a boy become a real man:

A parent figure who provides physical and emotional tenderness without being too controlling, and someone with a solid sense of values and work ethics whom the boy can look up to and believe in.

Okay, so these are the same ingredients that are essential to raising a real woman. They lead to the following definition:

A real man in American culture is a fairly responsible person who can stand alone when the occasion demands, but who can also be warm, comforting and kind; a person who doesn't need to prove his masculinity by trying to scare or intimidate others.

Of course, there are plenty of males who have none of these qualities, but appear to be total studs nonetheless. These are the guys who usually take their penises way too seriously. That's because the only way they can convince themselves that they are real men is by performing manly activities or drinking lots of beer or doing drugs, and then having a vagina nearby that they can stick themselves into.

While most of us resort to these behaviors on occasion, some guys make a lifestyle out of it.

Penis as Camouflage: Why It's Difficult to Be Satisfied by a Guy Who Takes His Penis Too Seriously

A hard penis is sometimes used to camouflage what's missing inside a man, as well as what's missing in a relationship between a man and a woman. Consider the following analogy from the world of surfing:

> A skilled surfer mounts his surfboard in a way that permits the ocean to cradle him with its fury and passion. If he is all hung up about his equipment, then the synergy between surfer and ocean is seriously compromised.

If a guy is all hung up about his penis being a symbol of his manliness or demands that it have a disproportionate amount of attention, then it gets in the way of his being at one with a woman. The same is true for a guy who needs to always play a manly role. He sometimes feels more warmth for his car or computer than for his wife.

Unfortunately, a lot of women grew up thinking that a distant, self-involved, dick-centered type of guy is what manhood is all about. As a result, they end up being attracted to guys whom they can never really get close to, and spend the rest of their lives bellyaching about what duds we men are.

Narcisso 'Gasms

Biologically, most women can have a couple of orgasms or extended wavelike pleasure runs to the average man's one. This is just fine with most men, since most of us would like to see our partners have as much pleasure as their hearts and loins desire. But for a man who takes his penis too seriously, orgasm giving sometimes becomes too important. His partner's orgasms become reassurance that he is a total guy. We all do this to some extent, but for some men it's a matter of narcissistic life and death.

If your man is like this, you may discover that your main function in life is to look good and have lots of orgasms. Or maybe it's just to look good. Consider yourself an offering to the great Dick God.

The Penile-Pumping Regatta

Some men lose emotional connection with a woman once intercourse begins. The woman starts to feel like a commodity, as though she has become the guy's masturbation machine. Sex becomes a virtual pumping regatta, with the man using intercourse to prove dick-worthiness. This can be really boring for both partners.

To give you an idea of how much insecurity is involved in all this, consider the words of a twenty-nine-year-old man who is starting to question why he takes his penis so seriously:

> It's like, I attack sex. I'm afraid of slowing it down. If I'm gonna be fucking, I'll fuck like crazy, gotta have a huge dick and fuck like crazy to avoid dealing with whatever's making me anxious. Women have always said to me, "God, you can't get enough." But I think the reason I can't get enough is that if I slow down, the fears start to crowd in on me. Does this woman really want to be with me? Is she going to leave? Is my cock good enough? It's hard for me not to use sex as a seal of approval. (In Harry Maurer's *Sex: An Oral History*, [New York: Viking Press, 1994])

Of course, there are plenty of women who have their own insecurities. For instance, is getting breast implants all that different from this guy's need to have a big penis?

The Diagnosis & Cure

How do you distinguish a man who takes his penis too seriously from one who doesn't?

The man who doesn't take his penis too seriously is able to be kind and caring and doesn't beg out when it comes to doing the dishes. He may have various passions in life, often sports, music, business or trying to fix things (sometimes successfully), but these usually help to center rather than isolate him. Sex with him is a natural extension of your friendship that makes all the sense in the world.

As for "curing" the kind of man who takes his penis too seriously, you can't. Hard as you might try, no human being has ever changed just because someone else wanted him or her to. It's something that has to come from within. Friends and lovers can sometimes help if they are willing to call the guy on his nonsense, but they can't make the changes for him.

Sexual Awareness: Hood Ornaments Vs. Wet Triangles

When it comes to sexual awareness, the penis is positioned like the hood ornament on a car. It's difficult to ignore what your hood ornament is telling you when it is sticking straight in the air. Sometimes we guys aren't even aware that we are sexually aroused until we feel ourselves starting to get hard.

Women are not conditioned from early childhood to associate sexual arousal with specific body cues in the way that men are. While their genitals often swell and lubricate, no flags get waved. Most of the changes happen on the inside and can be more easily ignored. Besides, "nice" girls are often taught to ignore their body's sexual cues.

While the penis can be a reliable indicator of sexual excitement, it does have its share of false positives and negatives.

Unwanted Wood

"For some reason, out of nowhere, your penis starts to get hard and it is extremely difficult to stop." *male age 25*

"It's totally embarrassing. You just want to get up and go, but you can't. So you start pulling on your shirt or sweater to try to cover up the bulge. You become very self-conscious; you think everyone is looking at your crotch." *male age 43*

"It's like being in an elevator with an umbrella that will not go down." *male age 42*

"It can physically hurt when your penis is trapped in your jeans pointing downward and it suddenly gets hard for no reason whatsoever." *male age 26*

"Most of my memories of unwanted erections were at school, generally during class, and I was terrified that someone would notice." *male age 24*

"I travel a lot for business and sometimes wake up erect after a flight. It's terribly embarrassing. If I can't think the damn thing down, then I have to go through the tricky maneuver of flipping it up, trapping it under my waistband without being noticed and then keeping my briefcase in front of me when I stand." *male age 25*

Women usually assume that the presence of a hard-on means that a man is sexually aroused, and that no rise in his pants means he isn't. Would it were that simple. Consider the occurrence of the unwanted hard-on. The average teenage male is capable of getting a totally unwanted hard-on in the middle of an algebra test for absolutely no reason, unless he is a member of that rare breed who finds polynomial equations sexually arousing.[1,2] When you are a young man, hard-ons just happen; nobody is more befuddled than the possessor of the penis. To say that all hard-ons are a sign of sexual arousal badly overstates the case. One reader took a bad grade in an early-morning high school class because he couldn't go to the board due to his unwanted erections.

In addition to getting unwanted hard-ons, there are times when a man can feel highly aroused, yet either fail to get hard or have it go limp when he needs it the most (floppus erectus).

---

[1]Fear of an unwanted hard-on might be one reason why teenage guys instinctively wear their shirts untucked. As for the issue of being aroused by polynomial equations, one woman recently recalled that her first orgasm as a teenager occurred spontaneously during a high school algebra test. She thinks it had more to do with the way she was sitting than the subject matter. She was so astonished and overwhelmed by the flood of sensations that she left the entire test blank, although she was an A-student and well-prepared. She suspects her female teacher understood what was happening, since nothing was ever said and she wasn't marked down. With more experience and self-awareness, this woman's earlier sense of being overwhelmed by her orgasms evolved into feelings of delight and amazement.

[2]Unwanted erections aren't helped by sitting, since sitting can cause the veins that carry blood out of the penis to be partially or fully closed.

THE GOOFY DICK GAME
Real Penises of Real Guys

Stephen

William

John

Clarence

David

Special thanks to Joe Sparling, Ph.D.,
whose real-life photos of male members
were used to make these illustrations.

Match Each Soft Penis on the Other Page with Its Erection on This Page

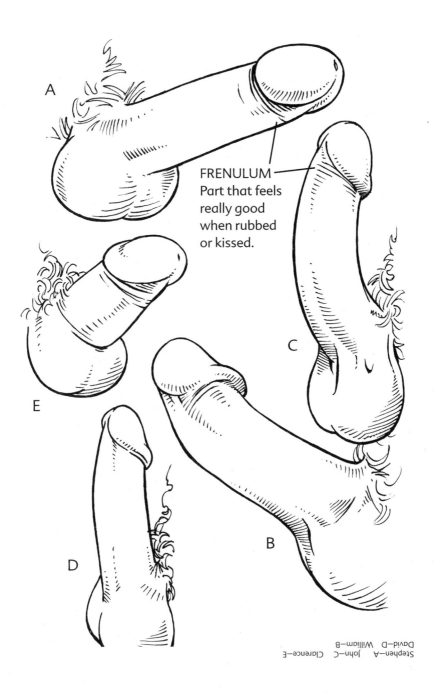

FRENULUM —
Part that feels really good when rubbed or kissed.

Stephen—A   John—C   Clarence—E
David—D   William—B

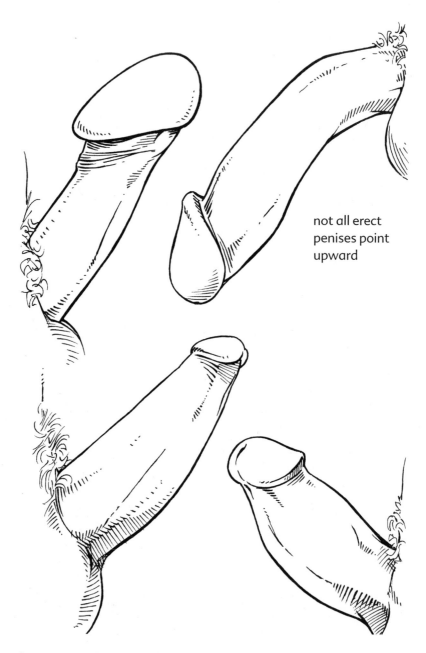

not all erect
penises point
upward

Shape: From these drawings of real-life erections, you can see that terms like "6 inches" and "normal" are somewhat meaningless. All of these penises are "normal," yet very different from each other.

Different Penises,
Different Erections

Size: According to a recent study at the University of California at San Francisco, the average length of a flaccid penis is 3.4 inches, while the average length of an erect penis is 5 inches. Most guys are within 2 inches of these figures.

False Negatives: When Gravity Dings the Dong

Confucius say: If limp dick is worst thing that happens to your relationship, you live charmed life.

Hopefully your lovemaking isn't solely dependent on the man's ability to get hard. If it is, your sexual relationship might be somewhat limited. It's also disconcerting to think that your entire sex life might be centered on the whims of the average penis, hard or soft.

Regarding the biology of erections, it is perfectly normal for a hard penis to partly deflate every fifteen minutes or so. Regarding the psychology of erections, be aware that hard-ons have been known to fly south for varying periods of time, from a single day to who knows how long.

The most unhelpful thing a woman can do when a guy can't get it up is to become defensive. Women often assume that erection failures mean the man doesn't find them attractive or that he might be gay. These are possibilities. But there are about a billion and ten other reasons for not being able to get an erection, from fearing that you won't be good in bed to what just happened on Wall Street. Given the stress of living in the modern world, it's a wonder we men are able to get it up as often as we do. And given the lack of tenderness or excitement in some relationships, an unerect penis might be a signal that the man and woman need to get closer emotionally before anything more can happen.

While most of us have been raised to think of a limp penis as a sign of failure, perhaps it might be more productive to view it as an opportunity to bring a man and woman closer. For more information, please see the chapter "When Your System Crashes," which discusses the penile nose-dive and other forms of male hydraulic failure. In long-term erection failures, one should first rule out physical causes which can range from the side effects of prescription drugs to failing arteries in the penis due to cigarette smoking or diseases that impact the circulatory system.

Betty on Dick

The following passage is from Betty Dodson's neat little book, *Sex for One* (New York: Harmony Books). In addressing the issue of misbehaving penises, Ms. Dodson speaks with welcome concern:

> Although I ran only a dozen men's groups, the experience helped me to let go of my old conviction that men got a better deal when it came to sex.... I thought they could always have easy orgasms even with casual sex, and I envied their never having to worry about the biological realities of periods or pregnancies. But the truth is that not all men are able to be assertive studs who make out all the time.... The most consistent sex problem for many men in the workshops was owning a penis that seemed to have a will of its own. An unpredictable sex organ that got hard when no one was around and then refused to become erect when a man was holding the woman of his dreams in his arms....

If this situation sounds familiar, tell your man that there probably isn't a woman alive who wouldn't be happy to receive a long, lingering back rub and oral sex in the place of intercourse. In other words, if his woody won't work, let him know in no uncertain terms that there are plenty of other ways to please you sexually. This guide's philosophy: *Never ever let a recalcitrant penis ruin your time or his!*

Dick at Dawn

Guys often wake in the morning with erections, which are usually left over from dream sleep. Contrary to what you might think, a man's first feelings upon waking with an erection often aren't sexual. They are more along the lines of "I wish this stupid hard-on would go down so I could pee," or "Damn, I hate having to wake up this early." While some men enjoy having sex first thing in the morning, not all men associate early-morning erections with horniness. In fact, a man who wakes up in a grumpy mood might feel seriously annoyed if a woman assumes that his early-morning wood is for sex. She may need to coax him into having sex, although his penis is rock hard.

Dear Paul,

My boyfriend seems to always wake up in the morning with an erection. But when we start having intercourse, it goes down. He doesn't have this problem any other time. What's up?   *Gretta in Marietta*

Dear Gretta,

Sometimes a dog barks when he's happy, sometimes he barks when he's upset. It's a wise owner who knows the difference.

Contrary to how it seems, the kind of erection your boyfriend has when he first wakes up is little more than a limp penis trapped inside of a raging hard-on. It happens because he wakes up while in the middle of a dream.

Dream-sleep erections occur no matter what a man is dreaming about. He could be dreaming that he's being chased by a pack of hungry wolves, the thing would still be hard as a rock. Appearances to the contrary, it's not the kind of erection that your boyfriend gets when he's been thinking about you all day.

Although it may look and feel like it's ready for action, treat it like a floppy penis that needs to be aroused. Try kissing or playing with it before jumping your boyfriend's bone(s). This will help transform it into a waking-state erection and should help prevent it from going down.

Since his erection was not born from sexual desire, don't assume that your boyfriend feels like having sex. He might feel better if he could pee and brush his teeth. On the other hand, he might feel just fine having sex with a full bladder and dragon breath.

A Wet Warning—Ain't Love Grand!

Every once in a while a girlfriend will ask a guy if she can stand behind him and hold his penis while he pees. This is a completely normal request born of completely normal curiosity.

But be forewarned that you are sometimes giggling so hard that the entire bathroom becomes a target. On the other hand, women sometimes do a better job of aiming the darned thing than we men. As for penile calligraphy skills, one female friend of this guide loves grabbing her husband's penis and writing their names in the snow with its amber stream.

Men Checking Out Other Men

Guys often have a powerful curiosity to check each other out. You might assume that this curiosity is greatest when they are kids and decreases as they get to be adults, but not according to a recent study by a group of Ph.D. students. These students hung out in restrooms at a San Diego Padres game and secretly studied a hundred different men who were peeing. They claim that nearly every guy made an attempt to check out the equipment of whoever was peeing next to him. Furthermore, guys who were well-endowed went out of their way to show their meat to the other men who were peeing. Of course these tendencies might be more true of Padres fans than, say, White Sox fans, who are usually too busy weeping in the men's room to check out anyone else's wood.

As for generalizations, if you are a guy who has ever glanced down at another guy's penis when you are peeing, you can take comfort in knowing that you're probably normal.

First Ejaculation

Before starting puberty, a guy can stroke his little pecker until it nearly falls off and his orgasms will mostly be dry except for maybe a few drops of clear, slick, slightly viscous fluid. Sometime during puberty, this changes. He starts to produce an adult-sized wad when he has an orgasm. Instead of being clear and thin, it's white and thick, and instead of being a drop or two, a teaspoonful or two shoots or oozes all over the place.

This process can be quite wonderful if you know what to expect and know that it's normal. It can be a little disturbing if a guy doesn't have a clue about masturbation except for knowing how to do it. It can be particularly disturbing if he has no clue about ejaculation and masturbates for the first time after entering puberty, since by then he's fully loaded and ready to shoot.

> "I didn't really know what I was doing. I was about eleven and discovered this new feeling when I rubbed this silky part of my blanket over my penis, so I kept doing it. Eventually, I got this intense feeling in my groin and then there was this goop everywhere. I was completely freaked and grossed out. I thought that I broke myself, but was too afraid to tell my parents." *male age 24*

> "I was sure anything that felt THAT good had to be sinful, and that my ejaculate was evidence that I was damaging my insides. Each time I'd masturbate (almost daily) I would feel horrible guilt afterwards and swear to God that I would never do it again." *male age 44*

> "I had heard about masturbation while sitting in the back of the school bus. When I tried it just the way the kid told me, it was almost like pain. For weeks I would stop short of actual orgasm for fear that I would do some sort of internal damage to myself. Finally, one day I kept rubbing through my fear and found that I enjoyed the hurting tremendously." *male age 25*

The Couch-Potato Penis

As they get older, many things start to petrify or harden. This is true for logs, fossils and the human brain. Unfortunately, it is not true for the human penis. In fact, as a penis approaches its fifth decade, it tends to petrify less fully than it did earlier in life. It also squirts less fluid during ejaculation. Some women will cling to this information like a ray of distant hope, while others will be a bit disappointed. Whatever your situation, it shouldn't make much difference. That's because as the bearer of the penis gets older, he becomes wiser in the ways of love. By then, he can hopefully compensate with wit and wisdom for whatever he loses in hardness or volume.

Also, older men seldom make an effort to stay in good shape. It's being out of shape, rather than increasing age, that often causes the couch-potato penis and decline in libido. However, age alone is responsible for changes in ejaculation, with the middle-aged man sometimes feeling nostalgic for his teenage genitals, which sometimes could propel ejaculate up to three feet.

Bebop & Squirt—Men & Multiples

Most males experience orgasm as an overlapping two-part process—sensation and ejaculation. Some guys have learned to separate the two events, experiencing a series of orgasmlike sensations before they finally ejaculate. According to Dr. Marian Dunn, who interviewed a number of men with this ability, the one common thread was that their partner remained in a state of high sexual excitement after the man's first feeling of orgasm. This seemed to provide an essential path of feedback that he could feel in his penis as it remained inside her vagina. Beyond that, some guys had small ejaculations with each orgasm, some didn't ejaculate until the final curtain; some had been able to do this all of their lives, others had learned it recently. Those guys who had always been able to do it assumed that all men could and were surprised when a sexual partner pointed out the difference.

While this ability may come easily for some men, it usually requires a great deal of practice. In some ways, it's an extension of the exercises mentioned in the chapter "Dyslexia of the Penis."

Most guys are perfectly happy with the way they come now, but if you want to explore further, here are some books to consider:

Liberated Orgasm by Herbert Otto (Silverado, California: Liberating Creations, 1999) ISBN: 0-9671181-3-1 To order, send $25.95 to Liberating Creations, P.O. Box 524, Silverado, CA 92676-0524.

The Multi-Orgasmic Man (Taoist sexuality) by Douglas Abrams and Mantak Chia, (San Francisco, California: HarperSanFrancisco, 1996) ISBN: 0-06-251336-2.

On Men's Hormones

Research indicates that men have mood shifts every bit as strong as women's, if not more so. This makes total nonsense of the myth that men are more emotionally stable than women. Researchers are also finding that sex hormones affect the moods of different men in different ways. Some men become irritable or depressed when their testosterone level is elevated. How men respond to the increase in hormone is an individual matter which probably has more to do with social conditioning than biology.

As for hormones and sexual desire, a certain level of male hormone is necessary for sexual arousal, but it isn't very high. Increasing the amount of male hormone above this level doesn't make men any hornier. The only time when added hormone increases a man's horniness is when his testosterone level is below the minimum to begin with. *Do not take things like testosterone and DHEA without first having your blood levels tested, and then under the direction of a skilled physician if lab results show a deficiency.*

Guys & Horniness

It is sometimes assumed that the average male wants to have sex each and every hour of the day as long as the opportunity presents itself. There are some guys for whom this axiom simply doesn't apply, at least around these parts. Maybe it's a problem with our masculinity, maybe we're latent homosexuals, or maybe we have nervous systems that are sensitive enough to be impacted by some of the really disturbing things that happen in the world around us. Or maybe we are really tired and simply need a good night's sleep. Whatever the case, it is sometimes difficult to drop everything and have sex. As often as not, it's nicer to cuddle up close to a sweetheart and simply enjoy falling asleep in each other's arms.

The Vicissitudes of Mercy Sex—Making a Man Come Sooner

Let's say you are getting your man off as an act of kindness and aren't particularly into it, or really need a good night's sleep but won't be able to until you've made his woody sneeze. Here are a few things you can do to help make a man come sooner:

Tighten the Foreskin Pulling the foreskin taut around the base of the penis can cause a man to feel more sensation when his penis is stimulated.

Focus on the Frenulum The frenulum is the most sensitive part of the penis. It's just below the head of the penis, on the side where the seam runs up the shaft. During oral sex, you might focus on this area. If doing him by hand, make sure that your fingers run over this area with a fair amount of pressure during each stroke. On the other hand, pumping too quickly may numb out the penis and be counterproductive. Also, using a well-lubricated hand rather than masturbating him dry will speed up most men's ejaculation if that is your intent.

Adding a Squeeze or Twist Try giving a well-lubricated hand job where your entire hand wraps around the penis and twists up and down it as though it were following the red stripe on a barber's pole. Try a similar twisting motion with your head during oral sex. Just a slight turn of the neck is all that's needed, nothing to give you whiplash. At the same time, work the area between his testicles with one of your hands.

Visuals If the man is turned on by your naked body, for heaven's sake, crank up the lights and park the parts he enjoys most in full view.

Play with Yourself Never hesitate to play with your nipples or vulva. Some men will be so turned on by watching you play with yourself that they will begin to masturbate and finish themselves off with their own hand.

Pleasure Toggles Some men have a spot along the part of the penis that is buried beneath their testicles or all the way back to the rim of their anus which deepens the degree of sensation when pressed upon. Knowing your man's sexual anatomy and keeping a finger on this spot may help move up launch time. Women who give superb blow jobs often work these areas with one hand while tending to the end of the penis with their tongue and lips.

📷 Nipples Some guys' nipples are quite sensitive; others aren't. If your man's are, tweaking them with your fingertips or caressing them with your lips and tongue can speed up arrival time.

📷 On or up His Rear A wet finger on or up a guy's anus can speed some men considerably.

📷 Etc. If he gets turned on by talking dirty to him, do it if you're in the mood. If he likes X-rated movies, load his favorite in the VCR. If you're having intercourse, try slowing down the thrusting rather than speeding up, or somehow change his pace. If he's thrusting shallow, have him thrust deep.

If His Weenie Goes Pop...

So let's say you are riding your cowboy in a sexual way and you suddenly fall off, or you rise up a little too high and cream his penis on the way down (not the fun type of creaming) or you are trying one of those ridiculous intercourse positions that some artist put on some Pharaoh's tomb. Or perhaps you've had a wicked week at work and the kids have the flu and the last thing in the world you want sticking inside of you is your partner's penis, but he has the nerve to insist nonetheless. Whatever the cause of the calamity, should your man's erection suddenly bend in a direction that nature didn't intend and makes a cracking sound or goes POP, get it to a hospital right away. Although rare, the pop might be from the snapping of a ligament in the penis that acts like the suspension cables on the Golden Gate Bridge. If it breaks, internal bleeding can result which might permanently damage the penis. Urologists can usually save the wounded soldier within the first few hours post-pop, but wait more than a day and your guy could end up going to the grave with a penis that's shaped like a deflated circus balloon, or worse yet, an Allen wrench.

An erect penis can also be damaged if it is repeatedly bent mid-shaft. This sometimes happens during sloppy intercourse and might eventually lead to Peyronie's disease. Peyronie's disease can cause painful and/or bent erections. Some physicians believe that Peyronie's disease results from patches of calcium that collect on the penis at points where it has been torqued. The calcium or plaque decreases the elasticity of the expanding penis, which is like pinching together the side of a balloon when you are blowing it up. This condition can be improved with vitamin E in approximately 30 percent of cases. Some urologists say that vacuum pumping can also help to straighten out a penis that is all bent out of shape.

Warning: The intercourse position that can cause the most potential damage to the penis is when the woman is on top. Be sure to use lots of lube and understand that it can damage your pecker if she pulls it out too far and then sits back down on it when it has nowhere to go. Any kind of genital pain that lasts more than ten minutes, whether it's caused by torquing your penis or a pop in the balls, needs to be tended to by a physician. Long-term damage can often be averted if you get medical help right away.

Dear Paul,
Why are guys always touching and grabbing at their genitals?"

Eva from Evanston

Dear Eva,

When the skin on the balls sticks to the thighs, and the skin on the penis sticks to the balls, you get a claustrophobic feeling. It's like if you had to keep your arms pressed against your sides all the time. Try it for just five minutes without lifting them. You just gotta dig to lift and separate. Body powder can help. Underwear that doesn't fit right can make matters worse.

Dear Paul,

When guys are peeing, why can't they aim it right? Would it kill them to get all of it in the bowl?

Nancy in Niagara Falls

Dear Nancy,

The problem is not with the aim, but with the unpredictable nature of the stream. It tends to break up about as often as the signal on a cellular phone. Sometimes a rebel tributary will appear and shoot off to the side, sometimes a healthy stream will suddenly turn into a spray, and sometimes it goes exactly where you aim it, but the toilet water splashes up and makes a mess on the rim.

Of course, this is no reason why a guy shouldn't grab a wad of toilet paper and clean up after himself (bowl, floor, walls, shoes, ceiling...). Also, I don't know if you are aware of the first law of fluid dynamics, but a man never pees on his pants leg unless it is one minute before an important meeting or job interview.

———————

Dear Paul,

The skin on the shaft of my husband's penis is a lot darker than the skin on the rest of his body. Is this normal?

Amber from down under

Dear Amber,

It's perfectly normal. Penises vary as much in skin tone as they do in size and shape. One guy's penis might be darker than his normal skin color, another guy's might be lighter, and a third guy might even have freckles on his. You can't predict until his pants are down.

———————

Dear Paul,

When my husband's penis is erect, it almost points down instead of up. Is this normal?

Diane in Bend

Dear Diane,

A lot of guys point up, at approximately a 30-degree angle from their stomach, assuming they don't have some big hanging beer belly. But plenty of guys stick straight out, and others point down. You might try an intercourse position where you are on top but facing his feet. From this position, he may be able to tickle parts of you that a guy with an "uppie" would miss. Most important is that you and he experiment with positions that feel good for both of you.

Dear Paul,

When it comes to pleasing guys, why are they so focused on their penises? There's so much of the body that feels good when it's kissed and touched, yet they seem to want everything to focus on the penis.

Flabbergasted in Frankfurt

Dear Flabby,

Let me start by asking you a few questions. Let's say you've just cooked your lover a romantic, candlelit dinner. You've gone to the gym, feel really good about the way your body looks, and are wearing a killer dress with your sexiest whatever on underneath. You want him to want you more than he wants his car, a new computer, or *Monday Night Football*. But when the lights finally go down, much to your surprise, his willy is nilly. No matter what you try, he's not able to have an erection. So tell me, what's going through your mind? Are you thinking that he's not interested? That he doesn't find you attractive? Let's say you call it a wash and go for it another time. If he still has no erection, are you thinking maybe he's a wimp? Gay? If you are married, do you start to wonder if he's having an affair?

The sad truth is, if a man can't get it up, there's no end to the negativity that follows. And as much as you aren't aware of it, you are just as focused on the penis as he is—as the ultimate indicator that you are attractive and that he is excited about you.

So once a penis gets hard, a guy figures he'd better start doing something with it ASAP. And if the thing suddenly goes down, especially if it deflates while your legs are wrapped tight around his waist and you've just cried out, "Fuck me harder," heaven help the poor boy. He'll be a big disappointment to you and an even bigger disappointment to himself. All of your hard work—the day, the beautiful dinner, the romantic evening—will be ruined because of the focus that you, he and the rest of us place on his penis. So while you make a point that I clearly laud, there's more to it than meets the eye.

I'm still simplifying this way too much. There are plenty of other issues involved, like the way many of us have learned to focus on our penises since it wouldn't be manly to do otherwise. Honestly, if you heard about a woman taking a leisurely bath and playing with her nipples for half an hour, you'd probably say, "Cool." So would most men. But what if you heard about a guy taking a leisurely bath and playing with his nipples for half an hour? I know what you'd be thinking. While guy nipples might be wired the same way as yours with the same potential for sensation, we certainly don't think of them in the same way.

And finally, whether it's due to our biology or simply the things we teach ourselves about sex, a man sometimes feels a strong need to ejaculate once he becomes aroused. This need is much more pronounced if he is in his teens or twenties than later in life. It makes us focus on doing something with that darned penis rather than being able to enjoy what's going on around us.

What's Inside a Girl?

Chapter 8

Most books on sex present female genitals as though they were a static entity that is easy to comprehend. They give you a few carefully illustrated diagrams and proceed to speak of women's genitals as one would a carburetor. This is a big mistake.

Of course, some people might say this puts women down since it implies their genitals are more complex or more mysterious than men's. Nonsense. Our goofy little brains aren't so totally fried that we don't value "complex" every bit as much as "simple." This is simply acknowledging that if a man approaches a woman's genitals in the same way that he does his own, he and his partner might be missing out on a lot of fun.

This chapter approaches women's genitals differently than most books on sex. It begins with a boy's quest to discover what's between a woman's legs. It then discusses some of the realities and myths about women's sexuality, although it is nearly impossible to separate the two in our society. Then it talks about various body parts and sexual sensations. It ends with women describing how it feels in their genitals when they are aroused or wet.

Instant Pussy

What follows is an experience that the author of this book had with women's genitals back when he was eleven years old and very, very curious.

He had been sent to the big city to visit relatives and it was now time to return home. Since the northbound bus didn't leave until noon, he got to spend the morning in the downtown area next to the Greyhound depot. That's when he found himself taking a leak in a big-city men's room, which was a far cry from the one-seater he had grown up with. For instance, right next to the towel dispensers sat three different vending machines.

One of the machines had men's colognes in it; you could spritz yourself with Old Spice or Brut for a dime. Next to that was a machine that contained a product which was totally baffling. And next to the mystery machine was a dispenser that said *Instant Pussy—2 Quarters*. To put this into proper perspective, back then candy bars weren't much more than a nickel, and two quarters amounted to a near fortune. But then again, the front of the machine promised a facsimile so exact that you couldn't tell instant pussy from the real thing.

For the next hour or so, the young boy pondered the ultimate existential question: ten candy bars or instant pussy, ten candy bars or instant pussy, ten candy bars or instant pussy. A rush of guy hormones apparently kicked in at this very moment and he returned to the porcelain rain forest with two shiny quarters in hand.

The rest of the day was spent in quiet anticipation, with thoughts of instant pussy overwhelming whatever interesting sights and sounds the big city had to offer. Finally, after he had arrived home, fed the dog and done his other chores, the anxious boy opened the small box and read the instructions. "Place capsule in a large glass of warm water." He spent the next half-hour trying to decide just how warm the water should be. He even took out the thermometer and tried to make it a perfect body-heated 98.6. Then came the big moment. He crossed himself and revved up his courage. With an Enola Gay-like swoop, his trembling fingers dropped the capsule into the glass. Then he waited. And waited. And waited.

To make a long story short, forty minutes went by before the gelatin capsule finally melted. The instant pussy was nothing more than a thin piece of sponge cut out in the shape of a cat.

What's Inside a Woman?

A fine way to learn about what's inside a woman is to hold her. For hours. Your skin against hers, the weight of her body and emotions pressing against yours. And if you really want to learn about a woman, consider having babies and raising them together. Hopefully you will like what you discover, although there are no guarantees for either of you. As for understanding a woman's sexuality, some women will let you deep inside of them; others will only have sex with you. It's no different than with men. Just because it's sex doesn't mean it has emotional depth, even if you are married and having intercourse the prescribed 2.3 times a week.

Myth #1 Men Are Hornier Than Women, & Men Peak Sexually in Their Late Teens Whereas Women Peak in Their Late Thirties

There is a silly notion in our society that young men are hornier than young women and that the cause is biological (hormones, chromosomes or the will of God). It is also said that women don't reach their sexual peak until they are in their late thirties.

It is interesting how these myths don't exist in cultures that are more accepting of women's sexuality than our own. Perhaps it's not until American women get into their late thirties that they start to realize what a crock of sanctimonious nonsense they have been swallowing all their lives about themselves and their sexuality. That's when they start to let go of their silly illusions about men being hornier and begin seeking their fair share of pleasure. Unfortunately, by that time a lot of their male contemporaries have gotten fat or are simply out of shape, which makes them less receptive to anything that requires physical effort and stamina.

Myth #2 Tampon-Related Insanity: Rosie the Riveter Has PMS?

The next biological myth, one that is more prevalent now that doctors and pharmaceutical companies can make a lot of money off of it, is that women become incompetent or emotionally unstable during "that time of the month." You know, PMS. To this day, PMS remains such a loosely defined concept that most men qualify as having it. Perhaps the concept of PMS has become so bloated that it no longer resembles reality.

During World War II, when the bulk of American males went to war, millions of American women manned the nation's industrial war machine. Our female-dominated workforce turned out an armada of planes, tanks, ships and guns that was unprecedented in history. It wasn't until the men returned from war and needed their old jobs back that the myth of women's so-called hormonal instability began to rear its head once again. It's a myth that fit well with our society's need to get women out of the workplace and back into the home.

One reason PMS is such a negative concept is that it helps fuel the notion that women as a group are flakier than men. Just as flaky, yes; flakier, no. While menstruation may not feel wonderful, it doesn't make a woman emotionally unstable unless she's fairly depressed or fragile to begin with, which most aren't. (Around 3 percent of women are emotionally unstable, the same number as men.) While most men don't menstruate, not officially anyway, we do have just as many mood swings each month as women.

The following quote from Harriet Goldhor Lerner helps put the hormone matter in proper perspective. This quote was found in Carol Tavris's excellent book *The Mismeasure of Woman: Why Women Are Not the Better Sex, the Inferior Sex or the Opposite Sex* (New York: Simon & Schuster, 1992):

> Let's face it. Do you stay off the streets at night because you fear attack from uncontrolled, irrational women in the throes of their Premenstrual Syndrome? Probably not. We stay home at night because we fear the behavior of men.

Myth #3 Wrestling with the Concept of "Womanhood"

People make all kinds of assumptions about womanhood, yet not many of these assumptions hold up to scrutiny. For instance, a conservative female's definition of womanhood might not have much in common with that of a radical lesbian feminist, which might not have much in common with that of a hetero-sexual feminist. And that's just the opinions of women; most of us men gave up trying to define womanhood sometime around 1970. Still, it might be instructive to consider some of the following contradictions about womanhood:

☕ Intuition is said to be a defining element of womanhood. Yet there is not a single respectable study on intuition that has ever shown women, as a group, to be any more or less intuitive than men. Besides, you don't have to know too many women who date and marry total jerks to have serious doubts about the assumption that women are the more intuitive gender.

☕ In the past, motherhood was thought to be an essential element of womanhood. Yet we all know plenty of women without children who are far from deficient in the area of womanhood, whatever womanhood might be.

☕ It is often assumed that women are the less aggressive gender and that men's aggression makes them more bullying or controlling than women. Yet what about those women who rule the domestic roost with an iron fist that redefines the word controlling, or the self-sacrificing matriarch who manipulates everyone around her by being the consummate martyr, or those women who nag, whine or criticize with an intensity that's the psychic equivalent of physical violence?[1] While women don't always do it with bullets and knives, there are just as many aggressive, controlling and unpleasant females as males. And when you adjust for the number of miles driven by each sex, there are just as many aggressive female drivers as male. Aggression, or the lack of it, is not a defining element of womanhood.

☕ One female-professor type recently penned a bestseller that claims there are significant style differences in the way men and women express themselves. Perhaps this is a defining element of womanhood. Yet when an interviewer noted that this woman's own style was more like the men she describes in her book, she fully agreed and added that her husband's style is more like a woman's. It's a good thing she didn't include herself and her husband in her studies.

☕ There are women who equate womanhood with desire in a man's eyes. In other words, if he wants her, she feels like a

---

[1] Statistics indicate that women initiate as many incidents of domestic violence as men.

woman. If not, she starts to feel sexless. So what do men think about womanhood? One totally normal heterosexual male said he wondered what it would be like to have women's breasts with sensitive nipples, apparently subscribing to the myth that all women's nipples are like detonators of nuclear bombs. Another straight man said he wondered what it would be like to have women's genitals, to have a penis inside of you during intercourse. A third man whose wife had recently given birth wondered what pregnancy would feel like and what it is like to nurse a baby who had grown inside you from the time it was a single cell.

Why do these men equate womanhood with having a woman's body, leaving out the social and political features that a professor of women's studies might include? Perhaps they are being insensitive clods, or maybe they have known and dated enough women to appreciate the huge range of personalities, capabilities and perspectives that different women offer. Perhaps the only unifying attribute they can ascribe to "womanhood" is having a female body.

Perhaps some of today's women feel equally challenged in trying to define womanhood for themselves. Hopefully you and your sexual partners will feel safe enough to be whatever you need to be, whether it is society's stereotypes of manly, womanly, boy-like, girl-like, passive, active, or bits and pieces of each.

Women's Sexual Anatomy — The Nerve of It All

In the late 1950s, a scientist named Kermit Krantz explored how women's genitals are wired. It is difficult to find a single research report on the topic of women's sexuality that is of more value than what Kermit Krantz discovered. What Dr. Krantz did is painstakingly dissect the genital regions of eight dead women. (Sorry, there's no other way of putting it.) Krantz found a great deal of variation in the way the nerve endings were distributed throughout the different women's genitals. While there tended to be a higher concentration of nerve endings in the clitoris, the amount varied significantly among the women; that is, some had more nerve endings in the labia minora (inner lips) than in the clitoris, and some women's nerve endings were highly concentrated in one area while other women had nerve endings that were spread out over a larger area. To quote Kermit Krantz:

The extent of innervation in different females varies greatly.

What this suggests is that no two women get off sexually in exactly the same way. Each woman needs to explore her own unique sexual universe, from where to touch to the kinds of fantasies that get her off. No matter how experienced her partner might be with other women, he won't know exactly what she likes until she tells him. It's not the sort of awareness he is going to assimilate during a one-night stand. A female reader comments: "Talking about this is as much her responsibility as his." A male reader comments about her comment: "Sex is a hundred times better when a woman can actually show or tell you what she wants."

Note: For a man, prior experience can be as much of a hindrance as a help. For instance, stimulating his current partner's vulva in the same way that used to drive a former lover wild could be about as effective as calling her by the former lover's name.

Show & Tell

Most guys know what other guys' penises look like. That's because male genitals stick out. You can't help but notice them when you have showered or peed together. On the other hand, women have no subtle way of looking at other women's genitals, even if they are buck naked. In addition, women have traditionally been discouraged from looking between each other's legs. It's not ladylike. One female reader comments: "While women speak to each other in graphic terms about things like menstruation, blow jobs and the ratio of penis size to male ego, we usually don't talk to each other about what our crotches look like, not that we'd necessarily want to."

Still, some women have found it reassuring to see what other women's vulvas look like. They are often surprised to find that there is a lot of variation. If you are a woman who would like to know what other women's vulvas look like, plenty of graphic displays can be found in men's jerk-off magazines. There are also a few photo books on vulvas which have been published by some feminists.

Interestingly, the muff shots in some of the politically correct beaver books have a clinically sterile edge that's not particularly arousing. In fact, these mug shots of women's crotches are every bit as unerotic as mug shots of men's crotches. Makes you wonder if it isn't the rest of the picture or the sexual situation, rather than just our genitals, that makes us sexy.

Perhaps the missing element in some of the feminist beaver books is an attitude that says, "What we have between our legs is a good thing. It's fun, it's sexy, we like it." Maybe that's the difference between a picture that's clinical and one that's erotic. Of course, some women will claim that men should value sour pusses every bit as much as happy ones. But some of us enjoy knowing that women find their own genitals to be sexy. Perhaps that's why a lot of us nearly ejaculate on the spot if a partner enjoys masturbating and lets us hold her or watch while she's doing it.

Note: In our culture the vulva is usually wrapped with anything from silk to spandex and leather to lace. This wrapping is known as lingerie. Lingerie is thought to give a sense of allure, like the wrapping that covers a precious gift. Or perhaps the allure is in knowing that the woman finds her genitals sexy enough to cover them in an erotic way.

Dear Paul,

My girlfriend thinks her genitals are ugly. Is there anything I can do to help her change her mind?

Bobby in Beaver Falls

Dear Bobby,

It's the strangest thing how even the most politically liberated woman can harbor negative feelings about the way her genitals look.

Even Betty Dodson, champion of female masturbation during the past three decades, used to feel that her genitals were deformed. She assumed they were deformed due to childhood masturbation. Finally, a male lover insisted that this wasn't true. He brought her porn magazines so she could see that her genitals were like other women's—and how much variation there could be in the way the lips are formed. Women's genitals are like human faces: all have the same parts, but no two look exactly alike.

We guys often assume that when women are naked together, like during P.E. or at the gym, they can see each other's genitals. But this isn't true. All they can see is the pubic hair that's on the top of their genitals. A woman would have to sit down and spread her legs for another woman to see her genitals, which is not the sort of thing that happens in most women's gyms, not around here, anyway.

So while it is totally normal for guys to know what different penises look like, it is not normal for a woman to see another woman's genitals. It's also unusual for a woman to give other women oral sex or to look at porn magazines. As a result, men end up knowing more about what women's genitals look like than most women.

Strange as it might seem, a lot of girls don't look at their own genitals until they are ten or even twenty years of age. The only way a guy would wait that long to look at his genitals is if he were born blind or was maybe paralyzed from the waist down and didn't know they were there.

Also keep in mind that our society doesn't want girls to be curious about their genitals. While it is natural for a child to fall asleep with a hand between his or her legs, parents often assume that this kind of self-comforting will turn an innocent girl into a slut-in-the-making. Heaven help a girl who is caught bringing her fingers to her mouth or nose after touching herself "down there." Talk about being threatened to within an inch of her life—all for exploring how she tastes or smells.

I recently received a video showing one of Betty Dodson's workshops where women explore the design of their genitals and help each other to evolve a more positive view of themselves. One of the women here at the Goofy Foot Press, who prides herself on her independence and liberation, felt uncomfortable when she first reviewed this tape. She knew that she would feel perfectly comfortable seeing men showing their penises, so she tried to relax and actually watch the tape. After getting over her discomfort, she said that the tape had a positive effect on her, and this woman is harshly critical of most of the videos we receive.

I would encourage you to get Betty's tape and watch it with your girlfriend. Together, you can see women dealing with their genitals in a positive way. These are not porn stars, just normal women discovering neat things about what's between their legs. The tape is called *Viva La Vulva—Women's Sex Organs Revealed* by Betty Dodson. You can get it by sending $43.00 to Betty Dodson, Box 1933, Murray Hill, NY 10156. Also, you can check out Betty's website at: www.bettydodson.com.

Vulvas, Vaginas, Beavers & Bear

While many of us can correctly label the male genitals, we usually don't know stem from stern about the female organs of sex. For instance, people refer to everything between a woman's legs as her vagina. Yet this is far from true. What sits between a naked woman's legs is her vulva.

You might ask, "What difference does it make if you call it a vulva or vagina?" One female educator answered this question by asking another: "What if parents taught their children that they had no eyes, ears, nose or mouth, but instead gave them one word for their entire face and called it 'tongue'?" This would be confusing and limiting. It might even suggest that parents are afraid of faces and all the wonderful things they can do.

For the record, a vulva is composed of:

☕ The outer lips.

☕ The inner lips and the clitoral hood.

☕ The tip or glans of the clitoris, if it's the kind that peeks through the clitoral hood.

☕ The urethral opening (peehole). Good luck finding it!

🍵 The opening of the vagina. (Spread the lips to see it.)

🍵 The mons pubis, a fleshy little mound that sits on top of the pubic bone and is usually covered by pubic hair, unless the woman has been trying to wear a string bikini with grace or simply likes to have her pubic area trimmed, close-cropped, or cleanly shaven. The mons pubis is a wonderful lovemaking ally that men sometimes ignore.

Lips, Lips, Lips

Wouldn't you know it, even the ancient Romans got it wrong. They named the outer lips "labia majora" (big lips) and the inner lips "labia minora" (small lips). But in a lot of vulvas, the outer lips aren't particularly prominent, while the inner lips fan out in all kinds of ways and shapes.

The outer lips often have hair on them, while the inner lips are bald as can be. For most women, the inner lips are more sensitive than the outer. In fact, a lot of women play with the inner lips or gently stroke them when they are masturbating. Perhaps one reason is because the inner lips connect to the hood of the clitoris. Tugging gently on the inner lips may provide a less direct and more pleasurable way of stimulating an extra-sensitive clitoris. And the lips are so grateful for the attention that they often swell and open when sexually aroused. Their color tends to deepen as they swell, which is nature's way of saying, "I'm ready for all the attention you can possibly muster."

For some women, the inner lips can be big players during intercourse. It seems that the inner lips might be pushed and pulled with each stroke of the penis, perhaps making them one of the mediums that helps transmit the message to the clitoris.

Clitoris—Point Guard for Women's Genitals

If you don't know a clitoris from a bunion, ask your sweetheart to show you. If you don't have a sweetheart, ask a female friend and then duck. Here's the definition of clitoris from the Goofy Glossary:

> **clitoris** — Latin for "darned thing was here just a second ago." The only organ in either the male or the female body whose sole purpose is pleasure, which from a biological perspective might indicate that the female genitals are more highly evolved than the male's. 2. Sometimes regarded as the Emerald City of women's orgasmic response. 3. Not to be approached in haste. 4. Sometimes wants to be caressed with vigor; other times can hardly tolerate being breathed upon.

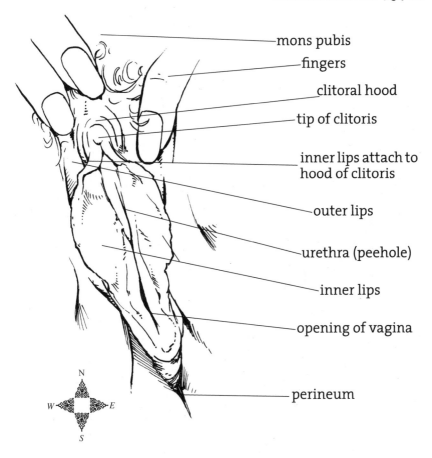

mons pubis

fingers

clitoral hood

tip of clitoris

inner lips attach to hood of clitoris

outer lips

urethra (peehole)

inner lips

opening of vagina

perineum

Some clitorises nearly pop out at you and shake your hand; others can hardly be seen. Some clitorises are extremely sensitive; others aren't. Some change sensitivity with the time of the month. Not to worry, the sensitivity of the clitoris has nothing to do with its size, which can range from 2 to 20 millimeters in diameter.

As a woman becomes aroused, the tip or glans of her clitoris often swells. The clitoris also has a foreskin or hood. Manipulating the hood of the clitoris is an art form that is discussed in the chapter "The Zen of Finger Fucking." **Note:** Newer theories describe the clitoris as being much larger than was previously thought. Some people now envision the clitoris as a wishbonelike structure, with the legs of the wishbone running beneath each of the labia.

Different Women...

...Different Vulvas

View from behind.
What? Aliens stole their anuses?

One way to find out how your vulva looks is to sit on a large Xerox/copy machine, lean forward and press the copy button. The cover is glass, so sit very gently, and be sure you have the permission of the machine's owner!

As the Clitoris Retracts...

As a woman approaches orgasm, her clitoris often disappears or seems to retract. This can be confusing for the man who is trying to stimulate the clitoris by hand or mouth. The confusion is in knowing whether to play Hercule Poirot and give chase, or to simply wait until the clitoris returns...

One researcher, Beverly Whipple, questions whether the clitoris actually retracts; maybe it simply gets lost in the swelling tissues that surround it. Also, as a woman becomes more aroused, she may want her partner to stimulate her in a different way or on a different spot. Discussing this with your lover makes a great deal of sense.

Incoming

The clitoris is seldom positioned to rub noses with an incoming penis. This is why a number of women enjoy the added stimulation of a finger or vibrator during intercourse, or they sometimes push the clitoris against the shaft of a sweetheart's thrusting penis or grind it against his pubic bone while his penis is all the way inside. Other women do just fine with thrusting alone. It all depends on how the man's anatomy interfaces with the woman's, where the particular nerve endings are located, how long the man is able to last, and the woman's level of arousal.

A Final Note on the Clitoris—How Do You Pronounce It?

One day the author of this book found that he had to address a classroom of students and might need to say "clitoris." There he was, with almost twelve years of college under his belt, not knowing how to pronounce the word "clitoris." To prepare, he wrote "clitoris" on one card and "penis" on another. He then asked friends of both sexes to say the two words out loud.

No one had any hesitation in pronouncing penis, but almost everyone approached clitoris with a perplexed look and said, "Well, here's how I've always pronounced it..." Some said cli-TOR-is, others said CLIT-or-is. As he was exploring his own usage of the word, he realized that the only time he had referred to it was in bed with a woman, and then he called it "it." (One dictionary says that either pronunciation is correct, although it lists CLIT-or-is first.)

Papa Freud & The Viennese Vagina

Not too long ago, Freudian psychiatrists proclaimed that women had defective egos if their orgasms didn't originate from deep inside the vagina. Sex researchers in the 1960s did society a huge service in showing that the majority of women's orgasms involve the clitoris rather than the vagina. However, they may have gone too far in discounting the vagina as a source of pleasure. In fact, some women feel that having something in the vagina (penis, dildo, fingers) during orgasm changes the character of their orgasm and makes it more of a full-body experience. It's not necessarily better, just different from an orgasm that's all clitoris.

Busy Little Beavers

People often view the vagina as passive or inactive. Not so. Consider the following:

☕ The human body is made up of many different tubes. The favorite tube of many straight males is the vagina, a hollow canal with walls that contain nerves and blood vessels. When not aroused, the walls of the vagina lie flat against each other like a firehose without water. When aroused, a vagina often straightens out and puffs up even more than an erect penis, often doubling in length or depth.

☕ When sexually aroused, the first third of the vagina becomes narrower while the back part expands and sometimes balloons open, a little like the bottom half of an hour glass.

☕ The first third of the vagina is often sensitive to touch, while the back two-thirds are more sensitive to pressure. The walls of the first third tend to have more tiny folds, while the back two-thirds tend to be smoother.

☕ For some women, the back part of the vagina expands before orgasm and then contracts. This might cause a longing to have something inside the vagina which the rear walls can grasp during orgasm. During this process, some women call out the names of various deities..

☕ We could try to map out a vagina for you, but why not make your own vaginal love maps? What nicer way to spend an afternoon than exploring the tender shoals of a lover's warm, moist vagina.

Variations in Preference

"I have orgasms fairly easily, but have never had one with a penis inside. I'm happy with that, but men seem disappointed that I don't need a penis."   *female age 57*

Some women like coffee first thing in the morning; others don't. Some like tomatoes; others find them slimy and odd. The same is true for intercourse: some women can't get enough of it; others prefer their crotches just as they are without a penis begging to enter. This has little to do with a woman's sexual orientation, but rather with her sexual perspective, which is determined by a combination of physiology, temperament and prior life experiences, or experiences from prior lives, if you are into that sort of thing.

As for variations, one woman might prefer oral sex to intercourse. Another might prefer masturbating while her partner either holds her or masturbates along with her. A third woman might not feel satisfied unless sex includes intercourse. And a fourth woman might prefer oral sex with John, but intercourse with Bill.

Variations in Wetness

When sexually aroused, some vaginas get so wet that the woman needs to wring out her underwear. Other women can be every bit as aroused, but their vaginas remain dry. Also, some women become wetter during certain phases of their menstrual cycle. Men shouldn't be so silly as to gauge a woman's level of sexual arousal on vaginal wetness alone.

Women who remain dry even when highly aroused are smart to keep a tube or bottle of water-based sex lube handy. Some women insert a glycerin suppository or similar product into the vagina to make it wet and sensually sloppy. Others find that glycerin-containing lubricants bring on infections. And no matter how wet the woman gets naturally, she should consider using lubrication when her partner is wearing a condom or is inserting a dildo or sex toy.

Aliphatic Acid Trip

Researchers have discovered that about one in three women has vaginal secretions that contain certain types of scent-producing aliphatic acid chains (organic chemical compounds). The scent of these women's vaginas varies with the phase of their menstrual cycle. For the other 66 percent of women there is no such vaginal scent, and the perfume of the vagina, or lack of it, remains the same no matter what day of the month a lover's face might find itself between their thighs. The researchers did not say if the added scent is encouraging or discouraging to the male of the species.

Four Scores & Seven Vaginas Ago

If you have had the good fortune to experience sex with a number of women and were of a clear mind when doing so, you may have noticed that not all vaginas are created equal. Not all penises are created equal either.

For instance, steam might be billowing out of your ears at the mere sight of a certain woman, but after having intercourse with her your penis complains that jerking off in the shower feels better. At the same time, a woman who seems quite plain on the surface may be the one whose vagina you remember most throughout life.

Also, you might find that some women's genitals lend themselves more to one type of sexual activity than another; for instance, you may love going down on Mary Jane, but intercourse with her is only so-so; the exact opposite might be true with Theresa. With one woman, the missionary position may rule; with another, it's some exotic position she read about in *Cosmo*.

Vaginal Farts

"My boyfriend was performing oral sex on me and fingering my vagina. When I sat up, all of the air in my vagina came rushing out and made a huge fartlike noise. I was totally embarrassed; it was completely unexpected. I looked at my boyfriend with shock on my face, and then we both started laughing." *female age 25*

Occasionally, air gets trapped inside the vagina and makes a fartlike noise when it comes it. This happens all the time and is nothing to be embarrassed about, given how both of you created the situation and hopefully had a fine time doing so.

Technically speaking, this is more likely to happen after you have had an orgasm and the rear part of your vagina which had ballooned open during arousal begins to collapse into its normal resting state. The Irish apparently utilized this principle to create the first foghorn.

The Cervix

The cervix is a fleshy little dome in the top rear part of the vagina. Nature put it there as a valve or gatekeeper that joins the uterus and the vagina. The cervix can be as small as a cherry in a woman who has not delivered a baby through her vagina, or it can be much bigger. It has a little dimple in the center through which female fluids come down and male fluids go up. It sometimes feels softer when a woman is ovulating. During that time, mucus passes through the opening in the cervix and bathes the vagina. This keeps it clean and more acidic, conditions which encourage conception. At the point when conception is most likely to occur, the mucus becomes clear and slippery. Danger! Danger!

The cervix has a space around it that is called the fornix. This is a delightful area to explore with a finger. It is also a good space to know about when the woman's vagina isn't particularly deep or her lover has a long penis. Such couples will want to find intercourse positions that encourage the penis to slither under the cervix and into the rear fornix. This will add an extra inch or two of runway space.

Rumor has it that some women find stimulation of the space around the fornix to be quite pleasing; others, of course, will surely hate it.

Birth Control Note: Diaphragms are little latex hubcaps that cover the cervix and attempt to block male ejaculate from sneaking through the little dimple in the center of the cervix.

Gynecology 101—The Wonders of Nature

There are two ways we know of to see a cervix. The first is the traditional way: using a speculum. This is a metal or plastic device that physicians insert into a woman's vagina to help push the walls apart. This allows the physician to see parts of a woman that most boyfriends and husbands never do. If you have a healthy sense of curiosity, get a speculum from your physician or medical supply store. Lubricate it with KY or contraceptive jelly, gently insert it into the vagina, and add the krypton beam of your favorite flashlight as well as the reflection of a hand-held mirror. This will give both of you a bird's eye view of the cervix.

Another way of seeing inside a vagina is to get an acrylic dildo with a view port that is optically designed to give you 5X magnification. The Xandria people sell one that's called "The Observer." It's not cheap ($75!) but might be neat to try. Once you insert it, the cervix should be in there somewhere.

A statement of disbelief that is often made upon seeing the small slit in the cervix is "A baby is supposed to fit through that?"

Ovaries—Gynecology 102

A man's testicles tend to announce themselves wherever he goes. Not so with a woman's ovaries. In fact, it's possible to have a long-term relationship with a woman and not even know her ovaries are there, except indirectly through events like pregnancy or menstruation.

Assuming you want to, the best time to feel a woman's ovaries is when she is lying on her back and is in an "It's okay if you feel my ovaries" kind of mood. Otherwise, don't even try. Rest one hand on her lower abdomen below her belly button. Place a lubricated finger or two from your other hand deep into her vagina. When you encounter the rear wall of her vagina, veer to the left or right and push up gently while pushing down with the hand that's on her abdomen. You will need to rely on her instructions from there. If a woman doesn't know where her ovaries are, she might ask her gynecologist to show her during her next exam.

While some women enjoy having their ovaries explored, others experience such attempts in the same way that a man does a pop in the balls. It might also depend on where she is in her menstrual cycle.

Menstrual Note: Highly astute males know that some women prefer different types of sexual stimulation during different phases of the menstrual cycle. This can be particularly true for nipple and breast stimulation. Learning about these variations can take months or even years, but good luck if you don't. And then, once you finally feel that you might have a handle on it, menopause begins and you need to learn it all over again!

Redboobs & Glamour Puss—Charms? Quarks? G-Spots?

Some people swear by the G-spot, others aren't so sure. Hopefully, as you read this section, you will appreciate that everyone's body is different, and what pleases one person might not please another.

The biggest problem with exploring for a G-spot area isn't whether you have one, but what your expectations are. If you are exploring just to explore, this is a fine thing. If you are exploring because you think you should have something that you don't, then you are sadly misleading yourself.

Just so you'll know, the writers at the women's magazines routinely call to ask about this spot or that spot—the G-spot, the C-spot or the X-Y-Z-spot. It's never enough for them if you say, "Sure, that might feel really good for some women, but not so good for others." These writers have been assigned to write a story that will validate the kind of cover copy that will sell the magazine—cover copy that is sometimes so misleading that you might as well go one step further and buy the *Weekly Catastrophe* that claims, "Jesus, Elvis and Pope Have Secret Meeting at Bloomingdales!"

The covers of women's magazines are designed to make you feel bad if you don't buy them. They want you to feel like you will surely lose your spouse to some other woman who did buy this issue of *Redboobs* or *Glamour Puss* and read, "The Ultimate Sex Spot—You Will Never Be the Same and Neither Will He!" or "The Hot New Sex Potion—Can It Change Your Life?"

So please, if you do want to explore different parts of your vagina, approach it as you would a game of Scrabble or Monopoly, and not as if you'll be sexually inferior if your this-spot or that-spot is no spot at all.

G-Spots & Chicks In Wheelchairs[1]

One theory about the G-spot that helps clear up the matter has been advanced by Drs. John Perry and Beverly Whipple. They think that women's orgasms are transmitted to the brain through two neural pathways instead of just one. This makes a great deal of sense when you consider the findings of Dr. Whipple's research with women who are paralyzed due to spinal-cord injuries. She found that a large percentage of these women are still able to have genital orgasms, which indicates that a secondary pathway to the brain exists for orgasms besides the one that runs up the spinal column.

It seems that feelings in the clitoris get to your brain by way of the pudendal nerve, while G-spot-area sensations are transmitted through the pelvic nerve. As a result, a clitoral orgasm travels to the brain by a different pathway than a G-spot orgasm. Perhaps this is why women who have G-spot orgasms describe them as being "deeper" in the body. It might also be why stimulation of the G-spot area makes a lot of women feel like they have to pee, since the same nerve that transmits G-spot sensations to the brain also transmits bladder sensations. (Can a woman have G-spot and clitoral orgasms at the same time? Heavens!)

Theoretically, the G-spot is made up of tissue that surrounds the urethra. This places it on the roof of the vagina about a third to three-quarters of a finger deep. Some people say the G-spot is

---

[1]For those of you who think that disabled people aren't just as sexually amped as the rest of us, please see the chapter, "Sex When You Are Horny & Disabled."

close to a small patch of vaginal tissue which might feel rough. The roughness is from several small folds in the tissue. Others refuse to get specific and seldom mention landmarks. Some people say the G-spot is small when unaroused (about the size of a pea), but grows bigger when fully aroused (about the size of a quarter). That's inflation for you.

Some women feel a slight discomfort or bladder fullness with G-spot stimulation. G-spot aficionados suggest that women let go of their concern about bladder fullness and allow their muscles to relax in order to enjoy the benefits. Why not put a towel down just in case? That might help her feel more relaxed. Also, it's best to wait until the woman is fairly aroused before exploring for G.

One way of stimulating the G-spot is by inserting a finger or two into a wet and awake vagina and making a "come here" motion. A woman who is exploring on her own might find it easier while squatting. In addition, there is an interesting vibrator attachment which is especially designed for G-spot stimulation. It can be ordered from Good Vibrations.

One intercourse position that you might try when exploring G-spot potential is as follows: the woman kneels on the floor next to the bed and leans on the mattress. She is leaning on her elbows and her upper body is diagonal to the mattress. Her partner enters her from behind. Experiment with various types of thrusting, shallow to deep. If it's more comfortable, she might try this standing, with her elbows resting on a table or dresser.

As for the feelings that accompany G-spot stimulation, some women enjoy them tremendously while others couldn't care less and some even find them to be obnoxious. Also keep in mind that sexual satisfaction is part of a much larger process. How you treat each other when you aren't having sex will probably impact your level of satisfaction far more than simply romancing a woman's G-spot.

If you are looking for more on the G-spot, consider reading *The Good Vibrations Guide to the G-Spot* by Cathy Winks (San Francisco: Down There Press, 1998). While we laud the cheap seven dollar price, it is hard to understand why the publisher printed the book with type so small your eyes ache from trying to read it.

Female Ejaculation Vs. Bum Bladders

For years, physicians have known that some women ejaculate following orgasm. Rather than trying to find out more about this, the doctors assumed that the fluid was urine from a leaky bladder. There are now plenty of people who dispute the leaky-bladder theory. They say that the fluid is similar to male prostate fluid, which provides the lion's share of male ejaculate. For instance, there is a pill you can take that makes your urine turn blue. They have given this pill to women who ejaculate and found that the ejaculated fluid isn't blue or is barely blue.

The biggest problem with female ejaculation is that women who do it sometimes feel embarrassed about it and try to stop it. As a result, they keep themselves from fully relaxing and enjoying the wonderful sensations. Most guys are happy to have a partner ejaculate when they realize it means she had a really deep orgasm.

There are now a number of X-rated videos that show female ejaculation. Some of the women in these videos expel fluid with the force of a busted fire hydrant. These female ejaculators claim that the pints of fluid they are shooting across the room were from tiny prostatelike ducts. Nonsense. Other women in the tapes spouted smaller amounts of fluid that may have realistically had a source other than the bladder.

Whatever the case, plenty of women squirt fluid when they come, especially if they have G-spot-type orgasms. Some women say they squirt right before having a G-spot orgasm.

If you happen to be a bed-drencher, please understand that there's nothing unusual about it. On the other hand, some of the tapes on female ejaculation get awfully evangelical about the subject, with some of the women who do squirt trying to make women who don't squirt feel inadequate. That's ridiculous.

Women & Multiple Orgasms

> "Usually I am too sensitive following an orgasm for any stimulation. But occasionally, when I've had a real shake-the-walls, body-mind-soul climax, I'm still in a state of high arousal and if my husband stimulates me again a few seconds later I go off with a bang. Sometimes this can happen two or three times in a row. It feels like a firecracker exploding without any prior warning, and we often start laughing at the surprise and delight of it." *age 47*

> "It feels like having a baby, except all the pain is replaced with pleasure." *female age 34*

> "It was very intense, almost too intense, like my body was out of my control." *female age 45*

Unfortunately, giving a concise definition of multiple orgasm is a problem. One hitch is that people usually associate "orgasm" with the ejaculation type of orgasm that men often have. Adjectives like "multiple" need to be added to make it fit the kind of experience that some women sometimes have, although multiples don't necessarily feel like a series of singles. Another problem in defining multiple orgasm is that the experience varies from woman to woman. Whatever the definition, here are a couple of reasons why some women are capable of having multiple orgasms. Please keep in mind that plenty of women are perfectly happy with their single orgasms and don't want or need anything more.

Anatomy Despite the extreme sensitivity that may follow her first orgasm, a woman's genitals often stay primed and ready for more. This gives some women the potential to have an extended wavelike orgasm or separate orgasms but with little time in between. Also, some women seem to have small ducts around the urethra that are larger than other women's. This may contribute to differences in experience among different women.

Physical Awareness Recent surveys of nurses and health-care providers show that nearly forty percent of these women have or have had multiple orgasms. This is much higher than among women who aren't health care providers. Perhaps familiarity and awareness of the body may contribute to the kind of orgasms a person has.

Emotions Gynecologist David Cheeks did a series of hypnotic regressions on a number of his women patients. One group of these women routinely enjoyed multiple orgasms, while another group had difficulty reaching orgasm at all. ("Hypnotic regression" means to explore early childhood memories while under hypnosis. Whether such memories describe what really happened or are simply metaphors for early emotional experience is a subject of much debate these days.)

The women who were able to have multiple orgasms could recall feeling wonderful sensations in their genitals that were present not only during events like baths or diaper changing, but also during moments of happiness and joy, especially when parents expressed love or acceptance for the child. These women had no memories of being scolded for playing with their genitals. This contrasted sharply with memories of the nonorgasmic women, who recalled few early associations between happiness or joy and sexual sensation. Under hypnosis these women could often recall being scolded for playing with their genitals.

It doesn't take a genius to figure out what this suggests. On the other hand, there are plenty of women with rather hideous childhood sexual experiences who love sex and get a tremendous amount of comfort and joy from it. Unfortunate or tragic early experience needn't shackle one for life.

Possible Parallels Between Girl 'Gasms & Giving Birth

Some people claim that a woman's sexual experience occasionally transports her into another dimension, one that incorporates aspects of Disneyland, the Taj Majal, and maybe an orbit or two around the moons of Jupiter. Perhaps some of the parallels between a woman's ability to bear children and her sexual response might give the latter extra kick. For instance, consider the following associations which were culled from the writings of an early feminist by the name of Niles Newton:

☕ During early sexual arousal and the first parts of

labor, a woman's breathing often becomes deep and slow. Then, at the point of orgasm and the second stage of labor, her cervix opens up and her breathing pattern becomes interrupted. Her face often tenses and strains, and she experiences uterine contractions. (Uterine contractions, whether part of orgasm or childbirth, are thought to be triggered by the release of similar hormones.)

☕ A woman's clitoris is usually engorged (swollen) during orgasm and immediately following birth, moments when most women experience a sense of joy and well-being. Some women have orgasmlike experiences after giving birth.

☕ During both sex and childbirth, a woman's behaviors and expressions become less inhibited. She is less aware of her immediate environment. If the sex is good, anyway.

☕ Uterine contractions and nipple erection often occur during orgasm and while nursing a baby. There are accompanying changes in the skin temperature of the breast during both orgasm and nursing, and it's not unusual for a woman to experience sexual pleasure while nursing. Some of the same hormones mediate both milk release and uterine contraction. Also, some babies respond to sucking on the breast with rhythmic movements and penile erection. Many of us grown-up guys do the same.

☕ Some women enjoy rubbing their clitoris while in various phases of labor. They report that it helps to relax them. This makes sense when you consider that orgasms help release the body's natural painkillers.

☕ Here is one that Ms. Newton may have missed: Some women who have really powerful orgasms push down as they are coming, perhaps a little like a woman who is pushing out a baby.

Perhaps these parallels allow a woman access to sexual feelings that might be different from a man's. Then again, the sexual journey could be an individual matter that has little to do with whether you are male or female.

Beware of Womb–Ovary Exorcism

If a woman in our society has her reproductive organs removed, no one takes much notice. It's an everyday surgical event. But if a man has his testicles removed, we gasp in shared pain. We are sensitive to the man's loss, but not to the woman's. It seems that American medicine has an inborn prejudice about women's reproductive organs. The prejudice is that women are better off without them — although unnecessary surgeries on the male prostate are on the rise, too.

In America, approximately 665,000 hysterectomies are performed each year. The average age of women having the surgery is 42.5 years. In her book *The Mismeasure of Woman*, psychologist Carol Tavris notes that many hysterectomies are unnecessary. Tavris quotes a university professor who is a second-opinion expert for Blue Cross as saying, "The patients who had the recommendations for the hysterectomies either had no pathology whatsoever or had pathology that was so minimal it was inexplicable to me how anybody could have recommended surgery." If a woman is told that she needs to have a hysterectomy, she should be sure to get a second opinion from a gynecologist who doesn't do surgery, especially if the reason for the hysterectomy is a precancerous pap smear. Perhaps a positive effect of managed healthcare will be a decrease in unnecessary hysterectomies and C-sections, since they will dent rather than enhance profit margins.

Readers' Comments

What does it feel like in your genitals when you are sexually aroused?

"Tingling starts in my clitoris and spreads to my labia. My whole vulva starts to throb, literally. The throbbing is extremely pleasurable. Then my vulva gets swollen and almost hot. Once it is swollen, every slight touch sends lightning bolts of pleasure all around my whole body."

female age 23

"Sometimes it's an ache not unlike having a full bladder. Other times, a sensation of heat and congestion in my labia, clitoris and vagina. If I'm highly aroused, or if my clothing is tight, I'll be able to feel my pulse between my legs. Sometimes I'll feel my tendons and muscles twitching as well." *female age 36*

"My labia feel swollen and tight; my clitoris becomes hard. Sometimes my clitoris feels like it's huge, and it sort of throbs. If I am extremely aroused, my whole vulva feels as though it's pounding, with my clitoris as the center."

female age 26

"You know the feeling you get right before your leg or arm falls asleep? I mean, before it's annoying or hurts. It's a really intense tingling feeling. It makes my whole body feel warm and excited. There are moments, however, right before my partner enters me, when my vagina actually aches." *female age 27*

When did you first make the connection between being sexually aroused and being wet?

"When I was around ten or eleven, while watching a sex scene in a film. My panties got wet, and I realized that was why. If I'm really turned on, I'll drip down to my ankles."

female age 25

"I first connected being wet with sexual arousal when I was 13. I was watching a silent, vintage erotic film with a friend. When I went to the bathroom, I was soaked!" *age 26*

"The first time I connected wetness with sex was when I was 9 or so and got all wet and throbby when I was watching a couple kissing at the beach. But I don't always get wet when I feel aroused; it isn't an indicator for me."

female age 38

"When I first masturbated, I only touched myself on my clitoris, so I was very surprised when I eventually felt my vagina and it was dripping fluid." *female age 23*

Comments about being wet...

"Being wet is hard to explain. I don't know if I can offer insight because it just happens. The most annoying thing is that if you don't wear panties and get wet, it tends to be very messy, but arousing!" *female age 36*

"For me, the degree of my wetness varies greatly from time to time and seems to be largely affected by how mentally 'into' having sex I am at that given time." *female age 34*

"If my boyfriend just starts kissing me and wants to have sex, I am not automatically wet. I need to be turned on. This could be by way of slowing down and paying attention to my body, or it could be by talking sexy, reading, looking at or listening to erotica." *female age 26*

"It does not work when my partner concentrates solely on doing mechanical things to get me wet. Yet a simple very tender kiss can do it, especially when the whole day is relaxed." *female age 48*

"I enjoy sex a great deal, but seldom get wet." *female age 32*

Dear Paul,

I am a 30-year-old sexually active woman. I was recently having intercourse with a gentleman of very large stature (big penis). I felt no pain, but started bleeding. I have had intercourse with other men, and assumed my hymen had torn long ago. Is it possible it didn't tear until now? My female physician didn't seem to know much about hymens, and said it might bleed some more.

Mary Anne from Mt. Hood

Dear Mary Anne,

It doesn't surprise me that your physician is hymen-challenged. Some of the better studies on hymens have only been done in the last couple of years, and some of these seem to contradict each other.

The hymen is a thin membrane that is located at the front of the vagina. Hymens are like dresses: some are nearly nonexistent, others cover everything. Most are somewhere inbetween.

Folklore has it that a woman's hymen stays intact until she has her first intercourse, during which time it supposedly bleeds. It has been said that in some cultures, the marriage could be called off and the woman even stoned to death if there was no blood on the sheets of the wedding bed. To this day, there are physicians who perform minor surgeries where the edges of the hymen are stitched together, creating the appearance of "virginity." One medical journal describes a surgery where a small capsule of bloodlike substance is attached to the hymen, assuring that there will be blood on the sheets the morning after. Women in the olden days would insert a blood-soaked sponge or a small fish bladder full of blood—several times a day in brothels that promised virgins.

A recent study has shown that the hymen isn't necessarily torn after intercourse. Nineteen percent of the sexually active women in this study had no visible abnormalities of the hymen.

Most physicians would have declared these women to be virgins—even if they had been boinking their brains out the night before. In its conclusion, this study states, "So-called rupture and bleeding of the hymen is not to be routinely expected after first sexual intercourse."

Some women are born without hymens and other women have hymens that tear or stretch long before they have intercourse. Hymens can also be torn or stretched during heavy petting, with nary a penis in sight. And contrary to what you might think, studies also show that tampon usage does little to stretch or tear a hymen.

For most women, the first intercourse causes very little hymen-related discomfort and/or bleeding. What usually causes the pain is lack of sexual arousal. Still, if you are worried about this and want to try stretching your hymen beforehand, wash your hands and make sure you don't have any lethal nails. Put some lube (KY, etc.) or saliva on a finger and slide it into your vagina. Gently push it down for a minute or so, and then ease up the pressure. Repeat this, and then insert two fingers. Gently push down and out toward the sides. Do this for a couple of days, and your hymen might be a happy camper when Mr. Penis comes barreling through.

You may also have heard that a hymen can be imperforate, meaning it covers the entire vaginal opening. This is not very common. It can lead to severe menstrual cramping, as the blood can't exit the body through the vagina. Treating an imperforate hymen is a simple outpatient procedure. Since it is usually done when a girl is in her early teens, it is important that the gynecologist carefully explain the procedure to her and her parents beforehand. It would also be helpful if the physician used a mirror to show the girl her hymen during the examination.

As for Mary Anne's question about her hymen bleeding after several years, this seems quite possible. The important thing is if you experience any discomfort or bleeding during intercourse, see a gynecologist to be sure that something else might not be wrong. Rarely, the small or large lips (labia) may have fused together and need to be separated if you want to have intercourse. This may have nothing to do with the hymen.

Finally, in case you were wondering what a hymen is worth, the courts in Korea ordered a hospital to pay a female patient $6,200 for tearing her hymen during a gynecological examination. This 40-year-old woman had requested $92,600. And for those of you with a bee in your bonnet, there is the *Journal of Hymenoptera Research,* as well as the International Society of Hymenopterists. This kind of Hymenoptera refers to a class of insects that we know as bees, wasps and ants, and would only relate to your genitals if you had ants in your pants.

Dear Paul,

I lost my virginity at 16, a relatively painless experience. I didn't really feel the tearing or separating that I have heard described. He just felt very large. Several years and several partners later, I noticed that something felt very different down there. Something inside was swollen. It turns out I had aggravated a "hymenal tag," or a remnant of my hymen.

This tag is just like any of the other folds of skin there, except it looks like a pointy little bit of skin where there probably should be smoothness.

My GYN said it could be snipped off with no major complications, just a bit of bleeding, but didn't recommend it if this was just one isolated incident. (No snipping for me!!) Apparently, hymen tags are fairly common, but most women never detect them because they are rather far up in there, and they don't feel any different from any of the other delicate folds.

Tagged in Tuscon

What's Inside a Girl?

Whoa... there's some things, baby, I just can't swallow
Mama told me that girls are hollow
Uh-uh... What's inside a girl?
Somethin's tellin' me there's a whole nuther world

Ya gotta pointy bra... ten-inch waist
Long black stockin's all over the place
Boots... buckles... belts outside
Watcha got in there yer tryin' a-hide?
Hmmmm?... What's inside a girl?
Ain't no hotter question in the so-called civilized world

Can't see it by satellite, baby that's cheatin'
The President's callin' an emergency meetin'
The King of Siam sent a telegram
Sayin' "Wop bop a loop a lop a lop boom bam!"
Wooeee... What's inside a girl?
Somethin's telling me there's a whole nuther world

Whatcha got... watcha got...   (chorus)
Watcha got in the pot?
Whatcha got... whatcha got...
Whatcha got in the pot?
In the bottom of your bottomless bodypit
You got somethin' and I gotta get it
Come onnn... What's inside a girl?

Like da itty-bitty baby takes apart his toys
I'm gonna find what's rilin' up the boys
Sugar and spice is just a bluff
You can tell me, baby... what is that stuff?
Come on... What's inside a girl?
That wavy gravy got my head in a whirl

Chapter Notes: While this chapter might not pay the usual homage to sex researchers of the 1950s, 1960s and 1970s, it was the work of those researchers that paved the way for books like this. Also, it is difficult to truly appreciate the prejudice and resistance that the early sex researchers faced. It is a resistance that continues to this day. ☕ Kermit Krantz' work arrived via a book titled *The Classic Clitoris*. Perhaps the sequel will be *The Postmodern Pussy*. ☕ Carol Tavris' book *The Mismeasure of Woman* was very helpful throughout this chapter. ☕ Thanks to Reay Tannahill for her *Sex in History*. ☕ Thanks to philosophy Professor Michael Russell from Cal State University at Fullerton for his work on Sartre and sex.

For a list of the latest resources on sex and Paul's weekly column *The Naked Truth*, please visit our website at
www.goofyfootpress.com

Sunsets, Orgasms & Hand Grenades
Chapter 9

"Define orgasm? It's somewhere between
a hand grenade and a sunset."

Mr. Billy Rumpanos, lifetime surfer
and early supporter of Goofy Foot Press

One of the many neat things about sharing sex is having orgasms, also known as coming. This chapter describes what an orgasm is and where it might come from. It talks about the sometimes fine line between pleasure and pain, styles of coming, faking orgasms, and how some people use orgasms for control rather than pleasure (orgasm dementia).

Perhaps it might be helpful to begin with a few comments from Dr. Frieda Tingle, the world's leading expert on sex:

Q. *Dr. Tingle, what do you think of sex in America?*

A. I think it would be a good idea.

Q. *Do you think Americans are too concerned about orgasms?*

A. Whose? Their own or their neighbor's?

Q. *In general.*

A. Orgasm is very important for many Americans because it tells them when the sexual encounter is over. Most of these people enjoy competitive sports, where some official is forever blowing a whistle or waving a little flag to let them know the event has ended. Without orgasm, they would be fumbling around, never knowing when it was time to suggest a game of Scrabble or a corned-beef sandwich.

Q. *What kinds of things affect a person's ability to have an orgasm?*

A. One important factor is diet. Many times I have been told that it is impossible to have an orgasm after eating an entire pizza. I assume this has something to do with the Italian religious taboo against sexual abandon. Another factor is the weather. Many patients have told me that if the window is open and they are being rained on, it is particularly difficult to have the orgasmic experience... (Dr. Frieda Tingle is the alter ego of Carol Tavris and Leonore Tiefer.)

Orgasm Defined

The best way to define orgasm is to put your hand in your pants and give yourself one. A more cumbersome way is to read the following definition:

🎺 Orgasms are extra-special sensations that people sometimes experience while being sexual, either alone or with a partner. They occur after a certain threshold of excitement has been crossed and can last from seconds to minutes or longer. A sense of well-being and relief often follows, perhaps because orgasms are thought to release pain inhibitors in the body. Studies have shown that people with arthritis sometimes get pain relief for three to four hours following orgasm.

🎺 Orgasms often feel as if they are being broadcast from the genitals or pelvic floor, although there is no reason why they can't originate from other parts of the body.

🎺 Some people experience orgasm as a single, tidal-wave-like surge of sensation with a couple of brief aftershocks; others experience orgasm as a series of waves, genital sneezes, or bursts of light, color, warmth and energy. Some describe orgasm as creeping up on them, slowly flooding their senses; some refer to it as a change in consciousness, and some experience it as a brief but potent explosion. People occasionally use the term "congestion" to describe the feelings in their genitals just before orgasm; this should not be confused with nasal congestion, unless it's the kind that makes you sneeze.

🎺 Some orgasms make you feel great; others can be wimpy and disappointing. Some orgasms are strictly physical; others are physical and emotional. Some reach into the body; others reach into the soul. Some are intense and obvious; others are diffuse and subtle.

🎺 The way an orgasm feels can vary with different types of sexual activity; for instance, oral sex orgasms might feel different

In our dreams!

from intercourse orgasms. Masturbation orgasms are often the most intense. One reason might be that there's very little anxiety or tension when a person masturbates, which isn't always the case when you are with a partner. Also, it's unlikely that a partner will be able to find the exact grip, pressure, movement and speed because they aren't getting the kind of instant feedback that you do when you are masturbating.

🔑 Orgasms with the same partner are likely to run the gamut from totally spectacular to downright disappointing. It depends on the particular day, and whether your worlds are colliding or are in sync.

🔑 Some people have orgasms when a lover kisses them on the back of the neck; others need a stick or two of dynamite between the legs. The amount of stimulation needed to generate an orgasm has nothing to do with how much a person enjoys sex. Orgasms which require more effort are sometimes more intense.

🎺 When shared with someone you love, orgasms and the feelings that follow often make it possible to experience a special kind of intimacy.

🎺 Some people feel pleasantly amped or energized following orgasm, while others feel mellow and might want to sleep. For some people, one orgasm begs for another or at least calls for more hugging and tenderness.

🎺 Genitals can become extremely sensitive after having an orgasm. Stimulation that may have felt wonderful moments before orgasm often feels painful or abrasive immediately after. It never hurts to ask your partner about this, since it's true for some but not all.

🎺 Some people are easily derailed on the road to orgasm. For others, the phone can ring, the earth can shake and a dam can break—they come no matter what.

🎺 An interesting and highly philosophical property of orgasm is that it may cause partners to become momentarily estranged. That's because when we are highly aroused, we enter our own private orbit, which might cause us to lose awareness of a sexual partner except as a generator of physical sensation. Many couples make up for this temporary separation by feeling extra-close right after orgasm.

🎺 It is not necessary or even desirable for partners to come at the same time. For instance, it can be wonderful to feel or watch your partner have an orgasm, which is difficult to do if you are coming simultaneously. On the other hand, it might be nice to occasionally blast off together. Just be aware that not many couples are able to pull this off.

🎺 Some people have orgasms with their legs squeezed together, while others come with their legs wide apart (innies vs. outies). People who prefer coming one way sometimes find it difficult to come with their legs the other way. Do you have a preference?

Your Partner's Orgasms

We often assume that a partner who has an orgasm is fully satisfied, while one who doesn't is somehow disappointed. This assumes that you want nothing more from sex than orgasms. For instance, most of us can give ourselves really intense orgasms when we masturbate, but not many of us can get feelings of closeness, friendship and love when we do ourselves solo. For some people, these latter feelings are the most important part of love-making. So try to be sensitive, but not too paranoid, about your partner's orgasms.

Note: If wanting orgasms were the sole reason for doing a particular sex act, not that many women would bother with intercourse. Only about thirty percent of women have orgasms from intercourse alone. Plenty of women who have orgasms during intercourse need extra clitoral stimulation in addition to thrusting, or they need the guy to ride high so his pubic bone rubs against their mons and clitoris. Lots of women prefer having an orgasm before intercourse. They say that the intercourse feels better after they've come.

Things that increase the chance of orgasm: being seriously into your partner, exercise and a healthy diet (these increase levels of hormones that enhance the sex drive), reading romance novels and seeing erotic images, and whatever else turns you on.

Things that decrease the chance of orgasm: being annoyed or angry with your partner, smoking (chemicals in tobacco constrict blood flow to the genitals and may lower the level of testosterone in both men and women), stress (notice how you tend to have more sex while on vacation), not sleeping enough, taking certain drugs (antihistamines will dry up more than just your nose, and there's a huge list of drugs that will dent your libido), and being Catholic (nearly sixty percent of Protestant women report they nearly always have an orgasm during sex, while twenty-six percent of Catholic women do). Perhaps one problem for Catholic women is the Catholic church's strident prohibition against touching yourself, which is how a lot of women learn to have orgasms.

Expressions, Decibels & the Way People Come in the Movies

People sometimes worry about how they behave when having orgasms. Some are self-conscious because they lose control, others because they don't. The answers? There are none. There is no correct way to come. Sexuality is an altered state of mind; what you do with it is strictly a matter of personal choice.

For instance, some people fear that they will look weird if they allow themselves to be overwhelmed by an orgasm. They fear that their partner will laugh or find them ugly. Quite to the contrary, it is far more likely that a partner will think something like the following:

"WOW! Her face got all twisted and contorted when she came. She looked like Whistler's mother on a really bad acid trip. She must have had a major orgasm. Maybe I'm not so bad in bed after all..."

Of course, there are plenty of people who have sensational orgasms but hardly show it at all. Their orgasms are an internal phenomenon that remains hidden from the outside world. Unfortunately, many of us assume that women are supposed to make a lot of noise when they are coming. Actually, there is little correlation between decibels and delight. Some women sound like freight trains when they come; others become rather quiet except for an occasional twitch and sigh. The same is true for men. If your partner comes in a quiet way and you would like to know more about it, why not ask?

Keep in mind that many of us learned to come quietly at a very young age. That's because there might not have been much privacy where we masturbated; letting out a large bellow would have informed the entire household. This was particularly true if you shared a room with siblings, and even worse if you had the top mattress in a bunk bed. The same difficulties are faced by people living in dorms, sororities, fraternities and military barracks, where roommates often sleep only a few feet away. In these situations, we pretend to be asleep when masturbating

—a funny notion when you consider that our roommates are probably doing the same thing.

The great sex-noise dilemma is also faced by moms and dads while making love (or trying to) when there's a household full of kids.

Is It Possible to Have Too Many Orgasms?

Some of the various Tantric types nearly hemorrhage at the notion of a man ejaculating more than once or twice every ten years. They think that the male body is seriously depleted when it ejaculates. As a result, they hoard the white sticky stuff like generals do weapons-grade plutonium. Some even teach themselves to have dry orgasms.

Is there much reality to this seed-spilling fear? It has been written that the Nazis pondered this same question. To test it out they forced a prisoner of war to masturbate every three hours, day and night, for the duration of World War II. Thanks to the Allied invasion, the prisoner finally got to stop jerking off. He apparently went on to father several children and lived to a ripe old age, certainly as old as most seed-retaining monks if they didn't fib about being 128 when they are really only fifty-five. As for other living examples, one male friend of the Goofy Foot Press is now in his early seventies, but his mind is incredibly sharp and he doesn't look a day over fifty. He currently has at least five ejaculations per week, down from the ten or so he has been having since he was a teenager. According to semen-retention theories, he should either be dead or a zombie. On the other hand, Doug Abrams, one of the healthier-looking guys on the planet, has co-authored a book that presents the Tantric position of coming without squirting. Doug clearly practices what he preaches, and it is our hope that his prostate doesn't suddenly explode one day.

Regarding women and orgasm: nobody in his or her right mind has ever worried about a woman having too many orgasms, except for the people who live next door or in the apartment below.

Where Does Coming Come From?

The following quote is from a woman who had a spontaneous orgasm while riding public transit — a rather scary thought if you have ever taken the bus in places like Los Angeles or Detroit:

> I've perfected this wonderful ability to orgasm without touching myself. It started one day on the BART train when I was ovulating, and I felt myself throbbing. I started running a fantasy in my mind and discovered I could bring myself to orgasm. The only trouble with a public place is you have to control your breathing.... (Words of a former high school homecoming queen who grew up in the Midwest, as found in Julia Hutton's helpful book *Good Sex* [San Francisco: Cleis Press, 1992].)

Sex therapist Herbert Otto writes about the time in college when he and his friends were talking about different ways of masturbating. One fellow said that he could ejaculate without touching his penis. Naturally, bets were made. The room became quiet and he pulled his penis out of his pants. After his eyes were closed for a while, his penis became erect. Eventually, he began breathing faster, and suddenly he had an ejaculation. This college student later became a well-known physicist.

Not only is it possible for some people to have an orgasm without genital stimulation, but it can even happen spontaneously without sexual thoughts. For instance, some women have spontaneous orgasms during highly charged debates or intellectual discussions that have nothing to do with sex. One female reader had her first orgasm as a teenager while her hair was being brushed, and as a forty-year-old she still has orgasms when her hair is brushed.

While not many of us are able to have orgasms without genital stimulation, the existence of hands-free orgasms does suggest that there is more to orgasm than genital contact. For instance, there are plenty of people who have suffered nerve injuries and can no longer feel sensation in their genitals, yet they learn to have orgasm feelings in other parts of their bodies, such as their faces, arms, necks, lips, chests and backs. They often find that these feelings are as satisfying as their former genital orgasms. This indicates that the power to experience an orgasm resides somewhere in the senses and not simply in the groin. (One woman whose clitoris and vagina were removed due to cancer surgery was able to experience the same kind of intense multiple orgasms after the surgery as before.)

People who have lost one of their senses do not suddenly grow new ones to compensate. Rather, they are forced to better use the senses that remain. This suggests that many of us could achieve greater sexual pleasure from other parts of our bodies if we learned to allow it. One way of doing this is mentioned later in this guide, where the woman stimulates her partner's penis with one hand while using her other hand or lips to caress another part of his body not normally associated with sexual feelings.

Orgasm Chapter Letdown

One of the failings of this book is that it doesn't define "orgasm" more broadly. For instance, in talking about a guy's orgasm, we assume that it's the kind that happens when his penis gets squeezed, stroked or sucked. But what if he's capable of having an intense full-body orgasm when his partner kisses his neck or sucks on his earlobes for an extended amount of time? In assuming that an orgasm needs to squirt out of our genitals, we keep ourselves from exploring other possibilities.

Unfortunately, to include the full range of possibilities would add another two hundred pages to this book, and if that doesn't make you cry out in horror, nothing will.

Pain Next to Pleasure

Receptors for pain and pleasure are located next to each other throughout our bodies. These receptors often fire at the same time. It is our brain's job to decide whether an experience feels good or bad. Some of the criteria that our brains use in making these decisions are hard-wired, like whether we are naturally ticklish or if we were born with lots of nerve receptors in a certain spot. Other criteria that our brains use are software driven, based on our collective life experiences. As a result, each of our brains makes its own unique decision about what is pleasurable and what is painful.

For instance, while one person might enjoy masturbating to the fantasy of seeing Johnny or Amber naked, the mere hint of Johnny or Amber's presence might make another person feel sick to their stomach. Or one person might find spanking to be painful and a turn-off, while another might find spanking to be painful and erotic. The stimulus is the same, but how we feel about it depends on how our brain interprets it.

The way we interpret pain is also impacted by our level of sexual arousal. For instance, people who enjoy an occasional slap on the rear during sex usually don't like the pain unless it's done when they are sexually aroused. Being aroused causes the brain to throw routine caution to the wind, converting feelings that are otherwise painful into feelings of pleasure.

One by Land, Two by Sea

As was mentioned on page 97, there seem to be at least two different neural pathways that transmit signals from the groin to the brain. Researchers John Perry and Beverly Whipple suggest that G-spot stimulation might be conveyed to the brain through one set of nerves, and clitoral stimulation through another. Perhaps the same is true in males for penis stimulation vs. prostate stimulation. This could explain why one type of orgasm might feel more intense in the area of the clitoris or penis, while another is not as well-defined but resonates deeper in the body.

Possible Assist for Women's & Men's Orgasms

When women are about to come they often pull in or tighten their pelvic muscles. Yet doing just the opposite, pushing out, might make their orgasms more intense. Some women will hesitate to do this from fear that it might cause them to pass gas, but what the heck, you'll both live if she does. And if you consider the gas-passing habits of men and women over the lifetime of the average relationship, chances are she owes him a few.

Whether you are male or female, you might occasionally experiment with relaxing the muscle tone in your pelvis when you come. For instance, some men find that they can prolong the feelings of orgasm if they relax their crotch and anus as orgasm is about to come. Other men find this to be uncomfortable.

What Was It Like?

Lovers sometimes ask each other if they came, but not what coming feels like. Granted, sexual experiences are hard to put into words, since they often exist on the cusp between physical and emotional sensation. But asking a partner to describe what it feels like when he or she comes might lead to some interesting insights and discussions.

Guys Faking Orgasm?

Back in the winter of '96, when the first edition of the *Guide* was published, the section on faking orgasms assumed that it was women who did the faking. Not anymore. It seems that up to 30 percent of young adult males are faking orgasms at one time or another. These are males in the middle of their so-called sexual prime.

Researcher Karen Yescavage found that guys fake orgasm for reasons like: "I was tired," "I faked it so she wouldn't see me go limp," "So she would think she was doing a good job," or "I wanted to get it over with." The reasons women gave for faking tended to fall into the "I was tired, bored, or it was hurting" category.

The good news is that even the people who admitted to faking orgasms didn't fake them very often. Also, a number of people who had faked felt that their faking had helped increase the intimacy in sex, and that the intimacy was more important than whether they really came or not. Other people feel that lying to a partner is wrong no matter what the justification. They can't see how you can lie and feel more intimate at the same time.

Interestingly, lesbians faked orgasms as often as straight white women, and straight white women faked orgasms twice as often as Hispanic women. Since the Hispanic women weren't having orgasms at a higher rate than the white women, it is possible that white males may expect their partners to have orgasms more than Hispanic males do, and so the white females felt more compelled to fake orgasms.

If Your Partner Fakes Orgasms

One of the worst things you can do when a partner fakes an orgasm is to try to help him or her to have one. This usually makes matters worse.

There is sometimes a fine line between helpful concern and obnoxious fretting, especially if the reason why you need your partner to have an orgasm is for your own reassurance that you are a good lover.

Rather than trying to help your partner have an orgasm, why not try to discover the things that give him or her physical comfort? Contrary to what you think, this might simply be holding each other for an extended time or not grabbing for your lover's crotch the minute you feel horny. If your partner has suggestions about technique, all the better, but this might not be where the problem lies.

While it is almost always a good thing to want to give your partner sexual pleasure, it can be counterproductive to assume that in a relationship, pleasure and orgasm are the same.

Far more relationships crumble from a lack of emotional pleasure than from a lack of orgasms. As long as you are able to give each other the former, there are plenty of ways to achieve the latter. This book lists several hundred.

Orgasm Dementia

Sometimes it's fun to count orgasms and go for it like pigs to mud. But for some people, orgasm production and/or procurement has a suspicious edge. Here are a few reasons why:

🦗 Some people get a sense of smug superiority by claiming how many orgasms they either had or "gave" a partner. They confuse sex with pinball.

🦗 Some people use pleasure-giving as a way of controlling a partner. They might hardly come at all while making sure that a partner comes several times. While this might not sound like such a bad problem to have, keep in mind that partners who won't surrender the reins sexually are sometimes very controlling in other aspects of life as well.

🦑 There are people who expect their partners to supply them with numerous orgasms. This can breed resentment over time.

🦑 Some people need to have sex or masturbate several times a day to help numb a chronic state of anxiety or ease feelings of deadness. Having a constant stream of orgasms can be their way of keeping an emotional funk at arm's length. Do not confuse this with sexual pleasure, even if they do.

Reinventing the Sexual Wheel—Marketing & Orgasm

In order to sell books and tapes on sex, publishers want us to feel sexually inept if we don't buy whatever kind of sexual experience they are currently hocking. For instance, during the last couple of years we were supposed to buy books and tapes on G-spot orgasms, female ejaculation, extended orgasms, one-hour orgasms, Tantric sex orgasms, extraordinary orgasms for boring people, and now, orgasms through herbal enhancement. It's only a matter of time before publishers start to sell *Better Orgasms for Your Dog and Cat,* and try to make you feel like a pet sadist if you don't plunk down $29.95 for the videotape.

Many of us would enjoy having bigger and better orgasms if we could. But sometimes the consumer simply has to say "enough is enough." On the other hand, sex can be a fun topic to learn more about. Since we are the physicians of our own sexuality, it wouldn't hurt to at least stay current.

Readers' Comments

For Men: What does an orgasm feel like?

"My knees get weak and I tingle everywhere. It feels like I am numb all over." *male age 21*

"Like an energy emanating in the soles of my feet, up the back of my legs, in and through my rear end, to my belly button, and out through my balls and penis. Awesome, warm, exhausting." *male age 26*

"When I'm getting close, it feels like every ounce of fluid in my body has been forced into my penis. My whole body is in anticipation of the moment when my penis can no longer take the incredible pressure and bursts. Flames envelope the entire thing and the shock reverberates throughout my entire body." *male age 25*

"Orgasm makes me feel very connected to my lover, like I'm becoming a part of her." *male age 39*

"It feels like all your vital matter collects in your penis and then shoots out of you!" *male age 22*

For women: What does an orgasm feel like?

"Every orgasm I have is different! Sometimes I feel like I'm just melting, floating away. Sometimes I feel like I'm running or pushing into the orgasm. Sometimes an orgasm will sneak up on me; other times I will be able to control its arrival and duration." *female age 45*

"All my orgasms seem to be the same beast, but with varying levels of intensity from 'Gosh, was that it?' to an ache so sharp it's almost hard to bear. My most intense orgasms tend to come from using a vibrator but, oddly enough, they're not always the most satisfying." *female age 36*

"Orgasms range for me from a simple response in my genitals, without much sensation and even some numbness, to a mind-blowing, explosive force of nature that permeates my whole body, mind and emotions, encircles my partner and fills the room around us. Sometimes it's the physical sensations that are the most intense part of orgasm; other times it's the emotional quality and being with my partner that take top billing. Even when the physical sensation isn't very intense, I generally feel much more whole and integrated after an orgasm." *age 47*

Your first orgasm...

"With a vibrator at age thirty-eight. Finally!!!" *female age 49*

"It didn't happen until seven months after my first sexual experience. I had no idea what was happening. We were through having sex. When I began to put my clothes back on, I started to tingle and fluids started flowing out. It felt great, but I was actually kind of scared and embarrassed."
female age 21

"I had an electric shaver that had an attachment which was a massager. After about an hour of moving it around on my clit (and praying that the pillow between my legs was muffling the sounds so my parents didn't hear) I had an orgasm. I'd already had sex many times with my boyfriend, but I felt like I was really sinning now!"
female age 25

"I didn't really know what I was doing. I was about ten or eleven and discovered this new feeling when I rubbed this silky part of my blanket over my penis, so I kept doing it. Eventually I got this intense feeling in my groin and then there was this goop everywhere. I was completely freaked and grossed out. I thought that I broke myself, but was too afraid to tell my parents." *male age 24*

"My first orgasm took place at age eighteen, when my fiance introduced me, despite my initial reaction of revulsion and disbelief, to the delights of cunnilingus. I thought he was depraved. I was sure I was going straight to hell. I couldn't wait for it to happen again!" *female age 55*

"I had my first orgasm during one of my first menstrual periods. The feeling of a clean pad against my genitals made me feel a warmth I had never experienced before. I rubbed against it to see if I could prolong the sensation, although I had no idea what the sensation was. I just knew it felt good!" *female age 45*

"I didn't know what was going on. My body felt like it was convulsing. I tried not to let the guy know this was happening. I didn't know at the time I was supposed to let myself go and enjoy it." *female age 26*

"The first one I had was clitoral—it tickled (I was probably ten). The second type of orgasm I had was when I was twenty. I felt it more in my vagina. It was overwhelmingly emotional and I came in a flood, and I do mean flood. I thought I had peed all over my partner. Now I have both kinds of orgasms. I get to pick, let's see, lobster or steak?" *female age 26*

"My first orgasm was when I was making out in the back seat of a car. I was on top of my boyfriend and there was a lot of bumping and grinding going on and I just climaxed, with my clothes on." *female age 49*

"I was surprised by how sensitive my clit was, but I wasn't sure the actual orgasm was an orgasm because it didn't seem nearly as explosive as what happened in the bodice-rippers I'd been reading. I couldn't believe I'd gone through all this work for that. Happily, many years of practice improved the results!" *female age 36*

"Age twenty. One morning before arising I was idly rubbing my clit and fantasizing, and from out of nowhere excitement began building more intensely than it ever had before. I rubbed myself quite vigorously and for a very long time, until suddenly there was a mind-blowing explosion. I was certain that everyone in the house figured out what I was doing. I was very embarrassed. However, I repeated the experience every night—it took over an hour of heavy-duty stimulation at first." *female age 51*

"My first orgasm was by a male friend (not a lover). I told him that sex was not that great. He used his fingers to teach me what it could feel like. I remember thinking 'Oh God, this is an orgasm!' " *female age 48*

Dear Paul,

I would like to know some techniques on how to make a girl have an orgasm. My girlfriend is like a brick and doesn't tell me nothing. What should I do?

Evan in Illinois

Dear Evan the Bricklayer:

I'm sitting here scratching my head, thinking back over the women I've dated, and I can't remember a single one who I could "make" do anything, let alone have an orgasm.

One of the worst things that ever happened to sex was the idea that we needed to give a partner an orgasm. It would have been much better if we had simply set our sights on trying to please him or her in other ways. Lord knows, that would have been challenging enough.

Wanting to give a partner an orgasm seems harmless enough on the surface. It's only when she doesn't cooperate that we start to get frustrated and our good intentions turn into something like "You'd better have this orgasm or it's going to make me feel like I didn't please you." Nasty, nasty, nasty. Likewise, guys who boast, "I never come before my partner does!" don't realize the subtle pressure they are putting on him or her to hurry up and come!

Another problem with the concept of giving a girl an orgasm has to do with ownership. If you are the one who is giving the orgasm, then it's not really her orgasm to have until after you have given it to her. So whose orgasm is it anyway? Hers or yours?

And finally, what if you feel the need to give her an orgasm, but she would rather you stroked her hair or gave her a long, involved foot rub? You know what happens. You'll do a half-assed job of stroking her hair or rubbing her feet because your dick won't stay hard forever or she might fall asleep from the sheer bliss of having her feet rubbed and you'll end up having to jerk off like some poor guy without a girlfriend. Get used to it, Evan.

You asked and here's what I suggest:

1. Stop trying to give her an orgasm.

2. Start trying to discover things that give her physical pleasure. For instance, does she enjoy it if you give her a foot or hand massage? Does she like it if you gently run your fingertips up and down her arms or legs? What about her hair? How about gently massaging her forehead and face, or planting tender kisses on her shoulders and back? When you are in the shower together, do you lather each other up and hug and kiss while your bodies are soapy and slick?

3. Do you relate to her physically without trying to get each other off? For some strange reason, a woman likes to know that a man can have a hard-on without always needing to plug up one of her body cavities with it. Maybe she needs to know that the two of you can hug and share moments of tenderness without it automatically leading to sex. Otherwise, she might start to tense up each time you are close or get wood.

4. If you are living together, it also helps to do your share of the vacuuming and dishes. There's no way she's going to let her body relax in a sexual way if she's holding onto anger at you for freeloading—although, as far as housework goes, the biggest slobs I've ever had for roommates were females, so I don't mean to perpetuate any myths in that area. Just keep in mind that guys who do their fair share of the housework get laid more often than those who don't.

Evan, you wrote to me about orgasms, and I'm responding with suggestions about foot rubs, romance and housework. Actually, I'm trying to broaden your thinking about orgasms, which is much greater than simply knowing what part of a partner's anatomy to rub or suck.

Dear Paul,

My current girlfriend doesn't like me to play with her breasts, and the only way she can have an orgasm is when I give her oral sex. My former girlfriend didn't like me to give her oral sex, but sometimes had an orgasm from breast stimulation alone. Both women enjoy sex, but seem so different. How come?

Confused in Kalamazoo

Dear Confused,

For some people, you play with their breasts and BOOM! their genitals are on fire. For other lovers, you are better off reading them their constitutional rights than tweaking their titties.

As for why the different responses, I'd like to share with you an idea that is being proposed by Herbert Otto, author of *Liberated Orgasm*. He feels that the kind of orgasms we experience are in part determined by what our culture teaches us to expect.

For instance, in the 1950s, a lot of teenagers enjoyed extended kissing and petting sessions, but intercourse before marriage was seriously frowned upon. So a woman who was a teenager in the 1950s might have learned to have orgasms from necking and nipple-play sessions in the front seat of a car—without a single touch or lick below the belt. This same woman's unmarried granddaughter pays no social price for messing around with her pants off. She has read *Cosmo* since she was twelve and feels that nothing short of a partner's mouth welded to her clitoris is going to give her an orgasm. And so her body responds differently than her grandmother's. Of course, this doesn't explain why your former girlfriend doesn't like oral sex, unless she's your current girlfriend's grandmother.

As for our current belief that the clitoris is the generator of all female orgasms, consider recent findings from the Sudan, where female circumcision is done to young girls to prevent them from masturbating or getting horny. In the Sudan, the clitoris, inner lips and part of the outer lips of the girl's genitals are removed.

What's left is then sewn together. You would think that if any woman on the face of the earth would not have an orgasm, it would be a woman who had experienced this kind of clitoridectomy. Yet in a study of more than 300 Sudanese women who had been circumcised, at least half reported having orgasms and sexual pleasure. It's clear these orgasms aren't being generated by some guy kissing their clitoris. (Oh please, if any of you honestly think I'm condoning female circumcision, use the energy to write someone else a nasty letter.)

There are dozens of other reasons why one partner might prefer attention above the waist while another prefers it below. I've focused on those above because they are important, but less obvious.

Now, did you ever wonder if your girlfriend has written in asking why YOU liked something one way and her former boyfriend liked it another way? Keep reading.

Sex Fluids
Chapter 10

I n order to enjoy sex, you need to feel okay about getting wet and slobbery. That's because no matter how you sort it out, sex is a wet adventure, an erotic monsoon of sorts. Various body fluids get sloshed around during sexual encounters. Some of these fluids, like ejaculate, arrive abruptly, while others, like saliva, sweat and lubrication, are more constant in flow. Also, menstrual fluids can double as sex fluids, but there's an entire chapter on lovemaking during periods later in this book.

Fluid Understanding

Sex fluids mean different things to different people. For instance, one woman might find it wonderful when her lover ejaculates. It leaves her feeling valued and powerful being the one who makes his fluids flow. Another woman might find her boyfriend's ejaculate to be a sticky mess that she would rather not have to deal with.

Men usually welcome women's sexual wetness, although there are exceptions. For instance, the author of this book can remember a conversation from his freshman year of high school with a fellow member of the track team who had just felt up a woman for the first time. The young man described "it" as being wet, sticky and yuckie, and indicated that "her thing" accommodated nearly half his arm. Considering this was a farm town, it seems likely that the woman in question may have been a cow.

Some young men who ejaculate for the first couple of times worry they might have broken something inside. Proper education about masturbation can help alleviate most of these fears. Single moms who want to explain ejaculation to their sons might find it helpful to know that prior to puberty, male ejaculate is clear and there is not much of it, perhaps a drop or two. After puberty it becomes white and there is more, about a teaspoonful. Whatever his age, it might be nice if a young man were taught to respect his own ejaculate as the catalyst for new life as well as a sign of his sexual maturity and pleasure—all three being good things that should bring pride as well as new levels of responsibility.

As for women's feelings about their own sexual wetness, most seem to enjoy it. However, young women who don't understand their body's sexual response may feel uncomfortable if they suddenly find themselves getting wet while having sensual thoughts.

Other Sex Fluids

Two other body fluids that switch-hit as sex fluids are saliva and sweat. These flow in steady and sometimes subtle ways, unless propelled by a sneeze or when making love when it's hot or humid and you are sweating like swine. Another body fluid that some people think of as a sex fluid is urine. People who view urine as a sex fluid are said to be into kink. (See "Golden Showers" in the glossary.)

Urine Note #1 Believe it or not, urine from most physically healthy humans is more sterile than saliva. In fact, urine is considered to be a mild antiseptic, although you might not want to replace the bottle of Bactine with it.

Urine Note #2: Some people, more than you might think, have trouble peeing in a public restroom. For instance, some men aren't able to use a urinal if other men are either going next to them or waiting in line. While some of these men are able to go in a closed stall, others can't even go then. The same is true for some women. This can be a source of great frustration. It can also make you feel socially inept, as well as isolated if your pee-shyness keeps you from attending certain daylong events. At the very least, you avoid having Cokes or beers while at football or baseball games; at worst, holding it all day can result in kidney damage. Whatever the underlying cause(s), most people with this problem would welcome even a 50 percent improvement. Unfortunately, there is no single therapy that has a consistently high batting average in curing the chronic pee-shy. Some people might find a lessening of symptoms with desensitization therapy or hypnotherapy; others might find help with psychodynamic therapy. Others continue to struggle with the problem no matter what they try, and for some, the situation improves with age, especially when the bladder can no longer hold fluids with the tenacity that it did in its younger years. (It would be interesting if any medications helped. If we hear of any, we will post it at www.goofyfootpress.com. Enter "pee-shy" in the Goofy search engine.)

Store-Bought Sex Lubes

There may be times when nature's own sex fluids aren't quite enough and you need a store bought assist (better sex through chemistry). Here are some of the basics.

Hand Creams (avoid) Most hand creams and moisturizers are designed to be absorbed by the skin so people won't feel like greased pigs after they use them. This means that the macro-molecules that make up moisturizers are designed to go flat fast. As a result, most hand moisturizers aren't adequate for sex or massage.

Jerking Off Whether it's for giving a super hand job or just jerking off, you'll want a super-slick potion that will leave a man's woody wet and slippery for as long as possible. If you want to spend a lot of money on fancy creams or lotions, go ahead. You might try one of the new water-based lubes with silicone. Otherwise, use an oil-based lubricant. On this score, the possibilities abound; from canola, corn and coconut oils to vegetable oil, mineral oil, almond oil, baby oil, various massage oils, and heaven only knows what. A popular and nearly legendary jerk-off lubricant is a facial cleanser called Albolene. A newer substance that is getting high ratings is called Men's Cream. It gets an A for the name alone. **Orifice Advisory:** Oil-based lubes shouldn't be used with latex condoms or in a vagina.

Women's Genitals Massaging the outside of a woman's genitals with oil-based lubricants is usually fine, but not so for the inside. Consider keeping a water-based lubricant handy for anything that goes inside a vagina—from fingers and dildos to penises and anything that's wearing a condom. Most water-based lubricants mix nicely with a woman's own natural lubrication, and a few drops of water or saliva can be added if they start to dry out. **Orifice Advisory:** Never use Vaseline (petroleum jelly) inside a vagina, as it blocks the ability of the vagina to cleanse itself and may result in infections. Scented lotions should be avoided because they can cause irritation, and some women get infections from water-based lubes that contain glycerin. Lubes that contain nonoxynol-9 may cause discomfort to some women.

Water-Based Lubes These are the latex paint of the lube world. They supposedly wash up with water, and don't have any pore-clogging oil in them. They don't harm latex condoms. KY is the grandmother of water-based lubes. It seldom rates highly among the boutique sextoy shops, but maybe that's because it's the one lube you can buy at your local grocery store and it's a lot cheaper than the others. Also, unlike most other lubes, it is made by one of the biggest pharmaceutical houses and is FDA inspected. **Orifice Advisory:** A few years ago, researcher Bruce Voeller analyzed a number of lubes and found chemicals that were not listed on their ingredient labels, e.g. mercury. Bruce recommended that people only buy lubes that were used for medical procedures or contraceptive jellies because they had to be produced under the highest FDA standards. Otherwise, you don't know what you are getting, as there is no government supervision and no set standards for companies that make sex lubes. Also, some lubes and moisturizers say they are water-soluble. These usually have oil in them and should never be used with latex condoms or in the vagina.

Silicone Lubes The "newest" kind of sex lube has silicone in it. You might say, "I've heard that silicone is unsafe in boob implants. Why would I want to stick it in private places?"

Chances are, if you've ever been on the receiving end of a penis that's wearing a prelubricated condom, you've had silicone inside of you. That's because the lube on prelubricated condoms contains silicone. As for the safety of silicone, silicone molecules are supposedly too large to be absorbed into the body. The problem with leaky boob implants is that the silicone gets trapped inside your chest. That won't happen with any body cavity that you can stick an object into.

Most silicone lubes are water-based, which means you can use them with latex condoms. The silicone keeps the lube from drying out, which is a problem with other water-based lubes. Although most silicone lubes are water-based, they won't dissolve nearly as quickly in water as other water-based lubes. Another advantage of using silicone is if you are having sex in the bathtub or hot tub. The water in tubs washes away the body's natural lubrication, making intercourse difficult. The silicone-based lube will help keep your piston pumping longer. Slop some on your genitals while they are still dry, and intercourse in water may be more enjoyable.

A possible problem with silicone lubes is their effect on silicone sex toys. The silicone in the lube gradually dissolves the silicone in the sex toy. If you are using a silicone lube, put a condom on your silicone sex toys first. Also, if you are into electric sex, the serious kind with probes and electrodes, do not use silicone-based lubes. The silicone acts as an insulator.

Lubes & Licks Most commercial lubes taste awful. There are exceptions. For instance, the folks at Blowfish (www.blowfish.com) highly recommend the For Play Succulents flavored lubes. They are said to taste good when mixed with vaginal juices. They come in a number of flavors including champagne cocktail, chocolate truffle, cinnamon toddy, egg nog, juicy fruit, lemon drops, navel orange, passionate pumpkin, peachy peach, pink grapefruit, watermelon and whipping cream.

Anal Intercourse You need a thick, goopy lube for anal play. Oil-based lubes are the standard, but you'll need to use them with polyurethane condoms and not latex condoms. You might also experiment with some of the new silicone-based lubes. They seem to share many of the good qualities of water-based lubes and oil-based lubes without many of the drawbacks.

Anal Fisting In a word: Crisco. Use nitrile gloves.

Vaginal Fisting Keep it water-based, but as thick as possible. Some people recommend Probe.

Dear Paul,

When I have an erection, it starts dripping like I've come before I actually come. Is something wrong with my penis?

Marty from Manitoba

Dear Marty,

Sounds like precum. Unlike your regular ejaculate, it's clear and sort of drips out gradually instead of shooting across your chest. It makes the head of your penis slippery and more disposed to slide kindly into the waiting vagina of the love of your life. It also helps make the urethra less acidic so your ejaculate is more likely to get her pregnant! You can tell precum from urine by touching it with your fingertip and then pulling your finger away. Precum will stay connected to your finger, making a cool-looking spindle or bridge, a little like bubble gum when you pull part of it out of your mouth. It can be there in the morning, before or after you pee, and can be a touch annoying if it starts flowing when you get an unwanted erection in the middle of a class or business meeting. Any other fluids of unknown origin that drip out of your penis, especially if they are a bit green or puslike, should be checked out by your healthcare provider.

The How-To Part
Chapter 11

There's one way that dogs do it, one way that sheep do it, and one way that each kind of bug does it. This is also true for elephants, lemurs and wildebeests. Unicorns need to be extra-careful when it comes to oral sex, and the female praying mantis eats her male sex partners—to death. So does the black widow.

The animal with the greatest potential for a varied sex life seems to be the human. Human brains are a bit beefier, which means that our minds and emotions, rather than our hormones, guide us in our sexual choices. We are also the only animals who do our sex indoors and in private, which makes getting it on somewhat of a mystery, in this culture anyway.

The upcoming chapters attempt to shed light on the mystery of sex. They describe various tips and techniques for giving your partner monster amounts of pleasure. Hopefully you will find these techniques useful. But first, it might be a good idea to mention a few things about give and take, shame and the *Guide's* policy on when to call it quits.

Give and Take

Author Julia Hutton interviewed eighty people about sex to find out how each person defined Good Sex. Needless to say, she got eighty different answers. According to Ms. Hutton, "The interviews suggest that sexual savvy depends less upon how-tos than on self-knowledge, which evolves slowly, awkwardly and through many different routes."

Please keep Julia Hutton's words in mind as you read the how-to part of this book. Also, people usually assume that if both partners are sexually amped, then all they need to do is get naked and good sex will follow. Would it were that easy... Even when the sex is great, it often takes time to feel comfortable with a partner. For example, consider the following quote from a 29-year-old kindergarten teacher whose comments appear in Julia Hutton's excellent book *Good Sex* (San Francisco: Cleis Press, 1992); Chris is her husband:

> With Chris, I like having him in me, that warm good feeling. I've discovered I can ask for what I like, that there's nothing wrong with wanting your nipples pulled taut. I've learned that keeping a vibrator by the bed is not a crime. I've learned that Chris can come, and then I can come, and we can both enjoy watching each other come—as opposed to having this simultaneous orgasm that's supposed to move the world. If we have intercourse that's fine, if we don't that's fine. Sometimes we come home weary from work and it's: what do you want? Do you want to masturbate? Do you think you can focus enough for intercourse? It's negotiation, which I never thought it would be. I always thought it would be this mystic experience, but it's become a verbal experience.

Again, while some couples have good sex from the start, other couples take months and sometimes years to find a satisfying groove. In addition, most couples report that their sexual desire for each other waxes and wanes, although sometimes it just wanes.

Shame between the Sheets

Because Ford never learned to say his original name, his father eventually died of shame, which is still a terminal disease in some parts of the Galaxy.

From Douglas Adams's *A Hitchhiker's Guide to the Galaxy*

Entire civilizations have been built upon the notion of guilt and shame. However, since modern psychology has become a new form of religion, the old standbys of guilt and shame have gotten a bum rap. No one is supposed to feel guilt or shame anymore, and everybody is supposed to have good self-esteem, whatever that might mean. Yet there is plenty in this world to feel guilt and shame about.

Still, some of us might do better in bed if we felt a little less guilt and shame about what turns us on sexually, assuming it does no harm to others. This is especially true for people who are too bashful to tell a partner what does and doesn't feel good.

When It's Okay to Go for It

Since this book is being used in educational settings, we thought it important to include a few words about relationship hygiene, or when it's okay to go for it and when it's not.

The Guide's Policy on When to Call It Quits

a. If a potential partner doesn't want sex every bit as much as you do, go home and masturbate. At least you will still have your self-respect. If the relationship is worth it, phone the next day and talk it over.

b. If you need to convince someone to have sex with you, then it's the wrong person, time or place. If someone needs to convince you to have sex with them, then it's the wrong person, time or place.

If you don't have that much self-control or the ability to know when another person doesn't want to have sex with you, nothing this book says is going to help. Still, here are a few answers to questions from inquiring minds: *To Mindy at the College of the Sequoias:* You say that you want him in the worst way and you can feel him getting hard, but it's no enchilada when you reach down and rub his crotch. He pushes your hand away. Just because a guy is hard doesn't mean that he automatically wants to have sex with you. Believe it or not, there are rare but important times when a man actually pleads with his penis to stay soft, but the thing goes BOING just to spite him. Mindy, there are reasons why we refer to genitals as "private parts." Maybe he has his reasons for not wanting your hands all over his. Did you ask? I'll bet you a milkshake and chili fries at Mearle's that you're moving way too fast. *To Mark at the University of Georgia:* Dude, when it comes to sex, we've all been misled (or led on) at one time or another. Some of us have even misled others. The fact is, we live in a society that is so weird about sex that it's not unusual for a person to appear incredibly seductive, but become confused or angry if you actually go for it. You end up feeling like some sort of pervert, when from all appearances it seemed like she wanted sex as much as you. In the future, why not make sure that it's your date who makes the first move—she kisses you first, she takes off your shirt before you reach under hers, and she unbuttons or unzips your pants before you touch hers. And while we wouldn't want to cramp your style, have you talked with her about the subject of sex when you both have your clothes on? *To LouAnne at Texas Women's University:* You say that you and he had been "slamming down Kamikazes in his bedroom and he was wearing blue jeans three sizes too small in all the right places and had on one of those little half-length T-shirts that was exposing each and every one of his washboard abs..." LouAnne, it wouldn't matter if he were buck naked and had a red tassel on the end of his penis, when he said "No more" you should have respected his wishes. None of us has a right to ignore another person's protests, no matter how hot, horny, hard, wet, willing, stoned, drunk, or sexually amped we might be. And even if a person has their tongue halfway down your throat for the better part of an hour, if they suddenly pull it out and wag it in a way that says "Stop," then you'd better be ready to stop. The same is true even if the two of you have been married for ten or twenty years.

The Zen of Finger Fucking
Chapter 12

❝ Rubbing lightly is what I do when I masturbate, so I like it even more when my boyfriend does it. I love it when he runs his fingers along my inner lips, up and down. I also love my genitals to be rubbed and tickled when I wear jeans or corduroy. I can come from that kind of stimulation."

female age 23

Some men, especially younger ones, take the term "finger fucking" quite literally. They think that a woman's idea of a good time is having a man cram his fingers up her vagina. Other men attack a woman's clitoris as if it were a hydraulic pump, believing that the more they rub it the closer she gets to the big "O." (The only "O" she sometimes experiences is "OUCH!" rather than orgasm.)

The truth is, finger fucking is not something a man does *to* a woman, but something he does *with* a woman. It's all of him: his smile, kiss, laughter, strength and tenderness focused in the ends of his fingers.

What follows is a great deal of information about pleasing a woman with your fingertips. Hopefully you will find some of this to be helpful, especially if you are able to leave your bulldozer behind and are willing to feel things with your fingers that maybe you've never felt before.

A Note on Terms of Art

In the pages that follow, this guide occasionally does minor violence to the English language by using words such as "masturbate" incorrectly. For instance, while masturbation is something you do with yourself, expressions such as "masturbating a partner" or "masturbating yourself" are sometimes used. This helps certain sentences to be more easily understood, although "masturbating a partner" is a contradiction in terms, and "masturbating yourself" is as redundant as saying white cow's milk.

Coaching, Patience & Practice

I had to learn how to touch her clit.... I can remember being clumsy about it early on. She'd have to stop me—I was going too fast, going too hard. I can remember her saying, 'You're in the wrong place.' Well, show me where. I mean physically, show me.... Rub so I can see it. Okay, now I understand. Over time, I've learned where the places are. I can find them in the dark now. But early on I couldn't. I'd say, 'Okay, show me. Are you sure?' Other times she would take my hand, or my finger, and she would put it right exactly where it was supposed to be, and she'd move it the way she wanted me to move it, and she would apply pressure to the back of my fingers, the amount of pressure she wanted, until I got the hang of it, and then she would take her hand away. If I got out of sync or something, she'd put her hand back and show me until I got it right. A few weeks later I might need some re-education, so she'd show me again. [From Harry Maurer's *Sex: An Oral History* (New York: Viking, 1994)]

A truly civilized way of learning how to get a woman off by hand is to make an agreement with her that she will provide lots of coaching and patience and you will provide an eager willingness to learn.

That's because hands that are used to throwing a baseball, holding a shovel or torquing down engine bolts tend to get a little frustrated when it comes to finessing a woman's genitals; and that's only part of it. There's the additional matter of knowing when to speed up, slow down, push harder or stay your course. For instance, some women might prefer that guys stimulate them with a constant speed and rhythm as they are approaching orgasm. This might not make sense to a man, since when we masturbate we sometimes speed up as we get close to coming. Other women cherish variety. They will want your fingers to go slow, fast, soft, hard, and have more speeds than a Kenworth big rig, or a Ferrari if you grew up on the rich side of town.

Differences in Attitude

"I've seen a couple of guys masturbate. I can't believe how rough they are with themselves!"   *female age 26*

Take this woman's comment to heart. The reason she can't believe how "rough" we guys are with ourselves is because she would never dream of finessing her genitals that way.

The best thing you can do when it comes to giving a woman pleasure by hand is to forget everything you know about giving yourself pleasure by hand. Do not even think for a moment about stimulating her clitoris in the same way you do your penis.

With a penis, you can slap it, yank it and nearly choke it to death, all it does is get hard or harder. In fact, think of how you squeeze or wag it when you are finished peeing. Try approaching a clitoris with that kind of careless abandon and you're likely to be a dead man.

When it comes to touching a woman's clit, assume that softer is better. Always err on the side of tenderness. Push just hard enough to move the skin back and forth over the shaft of the clitoris, assuming you can find the shaft of the clitoris.

In time, your lover may want you to be more vigorous. For instance, some women enjoy it if you put your fingers on the outside of the big lips and push all the way down so you can roll the entire vulva between your fingers. This is more like a deep-tissue massage of the entire crotch, but there can be a time and place for it if you know the woman well and her feedback is reliable and forthcoming.

Showing Instead of Telling

"When women moan or gasp, it encourages me to press harder or faster on the clit.... Always with poor results."
male age 41

Be aware that a woman's understanding of her own sexuality is sometimes on a body level and may have few words. Our society wants it that way and often teaches women from day one that they aren't supposed to tell men about their sexual needs. Getting all frustrated and yelling "Just tell me" does absolutely no good. She probably would if she could, but it's a little like asking someone to tell you the meaning of life. She may simply have to show you by putting her own hands over yours and guiding your fingers as they go. Or maybe she might say, "Please keep trying different ways—I'll let you know when it feels right" or "Maybe if you didn't press quite so hard..." or "Try it here." One reason why feedback is so important is because a woman might say "harder" when she actually means faster, or vice versa. And most guys make the mistake of thinking that if a little pressure feels good, a lot of pressure will send her through the ceiling. This is true, minus the metaphor. Guys also reason that if slow feels good, fast will feel even better. This kind of thinking is seriously flawed. If faster is what she wants, work together on establishing some kind of signal that will let you know.

Mix-ups will happen. You can get really frustrated or you can view this as part of the fun of exploration. After all, it's not like anybody's going to die or lose their job because you confused harder with faster!

Another suggestion is for a woman to use her partner's fingers or penis to masturbate with. That way he'll get a good feel for the different kinds of speed and intensity that she likes and the way she likes the process to unfold.

Intrigue Along the Inseam

> "I like to wait until I can't stand it and beg him to put his fingers inside of me." *female age 25*

Men make a big mistake when they forget to give their fingers a sense of humor. Fingertips that tease and dance will find an especially warm welcome between a woman's legs. For instance, gently running your fingertips up and down a woman's inner thigh is about a zillion times more enticing than shoving your middle finger up her crotch. When she's ready to have your fingers inside of her, she will let you know in no uncertain terms, and even then it's sometimes wise to hold back and tease and play some more.

Finger fucking is definitely more effective if your fingertips are playful and melodic rather than serious or hyper.

Zen Boot Camp—Learning Her Style

"It's not a dish of salted peanuts down there, don't just grab and hope for the best. It's very sensitive. Even the slightest movement can produce a reaction, good or bad."

female age 45

The latter part of this chapter is dedicated to special types of fingerplay that a woman probably doesn't use on herself when she masturbates. But first, it helps if you can learn how to stimulate her in the same way that she stimulates herself. (What if she doesn't masturbate? Then both of you can learn together.) With time, you will add your own special twists, but it's a big mistake to get fancy before you learn the basics—her basics. Give yourself at least a month or three in finger-fucking boot camp with your sweetheart as master and you as grasshopper. Assuming you currently have a partner, you might also ask her to put a small red heart in parts of this chapter where she thinks you could use a little brushing up, in the way that some restaurants flag menu items that aren't supposed to kill you nearly as fast as the others. Here are a few suggestions that might be helpful:

✍ **Your Fingernails** Make sure there are no rough edges.

✍ **Contradiction in Terms** Sorry, but finger fucking does not necessarily mean pushing your finger in and out of your partner's vagina. Much of the action occurs on the outer part of a woman's genitals.

✍ **Hand & Arm Placement** When a woman masturbates, she often rests her wrist on her lower abdomen just above the pubic bone. If this is what your partner does, try to do the same, since it will definitely influence the way your fingers feel on her vulva.

Hint Try lying parallel to your partner and reaching your arm over her body until your fingers touch her crotch. This allows your fingers to approach her vulva in the same way that her own fingers do when she masturbates. Another position that allows for a similar approach is for the two of you to be in a sitting position with her in front and you behind. (Illustration p. 145) The worst way to masturbate a woman is while sitting between her legs, facing her vulva. This can be a fine position to use for genital massage, which is discussed later, but it's ineffective if you are trying to imitate the way she touches herself.

✍ **The Proper Invite: Let the Vulva Come to You, Grasshopper** Guys who are more experienced at lovemaking often begin with a light, gentle caress that barely touches the inner thighs and pubic hair. They don't go much further until a woman's legs spread open and/or her pelvis begins to arch upward. They tease and caress until the lips of her vulva invite their fingers inside.

✍ **Forget Ground Zero** Too often, a guy's main focus is to get his fingers on a woman's clitoris and keep them there, or to go mining up her vagina, searching for that darned G-spot. Never hesitate to interrupt a bout of clit-play by running your fingertips up and down her inner thigh, or by massaging her mons, pulling on her pubic hair or reaching down a little lower and giving her inner lips a gentle massage or tug. Predictability is the hobgoblin of finger fucking.

📖 **Fingers on the Hood** Given how the clitoral area is often more sensitive than any single part of the penis, you don't want the rough skin of your fingers rubbing across it. This is why some men gently push and pull on the clitoral hood and labia (lips) when first touching a woman's genitals. Using the inner lips as leverage can provide pleasing stimulation without painful friction. Also, the inner lips attach directly to the clitoral hood, so tugging on them can provide a level of stimulation that's just right for some women, not too rough and not too light.

📖 **Lubrication** Does your partner use lubrication when she masturbates, such as saliva or baby oil? Do the same when masturbating her. Never be shy about using extra lubrication, especially if you'll be at it for long periods of time.

📖 **Wrist Motion** When men try to masturbate women, they often use just one finger. However, when a woman does herself she might incorporate a bit of wrist into the motion, even if only one finger is actually touching her vulva. This can be a subtle but important detail and may require practice.

📖 **Focus** A good reason for watching your partner masturbate is that it will help you to learn where she likes to place her fingertips. Does she like to dip her fingers inside her vagina? If so, this might not happen until she gets more aroused.

📖 **Favorite Side?** Find out if your sweetheart has a favorite side of her clitoris or labia that she likes to stimulate. Be sure to follow her lead. This is a lousy time to be dyslexic, but we all feel that way at times.

📖 **Don't Lose Sight of the Bigger Picture** Some books on sex are guilty of excessive clitoris worship, as though the female of the species were little more than a pair of arms and legs attached to a clitoris. While this may be true at certain moments for certain women, your lovemaking technique is going to be awfully raw if all you do is woo and lasso your lady's clitoris.

📖 **Pubic Bone** You wouldn't be worth a darn as a basketball player if you didn't know how to use a backboard. The same can be said for a lover who doesn't know how to utilize his lady's pubic bone—inside as well as out. It's a fine perch for a tired hand and offers all sorts of leverage when caressing a woman's genitals. The added bonus is that a woman's pubic bone is usually much easier to find than her clitoris!

🐱 **Mons Pubis** The mons is the little fleshy mound at the top of the vulva just above where the lips begin to open. It usually has hair on it. Men often ignore the mons pubis and head straight for the clitoris, yet women often use the mons when masturbating. For instance, some women masturbate by putting moderate fingertip pressure on the mons and making a circular or back-and-forth motion with it. If your partner is highly aroused, she might want you to do this while the fingers of your other hand are rubbing her clit or filling up her vagina. Some women enjoy it when a partner kneads the mons or taps on it with his fingertips.

🐱 **Retracting the Hood** Some women might want you to pull back the hood of the clitoris. This will allow for much higher levels of stimulation. But for a lot of women, especially those with hyper-sensitive clits, this is a finger-fucking felony. If you are looking for amplification, it's much wiser to pull up on the mons with the fingers of one hand while gently tugging on the inner lips with the fingers of the other.

🐱 **Imitations** An excellent way to learn more about pleasing your partner is to rest your fingers over hers while she is masturbating herself. Then do the reverse, with her fingers acting as guides for your own. A woman shouldn't hesitate to take a man's fingers and put them exactly on those parts of her body where she likes to be touched. Most men will appreciate the assist!

🐱 **Feeling Her Arousal: Body Cues for Changing Gears** Another advantage of having your arm resting across your partner's body is that it allows you to feel when she is tensing up, when her hips start to arch, and if her body begins to writhe or twitch as it sometimes does when highly aroused. These are important signals, because as a woman becomes more aroused she may need you to stimulate her in a slightly different way. This is the lovemaking equivalent of learning how to type without looking at the keyboard.

Range of Motion When they masturbate, some women direct the stimulation to just one spot. Others might stimulate themselves in a more global way, tugging and pulling on the surface of the entire vulva. Plenty of women use a circular motion when rubbing their genitals, while others move a finger side-to-side or up and down like plucking at a guitar string or turning on and off a light switch.

Tempo & Rhythm Most women appreciate it if your fingers achieve a certain tempo and rhythm as they traverse her vulva. This can change as she becomes more aroused. How to proceed can be confusing until you learn your partner's responses. Helpful indicators include the little sounds she makes, changes in her breathing, the way her body moves—especially her hips and legs—changes in her vulva, and her clitoris starting to retract. While one woman might want you to maintain the same rhythm and hand motion from start to stop, another might need an array of tempos because she quickly habituates to the same finger motion and it loses its effect. Finding the right rhythm and tempo may feel awkward and even hopeless for the first few months, but with time, you will learn when to mix it up and when to stay your course.

Fill 'r Up? Does your partner like to have something inside her when she comes? Your fingers, a dildo, etc.? Ask. Also, some women have sensitive spots inside their vaginas which they might love you to stimulate with the fingers of one hand while doing their clitoris with the other. Try doing the clitoris with whichever hand you use for writing, since stimulating a clitoris tends to require more fine motor skill than massaging a vagina. Simple pressure often works well in the vagina once you learn where to touch.

One Joint at a Time You never want to bogart a woman's vagina by shoving an entire finger into it. A more satisfying approach is to ease your finger in one joint at a time. For instance, once you get the signal that she wants your finger inside her, slide it in as far as the joint that's between your fingernail and middle knuckle. Use it to make sensuous circles inside her vagina, gently tugging the tissue this way and that. After a while, she'll give you a cue to up the ante. Then gently glide your finger in a little further until you reach the middle knuckle. Stop and play some more. At that point, she might want it to go all the way in, or maybe she'll prefer the added fullness of a second finger. She might want you to do an in-out motion with your fingers, or maybe she'll want you to stimulate the roof of her vagina. Perhaps she'll want you to jiggle your hand or pull upward with it as your finger makes an "L", with the fingertip part inside her vagina and inner knuckle part pulling up against the shaft of her clitoris. There are many different options; it's best to experiment, with her telling you what feels right.

Further Variations When lying parallel to your lover, try reaching across her body and resting the heel of your hand above her pubic bone. Then put your index finger on one of her labia and your middle finger on the other. Move one finger in an upward direction and the other downward so that her labia are gently rubbing against each other.

◌ **Nipple Ripple** Some women love having their nipples caressed, sucked on or pulled while being masturbated. The added nipple pleasure makes it easier for them to come. Other women find this annoying. Be sure to inquire.

◌ **Finger Variations** While lying next to your partner, rest your arm across her body with your fingers on her vulva. Separate her labia with your first and third fingers and stroke between her inner lips with your middle finger, bringing lubrication up from the bottom of her vaginal opening. If she isn't already wet, lubricate your finger with saliva or store-bought lube. And try to be gentle, since the belly of the clitoris is sometimes extremely sensitive. Some women like to have their vulvas tapped with fingers, and some even like to be lightly slapped on the genitals—but only a moron would try something like this if his partner hadn't requested it.

◌ **Lips** The outer lips often have hair on them; the inner lips don't. The outer lips are usually more prominent, although sometimes the inner lips are. Some women like to have the man clasp each lip between his thumb and forefinger and tug on it. Some like this to be done very gently, others with more force than you might think. Do this very gently at first, increasing the tension to the point where your lover finds it most pleasing.

◌ **Sunnyside Down** There are women who enjoy being touched from behind, when they are lying on their stomach or on all fours or while leaning over something. You simply reach between her legs from behind. This changes the angle that your hand makes with her genitals and can be a delightful change of pace. It's also a neat way to massage the roof of the vagina with your thumb!

🐾 **Wet Humping** There's no reason why a woman shouldn't lube up a favorite part of her lover's body and rub up against it with her vulva. Some women like to do this on a man's back or thigh. (There are women who think the penis would be more useful if it had been mounted on the front of a man's thigh instead of between his legs. There is even a special dildo harness that mounts a dildo on the thigh, achieving this very feat in an amusing way.)

🐾 **Using Your Head** Some women enjoy using the head of a sweetheart's penis for masturbating. This can be an invigorating experience for both partners. Keep in mind that even if the male doesn't ejaculate, unwanted sex germs can be passed on or the woman can get pregnant from such activity. You can greatly diminish these risks if the man is wearing a rubber that is well-lubricated with something like contraceptive gel or KY.

🐾 **Natural Lube** If pregnancy or sex germs aren't a consideration, some women like to use a man's ejaculate as a lubricant to masturbate with. This might be fun to do when he comes first. She might add some saliva or her own lube; otherwise it's likely to dry up fairly fast.

🐾 **Robot Alert** Some men follow the same protocol each and every time they have sex. It never hurts to experiment with new ways to touch your partner, both with your fingers and with your heart.

🐾 **A Special Note for Women** It may be difficult for a man to know when you are feeling pleasure as opposed to pain. Sometimes the noises for each sound identical, even if your experience of the two is very, very different. It's up to you to help your partner learn the difference.

The Extra-Sensitive Clit

Some women have a clitoris that is super-sensitive to touch. This kind of clit is simply too sensitive to be even the slightest bit forgiving, and if you don't appreciate the sensitivity of it you will start to assume the woman is way too finicky and not worth the effort. This is unfortunate. Read this chapter with her, and have her mark some of the things she thinks might work. Make sure she is highly aroused before your fingers go anywhere near her clit, and be mindful of how quickly it can go from being too sensitive to totally numbing out. Also, try to become a master of indirect stimulation, e.g. is it better if you caress her crotch when she's wearing blue jeans or underwear than when she's naked?

More Than a Peace Sign

In reviewing porn movies done by lesbian producers, author Jay Wiseman noticed that when lesbian performers feel each other up they almost always use two fingers—not one or three. Wiseman asked a number of women about this, and most replied that two fingers simply feel better. Some of this guide's women readers said they enjoy one finger, three fingers, an entire fist or even a big toe, but most agreed that two fingers is a fine number. The number of fingers a woman wants inside of her will also depend upon her level of arousal and sometimes upon her body's menstrual status.

You might consider wearing latex gloves when spending long periods of time with your fingers inside a woman's vagina. The smooth latex surface sometimes feels nice for the woman and helps to keep your fingers from stinging when they marinate in vaginal fluids, which are fairly acidic. Try putting a dab of water-based lube inside each fingertip of the glove and see if it makes any difference for you or her.

Female Readers' Advice on Fingers in Their Vagina

"I like it if he inserts one finger until the opening relaxes, then adds a second finger. When I begin to breathe faster, he should start flexing his fingers. The motion is similar to when you are signaling a person to 'come here.'"

female age 32

"When I am sufficiently wet, I enjoy two fingers. I like it when he puts them in gradually and 'fucks' me with them gently. But no fingernails and no rushing!" *female age 35*

"Start with one finger, then go up from there. To find the G-spot, put your thumb over my clitoris, then insert your first finger into my vagina and feel for the rough spot on the upper wall. Rub this spot!!!" *female age 26*

"I like a finger in there, but please, don't dig for China." *female age 48*

"I don't necessarily care for fingers in my vagina. I'd rather have a penis in there." *female age 43*

"I like him to rub the entrance of my vagina in a circular fashion, but don't particularly like a finger all of the way inside." *female age 30*

Playing the Over in Your Sweetheart's Under

There's a time to bunt and a time to hit straight away; a time to bring the infield in and a time to respect the hitter's power. It's no different with women's genitals; with a little skill and strategy, you're on your way. The next couple of pages offer techniques for knowing a woman's genitals in a way that can sometimes be profound. Most women will love the kind of detailed and caring attention that's involved.

Learning to Massage a Woman's Genitals

Giving a woman a genital massage differs from giving her traditional hand play in a couple of significant ways:

First: You sometimes use massage oil or lubricant.

Second: You sit facing her, either between her legs or to one side. The drawing on the next page is a good example.

Third: You are not trying to imitate the way she masturbates.

Fourth: What you learn about a woman's vagina from massaging her genitals can be used to increase her pleasure during intercourse. The sensitive spots or areas that you find in her vagina can sometimes be massaged with the head of your penis.

Fifth: Clocks. Think clocks. Close your eyes and imagine a clock—the old-fashioned type that has a big hand, a little hand,

Snow White and the Prince trying tips from this chapter while the Dwarfs are at work in the forest.

and a cuckoo bird if you must. There are six or seven clocks or pelvic time zones to consider when massaging a woman's genitals. An effective way to explore a woman's vulva and vagina is to image each part as having a clock face over it.

Working the Steps

What follows can take a day or it can take a year. Don't be a slave to protocol. If you have your finger at one o'clock and she suddenly starts moaning and her whole body contorts and writhes in pleasure, consider keeping it there. If you don't get to two o'clock for another week or two, who cares? Also keep in mind that points which bring subtle pleasure can be just as important as those which set off fireworks.

If you are using massage oil, nuke the stuff for a few seconds if it is cold, or rub it between your hands to warm it. Then put your hand over your lover's genitals and slowly drip the oil on your fingers so it seeps through them and onto her vulva.

✌ Sit facing your partner's crotch, either between her legs or on the side of her body that allows you to easily touch her genitals with whatever hand you might use for making obscene gestures.

✌ When massaging different parts of a woman's genitals, apply just enough pressure to move the skin back and forth over the tissue that's under it. Press harder if she asks.

✌ Place an imaginary clock face around your partner's clitoris. Then put your fingertip at twelve o'clock, press lightly, and stimulate as long as she likes. Do this at each hour on the clock face. Hopefully your sweetheart will let you know when you hit a fun spot by saying something profound such as "There!" You can then say "two o'clock?" and she might reply "try one forty-five." Go back and forth until you have it just right. Instead of having to say something out loud, she might prefer to hold your penis, ankle or big toe in the same way that kids use joy sticks. She can then squeeze this particular body part to indicate a direct hit.

✌ Explore the clitoral suburbs: When they masturbate, some women focus finger pressure on the smaller labia or on the inner part of the larger labia rather than upon the clitoris proper. Be sure to explore the parts that are clitoris-adjacent.

✌ Finding a man's peehole is not a particularly taxing exercise; finding a woman's can take a bit of work. Why would you want to? Because the little dome of tissue that surrounds a

Rolling the clitoris depends upon the size and position of the clitoris and how sensitive it is.

woman's urinary opening has sometimes been compared to the head of the penis. Some women might enjoy it if you stimulate this area; ask.

⚜ Lay your free hand over the lower part of your lover's abdomen. Experiment by applying different kinds of pressure with the top hand while fingers from your other hand are inside her vagina.

⚜ Think of the vagina as a tube that's about four inches long. Start at the rim (opening) of the vagina. Put pressure on each part of the tissue as your finger eventually makes a complete circle. Then move the imaginary clock face deeper inside and do the same thing all over again. Keep repeating this until you have done the whole thing. It helps to be extra thorough about clocking the first third of the vagina, because that is where it is most sensitive to touch. Pay special attention to the roof of her vagina between 9:00 and 3:00. A number of women report pleasurable responses in this part of the vagina.

⚜ Some women feel a certain dull but enjoyable sensitivity around the base or deepest part of the vagina, a full finger deep. This part of the vagina is more sensitive to pressure than touch.

⚜ A woman's cervix can usually be found in the upper rear part of her vagina. It is easily felt if she is on all fours or brings her legs to her chest. The cervix feels like a little dome of tissue that's fun to run your fingers around. It may also have a small cleft in the middle, like your chin. Carefully stimulate the area surrounding the cervix. Some women may enjoy this and want you to do it more often; others won't. Cervical sensitivity can vary with a woman's menstrual cycle; massaging it may release some blood if she is close to her period.

🐾 The urinary tube runs along the ceiling of the vagina from the outside of a woman's body into her bladder. It's a bit like an air-conditioning duct that is above a suspended ceiling. The urinary tube is surrounded by a special type of tissue that occasionally contains a multitude of nerve endings. Some women refer to this area on the roof of the vagina as the G-spot and find its stimulation to be quite pleasurable. One way of stimulating it is by making a "come here" motion with a finger that's put inside the vagina. See the illustration on page 150.

🐾 The perineum is the area between a woman's vulva and her anus. It really isn't a clock at all, but more like a mini football field with the end zones being her vagina and anus. Explore this entire area thoroughly, but try not to leave any divots.

🐾 The ring of the anus contains a multitude of nerve endings. Women and men who don't have aesthetic problems with anal stimulation might enjoy a clocking of their rectal areas. You may find that one part of it is more sensitive and putting a finger on it generates pleasure. But be careful about going from a woman's rectum to her vulva without washing your hands.

Massaging the mons.

Palms between her legs.

Palms Between Her Legs

Here is a form of genital massage with no clocks attached. Sit above or next to your partner's abdomen while facing her feet. Place a well-lubricated hand between her legs with your fingertips resting just below her vulva but not touching her anus. Pull the hand all the way up to her belly, with your fingertips gently separating her labia with each stroke. Immediately do the same thing with your other hand, alternating strokes like a dog does when he's digging a hole in your garden, but not nearly as fast. Sorry about the canine imagery.

The Lip Part of Erotic Massage

Women's genitals have two sets of lips—the labia majora, which form the outer folds of the vulva, and the thinner labia minora, which are the inner lips. The inner lips are particularly significant since they also form the hood of the clitoris. In erotic massage, much time is spent stimulating the inner and outer lips.

Tracing After applying lubrication, it might be nice to begin with one of the larger outer lips. Place the lucky lip between your thumb and forefinger, clasping it at the base where it attaches to the main part of your partner's body. Then run your fingers or fingertip from the lower to upper part of the lip, as though you were tracing one side of a parenthesis. Repeat this as long as your partner's feedback is positive. You can also make an upside down horseshoe pattern with a fingertip by starting at the lower inside part of one lip and finishing at the lower inside part of the other. It could be fun to do this with both inner and outer lips.

Off the Edge Another form of genital massage can be done by holding a lubricated lip between your thumb and forefinger. While squeezing just a little, pull your fingers straight away from the woman's body. Your fingers will end up in the air an inch or two above her body, as though you had pulled them off the edge of a table top or sheet of paper. If she likes this, repeat it many times.

What Did You Discover?

"My clitoris gets more sensitive, so when he hits just the right spot, I want him to stay there with his touch."

female age 34

It will take months to fully explore a woman's genitals. Maybe you will find one special place, or maybe you will find ten. You can then try to stimulate these spots while having intercourse or oral sex. Experiment with different positions that might allow you to reach them with the head of your penis. Or try stimulating an outer spot with your tongue while using your fingers to reach a spot that's deeper inside.

Obsession Alert

Hopefully you will approach genital massage in a spirit of playfulness and fun rather than as some sort of mission or quest. And while the sensations won't necessarily pack the kick of a mule, the overall effect can be quite pleasing when done for extended periods of time.

While this drawing makes a cool visual image, it misses the most fun part of taking a shower together—soaping each other up and hugging and rubbing your bodies together!

Hydropower—Aquatic Version of Finger Fucking

Many couples find it sensual to hug, hold and grope each other in the shower, hot tub or bath. Trouble is, the H_2O tends to wash away any kind of natural lubricant. For skin-to-skin play (nonintercourse), a good solution is to keep a plastic squeeze bottle with oil in it next to the tub. Stand and lube the outside of your dry genitals with vegetable oil, then ease your way into the water. This will keep your genitals slick and slippery and should greatly enhance aquatic hand play. For intercourse while submerged, try out a silicone-based lube, as mentioned on pages 134-135.

Two recent advancements in hydrotechnology have been a boon to aquatic sex play:

Hand-Held Shower Head If you don't have one of these gadgets, consider getting one. It shouldn't take more than fifteen minutes to install, unless your plumbing is really old and rusty. Hop in the shower with your sweetheart and try out the various settings on the shower head. Keep in mind that when you hold the shower head point blank against the skin it causes the water to bubble somewhat like the jet on a hot tub. This might feel good. Don't point the jet of water directly into a woman's vagina, as it might force air inside her body. This could be dangerous.

Some men enjoy the feeling of the spray against the side of the scrotum. Depending on your water pressure and how you hold the shower head, it's a sensation that can be on the cusp between pleasure and pain. This might have something in common with the kind of sexual experiences that some women report, where the line between pleasure and pain is a fine but pleasant one.

Also, different brands of hand-held shower heads create different kinds of spray. Some people might prefer one brand over another. You can often find them for under $30. Hardware chains generally put them on sale every month or so.

Powerjets in the Hot tub The possibilities for genital stimulation nearly cripple the imagination. Check with your hot tub repair person about fitting an extension hose on one of the massage jets so you can direct the flow where you want. Cut the air to the jets so none of it will get into the vagina.

Also, there are now waterproof vibrators. These are tiny things which only have one conceivable purpose, yet the box shows a woman in a tub using the point of the vibrator against the side of her neck!

Winding Down

"The first time I felt a woman's vagina was with my first love. We were taking things very slowly, and when I would ask if I could go down her pants, the answer was no. I respected her wishes and we always did something else, usually making out. One day she finally told me I could proceed below the waistline. It was warm and wet and very soft. The wetness of her vagina was the most exciting feeling I'd ever had." *male age 25*

For some men, putting their fingers between a woman's legs is a moment that has its own wonder or magic. They love feeling the woman's warmth and the start of her wetness, and how her body sometimes tenses and squirms.

Hopefully, you will keep in mind that there might be other parts of a woman's body where touch produces intense sensation. For instance, one reader reports that his lover has a small area on the lower part of her back that is so erotically sensitive that her knees nearly buckle whenever he strokes or caresses it. He once nearly caused her to have an orgasm in the middle of a busy hardware store by caressing the small of her back. Another woman reader is so sensitive to having her fingers touched that she has actually had orgasms while getting a manicure.

"It Just Snuck Up on Me!"

Sometimes the nicest orgasms happen purely by accident. Let's say you've been stroking those special spots on her body, playfully caressing her inner thighs and tugging on her inner lips for who knows how long, the morning sun creeping through the blinds, and suddenly one just sneaks up on her—and you. You weren't trying to give her an orgasm; you weren't stoking THE side of her clit; you were just kicking back, letting your fingers play and enjoy themselves, teasing, tugging, caressing, and suddenly one just sneaks up—out of nowhere.

Maybe it's not the most intense orgasm she's ever had, but it's totally unannounced and it's nothing but pure lazy delight.

Final Words about Caressing a Woman's Genitals

As kids we used to hold sea shells up to our ears to hear the ocean. As adults, some men find themselves pressing an ear against a partner's chest while pirouetting a hand and fingers over the sweet spot between her legs, listening to her heart beat as she starts to enter a state of bliss. It might not tell you the meaning of life, but it's a start. And that's what this chapter was all about.

Dear Paul,

How do you touch a woman between her legs? Based on my girlfriend's reactions, I'm clearly doing something wrong.

Klutz in Dinuba

Dear Klutz,

I still get confused about a woman's genitals. Sometimes they're too sensitive to be touched or even breathed upon; other times, your most valiant attempt at mouth-to-crotch resuscitation won't wake the thing up. So here's the sad truth: if your girlfriend and my wife got together, they'd probably be commiserating about what oafs we are when it comes to touching them down there!

To help me learn along with you, I pulled a video from the shelf titled *An Intimate Guide to Female Genital Massage* by Annie Sprinkle and Joe Kramer (Erospirit). While this was not done as a porn tape, it shows more up-close shots of women's genitals than any six editions of *Hustler.*

Klutz, if you learned how to do the things that they teach in this tape, you would be knee-deep in willing women. But herein lies the rub—with all the close ups of women's crotches, this isn't the sort of tape that most guys would watch if they wanted to be sexually aroused. And maybe that's part of the problem. If you touch a woman with the kind of pace that most of us want to see in a jerk-off tape, she will probably experience you as rude and inconsiderate. But if every once in a while you gave her a full-body massage and then gradually worked your way up to a light and intimate genital caress, things might start to change.

If your partner can trust that she'll be getting something good from your new approach, she might be able to relax more during sex. This might help her be more receptive than she currently is, and perhaps it will allow the two of you to meet in the middle.

We all need gestures that encourage us to achieve a better space with our partner. Otherwise, we get entrenched and give up. We might not leave, but we give up.

Dear Paul,

My girlfriend likes me to touch her genitals, but it takes a lot longer for her natural lube to flow than other women I've been with. Is there anything I can do to help the situation?

Sandy in Palm Desert

Dear Sandy,

I don't know if this has anything to do with your situation, but most of us guys start touching a woman's vulva near her clitoris. You are more likely to find lubrication near the bottom part of the vaginal opening, where the lips make a "U." Try dragging the fluid up from the bottom part of the vaginal opening with your fingertips. This assumes that you have spent plenty of time and effort to get the fluids flowing in the first place. Also, you might try using a water-based lube. I wouldn't recommend the lube in place of extra kisses and caresses, but in addition.

Hand Jobs: Different Strokes for Different Blokes
Chapter 13

The hand job is like the Swiss Army knife—a fine, multipurpose tool that is useful in many different situations. For instance, there's the classic hand job. Its goal is to bring the man to orgasm—rub rub, squirt squirt. This is usually most effective when you are able to do him in the same way that he does himself. He will think you are brilliant.

At the other extreme is the type of hand job where you use techniques that most men don't even know about. The goal of this type of hand job is to make every stroke an experience in and of itself, turning a man's entire body into one giant sex receptor. Rather than racing toward orgasm, the intent is to delay ejaculation while building erotic tension. In this type of hand job, there is no need for the man to have a full erection. It might be better if he doesn't.

There is a time and place for each—as well as mixing and matching with parts of both. That's what this chapter is about.

Learning from His—Uh—Mistakes?

"I could never move my fist that fast for so long. He really manhandles that sucker and it doesn't seem to hurt!"

female age 55

Let's begin by explaining how men masturbate. This can best be summarized with the following statement: *Grab it hard and whack it good.* Of course, there are variations, but this might help you appreciate the extent to which we men sometimes limit our range of sensual pleasure. This is something that sex therapist Herbert Otto drones on and on about:

It has been my experience that men, in general, are more rigid and less inclined to experiment sexually with their bodies than are women. Men appear to feel more insecure and easily threatened in relation to sexual matters, perhaps because of a perceived fragility of their manhood. (From *Liberated Orgasm* [Silverado, CA: Liberating Creations, 1999]).

Hopefully, that's one of the things you are here for—to help your man learn new ways of experiencing his body and his penis. Unfortunately, a lot of men view their body and penis as two different and sometimes unrelated entities, with the body merely being the chauffeur. Still, if you are going to find your way into a man's heart, the place to begin is by learning how to jerk him off. No matter how far you evolve past that point, being able to give a good old-fashioned hand job can be as comforting to a man as mom's home cooking, even if her biscuits were hard as rocks.

How Men Masturbate

While each man might have his own unique spin on it, there are two basic ways that men masturbate. One is by doing it dry; the other way is with lubrication.

Dry The man wraps one or two fingers around the penis at a strategically placed point, slightly below the head. He then moves the entire foreskin up and down with each stroke. Because the foreskin glides easily over the shaft that it covers, most guys clasp it more tightly than might seem comfortable. Much of the sensation occurs as the fingers move over the highly sensitive part of the shaft which is called the frenulum.

Lubricated Using lubrication results in a hand job that feels more like intercourse. When giving himself a lubricated hand job, the man often wraps his whole hand around the penis. The lubrication allows the hand to glide over the shaft and the head of the penis. Some men keep the foreskin retracted by pulling it taut around the base of the penis with their free hand.

Dry vs. Lubricated With lube, a man tends to get more sensation from the head of his penis; when doing it dry, more of the focus is on the front of the penis below the head. The lubricated hand job can be a more sensuous experience. However, plenty of guys prefer doing it dry and there are many times when masturbating dry is more practical. It's less of a production and it is easier to come into a tissue or sock, which requires less cleanup. You usually make more noise when doing it dry, though.

What Does a Penis Feel Like?

When a penis is soft it feels a little like human lips. The skin has a silky smooth, almost translucent texture that slides over the tissue beneath it. A soft penis is extremely flexible. It can be warm or cold to the touch and feels more like a squid than a hot-dog.

To know what a hard penis feels like, find a fairly buff guy who lifts weights and ask him to flex his arms. A hard bicep feels similar to a hard penis, although a hard penis won't be nearly as big around except in some guys' dreams. Poking a finger into a man's unflexed pecs will give you an approximate idea of what a semi-erect penis feels like.

Here are some women's recollections about the first time they touched a penis:

"It was sort of like 'Oh my God, what do you do with it?' I knew if you did something to it in the right way, that was good. I felt very, very careful, not sure what I was dealing with at all. It was like an alien creature that you were supposed to automatically know how to please. As I listen to myself describing it, I must have considered it as separate from the individual who it belonged to!" *female age 34*

"It was not a pleasant experience then, but it sure is now."
female age 42

"I had intercourse a number of times but never touched it. I didn't get into that until much later." *female age 26*

"I didn't like the way it felt when flaccid. A couple of years later I finally got around to making friends with it, and it became exciting.... When you make friends with a person, you make friends with his penis." *female age 21*

"It took me a while to figure out that you could really handle it, that it wasn't fragile." *female age 27*

Intent & Intensity

Some people say that the difference between giving a great hand job and a mediocre one is a matter of intent; if a woman isn't turned on by the situation, she can pump a penis till Tinkerbell commits a felony, nothing special is likely to happen. Other people say that giving great hand jobs is a matter of skill and endurance. Whatever the case, few women realize that they have the potential to control nearly every cell in a man's body with each stroke of their hand. Instead, they often just jerk away until things get sticky. One female reader comments, "Not true. Plenty of women are aware of the potential control they have, but choose not to pursue it."

Traditional Hand Jobs (THJ)

Taking the Jerk Out of Jerking Off

This section is about giving a guy a hand job without lubrication. Ways of doing it wet are described later in this chapter.

Some women give hand jobs that are jerky. This is understandable, since it might appear that when guys masturbate we use a single upstroke followed by a single downstroke, all in rapid succession. But that's not how we do it. We usually have a more fluid motion, so to speak. The hand doesn't stop or even slow down as it changes direction from up to down. The motion is smooth rather than jerky—which means the term "jerking off" is a misnomer.

Another potential problem occurs when a woman slows down or stops pumping as the man begins to ejaculate. While some guys may want you to stop right away, others will greatly appreciate it if you keep stroking for a few minutes after they ejaculate ("stroking through"). Some might even want you to proceed as though the penis were an udder, with you milking out each drop.

As the hand motion becomes more familiar, you might want to caress your man's testicles with one hand as you are jerking him off with the other. Your lover might also enjoy being kissed while you are giving him a hand job. And some people claim that orgasmic rapture is enhanced if you stare into each other's eyes as you are coming.

To find the optimal hand position, lie parallel to your man and reach across his body as he does when he is masturbating. Ask him to form your fingers around his penis in the same way he does when he's alone and thinking about you. The way he holds the penis and where he puts his hand on the shaft are more significant factors than you might think. Try to imitate the exact place where he grips himself. There are reasons for this. One of the most sensitive areas of the penis is just below the head on the side that's away from the man's belly when he has an erection. (See the illustration on page 57.) It shows good form to rub a finger—not fingertip—over this spot with each stroke, especially if you plan on getting this over with sometime before next Christmas.

Wrap your entire hand around the penis so your thumb and index finger would touch if there weren't a big sausage in the way. Your hand should be in the same position as if it were holding a cup of tea. That's how we guys learn to masturbate, by drinking tea.

If your fingers were a belt, try to buckle them on the side of the penis and not in the front. Otherwise, your fingertips would go over the frenulum, which can be uncomfortable. It would not be hand-job cricket.

Another reason to position your hand exactly where he does is because the foreskin is only so elastic—if he is circumcised, anyway. If your grip is too high or low on the shaft, the foreskin will be pulled beyond its stretching point. Again, much confusion can be avoided if you simply ask him to place your hand and fingers where he likes them. Then have him guide your hand up and down so you will get a sense of how high and low to stroke.

Variation Consider doing your man when he is standing or kneeling as opposed to lying on his back. This could be nice for both of you.

Pressure Chances are, your partner might want you to clasp or squeeze his penis more tightly than you were planning. Don't worry. It's unlikely you will choke it. It never hurts to ask if he wants you to squeeze tighter.

Ball Trick When masturbating, some guys push the little finger of the stroking hand against the lower part of the shaft near where the scrotum attaches. This causes the testicles to jiggle or vibrate with each stroke, which can

feel really nice. But it's always best to seek your man's input when first trying to do this, since your finger might inadvertently poke him in the nuts.

Ultimately, it's unlikely you will get your sweetheart's hand motion exactly right unless you have him show you. That's because each guy varies in terms of grip, stroke, and rhythm—not to mention anatomy. Don't be surprised if it takes a number of tutorials before you get it right, especially if your hand is considerably smaller than his. If your own man is too uptight to teach you, it's likely that any number of his friends will be more than willing to let you learn the basics on them, or maybe one of your girlfriends can demonstrate on her boyfriend... Then again, she might use a banana. It can be both fun and helpful talking to your friends about their own special techniques for getting guys off, although you shouldn't assume they know better than you when it comes to the guy you are with.

In his wonderful books *Tricks: 125 Sex Tips to Make Good Sex Better, Vols. 1 & 2* (San Francisco: Greenery Press) author Jay Wiseman lists several tips to make a traditional hand job more fun. For instance, he suggests caressing the penis and balls for ten seconds with your fingertips, followed by one quick up-and-down hand stroke. Then caress for ten more seconds, followed by two quick up-and-down hand strokes. After every ten-second period of caressing, increase the stroke total by one.

Extreme Hand-Job Techniques for an Extremely Good Time

It's time to up the ante and consider techniques for doing it with lube. The next couple of pages explain the various strokes you can use for both the penis and the testicles. Then we talk about ways to help your man enjoy a higher level of pleasure for a longer period of time.

Lubricating your hands and his genitals is essential when giving an extreme hand job. Any number of oils will work rather nicely, as long as you're thinking peanut oil instead of Penzoil and coconut instead of Castrol. It's a penis you are massaging, not a piston. Hand moisturizers absorb into the skin too quickly to be of much use.

This position is great for hand jobs with lube, but not
so good for doing it dry. Worse yet, her form is poor (fingertips on the
frenulum) and his penis appears to be detachable!

Lube Him Up

The first thing to do is to get your man completely naked.
This is usually not a difficult task.

The most civilized way of greasing a man's groin is to cup
one hand over his genitals and drip massage oil over it. Gravity
will pull the oil through your fingers and onto his genitals unless
you are in outer space. Make sure that your man's testicles and
penis are thoroughly basted with oil. Putting a plastic sheet or
a thick towel or two under him might be a good way to catch
the excess oil. Large plastic garbage can bags work really well.
If cleanup is going to pose serious problems, use less oil.

From Where You Sit

When doing him dry, it's best to sit by your bronco's side
so you can imitate the way he does it himself. When giving an
extreme hand job, you can do a fine job from wherever you sit
unless it's across the room. That's because you'll be using lube.

Different Massage Strokes

The strokes described below are simply possibilities. Perhaps one or two will seem fun to try. It can be nice to vary the pace by mixing and matching different strokes. You can certainly practice on a banana, but most guys would happily volunteer for beta testing.

Also, it is not necessary for a man to have an erection for this to feel great. Many guys remain semi-erect when receiving an extended penis massage. Some people think it feels best when the penis is from sixty to seventy-five percent erect.

Fists Going Up Be sure all skin surfaces are well lubricated. Wrap one hand around the base of the penis, squeeze lightly and pull it up along the shaft, over the head and into the air. As this hand is making its upward stroke, grab the base of the penis with your free hand, squeeze and do the same thing. Create a fluid motion with one hand constantly following the other. Be sure to slow the pace if the man shows signs of impending orgasm, lest he create fluid of his own. This technique is shown below. Some folks suggest giving a little extra squeeze or snap on the upward stroke just as your hand reaches the head of the penis.

Fists Going Up

🪶 **Fists Going Down** Same technique as above, only in the reverse direction with your hands going from the tip of the penis to the base. Downward strokes such as these usually require an erection. Otherwise, the thing just flops there in your hand. Also, use a more open grip so you don't shove the penis into the body,

🪶 **Thumbs Up** While facing your man's crotch, clasp your fingers together as you might do when praying that the check you just wrote doesn't bounce. The only difference here is that your hands are clasped around your man's penis. Use the pads of your thumbs to massage the front part of the penis where nature left the seam showing. Spend extra time rubbing the area where the head attaches to the shaft, or just below it, as this is usually the most sensitive part of the penis. (Some people compare the sensitivity of this area to that of the clitoris, although they are probably overstating the case.)

🪶 **Open Palm Rubbing Head of Penis** Some guys might like this; others won't. Hold the shaft of the penis in one hand so it is sticking straight out from the man's body (perpendickular). Open your other hand flat and rub it in a circular pattern over the head of the penis, as though you were buffing it. Make sure that the palm of your hand is well-lubed.

🪶 **Twisting the Cap Off a Bottle of Beer** Hold the shaft of the penis near the base. With your other hand, grasp the head of the penis as though it were the cap on a bottle of beer. Twist it as if you were opening a beer bottle, with your thumb and forefinger running along the groove under the ridge where the head attaches to the shaft.

🪶 **Wringing a Towel Dry** Grasp the lower part of the penis with one hand and the upper part of the shaft with the other. There should be no gap between your

hands unless mother nature mistakenly endowed your man with an elephant trunk instead of a penis. Twist your hands back and forth in opposite directions.

How to Pull the Foreskin Taut

The penis can usually be made more sensitive by stretching the foreskin. In fact, guys who masturbate with lubrication often use one hand to pull the foreskin taut while stroking the shaft with the other. This also helps keep the baggy skin on the scrotum from rising up onto the shaft of the penis. There are a couple of ways to achieve this:

Palm on the Side Clamp your thumb and forefinger or middle finger around the shaft of the penis nearly an inch above where it joins the testicles (scrotum). Pull the skin down so your other fingers and palm rest on the testicles. This will make the foreskin taut. If the man is uncircumcised, reach higher up on the shaft to pull the extra skin down.

Taut Variation When he's doing himself and trying to keep his foreskin taut, it is possible that your partner hooks his thumb around the shaft of his penis and uses the other four fingers to cup, squeeze or caress his testicles. Then again, if he's the outdoor type with a history of running power equipment, he may need to improvise, depending upon how many fingers he still has left. There are many variations on this. Sometimes just the ring and pinky fingers lie over the top of the testicles; other times it's the index and bird fingers.

Strokes to Try When the Skin on the Penis Is Pulled Taut

Owie Ouch Alert! Remember, you only pull the foreskin taut if you are doing him with lube. It's the ability of the foreskin to stretch that makes it possible to give a hand job without lube.

Penis/Belly Rub The penis should be lubricated and resting flat against the man's belly. Pull the skin taut at the base of the penis as mentioned above. Open your other hand and lay it flat on top of the penis. Then drag the hand up toward the man's chest, as if you were trying to push the good feelings out of his penis and onto the skin of his belly. Repeat. As with any of these strokes, feel free to vary the angles, pressures and grips to form your own unique style. And don't hesitate to do a series of one stroke followed by an entirely different type of stroke.

🔖 The Corkscrew or Following the Stripe on the Barber's Pole Pull the skin taut at the base of your partner's penis. Wrap your other hand around the base of his lubricated penis. Squeeze lightly, and twist it upward as though you were following a corkscrew or the stripe on a barber's pole. If his penis is hard enough, do a reverse downstroke which should return your hand to the same position where it started. If there isn't enough erection to make the downward stroke work, just do a series of upward strokes.

When it comes to giving either lubricated hand jobs or oral sex, don't hesitate to use a twisting motion up and down the shaft of the penis, especially on the ridge that's beneath the head.

🔖 Thumbs Up—Thumbs Down This may sound complicated, but it isn't. There are two ways to grasp a penis that is lubricated. One is with your hand facing up, so the little finger is toward the base of the penis and the thumb is toward the head. The other is with your hand facing down, so the thumb is around the base and your little finger is around the head end of the penis. It can be quite impressive when a woman alternates hand orientation with her stroking hand, so he never knows if the next stroke will be thumbs up or thumbs down.

🔖 Octopuss(y) Fingers Pull the foreskin taut with your lucky hand. Lay the palm of your other hand over the head of the penis and drop your fingers down along the sides of the shaft. (Your hand will look like an open parachute or an octopus when it swims.) Your fingers will stimulate the sides of the penis as you move your hand up and down. You can also twist your hand sideways, or do a corkscrew stroke that combines both motions.

The Man with Invisible Balls

Women often assume that the penis is somehow glued or stapled to the front of a man's pelvic bone. In reality, it runs beneath his testicles and anchors inside his pelvis. Some men enjoy having the "invisible" part of the penis massaged. Push into the space between the testicles with your fingertips and gently rub, or massage the flat space behind his balls.

Massaging Under the Testicles

If the skin over the testicles is tight, heat the room and put a warm washcloth over them. Let the scrotum warm up for a couple of minutes until the testicles hang freely. Press into the middle of the scrotum with your fingertips. They should be touching the part of the penis that is covered by the testicles. Massage this area all the way back to where the man's anus begins. There is often a single spot on this part of the penis where a number of ligaments, muscle fibers and nerve endings seem to converge. Putting fingertip pressure on this spot while massaging the "regular" part of the penis with your other hand can make the entire shaft—from the base of the pelvis to the head of the penis—experience a subtle, warm feeling that some men will find enjoyable. You might also try massaging this area when giving a blow job.

This part of the penis is smaller than a dime and is either tucked under the testicles or is in the area between his balls and anus. Also, it might be on one side of the shaft rather than in the middle. As for testicles that get in the way, do what we guys do: push your fingertips into the space that is between them or just behind them, or push them to the side.

A man's testicles will nearly cripple him with pain if they get hit, knocked or flicked, but not when a partner caresses and massages them. Being massaged in this area can feel like getting a really nice back rub, only it's between the legs. Still, be gentle at the start, and keep in mind that while some men find the sensation to be delightful, others don't like to be touched there.

Massage That Includes the Testicles

Here are a few techniques to try on the testicles, as well as some strokes that include the testicles and penis. None of these strokes should cause any pain or discomfort. If they do, stop.

📝 **Simple Testicle Massage** Explore with your fingertips the space between the testicles. Be gentle at first, and seek plenty of feedback. Once you find a form of massage that pleases the man, do it often. For some men, the sensation feels like it's part back rub and part orgasm. They might even prefer this to stroking their penis. Once you get it just right, try not to vary the pressure or finger position, since the margin between delight and no pleasure is small.

📝 **Penis Up, Balls Down** Be sure that your hands are well-lubricated. Grasp the lower part of the penis with one hand. Clamp the thumb and forefinger of your other hand around the base of the scrotum where it attaches to the groin. This should cause the testicles to pop out a bit and the skin covering them should become taut. Squeeze both hands lightly, and then do an upward stroke with the penis hand while the testicle hand pulls gently in

Penis Up, Balls Down

the opposite direction. Find a tempo that works for both of you and keep repeating these strokes.

Ball Rub With the thumb and forefinger of one hand, make a ring around the part of your man's scrotum where it attaches to his groin. Squeeze gently until his testicles are popping out a bit, but not enough to cause pain. Run the fingertips of your other hand up and down the sides of the scrotum with a light tickling touch.

Flat-Handed Doggy Dig Straddle your partner's chest while facing his feet. Lay his penis flat against his belly with the head pointing up toward his navel. Place one of your well-lubricated hands between his legs with your fingertips resting below his testicles. Pull the hand all the way up to his belly, dragging your fingers over his testicles and penis. Repeat with your other hand, rhythmically alternating strokes as a dog might when digging in the dirt. This same stroke is illustrated in the chapter "The Zen of Finger Fucking," but it is being done on a woman.

Cross-Modal Stimulation

There's never any harm in running a hand up and down a man's inner thighs or across his chest and stomach at the same time that you are stimulating his penis. For instance, you might make a complete "U" by going up one thigh, around his crotch and down the other thigh. The same is true for rubbing his chest and stomach with one hand while stimulating his penis with the other. And there aren't too many men who would mind receiving tender kisses while your hand is stroking or massaging their genitals. If your partner is the type who enjoys nipple stimulation, try kissing or caressing his nipples at the same time that you are massaging his genitals.

The Point of No Return

When doing an extreme hand job, you might want to keep your man highly aroused for long periods of time without letting him ejaculate. No, we haven't lost our minds, it is possible.

Think about a scale of 0 to 10 where 0 means no sexual arousal and 10 is an orgasm. Let's say your partner starts to ejaculate when he reaches a 9 on this imaginary scale of sexual excitement. Past that, there's no turning back. Try to keep him between 7 and 8 on the same scale for as long as possible before finally letting him squirt, an event that might be rather powerful when it finally occurs.

One way to keep your man at such a high level of excitement is to learn his body language for when he is about to ejaculate. As is mentioned in a later chapter, "Dyslexia of the Penis—Improving Your Sexual Hang Time," there are physical signs when the well is about to blow: the veins in his penis may start to bulge or his penis might give a sudden throb, the color of the head might darken, his testicles may suck up into his groin, his muscles may suddenly tighten, his hips may thrust and he might start to groan like a dying bull or invoke the names of various saints. Change the stroke or decrease the intensity when this starts to happen.

Some women find it very helpful if the man is able to report his levels of excitement by saying something like "6," "7," "8," or "9." Even the cues "more" or "less" are often enough. This will help you learn when to up the pace and when to back off. After a while you will become so familiar with his body language that you won't need him to actually tell you.

Ready, Set, Relax

It never hurts to begin an extended hand job by finding those parts of your partner's body where tension gathers. Who knows why, but the shoulders and back often become the body's collecting points for tension. There is no point in doing good work on a man's genitals when the weight of the world is parked between his shoulder blades. This is also true for women's bodies.

Some men believe that the only important part of sex is when a penis is being rubbed, sucked or fucked. They might not care about the tension in their shoulders or even notice. They will sometimes direct your hands straight to their crotch with the idea that an orgasm will help relax them. While this is true, think of how much more pleasure they could receive if they were relaxed to begin with.

If your partner is getting too penis-oriented for his own good, go ahead and fondle his testicles with one hand. At the same time, repeat your request that he close his eyes and relax, and inform him straightaway that you will do to his body what you like, when you like, and how you like. If he still objects, slap him upside the head and remind him what you are holding in your other hand!

Spreading The Excitement—Pavlov Between the Legs

Extreme hand jobs can be used to help a man link the sensations in his crotch with other parts of his body. For instance, Hindu/Yoga types might have you stimulate the man's genitals with one hand while caressing various chakras (e.g. upper abdomen, heart, third eye) with your other hand. It might help if he inhaled deeply, as though he were sucking the warm glow from his genitals into the upper part of his body.

Western-psychology types might suggest kissing or caressing your partner's neck, shoulders or chest while massaging his genitals. At various intervals, stop stroking the man's genitals but continue to kiss or caress the other designated body parts. If he were a dog and his name was Pavlov, he might eventually learn to have genital sensations when you caress these other body parts.

Likewise, he might learn to have pleasant sensations in other parts of his body when his penis is stimulated. The ultimate goal is to help a man experience greater sensation over his entire body.

FOR GUYS

Helping A Partner Learn How to Please You

A man can help both himself and his partner if he will turn the lights up, get naked and let her do an introductory physics lab on his genitals. The purpose is for her to tickle, squeeze, tug and prod each part of the man's sexual anatomy so she can become more confident in handling his genitals. She can begin gently, increasing the pressure until the man says something earthshaking such as "Ouch!" At that point, the woman eases up until he says "Ah, that's perfect!" Here are a few specifics:

Penis Have her tug it, yank it and squeeze it until she's able to distinguish your Ouch! zone from your Perfect! zone. Then help her learn how to grasp your penis to give you a hand job. Indicate how far up and down you like the strokes to go, as well as how fast to do them and how long you wish she would keep stroking after you come.

Testicles If the room is cold and your cojones are in frostbite mode, turn up the heat and put something warm over them until you have managed to coax them back down. Once they are hanging freely, let her tickle, caress and play with them, letting her know what feels good and what doesn't. Then have her slowly squeeze each testicle until you say "Ouch!" Also, have her put a finger or two in the space between your testicles and push in until she is massaging the shaft.

Prostate For couples who are either curious about or into anal stimulation, consult the chapter "Up Your Bum—Anal Sex" which explains prostate massage.

Readers' Comments

What did you think the first time you saw a guy ejaculate?

"I did it right! Good job! I was proud of me. Then I thought, 'Geez, I hope my mom doesn't come home early.'"

female age 22

"I remember being disgusted and oddly fascinated at the same time, and I couldn't believe how far that stuff could shoot out!" *female age 32*

"It just kind of oozed out. For some reason I thought there was supposed to be more of a stream." *female age 37*

"I was jealous he could actually project it from his body and I couldn't." *female age 23*

"I was kinda grossed out by the whole thing." *female age 45*

"I was proud that I made him ejaculate, but I couldn't believe that people actually would let that go in their mouths. I was a senior in high school." *female age 25*

"I was a little shocked. I was young, 15, and I don't think I understood exactly what was going on. It's also when I realized that tissues weren't just for noses anymore." *female age 27*

"I wondered what it felt like. I wondered what it tasted like. Also, I wondered what it would feel like to have that happen inside of me." *female age 25*

"I vaguely remember thinking, it's amazing how their bodily process is. Also, there is what is needed to help form a human being." *female age 36*

Dear Paul,

My former boyfriend liked it when I gave him hand jobs without lubrication; my current one wants it with lubrication. What gives?

Tina in Twin Cities

Dear Tina,

Some of us like to sleep naked, others wear pajamas. Some like the mountains, others like the ocean. The same is true for hand jobs, although I don't know why we have different preferences. I do know that most of us are extremely grateful when someone else's hand is doing the stroking besides our own.

Be aware that oil-based lubes are far superior to water-based lubes for hand jobs . That's because water-based lubes dry out and you have to keep squirting his penis with water or spit on it to keep the surface hydrated. Also, there's no need to buy an expensive lube. You can use anything from corn oil to coconut oil, as long as you remember to strain out the little brown pieces in case you've already used it to fry the chicken.

Try exploring different strokes that will keep your guy's gizzard going for a long time without letting it ejaculate. There's a fine video on this subject by a gay organization that will help any woman give amazing hand jobs, and who cares if it's a straight penis or a gay penis that's flopping all over the TV screen? Turn us guys over and we all look the same anyway, more or less. I do recommend this tape with the following caveats: 1. It takes itself way too seriously; 2. Watch it with the sound off and 3. Fast forward through the first third or so, until you see the two guys demonstrating the actual strokes. This video is called *Fire On The Mountain*. They show a few previews of the different strokes on their internet site. Go to www.erospirit.org or call (800) 432-3767. Another resource to check out for hand-job techniques is Jay Wiseman's *Tricks: 125 Sex Tips To Make Good Sex Better* from Greenery Press, (888)944-4434. Also, try Ray Stubbs's *Male Erotic Massage: A Guide to Sex and Spirit* (Tuscon: Secret Garden Publishing). It has more than 200 photographs.

Dear Paul,

What if a guy is uncircumcised? Do you give him the same kind of hand job as a guy who is cut?   *Tina from Troy*

Dear Tina,

There shouldn't be much difference when giving a dry hand job, except there's more foreskin so it will slide better. In fact, a lot of guys who are uncut never need to use lube when they masturbate, since the extra foreskin does the job. With an uncut penis, the head might be more sensitive, so don't retract the foreskin until he's fully erect; from there, you'll need to ask, e.g., will he want you to pull the foreskin back with your free hand while you run your lubed hand over the shaft and exposed head?

Chapter Notes: Thanks to the writings of Brooks Peters.

Balls, Balls, Balls
Chapter 14

Balls usually take a back seat to the penis. One reason is because the pleasure you get from them is more subtle than what you get from whaling on your wang. But just because the pleasure is subtle doesn't mean it should be ignored. As one reader comments, "When my wife caresses my testicles and runs her hands up and down my inner thighs, it's one part excitement, two parts relaxation, and six parts total bliss. I didn't appreciate this when I was in my twenties, but now I enjoy it every bit as much oral sex. The sensation is different, but just as satisfying."

Ball Rules

Testicles are far more rugged than you might think and can usually be handled with impunity, but pop them with a simple flick of a finger and you might have to peel their owner off the ceiling. Heaven only knows why. Testicles should feel a little like hard-boiled eggs without the shell, but they won't be quite that big unless your lover is related to the racehorse Secretariat.

As a man becomes aroused, his testicles tend to swell or become bigger. When he is highly aroused or just about to come, his scrotum and testicles will rotate and hug the shaft of the penis, like bungee jumpers on the upswing. Another thing to know about testicles is that they can easily go from feeling soft to feeling hard. It depends on the temperature and on the man's level of sexual excitement.

Testicle Embryology

In the womb, males and females start off with the same genitals. These are female. If the fetus is bathed with masculinizing hormones, the female genitals will turn into male genitals. If not, the fetus is born with female genitals.

Embryologically speaking, if your man hadn't morphed into a male while in his mother's womb, the skin that made up his scrotum would have remained the lips of his vulva. If you look carefully, you'll notice a seam along the center of his scrotum. That's where his fetal labia fused together to make a scrotum. This is a long-winded way of saying that a man's scrotum has about the same sensitivity as the lips of your vulva. And his inner thighs are just as sensitive as yours, a fact he might not have noticed because he's been so busy playing with his penis.

Ball Tending

The preceding chapter has an entire section on testicle massage. For now, there's no need to try anything fancy, just experiment and see what he likes. You might start out by placing your fingertips on the sides of his scrotum and caressing as lightly as you can. Let his verbal feedback guide you from there.

You might also try resting the palm of your hand over his penis with your fingertips pointing down. Experiment with lightly massaging the back part of the scrotum, where it attaches to his groin. Every minute or so, push your palm down against the penis. This should give his penis a pleasant, isolated jolt of pleasure, which might mix nicely with the more subtle sensations that your fingertips are providing his balls.

Some guys will also find it pleasurable if you caress their testicles while they are face down.

Intercourse Extra

You can handle a man's testicles during intercourse if you are in a position which allows it. The most direct way is if you are on top facing his feet. Different rear-entry positions may also allow you to reach between your legs and caress his testicles. Experiment and see what you and he like best.

Liking a Licking

Some guys enjoy it if you lick and suck on their balls. At least the guy in the illustration for the chapter "Oral Sex: Popsicles & Penises" sure seems to.

The Exquisite Brush-Off

Get yourself a makeup brush or a Japanese bamboo artist's brush, have your cowboy spread his legs and gently brush his inner thighs, testicles, penis and abdomen. Doing repeated circles around the outside of his balls can feel especially nice. The sensation is subtle, somewhere between a feather and a fingertip. It can feel relaxing and titillating at the same time. If you enjoy taking control, you can always tie him up first.

When brushing a guy, don't limit your strokes to just his genitals. Try his face, back, feet and hands. If you're lucky, he'll grab the brush and return the favor.

Same man, morning, noon and night?
Not quite. Different balls, different guys.

Perineum

There is a patch of anatomical real estate between the testicles and rectum which is often ignored but has the potential for much sensation. It is called the perineum. (Women have one, too.) Tantric and Hindu types get all excited about this particular area and regard it with the same kind of awe that we Westerners sometimes do the reset button on the garbage disposal. Place your fingertips on this area with just enough pressure so the skin moves over the tissue beneath it. Experiment and see what feels best.

Another Kind of Tenderness

If you are so inclined, don't hesitate to reach between your man's legs and cup or cradle his genitals at nonsexual times, like when watching TV or while falling asleep. Some men will find this to be extremely thoughtful and caring. Others will find it too arousing, and some may dislike this kind of tenderness.

Dear Paul,

When I was a kid I had the mumps and my testicles swelledup. I have heard this can cause sterility. Does this mean I am sterile?

Bill from Ball State University

Dear Bill,

Mumps is a virus that often causes swelling of the salivary glands (below your jaw) and sometimes swelling of the testicles (below your penis). About fifteen to twenty-five percent of guys who get mumps get swelling in one of their balls and sometimes in both. Even if your testicles were swollen due to the mumps, it is very unlikely that this would cause you to become sterile. Physicians use the words "rare" and "very rare" to describe the frequency of infertility from mumps.

While you probably aren't sterile due to the mumps, the only way to know for sure is to have your sperm analyzed or to get a woman pregnant. I encourage you to try the former.

Dear Paul,

My newborn son has an undescended testicle. What do you know about this?

Pam from Little Rock

Dear Pam,

The medical term for undescended testicles is "cryptorchidism," which is Greek for "hidden gonad." One way to get a case of hidden gonads is to go surfing during the winter; another way is to be born with them.

Contrary to what seems logical, the testicles in the male fetus don't form between his legs. Instead, they develop inside his abdomen and do not descend into his scrotum until a month or two before he is born. They make the journey from the abdomen into the scrotum through the inguinal canal.

Approximately 3.5 percent of male babies are born with an undescended testicle. This testicle often descends on its own without medical intervention, so that by one year of age, only one percent of males (1 out of 100 or 150) still have an undescended testicle. In ninety percent of these cases, it's just one of the testicles that is undescended.

If the testicle remains undescended after the boy reaches a year of age, the current practice is to treat it surgically. This is often done as an outpatient operation. Attempts to coax the testicle down with hormone therapy have unacceptable side effects and any gains are usually short-lived.

In any case, I would encourage you to get a second or even a third opinion from a pediatric urologist. As Dr. Joseph Dwoskin, a urologist from Texas Tech says, "There are as many opinions about testes as there are physicians who examine them."

Dear Paul,

My boyfriend was recently diagnosed with cancer of the testicles. Since it's hit so close to home, I try to tell guys to examine their testicles. Most just laugh. Maybe they'll listen to you.

Barb from Rock Island

Dear Barb,

The term "cancer of the testicles" is a misnomer. It should be cancer of the testicle (singular), given how it's usually only one testicle that gets the cancer. This is good news, since we guys only need one ball to be fertile and have a perfectly normal sex drive. The only reason for having the other ball is for playing pocket pool.

Cancer of the testicles is 97 percent curable if detected early enough. Unfortunately, the last thing a guy between the ages of fifteen and thirty-five thinks about is the possibility of getting cancer. After all, cancer is something that happens to people your parents' age, so it is beyond the average male's consciousness to check his balls every month for lumps or changes in texture.

Another problem is that a lot of guys would rather sit naked on a fencepost than call the doctor's office and say, "I'm concerned about my testicle and I'd like you to check it out." So they wait until the cancer has spread all over the place before getting care. This isn't good, since some forms of testicular cancer can double in size in less than thirty days and you won't feel a bit of pain as it's happening.

A third roadblock in detecting cancer of the testicles is the extra meaning that we attach to testicles, as in the term "He's got balls!" Ever hear anyone say, "She's got ovaries!"? On a symbolic level, it's a big thing when a guy loses a ball, and I'm not talking over the fence. Most of us would rather deny the possibility.

Interestingly, it is often a girlfriend who discovers the cancer. This can be a real lifesaver, so I hope women readers will learn how to examine their boyfriend's balls in the name of health as well as pleasure.

The most common symptom to look for is a small lump or nodule on the side or sometimes the front of the testicle. It's usually not painful when you press on it. Another symptom is hardening of the testicle. Mind you, testicles swell and shrink, but it's time to get it checked when the entire testicle starts to lose its spongy texture.

Less common symptoms include pain or discomfort in the testicles, back pain, swollen breasts (guy breasts), or a kind of heaviness or unusual discomfort deep in your pelvis.

There are a number of things that can look like cancer. Most of these aren't and can often be treated with antibiotics. So don't assume that your doctor is going to present you with bad news.

It's very wise to do a routine ball exam once a month. The best time is when the scrotum is warm and saggy, like after a hot shower. Follow the instructions in the Ball Check chart that follows.

For a more complete discussion about cancer of the testicles, please see our website, www.goofyfootpress.com. Enter "cancer" in the Goofy search engine. We include links to the websites of men who've had cancer of the testicles. Interestingly, a lot of guys who have lost a ball to cancer don't have it replaced with a fake one, and are quite happy with their decision.

BALL CHECK!

You need to do a ball check every 30 days or 3,000 strokes, whichever comes first.

The best time to do a ball check is after a warm shower.

Use both hands. Grab a ball. Roll it between your fingers. You are looking for any bumps or lumps. They can be smaller than a pea. Check the sides really well, and the top and bottom.

BALL NOTES If you ever get popped in the balls and the pain lasts for more than ten minutes, it's a really good idea to have them checked by a physician. If not treated quickly, ball trauma can cause your huevos to become sterile. Also, one ball is usually bigger than the other. Nature made them that way. When you are sexually aroused, your balls tend to swell.

NEW iMAC SCROTUM!
This is what your ball would look like if you had a see-through scrotum. There are a couple of spaghettilike cords that attach to each testicle at the back, toward the top. They form a structure that is shaped like a comma. These might be fuller if you haven't ejaculated in a while. It may feel a little weird, but check out your comma for any little nodes, lumps or changes since the last check.

Squeeze that puppy—gently. It should feel a bit spongy, although this varies depending on the weather and how horny you are. Be aware if the ball becomes unusually firm or tender or starts to lose its spongy texture.

 Grab your other ball, and have at it.

 If either ball has any nodes, bumps or lumps, take it to a physician for a checkup. Chances are, it's only a cyst or infection, but that needs attention, too.

 CONGRATULATIONS! You are done. Now go grab your favorite lube and reading material, and make sure your sperm are swimming fine.

Late-Breaking (Excuse the Term) Ball News

Physicians are beginning to find that some guys who are sterile as adults got that way because they were playing sports without a cup and took a significant knock in the nuts. Any guy who is involved in a contact sport should wear a cup, whether he's an adult or a kid. Ditto if he's playing catcher in baseball. Fortunately, they have soft cups these days which are a lot better than nothing for the weekend warrior, and they'll make you look like you are really well hung. See "cup" in the Goofy Glossary at the end of this book for tips on wearing a cup.

Doing Yourself in Your Partner's Presence

Chapter 15

A lot of women have never seen a man masturbate, nor have many men seen a woman masturbate. Yet plenty of us, male or female, would find it interesting if not highly erotic to watch a partner masturbate. That's what this chapter is about, masturbating together or in your partner's presence.

In Front of a Partner

For straight people, masturbating in front of a partner can sometimes take a lot of trust. That's because masturbation tends to be more self-disclosing than other types of sex. It can also leave you feeling vulnerable if your partner finds you doing it. ("Oh, hi, honey, I was just sitting here jerking off.") Still, most of us continue to masturbate even when we are in a relationship, and being open about it usually helps to expand sexual enjoyment for both partners. Here are eight reasons why:

⌐ There is often something erotic and even forbidden about seeing your partner masturbate. This is just as true for women watching men as for men watching women.

⌐ If your partner can see how you please yourself, it might help him or her understand more about pleasing you.

⌐ Orgasms from masturbation are sometimes the most intense kind of orgasm. It might increase the level of intimacy in your relationship if you can ask your partner to hold you while you bring yourself to orgasm.

⌐ Masturbating together is an excellent way to share intense sexual feelings without the risk of unwanted pregnancy.

⌐ People often have unreal expectations that a partner can satisfy all of their sexual urges. There will be plenty of times when one of you is in the mood and the other isn't. There may also be times when your partner is so pleasantly drained by what you have just done (oral sex, genital massage, etc.) that he or she curls up and falls asleep on the spot. If the two of you are comfortable about masturbation, then the spent one can simply offer to hold the horny one while he or she masturbates, or you can masturbate while your partner conks out.

🖐 There are times when people feel like doing it solo. If this is an accepted part of your relationship, you won't have to hide or feel like some sort of weirdo when you want to control your own orgasmic destiny.

🖐 Sometimes your partner may want to lie down beside you and masturbate too!

🖐 Summers in the East, South and Midwest are sometimes so miserably hot and muggy that the last thing you'll want to do is hug an equally hot and sweaty partner. Masturbating together is one way you can share sexual pleasure without full body contact.

When you do masturbate in each other's presence, don't forget that a partner's pleasure might be greatly enhanced with a special assist on your part. For instance, a man might enjoy it tremendously if his partner caresses or massages his testicles while he masturbates, and a woman might find it delightful if her partner licks her nipples or whispers sweet but nasty things into her ears while she masturbates. The possibilities abound.

Virgin Birth Alert! If you have your partner's ejaculate on your fingers, be sure to wash your hands before touching your vulva. One woman actually became pregnant from masturbating right after giving her high school sweetheart a hand job.

Readers' Comments

"I wish he would do it in front of me more often.... I've even named his penis Squeegy Loueegy." *female age 37*

"I never realized it was possible for a guy to be turned on by seeing a woman touching herself. Needless to say, once I figured this out about him, I put on a good show."

female age 45

"It took a while for us to get comfortable with it, but I like to watch my husband stroke his penis. He enjoys watching me, too. I often masturbate as part of our loveplay because I like stimulation in more places at once than two hands are capable of doing." *female age 47*

"During intercourse one of us always has to touch me so I can have an orgasm, so in that respect, he's seen me do it. And we both chat about how we masturbate when we are alone sometimes." *female age 30*

"It's very intimate, sort of like sharing your most personal thoughts! And it's very arousing." *female age 26*

"I masturbate in front of my husband, mostly with a vibrator. I still find it a bit embarrassing." *female age 35*

"We never masturbated together until my wife bought your *Guide To Getting It On!* After reading it, we now talk freely about masturbation. We've both had some wonderful orgasms this way!" *male age 38*

"I have watched her masturbate and even helped her, and she has done the same with me. It is fun and important for both of us." *male age 70*

Dear Paul,

I sometimes wake up in the middle of the night to find my boyfriend masturbating. He thinks I'm sleeping and don't know about it. Why would he be doing this after we just made love a few hours earlier?

Ann in Cheyenne

Dear Ann,

There could be lots of reasons, and maybe I'll be able to nail one or two in the paragraphs that follow. But first, let's talk about masturbation within a relationship.

Many of us have the fantasy that once we get into a relationship, we won't be playing with ourselves anymore. In some relationships, that's how it is for the first couple of months or years. You either don't have the urge to masturbate, or can't remember why you used to do it so often. In other relationships, which can be just as satisfying, you don't really stop masturbating.

More often than not, it's impossible for us to fully satisfy each other's sexual needs. For instance, you might be worried about a project that's hanging over your head and the last thing you feel like doing is having sex. Or maybe there is nothing you are worried about—you just don't feel like getting physical. That's when it is really helpful if your partner feels free to masturbate.

As for your current situation with your boyfriend, here are some things to keep in mind:

It is possible that he loves having sex with you, but wakes up horny and feels bad about waking you up, so he takes care of matters himself.

It's possible that he wakes up in the middle of the night and can't get back to sleep. Plenty of us use masturbation as a natural sleep aid.

It's possible he masturbates several times a day to help with anxiety or depression. If that's the case, it's best for him to get some therapy.

It's possible he feels the same way as some of the people who answered our sex suvey on the next page.

Also, some guys aren't able to come with a partner, but are able to do so by masturbating. They might learn to fake orgasms so their partner won't think there is something wrong.

Whatever the reason for your boyfriend's midnight masturbation, it might help if you could talk to him about it. Otherwise, you will think there's something weird about the situation when there probably isn't.

The last thing I would do is confront the issue directly. Instead, try to create an atmosphere where it's safe for the two of you to disclose really private things about yourselves. For instance, you might raise the issue of masturbation in general, asking him if he would hold or maybe watch you while you gave yourself an orgasm. Most guys would think they had died and gone to heaven. Perhaps this would help make the subject of masturbation safe for conversation. Eventually, you can ask him how he does it and if he enjoys doing it in addition to the sex that the two of you have.

We recently asked the following question on our sex survey at www.goofyfootpress.com:

Is masturbation an important part of your life? If you have a partner, does she or he know?

Nearly ninety percent of the men and women who are in sexually satisfying relationships answered "Yes" and "Yes." Here are some of the typical responses:

"How often? About three times a week, give or take. My partner does know, and we openly masturbate in front of each other." *female age 20*

"I masturbate regularly because in the fourteen years that I have been sexually active I have never received an orgasm from intercourse. The only way I can come is from a vibrator or by my husband performing oral sex on me. Sometimes I masturbate privately, other times in front of my husband right after intercourse." *female age 35*

"Masturbation is the act in my life that keeps me sane. My wife even helps me sometimes...." *male age 38*

"My partner probably knows, but I do it more than he thinks." *female age 21*

"I masturbate several times a week, and if she doesn't know after twenty-five years, well I'd be surprised." *male age 48*

"Sometimes, you just want to come and not have intercourse with your partner. It makes sense because you know how to make yourself get off better and faster than anybody else. You might also get to know yourself and discover new techniques." *female age 26*

"I love to touch myself, even if that means just holding the palm of my hand between my legs on top of my jeans. I just like the warmth and the comfort." *female age 22*

Nipples, Nipples, Nipples
Chapter 16

This chapter talks about ways of using your fingers and mouth to tweak your partner's titties. Plenty of women and men have mega nerve endings in their nipples. The sensations they transmit can be both pleasant and annoying.

For instance, one woman might find it heavenly when a lover barely breathes on her nipples, but convulses in pain if he is the slightest bit rough. So the guy learns to traverse her tender nipples like a butterfly and becomes a master at the art of subtle stimulation. Another woman might want her partner to handle her nipples with authority and doesn't find it erotic until his lips latch on like an industrial vacuum cleaner. Also, some women's breasts become more sensitive during certain stages of their menstrual cycle, especially if they are taking birth control pills. Know your lover's body, and be sensitive to this.

In our society it is assumed that men are the ones who stimulate women's nipples instead of its being a mutual experience. Too bad. Guys have the same variation in nipple sensitivity as women. Some men get an erection and nearly come when their nipples are caressed.

No matter what the sex of your lover, here are a few things to consider when kissing and caressing nipples and chests. Keep in mind that you may feel clumsy the first umpteen times.

Size vs. Performance As with a clitoris or penis, the sensitivity of a breast has nothing to do with its size. Small ones can be like lightning rods, while big ones might not be sensitive at all.

Making the Nipple Taut Place your fingers on each side of the nipple, not quite touching the nipple but around the perimeter of it. Push down lightly and pull or slide your fingers apart. This will make the nipple taut. Begin licking or sucking.

🐄 **In and Out** Pucker up your lips and use them to make a gasket around the nipple. Then suck in and out without breaking the seal—so the nipple feels alternating currents of vacuum and pressure. This method is described in more detail in Ray Stubbs's book *The Clitoral Kiss* (Tuscon, Arizona: Secret Garden). It also works well on earlobes and the clitoris. However, if you are sucking earlobes in this way, be sure that earrings are removed first. As for jewelry in the nipples or clitoris, what's a boy to do?

Five-Finger Nipple Grab This works best if the breast and your hand are lubricated with massage oil. Rest the palm of your hand over the breast with your fingertips around its circumference. As you lift your hand, let your fingertips caress their way up the sides of the breasts until they are clasping the tip of the nipple. Pull on the nipple just a little or a lot, depending on what your partner likes and her level of arousal.

Nipple between Your Index & Middle Fingers The ability to do this will depend upon the size and shape of the nipple. Cup your hand over the breast in such a way that the tip of the nipple rests in the space between your middle finger and index (or other) fingers. Squeeze the fingers together so that when you lift your hand the nipple follows, pulling the rest of the breast up with it.

Nipple and Penis Some women find it highly arousing when a man caresses their nipples with the head of his penis. If he pulls apart the opening of his penis, he can sometimes stick the tip of an erect nipple into it. This is particularly true if he is uncircumcised.

The Whole Enchilada Women who like having their breasts and nipples caressed sometimes complain that men don't spend enough time doing this. It's hard to lavish too much attention upon your partner's breasts if she enjoys it. Also, consider licking and sucking the entire breast and not just the nipple, and remember to alternate breasts every once in a while.

Hand and Mouth Chances are, your partner has two breasts and you have only one mouth. Perhaps she might like it if your fingers are caressing one breast while your lips are tending to the other. Or maybe she'll find this distracting, or perhaps she would prefer your hand to be caressing some other part of her body. The best way to find out is to ask.

Variations in Sensitivity Sometimes one breast or nipple is more sensitive than the other. Find out if your partner would like you to spend more time on the sensitive side.

🐐 **Different Temperatures** An ice cube in the mouth can be a rousing way to greet a partner's nipples. Or for nipples that are already cold, drinking something warm just before licking or sucking them can feel quite exquisite.

🐐 **Playful Plate** Fruit salad, all kinds of fruits, dessert foods, and certain liquors can be served on nipples, chests, abdomens, backs and other body parts with extremely pleasing results. Do what you can to keep sugars out of the vagina. Also, you might check out the definition of "body shots" in the glossary at the back of the book.

🐐 **Getting to Watch** Some people find it highly erotic to watch while a partner plays with her (or his) own nipples and breasts. So if you enjoy playing with your own nipples, there's no point in keeping it a secret.

Hard-Nipple Alert

Let's say you are playing with your partner's nipples and they get hard, is this a good sign? Sometimes yes, sometimes no. Until you learn more about your partner's body, don't assume that hard nipples mean happy nipples. Nipples can get hard from unpleasant stimuli such as roughness, abrasion, and cold—so be sure to ask your partner if he or she likes what you are doing. Also be aware that what a person wants in terms of nipple play can vary with their state of sexual arousal.

Readers' Comments

"Kissing my breast depends upon my mood. Sometimes I like being touched gently with fingertips and then gentle circles of a tongue followed by a very light sucking on the nipples." *female age 27*

"Most of the sensitivity is in the nipple, but there are good feelings from having the whole breast caressed and sucked. Swirling your tongue around the nipple is good. Sucking the nipple is great! Biting the nipple is a MAJOR no-no." *female age 34*

"Depending on how aroused I am, I like to be sucked hard and even gently bitten on the nipple." *female age 45*

"There doesn't seem to be any logical pattern or reason behind it, but sometimes even touching the breast area can hurt. Other times, pretty much of anything is okay." *female age 32*

Dear Paul,
My girlfriend has killer boobs, but I don't have the hang of how to please them. Any suggestions?
Harry from Hootersville

Dear Harry,

May I point you in the direction of a wonderful, easy-to-read book by author Meema Spadola titled *Breasts—Our Most Public Private Parts* (Berkeley: Wildcat Canyon Press, 1998).

🐑Here's one quote from *Breasts* that plenty of couples can relate to: "For many women, what turns us on varies from day to day. My preferences vary constantly. What feels pleasurable one moment can feel annoying the next. Sometimes I hit sensory overload and can barely stand to have my breasts touched."

🐑Cecilia, from *Breasts*, says, "My nipples are very sensitive and I could be aroused almost to the point of orgasm just by touching them, but only very gently, almost not at all." At the other end of the spectrum is Heather, who prefers a very firm touch that includes clothespins and biting.

🐑Ms. Spadola tells about Carrie, who was known as the girl with the big boobs. "Guys were sometimes more attracted to my boobs than to me." One day when Carrie was wearing a large rain slicker which hid her breasts behind a wall of thick yellow plastic, she met a guy from out of town and they seemed to hit it off. They talked on the phone and wrote letters for the first year of their relationship, with him never knowing that her bras were the size of saddlebags. Assured that he liked all of her and not just her mammaries, she eventually married the man.

🐄Breast negative: Ms. Spadola quotes a woman who says, "When a man touches my breasts, I feel a little removed from the whole experience—as if he's on a date with my breasts." Another woman says, "My boyfriend loves to suck on my nipples, but sometimes I get this sense that he is focusing on them and tuning me out, and I can feel a wave of resentment, almost jealousy, when he latches onto my breasts." (Guys, can you imagine feeling jealous of your penis if a woman was constantly latching onto it with her lips?) A third woman says, "I would feel like I had this 180-pound baby in my arms, and occasionally he'd fall asleep there [sucking her breasts]. I'm sure he thought he was giving me great pleasure, but it just didn't do it for me."

🐄Breast positive: There are women who describe their breasts as being "a place of warmth and love," and "Without breast stimulation, sex is purely physical with no emotional component." Another perspective comes from Scarlet, with 38DD breasts, who says, "I can't wait to take my clothes off in bed because I know that men will get excited; they always want to suck on my breasts. They think that I get incredibly turned on by it, but my breasts aren't as sensitive as men expect. Honestly, I could be balancing my checkbook while they're doing it. It's really not a big deal. But I do get turned on seeing them getting very turned on."

🐄And finally, Ms. Spadola quotes a woman who has had sex with both men and women: "The men didn't seem to grasp that twisting them like radio dials does not work. They treated my breasts as something separate from my body. Women seem to know instinctively what to do with breasts. Women sense that there are times when you want your breasts to be touched, and times you don't. It didn't seem to occur to the men I was with that there might be mental and cultural baggage wrapped up there."

With all of this in mind, I have a suggestion for female readers: Even if your guy has a big hairy chest, tell him you're going to touch and kiss his "breasts" the same way you like to have yours kissed, and then do it. If there are times when you like it gentle, tell him, "This is what I like when I say gentle." If there are times when you like it extra-rough, grab a pair of vice grips and let him know what you mean when you say rough. If you like your nipples tugged, show him exactly how and for how long. And please, don't get all bent out of shape if he requires refresher lessons. The learning process is not nearly as straightforward as you might think.

Men and women alike are encouraged check out Meema Spadola's nifty book. You can purchase it from your local book-store or order it directly from Wildcat Canyon Press, (510)848-3600. ISBN 1-885171-27-7.

Dear Paul,

No matter what I do, I can't get my wife to examine her breasts for breast cancer. She seems to be in denial that the possibility of cancer even exists. What should I do?

Syd from Sheboygan

Dear Syd,

Ask your health-care provider for info on doing breast exams. Perhaps you can do them on an ongoing basis without her knowing, or maybe she'll let you do them if she can be totally passive and uninvolved. Don't expect gratitude, but maybe she'll let you do it. On some level, she might even feel relieved.

A few things to consider when doing a breast exam: Breasts tend to be lumpy, and the lower curve of each breast often contains firm tissue. Since the geology of each breast fluctuates with the woman's menstrual status, it is a good idea to do breast exams at the same time each month, preferably after a woman's period. That way you'll establish a baseline reading. With the woman's arms raised above her head, feel each part of her breasts with the pads of your fingers as opposed to your fingertips. Check all the way to the armpits. Things to look for are lumps that are hard, don't move, or feel connected to the breast itself.

Contrary to what you might think, women in their twenties can get breast cancer, so start doing those exams now!

For those of you who would examine your breasts more often if only it were fun, we gladly present, "Boob Check"....

BOOB CHECK!

①

You gotta check your boobs, right? While it's good to do it the American Cancer Society way, you can also mix it up at times by making it part of a fantasy.

Either way, breast exams need to be done every month, even if you are only twenty. But it doesn't have to be like a trip to the gynecologist.

Here's one way of spicing up the monthly breast exam...

②

You have nothing on except one of those skimpy little paper gowns. You hear the door to the examining room open. Suddenly, your view, which until now has been of white ceiling tiles, is interrupted by the smile of a doctor. You quickly do a double take—this guy is seriously cute!

He apologizes for having to meet you this way, and asks if you will stand and open the gown. He tries to look calm, yet he pauses and breathes deep. He has you do all sorts of rude things with your arms—hold 'em up, put them on your hips, bend forward and finally relax. With each change in your posture, you can feel his eyes on your breasts, hungry and alert for any changes in the color or texture.

③

Now he asks you to lie flat on your back with your right arm behind your head.

④

Your body tenses as the pads of his fingers (your left hand) begin to examine every inch of your chest. You moan quietly as he moves his fingers in small circles, the size of a dime. You think you hear him moan too. He pauses to put talc or lotion on your breasts, to help his fingers glide smoothly from one spot to the next, making little circles, as if he were finger-painting a string of pearls across your breast. He repeats every circle several times before moving his fingers forward, varying the pressure from light to hard, feeling every creamy, sensuous layer. His fingertips move slowly.

⑤

He grasps your wrist and places it by your side. His fingers gently probe the warm moist crease between your breast and arm, searching for lumps, bumps and swelling. How can something as unattractive as an armpit suddenly feel so good?

⑥

His fingertips reach for your nipple, hard from delight not cold. He squeezes for discharge. Your hips lift; a moist longing between your legs begins to spread. His breathing stops—then starts.

⑦ He clears his throat and tugs his white coat closed. He asks you to lift your other arm...

Dear Paul,

    I am a twenty-year-old female and had to have a breast biopsy last year for a lump. I had not thought of my breasts as pretty before. They have always seemed too small compared to what all the boys were paying attention to. With a gain in self-esteem and self-respect and with the help of my current boyfriend, I've found that I really do think of my breasts in a whole new way, especially after going through the experience of surgery. My lump was benign, but it made me think about myself in a new way and what I really have to appreciate.

DD from Boulder

Dear Paul,

    When I was a girl, my dad and I used to play and wrestle a lot. These are some of my fondest memories of childhood. Then, when I became a teenager, our physical closeness seemed to suddenly stop. Now that I'm older, I think it might have been because my chest started to develop and he began to feel uncomfortable. Is this possible?

Bella from Bellingham

Dear Bella,

    I suspect you have hit the proverbial nail on the head. Growing breasts come between a lot of dads and their preteen daughters. Hopefully, dads will become aware of this and understand the huge loss to their daughters. Dads can gradually transform the physical closeness by being involved in other ways—with everything from playing catch to taking their daughter someplace special each week like a museum or out to lunch. The important thing is to maintain the intimacy which is so important to most daughters and dads while moving the physical relationship into something that's a bit more age appropriate.

Oral Sex: Popsicles & Penises
Chapter 17

Some women truly enjoy giving oral sex to a man. It provides them with feelings of intimacy and closeness that can be both soothing and erotic. It also gives some women a feeling of power and control. Other women don't find anything special about doing oral sex, but will go down on a guy if he enjoys it. And some women would rather suck on a rusty old pipe than let their lips stray south of a man's beltline.

Whatever your preference, this chapter offers tips and techniques about giving oral sex to the male of the species. It starts with a candid discussion about male ejaculate and then offers various techniques for giving splendid blow jobs. It also includes a series of suggestions for the man who is receiving oral sex—things he can do to help make it a neat experience for both partners.

When Gay Guys Blow

Straight women often get the feeling that they need to swallow a guy's ejaculate in order to give a truly fine blow job. If this were true, you'd think it would apply just as much in the gay community, where the giver of the blow job knows exactly what it feels like to receive a blow job. But that's not true. Gay guys usually don't swallow when giving blow jobs. As one gay male reader says, "No way am I going to do all that work getting a partner to come and not watch him ejaculate. Besides, I don't exactly love the taste."

Of course, you might love swallowing whatever your man can pump. But do it only because you want to and not because there's some Emily Post of Blow Jobs who says it has to be.

To Swallow or Not to Swallow—That Is the Question

Considering what happens if you suck on a penis for long enough, a woman who gives oral sex eventually has to decide if she wants to swallow ejaculate. While some women don't mind swallowing, others find it weird. For many women the salient factors are how they feel about the guy and how they feel within the relationship. For others, it's a matter of taste and texture.

Different guys come in different flavors. They also have different textures and volumes. For instance, one man's ejaculate might be viscous while another's is thin. One man might taste good while another tastes bitter or salty, or as a female reader states: "My current lover tastes great, I like swallowing his ejaculate. But when my former boyfriend came, it felt like battery acid in the back of my mouth." Another reader comments that she has no problem with the taste or texture of male ejaculate, but that it sometimes upsets her stomach. A British sex expert with a Margaret Thatcher-like voice says that male ejaculate is an acquired taste, like swallowing raw oysters. She says it's nothing to get worked up over. We're not so sure, given how nobody around here likes swallowing raw oysters. As for the smell of male ejaculate, it's like a weak solution of Clorox—original scent rather than Lemon Fresh or Spring Rain.

Who knows what to advise about swallowing male ejaculate, except to say that a man shouldn't push the issue unless he is willing to swallow a mouthful of his own, although the actual amount is closer to a teaspoonful. Suggestions for how to give a really good blow job without swallowing are listed later in this chapter.

To Swallow or Not to Swallow: Hormonal Considerations

Women sometimes wonder if they are going to get a dose of male hormones when they swallow male ejaculate. Not to worry. While the testicles produce the lion's share of male hormone, these hormones are not released into a man's ejaculate. Instead, they are dumped directly into the bloodstream, where they can have an impact on the rest of his body. A woman is not going to sprout a beard or grow a big Adam's apple from swallowing her partner's cum. She will get more male hormone from giving him a hickey. As for the question of calories, the only way you will gain weight from male ejaculate is if it makes you pregnant, and it is biologically impossible to get pregnant from oral sex alone.

Regarding the issue of health, ejaculate from a healthy guy has far fewer germs than saliva. It seldom causes an allergic reaction. The main health concern about male sex fluids is whether the man has a sexually transmitted disease. For more on STDs, see the chapter, "Birth Control & Gnarly Sex Germs."

Quick & Easy

Going down on a man isn't as much a mystery as going down on a woman, given how the penis is pretty much in your face from start to finish. The childhood experience of sucking on popsicles will give you an idea of how to begin. However, popsicle sucking does not make for an excellent blow job unless your man keeps his penis in the freezer.

There are many different kinds of blow jobs. Some women like to give blow jobs that include lots of kissing and licking; others mainly suck on the thing and do fine at that. Using your hands while giving oral sex adds an extra dimension.

It never hurts to ask your partner what he likes, but these discussions are usually more productive after you've been down on him a time or two. The shared experience provides both of you with a point of reference. Then he can say, "I really liked it when you..."

Dozens of tips are listed in the pages that follow—just about anything you'd ever want to know about giving a really good blow job. But if the doorbell is ringing and you need a quick primer in ten lines or less, you might start by tossing the lucky guy on his back. Lick his penis to get it wet with your saliva. This provides pleasure and lubrication. Then, make a ring around the penis with your lips. This will create a gasket. Slide your head up and down, but only as far as you feel comfortable. There is no need to suck. Each time you pull your head up, suction will build naturally in your mouth. But please don't take our word for it. Try it first on one of your fingers. Notice how good this makes your finger feel!

Of course, there are about a hundred other factors to consider, from what to do with your saliva to keeping yourself from gagging.

Gag Prevention

Some women complain that they gag when giving blow jobs. When asked if they ever bothered to tell their partners about this, the gagging girls usually reply no. Perhaps their male partners were inconsiderate oafs, or maybe these men had trouble reading the women's minds. Whatever the case, many men would do back flips to please a partner if only they were told what she does or doesn't like. The last thing most men want is to hurt or displease a woman sexually.

What follows are four suggestions to help keep yourself from being gagged while giving a blow job, but the most important and intelligent suggestion is clearly the first:

🦊 **Tell Him!** If he thrusts and it gags you, let him know. Tell him that the two of you need to work on it, because you enjoy giving him blow jobs except for that part. Be specific! If a little thrusting is okay, help him recognize the difference between good and painful thrusting.

🦊 **Fist on Shaft** Make a fist around the shaft of your lover's penis, with your little finger resting on his pubic bone. This will give you four knuckles' worth of washer or buffer. If your man has an average-sized penis, there should be less than three remaining inches to go into your mouth. If your man is luckier than most, use two hands instead of one, as you would if swinging a baseball bat or even a golf club. As an added benefit, keeping your fingers around the shaft can be nice for him if you use them to pump the foreskin or pull it taut. More on the pleasure aspects later.

On His Back Some guys thrust involuntarily when they come. To deal with this, keep your bronco on his back and position your body between his legs. When he is close to coming, keep both of your hands around the base of his penis and your forearms flat against his pelvis. The weight of your body distributed against his pelvic region will help discourage any unwanted thrusting, and if he does thrust it will pull you up with him.

Balls Clamp your thumb and forefinger together around the upper part of the man's scrotum where it attaches to his groin. This will place the testicles in the palm of your hand. Some men find this pleasurable, especially if the woman gently pulls downward. Then, if he thrusts more than you want, increase the downward pull, as though you were pulling back on a horse's reins.

Positions for Penis Sucking

A highly effective position for doing oral sex is to place yourself between your partner's legs, facing his body. This gives your tongue direct access to the most sensitive parts of his penis and scrotum, and the angle minimizes the tendency of the head of the penis to bang against your molars. It's a comfortable position for most women, and it lets a man watch you giving him head, which some men find to be reassuring, loving and a turn-on. Another variation is to sit, kneel or crouch in front of your partner while he is standing or sitting.

Some couples like the woman to straddle the guy's chest. In this position, she faces southward as she would if the couple were doing 69. This can be particularly nice for the guy if staring at his sweetheart's crotch and rear end provides an extra turn-on.

But it places her mouth in a lousy position to give his penis maximum stimulation, as it puts her tongue in contact with the back side of the penis, which isn't as sensitive as the front.

In the positions mentioned so far, the guy lies still and the woman provides the up and down motion. Another way of doing a blow job is where the woman keeps her head still and the guy moves his penis in and out of her mouth. The fancy term for this that nobody but the pope ever uses is "irrumation," which is Latin for "altar boy, hold still!"

The position the woman usually takes in irrumation or "face-fucking" is on her back with her head propped up on a pillow. The man sits astride her upper body and gently thrusts his penis in her mouth. The woman lets the guy do some of the work and she has good access to his testicles and rear end, or she can easily masturbate while he's receiving the blow job. The couple can also alternate penis thrusting with French kissing. On the other hand, some women become bored or feel claustrophobic giving a blow job with the guy on top, or they fear that the man might be rough or thrust too deep. Putting your hand around the shaft of his penis while he thrusts will greatly decrease any chance that he might thrust too deep.

A final position that some couples enjoy is where they lie side by side, with the woman's mouth in front of the man's genitals. She can lay her head on a pillow and do the up-and-down motion by moving her neck or he can thrust with his hips. On the other hand, one of her arms may be out of commission because she's lying on her side, and her head motions are limited.

Deep-Throat Myth—Where to Suck and Where Not To

You wouldn't stick an entire popsicle down your throat, so why try it with a guy's dick? Truly great blow jobs have nothing to do with deep-throating a man. Deep-throating is more of a novelty than something that makes a penis feel great. If your man insists that you deep-throat him, go to the market and buy a vegetable that's the same size as his erect penis, hand it to him and say, "Okay, let's see you shove this thing down your throat!"

Also, don't confuse a penis with a clitoris and think that every square centimeter is packed with thousands of nerve endings. As was said in the porn film *How to Perform Fellatio:* "The most sensitive part of the penis is the top part, so stop wasting your time on the bottom," and the male actor who uttered this profound statement had a penis with a great deal of bottom part to suck if he had so wanted.

The average penis has certain parts that are sensitive and other parts that are mostly for show. For some guys, especially those who are uncircumcised, the head might be really sensitive. Work out with your man if and how he likes you to suck or lick the head. Also, there is a sensitive nickel-sized area just below the head on the side of the penis that's away from his body when he has an erection. It's called the frenulum, and some guys can be brought to orgasm from stimulating this area alone. The seam of the penis that runs from the scrotum to the head usually responds to tender kisses, as does the entire scrotum.

If you still insist on deep-throating your partner, two resources to consider are the videotape *How to Perform Fellatio* with tonsil-aerobics host Karen Summer, and the book *Ultimate Kiss* by Steve and Jacqueline Franklin. Do not get the video by the same name, as it has nothing to do with the book and is truly dreadful. It might also help if you position your body so you are either on top of the man in a 69-type position or are lying on your back with your head over the edge of the bed. These positions will help to straighten the pathway down your throat. They are better for deep-throating but not nearly as good for regular blow jobs.

Blow-Job Basics

Several tips and techniques are listed in this section for giving a really good blow job.

Slobber People who are neat freaks often try to swallow all of their own drool when giving blow jobs. Such people have been known to nearly drown. Smart women let gravity carry their saliva down a lover's penis. They can also use it as a lubricant for pumping the bottom part of the penis with one hand while doing the upper part by mouth. Don't hesitate to toss a towel under the man's rear or to wedge one beneath his testicles; that way there won't be a big wet spot or stain on the mattress or couch.

If It's Still Soft Some women enjoy sucking on a soft penis and feeling it grow inside their mouth. Just because it's soft, don't think for a moment that each kiss, lick and suck doesn't feel exquisite. One of the few times when a man can be totally passive and feel no need to perform sexually is while he is receiving a blow job. Don't assume it's a negative sign if it takes a while to get hard or if it doesn't get hard at all. A guy can still have a really enjoyable orgasm with a soft dick.

Lubrication for Licking When you first lick a man's genitals, coat your lips and tongue with extra saliva. This will make it feel better. Honest. If you suffer from the dreaded pre-blow-job dry mouth, try sucking on a mint beforehand to help kickstart your salivary glands.

Teeth Some women wrap their lips over their teeth when giving a blow job, given how the mere hint of teeth on the penis scares the tar out of some men. However, a set of sexy choppers can sometimes feel erotic, assuming you're not in a pit-bull kind of mood. Ask, experiment and see what you come up with.

Little Kisses & Flickering Tongues Never hesitate to lavish your man's genitals or any other part of his body with neat little flicks of the tongue or sweet little lip-locks. The kisses not only feel nice, but allow you to rest your jaw without totally stopping the action. It usually works better if the area you are flicking your tongue over is already lubricated with saliva or massage oil, so get it good and wet.

Twisting Your Head Twisting your head when going up and down the penis (in a corkscrew pattern) provides a higher level of stimulation, especially when focused on the upper half of the penis. Try it on your finger.

Further Twisting/Corkscrew Action (for the experienced) While on the upstroke, wait until you are halfway up the shaft and put the tip of your tongue under the ridge of the penis head. Not only does your tongue press against the sensitive frenulum while your head is twisting, but the tip of your tongue adds extra stimulation to the sensitive ridge.

📿 **The Shirley Temple** You can lick the penis with the pointed end of your tongue, or you can soften your tongue and give it a long flat lick that covers more real estate. The latter is called a "Shirley Temple" because it's similar to the way a person licks a big lollipop.

📿 **Uncut** For Partners Who Aren't Circumcised: Without retracting his foreskin, stick the tip of your tongue inside his foreskin and run it in a circle around the head of his penis. You can pull the foreskin down with your fingertips. NOTE: Guys who are uncut usually have a more sensitive penis head than guys who are circumcised.

📿 **The Long Lick** Mother nature left a seam on the penis that runs from just below the head to halfway down the scrotum. Never hesitate to take a long, wet lick from beneath your partner's testicles all the way to the tip of his penis, along the length of the seam.

📿 **Making the Foreskin Taut** Using your hand to pull the skin taut over the shaft of the penis can sometimes enhance the pleasure of a blow job. It might also encourage the man to come sooner if that's what you want. The way you do it is by wrapping your thumb and forefinger, or your entire fist, around the shaft of the penis an inch or so above the base. Then pull it down to the base. This makes the skin tighter on the penis and usually increases the sensitivity in the upper part of the penis.

📿 **Pumping the Shaft** While your lips are focusing on the upper part of the penis, there's no reason why you can't be pumping the bottom part of the shaft with your hand or fingers. Let your saliva flow down the shaft, lubricating both it and your hand, and start pumping.

📿 **Pumping the Shaft, Part II** Some women synchronize the shaft pumping with their head bobbing, so their hand follows just beneath their lips at all times.

📿 **The Vacuum Factor (Hoover Fellatis)** Some men will like it if you draw a light vacuum with your mouth. One way to draw a vacuum is to take as much of the penis in your mouth as feels comfortable, make a seal around the shaft with your lips and suck some of the air out of your mouth. Then, as you pull your head back, a vacuum is created.

Na-Na-Na-Nipples Some guys have nipples that are highly sensitive. Caressing them with your finger while doing oral sex might add to the man's overall pleasure. The best way to find out is to experiment and seek feedback.

Inner Thighs and Other Places The inner thighs of both men and women can be extremely sensitive. There's no reason why you can't lick and suck on your man's inner thighs, or caress them with a free hand while giving him a blow job.

Fingers in His Mouth When you are blowing him, you might try sticking your fingers in his mouth. Some guys will find this added touch to be very erotic.

Perineum (Between the Testicles and Rear End) There is an area behind the testicles called the perineum that is often overlooked but has the potential for wonderful feelings. Licking this area can light some guys up. A gentle finger massage down here can also add an extra dimension to oral sex.

The Blow Hole This is the little slit in the head of the penis where the ejaculate comes out. It might be fun to explore it with the tip of your tongue.

Rear End Some men find that a finger on or up the anus when receiving a blow job can feel wonderful. Some men claim that the most intense orgasms they have ever had occurred when a woman was giving them oral sex while massaging their prostate. Other men hate this sort of thing. Also, a small vibrator up the rear might catch some men's attention, and some couples enjoy rimming (oral-anal contact). For more on playing with his bum while giving him oral sex, see the chapter "Up Your Bum."

Visual Glee There are plenty of men who enjoy watching a woman give them head. Some women might be offended by the notion, thinking that this has something to do with submission. If the truth be known, the chances are that the man is way too appreciative to be thinking anything other than adoring thoughts.

In her video on how to give blow jobs, porn star Nina Hartley comments, "It took me a long time to be able to do a blow job in the light and not get embarrassed." She apparently got over it.

🐊 **Oral Intermission** If your mouth gets tired, do your man by hand for a while, or run your hair over his genitals. You might also masturbate for a bit, giving him the treat of watching you do that. Some women say that they give their best blow jobs when they are just as turned on as their partners. Don't be afraid to let him know about it if you are. It may help speed things up.

🐊 **Tap & Hum** It might enhance the feeling of a blow job if you occasionally hum or tap the shaft of the penis when the head and frenulum are in your mouth.

🐊 **Hot, Cold, Etc.** Don't hesitate to suck on ice cubes to make your mouth cold, or drink hot liquids to make it extra-warm before and during oral sex. The same applies to licking nipples.

🐊 **Going Down after Intercourse** Some women enjoy giving blow jobs after intercourse. They find it highly erotic to suck on a penis after it has been inside of them. Other women aren't as eager.

🐊 **Size** Oral sex may be problematic if your man's salami is on the enormous side. Never fear. The illustration on the following page shows how you can still lick and kiss it into submission. Use your hands to pump the shaft while focusing your efforts on the frenulum and head. Also, the chapter "Techno Breasts & Weenie Angst" lists a number of tips for having sex with the extra-well-endowed.

🐊 **A Little Help from Your Friends** If you have a friend who is more experienced at giving blow jobs, consider asking her (or him) for pointers, but keep in mind that you will soon be evolving your own personal style. What you do will also vary depending on the guy you are doing it with.

Cojones

What you do with your hands sometimes separates the good blow jobs from the great. Better blow jobs often include lots of finger and hand work. For instance, at the same time that your

An Effective Way to Get Him Off Orally without Swallowing

This feels so good that a lot of guys won't be able to tell that you aren't swallowing unless they are actually looking. The trick is to focus your lip action on the sensitive frenulum area while cradling the penis with your hand. This area is just beneath the head of the penis. Use lots of saliva and put plenty of tongue into it—almost like you are French kissing this part of his penis. Occasionally fill your hand with your hot steamy breath. This also works well if your lover's penis is a little on the huge side and you'd more easily fit a zeppelin in a one-car garage than get it in your mouth.

---

mouth is on his penis, consider caressing your partner's testicles. Also, there might be places along the lower shaft of the penis—the part that is covered by the testicles—that respond nicely to fingertip massage. Massaging this area with your free hand when giving a blow job can substantially increase the sensation. Make hand play an active part of the blow job, and he's not as likely to notice when your lips need a rest.

Two Balls, One Tongue

"I love my boyfriend's testicles. I like taking them into my mouth one at a time and sucking on them. The skin on the sack is really soft and feels great in my mouth."

female age 23

Some men will feel highly appreciative if you take one or both of their testicles in your mouth. Don't fear doing this. Just go slowly the first couple of times until you get the hang of it. The skin around the testicles (scrotum) also loves being licked and kissed. The sensitivity of the scrotum has been compared to the outer lips of women's genitals.

If he doesn't have an erection, you might be able to fit his testicles in your mouth as well as his penis.

Sage Blow-Job Advice

In the video *How to Perform Fellatio,* porn starlet/host Karen Summer encourages women to listen to the man's body. Ms. Summer says that if the man moves, move with him, but once he starts to moan or grunt, keep doing exactly what you were just doing, because it's working extremely well.

Right before He Comes

There might be certain things that you can do just before a man starts to come that will increase his pleasure. Some women wrap a hand around the bottom part of the penis so the entire shaft feels like it's inside a vagina. Others place their fingertips along the seam on the front side of the penis and apply a bit of pressure. They might be able to feel the ejaculate surge through the penis when they do this. Some men might appreciate it if you increased the vacuum in your mouth as they are about to come. Others enjoy it if you hold or caress their testicles or massage the part of the shaft that's beneath them. Since this is a highly individual matter, issue a warning that you would like to experiment with a couple of new things and seek his feedback.

Note: An extremely intelligent and highly experienced prostitute who consulted on this chapter said she finds that many men like to have their nipples pinched as they are about to come.

Learn When He's Coming

If you know the right signs to look for, you can often learn when your man is about to come. This will give you options if you don't want to swallow.

While it's not like Mt. St. Helens, there are definite signs. Until you learn his body's signs, ask him to tell you when he's about to come. But after a while, you'll hopefully notice that his Little Willy starts to swell and contort just before it spurts. You can feel this in your mouth. Also, a hand over his testicles may also be a good source of information, as they tend to draw close to his body when he is about to squirt. In addition, his body might tighten up or his hips might give a small thrust when coming is inevitable.

If You Don't Like the Way He Tastes

If you know you're not going to swallow, keep a hand around the base of his penis while you are sucking on the upper half. As the signs of ejaculation present themselves, free your mouth from the line of fire, slide your hand up the shaft, to just below the head, and start pumping for Old Glory. Be sure your grip is firm and pump fast and furious. This is no time for a gentle touch.

Another way of bringing him off without swallowing is shown in the illustration two pages back. Here are some other suggestions that you might find helpful:

🦊 **Tartar Control** Sticking a bit of toothpaste in your mouth before inserting a penis can improve the taste greatly. The same is true for sucking on a mint beforehand. The flavor of blow jobs can also be enhanced by sipping on your favorite sherry or liquor, or by glazing your man's yam with things like honey, jam or whipped cream. Champagne blow jobs can also be fun. While you might enjoy experimenting with minty liquors such as creme de menthe, be sure to do a small test patch on the side of the penis beforehand. While a little menthol on the skin can feel great, especially when you blow on it, too much can burn. It takes a few minutes for the full intensity of the burn to peak, so wait awhile before declaring your test a success.

Bag It A competent prostitute can slip a condom over a man's penis with her mouth alone and he will never know it is there. This suggests that the problems some guys have with wearing condoms might be psychological. (So what else is new?) Here are two highly acceptable approaches to consider if you want your man to use a condom while blowing him but he balks. 1. In a loud and clear voice, say, "Forget it, Charlie! If you think it tastes THAT great, suck on it yourself." Actually, he probably would if he could, and maybe even tried a couple of times when he was a kid. 2. Try making the whole process of oral sex more fun and pleasurable for both of you. If he knows that the blow job is going to be lots of fun, putting a condom on won't be such a big deal. **Condom Tip:** You might try sticking a drop of water-based lube or contraceptive jelly on the head of a man's penis right before bagging it with a condom. Once you have rolled the condom over his penis, squish the lube around the entire head. Some guys say that sloshing around in a rubber that's been lubricated on the inside feels better. If you don't have any lube handy, hock a small wad of loogie on the head of his penis before putting the condom on. If you use a condom for oral sex, try finding ones that aren't lubricated. Condoms with lubrication often taste bitter. There are also varieties of condoms made of flavored latex. At the time of this book's printing, a condom that many people favored for blow jobs was the unlubricated Gold Circle. Saran Wrap: If you're in a jam or don't exactly cherish the taste of latex, you might experiment with Saran Wrap. It's neat because you can see through it, and you'll probably like the feel of it better than latex. You can lay it over the penis if you're using the technique that's illustrated earlier, or if you decide to tent the penis with it, put the gathers on the side of the penis that's away from the frenulum and faces his stomach when he's got an erection.

Slobber and Punt When Old Faithful is about ready to blow, start to mobilize a pool of slobber in your mouth. When he comes, let the floodgates loose. The saliva will help thin the ejaculate, making it run out faster. And for heaven's sake, don't worry about the mess. The more goo and slime running down the shaft, the better.

➵✑ **To the Rear** If you are going to swallow but want to decrease the taste, place his penis as far back in your mouth as you can while still being comfortable. Then start swallowing fast. Unless he comes in buckets, it should decrease the amount of ejaculate that hits your taste buds.

➵✑ **Sublingual Ejaculation** The following tip is mentioned in the excellent book *Tricks—125 Ways to Make Good Sex Better* by Jay Wiseman: When it feels like your man is close to coming, put your tongue over the head of his penis so the ejaculate does not squirt directly on the taste-bud side of your tongue.

➵✑ **Let Him Help** Some guys won't mind finishing themselves off with their own hand if you have taken the time and energy to give them a really good blow job. It might be a special treat if you kiss or suck on their testicles while they pump themselves to orgasm.

After He Comes

The head of the penis can become extremely sensitive immediately after orgasm. If you keep his penis in your mouth while he is coming, be sure to find out what he wants you to do while he is coming as well as after. Some guys might want you to keep it in your mouth, but to slow the action way down. Others will want you to stop completely at some point, and some might want you to keep going full force. Another option is to stop the sucking action, but to keep pumping the shaft with your hand.

The trick is to know when to stop or switch gears. The only way to learn this is from experience and plenty of helpful feedback on his part.

What If He Doesn't Come?

This is a situation where one woman's blessing is another woman's curse... Some guys don't come from oral stimulation alone. This doesn't mean that they didn't love every minute of your blow job. It doesn't mean that you haven't given a great blow job. It just means that they don't come from lip action alone.

Beginner Jitters

Some people who are new at sucking on penises, as well as some seasoned veterans, experience a brief paralysis or mini-dread right before the thing ejaculates. There are two things that might be helpful: reread the preceding section "If You Don't Like the Way He Tastes" and try to talk to your partner about it. Maybe he can give you plenty of warning so you can stop sucking and start pumping by hand long before the sticky stuff starts to ooze. With time and experience, it's likely any dread will go away.

Hands on Your Head

Men will often put their hands on a woman's head when she is giving oral sex. For most guys, this is a very loving gesture which can also be used to let a partner know what feels good and what doesn't. However, some men will put their hands on a woman's head and attempt to forcibly push it down onto the penis. Not only is this rude, it's a form of assault.

Counterpoint: One woman says, "This can be particularly exciting, when a man pushes my head down on his penis. But then again, I would never have sex with a man who I didn't love going down on. Also, you make a joke out of it when a woman grabs a man's head and pulls it into her crotch [next chapter under "Feeling Like a Crash-Test Dummie"] but call it assault when a man does this to a woman. You present a double standard that says we women are either more fragile than men or more easily offended when it comes to sex."

Research Findings

One of the more interesting research findings of all time is in an article about the hazards of oral sex. It was written by a group of dentists and published in a medical journal (Bellizi, Krakow and Plack, *Military Medicine* 145 (1980):787—honest, his name is Dr. Plack and he's a dentist). The article is titled "Soft Palate Trauma Associated with Fellatio."

The article tells about the daughter of an officer who was taken to the base hospital because she discovered a black-and-blue blotch in the back of her mouth. Several dentists eventually converged on the mystery blotch, trying to discover its origin. After eliminating all other possibilities, the dentists finally asked the officer dad to leave the room and then popped the big question:"Gotta boyfriend?"

In the back of the mouth near where the tonsils hang is a highly vascularized mass of tissue (highly vascularized means lots of small blood vessels). An erect penis hitting against this rather sensitive tissue can cause a bruise.

This isn't a common injury. It goes away like any other bruise, but it is a reminder that the woman, and not the man, should control the level of movement during a blow job. For instance, it's fine if she wants a lover to thrust in and out of her mouth, but the choice needs to be hers.

Ejaculate-Related Sinus Infections

When some women give blow jobs, they like to create a slight to moderate vacuum around their lover's penis. Men who enjoy this kind of sensation find it to be heavenly. However, a problem can occur when a man comes with the head of his penis in the back part of a woman's vacuum-pulling mouth. Apparently, the vacuum can sometimes draw ejaculate up into the woman's sinus cavities, creating what might be a cum-related sinus infection. If this is the case, the woman and her partner need to work on keeping the head of his penis in the middle part of her mouth when he is coming. Another solution, of course, is for him to wear galoshes (a condom).

Lasting Shorter (As Opposed to Lasting Longer)

"Why is it when you are giving men head, they take forever to come, but are so much faster when having intercourse?"
female age 29

During vaginal intercourse, most guys make an effort to last as long as their partners want, sometimes successfully. While this might be a noble gesture during intercourse, it is not appreciated nearly as much during oral sex. That's because oral sex tends to tucker out the mouth of the giver. So if the purpose of the blow job is to get the man off, he shouldn't necessarily try to hold back his climax just to show what a stud he is. On the other hand, some guys love oral sex but can't come from it. The best course of action is to discuss this matter with each other. If the male is one of those lucky guys who can pretty much come at will, he and his partner might devise a signal for when she'd like him to come. For the rest of us, the woman can ease up if we are approaching orgasm too fast, or she can try some of the measures listed on pages 66-68 to speed us up if her jaw is about to drop off.

Do Men Blow Men Better Than Women Blow Men?

In researching different sexual techniques, we have reviewed many videos on sex. Videotapes made by women, many of whom are bisexual or lesbian, are often (although not always) a good source of information. The absolute worst source of information is traditional straight pornography.

It wasn't until this book was nearly finished that we took stock of the fact that no gay male videos had been reviewed—except those on male genital massage, which were very informative. With this in mind, the following question about oral sex was posed:

*Is it possible that gay men give better blow jobs
than straight women?*

Armed with several gay videos, this question was examined by a small group of straight men and women, with the men being somewhat uncomfortable and the women being highly curious. Of course, the videos themselves caused a few unanticipated comments.

Most of the actors in the gay videos were exceptionally good-looking and appeared totally straight. At the very least, these men were far more buff, attractive, and likable than many of the actors in traditional straight porn movies. Upon making these discoveries, one female reviewer exclaimed, "It's a straight woman's nightmare: five naked men who are physical gods and I couldn't get one of them to look at me if his life depended on it!" Another woman viewer stated: "It's one of the few times in my life when I wish I had a penis. I'd let that cute blond guy with the dimples and shoulders suck on it all night long."

As for conclusions, it seemed that these men handled each other's bodies with a kind of skill and effectiveness that some straight women might do well to imitate. However, the actual difference in doing oral sex wasn't so much in technique but in intensity, although the gay men did seem to use their hands more than most women do when giving blow jobs. It's difficult to put into words, but viewers had the feeling that the gay males (or gay male actors, anyway) seemed to form an intense relationship with the penis itself. No matter how much they might enjoy doing oral sex, few women make an emotional connection with a man's genitals in quite the same way as these gay men appeared to.

Granted, few people who have ever worked with actors consider them to be representative of average people. And this guide's methodology is clearly lacking in scientific rigor, but the conclusion is, yes, it's quite possible that gay men blow men better than women blow men, at least in porn movies.

In turning the question around, it can be asked if women do a better job of giving oral sex to women. The answer? Who knows, although one female reader who is bisexual was kind enough to offer the following comment:

"Having received oral sex from many men and women, I believe women's superiority at this activity is mostly myth."

An Oral-Sex Postscript over at the Beta House

Let's say a very straight, homophobic college fraternity man who prides himself on his conquests with women has just volunteered to take part in an experiment on sexual response. The researchers put EKG leads on his chest, blindfold him, restrain his hands and inform him that he is going to receive a blow job from "a very sexy blond." After receiving the blow job, he responds that she seemed to know more about how to please him orally than any sorority girl he's ever dated, and pleads for "her" phone number. The researchers then inform him that the sexy blond is a male who starred in one of the previously mentioned gay videos, and show him a tape of this sexy blond doing him. Suddenly, our fraternity brother's enthusiasm isn't quite the same and he's not sure if the blow job was all that exceptional. More importantly, if this subject had been told the true identity of the sexy blond ringer before receiving the blow job, it is quite possible that he wouldn't have been able to get an erection or ejaculate.

In this hypothetical experiment, our subject's pleasure was determined as much by his fantasy of who was giving the blow job as the reality of it, assuming the blow job was competently done. MORAL: Never underestimate the role of the human mind in determining what does and doesn't work sexually.

Things a Guy Can Do to Help a Woman Who Is Trying to Give Him Oral Sex

Careful Reread the preceding pages about bruising, gagging and not lasting as long. Also try reading this chapter with your partner. The keys to a really good blow job are being willing to explore and give each other feedback.

Clean Keep in mind that most women won't go down on guys who smell rank. Whether you are going out on a first date or have been married for twenty years, here are a few things to keep in mind: Clean #1: Shower at least once a day, unless you are seriously into grunge or are a holdover from the court of Louis XIII, in which case bathing is irrelevant. Clean #2: Don't wear the same socks or underwear for more than one day without washing them. If everyone including the dog and cat runs out of the room when you take your shoes off, use foot powder or spray. Clean #3: While not particularly popular with the organic crowd, deodorant can be a wonderful thing. Clean #4: Brush and floss your teeth often. Clean #5: Cut your fingernails and toenails often. Clean #6: If you wear cologne, ask your partner or a woman friend how she likes the smell of it, as well as how much you should use. Maybe she will prefer you without cologne. Some guys smell great from just bathing alone. On the other hand, she might like you marinated with a bit of citrus or spice.

🐾 **Pube Tug** Tug on your pubic hair ahead of time so you'll pull out the strays that might end up in her mouth.

🐾 **Attitude Issues #1 Arrogance** Don't assume that a woman automatically wants to suck on your penis just because you like the way it feels. (How would you like to suck on some guy's dick?) Never take blow jobs for granted, and be thankful whenever you get one, even if your partner loves doing it. Tell her how good it feels. Also, it never hurts to ask yourself, "What have I done lately to deserve a blow job?" Did you give your partner a long lingering body massage? Did you help her with a project she's been struggling with? Did you do more than your share of the housework? Did you respond kindly in a situation where most men would have been jerks? Are you a loving partner and good friend?

🐾 **Attitude Issues #2 Downfield Coverage** Think of what a catastrophe it would have been if Joe Montana or Steve Young had never discussed patterns and coverage with Jerry Rice. Oral sex requires a doer who is willing to accept helpful feedback and a receiver who is willing to give it.

🐾 **Attitude Issues #3 Mutuality** Never, ever cop an attitude such as "My last girlfriend blew me really well. Why can't you?" There are reasons why you aren't with your last girlfriend. Giving and receiving great blow jobs is a shared responsibility. With enough mutual caring, love and experimentation, the chances are excellent that you will soon be getting fine oral sex, but don't expect it to happen magically without your help.

🐾 **Attitude Issues #4 The Deep Throat Fantasy** Ever since the *Deep Throat* movie, some men have been all hyped up over the notion of having a woman do a sword-swallowing act with their penis. Get over it. A throat is not a vagina, and any extra thrills you might get from this are mostly psychological. Besides, why would you encourage your partner to do something that might trigger a natural gagging reflex? And if she gags on your penis, do you really think she's going to be excited about putting it in her mouth again?

Attitude Issues #5 He Who Gives, Gets A fine way to get great oral sex is to give great oral sex. This assumes that the rest of your relationship is in good shape. Some guys are great in bed, but total jerks otherwise. Do not expect that being a great lover will make up for being a selfish person. Some women will overlook bad manners and social lunacy for a good lay, but they tend to have their own emotional problems and will make your life a living hell in other ways.

Asking vs. Not Asking Every once in a while you might have a really horrible day or week and are totally frazzled and in desperate need of a blow job lest you decompensate even further and have to be hauled off to the loony bin. If you don't abuse the privilege and have a loving partner who hasn't had an equally bad day or week, she will usually do the mercy blow job even if she's not particularly into it. For this type of situation, it is fine to ask (okay, beg) for a blow job. However, in the course of normal lovemaking, it might not be such a good idea to routinely ask for oral sex. That's because some women don't take well to being pestered for blow jobs. Granted, they might love blowing you and will do so often, but only if it's on their own initiative. Of course, there are other women who are just fine with being asked.

Improving the Way Your Ejaculate Tastes Some people claim that vegetarians, both male and female, taste better than their carnivore brethren. However, it is likely that this is mere propaganda from the cows and chickens; e. g., red meat makes some men taste strongly and dairy products make ejaculate taste bad, but not nearly as bad as asparagus. Also, smoking and/or drinking coffee might cause a guy's ejaculate to taste strong or bitter. Perhaps Starbucks can formulate a new blend of beans and call it "Ejaculate Lite." Regardless of their impact on the taste of semen, the combination of smoking and drinking coffee makes for hideous-smelling breath.

One common suggestion for improving the taste of male ejaculate is to eat fruit or celery each day, especially pineapple and apples. The sugar in the fruit is supposed to give a guy's ejaculate a bit of a sweet edge. Perhaps this is just useless folklore. However, if this is what a partner requested before doing more blow jobs, most guys would go to work each morning munching stalks of celery and finishing their lunches with slices of fruit. Whatever the case, if your partner is willing to be the taster, experiment with different combinations of food. Does ingesting a little cinnamon make any difference in the way you taste? What happens if you drink less coffee or eat less broccoli or garlic?

🐊 **Bitter Taste Due to Infection** If your partner says that your ejaculate is really bitter, consider seeing a urologist to screen out the possibility of an infection in your prostate or urethral glands. Although you might not be feeling any pain, it's still possible to have an infection. Unfortunately, in this day and age of HMOs, you will probably need to see a family physician or internist first, and might be a bit embarrassed saying, "Heather says my cum tastes bitter." Urologists, on the other hand, see genitals all day long, and it's usually easier to say something like that to them. In either case, rather than telling the receptionist or nurse the exact reason for the appointment, you might just say that you suspect having a prostate or urinary tract infection. Then tell the physician the real reason once you see him or her in private.

Readers' Comments

"I am certain that women would give more blow jobs if they didn't feel like they had to swallow!" *female age 43*

"Cum is not a gourmet treat, but not unpleasant either. I'd rather be eating mocha chip ice cream, but getting there isn't half as much fun. My partner's orgasm is often a total turn-on for me, and occasionally just a relief that the blow job is now over with." *female age 47*

"I don't find oral sex repulsive in the least if he is conscious of good hygiene. If he smells bad down there, it's a turn-off for me." *female age 34*

"I swear by pineapple; it helps take the bitter taste away."

female age 24

"It feels funny when he squirts in my mouth. His cum often gives me an upset stomach so I usually spit it out."

female age 23

"If I'm in the mood it's really sensual. If I'm not it's like a job." *female age 43*

"It is a major power trip for me if he comes in my mouth. I like knowing I have the ability to take this big strong man and turn him into a sack of Jello." *female age 37*

"It is great! I like running my tongue around the head and sliding it in and out of my mouth. I like to take his penis in my mouth as far as possible and rub my tongue on the underside of it, pushing the head into the roof of my mouth. It seems to drive him crazy!" *female age 37*

"More than anything it feels so good because I am in control." *female age 23*

"When it comes to blow jobs, let the lucky son of a bitch treat you like a queen, honey, because you are."

female age 48

"I have to open my mouth wider than normal and it gets tired pretty fast. I don't really like it much, but he loves having it, so it makes me feel really good and loved to be giving him oral sex." *female age 32*

"I never was very good at blow jobs until I had a lover who had a small penis. Then I felt comfortable with him in my mouth." *female age 45*

"I like to give head, so I don't need much persuasion. I get really wet from giving someone that kind of pleasure, and I always feel so powerful when I do it." *female age 23*

"It feels very sensual if he lets me take it at my own pace. I think the penis has the most wonderful velvety skin."

female age 38

"I only like it if I can keep the hair out of my mouth. I enjoy it only because I know he enjoys it so much." *female age 35*

"I like it. I especially like the little leaks before he comes; it gets me excited to know he is so excited. I think cum has an interesting taste, sort of fizzy." *female age 38*

"I have discovered that we both find it erotic to have him come on my face or on my breasts when I give him head. I don't care for the taste of his semen." *female age 22*

"I find it helpful to open my mouth a bit when he's coming, then swallow quickly." *female age 26*

"I really don't like it when he comes in my mouth. I kind of gag on it." *female age 26*

"I used to tell my partner that I was semen-intolerant." *female age 26*

"It's okay as long as I can spit it out. I don't like to swallow it." *female age 43*

"It's fun to take a limp penis, put it in your mouth and suck on it until it hardens." *female age 37*

"One thing that's really neat about sucking on a guy's cock is watching it change shape and color and get harder as it get's more aroused. You're right up there in the front row! You don't get that with intercourse." *female age 42*

"I've observed that not all guys come as much: some have very little, and others lots and lots!" *female age 27*

"Never forget to caress and tickle the balls." *female age 44*

"Usually it's very erotic and sexy, especially if I'm particularly in the mood to suck him. Sometimes (rarely) it feels too much, invasive." *female age 48*

"My lover likes to hold my head and slowly slide in and

out of my mouth. I trust him to do that without going too deep or choking me." *female age 37*

"My mouth and hand work as a team. As I pull away with my mouth, I twist my hand almost like a corkscrew."

female age 26

Advice for Men from Female Readers

"Be very clean. Feel free to moan when you feel pleasure. Speak up if there is something I am missing."

female age 30

"Keep your genital area clean and pleasant smelling."

female age 34

"Tell me what you like. If you want to grip the shaft or caress your testicles while I am sucking, go ahead and do so." *female age 37*

"I love to give head, but I hate to feel pressured into doing it. Also, remember what goes around comes around. If I'm the only one going down, I'll be less likely to do so again."

female age 26

Advice for Women from Male Readers

"Please don't do it like they do in the porno flicks, where the girl just about bobs her head off. Not a turn-on."

male age 46

"Don't be fooled by the name. Blowing has nothing to do with it." *male age 26*

Oral Sex: Vulvas & Honey Pots
Chapter 18

Having powerful feelings for a woman can leave some men with an insatiable need to kiss and lick her genitals. It's hard to explain why, but it's a primal need that can be triggered by a mere wink of her eye. Other men are happy to give a woman oral sex because it pleases her sexually, but aren't fully into it. And some men would rather eat a cat.

Whatever your preference, this chapter is loaded with tips and techniques for giving a woman all of the oral pleasure her heart and thighs could possibly desire.

Talking to Elvis from between Your Sweetheart's Thighs

It's a funny thing about oral sex, at least when you are a guy on the giving end. The woman whom you are giving oral sex to, a person whom you know and often love, sometimes just disappears. All that's left is a strange, twitching, moaning proto-plasm which only partially resembles the person who was there just minutes ago. You are left virtually alone, with your tongue feeling like it's running the Boston Marathon. You might as well be talking to Elvis. After it's over, you might want to ask, "Hey, where did you go?" but you learn not to because she'll usually just give you a big smile and want to curl up in your arms.

A female reader offers a possible explanation. She says that when she is receiving oral sex, she isn't as aware of her partner's presence, so it's easier to let her fantasies run wild. She wouldn't necessarily want to tell him "where she went," since her fantasy might have been with someone else. Little does she know, guys who are sexually secure might get off on hearing about her fantasy escapades, even if they're with someone else.

The Way Women Taste

The previous chapter on blow jobs begins with a discussion of how guys taste. This chapter turns the tables and talks about the way women taste.

Most guys who enjoy going down on women know that some vulvas taste great, while others don't leave fond memories. Beyond that, men are fairly useless when it comes to discussing genital taste. Lesbian and bisexual women, however, will talk your ear off about the subject of how women taste. What follows are some of their comments. But first, a brief discussion about female genital chemistry.

While most of the skin on the human body has a pH between 6.0 and 7.0, the optimal pH of the vulva and vagina is between 4.0 and 5.5. Vaginal secretions contain lactic acid, which helps to maintain the lower pH.

A lower pH helps eliminate unfriendly bacteria which can cause anything from a rank odor to vaginal infections. Unfortunately, most body soap has a pH of between 6.0 and 14. This can raise the pH of the vulva and may challenge nature's system for eliminating unfriendly bacteria. It might be why women who bathe more than once a day tend to get more vaginal infections.

Fortunately, there are now low-pH soaps with lactic acid that are made especially for women's genitals. They contain none of the artificial deodorants or scents that are in some products that go between a woman's legs. One woman who has been using the soap for almost a year says that it allows her genitals to stay fresh for a full twenty-four hours. Another says she no longer hesitates to let her husband go down on her twelve hours after her last shower. Physicians especially recommend this soap for women who have frequent infections.

Unfortunately, these soaps are mainly being sold in France, Italy, Switzerland and Ireland. Gynecologists in those countries can't agree on exactly which pH is optimal, so the soap is made with a slightly different pH in each country. (The fights in the gynecological journals must be interesting, with the Italians claiming to have invented love, the French claiming to have perfected it, the Irish raising a glass to it and the Swiss declaring neutrality on the matter.) One reader who started using a low-pH soap for her Canadian crotch now uses it from head to toe. She says it's helped to cure her dry skin!

There are two low-pH soaps that North American women can find if they look hard enough: Nature's Plus Natural Beauty Cleansing Bar (800) 937-0500 and Sebamed Liquid Face and Body Wash (877) 732-2633 at www.sebamed-in-canada.com. Neither are just for crotches, but a number of readers have tried them and would swear by them if they weren't so busy receiving oral sex.

Soaps aside, here are a few comments that bisexual women and lesbians had to say about the taste of their female lovers:

"One woman who I loved going down on suddenly began tasting different—not nearly as good. As it turned out, she had started taking vitamin pills. It was never a problem if she took herbs, but vitamin pills would ruin the way she tasted."

"A former girlfriend was a tennis pro. Sometimes she would play tennis for a few hours and I could go down on her without her taking a shower and she would still taste sweet. There are other women whom I have gone down on right after we showered, and they still didn't taste good. In making my own inquiries, I found that the sweeter tasting women didn't eat red meat."

"I watch my diet carefully, but I have to admit, the sweetest, best-tasting lover I ever had was a meat-eating, beer-drinking dietary disaster."

So much for consensus. Finally, a thought from the cleanest lesbian in all of Hackensack, New Jersey:

"Some women spend more time filing their toenails than they do taking care of their pussies. When I'm in the shower, I always separate the lips of my vulva and use a wash cloth to clean between them. I'm also careful about little bad-tasting pieces of gunk that might collect under my clitoral hood. These are what uncircumcised males get under their foreskin if they don't pull it back and clean it."

A Q-tip dipped in mineral oil works well to get rid of any "little pieces of gunk" that stick under the clitoral hood. As for how you taste and what to do about it, aside from perhaps trying a low pH soap, keep in mind the following tip from a bisexual woman from South Bend, Indiana: "A crotch in a spandex leotard is an unhappy crotch; nature meant for it to breathe." Nature also meant for it to get love, and that's what the rest of this chapter is about.

Talking With Tongues—Suggestions for Pleasing a Woman With Your Mouth

According to some women, a smart and loving tongue between their legs can offer feelings of pleasure that fingers or a penis simply can't. Yet many a male merely pushes his face into a woman's crotch, sticks his tongue out like when the doctor asks you to say "ahhh" and wags away. What follows are suggestions to help cure a chronic case of tongue wagging.

On the Tip of Your Tongue

The human tongue, like the penis, can be made hard or soft. To understand the difference between a soft and a hard tongue, spend a few minutes licking the palm of your hand. This may not be as much fun as when Lulu Belle sits on your face, but a moment's practice on the palm of your hand can be a good way to learn about subtle variations in oral-sex technique.

First, if you've just been installing a new head gasket or fertilizing the lawn, it might be a good idea to wash your hands. Then, pretend your palm is a woman's vulva and give it a good licking.

Notice how quickly the end of your tongue goes dry. So much for the fantasy that the human tongue is automatically wet. A dry tongue creates drag or friction. Nature did not create the clitoris with a high tolerance for friction. In fact, nature did not create the clitoris with any tolerance for friction. None. Nada.

This is why you'll need to coat your tongue with saliva before licking a woman's private parts. Not so much that you drool, but enough to blow a good-sized bubble. After a few minutes, saliva from your mouth will automatically run down your tongue and keep everything well-lubricated, but not at the start.

Try licking your hand again. You may find that your tongue is somewhat taut with the tip hard and pointed. Try to let it go soft, in a way that would cause you to slur your words if you were attempting to speak. You may need to push your hand closer to your face, since a soft tongue is not as long as a hard tongue. Some women will prefer a softer, more rounded tongue when you are licking the underbelly of the clitoris, given how it isn't insulated by the clitoral hood. A harder, more pointed tongue can be a fine choice when licking the side of the clitoris or clitoral shaft, as these are protected by the clitoral hood and your tongue won't be making direct contact with the clitoris.

This may all sound like French if you have yet to go down on a woman. Not to worry; no matter how experienced you might be, she will still need to teach you where and how she wants you to lick. This can take weeks, months or years. Also, it's normal to feel clumsy when you are with a new lover or if you haven't done oral sex in a while.

The Initial Approach—Getting There

"Gentle teasing brings me to an orgasm. I like him to start off gently, with light licks and kisses all over my vulva. I can't take too much pressure on my clitoris, though, and sometimes that ruins it for me." *female age 23*

When you are shooting a free throw, you don't want to hit the rim. When you are landing a plane, you don't want to brush the treetops. When you are going down on a woman, it's an entirely different story. The best approach to a woman's genitals is anything but direct.

Once you've been with a woman for a while, you'll discover what body parts she likes to have licked. For instance, one woman might love it when you kiss her inner thighs or rear end, but hate it if you kiss her abdomen. Another woman might want just the opposite. Find the body parts close to her vulva that she likes having kissed, and spend plenty of time on them. Plant occasional kisses on her vulva, but only as a preview of what's to come.

An indirect approach helps assure a warm welcome when your tongue finally drops into your lover's saddle.

Your Goal: Orgasm or Pleasure?

Some guys think they haven't pleased a woman unless they have given her an orgasm. That would be fine if sex were football and orgasms were touchdowns, but this kind of philosophy can spoil your love life. Instead of trying to delight your lover's senses, you'll always be playing to her clitoris. This can get tedious.

Of course, there are times when it's important to be single-minded about a woman's orgasm, but not as a rule. You'll do a lot better if you let yourself have fun, be close and want her dearly. If your lips convey this when they are between her thighs, you'll have a leg up on most guys.

Avoiding Beard Burn

When it comes to receiving oral sex, one thing that women often complain about is men's beards. Their advice: grow a full beard or keep your face clean-shaven. Grunge does not feel good on a woman's thighs.

If you're the kind of guy who grows a five o'clock shadow ten minutes after you shave, find a favorite set of towels and drape one over each of her legs, like mechanics sometimes do on the fenders of cars when they are working on the engine.

Three Oral Sex Caveats

Until shown otherwise, do not assume there are any similarities between the way you like your penis sucked and the way your partner likes having her genitals licked.

If your main exposure to oral lovemaking has been through watching porn videos, forget all you have ever seen. Rather than showing the back of a man's head buried between a woman's thighs, the porn industry has invented its own version of oral sex. In porn oral sex, a woman sits with her legs about six miles apart while some guy tries to lick her vulva without blocking the camera shot. While this is good for the cameraman, it's not necessarily going to please a woman.

A mediocre lover always knows what a partner wants without having to ask. An accomplished lover is a wise grasshopper who implores a partner to give him copious amounts of advice.

Body Positions

There are some oral sex positions that might look great, but don't work as well as others. What follows is a description of oral sex positions where your bodies are both pointing in the same direction. These provide the best face-to-vulva alignment, where your tongue has clear access to the tip and shaft of the clitoris. In this alignment, you will be licking in an upward direction. This gives you the most options, especially if she likes you to retract her clitoral hood once you get to the later innings.

To start with, imagine that you are standing in a swimming pool and the lucky lady is sitting on your shoulders. Only she is turned around so you are staring into her stomach and her feet are dangling over your shoulders, resting on your back. You are getting a mouthful of bathing-suit crotch material and can't see a thing, but this beats the heck out of anything you ever learned in Red Cross swimming lessons. Envision yourself falling forward, so she lands on her back and you are on your stomach. You will be staring up at her navel, unless she hasn't been to the gym in about a hundred years, in which case her navel may be resting on the top of your head.

One disadvantage of this position is that your neck has to bend backward, which can be really uncomfortable.

For the second oral sex position, which might be far more comfortable than the first, go back to the swimming pool and imagine the two of you falling to one side or the other. You land on your sides, with your body in back of hers, except for your head which is between her legs. Your mouth is on her crotch, and her inner thigh becomes a pillow for your head. Your neck doesn't have to bend backward as it does in the first position, since you can move your entire body to form more of a right angle to hers.

One disadvantage of this "sides" position is that you don't have the full access and degree of control that you do when her legs are spread apart. So some guys will start off in the first position, when her clit is more sensitive and mouth and tongue control is more critical. Then they ask the woman to roll on her side so they can get into a more comfortable position and keep at for as long as she likes.

In another oral sex position, she is "sitting on your face." Go back to the swimming pool and imagine that you fell straight back. You end up on your back and she's above you on all fours. The term "sitting on your face" is rife with deception. While it might look as if she is sitting on your face, she shouldn't be. Also, while it might feel good to have her in this position over your face, the human face isn't the most comfortable object to sit on, unless you've been taking a lot of steroids and your face is starting to look like a park bench. As an alternative, she might want to stay on all fours, with you propping your head and upper body on a bunch of pillows to give your lips the necessary altitude.

She can sit in a chair or on a stool, with you sitting or kneeling between her legs. She'll need to slouch so you don't get a mouthful of chair cushion, oak or leatherette.

There are other oral sex positions, like the ones you would use if you were doing 69. In these positions, your head is pointing in the opposite direction from hers and the alignment is not optimal.

With time, you may evolve your own variations, but these are excellent no matter how experienced you are.

Ground Zero

Perhaps you are a total pro at giving oral sex, or maybe you know more about the dark side of the moon than licking a woman's genitals. Regardless of your experience, what follows is a blueprint for giving really good oral sex—as long as you get reliable feedback from the woman you are doing it with.

🐾 The tongue can be an abrasive little organ unless it is lubricated. Coat your lips and tongue with extra saliva as you approach your lover's vulva.

🐾 Doing oral sex tends to make your salivary glands sing. Instead of swallowing or letting it pool in your mouth, try allowing your slobber to flow wherever gravity wants to take it. That way, you're less likely to drown and you won't have to worry as much about pubic hairs wrapping themselves around your tonsils each time you try to swallow. Putting a towel under your sweetheart's rear will help to keep the mattress from turning into a giant sponge. Some women will appreciate it if you push an edge of the towel against the area that's just below their vulva so the saliva doesn't trickle down their butt crack.

🐾 When a woman flexes her legs, her pelvis arches forward. This will provide the access a partner needs to give good oral sex. A lot of women will do this themselves by putting their legs over your shoulders, or by planting one or both feet on your shoulders. Some pull their legs up to their chest. The guy can also wrap his arms around the back of the woman's thighs and push them forward.

🐾 As a woman becomes more aroused, she might want to change her leg position or flex her thighs in ways that help to get her off. This might limit your access to her vulva, but if it's what does the trick, so be it.

🐾 As with any kind of sexual activity, a strategically placed pillow under your partner's bum can provide better access to her genitals. And don't hesitate to put a pillow under your head if it makes you more comfortable.

🐾 Some women provide all the oral access a man needs by simply spreading their legs. On the other hand, you may want to separate the outer labia with your fingers. This gives your mouth better access to the inner lips, and can sometimes feel like the difference between kissing a woman whose mouth is open and smooching with lips closed. Some women will offer a helping hand by separating the lips themselves. This can be highly erotic.

🐾Lavish the outer lips with licks and kisses. Then try running the tip of your tongue up and down the furrows between the outer and inner lips of your lover's vulva.

🐾The mons pubis is the little mound of flesh that sits directly above the labia. It is where the bulk of the pubic hair grows. Some women enjoy it if you rub the mons in a circular pattern. Also, pushing or pulling up the mons while doing oral sex can heighten the intensity for some women.

🐾Some women will enjoy it if you run your fingertips through their pubic hair, and some will particularly enjoy it if you tug lightly on it or nibble gently on the mons.

🐾The inner lips of women's genitals tend to be longer around the vaginal opening. Some are prominent enough to clasp between your fingers and tug upon gently. When a woman is highly aroused, she may enjoy this tremendously. As with everything else, be sure to ask!

Her Clitoris

"Don't immediately dive into the clitoris and stay there. Warm up by licking all of the vaginal area. Suck on the labia. Then turn your attention to the clitoris. I like my clitoris to be licked, flicked and sucked. Sometimes I get off faster if my partner licks lower on the clitoris, rather than at the top of the hood. It makes for a different kind of orgasm." *female age 25*

No matter how small your penis is, nobody's going to have trouble finding it. No matter how large her clitoris is, nature designed it to play a mean game of hide 'n' seek.

After you kiss and caress the other parts of the vulva, most women will appreciate it if you focus your oral efforts in the vicinity of the clitoris. "Vicinity" might mean simply in the neighborhood, or it might mean knocking on the front door. Here are some landmarks describing different parts of the clitoris.

🐱〜The shaft of the clitoris runs from the top of the labia to the tip of the clit. It might be anywhere from under a half-inch long to more than an inch. Pushing the labia apart and upwards with your fingertips will help to expose it.

🐱〜The shaft of the clitoris wears a thin little wetsuit called the clitoral hood. This hood is similar to the foreskin on a guy who is not circumcised. It protects the shaft from the rigors of crotch life. Oral sex pros manipulate it to great advantage. With practice, the clitoral hood will be your friend.

🐱〜The glans or tip of the clitoris is somewhere near the juncture where the clitoral hood splits into two. The tip of the clitoris can range from the size of a pen tip to a small finger, depending on the woman. Its sensitivity has nothing to do with its size. The tip is usually more sensitive to your tongue's caress than the shaft because it's easier to expose than the shaft, which is covered by the clitoral hood. This is why some women prefer it if you use a softer, more rounded tongue against the clitoral tip. Others will want you to lick with authority.

🐱〜Sometimes all it takes to expose the tip is a single finger to pull the hood up. Sometimes it takes both hands and a litany of prayer.

🐱〜To find the tip with your tongue, separate the outer lips with your fingers. Make sure your tongue has plenty of saliva on it for lubrication. Take a long slow lick from the bottom to the top of the vulva where the big lips meet. Somewhere along the way you will most likely feel a small knob or slight protuberance. Find out from your partner if this is the tip of her clitoris. Have her explain to you exactly how she likes it licked.

🐱〜As your sweetheart becomes more aroused, it is likely that the tip of her clitoris will swell. Some swell predictably; others don't. This process can be challenging until you become more familiar with the way her clitoris changes, and changes and changes. In fact, with some women, you learn to lick on a specific spot rather than relying on finding her clitoris with your tongue. You simply have faith that after a while it will appear.

🐱~You might think that the surest way to arouse a woman would be to start at the tip of the clitoris, since that's where so much of the action seems to be. But this is not the way it usually works. For most women, you don't even approach the clitoris until you have planted plenty of kisses in the surrounding area. Then you might focus on the clitoral shaft, working the hood with your tongue and avoiding the tip until she is more highly aroused. With some women, you don't touch the tip at all. Of course, these are just suggestions. If your lover wants you to start by throwing a liplock on the tip of her clitoris, far be it from this guide to suggest anything different.

🐱~Some women enjoy it if you kiss their vulva in the same way that you do their mouth. Some crave a gentle nursing action on the clitoris. Some like it if you flick the tip of your tongue over the clitoris in a sideways direction; others prefer an up-and-down motion as though you were rapidly turning a light switch on and off with your tongue, and some enjoy a circular motion. These different motions may seem awkward at first, but you will eventually learn to flick your tongue back and forth (or is it hither and yon) with enough grace to humiliate the average humming-bird. Also keep in mind that some women will want you to speed up or change locations as their arousal grows, while others prefer a constant and steady mouth motion. *Once some women reach a certain threshold of arousal, they can't tell which direction your tongue is moving in. All they know is if it feels good or not.*

Note: Be sure to pay close attention to your partner's body language as your tongue touches her exposed clitoris. If her body suddenly convulses or jolts, you have probably hit the right area but too early or with too much force. It never hurts to retreat and find a safe spot along the clitoral shaft that's protected by plenty of hood. She will usually let you know when she wants more tongue. The ways she might do this include telling you, pulling your head into her body with her hands, or grinding her crotch into your face. Hopefully she won't grab you by the ears, although men's ears make fine rudders for oral sex.

〜Your partner might have a favorite side of her clitoris where she wants you to lick. To help improve access to the favored side, she might try flexing one leg while the other lies flat and a bit to the side.

〜The clitoris sometimes disappears right before orgasm. This might be because it retracts, or because it simply gets lost in the swelling labia that surround it. This can be discouraging, because you may have just spent the last twenty minutes finding the thing. With helpful input from your partner you will eventually learn how to respond; in the meantime, you will simply need to let The Force guide you. **Note:** When a clitoris disappears on you, you might try giving a little suck to pull it back out.

〜After learning more about your partner's responses, you might experiment by puckering your lips around her clitoris and making a light vacuum. You can then push the clitoris in and out of your mouth either with your tongue or by reversing the suction every couple of seconds. Tricks like this can be found in Ray Stubbs's book *The Clitoral Kiss* (Tuscon: Secret Garden Press).

〜You might find that your partner's clitoris or the area around it begins to pulse once she is highly aroused. This is probably an indication to stay your course without making the slightest variation in speed, tempo or rhythm. Problems start when you assume that if she's pulsing at this speed, she'll love it even more if you double the tempo or do it harder. WRONG! These pulses happen every second or so and seem to be in direct response to the stimulus of your tongue. If you speed up, you quickly lose them.

〜The contractions of orgasm are said to happen every seven-tenths of a second. Some men say that the best way to simulate a woman's clitoris either by mouth or by hand is to use strokes that last seven-tenths of a second.

〜Some women prefer different kinds of stimulation depending on the time of the month. For instance, at one point in her menstrual cycle you avoid the tip or glans, but two weeks later you know to lick the tip silly. It's nothing you're going to learn in a one-night stand, and these changes don't apply for a lot of women.

Her Vagina and Beyond

🐱~Using terms like "urinary meatus" or "the area around her peehole" can cause an aesthetic flat tire. However, the part of a woman's vulva between her clitoris and vagina which contains the urinary meatus is definitely worth exploring with the tip of your tongue. For some women its stimulation might be the difference between good oral sex and great oral sex. If you have aesthetic problems with this notion, think about what your lover dips the tip of her tongue into when she is sucking on the head of your penis. Also keep in mind that urine and the urinary passageway are more sanitary than the human mouth and that kissing her down here is far more hygienic than kissing her on the mouth.

🐱~The opening of the vagina can be found in the lower half of the woman's vulva. A man might occasionally be swept away by an urge to stick his tongue far into his lover's vagina. This, of course, is ridiculous unless he has the same gene pool as Lassie. Still, it's a nice thing to do, or want to do. Realistically, your tongue will be able to stimulate the outer edges of your partner's vagina and maybe an inch or two inside of it. Reaching too far inside a woman's vagina can cause your tongue to get a nasty cramp.

🐱~Some women may treasure a finger or two inside the vagina when you are doing oral sex, but usually not until they have reached higher levels of arousal. As for what to do with your fingers once they are inside, you will need to ask. Some women like them to stay perfectly still, while others will enjoy it if you twist, jiggle or thrust your fingers in and out. Also, there might be special spots in her vagina that your partner enjoys having stimulated.

🐱~The inner part of a woman's vagina often balloons open when she is sexually aroused. A number of women enjoy having this filled up. While a man's fingers will usually do the job, some women find that a silicone dildo works better. For some couples, inserting a dildo during oral sex can be quite a turn-on. Also, a woman might fantasize about having one man's penis inside her vagina at the same time that another man is licking her clitoris. Using a dildo while receiving oral sex can help satisfy this fantasy unless you are actually into threesomes. (Believe it or not, there are special oral sex dildos that strap on a guy's chin!)

One highly athletic advisor to this guide so loved doing oral sex on his women friends in high school and college that he was considered an important resource off the court as well as on. His secret? When a woman was about to have an orgasm, he would gently insert a fingertip into her rectum. He says this would invariably launch a cascade of pleasure. If you want to try this, there is no need to stick your finger in very far; just putting pressure on the rim around a lover's anus might light up thousands of nerve endings whose sole experience to that point has been to endure methane storms and toilet paper abuse. A variation is to insert a small, well-lubricated vibrator in the woman's rear while doing oral sex. Just don't put this or your finger in her vagina afterward.

You can always go for a triple play: lips on her clitoris, one finger in her vagina and one up her rear.

Some women push a man's head away from their vulva after they begin to come. Other women pull it in tighter. Don't fret if she pushes it away. This will give your tongue a well-earned rest. Also, some women are extremely sensitive after orgasm, when barely breathing on their genitals can feel overwhelming.

If She Starts Bucking

It's not unusual for some women who are receiving oral sex to start bucking their hips with pleasure. This kind of motion can knock a guy off the mound.

While it is important to discuss this with your partner, a response that some women seem to appreciate is as follows: Wrap your arms around her thighs from behind, as in the illustration earlier in this chapter. Put your hands firmly on her hip bones. The female hip bones provide a perfect handle and were clearly put there by Mother Nature for this very purpose. Flex your arms so that she has to lift the weight of your upper body in order to buck. This shouldn't hurt her at all and will keep her pelvis still enough so you can give her more of what's causing her to buck in the first place.

Fun at the Y—Random Tips & Techniques

Find out if your sweetheart likes you to reach up and play with her breasts or other body parts while you are going down on her. One reader loves her partner to squeeze her toes when she's receiving oral sex—it can be the difference for her between coming or not.

One female reader suggests writing each letter of the alphabet with your tongue on your partner's vulva. Before long, she might start requesting specific letters or whole syllables!

Here is a game suggested in the helpful book *Ultimate Kiss* by Jacqueline and Steven Franklin. Bring your lover to the edge of orgasm with oral sex and then pull your mouth away for a count of fifty. Then bring her to the edge of orgasm again and pull your mouth away for twenty-five seconds. Then bring her to the edge of orgasm and pull your mouth away for ten seconds. Do this once more, pausing for just a few seconds. Be sure to explain this game beforehand so your partner doesn't become seriously annoyed when you stop for the first fifty-second pause. Also, one female reader suggests that this kind of game can work equally well when masturbating a woman.

Sometimes it is fun to give a woman oral sex when she is still wearing her panties or bikini bottom. Start with your lips on her inner thighs, work them up to her crotch, and then sneak your tongue under the material and into her vulva. Eventually, you might want to push the material to one side with your tongue, teeth or fingers. This will provide more working room.

Some women might like it if you blow warm moist air through the front panel of their underwear; others won't. But never blow air directly into a woman's vagina.

Consider pulling your lover's panties off with your teeth. But be careful not to leave any holes or rip the material, given how fancy little underthings often cost an arm and a leg; it's best that she not remember you as the one who destroyed her favorite undies.

It is next to impossible to do oral sex on a woman who is standing. The access is just too limited. Think nothing of crawling under her dress when she is standing to plant tender kisses in places where other guys only dream of touching, but she'll need to sit or lie down to receive your oral finest.

After the woman is highly aroused, place the tip of your tongue on the side or bottom of her clitoris. Then push the tip of a small vibrator on the other side of your tongue.

Separate the outer lips with your fingers and lay your tongue flat against her vaginal opening at the lowest part of her vulva. Take a slow, long, wet lick that lasts for about sixty seconds. This way, her clit gets a long, slow protracted licking as your tongue creeps its way up her vulva like a red-hot glacier.

Some women like so many pillows under their rear ends that their entire body is on an incline with their crotches angled up in the air. This provides wonderful access as well as an intriguing view. It may also cause lots of blood to rush into the woman's head.

A more subtle way of making your tongue vibrate is to hum while placing it on your partner's clitoris. A well-hummed aria can push some women into orgasmic orbit. Others will start laughing hysterically.

On a hot muggy day, ice cubes can always spice up any kind of sex play. Some women enjoy an occasional ice cube in the vagina. If you try this, use small cubes that won't cause frost burn. During the cold of winter, sipping a warm drink before kissing a woman's vulva can leave her with warm and sensual feelings.

Some couples enjoy placing a slice of banana, mango or papaya inside a woman's vagina for the man to retrieve with his tongue. Honey and syrup should be used with caution. While they are fine on nipples and other parts of the body, residual sugar in the vagina might inspire its resident yeast cells to procreate with painful delight. This may not be a problem for most women, but is worth noting. Also, you may need to douche to get out any remaining fruit if your man is a sloppy eater.

There are special swings that are great for doing oral sex. They can be hung from a doorjamb or ceiling rafter. The swing spreads the woman's legs and places her at the perfect height for a man to give her oral sex while he is sitting upright. Beware that most swings are poorly made and uncomfortable. Check our website at www.goofyfootpress.com for updates on sources for good swings.

Some couples occasionally pour champagne into a woman's vagina when her legs are elevated. (Vamosa?) Her partner then licks out the champagne, although this is not recommended for men in twelve-step programs or for women whose vaginal tissue might become irritated. (She should check with her gynecologist.) An extremely dry champagne with low residual sugar is preferable. Avoid putting cold duck in a woman's crotch, although a loving goose on her rear is usually welcome.

Some women have a problem with being kissed on the face after being kissed on the crotch. If that's the case in your household, consider keeping a wet washcloth handy. Run it across your face before kissing above after kissing below.

Blowing air on the genitals can feel refreshing, but never blow air into a woman's vagina.

Safety Note: It can be very sexy to blow warm moist air over your lover's vulva, but very dangerous to blow air into her vagina. Never lock your lips on your partner's vulva and blow air into it, unless your partner is made of plastic and gets inflated that way.

Female Ejaculation

Some women who are highly aroused ejaculate fluid around the same time that they have an orgasm. One female reader who ejaculates says that her male partner finds it exciting. Guys who are ejaculate-shy should discuss it with their partners and explore ways of ducking when the tsunami begins.

If your partner ejaculates and you have a problem with it, take solace in knowing that you've done something incredibly right to get her to that point. For more on female ejaculation, see the index.

Feeling Like a Crash-Test Dummy

Some women are not particularly subtle when it comes to signaling their oral sex wants and desires. In fact, it is not unheard of for a woman in the heat of oral passion to suddenly grab a man's skull and yank it one way or another with enough force to cause whiplash.

If she grinds your face into her crotch with a nose-flattening swoosh, she probably wants you to up the tempo a bit. But don't be silly and let your tongue go full throttle, because this might cause her to whip your head in the opposite direction. Learning to shift tongue-gears gradually can add years to the life of your neck and spinal column.

Neck Pain, Lock Jaw & Tongue Cramping

Tongue cramping and jaw paralysis are common side-effects of giving oral sex. These usually occur just moments before the woman blurts out "There, that's perfect, don't stop!" Being able to continue when every ligament and muscle fiber from your neck up is screaming for mercy is what separates the oral sex men from the oral sex boys.

With experience, you will discover which positions land you in traction and which don't. Do not suffer in silence. Discuss this with your partner so you can find oral sex positions which are mutually pleasing. That way you'll be able to give her more of what she likes.

Also, if your jaw is jamming, don't hesitate to give it a breather by gently replacing the tip of your tongue with the tip of your finger.

Damn Those Dental Dams & Latex Beaver Tarps

About ten years ago, when the AIDS concern reached full steam, some bozo decided that a way to safely go down on a woman was to spread a dental dam over a woman's crotch and lick away. While dental dams work great for dentists, we challenge any loving couple to enjoy oral sex through a dental dam. Why not just use neoprene or Naugahyde?

Lately, they've come up with an alternative that's supposedly thinner and more lick-friendly. Hogwash. It may be made for vulvas instead of molars, but good luck. First of all, you have no clue to what you're licking. It might as well be the President's face that's under there, for all you can tell. And then there's the texture problem. Try whipping your tongue back and forth over latex. No matter how much slobber you throw on it, your tongue drags and your RPM rating goes straight to hell. Giving a woman oral sex through even the thinnest of latex barriers makes you appreciate how much subtlety is involved when making her little lips sing.

A far more satisfactory barrier is Saran Wrap. You can see through it, it doesn't slow your tongue action, and you can always use it afterward to cover the Peach Melba or Apple Brown Betty.

When a Woman Doesn't Like Her Own Body

"I have a lot of hang-ups about oral sex because I think the guy wants to get out of there as soon as possible. So I need to be reassured you really enjoy it. The orgasm I have with oral sex is the most wonderful, but it often takes a long time and would try the patience of anyone." *female age 38*

Some women don't like their bodies and are uncomfortable when a man has a close-up view. If this is the case in your relationship, it might help ease your partner's mind to do oral sex with the lights out. On the other hand, if your partner is looking for an excuse to feel bad about herself, she will assume that you turned the lights out because you find her body ugly. Either way, it never hurts to talk about this.

One possible solution is to start doing oral sex when the two of you are in the shower. She might feel more comfortable with this, reassured that she is clean enough for you to enjoy.

Maintaining a Hard-On While Giving Oral Sex

If a guy is giving his sweetheart oral sex, it might be nice if he kept doing it long enough to at least get her off. But once he feels his hard-on starting to go, a man will sometimes surface from between a woman's legs and try to have intercourse before it's "too late." Otherwise he feels unmanly about going soft.

So why does a man sometimes lose his erection while going down on a woman? First of all, doing oral sex requires the kind of concentration that isn't always conducive to maintaining an erection. It's a little like playing catch or strumming a guitar, things that are immensely enjoyable but don't necessarily make a guy hard. Also, for some men, doing oral sex on a woman can bring up all sorts of primal feelings that aren't fully in sync with getting a hard-on. These can be pleasant and even deeply moving feelings, but they might not be the stuff that erections are made of. For other guys, it's instant wood when tongue touches thigh.

There is also the matter of mouth fatigue. It's not easy to keep a hard-on when your tongue and jaw start cramping. On the other hand, it's kind of fun to see how far you can lick a lover into an altered state of consciousness even if you can't talk too well afterward.

Whatever the cause, it's not unusual for a man to lose his erection when he is going down on a woman, but not because he is unhappy or a wimp. Women might consider what a drag it would be if they had to stay hard while doing oral sex. Nobody ever gets on their case for losing an erection.

Things a Woman Can Do to Help a Partner Who Is Going Down on Her

Here are a few suggestions for the woman who likes to receive oral sex:

Tugging on Your Bush Stray pubic hairs in the mouth can sometimes put a damper on wanting to lick a woman's genitals. Take a moment to tug on your bush before your man goes down. You'll pull out the lose hairs that would otherwise end up sticking to the back of his throat.

Trimming Your Triangle While some women feel that trimming the triangle defiles the natural appearance of the female body, others take pride in showing off more of their genitals. A woman so inclined shouldn't hesitate to put her lover in charge of muff maintenance and coiffure. Many men find this a joyful duty and take the responsibility quite seriously.

Labia Laundering Separating the labia and washing between them once a day will help to keep your genitals clean and tasty. Douching usually isn't necessary or advisable.

Not Helpful Women who think that their own genitals are dirty or not likable seldom do themselves any favors when it comes to oral sex. For instance, a guy might be having a wonderful time kissing and caressing his partner's genitals when she suddenly pulls him up because she's decided that he surely can't be enjoying something "as gross as that." If a woman fears that her genitals don't taste good, she should ask her partner. And if she feels there is something bad about her genitals, she should tell her partner lest he feel hurt by her rejecting behavior. Perhaps his reassurance will be helpful. (What if he brought her roses and she said "Yuck" or made him return them? He would feel no different if she responded this way to his genital kisses, assuming he wasn't a total klutz about it.)

Information As long as it's done with sensitivity, most men will appreciate any input or suggestions that a woman has about giving her oral pleasure. If you feel shy, hand your lover a copy of this chapter and ask if he'll read it with you. And if your man's ego is so fragile that he can't handle your input, perhaps he would do better with a mindless partner who has no input to give. If you aren't equal partners in sex, you aren't equal partners period. Is that what you want?

Masturbating Don't hesitate to reach down and masturbate while your partner is doing oral sex. Of course, this may be more easily said than done, so be sure to let him know that you want him to keep licking while you masturbate. While this can be fun, it may require some interesting tongue-finger logistics.

Attitude Issues There is a section at the end of the preceding chapter on blow jobs that is similar to this, only it is addressed to men. You might look over the parts titled "Attitude Issues." If the shoe fits...

Humor. Next to bathing, humor is the most important sex aid there is. Try not to forget this.

Oral Sex during Menstruation

Some couples are fine with oral sex while the woman is menstruating; others wait a few days until the menstrual flow has stopped. Here are four possibilities if you don't want the mess but don't want to wait:

🎵~Instead. It's the name brand of a new tampon alternative that fits over your cervix in the same way as a diaphragm. Pop one in before oral sex and it will catch most if not all of the bloody flow. You can get them at your grocery store. **Note:** These are not for birth control.

🎵~A woman who is menstruating can douche and insert a couple of tampons before a man goes down on her. The tampons will usually catch most of the flow, assuming that you don't attempt to tickle the woman's cervix with the tip of your tongue. If you douche, which might do more harm than good, consider using a gentle solution with a lower pH.

🎵~Some women get a diaphragm for the sole purpose of having sex during their periods. The diaphragm becomes a barrier that traps the menstrual flow. Some couples use the diaphragm for oral sex but not for intercourse, since menstrual secretions can help make intercourse feel extra nice. If you do this, be sure to use an alternative method of birth control.

🎵~A simple way of dodging menstrual flow is by putting plastic wrap over the woman's vulva before going down on her.

For couples who are concerned about AIDS transmission: Whether AIDS can be transmitted through oral contact is still not known, but why take the chance? Also, you should never do unprotected oral sex on a partner if you have a chancre sore or active oral herpes in your mouth, or if your partner has a herpes outbreak on his or her genitals.

69

69 is when a man does oral sex on a woman at the same time that she does oral sex on him.

There are plenty of couples who enjoy oral sex but don't necessarily like doing 69. That's because when a person is on the receiving end of oral sex, he or she might want to kick back and not have to worry about getting the other person off. 69 should also be avoided if the female partner involuntarily clenches her jaw during orgasm...

On the other hand, there might be times when 69 is great fun. Some couples enjoy it as their favorite way of having sex. They love the feeling of simultaneously sucking and being sucked. 69 might also be good for people who can't tolerate receiving pleasure without giving it at the same time, or vice versa.

Readers' Comments

Advice on Giving Oral Sex

"Lick around the area of the clitoris, not directly on it, until I am more aroused and then only part of the time."

female age 35

"Get a good rhythm going, don't suck or lick too hard on the head of the clit. Also, either be smooth-shaved or have a beard, but no in-between. Razor burn really kills down there!" *female age 45*

"Stubble on the face is not welcome in tender areas down below." *female age 48*

"Please quit when I say so; it gets really tender and ticklish after I come." *female age 43*

"Start out slowly, working around the outer area with your tongue. Don't just push in. Do a lot of gentle rubbing and caressing on the insides of the leg. Gradually probe the vulva with your tongue. Develop a rhythm and keep going until I come." *female age 32*

"If my partner's tongue gets tired, he uses his finger and sometimes it feels the same." *female age 25*

"I like a man to first shave me smooth, then gently kiss and finger me." *female age 34*

"It's great when he puts a finger into my rear while giving me oral sex. It makes for quite the explosion!"

female age 38

Massage, Back Rubs, Body Rubs
The Ultimate Tenderness
Chapter 19

In doing research for this book, almost every way that human adults get each other off was considered. Attempts were made to view sex through the eyes of mate-swappers, Tantric sex masters, gays, lesbians, conservative born-again Christians, bondage enthusiasts and even those whose sex lives are really boring. Having left no sexual stone unturned, one and only one universal truth about human sexuality emerged:

No matter what your sexual beliefs, fantasies, kink or persuasion, nothing beats a good back rub.

Nobody, absolutely nobody, had a single bad thing to say about a good back rub. Ditto for foot massage.

Hard vs. Soft? Male vs. Female?

Just about every book ever written on sex loves to state that men touch women too hard, and that women touch men too soft. Baloney, says a straw poll taken by the Goofy Foot Press. Here are two types of touch that both men and women like a great deal:

Feather-light to Light: This is where the fingertips lightly dance across the surface of the skin, resulting in a delightful tingling sensation that may or may not raise goosebumps. It can also be done with the flat of the hand doing light, long, gentle strokes. Optimal feather-light touch time: from five to fifty minutes. Some people who were held down as kids and mercilessly tickled might not like this kind of touch.

Deep & Hard: This is when muscles are kneaded with a strength and authority that chases away stress and tension. The men commented that they often fear they are doing this too hard, but their female partners almost always say it's just right or to do it harder. Optimal deep-and-hard massage time: from half an hour to however long the giver wants to keep doing it.

Fortunately, numerous books on touch and massage have been published in the last twenty years. There are also several nicely done videos on the subject of massage. An hour spent reading one of these books or watching a tape will probably do more for your relationship than a lifetime of looking at *Playboy* or *Penthouse*. Pay special attention to the chapters on foot rubs, hand rubs, and scalp and facial massages. These body parts are often ignored because they aren't considered blue-chip erogenous zones.

Spectators vs. Participants

Some people struggle to get fully into their bodies. Some are perpetually stuck in "prepare to defend" mode and have trouble relaxing enough to enjoy what is being shared with them sexually. They need to be hypervigilant about what is going on around them. The same thing happens when a person always needs to perform and has difficulty becoming passive enough to allow sexual things to happen to his or her body.

Learning to massage and be massaged is one way that might help you to relax your body's armor. This might be anxiety-producing at the start, so go slowly and try to enjoy the gains you are able to make.

Combining Sex & Massage

One reader comments: "My husband often massages my shoulders while I'm giving him head. It feels wonderful and serves to relax me so I can become more easily aroused." Another reader ties her naked partner's hands together above his head, lets him watch as she slowly removes her satin underwear and then caresses his entire body with them. A third reader drags her long hair across her lover's naked body and eventually wraps it around his genitals. One man reports that the best way to drive his partner into total ecstasy is for him to brush her hair or massage her scalp with his fingertips. Another couple takes long, candlelit showers together, shampooing each other's hair and soaping each other's body.

Perhaps you have your own favorite ways of combining massage with sex play. Whatever your inclination, if there is only one thing you take from this book, take the resolve to make massage and body rubs an integral part of your sexual relationships. Touch and massage might be the most important aspects of human sexuality, outside of the occasional need to replenish the species.

Intercourse Alert

There are a number of fun, exciting and highly satisfying ways of sharing sexual pleasure besides vaginal intercourse. Many are listed in this book.

If you are not fully prepared to become pregnant, to support ($$$) and parent a child for the next eighteen years, to give your baby up for adoption or to have an abortion, then you shouldn't be having vaginal intercourse. [1]

Even the best birth control methods fail. In our culture, we value the creation of human life too much to ignore the responsibility and consequences of what may follow.

Intercourse is also the most common means of passing on sexual diseases.

---

[1] Unless you are past menopause!

Horizontal Jogging (Intercourse)
Chapter 20

closed caption

Intercourse can mean different things to different people. As presented in this chapter, it's an intensely private, delicious act. You can use it to honor and expand your relationship at the same time that you are doing really nice things with your body. It's also what couples do when they want to create new life. We don't take it lightly, and we try to present it with a level of feeling and intelligence not normally found in popular books on sex.

Dick, Laura & Craig

To learn more about the role of intercourse in sexuality, this book has invaded the privacy of three young adults, Dick, Craig and Laura. Laura used to go out with Dick, and now she's involved with Craig. Here are their goofy stories:

DICK

Dick is a very nice-looking guy who won his fraternity's "Mr. All-America" title two years in a row. Dick has a nice job, a nice social manner, drives a nice sports car, wears nice clothes, has nice biceps, triceps and pecs, and goes out with nice women. Since this is a book about sex, you might as well know that Dick has a tree trunk of a penis that stays rock hard from dusk to dawn. A former girlfriend referred to it as "the sentry."

CRAIG

Craig is the same age as Dick. Craig's a sportswriter. Craig is no longer eligible for the Mr. All-America contest. During a football game a few years ago, Craig went airborne to catch an overthrown pass. On the way down he got sandwiched between two spearing linebackers. Craig's spinal cord snapped and he hasn't been able to walk or have an erection since.

LAURA

Laura is a fine young woman who just left a big corporation to form her own company that makes sporting gear. Laura's had sex with both Dick and Craig. Let's see what Laura has to say about these two different men.

"Dick's the kind of guy that many American women have been raised to worship. Parading him around your friends or taking him home to your parents would win you the female equivalent of the Breeder's Cup.... I've always really enjoyed sex, and until recently I could never understand why a woman would want to fake an orgasm. But it didn't take too many nights with Dick before I started faking orgasms. There was Dick, Mr. Right Stuff, making all that picture-perfect love. I didn't want him to think there was something wrong with me since I couldn't get into it like he was, so I started faking orgasms."

"Craig is nowhere near as perfect as Dick, but he has a great sense of humor and he is genuine. Craig is able to laugh at himself, which Dick never could. Craig has taken the time to learn exactly how to kiss, touch, and caress me, and the sex I have with him is great. When I'm with Craig I don't need to fake a thing."

"This may not seem relevant to your question about sex, but I work in a totally male-dominated business. I have to think like a guy from morning to night. Sometimes it leaves me feeling alien from my femininity. With Craig it's easy to find it back again.... Craig never wakes me up at 3:00 a.m. with a hard-on poking in my back, but he feels just as masculine as Dick. With a lot of guys there's a huge difference between how they treat you in bed and how they treat you the rest of time; with Craig that's not the case. Maybe that's another reason why sex is so nice with him, even if it's not intercourse."

Okay, so here we have Dick, more functional than a Sidewinder missile. He fulfills everybody's definition of what a true sexual athlete should be. Then we have Craig, who redefines the term "sexually dysfunctional." If Craig had the same erection failure but no spinal cord injury, a bunch of psychologists and sex therapists would collect a small fortune trying to make him "normal." At the very least, they would have him munching down Viagra pills as if they were M&Ms. And probably Prozac, too.

And finally, there's Laura, a woman who enjoys sex a great deal. She's saying that the guy who can't get it up is a more satisfying lover than Mr. Erectus Perfectus.

In telling you about Laura, Dick and Craig, the intent was not to dump on intercourse. Intercourse, when it's good, can be one of the sweetest things there is. What this book is dumping on is the assumption that intercourse is good just because it's intercourse and that a man is a man because he can get hard and fuck, or that a woman is a woman because she can get wet and fuck him back.

When Ms. Dworkin Has Intercourse

These days, certain groups of women are referring to any and all kinds of intercourse as evil. They say that even if a woman wants intercourse badly, it's only because she has been brainwashed by men into thinking it is pleasurable. To explore this issue in greater depth, we asked our women readers the following question: "What does it feel like when you have intercourse?" Mind you, these women are describing intercourse with partners whom they care deeply about.

What Does It Feel Like When You Have Intercourse?

"Oh God—It's like describing the universe. It feels like I might explode and can't wait to but at same time want it to last forever. Breathless, hot, turned on in the extreme. I want to engulf and squeeze his penis, get it in me as much as possible. I love the connection of it." *female age 48*

"When his penis first enters me I want to feel every inch of it because it is exquisite. I feel like I need it inside me and I don't know if I can describe that. The actual sensations of his penis sliding in and out of me are sometimes overpowered by the pleasure I feel all over my body, so I don't necessarily concentrate on the intercourse."

female age 23

"As he enters me I feel myself spreading open to accommodate him. Emotionally it feels right that he is inside of me. I have a feeling of fullness when he is inside me. I can feel the head of the penis as it slides in and out and can feel my vagina collapse or expand around him. If he plunges deep I can feel the head of the penis bump my cervix, a not altogether unpleasant feeling. From rear entry I can feel the penis more acutely rubbing the top of my vagina." *age 37*

"It feels different everytime. Sometimes it is very satisfying. Sometimes it hurts inside my vagina if I'm not lubricated enough. And sometimes when his penis hits my G-spot it takes my breath away!" *female age 34*

"At first I feel the light pressure of my partner's penis against my unopened vagina. It is often deeply pleasurable to feel the head penetrate, and then a slow, smooth slide all the way in, and a jolt of excitement when my lover's penis is completely inside me. The most sensation is around the outer part of the vagina, but there is also a pleasurable feeling of fullness when he is fully inside me. My hips want to move and match his strokes, or create my own rhythm for him to match. Different types of strokes and rhythms create different sensations." *female age 47*

"The first thrust is the most vivid for me. I like to slowly slide down his cock and feel it go up me. I love it when he is trying to hold back from coming; I can feel him get more swollen and hard and I get very excited when I feel that. It actually is the time when my vagina gets the most pleasure from intercourse." *female age 23*

"It depends on how sexually excited I am and whether I'm in the mood or if I'm just doing it because he wants to. If I'm into it, it's like ecstasy!" *female age 43*

"I enjoy the pumping and grinding a great deal. I love it when we are rubbing our pelvic bones together and when the penis is in deep." *female age 21*

"My favorite part of intercourse is when he comes, his entire body stiffens." *female age 55*

"I'm strictly a clit person. I love having sex with men, but I don't like intercourse." *female age 36*

At the Start—New Relationship or New to Intercourse

For a lot of couples it takes time and familiarity for intercourse to get that kind of sloppy-intimate-erotic edge that makes it so much fun. This means that intercourse won't necessarily knock your socks off at the start. It may not even feel as good as masturbation.

Also, each partner brings his or her own hopes and expectations, as well as physical anatomy and body rhythms. Patience can be a virtue. For instance, some couples who are having dynamite intercourse during the fifth year of their relationship had lousy intercourse during the first year. And even if the sex is great at the start, chances are there will be periods in any relationship when sexual desire falls flat. Hopefully you will continue to grow as a couple during those times.

Your First Intercourse

In a recent study on first intercourse that included 659 college students, researchers Schwartz, Sprecher, Barbee and Orbuch found the following:

☞ While seventy-nine percent of the men reported that they had an orgasm during their first intercourse, only seven percent of the women reported having an orgasm.

☞ Males had far more overall pleasure than females.

☞ The mean age for first intercourse was sixteen and one-half years, although those who waited until they were seventeen or older reported having a better experience than those who were younger. Not that anything gets better with age automatically, but sometimes a year or two of added life experience can go a long way when you are only sixteen.

☞ Both males and females reported more pleasure if they had intercourse for the first time in a more serious or long-term relationship than in a casual or brief one.

☞ Individuals in long-term relationships reported having less guilt during their first intercourse than those in more casual relationships, although they experienced more anxiety, perhaps from having more at stake.

☞ People who used alcohol during their first intercourse (about 30 percent of the total) reported significantly less pleasure and more guilt than those who did it sober.

☞ Individuals who used contraception reported more pleasure than those who didn't.

BIRTH CONTROL NOTE FOR POTENTIAL FIRST-TIMERS: It's easy to get pregnant the first time you have intercourse. You can also become pregnant from having intercourse during your period.

This edition of the *Guide* has an entire chapter titled "The First Time–Not What You'd Think." There are also readers' suggestions about your first time at the end of this chapter.

The Approach

Sometimes you're both so horny that you hardly get your shoes and socks off before you are doing the wild thing. But a lot of the time, one of you is ready for intercourse before the other. Now if it's the man who isn't ready, it's a no-brainer who needs to get turned on a bit more. And if his erection detonator remains in shutdown mode, then it's time for him to pull out his trusty tongue and dive. Muff dive. (Why ruin a perfectly good night of sex just because a penis won't get hard?)

If he's the one who's ready first, it wouldn't hurt a bit to tease his partner until she's more or less pleading to be entered. You can always get a little extra mileage before taking the big plunge by letting the head of your penis caress the lips of her vulva.

She'll know it's there, but she won't know when it's going in. One problem with this is if the big dude is worried that his little dude won't stay hard.

Some women are able to enjoy intercourse more if they have an orgasm before the penis goes in.

One in the Hand... Who Sticks It In

"I generally prefer to put it in; otherwise we seem to miss a lot." *female age 32*

"I always want him to put it in." *female age 25*

"I like to put his penis in me because it seems no matter how many times we have had sex, he still misses a little bit when aiming. Also, I find it exciting to hold him while he thrusts into my vagina." *female age 23*

"It's really whoever grabs ahold first." *female age 36*

"He prefers to put it in, because if I do, he thinks I think he doesn't know where in the heck that hole is." *female age 38*

"She always does. No matter how many years we've been doing this, I still manage to miss!" *male age 43*

This may seem like a dumb thing to talk about, but the issue of who sticks the penis into the vagina can sometimes be significant. A rule of thumb, so to speak, is that the woman should be the one who sticks it in—at least for the first few times until both partners have their signals in sync. That's because only a woman knows when she is ready to have a penis inside, and all those years of inserting tampons have taught her exactly where the head of little Tonto needs to go. Of course, some women might be shy about grabbing a guy's penis and guiding it in for a landing. This kind of reticence is silly, but understandable.

If it's the man's job to put the penis in, he should wait until getting a go-ahead signal. At the very least, he should check out the readiness of his partner's vagina with a finger. If it's not particularly wet but the woman still wants him inside, he should lube himself up with a water-based lubricant such as KY or contraceptive jelly. Also, a wad of saliva slapped on the head of the penis is a time-honored antidote for a willing but arid vagina.

If you are using a water-based lube and it dries out with extended thrusting, add a few drops of water or saliva rather than more lube. A drop or two of water will give it new life, while more lube will just gum things up. The women at Good Vibrations suggest keeping a water pistol handy for just this purpose, although women without humor will find this to be offensive, and wives of NRA members should be careful not to grab the Uzi by mistake.

The First Thrust

As we were reading the questionnaires of our women readers, an amazing pattern emerged. A large number of women said that the part of intercourse they liked best was the first stroke. For a lot women, it seems like the first stoke is a nearly religious happening, assuming they're primed and eager for the thrusting to begin.

Do not hesitate to ask your sweetheart how she likes you to do your first stroke. Does she like you to start by teasing her with a series of short little thrusts, going in only an inch or two? Or does she like one big straightforward glide for the gold?

Legs Bent or Straight, Open or Closed

The Physics of Intercourse Part 1 The biggest single variable in the physics of intercourse is often the position of the woman's legs—whether they are straight or bent, open or closed, over your shoulders or in your face. For instance, when the woman's legs are straight, penetration is not as deep, but the clitoris tends to receive more stimulation. When a woman bends her legs and brings her knees closer to her chest, the penetration is deeper. This can be nice if she likes more pressure in the back part of her vagina, although this sometimes pulls the clitoris away from the penis. It also changes the angle of the penis in the vagina, causing a different feel for both the man and the woman.

If the woman's legs are together, the penis is hugged more snugly. This might offer better clitoral stimulation, because the added snugness may push the inner labia more tightly against the shaft of the penis as it goes in and out. When she opens her legs, there is greater skin-to-skin contact between her vulva and the man's genitals. This can also result in more bouncing-testicle action if the man is on top.

Some couples enjoy intercourse with one leg straight and the other flexed. And some women compensate for decreased clitoral contact by reaching between their legs and pushing the clitoris against the penis with their fingers. Got all of that?

And if this isn't confusing enough, some women keep their legs straight and together while flexing their thighs to help push themselves over the orgasmic top.

Legs Bent or Straight: Anatomical Consideration

A woman's decision to keep her legs straight or bent might also vary with the length and thickness of the man's penis. A woman whose partner has a really long penis may find that she gets poked in the cervix if she opens and bends her legs during intercourse, while a woman whose man has a short penis might prefer the feeling of deeper penetration that bent knees allow.

Porn star Nina Hartley has a shallow vagina and can't take guys who are really long. Mind you, "shallow" and "long" are defined differently in the world of pornography than in the average bedroom. Ms. Hartley suggests that women can add another inch or two of thrusting room by using positions that allow the penis to move into the space behind the cervix that is called the fornix. You will need to experiment on your own–Nina doesn't say what these space enhancing positions might be.

Apologies: Sex books these days don't use the term "short penis." Instead, they say a penis that isn't overly long. The latter phrasing is meant to protect the allegedly fragile male ego, yet this guide hates to think that today's male is so fragile that he can't say "I've got a short one" without experiencing a crisis of character. As for the sentiment expressed by the 20 Fingers hit song "(Don't Want No) Short Dick Man," consult the chapter "Techno Breasts & Weenie Angst."

Thrusting—Shallow vs. Deep

The Physics of Intercourse Part 2   The walls of a woman's vagina change shape with each thrust of intercourse. This means that with each stroke, thousands of nerve endings are being pulled and tugged, which, neurologically speaking, can feel extremely nice. (This doesn't feel half bad for guys, either.) The most sensitive part of the vagina is usually at the opening, up to an inch or two deep. This also becomes the snuggest part of the vagina when it is aroused.

Shallow thrusting encourages the snuggest part of the vagina to wrap around the most sensitive part of his penis, just below the head. Shallow thrusting also allows the ridge around the head of the penis to stimulate this sensitive part of the vagina. An exception might be if the man's penis has a compact head and is thicker around the middle part of the shaft, in which case the woman may prefer the thicker part to be in the vaginal opening.

Deeper thrusting offers its own advantages: 1. Unless the man's penis is really long or the woman's vagina is shallow, deep thrusting can help to position his pubic bone in direct contact with her clitoral area. Rubbing against a man's pubic bone helps some women to have orgasms during intercourse. 2. Deeper thrusting may allow the penis to pull on the labia minora (inner lips) for a longer period of time, providing more simulation to the clitoral area. 3. The deeper part of the vagina is often sensitive to pressure. As some women approach orgasm, they find it pleasurable if there is a penis or penislike object in the back part of the vagina which it can contract around.

The Zen Police Talk Thrust

Some Tantric and Oriental sex masters caution about deep thrusting during intercourse. They feel that the vagina does best with a ratio of five-to-one or nine-to-one shallow-to-deep thrusts. This is an interesting observation, given how they don't allow women to be monks or masters and they don't even allow them to enter business meetings unless it's to bring tea, but they have no shortage of suggestions for pleasing them sexually.

Anyway, the nine shallow for every one deep thrust is a pattern that pretty much wins you the Tantric intercourse exacta. Then, as your partner becomes more aroused, increase the ratio to two deep for every four shallow, or live dangerously and go for one shallow to one deep.

This is definitely something to experiment with, but if your partner starts threatening you with serious grief if you don't knock off the shallow stuff and start thrusting deep, you can safely assume she wasn't an Asian princess in a past life.

Battering Ram or Pleasure Wand? Mosh Pit or Symphony?

Some men use a penis as a kind of battering ram, believing that women enjoy being slammed during intercourse. Other men, perhaps a bit more sensitive or experienced, realize that there are different thrusting rhythms that can help make intercourse feel more symphonic than metallic. A lot of it also depends on what style or styles of thrusting the woman enjoys. Maybe she will like it slow at the start but strong at the end.

An excellent way to find out what works best during intercourse is when the woman is on top. That way the man can feel what she does with his penis, how she moves up and down on it and what parts of her vagina she focuses the head on. For instance, does she thrust rapidly with it, or does she keep the penis deep inside of her and rub her clitoris on the man's pubic bone? Does she like to massage her clitoris or breasts while a penis is inside of her, or would this be an unwelcome distraction? Where does she like to look, and what does she do with her mouth?

Eager for Beaver—Intercourse as Two Separate Acts

If you are feeling terminally reflective and have nothing else to do, it might be helpful to think of intercourse as two separate acts—the thrusting or rocking part and the orgasm part. If the sole purpose of the former is to achieve the latter, then the intercourse might not have much emotional depth to it. That's because it is during the thrusting part of intercourse (before orgasm) when feelings of love, friendship and gratitude are often shared.

Most couples have a variety of thrusting modes—hot and furious, fun and playful, giggly, tearful, passionate, powerful, passive and maybe even angry at times. This becomes part of the private language that lovers share.

Using Your Head

Keep in mind that the first inch or so of a woman's vagina is sensitive to touch. That's why a bit of gentle finger or penis-head action around the rim can be a nice way to begin. The art, of course, is in making those shallow little thrusts without pulling out too far and having your dick fall out. If it falls out enough times, she'll start thinking your middle name is "Goober."

Beyond the first inch or so, you need to start thinking pressure. That's because the back part of the vagina feels stretching and pressure more than it does light little touches. This is when it's wise to learn which parts of her vagina respond best to pressure, that is, the kind that happens when the head of your penis pushes against it. If you pay close enough attention, you'll find that you can combine certain positions with certain angles to pressure almost any part of her vagina that she likes.

A good way to learn about a woman's genitals is with your fingers as well as with your penis. This will give you a better under-

Studies show that guys who help out around the house get laid more often than guys who don't, causing speculation that Windex and 409 are better aphrodisiacs than oysters, expensive cars and a medicine chest full of Viagra.

standing of what needs to be done with your penis. (As one female reader says, "It wouldn't hurt for women to know this about themselves.")

Popping Out

During some orgasms, the vagina contracts so much that it can expel a penis. When asked about this, most women advise, "Push It Back In!!!" With this kind of contraction, it feels good to have a penis deep inside a vagina, even if it might take quite a thrust to keep it in or get it back in.

Thrustless in Seattle

Some couples don't thrust at all during intercourse, but move their entire bodies in sync or the man might do a circular motion with his penis or pelvic bone pushing against the woman's clitoris. And some couples occasionally stay really still during intercourse and simply try to coordinate their breathing. For instance, one partner breathes in at the moment that the other breathes out.

You don't have to be a yogi master to achieve wonderful experiences with breathing instead of thrusting. You don't even need to meditate six hours a day or stand on your head while chanting some mysterious incantation. All you need to do is be in sync with each other.

Another interesting way of enjoying intercourse without thrusting is to play "squeezing genitals." It is based upon the anatomical fact that when the male squeezes or contracts his erect penis it momentarily changes diameter, and when the woman squeezes her vagina it hugs the penis—sometimes rather snugly and with memorable results. To play "squeezing genitals," partners alternate squeezing their genitals. This can be extremely satisfying if your pelvic muscles are in really good shape, and it doesn't require a particularly high I.Q. or daring sense of adventure.

Riding High—Tom Landry Remembered

Each year a new book comes out that promises to reinvent the wheel sexually. For instance, a recent entry talks about a radical "new" way of having intercourse. The couple starts by assuming the traditional missionary position with the man climbing on top. Right before the thrusting begins, the man makes a quick shift toward the head of the bed, like the Dallas Cowboys used to do at the line of scrimmage before the set call, back when they were America's team and Tom Landry was coach.

During this quick shift, the male pushes his entire body a couple of inches forward over the head of the woman. Not only does this tempt a man to obnoxiously rest his chin on his partner's third eye, but it puts him in the position of being able to say, "Honey, your roots are showing something awful, time for a new bleach job." This new intercourse position is supposed to bring the man's penis in more direct contact with the woman's clitoris, assuming his poor weenie doesn't snap off between the down and set call.

There is no in-out thrusting motion in this new form of intercourse. The couple simply move their hips back and forth in synchronized form, like those women swimmers at the Summer Olympics. Fortunately, the founder of this new position says nothing about wearing ugly swim caps, or Dallas Cowboy football helmets for that matter.

This intercourse position does attempt to maximize clitoral stimulation by making the man "ride high." Guys who are sensitive lovers figured this one out long ago, although an occasional man may have had the knowledge forced upon him by a rambunctious lover who rode so low that she made him wonder if his penis would survive the night. Her low riding is the equivalent of his riding high. Again, a good way for a man to learn what angles his partner prefers is to pay close attention when she's on top. Or ask.

Nasty Reflections

Watching your genitals at work or play during intercourse can be an amusing and fun way to pass time. "Sexy and hot," adds a woman reader. There are several positions which allow one or both partners to watch the vagina swallowing up the penis and then spitting it out again—oops, passionately enveloping it. A good-sized hand mirror can offer a nice view of genital play until one of you accidentally kicks it over. Also, try using the magnifying side of the mirror. It will make you look huge! A woman reader comments: "That's a frightening thought."

Some couples also like to pull out the Camcorder and tape themselves when having intercourse. Entire books have been written on this subject. Precautions for making home movies are mentioned in the fantasy chapter, such as putting a big X on the cassette and keeping it in a separate place from the movies that go back to Blockbuster. There are also special video locks that can be put on tapes of mom and dad having sex so the kids don't accidentally watch and suddenly have the ammo to blackmail you out of every last dollar in your retirement fund.

Kissing When Thrusting—Size vs. Intent

Sometimes there's nothing nicer in the world than kissing passionately when your genitals are locked in a loving embrace, but this simply isn't possible for some couples. For instance, if a woman is 5'1" and her partner is 6'4", there is no way her tongue is going to comfortably play inside his mouth at the same time they are having intercourse unless she has a really deep navel or a foot-long tongue.

One reason why it's impossible to make recommendations regarding intercourse positions is because different couples come in different sizes. For instance, some positions will feel better for certain couples who are relatively the same height and weight, while those same positions might be a total disaster for a union between Twiggy and the Jolly Green Giant. Likewise, certain positions will feel better or worse depending on the size and angle of your respective genitals. And some positions that feel best during the first part of a woman's menstrual cycle might give way to other positions during the later part of her cycle. And that's just physical differences. It really gets complicated when you factor in each partner's emotional desires and needs.

Ends & Odds

Here are some observations on intercourse that you might find helpful:

🌸 Some couples enjoy it greatly when the woman uses a vibrator during intercourse. The sensations can be very pleasing for both partners. You can do this in any number of positions that actually feel comfortable, or you can get all artsy and try doing it like the couple in the illustration in the vibrator chapter.

🌸 A woman who is on top and facing her man's feet can easily watch his penis as it bebops in and out of her vagina. She can also reach forward and play with his little piggies, or reach down and play with his big piggy and testicles.

🌸 Rear-entry positions allow the head of the penis to focus on the upper front wall of the vagina, a place that some women find extra-sensitive. Rear entry also provides extra padding, which can be very welcome if one or both of you is really bony.

🌸 Rather than thrusting, some couples find that rocking back and forth with a penis inside can feel quite pleasant.

🌸 Some couples enjoy taking an intercourse break in order to have oral sex (oral intermission); other couples like to have oral sex after intercourse, and some women have their orgasms by receiving oral sex before or after intercourse.

🌸 In Veronica Monet's video of women masturbating, some of the women used dildos. However, they used the dildos differently than men use their penises during intercourse. For instance, it was not unusual for the woman to run the dildo between her labia rather than plunging it into her vagina. Some women enjoy a well-lubricated penis moving between their labia in this way, like a hot dog going back and forth through a hot dog bun, although you might skip the relish and mustard. The ridge around the head of the penis can feel especially nice as it glides back and forth over the clitoris. The woman can increase the pressure by pulling the penis tighter against her vulva with her fingertips. This is also called femoral intercourse.

☞ In the highly recommended book *Tricks — More Than 125 Ways to Make Good Sex Better*, author Jay Wiseman suggests having the man lie on his back and the woman place a pair of her panties over his penis. The penis sticks through a leg hole, with the panties draping down over his testicles and between his legs. The couple then has intercourse with the woman on top. If the panties are silky or rayonlike, the material might stimulate him each time she moves up and down.

☞ Some couples find a well-trimmed and freshly bathed big toe to be a fun penis substitute. Also, the pad of the big toe or heel can be used rather nicely to stimulate a woman's genitals.

☞ There are couples who like to gently bite each other's shoulders or run their teeth along each other's skin while having intercourse. This works best when the skin is well-lubricated and the lovers let each other know when it starts to hurt.

☞ Some men and women particularly enjoy the feeling of intercourse after a woman has had an orgasm.

☞ If for some reason a vagina doesn't get as wet as a couple might want, be sure to keep some water-based lube handy, or pick up glycerin suppositories from the drugstore that can be put into the vagina ahead of time. (If vaginal infections are a problem, you might experiment with water-based lubricants that have no glycerin.) As the former baby boom generation hot flashes its way into the next century, a plethora of pricey new "personal moisturizers" will flood the market. To understand more about them, see the sections on store-bought lubes at the end of the "Sex Fluids" chapter.

☞ Women might not lubricate very well for the first couple of months following pregnancy. Extra lubrication can also help if the woman is taking certain drugs such as antihistamines, alcohol or pot, and if the man is wearing a condom or the couple is playing with sex toys.

☞ Why not try feeding each other while having intercourse? That's what nature created papaya for...

🖐 Some couples enjoy a finger, thumb, small vibrator, gerbil or butt plug on or in each other's anus during intercourse.

🖐 Most sex stores sell little plastic thingies that fit over a man's penis and provide extra stimulation to the woman's clitoris when she rubs up against his pubic bone. There is also a plastic device called a vibrating cock ring that some couples enjoy using, and a special vibrator in a harness can be strapped in place over the clitoris for use during intercourse.

🖐 Some vaginas make fartlike noises during intercourse. This is due to air that has been pushed into the back of the vagina. If you get embarrassed about these sounds, it might be helpful to remember that it wasn't just one of you who "farted," that the noise was the result of the two of you doing wonderful things to each other.

🖐 There is one position where the man sits on a chair and the woman sits in his lap, wrapping her legs around his waist. While this doesn't work for heavy-duty thrusting, the penetration can be really deep. Sitting up also allows more blood to pool in the pelvic region, which can help some men get better erections. You might try a similar position where the man sits in the chair and the woman sits on his lap but facing away from him (sitting spoons position?).

Signaling

Sex seldom works well when one partner is too passive or inhibited to let the other know what feels good and what doesn't. Fortunately, signaling during intercourse doesn't need to include words, because hands on a partner's hips or rear end can be great rudders—as long as the partner with the hips is hip to the hands.

To Come or Not to Come...

People have this silly notion that women are supposed to come during intercourse and by thrusting alone. The fact is, way fewer than 50 percent of women have orgasms during intercourse.

One reason is because the clitoris does not usually receive direct stimulation from the penis during intercourse.

As you will see from the comments below, many women who do come during intercourse need a little help from either their own or their partner's fingers.

> "I very rarely have orgasms with intercourse, unless I'm playing with myself at the time. The best way for me is oral sex or using a vibrator." *female age 36*

> "I don't usually have orgasms during intercourse. In a very open relationship, I can have an orgasm after intercourse by manually stimulating my clitoris or by rubbing myself on his flaccid penis." *female age 26*

> "I usually have them with intercourse if my husband is rubbing my clitoris or using a vibrator while he is thrusting. Sometimes when I am really excited, I can have one just with thrusting." *female age 35*

> "I come faster sometimes when he's inside me, but I always have to rub my clit to climax." *female age 25*

In case you think these women don't like intercourse, think again. A woman can love the feelings she gets from intercourse, but still not have orgasms from it.

When Is Intercourse a Success?

Most books imply that intercourse is a success if you give each other orgasms and a failure if you don't. Hardly. This guide takes the position that intercourse needs to convey certain feelings between partners that are too primal for words alone. These feelings rest on the boundary between body and soul and are transmitted from one person to another in many different ways. If orgasm is part of that process, fine, but simply having an orgasm is no guarantee that anything special has taken place. At the same time, it's possible to have intercourse with no orgasm at all and experience it as being wonderful or enchanting.

When is intercourse a success? Intercourse seems successful when it leaves you feeling a little more solid, less grumpy, more able to face the day, and less afraid of the world when it's an overwhelming place. Intercourse is successful when it allows you to both give and get something from your partner that makes you feel more whole or wholesome and secure.

When is intercourse a failure? This book's criterion for failure is waking up at three or four in the morning, looking at the person who's sleeping next to you and thinking "I wish I were home in my own bed, ALONE." This can be a particularly nasty dilemma if you are married or living together. Also, intercourse that conveys less pleasure than when someone leaves you a free hour on a parking meter is not necessarily worth having.

Pillows on Parade

Don't underestimate the power of a pillow to help enhance intercourse. For instance, consider trying a pillow under the rear of whoever is on the bottom. For some couples, the change in angle increases sensation. Depending on who's doing what, optimal pillow placement might be higher above the tailbone or further down under your rear. Experiment to find what placement, if any, is good for you.

If you like intercourse from the rear, keep a lookout for the right big pillow that might provide support and raise the woman's rear end to an angle that is both comfortable and inviting. The more humongous the pillow, the more fun. Experiment with bolsters and oddly shaped pillows.

Environment

If intercourse is seeming a bit stale, it might help to start doing it in a new location. Of course, it never hurts if that new location happens to be a four-star hotel somewhere in Europe, but if you haven't saved up quite that many frequent flyer miles, here are a few other possibilities:

🐾 **The Kitchen** Always a fine place for intercourse until you have kids. But once the kids reach school age, the kitchen is usually free for an occasional nooner.

🐾 **In Front of the Fireplace** There's nothing quite like doing it in front of the fireplace, until the woodsman delivers wet pine instead of seasoned oak and a slew of hissing, burning embers shower your naked back and rear end.

🐾 **The Yard** It's a shame to spend all that time and money making the grass grow and never fuck on it. Go ahead, give the gophers a show.

🐾 **In Water** Hot tubs, bathtubs, pools and other large bodies of water can be great places for people to do all sorts of nasty things to each other. But intercourse in water provides its own unique hazard because water washes away natural lubrication. The best solution is a silicone-based lubricant. Another solution is to slip the penis inside the vagina while both sets of organs are outside the water. Then slither your way under the surface, penis-in-vagina. Aquatic intercourse is now possible if you limit yourselves to a muted kind of thrusting. Also, to help facilitate underwater hand play and other forms of sexual groping, coat your genitals with something oily while they are still dry-docked. But oil-based lubricants can be unhealthy for a vagina if you then have intercourse.

🐾 **Sex at the Office** Sex at the office often has the right elements of risk and mischievous fun. One reader is a commercial real estate agent who has keys to some of the finest offices in all of Los Angeles. When he and his girlfriend want a dramatic change of scenery, they check out the upper floors.

🐾 **Candlelight** An old standby for erotic ambiance is candlelight. Make sure that the candle wax doesn't drip on your carpet, because it will cost you a fortune to have it commercially removed. Also, one reader cautions that some types of candleholders get hot enough to scorch furniture.

After Intercourse—The Drip Factor

Unless a guy is wearing a rubber or pulls out and squirts to the side, he usually leaves ejaculate inside a woman's vagina following intercourse. Okay, so where does the ejaculate go?

"Runs down your leg," says one female respondent. "It usually drips out," replies another. "Like water in a cup that's turned upside down," says a third. This might not be a problem if you are going to sleep, except for the wet spot on the mattress, but what if you had intercourse in the morning or at lunchtime? "You can usually get it out in the shower" was one response, while another woman says, "Not true. It tends to drain out at its own pace, and all the showering in the world isn't going to hasten it along." Either way, what if you already took a shower or don't want to take one just then? "Sometimes I'll wear a panty liner," said one woman, "but it's not worth a tampon." All of the women who were asked said they know of other women who douche right after intercourse even when they have it at bedtime. Most thought this was silly and unnecessary. As one woman said, "It's not dirty; I put the stuff in my mouth!" Another woman said, "I don't have sex with a man unless I really care about him.... While this might sound a little weird, I find the occasional dripping to be a sweet and sometimes exciting reminder that he's been here."

Top Dog

It has been said that people who always need to be on top during intercourse are basically insecure, while people who have it more together are happy to switch off. If this is true, then intercourse is no different from life in general.

Also, feminists claim that intercourse usually follows a prostitute model of sex— once the male comes, the sex is over. Maybe this book is terribly out of step, but it seems like a shame to end that way. It's also rude. Perhaps the two of you can talk about ways to help the woman get her share of pleasure if the man comes before she's ready to stop.

On Not Pulling Out

Staying inside your sweetheart after the thrusting is done can sometimes feel magical. Since most men lose their erections after coming, the two of you need to be somewhat clever, keeping the fading member in while getting comfortable enough to stay in each other's arms. Some couples like to fall asleep this way.

The desire to stay inside your sweetheart after ejaculation is one of the downsides of using a rubber. A man who is wearing a rubber needs to pull out soon after he's come. Otherwise he might leave the rubber inside his partner.

Too Early, Too Late

Men who have trouble coming tend to pump faster during intercourse, hoping this will provide extra stimulation to help them ejaculate. This is a bad idea. The rapid thrusting desensitizes the penis even more, and it's possible the female partner won't be able to walk right for a few days afterward. This is discussed further in the chapter "When Your System Crashes."

While some women wish they had a partner who had trouble coming, it's a problem that is often more difficult to deal with than premature ejaculation, which is the topic the chapter "Dyslexia Of The Penis—Improving Your Sexual Hang Time."

Passive Intercourse vs. Masturbation

This section was included with an awareness that only some couples might be interested. Other couples will find that it has no place in their relationship or that it might even seem perverse.

Let's say a woman wakes up at 5:00 A.M., horny as can be and would like to have something approximating intercourse. Her partner, on the other hand, is not a morning person and is pretty much comatose until noon. Assuming he's not the type who is an early-morning grouch, he allows her to stimulate his penis to a point of erection, or maybe he's already got an early-morning (REM-state) hard-on. They then have intercourse in a position where he can be passive while she is active, or she massages her clitoris while his penis is inside of her. In a sense, she is using his penis as a dildo.

Or let's say it's nearly midnight and this woman's partner is feeling sexually amped, but she is pretty much dead to the world. She doesn't mind his using her vagina for intercourse, but doesn't want to have to be into it either. So she rolls on her side and allows him to have rear-entry intercourse. (Women have been doing this sort of thing for years, but the difference here is the lack of false pretenses. She doesn't need to pretend that he is giving her an earth-shaking orgasm. It also helps if the form of birth control is the pill, an implant, a condom or an IUD, rather than something she has to make an effort to prepare or insert.)

Ah, you might say, why didn't the horny partner simply masturbate instead of bothering the one who is zoned out? Sometimes a partner honestly doesn't mind being "used" for sex as long as he or she isn't expected to get all turned on. He or she might even enjoy the partner's pleasure. However, it is essential that the passive partner feels comfortable saying, "Naw, not now," and the horny partner should be willing to masturbate if that is the case. And it requires a sex life that is fairly rich at other times, given how an entire diet of passive sex might leave the active partner feeling unvalued or the passive partner feeling used.

What's the Frequency, Dan?

When it comes to frequency of intercourse, people who ask "What's normal?" usually aren't asking the right question. For instance, if you are in a relationship, good questions to be asking are "Do we have intercourse as often as each of us likes?" "Do we have intercourse more often than one or both of us likes?" The reason these questions are far more important than "What's normal?" is because the only thing that matters about sex is what feels best for you—whether it's three times a day or three times a decade.

Betty on Intercourse

What better way to wind down a chapter on intercourse than with a few passages from feminist writer Betty Dodson's book *Sex For One?* These quotes refer to things that transpired during Ms. Dodson's sex groups for women. Part 1 is a summary of women's experience with orgasm, part 2 describes a role-playing exercise where Betty Ann had the women take the man's role in intercourse, and part 3 includes general comments on intercourse.

1. On Orgasms

Some women had good orgasms with oral sex but not with intercourse. Others could come with intercourse but couldn't get off alone. Still others were having orgasms with themselves but not with a partner. All of the orgasmic women agreed on one thing: Their experiences of orgasm varied greatly from one orgasm to the next...

2. On Pretending You're a Guy during Intercourse

One amusing and informative exercise was called "Running a Sexual Encounter." It involved reversing sex roles with the women on top. We made believe that our clitorises were penetrating imaginary lovers, and we had to do all the thrusting. I would set the egg timer for three minutes, a little longer than the Kinsey national average. As the fucking began, I would participate and at the same time comment on everyone's technique. "Keep your arms straight; don't crush your lover. You're too high up; your clitoris just fell out. Don't stop moving, you'll lose your erection. Don't move so fast; you'll come too soon. And don't forget to whisper sweet things in your lover's ear between all those passionate kisses."

Watching the egg timer, I coordinated my theatrical orgasm with the ding of the bell, frantically thrusting for the last ten seconds. Then, falling flat on my imaginary lover, I muttered, "Was it good for you?" and promptly began snoring loudly. It was always hysterically funny. Panting and exhausted, [the women] all exclaimed, "How do men do it?" Complaints included tired arms, lower-back pain, and stiff hip joints. Most of the women had fallen out long before the bell went off. After that, there was always more empathy for men, and the women showed an increased interest in other positions for lovemaking....

3. Odds & Ends

Some of the women talked about experiencing pain with deep thrusting intercourse, while others claimed to want a hard fuck. In my youth, I'd confused hard pounding intercourse with passion, and experienced internal soreness afterward. I explained that I felt a sensitive lover would never thrust with violence. While I enjoyed a strong fuck when we were two equal energies in sync, I also loved the slow intense fuck.

Another problem the women complained of was lack of lubrication and the pain of dry intercourse. Some women felt inadequate if they weren't wet with passion. My experience varied; sometimes I lubricated when I wasn't even thinking about sex. Other times I could be dry even though I felt sexually aroused.... (Betty Dodson, *Sex for One* [New York: Harmony Books])

Readers' Comments

Some of your favorite positions?

"My favorite position is doggy style, with me on my hands and knees, and him behind me. I like this best for two reasons: my vagina is tighter this way, and I can easily rub my clitoris and have an orgasm. I also love to sit on a guy while he is sitting up. This just feels wonderful. Our bodies are so close." *female age 26*

"Good old missionary, with me on the bottom and him on top!" *female age 32*

"One of my favorite positions is sitting in his lap in a chair. He can kiss my neck or armpits, which drives me nuts, and I can move freely. If we are on the bed, I can also lie back and touch my clit if I want." *female age 38*

"My favorite position is sitting on top of him. That way I can stroke my clitoris or I can watch him do it." *female 43*

"I enjoy having him on top but recently discovered that if we lie on our sides with me in front and I throw my upper leg over his, he can enter me from behind and it's very exciting." *female age 45*

"I like it best when we're doing it doggy style and I hold the vibrator and rub my clit with it. The sensation is wonderful!" *female age 25*

"I like to bend over a table and have my partner insert his penis from behind. We get great penetration this way, and he is also able to hit something in there that makes me feel really good!" *female age 34*

"I like to be on my back with my legs up while he is on his knees entering me and rubbing my clitoris. We started using this position when I was pregnant and I still like it best." *female age 35*

What do you like the most about intercourse and what do you like the least?

"Worst part—the big wet spot. Best part—making the big wet spot." *female age 27*

"It is wonderful when we first start having intercourse and I love the cuddling after. I don't like how, if you don't clean up afterward, the ejaculate runs out of you (sometimes cold) and drips down your butt onto the sheets." *female age 30*

"I like it when he first inserts his penis into my vagina the best. The thing I like least about sex is having to really work for a long time to get him to orgasm when he's had too much to drink." *female age 34*

"I like the beginning the most and orgasm, of course. If somebody takes too long, the middle gets dull." *female 25*

"The first moments of penetration are the best. The wet spot on the bed, the worst." *female age 44*

"The part I like best is when my man spends a long time getting me hot until I want him so badly I can't wait and he finally sinks his penis into me. It's such a relief to finally be joined together. I like it least when he enters too soon and comes too fast and says, 'I'm sorry' when I had my hopes up for more." *female age 38*

"I love feeling him on top of me, kissing and caressing, and I love the feeling of his penis inside me. The part I don't like is the mess." *female age 35*

Women readers offer their suggestions about having intercourse for the first time

"Make him read the *Guide To Getting It On* first!"
female age 30

"Use protection!!!" *female age 26*

"Be choosy. Take your time. Touch and explore everything, maybe tie him up and you take total control; it's amazing the feeling you get by doing that." *female age 36*

"Make sure you really want it and it's not about being pressured. Masturbate together first. Be comfortable together. My first time was painful and humiliating; there's got to be a better way." *female age 38*

"It was very hard to do, but I waited until I was 18 to have intercourse. It was with a guy who I know cared deeply about me, which made my first experience very fun and comfortable." *female age 36*

"Relax and don't expect it to be like the romance novels."
female age 32

"Make him go slowly and be sure that you are aroused sufficiently before you let him enter you because it will probably be a little uncomfortable the first time. If he rushes, it will hurt and you won't enjoy it at all." *female age 35*

Dear Paul,

Currently I'm not having inter-course with anyone, but in the past I've always wondered what is the "proper way." Am I supposed to pull away as he pulls his penis out and move toward him as he thrusts in?

What do guys really like or does it depend on the guy?

Minnie at the University of Minneapolis

Dear Minnie,

There are a couple of ways to go about it. You can pull back at the same time he does, but if you pull out too far, his penis will keep flopping out of your vagina. You can also move with him, rotate your hips or stay still while he does the moving. Intercourse will feel pretty good for most guys no matter what you do, as long as you are both enjoying yourselves.

There are subtle changes you can make that will help his penis touch different spots in your vagina. For instance, putting a pillow under your rear end will change the angle of your pelvis. This might allow the head of his penis to massage a special place inside of your vagina that provides more sensation for you.

Also, different positions offer different levels of intimacy. You might be in a mood to have Joe Bob's entire body pushing down on yours like what happens in the missionary position. The pressure can feel intimate and reassuring. Or you might feel like being on top, or have him enter from behind where you have less skin contact but his big old testicles bang against your clit. Your mood and emotional needs at the moment can be a large factor in determining how much skin contact you want to make and which one of you is on top.

Most guys will be very turned on by your desire to explore variations like this. They will also be grateful to know what feels best for you. It's a partner's ability to give you pleasure during intercourse that often gives him the most pleasure.

One thing to avoid is to lie there like a corpse. All you need to do is let him know with a few words and sounds that you are very much into what he is doing. Or if you can't let yourself do that, try digging your fingernails into his back once or twice. This usually doesn't hurt him, and it has the extra benefit of increasing his standing with his roommates or the other guys in the dorm when he's on the way to the shower.

Letting him know it when he is pleasing you will make him feel good. It's no different from how you feel when the tables are turned and he lets you know how much you are pleasing him.

Trying to improve your position? Try Kenneth Ray Stubbs's *Secret Sexual Positions—Ancient Techniques for Modern Lovers* (Tuscon, Arizona: Secret Garden, 1998) ISBN: 0-939263-15-7. Nearly all books on intercourse positions are basically a poor excuse for jerk-off material. Finally, there's a book on intercourse positions that is worth recommending. It isn't a book that's going to instantly make you hard or wet, but it is a fun book that couples can comfortably share. Each position that is shown includes comments from readers. It is the kind of book where you can put Post-It notes on certain pages for your partner to see. "I'd like us to try that one." Some of the positions are ridiculous, but others are really quite helpful, and the reader comments for each position are honest and helpful.

Warning: This can hurt you!

Certain kinds of intercourse injuries can cause your penis to forever bend in a strange way. Most of the injuries occur when the woman is on top. Urologists strongly suggest that when using this position, the woman is well-lubricated and she restricts her up-and-down motion. This helps decrease those instances where she sits down on your penis, but at a funny angle, or when it comes out on the upstroke and gets crunched on the downstroke instead of sliding in easily the way it's supposed to. A good way to compensate for the decreased thrusting is to put a pillow under the man's rear end. This can help make his pelvic bone more accessible, and his partner might delight more in pushing down against it (grinding) than in moving up and down. That way she's got the penis deep inside and gets her clitoral area worked too. She might also try squeezing, as if she's peeing and trying to stop the flow.

Up Your Bum — Anal Sex
Chapter 21

The following recollections are those of a seventy-one-year-old woman: "I grew up in the country.... We had neighbors, Amos Wheatley and his wife. One night while washing dishes, Mrs. Wheatley told my mother that she let Amos 'use the other hole.' Then they had a baby girl, and I heard my father comment that Amos must have got it right at least once. Sometime later, Amos, who was uneasy about the expense of having a new baby, told my father he'd rather have had a team of horses. My father said, 'Isn't that expecting rather a lot of Mrs. Wheatley?'"

As told to Julia Hutton in her wonderful book,
Good Sex: Real Stories from Real People (San Francisco: Cleis Press, 1992)

Anal Sex — Statistical Lowdown

Some couples would rather drink goat sweat than try anal sex; others enjoy an occasional rectal soiree. The reasons for doing it, as explained later, have more to do with stimulating various nerve pathways than just with the perverse thrill of it all. This is why a number of heterosexual women and men, as well as some gay guys, like having their rear ends plowed.

Anal sex—*Penis into Rectus*—is often associated with homosexuality. However, according to various statistics, 30 percent to 40 percent of all heterosexual couples in this country have tried anal intercourse, with up to half of these continuing to do it on an occasional basis. While two to five million straight American couples are said to practice anal intercourse with regularity, only about 50 percent of gay males are into backdoor sex. Of course, straight or gay, these statistics refer only to anal intercourse. The following reader comments indicate there are other ways to tickle your hemorrhoids than with just a penis:

"My boyfriend likes me to rub a finger on his anus while I give him oral sex. Gentle pressure and a rotating finger add a lot to his pleasure." *female age 23*

"I hate admitting this, but I like it when Dave wets one of his fingers and slides it into my anus. It is a huge turn-on, and there are times when it makes me orgasm. The only problem is pulling out. It always hurts coming out and usually throws off my bowel movements for the next few hours. It feels like I have to go...." *female age 26* [Editor's note: You didn't think we'd leave out the last part, did you?]

Whether you are straight, gay, or somewhere in between, the chances are good that at some point in your life you might try anal sex. That is why the topic is covered in this book, although it may catch severe grief from the self-righteous and anally oppressed. Please be aware that this guide couldn't care less whether you do or don't practice anal sex, but it does have a few suggestions in case curiosity nips you in the rear.

Why Do People Do It?

Why do people have anal sex? Some women offer anal sex as a way of keeping their virginity. Some men offer anal sex as a way of getting work in the entertainment industry. Some couples like anal sex because it's forbidden. But the most obvious reason why people do anal sex is because they enjoy the way it feels.

"Anal sex helps me feel a whole different part of my vagina and vulva. The fact that it is so tight and kind of nasty is a turn-on to me too." *female age 23*

"My wife asks for anal intercourse on occasion, usually late at night when she is very aroused and her inhibitions are down." *male age 41*

"I can come from anal intercourse, but not from vaginal intercourse." *female age 32*

"When Hillary is all worked up, she sometimes really likes me to massage her anus. When I slip a lubricated finger inside her, it is often the thing that puts her over the edge. If I have a finger inside her vagina and one in her anus, she reacts very well to the sandwiching of the wall when I press the two together. Other times, she really hates it when I touch her there. I can never quite guess when it's going to be a green light." *male age 25*

"Both of us like it. I will sometimes put a finger in her anus while we are having intercourse. It's very exciting for her, and I can feel my penis through the wall, which I find to be very erotic." *male age 39*

A lot of people have the notion that the only reason women do anal sex is to please a male partner. Not a single woman in our survey who does anal sex mentioned anything about pleasing a partner. Each one said she did it because she liked the way it feels. Aside from the obvious reason, which is that the anus is filled with lots of nerve receptors, it seems that the wall between the vagina and rectum may swell when the woman is sexually aroused. This wall might tug on the same nerve that transmits G-spot orgasms to the brain. As a result, some women experience extra-pleasant sensations on the wall between the rectum and vagina during anal intercourse that they don't get otherwise. Some women report getting an extra-intense orgasm when they stimulate their clitoris at the same time that they are having anal sex. This makes sense, since the extra anal stimulation might intensify the orgasm signal that is going to the brain, as well as providing extra stimulation to the pelvic nerve.

As for men's pleasure, some enjoy having their anus massaged or penetrated, and some report having their finest orgasms when their prostate gland is being pressed. This could be, in large part, because the nerve pathway from the penis to the brain runs through the rectum. One large nerve bundle is located beneath the prostate. Another reason why an anal-assisted orgasm might feel "deeper" is because the nerve that transmits sensations from the bladder to the brain may also be getting extra stimulation.

A final reason that some couples do anal sex is for birth control. Anal sex is practiced as birth control in some South American countries that take seriously the Catholic Church's opposition to contraception. Perhaps this isn't what the Vatican had in mind. Or maybe anal sex is simply a hot concept down in the Southern Hemisphere. Is anal sex an effective means of preventing pregnancy, or can ejaculate run out of the anus and into the vagina? Pregnancies from anal sex are common enough that the term "splash conception" is used to describe them. Perhaps this is how people with anal-compulsive personalities are conceived.

Big Mama Nature & the Human Backside

When Big Mama Nature designed the female body she gave it a vagina that's rough, tough and durable. She made the walls of the vagina so they would stretch, swell, lubricate and straighten out at times of sexual excitement. This allows objects of desire to slide in and out with a fair amount of ease and enjoyment.

Mother Nature was working from a different set of blueprints when she built the human rectum. That's because the rectum's main purpose is for elimination rather than romance. As a result, the walls of the rectum don't stretch and lubricate like those of the vagina, although they comfortably fit objects that are even larger than a penis on a nearly daily basis. Think about it. Reports that anal sex will damage your rectum are not backed up by medical fact as long as you use lots of lubrication and leave your crowbar in the toolshed.

Another difference between the rectum and the vagina is that nature included a pair of pugnacious sphincter muscles to guard the gates of your anus. These muscular rings were designed to facilitate outgoing rather than incoming objects, although they can be taught to yield in either direction. The anal sphincters are two of the most important muscles in the human body as long as you plan on living and working in the vicinity of other human beings.

A Brief Historical Summary of the Structure & Function of the Human Rectum from the Time of Cro-Magnon Man until the Founding of Ancient Greece

If you consider the history of the human rectum, say from the time of Cro-Magnon man until the founding of Ancient Greece, its sole purpose was to hold things in. It wasn't until the Ancient Greeks invented sodomy that our bums became multi-purpose. (In giving credit where credit is due, the Old Testament may have had an interest in the subject of anal sex that possibly predated the Ancient Greeks. At the very least, one of the early Biblical plagues visited upon the Egyptians apparently included hemorrhoids.)

Down & Dirty at the Acropolis

Thanks to the inventiveness of the Ancient Greeks, we now have things in our lives like politicians, lawyers, doctors and anal sex. The only one of these that should never cause you any pain is anal sex. If it does, you are doing it wrong, says psychologist Jack Morin, who has written an entire book on the subject called *Anal Pleasure and Health* (San Francisco: Down There Press, 1998). It is doubtful that you will find this title at your local B. Dalton.

The key to pleasurable anal sex is training the anal sphincter muscles to open for incoming objects. One set of these muscles is under conscious control. It's what people use to maintain their dignity when waiting to use the bathroom. The second set of

310 Up Your Bum — Anal Sex

sphincter muscles is a total free agent that automatically closes whenever something pushes against it. In order to have comfortable anal sex, the second set of sphincters must be taught how to relax when you ask.

Rectal Aerobics — A One and a Two and a...

"I like it when a guy stimulates my anus with his fingers or a dildo before entering it with his penis. It's much easier to take him that way. It's a very intense feeling, and can be very pleasurable, but it has to be slow and gentle; otherwise it's too painful." *female age 26*

This section has been written as if the male is doing the inserting and the female is receiving. Far be it from this guide to say how it is in your own relationship. Make sure that your fingernails are trimmed and your hands are washed. Wearing a latex glove and/or condom is recommended. Also, some people prefer to give themselves a quick enema ("short shot") with a bulb syringe or a prepared store-bought solution before having anal sex. Others might equate this with removing the patina from the Statue of Liberty.

Psychologist Morin suggests the following technique for teaching your rectum to relax: Each night for a week or so the male partner lubes up a clean finger and gently inserts it in the female's rear, pushing very softly and slowly.

Rectal expert Erik Mainard—known as the Avatar of Ass— encourages a gentle massage of the anus and suggests angling the finger slightly upward toward the tailbone, since that's how the rectum curves. He says to push in quite slowly and only as the resistance eases. This kind of digital exploration should feel very good for the receiver; otherwise the person who is inserting the finger is either rushing it or being a brute.

One way to help relax the anal area is for the receiver to push down as though she were trying to move her bowels. In addition to relaxing the sphincters, this adds a bit of suspense to the exercise. However, anal purists say that with the help of a patient, caring partner, one needn't trick the sphincters into relaxing.

The receiver should feel comfortable with finger penetration before attempting any further unnatural acts. It is also suggested that the receiver try inserting her own finger, for instance, when she is in the shower, so she can get a better sense of how her second sphincter works (aka digital-rectal bonding). It is not until the second sphincter learns to relax that anal sex will feel comfortable, and if it doesn't feel comfortable, you shouldn't be doing it. If there is any discomfort other than a feeling of fullness which shouldn't be painful, spend an extra week doing the finger exercises or give up the concept of anal intercourse entirely.

Butt...

"I like to have my anus stimulated when I'm receiving oral sex. I like to have one finger inserted, but it doesn't have to be very far—just past the sphincter muscle will do. And rather than sliding all the way in and out, it is better if there is just a slight tugging movement. It adds one more sensation to the myriad of sensations involved in oral sex."

female age 37

If you want anal stimulation, you need to ponder the profound question of exactly how you want it. Do you want it thin like a finger, or wider like a penis or dildo? Do you want it to move in and out, or do you want it to go inside and stay there? When it comes to purchasing sex toys, the former activity would call for a dildolike object; the latter would be best be served by a butt plug. When it comes to toys for anal sex, you have more choices than at a Marks & Spencer After-Christmas Sale. For more on sex toys, see the chapter "Oscillator, Generator, Vibrator, Dildo."

Rear-end connoisseur Erik Mainard claims that people tend to stick fingers or a penis into a partner's rectum ("rosebud") when they would be better off spending more time massaging and caressing the external butt and anal parts. Until watching Mr. Mainard's *Rosebud Massage* video, we'd always assumed that a man either left his sweetheart's rectum alone, which seemed like a fine idea, or tried to stick a finger or penis up it, assuming that's what she wanted. But Mr. Mainard teaches several different ways of massaging a partner's anus which seem pretty interesting if the two of you are into backdoor stimulation. For information on Mr. Mainard's videotapes, contact EroSpirit, which is listed at the rear end of this chapter.

Romancing the Rear

Any kind of anal play, be it using a butt plug or a real-life penis plug, goes best with relaxation. Make sure the receiver receives a long, lingering massage, a candlelight bath or whatever it is that you do to get really relaxed. That's because one of the places in our body where we tend to carry a lot of tension is between our butt cheeks. If you are going to do anal sex, you want that area to be as relaxed as possible before anything goes in. That could well be the difference between an experience that is pleasing and one that is painful.

Anal Sex Tips from Lucas, May He Rest in Peace

The rectum isn't encased with muscle except at the very end. This means that it can't hug a penis as a vagina might. Aside from possible pain and aesthetics, this is may be one reason why some couples only try anal intercourse once.

One suggestion for having a good time rectally is to have the receiver occasionally contract her upper thigh muscles. This helps to massage the penis, and the woman might enjoy the added sensations too. This may make it unnecessary for the man to thrust in and out. Also, it is recommended that the receiver be the one who backs into (or lowers herself onto) the penis or penis substitute, at the start anyway. And always apply massive amounts of lubrication.

Playin' the Back Nine? Bag It

Straight or gay, single or married, monogamous or slut from cyber-hell, you are always wise to use a condom when having anal sex. There are really good reasons for this that extend way beyond concern about AIDS.

Fluids deposited in the rectum are absorbed more easily into the body than fluids deposited in the vagina. In other words, deposit a wad of male ejaculate up a partner's rear, and chances are her hungry colon is going to slurp it up. Heaven only knows how her immune system is going to respond, but there is some speculation that it's not a healthy process. Again, this has nothing to do with AIDS. If you bag the penis before it goes up her bum, you've eliminated a legitimate source of concern.

Also, some males get urinary tract infections from having anal sex without wearing a condom. In addition, no matter how hard you wash your penis after a rectal rendezvous, little pieces of poop still remain inside the urinary opening. This is not good for either of you, and at the very least can give her an infection if you follow with vaginal intercourse. When it comes to condom use up your bum, here are some possibilities:

Avanti or Trojan Supra: These polyurethane condoms should be a butt pirate's dream; however, they have not been approved for anal-sex usage by the FDA. These are made thinner than traditional latex condoms and can be used with oil-based lubricants. On the other hand, they may have a higher rate of breakage than the old latex war horses.

Latex condoms with silicone water-based lube: Silicone lube is the water-based lube of choice for anal sex. It won't harm latex condoms and you get a lot more slide for your buck than with KY or other water-based lubes. It also won't dry out as fast as most water-based lubes.

Femidon: This is the new female condom that was designed to be used in a woman's vagina, but what the heck. Some women like it for anal intercourse. It can also be used for rimming. Unfortunately, sticking the bottom ring of the Femidon condom up your bum may be a challenge. Also, the FDA has not approved Femidon for the rear.

Do not used ribbed or studded condoms for anal sex. It's always a good idea to put a new condom on any sex toys that go into the rectum and to wash the toy afterward.

Beware the Butt-Fuck Video

If you like the thought of doing anal intercourse, the chances are good you like to watch anal-sex videos. In her book *The Ultimate Guide to Anal Sex for Women,* Tristan Taormino warns that anal intercourse requires lots of patience and a slow, relaxed approach. This is the part that the anal-sex videos leave out. Even when making X-rated movies, they don't just go plowing some porn starlet's rear end without lots of preparation and anal fore-play—none of which the viewer actually sees in the video. So while it's fine to enjoy the hot action shown in *Anal Invaders Number Six Million and Thirty-Two,* don't for a moment try to replicate it in real life with a real partner, unless she's inflatable and has a vinyl rectum.

In Slow—Out Slow

No matter what you are putting inside a rectum, it needs to go in very slowly and come out very slowly.

Most people have no difficulty grasping the former, but they don't realize that anything being pulled out of a rectum, whether it's a finger, penis or butt plug, needs to be pulled out slowly. Otherwise, extreme discomfort and even physical damage can result.

Anal Intercourse Alternatives

One of the most sensitive parts of the human body is the skin that surrounds the outer rim of your anus. It's easy to stimulate this area with a thumb, finger, tongue or butt plug without sticking a penis all the way up it. For instance, some women who are receiving vaginal stimulation enjoy it when a partner puts pressure on their anus with a thumb or finger. Just be sure to avoid putting something that's been up an anus into a vagina.

All Things Considered: Zucchini Revenge

It's only fair that if a guy wants to stick his penis up a part-ner's rectum, she should be able to stick something of comparable size up his. If vegetables are used, don't forget to check with your grocer or family doctor as to which are safest and most suitable.

You don't want a vegetable breaking off and taking up permanent residence inside your man's rectum, do you? Couples who are less organically inclined might use a silicone penis substitute known as a dildo or butt plug.

Butt Plugs Galore

Butt plugs are dildolike objects made specifically for the rear end. They have flared bases to keep them from getting lost on the Hershey highway (Hershey is a well-known brand of chocolate in the Colonies). Butt plugs come in many different sizes, and some even vibrate. People use butt plugs to give their rear ends a feeling of fullness. They are much better suited for this purpose than a dildo, which is made for thrusting.

Dildo Deluxe

Okay, so you thought you finally had this sex-toy thing under control when suddenly your old man informs you he wants you to fuck him up the rear. What's a girl to do? Pull out her real-life soft rubber version of porn star Jeff Stryker's monster dong? Or does she use her silicone Rocketeer, or what about her Billy the Kid with the vibrating head?

When it comes to violating a loved-one's rear end, wisdom has it that a dildo which curves upward is the way to go. That's because our rectums tend to curve. The nice thing about using a dildo instead of a real-life penis is that you can turn the dildo upward or downward to hit the right spot. Check out places like Good Vibrations or Blowfish to find which dildos are best for anal penetration. They'll also be able to tell you which dildo will fit into your new Malibu two-strap harness. (Your Jeff Stryker dildo won't—it's too big!)

If you plan to use a dildo for both vaginal and anal recreation, it is a very good idea to get a separate one for each port of entry. Having dedicated dildos helps decrease the chance that fecal matter will get into the vagina.

"Bend Over Boyfriend"

"My boyfriend of five years actually made the suggestion that I penetrate him anally. I lubricated the finger with the shortest nail on it and slowly slid it into his anus. He enjoyed it so much that he asked for two fingers and then three. While doing this, I also alternated sucking and manually pumping his cock with my other hand. He had a mind-blowing orgasm. He tells me it's the kind you feel deep down to your toes.... I'm now looking for a strap-on that stimulates me as well as him!" *female age 40* [Editor's note: May we suggest the new and totally cool Nexus double dildo from Vixen Creations. It's the only double dildo designed to fully stimulate the wearer as well as the receiver.]

Some people feel that only gay guys like things up their rears. Yet straight men have rectums that are every bit as sensitive as those of gay men. While plenty of straight guys would just as soon be boiled in oil as have a dildo or butt plug put up their rear, other manly guys enjoy the feeling tremendously. In fact, there's a popular new series of straight adult videos titled *Bend Over Boyfriend*.

As for penetrating their men anally, some women hold a dildo with their fingers; others put it in a dildo harness and propel it with their hips. A dildo harness looks somewhat like a jockstrap and holds the dildo in the same position as a man's erect penis. This allows the woman to thrust in and out, more or less. Learning how to use a dildo in a harness is an acquired art that takes time and patience. Also, keep in mind that a man's anal sphincters need just as much rectal foreplay as a woman's.

Consider trying a harness that straps to your thigh. It might be easier to control than the model that goes over your crotch.

Toy Precautions

Contrary to what you might think, rectums are hungry little orifices. Make sure that anything going up them is firmly anchored on the outside of the body so it can't get sucked up inside. Dildos or butt plugs with flared bases are best for anal play, as it is unlikely you will need the assistance of an emergency room crew to get them out.

🐑 Be sure that anything inserted into the rectum is smooth with no points or ridges.

🐑 Anal beads consist of five large beads on a string. They resemble worry beads, but each bead is held in place on the string so it doesn't slide. While anal beads can certainly be used to count your worries on, people usually stick them up their butt. They are slowly pulled out, often at the point of coming, which is said to make for a kick-ass orgasm. Anal beads can be as small as mothballs or as big as tennis balls (okay, golf balls). If the beads are plastic and have sharp blow-mold edges, be sure to file them down first. Also, it is wise to encase them in a condom before inserting. That's because they are very difficult to fully clean.

Prostate Stimulation

A number of straight men experience pleasant sensations from rectal stimulation, especially in the area of the prostate. Yet the only time most straight men get anal stimulation is during a physical exam. Then and at tax time.

If prostate stimulation is what you would like to try, consider the following, some of which was suggested by Kenneth Stubbs in his excellent book *Romantic Interludes* but translated into this guide's own homespun style:

For hygiene and comfort, wear a well-lubed latex exam glove. With your cowboy naked and on his back, sit to one side or between his legs. Spend some quality time massaging his penis. Then work your hand down to the perineum area, which is between his testicles and anus. Using the pads of your fingertips, press and rub in a circular way so that the skin moves over the tissue that's beneath the perineum. This is the equivalent of rectal foreplay. Eventually, slip a well-lubricated finger with a nonlethal fingernail over his anus. Massage it in a circular pattern, a bit like the Indians did when circling a wagon train. Gradually ease the finger inside, with the same gentleness and tenderness that you wish men would use when sticking fingers inside you. Once your finger is fully inserted, make a "come here" motion. This should put your fingertip in the immediate vicinity of the prostate. The prostate of a young man feels like a walnut-shaped minimound of gristle, but in older guys it can grow to the size of a baseball. Let your finger gently explore and massage the prostate gland and the area around it. With patience and feedback you should be able to generate some very pleasant sensations. You can also give your man a blow job or masturbate him with your other hand while stimulating his prostate. This can result in a very intense orgasm which gay men refer to as "a gusher." If you are really adventurous and have nothing better to do, you might try intercourse at the same time that you are tickling his prostate, mounting him while facing his knees so you can reach between his legs without dislocating your finger. Be sure to stop if there is any pain or discomfort, and don't even think about doing any of this if your lover has a pair of big old hangin' hemorrhoids. If you have any questions at all, be sure to ask your family doctor or nurse practitioner, and don't forget to tell them that Goofy Foot Press sent you.

Men who are curious about feeling their own prostate can do so by reaching between their legs and sticking a well-lubricated finger up their own wazoo. It can be both weird and neat to feel a part of your body that you've never touched before. Pressing on the prostate will probably cause a dull, subtle sensation in the penis. Some men find that the physical contortions necessary to reach their own prostate can result in unanticipated trips to the chiropractor. To avoid this, you can purchase specially curved sextoys that help a guy to stimulate his prostate comfortably.

Rimming

Rimming is a slang word for kissing ass, literally. It means sticking your tongue up or around your partner's deep-space nine. Keep in mind that it's probably not a good idea to rim just anyone, unless he or she is your boss or the chair of your dissertation committee. One reason to avoid indiscriminate rimming is that it can be an effective way of getting hepatitis and various parasites. It's the sort of thing to save for long-term relationships if you are so inclined, or cut a condom lengthwise and lay it over the person's anus before licking. Good hygiene is also a plus.

One gastroenterologist has said that by the time a couple has been together for a couple of years, they pretty much share the same anal flora. This means you probably won't get anything more from licking your partner's asshole than you would from licking your own. On the other hand, if you are in anything that even resembles a casual relationship, use a barrier before licking ass. For the latest information on the medical advisability of rimming, call your local gay and lesbian health center or call one of the sex-information hotlines listed on our website.

Anal Fisting

Yes, Martha, there is such a thing. It can be very dangerous if done by the inexperienced. If you absolutely must have someone else's fist up your ass, the best book on the subject is said to be Bert Herrman's *Trust: The Hand Book—A Guide to the Sensual and Spiritual Art of Handballing* (San Francisco: Alamo Square Press, 1991). Be sure to check with a physician first, perhaps one from your local gay and lesbian health center. Even if you're not gay they are more likely to know about the practice than a regular family practitioner.

Rules of the Rear—A Pocket Guide

Here's a list of precautions for anal sex:

🐑 Straight or gay, married or in transition—if you are doing anal intercourse, use a condom.

🐑 Make sure that anything about to go up your rectum is both clean and well-lubricated. Reapply the lubrication often.

🐑 The human rectum curves in a funny way and your partner won't know which angle feels best unless you specify. This means that you'll need to discuss which positions and angles feel best. Positions are similar to those used with vaginal intercourse.

🐑 Remove anything you have placed in the rectum very slowly. This includes a penis.

🐑 Don't stick a finger, penis or other object directly into a vagina when it's just been up an anus. Wash it first with soap and water. Make sure that your nails are well-trimmed.

🐑 People who have anal intercourse should occasionally get a rectal swab done to check for VD, yet few individuals want to own up to doing anal sex, so they don't tell their doctors. It might be easier if doctors simply asked, "Have you ever tried anal sex?" but it seems unlikely that the answers given would become a barometer of truth.

🐑 Never, ever have anal sex unless your rectum is in 100 percent good health. Do not do anal sex if it is painful. Unless you are sure of what you are doing, check with a physician or qualified sex expert first.

The author of this book went to a university with a top reputation in the sciences. Many of his classmates became medical doctors. A number of these did not seem equipped to deal with questions about sex, anal or otherwise. If you have medical questions about any kind of sex, it is possible that you won't be comfortable asking your private physician. An alternative is to call your local free clinic or national sex hot line. And while you may not be homosexual, a good place to call with questions about anal sex might be the nearest gay and lesbian health center.

Additional Anal Tips

Instead of simply sticking a finger into a partner's rectum, rest the pad of your finger over their puckered opening. Massage gently. Eventually, slide the tip of your finger in, assuming it is well lubed. 🐑 Make sure the receiver is aroused in other parts of his or her body before knocking on the backdoor. One of the keys to enjoyable anal sex is having your entire body relaxed and receptive to sex. 🐑 Do not hold your breath. Breathing deeply will help you to stay relaxed. 🐑 Once your get your finger, penis, dildo or whatever inside your partner's rear end, don't start thrusting with it. Leave it in place and gently start making circular motions. If and when your partner wants you to start thrusting, pull out slowly and as far as possible, and add more lube. Then you can start thrusting slowly. A woman might like her clit being massaged at the same time she is having anal sex, as it may extend the feeling throughout her pelvis. Or maybe not. Ask and see. Using a latex glove helps fingers slide in more smoothly, using a condom helps a penis slide in more smoothly. You might try inserting an anatomically shaped butt plug and then applying a strong vibrator to the base of it. Don't have anal sex when you are drugged or drunk. Your rear end is more easily damaged by sloppy sex than other body parts. Anal sex requires that the driver as well as the passenger be alert and sober. If you are into enemas as part of anal sex, use plain tap water and make sure it's not too cold, unless you enjoy giving yourself cramps.

Recommended Resources

If you are into anal recreation, consider the following:

Jack Morin's *Anal Pleasure and Health* (San Francisco: Down There Press, 1999). To order visit the Good Vibrations website: www.goodvibes.com.

Tristan Taormino's *Ultimate Guide to Anal Sex For Women* (San Francisco: Cleis Press, 1998). In spite of its title, this book is just as informative for men as for women. To order, see their website: www.cleispress.com.

For a videotape on self anal stimulation, there's EroSpirit's *Uranus*. You can also order Erik Mainard's videos, which were made for a gay male audience, from Erospirit. However, if you don't mind seeing a bunch of male buttholes, the massage information works just as well on women. Their internet site is: www.erospirit.org.

Chapter Notes: If anal sex puts people at higher risk for AIDS, why do a chapter on it? Driving a car puts most straight couples at far greater risk for death than having anal sex. This guide would be more reckless asking most of you to start your car than writing on anal sex. Thanks to the late Dr. Bruce Voeller, Mariposa Foundation, for help.

Playing With Yourself
Chapter 22

Before the 1960s, people who wrote books on sex stated with an almost religious fervor that playing with yourself (masturbation) was a very bad thing to do. Today, people who write books on sex speak with the same kind of religious fervor, only now they are saying that playing with yourself is a very good thing to do.

It doesn't seem as though anything has changed. That's because none of the so-called experts are asking you what you want to do. When it comes to the question of whether you should or shouldn't be masturbating, this book doesn't have any answers. It's your hand and your pants; if you want to stick one into the other, that's totally up to you.

What we can tell you is that teenagers sometimes feel that masturbation is an adolescent thing, something they will grow out of when they become adults. Not true. There are times when you may do it a lot, and times when you'll hardly do it at all; times when it feels great, and times when it's a letdown. Whatever the reason for doing it, masturbation can usually be counted on to help take off some of the edge. It's also a wonderful nighttime aid that helps ease the transition between wakefulness and sleep, and contrary to what you might think, it can play an important role in relationships even when the sex between partners is totally satisfying.

"If I have a test to study for and am getting burned out, sometimes I'll masturbate just to take a break from it. After I'm done, I'll be relaxed and ready to work again. I'll masturbate as a way to get to sleep. I'll masturbate when I'm having a bad day or am bored. And of course, I'll masturbate when I'm feeling sexually aroused." *male age 20*

Playing with This Chapter

Playing with yourself can be a way to explore and pamper your body, as well as to explore the sexual feelings that you might be having about someone else.

Some people find that their bodies simply work better if they have an orgasm every day or two, with masturbation being a natural way to help this happen. Do you ever get into a certain state of mind where you need to masturbate just to relax enough so you can get the rest of your work done?

Whatever your motivation, if you are going to get yourself off by hand, why not try to get the most out of the experience? That is the focus of this chapter.

Vital Statistics

The following was told to Harry Maurer by a young woman for his book titled *Sex: An Oral History* (New York: Viking Press, 1994):

"My mother has a vibrator that my father gave her one year. When I used to come home from college, I knew where she kept the vibrator, and I knew they never used it, so I would put it into my room and use it for the vacation. One summer I came home and it wasn't there. I was going crazy, I'm really a vibrator addict. Finally I was just so horny I said, 'OK, Mom, sit down. Where's the vibrator?' She's like, 'What!' I said 'Look, here's the deal. I've been stealing your vibrator for three years, and I need it now.' She was blown away, but she goes into her room, comes back with the vibrator, and says, 'By the way, have you ever used the jet in the hot tub?'"

According to just about everyone who has ever researched the subject, somewhere between 80 percent and 95 percent of guys eventually masturbate. Depending on whose statistics you look at, between 50 percent and 80 percent of women do the same.

Contrary to what you might think, people don't masturbate any less as they get older. In fact, many people who are married or deeply involved in a sexual relationship still get themselves off by hand. Masturbation doesn't decrease a person's desire for shared sex. For some people, it increases it.

How often do people masturbate? It varies from a couple of times a day to sometimes never. As for the number of orgasms per effort, researcher Thore Langfeldt interviewed children in Norway from kindergarten through high school about sex. Langfeldt found that the younger boys and girls could give themselves multiple orgasms when they masturbated. But as they got older, the boys started reporting fewer orgasms per attempt, while the girls reported more. This is a trend that continued with increased age and experience.

What the Sandman Knows about Masturbation

"In my younger years, it usually took an hour or so before I had an orgasm. Now, if I'm especially hot, five minutes with a vibrator can do it, or about fifteen to twenty minutes by hand. Sometimes I like to keep things slow; I prolong it by starting and stopping. Other times, I just want to get off as fast as I can. Sometimes I masturbate, but not to orgasm. It feels good and relaxes me without wanting to come." *female age 47*

According to the Sandman, the most common time when people masturbate is at night before they go to sleep or before taking a nap. He says it makes his job much easier. People get themselves off at other times, too. For instance, it sometimes feels good to masturbate after a workout, since workouts can be sexually arousing. Plenty of people masturbate as a study break or when they have to spend long hours doing a paper or a project. It helps them refocus and return to the work at hand. Some people masturbate before a date so they will be more intellectually present. Women sometimes masturbate during their periods to help relieve cramping, or before intercourse to help it feel better. Some people wake up feeling really horny. They sometimes masturbate early in the morning, when the cock crows, before having their Wheaties®.

Note: It should have read Corn Flakes instead of Wheaties, since Kellogg's Corn Flakes were created to give children more stamina so they wouldn't want to do horrible things like masturbate. John Harvey Kellogg, M.D., founder of the flake, thought masturbation to be so evil that he encouraged parents to lift their sleeping children's nightshirts to make sure that no little fingers strayed into private places. To keep Dr. Kellogg spinning in his grave, this book encourages its readers to occasionally masturbate while eating a bowl of Kellogg's Corn Flakes.

How Guys Learn

"When I was ten, an older friend showed me how to masturbate. He had a full ejaculation; nothing came out of my penis except for a few drops of clear fluid. This was back in the 1960s, when astronauts first orbited the earth, and I believed that technology could fix anything. So I pulled out my erector set and decided to create a jack-off machine. Planning and building it kept me busy for days. Unfortunately, it didn't make anything more come out of my penis than my hand did. Time, rather than technology, was the answer to that problem...." *male age 45*

A lot of guys learn to masturbate from other guys, often a big brother or friends. One shows the other how he does it, or the experienced whacker might put his hand on the novice guy's penis and jerk it off for him. Guys who don't learn about jerking off from other guys eventually learn on their own. That's because a teenager has to be pretty numb to himself to miss the obvious connection between soaping the thing up in the shower and the nice feelings that result. Also, when lying face down on a mattress with a hard-on, most guys are eventually compelled to hump. Males eventually learn to masturbate because the penis, of all human organs, is the only one that pleads to be yanked, stroked, lubed and squeezed.

Of course, if they haven't been taught about ejaculation, some guys will experience anything from concern to terror the first time they ejaculate, e.g., "Oh no, I broke something," to "Please

God, I'll never ever do it again! I promise, just make it okay." For more on this, see the end of the chapter "Sunsets, Orgasms & Hand Grenades."

The Group Thing

"I can understand all sorts of things about guys' sexuality, except why they jerk off together. It seems so gay. Why do they do it?" *female age 23*

Good question. Maybe it has to do with the maturation process. Most young guys need little encouragement to take their pants off and explore. Getting naked can be so exciting for some boys that they get hard-ons from that alone. It's also natural for boys to share experiences, whether it's checking out an abandoned house or cave or showing each other the things you do with your dick. After all, you'd want to show your best friend the model you just built or take turns doing the latest skateboard trick, so why wouldn't you want to jerk off together and see what happens when you get hard or come?

"When we became teens, some of us boys would get together for a masturbation meeting in the treehouse, but it was more the thrill of something exciting and forbidden than anything else." *male age 26*

Of course, plenty of guys will shake their heads and say, "No way. You'd never catch me jerking off with another guy when I was a kid." Perhaps they represent the majority. Other guys will say, "Sure, that's how I learned" or "That's how we did it." And some might even say, "It was neat back then, simpler and a lot of fun."

As far as masturbatory etiquette goes, some males have guylike tea parties called circle jerks where everybody stands around and masturbates. There might be games connected with this, like who shoots the farthest or who comes the fastest (it's interesting how priorities change as you get older!). It's even been said that some young men feel terribly excluded until they have been allowed to beat off with members of the local gang. The urge to beat off together seems to peak before high school age and drops off significantly after that. However, there seem to be plenty of adult males who, while identifying as heterosexual, enjoy beating off together.

The following answers to a survey in the newsletter "Sex & Health" help summarize some of what's involved:

"While partying with fraternity brothers, someone suggested a contest to see who could ejaculate the farthest. Each of the five of us took our turn in a tiled shower room. Surprisingly, the least endowed among us won!"

"Sometimes when I'm camping with a couple of my buddies and our girlfriends are otherwise occupied, we get to joking about sex. We soon get so aroused that when one of us whips it out to pee, we start joking and the others whip theirs out, too. Then we just start stroking ourselves and talking about our favorite techniques. We don't touch each other, but we do comment on each other's members and may cheer one another on to climax. We're all good friends and have become much closer sharing our sexuality this way."

Before its publisher drove it into the ground, "Sex & Health" had a large straight male readership. Here's a summary from a survey they did two years ago:

"Ninety-five percent of the men who responded to our survey characterized themselves as strictly heterosexual; most were married and many had children. Eighty-four percent reported fantasizing about masturbating with or in the presence of other men, e.g., 'Although I'm happily married with two children, I do sometimes fantasize about masturbating with friends. I've thought about asking one friend in particular, but I haven't had the nerve.'"

Before you start saying, "That guy's a closet case," consider that the key part of straight-male porn flicks is the "money shot," where the guy pulls his monster schlong out of whatever female orifice it's been parked in and then strokes himself to ejaculation—with a full camera close-up. Perhaps it's acceptable to be curious about another guy's ejaculation if he's just had his penis in a woman's body, but not acceptable if it's just two guys together.

How Girls Learn

> "When I was young, climbing a flagpole always brought on such intense tingling feelings that I was only able to hold on tight and my legs would clamp around the pole. When the feelings subsided enough, I would resume climbing."
>
> *female age 37*

> "It was my freshman year of high school. I was kissing this guy and was getting really turned on. He put his hand on my inner thigh and I was going crazy! This was my first heavy petting session. I didn't quite know what to make of it. When I got home, I went to the bathroom. My underwear was very wet. I went to touch myself and BAM!— instant orgasm! My very first. I've never had it that easy since." *female age 27*

> "When I had my first orgasm I kept saying, 'Oh my God!' over and over. I was really shocked because I didn't know I could do that to myself!" *female age 25*

Girls don't do the "show and tell" game nearly as often as boys. They tend to learn about masturbation on their own or by reading about it. Sometimes women learn how to masturbate from the sensation they experience while cleaning or wiping their genitals, from climbing trees, poles or ropes, while on swings or when riding bicycles. Sometimes they learn by putting a pillow between their legs or by leaning up against something such as the washing machine when it's on the spin cycle. It might also happen when they have a sex dream and wake up before it's over—the sensation is still alive in their genitals and all they need to do is reach down and rub. One woman reported learning to masturbate by pushing a sanitary napkin against her vulva; another by stroking the shaft of her clitoris with a pencil. The possibilities for discovering how to masturbate are way too many to name here.

Tools of the Trade—Girl Variations

"I did it in front of a mirror with a condom-wrapped candlestick, and another time with the end of a comb."

female age 21

"Bathtub, vibrator, boyfriend's fingers (my own don't work). Electric toothbrush handle, my ex-husband's hammer (the handle), even celery once." *female age 26*

"I get the most intense orgasm by leaning on a hard surface like a counter and wiggling around till I come. I also use a dildo, and I use my fingers to massage my labia and clit, occasionally fingering my vagina." *female age 37*

"I use a finger, then fingers." *female age 49*

"Occasionally I use my hands, but usually I use a running faucet before I take my bath." *female age 19*

"I rub my clit in a circular motion with my fingers or use a trusty old Prelude 3 [vibrator]. I've tried putting things inside my vagina, but so far that's been a very neutral experience — I need my lover's hand or torso to be attached to what's going inside. Sometimes I gently rub my chest as I masturbate, or run a soft piece of cloth over my nipples."

female age 47

"I do it while reading a book or having a fantasy. Usually I stimulate my clit directly with one or more fingers. Only rarely do I put anything inside my vagina, although I do like the feel of a tampon. I also like anal stimulation. That will make an orgasm more intense and more diffused."

female age 36

It is virtually impossible to list all of the different ways that women masturbate. A lot of women use their fingers while lying on their backs or sitting in chairs. Some do it on their sides, or while lying face down so nobody can see what they're doing. Some women may even occasionally prefer to squat.

Men sometimes have the fantasy that a woman who is masturbating sticks her fingers inside her vagina. Some women do, but many don't. Instead, some women like to squeeze together the lips of their vulva or push against their vulva in ways that create pressure rather than penetration.

Plenty of women use lubrication when they masturbate, either their own (vaginal or saliva) or store-bought. Lots of women like to use vibrators for masturbating, and some use dildos.

Some women like to masturbate by using the faucet in the bathtub. After you get the water temperature just right, lie down in the tub and push your bum against the wall of the tub where the faucet comes out. It might help if you have an inflatable pillow to put under your rear to get the angle just right. Some women say it works better if they spread their labia open with their fingers so the water cascades onto their awaiting clitoris. **Water Safety:** When masturbating with a water jet in a whirlpool or Jacuzzi, sit back at a distance and aim the jet toward your genitals. The current might be stronger than you think, so approach slowly. Some women like to pull their labia apart; others don't. Do not get extremely close to the jet and don't aim it up your vagina or rectum.

A woman who has responsive nipples may make nipple stimulation an enjoyable part of her masturbation.

Thigh High

Some women are able to masturbate by squeezing their thighs together. The woman writer who contributes to the female part of www.JackinWorld suggests that some women can teach themselves to come by squeezing their thighs together. She suggests that you start by masturbating in the normal way, but press your thighs together when you start to have an orgasm. After a few weeks of doing this, masturbate yourself to the point where you almost have an orgasm, but pull your fingers (or whatever) away at the last minute and try to finesse yourself into orgasm by squeezing your thighs together. Once you are able to do this successfully, start with the thigh-squeezing action a little earlier each time. Some women might prefer doing this with tight jeans on so they get an assist from the seam in the crotch.

Additional Ways

One of us knew a woman who could have an orgasm by doing thirty-seven stomach crunches (mini sit-ups). What an incredible incentive for keeping your abs in shape!

Other women get off by humping pillows or water bottles, swinging on swings, tugging on underwear, rubbing up against things, using peeled cucumbers and riding a bike down bumpy roads. Some like to stimulate their anus, either by putting pressure on it or by sticking a finger or butt plug inside it. Some like to look in mirrors, some get turned on by wearing their boyfriend's or girl-friend's shirt or underwear. Heck—fill in your own blanks.

Say It Ain't So!

Tennis elbow is a form of tendonitis. One reader, a female phy-sician, suspects that some of her patients with tennis elbow actu-ally got their tendonitis from—gulp—the number one repetitive finger motion that many women do. So if you are having tendonitis or repetitive stress syndrome on the arm that you masturbate with, try using a vibrator for masturbating and see if the problem doesn't improve. Ditto for lovers who routinely masturbate their female partners. This physician adds that guys with unexplained tendonitis might try masturbating differently, too. If you do it dry, you might try using lube. The hand motion can be quite different.

Rubbing the Nub? Beating the Bush? Giving Girl-Masturbation a Name

There are numerous slang terms for male masturbation. This is not the case with female masturbation (Diddle? Jill off? These are not exactly universal terms). Since women don't usually masturbate together, they haven't needed to establish slang to convey what they are doing. In fact, it has only been during the last thirty years that our society has even acknowledged the existence of women's masturbation. Maybe it's time that women adopted a universal slang term for masturbation. Perhaps one of the women's magazines could have a contest, or maybe the First Lady could announce what she calls it.

Women Rock'n'Rollers Touch Themselves

While there are several rock'n'roll references to male masturbation, there seems to be only one song that mentions women's masturbation (on a major record label, anyway). This is a 1980s song by the Divinyls about a woman who touches herself when she thinks about her lover. Blessed with a great melody and steamy vocals, the touching-herself song became an instant megahit. According to the lyrics of this song, the woman is so into her man that she doesn't seem to have much of an identity without him. This amplifies an age-old double standard: guys can masturbate because it feels good, but women need to frame their sexuality with love for a man.

Goofy Music Note: In a *Rolling Stone* interview, Christina from the Divinyls says that the song doesn't refer to masturbation. Perhaps she hasn't seen her own video. A reader disagrees: "First, I think the song is speaking of how thoughts of her man make her horny. Second, I fail to see how the song implies that she doesn't have her own identity without him. Do you think you might have read too much into the lyrics?" Editor's note: We stand by our guns. Unfortunately, the song is owned by four different publishers, one of which wanted an obnoxious amount of money for print rights. So if you are interested, you will need to listen to the "Touch Myself" song on your own.

Women, Masturbation & Intercourse

Some women give themselves orgasms during intercourse by pushing against a partner's pubic bone or by reaching down with their fingers and playing with themselves while the penis is inside of them. Is this masturbation, intercourse or both? It doesn't matter, given how it happens often and is totally normal.

Also, it's not unusual for a woman to masturbate before intercourse to help her genitals be more into it, or after inter-course because she needs more stimulation or simply enjoys the feeling. It is unfortunate that women often hide this and that their partners might not want to know about it. It seems like a sign of a good relationship when a woman feels free to finish what we couldn't, or when we help her get started and she takes it from there.

It's also nice when a partner feels free to masturbate on his or her own. Far from being a sign of deficit, this might be an indication there is a great deal of love and understanding in the relationship.

As a cultural aside, some Eastern religions seem to encourage female masturbation. From their perspective, a woman's energy, like her orgasm, is considered to be infinite and life-affirming. The whole world is thought to be a better place when she mastur-bates.

Girls, Their Horses & the Fifty-Minute Hour

"My first orgasm? I was riding my horse and I felt a strange sort of pleasure between my legs. I felt like I wanted it to stop so I could concentrate on my riding, but it felt so good...." *female age 18*

"I was standing in the barn with my horse when I had a spontaneous orgasm. I gushed and everyone laughed at me for peeing in my pants. I was fourteen or so. I didn't discover masturbation until I was twenty, and then I thought orgasm was so incredible, I wanted one every day." *female 37*

Having grown up in a farm town, your author knew from a young age that it was unwise for any man to come between a woman and her horse. But can you imagine his amazement years later when an occasional female patient would describe the euphoria she gleaned from the back of her favorite gelding? It's information that's usually relayed in hushed tones of revelry and delight—warm, pleasing, primal sensations with one of nature's most magnificent creatures between her legs. Women rarely speak about their husbands or boyfriends with the kind of knowing sensitivity that is reserved for their favorite horse.

From Trigger to Hitachi...

After having an orgasm, women's genitals often stay primed longer than men's. Since their genitals stay pumped up, some women experience waves of orgasm that can be finessed for the better part of an hour. Other women find a single orgasm to be very satisfying.

Because of the different possibilities, one woman might masturbate on and off for an entire evening, reaching between her legs every page or two while reading a book. Another woman might masturbate with the sole purpose of reaching a single, discrete orgasm, going from beginning to end without pause.

Of course, there are plenty of women who don't like to masturbate. Some never feel the urge. For others, touching themselves implies an uncomfortable investment in their own sexuality. While it may be perfectly fine to enjoy sex with a man, masturbation might feel dirty. This might be true even if their body badly needs an orgasm to help it unwind. There are also women who like to masturbate but don't like to touch their genitals. They might use a vibrator or masturbate with their fingers on the outside of their underwear.

The Limitations of a One-Grip Rhythm (For Both Sexes)

If you always use the exact same touch and rhythm when you masturbate, you might be teaching your body to expect that and only that. Given how it's difficult for someone else to do you in precisely the same way that you do yourself, you might consider occasionally mixing it up. For instance, if you usually get yourself off dry, you might try it with lotion. If you use your right hand, experiment with your left. Women might try it with a vibrator one time and another time in the bathtub, but not with a vibrator in the bathtub unless your vibrator is waterproof.

On Sucking Air (For Both Sexes)

Learning to breathe right is an essential part of being an athlete, unless maybe your sport is billiards. It's no different with sex.

When you are in the process of having sex, be it solo or with a partner, you might occasionally pay attention to your breathing. The Tantric types encourage taking long, slow, deep breaths where you imagine pulling the air all the way into your groin. This helps some people to have a more intense experience. From this book's more geriatric perspective, the extra O_2 helps keep us from having a coronary.

Guy Tricks—"First, Nuke a Jar of Miracle Whip, Then..."

"I made a false pussy out of bicycle tire inner tubes, and it worked quite well. I have also used banana peels, watermelons, and a hole in a piece of wood." *male age 42*

A lot of guys use their hands to jerk off with. Some do it dry and some add lubrication which includes saliva, soap, hair conditioner, Vaseline, vegetable oil, coconut oil, baby oil and anything else under the sun that can make their pecker slick. Guys do better using an oil-based lubricant, and some even use a special type of facial cleanser called Albolene which is greatly admired for its jerk-off properties. The trouble with standard moisturizers is that they dry up quickly, as do water-based lubes when exposed to air. If you use a water-based lube, try adding a few drops of water

This young buck is taking his time.

or saliva as it dries instead of adding more lube. Otherwise, you might end up with two sticky messes instead of one.

A lot of guys masturbate in the shower using soap as a lubricant, but that's kind of iffy because the soap can get up your peehole and irritate the living daylights out of you. A fine substitute is hair conditioner, or you might start each stroke by grabbing your penis around the base and pulling outward only. As soon as one hand reaches the head, grab the bottom of your penis with the other to keep an uninterrupted rhythm going. The hand motion is the opposite of what you would be doing if you were pulling in a rope.

Another way that guys sometimes masturbate is by lubricating the inside of a condom with a water-based lube like KY. They slide the condom on an erect penis, wrap their fingers around it and pump away. A variation of this is to lube up the inside of a Baggie or plastic bag and put it between your pillows or mattress and box springs. You then get on your knees and hump the bag, being careful not to get your mattress pregnant.

Note: If you make an artificial vagina and heat it in a micro-wave, be cautious. It could feel nice and warm around the outside, but could sizzle your little pecker when you stick it in the center.

Rushin' Roulette (For Men)

Guys tend to rush themselves when they are masturbating. There are a couple of reasons for this. First, a man who is jerking off often wants to get to the heavy duty pleasure part as soon as possible. Second is the matter of privacy, or lack of it, when you are growing up. The last thing most guys want is for someone to walk in on them when they are stroking themselves, so they teach themselves to come quickly and quietly. Also, if they are doing it in the shower, the extra speed helps them finish before the hot water runs out.

In employing the basic theorem of jack-off relativity, $M = Q^2$ (masturbation = quick x quiet—Betty Dodson from her book *Sex For One*), the body becomes numb to anything but the rush of coming. This might desensitize a man to some of the more subtle sensations that can feel so wonderful when he is sharing sex with a partner.

Learning to Live in the Zone of Subtle Sensation

Taking extra time when masturbating might help a man learn about subtle sensations that he won't notice if he's red-lining it. For instance, if he slows down as ejaculation approaches, he might discover a rush of feelings in his stomach, bladder or rectum. Instead of going for the big squirt, he might try to back off a bit, teaching himself how to live in the zone of subtle sensa-tion. If allowed to emerge slowly, pre-squirt feelings can be quite intense and last for long periods of time without becoming an actual ejaculation. Learning to stay with these feelings might help a man experience deeper levels of intimacy when he is with a partner.

Also, instead of reaching for his crotch each time he mastur-bates, a man might start by touching or massaging other parts of his body: scalp, face, neck, shoulders, chest, hands, feet, etc.

This can be a way of reminding himself that sex is a full-body activity rather than something that just happens between his legs. (One female reader suggested that this section should have been written for women as well as men.) For new ways of stroking yourself that you might not have thought about before, check out the "Extreme Hand Job" part of the chapter "Different Strokes for Different Blokes."

Intercourse Spoiler

Guys tend to grip themselves tightly when masturbating. Yet few vaginas can even come close to generating that kind of squeezing action. This might be one reason why some guys have more intense orgasms when they masturbate than during intercourse. One way around this is by masturbating with a light grip, at least occasionally.

Socks or Tissue?

In case you were wondering, "Sex & Health" reports that younger men tend to use socks to jerk off into, while older men prefer tissue. Now that guys are wearing darker underwear that doesn't show cum stains, it is likely that more socks are being spared during bedtime masturbation by guys who sleep in the buff and use their shorts for cleanup.

Warnings

URETHRA SAFETY Some people, both men and women, are tempted to stick things up their urethra (pee hole) when they play with themselves. This can be a dangerous thing to do. It may end up requiring an embarrassing visit to a hospital emergency room and maybe even surgery if the object gets lost in your bladder. If you absolutely must do this, find a physician or nurse who can show you how to correctly use a catheter and get sterile ones from a medical supply house or one of the mail-order houses that include fetish and kink. Even then, you might end up getting infections.

BUTTHOLE SAFETY Some men and women enjoy sticking things up their butt holes when they play with themselves. Be sure it is well-washed and has no sharp edges. The advantage of using a finger is that it's not likely to get lost up where the sun don't shine. Always wash your hands ahead of time and make sure that your fingernails don't look like Elvira's. A good alternative is to use a butt plug.

REALLY TWISTED STUFF   Over the years, people have tried some seriously dangerous and life-threatening ways of jerking off. If you are into that sort of thing, there are two ways to go. Maybe you need to act out various scenes or kinds of kink that are best done in the company of people who know how to do it as safely as possible. The other way is to get yourself some therapy from a sex positive therapist or a positive sex therapist.

Readers' Comments

Have you ever needed to masturbate while away from home?

Guess which answers are men's and which are women's!

a. "I have done so occasionally in the car, while driving. Tricky, but doable." *age 37*

b. "I would pretty much masturbate anywhere if I could. I know it sounds silly, but when I am on the beach or catching a killer wave I get kind of horny." *age 23*

c. "Yes. Although never at my current job, I have masturbated at work." *age 26*

d. "Yes. I've masturbated driving in my car; the urge was just too great and I had to deal with it right then." *age 36*

e. "It has happened. I feel pressure like I'll go nuts if I don't get relief, and I'll sneak off." *age 38*

f. "Except for when I was on a long vacation, I've always been able to wait until I got home." *age 26*

g. "One time I was driving and I had a terrible urge, so I brought myself to orgasm. I've also done it at work once." *age 43*

h. "I was once on a long-distance bus trip and a teenage boy was next to me. I don't remember why, but I got very aroused, so I put my coat over me and masturbated while he slept." *age 45*

i. "While my partner lived in a different city, I used to all the time. I would lock myself in the bathroom and put my feet on the wall while sitting on the toilet, with my legs bent and above my head. It was most satisfying this way." *age 37*

j. "I was using the computer at my brother's house when no one was home. While on the net, I was talking to someone who was so hot that I had to masturbate to release enough tension so I could keep talking online." *age 27*

a. female b. female c. female d. female e. female f. male g. female h. female i. female j. female Darned stereotypes...

Oscillator, Generator, Vibrator, Dildo
Chapter 23

Some people claim that the light bulb is the most important electrical invention of the last 150 years; others say it's the vibrator. This chapter is about vibrators and dildos. Its emphasis is on the use of sex toys by couples as opposed to individuals, although many people use these toys for solo sex. Please keep in mind that there are lots of people who don't like to use sex toys. They should be spared the sometimes evangelical prodding of sex-toy enthusiasts.

Confusing Vibrators with Dildos

People often confuse the vibrator with the dildo, which is like confusing a rhino with a giraffe. Both are native to the bush, but that's where the similarities end.

Vibrators are valued for their buzzing properties and are usually rested on the outside of the genitals rather than placed inside them. Dildos are penis-shaped and are used as such. They don't vibrate like a vibrator, but are made to be kept inside the vagina to give a feeling of fullness or to be thrust in and out. They can also slide up and down between the lips of the vulva.

The common battery-operated plastic vibrator is sometimes thought of as a dildo. While some women use them as such, the vibrating part of these little devices is usually located on the tip, which means a woman can't insert it deeply inside her vagina and expect it to keep her clitoris happy. These are also made of hard plastic, and they don't pack much of a wallop compared to the more adequately appointed AC models. While fine for business trips or weekend camping, these devices aren't in the same league as a well-made dildo or vibrator, although some highly devoted users would clearly disagree. One of these is illustrated on the next page. It is to the right of the dildo.

Vibrators, Dildos & Couples

Most guys have no problem with a partner who uses sex toys; many find the situation a total turn-on. However, some males worry that their sweetheart will start preferring the vibrator or dildo to them.

On the surface, this is not an irrational fear. First of all, the vibrator keeps running long after most men have delivered the mail, and nobody's ever heard of a dildo that couldn't get it up. Also, women can put the vibrator or dildo anywhere they want and totally control the proceedings. But strangely enough, if you are a considerate, caring, real flesh-and-blood guy, most women will still want you regardless of how often they fire up the old magic wand. In fact, it's hard to have a meaningful conversation with a vibrator, and no dildo has ever played catch with the kids or gotten up in the middle of the night to feed the baby. Also, sex toys aren't the sort of thing that you can cuddle up next to and feel safe with—not that you can with all men, either.

In purchasing a new vibrator or dildo, a woman who is in a relationship should consider making her partner a part of the selection process. This way, her partner won't feel left in the dust, resentful or inadequate. Perhaps it might not hurt to show him this chapter, which encourages men to take pride in a woman's sex toys. It might also help to let him know that women who buy vibrators and dildos are often extremely happy with their male sex partners.

Making Friends with Your Lover's Toys

Rather than feeling at odds with your lover's vibrator or dildo, ask her to show you how she uses it. Hold her tight while she's getting herself off with it. If she has a vibrator, let her use it on you. And for heaven's sake, be sure to have her use it during intercourse. Some couples find the sensations to be sensational. It's even possible to combine vibrator play with oral sex. The man pushes a small battery-operated vibrator against the bottom of his tongue while the tip of his tongue is touching his partner's clitoris. Or the man can gently push a dildo in and out of her vagina while planting warm wet kisses on her clit.

Vibrator Bits & Pieces

Here are a few vibrating facts that might be helpful if you have never used a vibrator before. (People with medical conditions such as phlebitis should check with a physician before using a vibrator.)

Coil vs. Wand There are two different types of vibrator design: wandlike vibrators with longer bodies and large heads, and coil vibrators with compact heads. Each type delivers a unique sensation. For instance, coil vibrators are smaller and nearly silent. The sensations they produce tend to be more localized. The more popular wand vibrators are bigger and make a distinct humming noise. Newer models are rechargeable and will hum for up to an hour per charge. Some come with two heads which can be used for a variety of purposes, including on your genitals and bum at the same time, or for up and down your spinal column. The new

Windmere coil vibrator was specifically designed for sex play and its vibrations are a bit more gentle than the Wahl or Sunbeam.

Be a Brand-Name Snob While some people swear by the little battery-operated cylinder vibrators, plenty of other people swear at them. The beefier AC-powered vibrators, such as those crafted by Hitachi, Oster, Wahl, Panasonic and Windmere, deliver more bang for the buck and won't let you down at critical moments. They are also well made and have warranties. **Note:** If you are new to a vibrator, be sure to use it on the lowest possible speed at first while you learn to navigate the head around your pubic bone. Some new users have actually bruised their pubic bones by plopping the head of a vibrator on a bony pelvis.

Geography Some women move a vibrator around the entire vulva rather than parking it in one particular place; others find a favorite spot and leave it there as though it were welded.

Muffled Sensations Some users like the sensations of a vibrator full blast; others like to muffle the vibrator with a towel or even a pillow, and some hold the vibrator in a way that allows their fingers to transfer the vibrations. Some of the wand vibrators have variable speed controls, and many vibrators have a low and high option.

Hands Some vibrators strap on the back of your hand. Your fingers deliver the vibrations. These can be great fun to use, but they do tend to numb out the fingers (only temporarily).

Fingers The new Fukuoko 9000 fits on your finger. It is incredibly small and almost unnoticeable.

No Hands Some women rest a vibrator between their legs so they can use their hands for other things such as holding a book, playing with their nipples, touching a partner's body or channel surfing. There are also special harnesses which hold the head of a vibrator snugly between a woman's legs. There is even a small vibrator with built-in straps that is sometimes called Joni's Butterfly. It can be worn during intercourse, in public, at work, on a date or wherever a woman might want to get her own private buzz in a public place. However, this type of vibrator can sometimes be heard in super-quiet places like elevators or libraries, so plan accordingly. (One woman says that when she gets really bored she tucks a vibrating pager in her underwear and phones herself repeatedly....)

〰️ **Positions** Unlike most men, vibrators are meant to be abused. Be sure to try different positions with it on top of you, with you on top of it, with it between your legs and as you lie on your side.

〰️ **Vibrator Vacations** People sometimes worry that a woman will become used to the vibrator and want only that. This seldom happens, but if you are worried about it, consider taking vibrator vacations for one week every month, or alternate with different ways of getting yourself off.

〰️ **Attachments** There are a number of vibrator attachments for both coil and wand vibrators. These have names such as the G-Spotter, Clitickler, Twig and Wonder Wand Plus. They can deliver a finger of vibration to any specific location a man or woman wants.

〰️ **Vibrators and Boys** Women aren't the only ones who appreciate an occasional mechanical assist. For instance, some boys learn to wrap a towel around their dad's hand-held vibrating sander and hold it against their genitals for a quick and easy orgasm. In fact, just about anything around the house that vibrates will eventually find a young man leaning against it to see how it feels. Likewise, a number of girls first learn about good vibrations by leaning against the washing machine when it's on the spin cycle. Leaning against the handles of some vacuum cleaners can also be enlightening.

〰️ **Vibrators and Men** Given how many times the average male masturbates during his lifetime, it makes a certain amount of sense to try out a couple of gadgets and special sleeves that are made for that purpose. Some are interesting, most are disappointing, and few are anywhere near as convenient as simply using your hand. For instance, there is a special attachment for certain types of vibrators called a come cup which fits over the head of the penis. (Be sure to lube up the cup first.) To make a come cup of your own, push the head of a vibrator against your hand as it is holding your penis. Some men wrap a vibrator with a towel and lean into it. The towel helps to muffle the sensation, since vibrators numb some men out (temporarily). There are even special vibrating sleeves that a penis can fit into. If the establishment that you buy from is reputable, the salesperson should be able to tell you which of these works best. Beware of sleeves that vibrate or suck, though. We tested one that sells for $625; it didn't come close to using our hands and five cents-worth of lotion. We also tried a passive vagina substitute that's called the Flesh Light. Sticking your penis into cold mud would have been more fun.

🕊️〰️ **Battery-Operated Personal Massagers** There are many different vibrators crafted in every possible shape known to woman, from cute little lady bugs to vibrating silver bullets and even vinyl hummingbirds. While some of these are made by reputable companies, few deliver the kind of sensation provided by those that plug into the wall. However, a new family of battery-operated massager was recently designed by Candida Royale. It is called the Natural Contours vibrator and it's getting rave reviews, both for its neat nondildolike design and for its quality.

🕊️〰️ **Flying High** When viewed through X-ray, some vibrators resemble detonating devices on bombs. As a result, airport security people might make you open up purses, briefcases and suitcases that have vibrators in them. Resist informing them about what your vibrator does and doesn't detonate.

Dildo Logic

Vibrators have become so socially acceptable that most department and drug stores prominently display them. Of course, few stores or manufacturers mention the real reason why people buy the vibrators, although most of the boxes show scantily clad women using them on their calves. With dildos, there are fewer options for subterfuge and denial. Big stores would be hard-pressed to advertise that dildos help relax tense muscles, although they clearly do. And if people hear a woman say the word "dildo" in a public place, they are more likely to think that she is referring to a male member of Generation X than something that gives her pleasure.

The next couple of pages offer enough information about dildos so you won't be in the dark even if you use it in the dark.

Dildo vs. Penis

It is a known biological fact that the human penis when fully anchored to the human crotch imposes certain limitations upon a woman's sexual pleasure that the silicone dildo does not. For instance, a real penis can't be radically flipped upside down without necessitating a trip to the hospital for the man whose body it is (or was) attached to. There is also the matter of hardness:

the male penis isn't always hard when a woman wants it hard, nor for as long as she might desire. And finally, a penis is not like a car that you can trade in every couple of years. Even if her spouse's penis might not be the best size and shape to fit her psyche or anatomy, a married woma is pretty well glued to it till death or divorce does them apart. Fortunately a woman needn't ditch the man she loves just because she prefers a Chevy-type penis when nature gave him a Ford or, gulp, a Yugo. She can purchase a dildo instead.

In Search of the Perfect Dildo

Dildos are made from a large variety of materials, including jade, acrylic, alabaster, latex, leather, glass, brass and wood. However, the most highly regarded dildo material is usually silicone. Silicone has a soft but firm texture with a smooth surface that is durable and easy to clean, although it doesn't stand up to cuts too well. The silicone material also warms up rather nicely, which is an added plus unless you like cold things in your vagina.

Since there is a fair amount of craftsmanship involved in producing a high-quality dildo, be sure to purchase dildos from places that carry only proven products and take pride in pleasing their customers. One such place is Good Vibrations in San Francisco, where all the products are approved by a member of the staff before going on the shelf. As for dildo particulars, here are a few to consider:

Price Expect to pay from $45 to $90 for a good-quality silicone dildo. Vinyl or rubber dildos are much cheaper, but each has its own set of drawbacks. For instance, rubber dildos have little divots in the surface which make them next to impossible to keep clean. You should always use a condom over rubber dildos.

Size The most important consideration in sizing a dildo is width. One strategy for determining which width is best for you is suggested by the women at Good Vibrations. They say to buy a couple of different-sized zucchinis, carrots or cucumbers that have an inviting width. Steam or nuke them for just a few seconds so they won't be cold, wash them, and put condoms over them. Add lubricant and then try them in your vagina. Don't hesitate to use a vegetable peeler to fine tune the width. When you find one that feels just right, cut it in two and measure the diameter, which will most likely be somewhere between one and two inches. If you are the one who will be inserting the dildo, order one that's sized just right. However, if a friend will be doing the inserting, consider getting a dildo with a slightly smaller diameter. As for length, a four- to five-inch-long dildo should be just right if you plan to keep it stationary inside your vagina, while a six- to eight-inch length might be easier to handle if you like thrusting.

Shape When it comes to dildos, there are plenty of variations within a basic theme: Some dildos are made to look like penises, complete with veins and testicles, some look like dolphins or bears, and some have ridges. Dildos also have different-sized heads. With a small amount of effort, you are likely to find the dildo of your dreams.

Lubrication No matter how wet you might be, it's best to lubricate both the dildo and yourself before inserting, but don't lose track of where you put the tube of lube. You may need to add more as you go.

What to Do with It Contrary to what most people believe, women don't necessarily use dildos for thrusting in and out. For instance, she might like a dildo to be stationary inside her vagina while she uses her fingers or a vibrator, or while a partner provides her with oral or anal attention. Or she might enjoy running the dildo up and down between her labia.

Numbers Some women have one favorite dildo; others have dildos of different shapes and sizes for every day of the week.

Clean Dildos should be washed and dried after each use or used with a condom over them. If not properly cleaned, the porous surface of some dildos will grow microorganisms that are best not introduced (or reintroduced) into you body. If you are sharing sex toys, sterilize your dildo with hydrogen peroxide, rubbing alcohol or a light bleach solution (nine parts water to one part bleach).

Anal Play If you use the dildo in your own or your partner's rectum, be sure to wash it with soap and water before putting it into a vagina. Better yet, slap a condom on it before it goes up anyone's rear. Also, it is wise to limit your anal play to dildos with a flanged end or use a butt plug which won't get lost up your rear end. (Bum bummer.) People who enjoy both anal and vaginal penetration are wise to have dedicated dildos for each orifice.

Dildo Harnesses for Outer Wear Dildos with a flared base can be worn in harnesses which make them appear somewhat like erect penises. With a moderate amount of skill and effort, the person wearing the harness can use the dildo to penetrate a partner. This can be disappointing, though, because the dildo isn't connected to the wearer's nervous system like a real flesh-and-blood penis and she can't feel what the dildo is feeling. (Talk about an existential crisis!) Nonetheless, there are plenty of couples, both straight and lesbian, who enjoy using a dildo in a harness. The best harnesses are made of leather or nylon webbing. The actual geometry of harness construction and fastener application can be tricky; the catalog of Good Vibrations is full of advice about the dos and don'ts of dildo-harness buying and wearing. Also, there are other kinds of dildo harnesses such as those that fit on the thigh. Users of these marvel at the versatility of such an arrangement and claim that the human penis should have been attached to the thigh of the male rather than between his legs. There is even a dildo mounted on a beach ball that a person can bounce up and down on.

Dildo Harnesses for Inner Wear So let's say you're shopping at the supermarket or have a hot date and want to spice things up a bit. No matter where you go or why, you can do it with your favorite dildo sticking inside of your vagina and no one will ever know. That's because they now make dildo harnesses that hold the dildo inside a vagina so it won't pop out when you are at WalMart or when making a special presentation to that hugely important foreign client who just flew in from Algiers.

🪱〰 **Doubles?** A double dildo is worn in a harness, with one end going up the wearer's vagina and the other end sticking out in front like a penis. The highly rated Nexus double dildo from Vixen Creations is the dildo to beat if you are shopping for doubles. It is the top in its class.

🪱〰 **Techno Dildo** Some dildos are motorized and move in circles, as well as having a vibrating appendage that can be parked over the clitoris.

🪱〰 **Beware of Gumby-Like Dildos** Some dildos are embedded with wire rods to help keep whatever shape the person bends them into. Be aware that if the wire separates from the dildo material, it will become embedded in the wall of your vagina or rectum.

🪱〰 **Menopause** Masturbating with a dildo fully inserted might help some menopausal women without partners to keep their vaginas in good shape.

🪱〰 **Full-Court Press** Some women like to be penetrated in both the front and the rear at the same time. In lieu of doing a threesome, the dildo can penetrate one gate while her partner fills the other.

🪱〰 **Suction Cups** There are even dildos with suction cups on the bottom so the woman can stick them on a wall or the floor while she moves her entire body up and down or forward and back while the dildo remains stationary. These can also be planted on the wall as decorations for your home or office.

Sex-Toy Layering—Dildos & Vibrators

Some women who have never enjoyed masturbating with their fingers or a vibrator go to town once they get the right dildo. The dildo provides an internal fullness that makes it much more satisfying when they stimulate the vulva with their fingers or a vibrator. Some like to rest the head of the vibrator on the end of the dildo. Other women consider this to be sex-toy overkill, and do just fine with their fingers or vibrator a cappella.

Backdoor Men & Women

Good Vibrations reports that about half of the dildo harnesses they sell are to heterosexual couples in which the woman wears the dildo to do her man in the rear. So much for the notion that only gay men like an occasional rod up the rear. More on rear-end romance in the chapter "Up Your Bum—Anal Sex."

Quality dildo and vibrator shopping can be done online at places like Good Vibrations [www.goodvibes.com] and Blowfish [www.blowfish.com]. Our website has listings for many other places where you can shop for vibrators and dildos [www.goofyfootpress.com]. We do not get a commission or kickback from any site that is listed on our website. They are strictly there as a public—and pubic—service.

Dear Paul,

Our holiday edition is coming up. Please write an article for us on buying your partner a sex toy.

Pam, editor of the Colorado Daily

Dear Pam,

If you are trying to get a sex toy for a partner, the first thing to do is to think about the kinds of things that turn him or her on. If your gift doesn't resonate with some inner fantasy, it will end up being just another buzzing piece of plastic or strange suggestive object without any sexual oomph.

Another thing to do is to ask yourself, "Would my partner prefer flowers and the latest book by her favorite author?" "Would he like it better if I got him a new modem or brake cable for his mountain bike?" If the answer to either of these questions is yes, consider dumping the sex-toy idea. You will end up having better sex if your partner knows that you went out of your way to get something that he or she really wanted.

As for sex-toy specifics, let's say you are a woman who is trying to rev up her partner's interest. You could be uncreative and buy one of those sleeve things that he sticks himself into, but even the best of these feel cold and strange and will only be used once unless he has a secret thing for sex with dead people. Instead, what about giving him a gift that helps create a shared adventure?

There are plenty of great sex toys that hardly cost anything. For instance, you can make a series of coupons that you give your partner. Each lists a special thing you are willing to do, from giving her a special bath and full-body massage to things we can't even print in the *Colorado Daily*. She gives you the coupon when she wants you to do what it describes.

Another idea is for each of you to describe a sexual scene that is a personal turn-on. Then go shopping for various props to make the scene happen. For instance, if one of you has the fantasy of being stopped and frisked by an officer in uniform, you can go to a used-clothing store and buy the perfect uniform for acting out the scene, perhaps including handcuffs. If the fantasy concerns a visit to the doctor, do your shopping at a medical supply house.

If you don't like that idea, try surprising your partner with a sex toy that's found at your local pet store. When your lover comes home, you can be standing there in your underwear with your new dog collar around your neck; hand her the leash and say, "I'm yours for the night!" But don't forget to attach a bow to the collar, as they do at the fancy pet groomers, and pray that she isn't bringing her parents home for a surprise visit.

There's a new world of erotic books and literature that you and your partner can read together or to each other. Collections of short stories by competent writers abound. The quality is leagues above the typical letter to *Penthouse;* think *Vanity Fair* or the *New Yorker* instead. Some will get you going, others will fall short, but it's nowhere near as bleak as it used to be. A collection of erotic short stories might be the best sex toy you ever gave or got!

If your partner feels his penis is adequate, consider getting a kit from your local art supply store that allows you to make a mold of his little soldier. Best to tell the clerk that you want to make a mold of your son's foot or hand. It's the same kit and won't cause you unnecessary embarrassment. You and your lover will be laughing yourselves silly as you make the mold and the whole thing becomes an adventure. He might even be paralyzed with excitement when you use the finished product on yourself or place it proudly on your bookshelf.

You can find a kit to mold your man's penis on the web at www.artmolds.com. Put the words "intimate" or "penis" into their search engine once you reach their site. And finally, the real experts in making castings of the male member are the boys at Hard Art. They send you the molding material to do at home or you can stop by their studio in Los Angeles (323)667-1501. They will then craft the little masterpiece to your specifications. These guys can even do your lover's schlong in ethnically correct skin tones, but maybe you'll prefer purple or chrome.

If you are still sold on getting traditional sex toys, make a deal with your partner: she selects a toy for you to use on her, and you select a toy for her to use on you. Then go shopping together.

The neat thing about using toys in this way is they help you reveal new things about yourself to your partner, and vice versa. Sex can get boring when you think you know all there is to know about the person you are sleeping with.

Chapter Notes: Is David Bowie's "TVC-15" about a vibrator that was made in the UK? Special thanks to the Good Vibrations catalog for technical help, to the *Good Vibrations Guide To Sex* by Cathy Winks and Anne Semans (San Francisco: Cleis Press), and to those movers and shakers who shared their personal tips.

Basic Brain Weirdness & the Mind-Body Interface
Chapter 24

This chapter is about mental events that can get in the way of having a good sex life, or just having a good life period. Some people would call these mental glitches; others might say they are a normal part of the human condition.

Shyness

Shyness is a funny thing. Sometimes it sits like a shroud over everything you do. Other times it is highly selective, making only certain parts of your life sheer hell. Shyness can take many different forms and can be a great deal more mysterious than people give it credit for. For instance, shyness can make you babble like a fool and say really stupid things or it can make you seem cold and aloof when you're really not.

To illustrate what happens when shyness gets the better of you, consider the following true story of a former high school student whom we will call Andrew.

It was a beautiful spring day about a month or two before the beginning of a somewhat magical time that later became known as the Summer of Love. This was the same year when nearly half a million young people gathered at a now-famous farm in upstate New York for three days of rock'n'roll that became known as Woodstock. It was also a time when other people gathered on other farms throughout the country to do more mundane things like milk cows and tend crops. Andrew was more than three thousand miles away from that very special farm in New York. As for the Summer of Love, he had never even put his hand up a woman's shirt.

None of this stopped him from having an overpowering crush on a very popular young woman who was older than he. (Back then, younger guys rarely dated older women.) This female heartthrob just happened to be the local homecoming queen, or first runner-up, or Future Farmers' Princess, or whatever it was that a young woman became in a small town when everybody claimed to like her. She was so special that he was too embarrassed to tell even his best friend about his lick-the-mud-off-her-shoes-if-that's-what-she-wants crush. Instead, he focused his energies on trying to act cool whenever she passed by.

To make matters worse, the young goddess was constantly surrounded by senior guys who had their own cars, lettered in football and baseball, and got drunk and never even threw up. He, on the other hand, saw himself as just another underclassman who had less than a snowball's chance in hell of attracting this woman's interest.

One day about an hour after school, some strange and peculiar force caused this special young woman to toss her books and pompoms into the back of her car and aim it for the very address where this young man lived. When the doorbell rang he figured it was probably the paper boy or a Jehovah's Witness selling "The Watchtower." When he walked outside and saw who it was, his lower jaw dropped so radically that a big wad of drool nearly fell out of his mouth. All things considered, he did well to maintain bladder control.

He stood staring at this babe like a deer in front of headlights. He felt so paralyzed that he couldn't even mobilize the words to invite her inside. When he did start talking, it was in an almost glib way that didn't allow the slightest bit of closeness. He was clearly blowing it. After about ten awkward minutes of trying to deal with the situation, the young goddess blew the baffled boy a puzzled kiss and drove away never to return.

Many years have passed since this fellow botched the Summer of Love. He still feels just as clumsy and awkward when he meets a woman whom he is really attracted to.

One-Night Stands & Back-Seat Bangers

You will simply have to find out about things like one-night stands on your own, and even then you may disagree with this book's stand. But working up a good fantasy and getting yourself off by hand tends to be less of a headache and is often just as satisfying as most one-night stands. The fantasy of a one-night stand is usually better than the reality of it.

Counterpoint: One reader from London clearly disagrees: "A one-night stand can be an immensely exciting and rewarding experience which you may remember your whole life."

On Being a Sex Object

People usually associate "being a sex object" with being a woman. However, this is about a guy named Steve whom women treated as a sex object. Steve was tall, blond and blue-eyed and had a perfect body. In addition to being a fine surfer, he was a male model who was actually straight.

Everyone was thrown into total shock one night at Steve's tearful lament that he wished women would stop wanting him just for sex. It's a problem none of us could relate to. Steve was in a total funk because women were constantly diving for his crotch.

It's difficult to imagine that physical attractiveness can get in the way of leading a happy life, but people who are physical 10s are sometimes rather lonely. Friends of the same sex are often envious and sometimes feel threatened by the attention that the 10 seems to get. Members of the other sex tend to stare or else act bizarrely. People who are extremely attractive sometimes marry simply for protection.

What's Wrong with This Picture?

The opposite problem is being less than beautiful and having someone who is drop-dead gorgeous show a romantic interest in you. Instead of responding romantically, you might be saying to yourself, "Naw, can't be true. Big mistake here." While the physical 10 may be begging for romance, the less-than-10 is turning a great opportunity into a self-fulfilling prophecy of doom.

People Who Claim, "The Opposite Sex Is Worthless"

Some people choose sexual partners who can't supply any of their emotional needs. It's as if they would be horribly overwhelmed to find someone who could be both a friend and a lover, and therefore not quite so "opposite." Perpetual victims such as these claim that they are more mature and able to love more than their moron partners.

The fact is, people who have a healthy self-regard do not suffer the presence of fools and jerks, let alone sleep with them. The perpetual victim is just as immature and has as many problems with intimacy as does the jerk whom he or she dates or marries. Neither has much to brag about.

Giving Friendship a Chance

The only male-female relationships that we usually teach our children to value are those with romantic potential. As a result, men and women tend to approach each other as potential sex partners rather than as potential friends.

Platonic male-female friendships are a wonderful thing, but they sometimes become endangered if one person starts to feel sexual and the other doesn't. A lot of male-female friendships never happen because people are unable to work it out when one of them wants sex or romance and the other just wants friendship. Knowing that a friend wants romance when you don't can be uncomfortable. However, if he or she were given the time and understanding to cool his or her jets, the nonsexual friendship might be able to flourish for years to come. As for the person who feels smitten and then bitten, keep in mind that a platonic friendship often lasts for years, while that is not always the case with romantic affairs. You might be losing out on something special if you aren't able to accept the person as a friend instead of as a lover. (Another factor that often destroys male-female friendships is jealous partners.)

Counterpoint: One reader comments, "This is a cursory and shallow discussion of this issue." We apparently struck a nerve. She's right; the matter is often far more complex than what's presented here. Sometimes it is filled with all kinds of hopeful expectations and excruciatingly painful disappointments, when one person feels romantic love and the other feels "only" friendship.

Initiating Sex When Holding Is What You Need

Some people find it hard to acknowledge that they simply need to be held, since asking to be held might make them feel weak, wimpy, vulnerable or frightened. Instead, they sometimes initiate sex when what they really may have wanted was physical tenderness and comfort. Fortunately, the desires for sex and tenderness often overlap, which allows them to receive both at the same time. But sometimes they need more of one than the other. Hopefully you can evolve a set of clear signals that will help your partner know what it is that you need, assuming you know yourself.

In Love but Out of Sync

It's the saddest thing in the world when people have powerful feelings for each other but can't make their relationship work. For instance, one of you might become more settled and grounded earlier in life than the other. You may feel like putting down roots or becoming established while the other is still an emotional tumbleweed who needs to experience the outside world and soak in whatever it has to teach. The lack of synchrony forces a breakup. While you may not have any desire to get back together, there might always remain a place in your heart for the other person.

Breaking Up

Breaking up is the sort of thing that you write a whole book about, or not much at all. Otherwise, you risk being trite about a phenomenon that can leave even the strongest of hearts and minds crippled for months, if not years.

The one thing we will mention is that breaking up doesn't always happen with a big fight or hell storm of hostility. In fact, sometimes you spend your last hours together holding each other tight, with tears flowing and a kind of desperate, profound sadness in both your hearts. And even if you are the one who is doing the leaving, the final steps toward the door can sometimes feel horribly lonely or empty.

Forgiving Yourself

Every once in a while we say or do something so stupid that even friends talk about having us committed. This can be particularly devastating when it results in the loss of friendship or love.

The best thing you can do in these situations is to figure out how and why you messed up. Then do what you can to mourn the loss and get on with your life. While there is much to be gained from introspection, there is little to be gained from beating yourself up. On the other hand, if you suffer from a perpetual case of foot-in-mouth disease, it is possible that there is some kind of chronic confusion or anger in the depths of your soul that prevents you from using good sense. In that case, the input of a respected friend, teacher, colleague, relative or even therapist might be an important thing to seek.

Stupid Mistakes—Young vs. Old

If anyone ever tells you that making stupid mistakes is a part of being young and will pass as you get older, don't make the really stupid mistake of believing them.

True, you usually don't make as many mistakes as you get older, but that's only because your brain doesn't work nearly as fast. As your brain slows down, you simply don't have the opportunity to make mistakes with the same lightning speed that you once did.

The Fantasy of Love & Commitment

When you feel particularly empty inside, it's easy to labor under the illusion that things will be better if you can just find someone to love.

Love is a special way of sharing friendship that can bring tremendous joy. It allows you to think and worry about someone other than yourself, which can be a much-needed relief. It also lets you know that there is someone who believes in you when you don't particularly believe in yourself. But in spite of all its pluses, it's unlikely that love will take away your personal fears and insecurities, organize your chaos, cure your bad habits, help you lose weight, stop smoking or get in shape, or turn you into a better human being—not in the long run anyway. These are personal demons that we need to conquer on our own.

The Dark Side — Nights of Quiet Despair

Sometimes you get hit by a certain mood, one that's a quiet mix of frustration, hopelessness and despair. It's when something deep inside you isn't working right, something incredibly human, but you can't put a finger on it.

Being in a relationship does not always help the bad feelings to go away.

Sometimes it becomes a contest between you, the despair and the beer, pills, sleep, food, sex or whatever it is that helps make you feel better. Presidents' wives tell you to just say no, the disc jockey on the all-night radio station never plays the song you need and a river of pain cuts your heart in two.

Nights of quiet despair sometimes go away by morning.

Readers' Comments

One-Night Stands vs. Long-Term Relationships

"Not to sound like a dick, but a 'one-night-stand' is all about me. I am there to get and to be fucked. Sex in a relationship is about both of us. Adding in love and respect makes sex in a long-term relationship better." *male age 25*

"In 'one-night stands,' the expectations far exceed the experience. I'm not in tune to what turns my partner on sexually as I would be in a long-term relationship." *male age 39*

"'One-night-stand' sex can be exciting because you just don't know what you're gonna get." *female age 25*

"Sex in a 'one-night stand' has its own excitements. But most of those are related to the 'naughtiness' of the situation and having to live with the thoughts and fears of possible exposure to STDs, as well as guilt concerning 'what type of person do I want to be.' " *female age 37*

"I am a very horny person and I was surprised that I could not get wet when I was with a 'one-night stand.' It was almost like a business deal. I felt no release and passion that I do in my relationship with Chris." *female age 23*

"My 'one-night stands' have varied; some guys pass out drunk, or they plain just can't get it up no matter what you do. I really haven't had much luck with one-night stands." *female age 36*

How Does Sex Impact Your Long-Term Relationship?

"I find that if we go without sex for a few days it throws my boyfriend and I off and we lose our common wavelength. After sex we are right back in tune with each other, and there's nothing like that." *female age 23*

"Sex enhances just about everything in my life. It relieves my stress and anger, and it increases our love and romance. It leaves me happy and with a certain glow. It's as though I can conquer anything!" *female age 36*

Dear Paul,

Ever since I graduated from college my sex life has taken a big nose dive. I have had sexual intercourse ONCE between 1994 and today! I had a healthy sex life in high school complete with true love and several short-term physical relationships. That was when I wasn't even legally an adult. Now I am almost 30 and for most of my twenties my sex life has been NO life at all. I am not at all physically unattractive, although I am somewhat shy and keep very busy. I think my problem is not meeting women. I dislike bars.... I do not feel my sex life is representative of a mature, healthy adult male, and the lack of physical intimacy bothers me considerably. Both of my house mates have the same problem and I know many other guys do. Paul, what is up with this problem, and besides offering your own valuable suggestions, can you direct me to some resources that might help me locate and meet available women?

Blue in Boulder

Dear Blue,

High school and college may not fill our lives with happiness and bliss, but they do provide an important social safety net. I can remember my own horror at finally having to leave college. I hadn't gotten into medical school, I didn't feel like doing grad work, and my girlfriend had just given me the boot. I didn't know it was possible to feel so awful. I got a job waiting tables—which is the equivalent of leaving school but not really. I wrote and floundered for a couple of years until I finally went back to graduate school when I was about your age. I don't remember getting laid much during that time. I also made the huge mistake of doing what you are doing—trying to find ways of meeting women. There is no shortage of books or manuals on that subject. But I'm not so sure they will help, and I don't know if they are what you need. In fact, I strongly encourage you to do something else with your time than trying to meet women.

Please take a moment to imagine that you only have a couple of hours to live. I am willing to bet that even if you had been a stud lover and had created wet spots on mattresses all over Boulder, memories of your love life would bring you zero solace in the face of death. It's not how often you've had sex or who you had sex with that would make you feel like your life had been worthwhile. What's more important are the contributions that you've hopefully made in life.

For instance, if you had volunteered in a program where you helped people learn to read, I bet you'd get comfort from remembering some of their smiling faces when they read their first sentence. If you coached a baseball team and helped keep kids out of trouble, or helped build a park, or did something that makes your community a better place, those are the things that will give you solace. If you created something that is helpful to others, that's what will be important in your waning moments. It's what you have done to make yourself a better person that counts the most in life. So instead of wasting your time trying to find a bed partner, why not do things that will make you a better person? Please, don't think I am suggesting that you do altruistic-appearing events as a thinly disguised sham for meeting women. There is nothing more obnoxious than people who volunteer for things with the ulterior motive of trying to find love or sex.

Improve yourself, and maybe love will come. Maybe it won't. But it seems that people who are vitally involved in life tend to have an energy that attracts others. This is not as true for people who spend their evenings in front of a TV set or who think mostly of themselves from morning to night.

Not to overdo the death thing, but the best advice I ever received after the age of thirty had nothing to do with sex. It was just three words, "Grow or die." It's something I remind myself of often, especially when the couch potato in me threatens to take over. Since there is nothing about cruising for women that is particularly growth-promoting, my advice is to go for the bigger picture. Do what it takes to improve yourself as a person. Hopefully, the other things in life, like finding relationships, will fall into place. [You can find more columns at www.goofyfootpress.com.]

Men's & Women's Experience of Sex
Chapter 25

Men's and women's genitals are generally found in the same location: behind the buttons of a person's blue jeans. But what about the way we experience sex? Do men and women experience sex differently? That's what this chapter is about. But first...

Forget Everything Else!

Forget penises, vulvas and chromosomes. The biggest difference between male and female sexuality throughout the ages has been the fact that men don't get pregnant and women do. Forget the "behavioral influences" of estrogen and testosterone — instead, consider how differently we might approach sex if men were the ones who got knocked up and had to carry a baby inside themselves for nearly ten months, and if men were expected to be the child's primary caregiver for the next eighteen years.

Of course, there are other factors that influence men's and women's experience of sex. While most of these have to do with cultural roles and expectations, some reflect differences in biology. For instance, there are subtle differences in brain anatomy which may influence behavior. Consider how the female brain responds to the smell and taste of chocolate. Think of how different life would be if the female brain responded to the penis with half as much craving as it often does for chocolate.

There are also claims about differences in the behaviors of male and female newborns. The author of this guide spent a number of years in graduate school holding and studying babies, from two-pound preemies to drug-addicted newborns of crack-smoking moms. He can assure you that the only difference between boy babies and girl babies that means a single thing is how the babies pee. Boy babies have the capacity to wipe out your favorite shirt, tie, glasses and note pad, while girl babies are more forgiving pee-ers. Working with boy babies requires a quickness of hand which some women report is just as necessary when working with the babies' adult fathers.

Perhaps a more relevant finding of infant research is that girl babies are every bit as strong and healthy as boys at birth, if not more so. Yet we often treat girl babies as though they were more fragile. For instance, researchers have dressed the same baby as a boy and then as a girl. When caregivers thought that the baby was a girl, they said things like "Aren't you pretty and dainty." When they thought it was a boy, they said, "Aren't you a big one; look at how strong you are." Furthermore, if you want to know the sex of a baby from ten yards away, just observe how its daddy plays with it; girl babies get an abundance of hugs and kisses while boy babies get the rough 'n' tumble. With such profound differences in the way we raise our children, it's hard to imagine how subtle variations in neurology or genetics even matter.

Note: We use the term "opposite sex" when comparing men and women, yet there is not a single psychological test battery that can distinguish male from female test takers.

Typical Male Porn vs. the New Female Porn

What happens to these babies twenty years later when they are having sex and maybe even thinking about making babies of their own? Do the women's experiences fall into the "pretty and dainty" category? Are the men's "big and strong"? Perhaps not, but our culture does have specific insults that it hurls at women whose sexuality appears to be "big and strong" and at men whose sexuality is "pretty and dainty."

To help illustrate possible differences in men's and women's experience of sex, we have included a few samples of pornographic writing. The following is a typical letter to a male magazine that is commonly used for masturbation. It has a monthly audience of around five million people:

> It wasn't long before a wet area began to appear in the front part of DeAnne's bikini panties. I slowly started to pull them down, at first revealing a neatly trimmed patch of silken blonde down, then the glistening tip of DeAnne's

swollen clit, and finally the rest of her hidden steamy treasure. The mere sight made me so hot I nearly exploded.

DeAnne must have sensed my excitement. Without saying a word, she ripped open my bulging blue jeans and started ravaging my nine-inch cock with her pleading lips. Within seconds I was filling her hungry mouth with load after load of white hot cum. DeAnne kept sucking and slurping on my throbbing rod until she milked my big balls dry.

Okay, so getting your rocks off is the name of the game in traditional male porn, with the focus being on the particular body parts that get you there the fastest.

Typical male porn holds the premise that within every woman sits a raging nymphomaniac begging to wrap her lips and legs around the teeming bulge of the nearest available guy. There is little concern that a woman's idea of fun might not include deep throating her teacher's nine-inch penis, that she might need a plumber for something other than a hard pounding fuck or that she might find it less than pleasing when an out-of-shape salesman with muttonchop sideburns starts coming all over her face and chest.

The next two passages are from *Erotic Interludes*, a collection of women's pornography—ah, erotica—edited by Lonnie Barbach (New York: Harper & Row, 1986):

J.B. tenderly caressed my breasts until I could feel the space between my legs grow warm and wet. His kisses were different than ever before, long and slow at first, then his tongue licked mine like fire dancing in the dark. His long, slender legs gradually, rhythmically inched mine apart. The tip of his cock played on my belly, and I couldn't resist rising up to meet him, opening my legs as far as the backseat would allow. A soft flash of red filled my vision when he entered me, his kisses wild on my face. I remember only the sense of infinite motion that followed. (Written by Sharon S. Mayes)

Amy groaned with pleasure as his large hand cupped her gently and his third finger came to rest on the one sweet spot he knew so well. As he touched it she felt an electric current flow from his hand into her. His energy swirled inside her till the whole universe seemed to start spinning around.... The spinning sensation rose up and flooded her whole body, pushing at the boundaries of who she thought she was.... Finally, unable to hold the energy back any longer, she let it explode through every cell in her body, cleansing her with light and pulsating out into the room. (By Udana Power)

Blinding light? Infinite motion? Spinning senses that rise up to flood her whole body, pushing at the boundaries of who she thinks she is? This has a different edge than "Within seconds I was filling her hungry mouth with load after load of white hot cum."

On the other hand, one female reader protests that the samples of women's porn "left me bored," while she found the male passage to be "erotic for me until he wastes his cock in her mouth." Several female readers have echoed this same sentiment, but with phrasing that is somewhat more delicate. At the same time, a male reader says that he finds the women's passages to be more erotic. Perhaps it's not so easy to generalize about the preferences of men and women, although the samples could easily be tagged as typical male or typical female.

Is It Really Different?

Are men's and women's experiences really different, or do they just use different words to describe them?

Researchers asked men and women to write a paragraph describing their experience of orgasm. A panel of judges could not tell the women's descriptions of orgasm from the men's. So much for those charts on orgasm that make men and women look like they come from different planets. Nonetheless, studies have shown that there are some sex-related differences in the attitudes of men and women, but mostly when they are with members of the same sex. These differences decrease greatly when men and women are in mixed company.

But this isn't what Madison Avenue wants us to think. Advertisers work hard to make us believe that men and women are very, very different. That's because manufacturers can often charge more for products that are targeted to a specific sex, such as cigarettes, deodorants and even hemorrhoid ointments which are for one sex only. It's a little surprising that we haven't seen toilet paper that's made just for a man's or woman's "special needs"—although one manufacturer, Kleenex, did try to sell man-sized facial tissues, which, by the way, really were better for jerking off into than normal-sized tissue.

How Men and Women Experience Visual Pornography

It is often said that women aren't as turned on as men by X-rated movies. However, research is showing that rather than being turned off by visual pornography, women are mainly turned off by the premise of most male pornography, which portrays females as submissive bimbos. When shown X-rated movies which are smart and fun and where the sexuality conveysaffection, both male and female viewers prove to be highly aroused. (If men were the ones who risked pregnancy during sex, perhaps traditional male porn might have a more caring premise!)

In research on pornography, college students were hooked up to devices that measure blood flow in the genitals. They were then shown X-rated movies. Although these devices indicated that the groins of the female students were as sexually aroused as the males, several of the women were not consciously aware of their arousal. This may have been due to an experimental glitch. On the other hand, it might reflect how women are often raised to ignore their body's sexual cues. Also, it is possible that males wouldn't be nearly as conscious of their own sexual arousal if they didn't have a penis that's difficult to ignore when it gets hard. Whatever the case, women do rent about 40 percent of adult videos, with the absolute number of X-rated rentals being staggering.

Role Reversal—Fingers Up Men's Rear Ends

Getting a finger up the rear during a routine physical exam makes many guys feel like they've been raped, yet they don't think twice about sticking their own fingers up a woman's vagina. It's possible that a woman's experience of sex might feel more private than a man's since her body is the one that is usually being penetrated. One woman reader comments:

> "Even if he's wearing a condom, it still feels like a man leaves something inside of me during intercourse. He's got to have something I really want inside of me, or I won't do it."

One of the few times when a woman gets to stick something of hers inside a man is during French kissing. Some men love the feeling of a woman's tongue inside their mouths, while other men are only comfortable with French kissing if it imitates intercourse, with the male's tongue doing the thrusting. Also, some couples are into certain kinds of anal sex where the woman penetrates the man's rear with her fingers or various kinds of sex toys.

Intimacy—Men vs. Women

In our society, we often assume that women are better at intimacy than men. Is this true?

The answer depends upon how you define intimacy. While women are often better at some levels of intimacy (sharing feelings, talking about how the day went, etc.), neither sex fares particularly well when it comes to getting extremely close. Psychologist David Schnarch speaks to this issue in his book *Constructing the Sexual Crucible* (New York: Norton, 1992):

> Popular wisdom suggests that women are more interested in intimacy than men.... However, sharing feelings is not the same as open self-confrontation in the presence of the partner. When the focus is intense intimacy, there is no consistent gender difference in intimacy tolerance: almost no one wants it.... When intimacy is distinguished from dependency and fusion, many women don't want it either.

A Final Perspective

Some evolution experts believe that nature has programmed men to ejaculate into each and every available vagina (the victory plunge), while women are programmed to couple with males who will offer the best chance to successfully raise a family (relationship material). The people who take these theories most seriously are the evolutionists themselves, but there is little in this chapter that contradicts such a premise.

On the other hand, a man who is straight and masculine-appearing might experience sex in a way that we would typically expect of a woman—sensitive, monogamous and intimacy seeking, while a very feminine-appearing straight woman might enjoy sex with numerous men, value it for the rush of sensation that it offers and avoid long-term relationships. It's also possible that what we want at one point in our lives may be totally different from what we want at another. In other words, it's dangerous to generalize about how any of us, male or female, experience sex.

The most important thing to be aware of about sexual differences is that your partner might experience sex differently than you do. Instead of pretending to know what that might be or making silly assumptions based upon even sillier generalizations, why not ask, explore and find out for yourselves?

Also, as we get older, life keeps presenting us with opportunities for growth and change. Hopefully, you will be able to use these opportunities to increase the intimacy and satisfaction in your relationships, even if it means being more "male" or "female" in bed than your gender's stereotype currently allows.

Some days you're the mouse, some days you're the elephant.

What's Feminine, Masculine & Erotic
Chapter 26

When a human male walks into a classroom of human females, he can't tell which ones are ovulating (able to get pregnant). Few of the women know themselves. However, when a male gorilla walks into a room full of female gorillas, he automatically knows which ones are ovulating. That's because the rumps of female gorillas turn red and they put off an irresistible sex perfume that makes male gorillas weak in their big hairy knees.

Most animals are highly influenced by the reproductive cycle of the female, except for us humans. One reason is because we have bigger forebrains. Our souped-up forebrains allow us the choice of having sex when we want, how we want and with whom we want. We also rely upon cultural cues in deciding what is masculine, feminine and erotic.

Does having bigger forebrains mean we have it better than the other animals? Not really. While gorillas may not have as much choice about sex, they don't sit around reading books about it either. Nor do they seem to experience as much sadness and anguish as we humans.

Linebacker-Dad Likes What?

In defining what's masculine and what isn't, let's consider Dave, the prototypical manly guy. Dave plays football, hunts, is a great dad and beloved husband. And there's one other thing. Every month or two, Dave gets together with an old friend who gives it to him up the rear. You know, anal sex. So what happens now to his rating on your scale of what's masculine? Does it drop some? A lot? Just a tiny bit? None?

Even if you said, "Just a tiny bit," please be aware that your definition of masculinity includes "what goes in and out of a guy's butt": 100 percent feces = 100 percent real man. Less than that, and he's not a real man. That's how many of us define it.

What Society Finds Erotic

Each culture has its own definition of what's erotic and what isn't. Here are some examples of how these definitions differ from culture to culture year to year:

🦇 Women in Muslim cultures cover themselves from head to toe when appearing in public. Women in Hollywood appear in public wearing a few molecules of black spandex, designed more to tease than to cover. The women in Hollywood claim that their Muslim counterparts are sexual prisoners. The Muslim women feel that the real prisoners are the females in Hollywood. A neutral observer might call it a tossup. One female reader says that neither women are sexual prisoners, since they both use sex to control the people around them!

🦇 In Japan, it's a common practice for people to strip naked and bathe together. Nobody finds this kind of public nudity to be erotic or shameful, but Lord help two Japanese who kiss in public. In our society, it's nearly the opposite, with kissing being fine but public nudity being a legal offense.

🦇 Kim Edwards is a woman who taught English in a rigid Islamic country for two years and then moved to Japan. In the Islamic country, an exposed female body is considered to be the tool of the devil, and women cover it from head to toe to save the souls of men. After a few years in a rigid Islamic country, Ms. Edwards literally started hating her own body. When she finally moved to Japan, she was shocked to find herself treated as a normal person no matter what she wore. She could even bathe naked in public bathhouses, while she could have been stoned to death for doing this in an Islamic country. (Kim Edwards's story is told in her work "In Rooms of Women," published in Laurence Goldstein's *The Female Body: Figures, Styles, Speculations* [Ann Arbor: University of Michigan Press].)

🦇 During the Summer Olympics, male gymnasts from the Russian team often celebrated good performances by kissing other male team members on the lips. Our U.S. male gymnasts wouldn't be caught dead doing that, not in public anyway.

🦇 In America, many straight women now wear their hair

Who is the "Sexual Prisoner"?
a. The Muslim Woman
b. The Western Woman
c. Neither
d. Both

short, and straight men wear their hair long. Forty years ago this meant that you were homosexual. And think of the public outcry if a 1950s professional baseball player appeared in billboard ads wearing a pair of red bikini briefs; or if his 1950s beehive-coiffed girlfriend went to the grocery store wearing Doc Martins and a pair of male boxers. Or what if a straight American male tried wearing a pierced earring before the 1980s?

━━ In America, there is nothing unusual about an unmarried 18-year-old woman having sex; but among more traditional Arab-Muslims, Christians, Druze and Israelis in places like the Gaza Strip and the West Bank, such a woman risks being brutally murdered by her own brother for harming the honor of her family. This type of murder, which is called "honor killing," is supported by the girl's family as well as the rest of the village. Even the girl's mother and sisters support the murder because it protects the family name. In one village, they favor throwing the accused girl off the minaret of the local mosque; in other areas the brother, father or a close blood relative murders her with an axe or a knife, strangles her or burns or buries her alive. All of this for having sex while unmarried, which millions of American women do by the age of sixteen or seventeen.

━━ In Africa, nearly 80 million adult women had their clitorises and inner labia crudely cut out of their bodies as children. This type of "surgery" is considered an important passage to womanhood which many African mothers have done to their young daughters. In the Western world, a mother who did such a thing to her daughters would be put in prison. Of course, African women might claim that the clitoridectomy is just as cosmetic and feminine as our Western penchant for mutilating female bodies with breast implants. Mohammed only knows what an African woman might say about liposuction.

━━ In the Hispanic culture of East Los Angeles some males don't feel masculine until they have gotten a woman pregnant ("given her a child"). Likewise, some Hispanic females don't feel good about themselves until they have borne children. Twenty miles to the west, in Pacific Palisades and Malibu, the last thing a teenage couple wants to do is get pregnant. They often seek an abortion if it happens. Also, a Malibu woman who is pregnant often worries about losing her hard-earned, occasionally anorexic shape, while the pregnant Hispanic woman might relish the feeling of fullness that pregnancy offers.

Until the last couple of decades it was considered unfeminine for women in our society to enjoy sex as much as men. Valuing sex was a masculine trait, and some women even believed that it was unladylike to have orgasms. Yet there are plenty of other cultures which take it for granted that the sex drives of men and women are equally intense. In some cultures, parents even teach their children about enhancing sexual pleasure.

Masculinity & Femininity

Masculinity and femininity are concepts that make all the sense in the world as long as you don't try to define them.

For example, people in this country think of masculine as being rough-and-tumble, and feminine as being dainty and nurturing. Yet this isn't nearly as true in preschools that require little girls to wear the same kind of clothes as little boys. Once freed from wearing dainty outfits, little girls get rough-and-tumble too. Likewise, if little boys had to wear precious outfits that needed to be kept clean, they would probably act more daintily.

Equally puzzling are all those rough-and-tumble men who become extremely nurturing and maternal when it's time to feed the baby. Do their aggressive male hormones suddenly dry up at dinner time? Do their brains change shape? And if you assume that women are less aggressive or the more nurturing sex, try talking to a random group of female lawyers, advertising execs or women in entertainment.

While hormones may have some impact in determining male and female behaviors, what we learn from culture about our respective sex roles is clearly the larger force in shaping the way we behave. That's why it is hard to talk about the definitions of masculine and feminine unless we also know the particular country, culture and year.

Ethics vs. the Law

There is sometimes a big difference between laws and ethics. For instance, there are groups of professional people who have drawn up codes of conduct which they sometimes refer to as "ethics." As a result, it is unethical for certain professionals to have sex with the people they serve. It is important that these ethics be upheld in order to maintain the fabric of society. On the other hand, many states have laws telling married couples what they can or can't do in bed. Laws like these are silly.

Hypothetical: State trooper pulls over a speeding motorist. Motorist says, "Betcha' never had a blow job on this stretch of highway before." Officer lies, says, "No, I haven't. Maybe we should do something about that." Which person, cop or motorist, is being unethical? Hint: The last time you took a driver's test, did you have to pledge that you would never offer sex to get out of a speeding ticket? Sometimes it's not unethical to offer, while it is unethical to accept. Also, while not unethical, it might be against the law in some states to offer a blow job to get out of a ticket (attempting to bribe an officer of the law).

Upcoming Chapters

From this guide's perspective, any culture's definition of masculine, feminine and erotic is arbitrary, transient and often artificial. Nonetheless, people take these definitions seriously and get really bent out of shape if you ignore their local customs. In some of the chapters that follow, we consider society's sacred-cow rules and traditions, as well as the perspective of people who don't abide by them.

Counterpoint: One reader from France writes, "You have done a great job in this chapter explaining cultural differences, yet you blow it with the first sentence of your final paragraph. In my mind, it's a culture's rules and definitions that make it unique. It would be a very boring planet if we were all the same, and especially if we were all like Americans."

Gay & Bi
Chapter 27

Let's face it, ours is a culture based on the great hetero-sexual dream—marriage, kids, own your own home and a rock-solid pension plan. Straight or gay, people who don't fully subscribe to the great heterosexual dream tend to feel left out. This is particularly true for teenagers who are gay, many of whom are desperately trying to fit in and behave like future breeders.

This chapter is about people who are turned on by members of the same sex, people who often feel left out in a big way. But first, the following is from the very funny book *Who Cares If It's a Choice? Snappy Answers to 101 Nosy, Intrusive and Highly Personal Questions about Lesbians and Gay Men*, by Ellen Orleans, (Laugh Lines Press, 1994):

At What Age Do You Know You're Homosexual?

As you might imagine, this varies greatly. Guys seem to be aware of their sexuality early on. A single erection while watching Batman free Robin from the clutches of the Riddler provided many young men with their first clue. One gay friend told me that his childhood role models were Bert and Ernie. For others, it was Skipper and Gilligan.

Women seem to discover their sexual orientation more from personal experiences. Although I didn't realize it at the time, my first clue was when I zipped up Bobby Wolin-sky's fly for him in the second grade. My teacher said this was not proper—that that was a boy's private area. At the time, I didn't see what the big deal was. Guess I still don't.

One man in *Frontiers Magazine* said he knew he was gay when it became clear that he preferred masturbating to the men's underwear part of the Sears catalog instead of *Playboy*.

Gay, Straight or In Between?

What's straight and what's gay? The following is a traditional definition; it tends to simplify matters a bit much:

Straights are turned on by people who have genitals that are shaped differently from their own. *Gays* are turned on by those whose sex organs are cut from the same cloth. *Bisexuals* are people who don't fit neatly into either category.

As for statistics, it is estimated that at least sixty percent of the population is straight, that five percent to thirty percent or more might be bisexual, ranging from barely bi to full-blown bi, and that two percent to seven percent of the population is gay. The numbers derived from different sex surveys vary hugely, depending upon how the questions are worded and how each category is defined. For instance, how do you categorize someone who occasionally fantasizes about having sex with a member of the same gender but would never want to actually do it?

Of the various sexual orientations, which is best? We have no clue. There are times when life and relationships totally suck no matter what your sexual orientation; being straight is no guarantee of happiness. Nonetheless, it's what the majority of people are, and it is usually easier to be part of the majority no matter what the subject. Easier, but not necessarily more satisfying.

Most studies measuring the satisfaction of straight, gay male and lesbian couples find few differences, although the data often suggest that lesbian couples are likely to be more satisfied than their heterosexual or gay male counterparts.

When Your Minister & His Wife Have Anal Sex

While it's one thing to feel uncomfortable about another person's sexual orientation, it's quite another to make fun of them, occasionally beat them up and pass laws that discriminate against them. Yet that's what a number of straight people do to gays.

Consider the following: Straight or gay, most men enjoy having their penises sucked. If you are straight, you prefer that a woman does the sucking. If you are gay, you prefer that a man does the sucking. What's the difference? Did some prophet come down from the mount and announce that a woman's mouth is better suited to suck a penis than a man's? Are her molars more penis-friendly than a man's? And believe it or not, just as many heterosexual couples in this country had anal sex last night as did gay couples. Maybe even your minister and his wife enjoy anal sex, not to mention some of our country's ultraconservative senators and congressmen. Are they bad people because they enjoy an occasional butt fuck?

Human beings have a long history of being uncomfortable with perspectives that differ from their own; as Americans, we have a history of being squeamish about sex. It makes sense that so many straight people feel uncomfortable about gay sex. Still, why should someone else's sexual preference cause a hostile or fearful reaction?

Gay Bashers & Reaction Formation

The University of Georgia is one of the finer institutions of higher learning, and not simply because they use the *Guide to Getting It On!* as required reading in their sex education classes, although it does speak well of them. The University of Georgia did a fascinating study on homophobia.

Psychologists gave a questionnaire about homosexuality to a group of sixty-four men. Based upon their responses, the men were divided into two subgroups: those who were homophobic and those who were not. The testers then showed the subjects hardcore X-rated videos of men having sex with women, and men having sex with men. They did this after placing sensors on the guys' penises to see if they were having erections while watching the different videos.

When watching the tapes of gay guys, eighty percent of the homophobic men had penile arousal, while only thirty-four percent of the nonhomophobic men did. This means that eighty percent of the men who strongly disliked gays or gay behavior became sexually aroused while watching men having sex with men. Get the picture? Perhaps they protest too much.

Naturally, almost all of the homophobic men denied feeling aroused while watching gay guys having sex.

Heather & Cher's Place

While this guide doesn't care what your sexual orientation is, it does care that you respect your sexuality. This puts it at odds with what has been happening in some of the more visible parts of the gay male community.

For instance, several years ago the author of this book moved to Los Angeles for graduate school. That's when he joined one of the glitzy health spa chains whose spokespersons were celebrities like Cher and Heather Someone. Being a person who loved taking a steam bath after a workout, it's also when he discovered that the men's steam room at Heather and Cher's place was where some of the local actor-wannabe types congregated to jerk off.

Call it provincial, call it petty, but there's something really annoying about taking a steam bath and having to worry about sitting in a puddle of actor-wannabe cum. This was before people knew much about AIDS, so the complaint was strictly aesthetic.

Livestock sexuality can be a lonely thing. This is just as true for straight people as for gays cruising locker rooms with pumped-up dicks hoping to attract the hand or mouth of a nameless, faceless stranger. On the other hand, if you consider the history of homosexuality in America, being able to troll inside of Heather and Cher's locker room is quite an achievement. That's because before the 1960s, being a homosexual in America was a greater crime than being a robber or a rapist. Having gay sex in the privacy of your own home could land you in jail and leave you branded as a sex offender for life. Even today it's illegal to perform a homosexual act in more than twenty states, in spite of the fact that approximately one out of five Americans will take part in a homosexual act at some point in their lives.

Given this rather frightening history of oppression, it's easy to see why gays may have viewed the freedom to jerk off in Heather and Cher's locker room as a tremendous victory. But there comes a time to stop measuring the present strictly against the past.

Instead of encouraging its members to respect their sexuality, the gay community in the '70s and '80s went out of its way to sanction the practice of livestock sex. The implied message became "Love me because I'm gay," which is about as dumb as saying "Love me because I'm straight."

Of course, one doesn't criticize this sort of activity without being called homophobic or anti-gay. But maybe it's possible that this section was included out of love and an awareness that whether you are gay or straight, life is even more difficult without a sense of dignity and self-respect.

Some people might argue that this perspective is out of date, and that anonymous trolling in the gay community is a thing of the past. If that's true, is the reason due to increased self-respect or simple fear of the plague? If AIDS were to disappear tomorrow, how long would it be before '70s-style cruising would return?

Postscript—That's Entertainment

Recently, the author walked past a group of young women who were swooning in front of the poster of a good-looking actor who has made it big in the last couple of years. This actor has had quite an impact on the American public—women want to sleep with him; their boyfriends wish they could be him.

Your author couldn't help but chuckle because he rarely forgets a face, even if it was through the fog in the steam room of Heather and Cher's gym several years ago.

Straight Male Friends Can Be Important

Contrary to what some heterosexuals fear, the last thing most gay men want is to have sex with a straight guy. While there are exceptions, most gay men would be bored by the concept. And if you are a straight guy who gets hit up for gay sex, it's quite easy to say, "Sorry, but I'm one of those boring breeder types."

Straight men should also be aware that within the gay community, conversations sometimes boil down to one of three topics: sex, AIDS or gay politics. This is one reason why some gay men value their friendships with straight men. With straight men they are only friends and not potential sex partners, and they can have conversations about things like baseball scores and new car tires without the added postscript of who just died. Furthermore, their straight male friends aren't invested in the sometimes vicious politics of the local gay scene. Likewise, there are plenty of straight men who can use help with fashion, design or advice about women from their gay male friends.

Straight or gay, most men prefer to be known for what they are rather than whom they fuck. Yet there are large portions of both the gay and the straight communities where this is not possible.

A Sad Note about Teenage Runaways and Suicides

Statistics show that more than 50 percent of runaway teenagers living on the streets of New York City are gay or bisexual. A disproportionate number of teenagers who commit suicide are also gay, and that's only counting the ones who had come out before they killed themselves. Is there something about being gay that predisposes kids to be depressed or unhappy in their own homes? Does it make them unlovable or antisocial? Or are these statistics an indicator that being gay is so alienating in our society that it disrupts even the bond between parent and child.

Whatever the case, this is an indicator that teenagers can most certainly benefit from contact with healthy role models, both gay and straight. Unfortunately, we don't like the idea of our children having contact with gay men and women, especially gay Boy Scout leaders.

Going Both Ways—Bisexual Considerations

At one time or another many straight people have a homosexual feeling or ten. It's no big deal unless you are also homophobic, in which case your mind has to perform all sorts of mental gymnastics so you can live with yourself. Likewise, there are plenty of homosexuals who have heterosexual feelings. And then there are people who have their primary relationships with members of one sex, but also have pronounced desires to get it on with members of the other sex.

As you can see, there are many degrees of bisexuality. For some people, the extent of their bisexuality is simply to enjoy bisexual fantasies, while others want and need real sexual contact with both male and female partners.

People who give full rein to both hetero and homo desires are called switch-hitters and are said to go both ways. While the ability to switch-hit might win a baseball player an added bonus, this is not the case when it comes to human sexuality. Both the gay and straight communities regard switch-hitters with suspicion, and the switch-hitter often feels alien with both straights and gays. This is especially true in parts of the lesbian community, where a good lesbian isn't supposed to even think about having sex with a man and where it is poor form if you refer to a dildo as a penis substitute. It's also true on college campuses, where studies show that students regard bisexual males even more negatively than they do homosexual males.

While bisexual women might by shunned by ardent lesbians, they fare better overall than do bisexual men. For instance, a former hit song by female singer Jill Sobule is all about how she kissed a girl. Do you think that a song like this would have ever been cut, let alone become popular, if it had been performed by a male singer and were titled "I Kissed a Guy"? Perhaps one reason for the discrepancy is because a large number of straight males get off on the notion of two women making love, with a common fantasy being to watch their wives or girlfriends make it with another woman. On the other hand, not many women fantasize about their husbands making it with another man. Whatever the case, the following words of a bisexual woman might be helpful in explaining how some bisexual people experience their sexual feelings:

> It's funny to talk about the difference between male and female partners, because we did a lot of the same things. If I've got the emotional, intellectual connections, then the physical stuff can be about the same.... There's a chemistry that happens, and I don't know if it's going to be with a man or a woman. From Julia Hutton's *Good Sex* (San Francisco: Cleis Press, 1992).

Resource: A book on bisexuality that many people speak well of is *Bi Any Other Name: Bisexual People Speak Out*, edited by L. Hutchins and L. Ka'ahumanu (Boston: Alyson, 1991). There is also an extensive list of bisexual resources on our website: www.goofyfootpress.com.

Life As a Lesbian, As If We Had a Clue...

People often think of gay men and women as being similar just because they are both homosexual. Silly them. To give you an idea of how dissimilar gay men and women can be, consider these statistics: while the majority of gay males in this country will have sex with at least a hundred different partners in a lifetime, the average gay woman has sex with a lifetime total of two to five partners. And while less than 20 percent of gay males have had sex with a woman, more than 80 percent of gay women have slept with a man.

Setting a stereotype for gay women is not possible, says sex researcher Ira Reiss. While common personality traits and pathways to homosexuality have been found among some groups of gay males, Reiss has found few among gay women.

Lipstick Lesbians

People sometimes think that all lesbians are bull dykes or motorcycle mamas. This guide is willing to bet its left foot that there were as many lesbians entered in last year's Miss America Pageant as were on the women's professional golf tour. Lesbians are just as feminine (or unfeminine) as straight women. A number of very hot-looking actresses and models are lesbians.

Equally off base is the notion that gay women make love in a delicate or particularly poetic way. Gay women get it on with as much passion (or lack of it) as straight women.

Beyond Brown & Yale

In the past, women who preferred women still dated and married men. And women who had lousy experiences with their fathers often replaced them with equally difficult boyfriends or husbands. In fact, it was usually expected that women should remain in heterosexual relationships even if they preferred being with women. There are at least five reasons why this is not necessarily the case anymore:

1. Mothers used to teach their daughters that it was hugely important to marry a man and have his children. This is not as true as it used to be. 2. Appealing lesbian role models used to be few and far between. There now exists a group of very appealing, successful, high-profile lesbian role models in sports, business, rock 'n' roll, and entertainment. 3. It is now acceptable for lesbian couples to have children by artificial insemination, spawning a whole new market for turkey basters. 4. It is now the height of academic chic for angst-filled coeds to have lesbian affairs at schools other than just Brown and Yale. 5. Straight women get no respect at the Dinah Shore Golf Classic.

Mistaken Identity?

Women in our society can hug, hold hands or dance together and it is not considered a sign of homosexuality. As a result, they can have homosexual feelings without acknowledging them as that. The following statements by two lesbians help describe how this lack of labeling can impact female homosexual thought, from *Women's Sexual Development*, edited by Martha Kirkpatrick, (New York: International Universities Press):

> "I never thought of homosexual as relating to women, only to men...."

> "Our sexual relationship we kept to ourselves, and I was more excited about it than anything else. I thought it was just a delicious secret. And at the same time I had a mad crush on a guy."

Avoiding a label of straight or gay seems like a refreshing idea in this current age when one's sexuality is considered part of the community agenda. On the other hand, there are times when it is important for people who are gay to band together en masse, especially when their civil rights are endangered.

Lambs & the Biology of Sexual Orientation

Much has been written in the past few years about how sexual orientation might result from biological factors. For instance, researchers have injected sheep with hormones that cause male-type behaviors. The female offspring of these sheep turned out to be stud-muffin lambs who displayed so many stereotypical male behaviors that the other sheep treated them like males. These lady lambs even mounted other females, giving rise to speculation that lesbian lambs had been created by the injection of maleness-inducing hormones.

Other researchers are claiming that there are differences in certain structures of human brains which they believe cause homosexuality. Stories like these tend to make headlines, yet there are plenty of researchers who say that we still have a long way to go before anyone will be able to demonstrate that homosexuality in humans has a strictly biological origin.

The sad thing about these studies is the way some people use them as an excuse for being gay, e.g., "My son had no choice about being gay." Does one need an excuse for his or her sexual orientation? Whose business is it anyway?

When it comes to needing excuses, the vast majority of serious crimes in this country—from violent attacks and child molestation to bank fraud and illegal drug importation—are committed by heterosexual males. If anyone needs excuses, it's the straight males who commit these crimes and the parents who raised them.

Chapter Notes: Are you a straight woman in love with a gay male? The best advice ever written on this subject can be found in Cynthia Heimel's wonderful book *Sex Tips for Girls*. There are also books for when your husband comes out of the closet. These are listed in the resources part of our website: www.goofyfootpress.com. We know of no books for husbands whose wives come out of the closet, although there are plenty of flabbergasted men who could use one.

I Knew the Bride—
Long-Term Relationships
Chapter 28

This chapter is about marriage and long-term relationships. It doesn't pretend to be comprehensive, but it does speak about weddings, tradition, sex in marriage, fights, kids and divorce.

I Knew the Bride

I can see her now in her tight blue jeans
Pumping all her money in the record machine
Spinning like a top, you should have seen her go
I knew the bride when she used to rock 'n' roll

"I Knew the Bride" performed by Dave Edmunds, written by
Nick Lowe, Anglo Rock, Inc./USA, RockMusic Co. LTD/The World

One of the fun things about weddings is watching the white-laced bride taking her vows of marital bliss and wondering if she has ever handcuffed the groom and done some of the outrageously nasty things to him that she once did to you. The memory puts a smile on your face and maybe even makes you blush. But it's not the kind of question you ask as you are working your way through the reception line—not with everyone's parents standing there with an array of cold, clammy hands hanging out of pastel gowns and rented tuxedos waiting to shake yours.

Weddings—What's Love Got to Do with Them?

You don't have to go much farther than the average magazine rack to realize that weddings are big business. Plump, glossy zines with names like *Modern Bride* nearly bite your arm off as you walk by. The ads in these magazines reflect the many segments of our society that thrive on marriage-related businesses — bridal-wear shops, tuxedo rental centers, wedding gift registries, boutiques, kitchen appliance stores, caterers, florists, bakers, wedding coordinators, ministers, priests, rabbis, justices of the peace, churches, synagogues, reception halls, hotels, resorts, diet plans, etc.

In our society, traditions like marriage (and Christmas) have become an economic spectacle rather than a symbol of love and commitment. Today's marriages are so choreographed that you seldom get a feeling that two people are making a promise to be there for each other no matter what, to be inseparable partners on the great rock climb of life. Instead, what you often get is the all-too-familiar bride-to-be psychosis, where the future bride and her mother become so savagely obsessed about things like table centerpieces and bridal gowns that any sense of love and devotion is pretty much out the window.

What if couples put as much effort into improving the level of intimacy and fun in their relationship as they do into selecting wedding invitations? And what about those bizarre, adolescent feeding frenzies known as bachelor parties? If guys need to see high-priced women getting naked or want to lick whipping cream off silicone-filled breasts, why not just do it? Why use weddings as the excuse?

Marriage is a big step, an important step. Hopefully you won't get caught up in our culture's expectation of marriage as a generator of crippling debt, and will instead work to make your union a safe haven in a world that is sometimes anything but.

And what if couples took the money they spent on weddings and set it aside for one long weekend each and every month, just to be with each other and have fun? No cell phones, no pager, no work, just an extended three-day weekend each and every month.

Sex after Marriage

Studies show that within a year of saying "I do," most couples start saying "I don't want to." A recent study by Call, Sprecher and Schwartz investigated factors that influence levels of sexual activity in marriage. Contrary to what they expected to find, the authors state:

> Couples who want to make time for sex do, even with the obstacles of schedules, fatigue and work-related emotional complications. The DINS dilemma (double income,

no sex) may be a myth.

The authors of this well-designed study about sex in marriage suggest that one reason why sex declines within a year after the wedding is because marriage makes sex legitimate. This might cause it to lose some of its erotic edge. It also seems that once the wedding ring is welded to the finger, people are less inclined to use sex to help make things better.

Styles of Problem Solving

Besides feeling love and friendship for each other, an important ingredient in keeping a relationship happy is a couple's ability to solve conflicts. Couples with a knack for problem solving tend to have happier marriages. (Duh...)

Such couples approach conflicts with a willingness to talk things over and work them out, and we are sure that such couples exist. Somewhere. The rest of us occasionally resort to sarcasm, name-calling, stubbornness, making threats, automatically giving in, taking blame needlessly, becoming silent or pretending that there is no conflict when all hell is about to break loose.

Contrary to what you may have heard about the value of releasing anger, trying to resolve a conflict when you are still fuming at each other is not always productive. Sometimes it is best to wait until cooler heads prevail. Of course, some people will use this as an excuse to avoid confronting a partner altogether. Then nothing ever gets worked out.

The Good, Bad & Ugly

When you enter into a marriage or long-term relationship, the chances are good that you will discover hidden but wonderful aspects of your partner's character. Cherish, respect and admire these. To deal with the less fortunate parts of your sweetheart's character, consider the following:

1. Learn how to fight constructively. This means that no matter how nasty or unpleasant your fights might be, try to keep them issue-oriented so you can work your way toward a solution or compromise. This is quite different from fights that revert to name-calling or rehashing past hurts. These accomplish little, except to degrade whatever dignity you once may have had.

2. Fighting is preferable to indifference, unless you are getting violent.

3. Every once in a while, when you feel like wringing your partner's neck, do something really nice for him or her. This could end up being far more satisfying than fighting, and it might even get you laid.

WE SOMETIMES FORGET ABOUT THE POTENTIAL OF SEX TO CREATE NEW LIFE, SUSTAIN LOVE AND OFFER HOPE.

The illustration above was in the first edition of this book. But some people got all worked up over the notion that the couple might be doing the nasty while holding junior, so we now include this revision in addition to the original.

4. Instead of blaming your partner for things that are going wrong or wishing that he or she would somehow change, try to eliminate ways that you might be setting your partner up to be the bad guy. Also try to make changes that will help you to be a better or more effective person. This doesn't mean that you should stay in a relationship that's no longer working, it just means that the things you control most in a relationship are those that you put into it. If your efforts to change yourself don't inspire changes in your partner, then there's not much more you can do.

Birds of a Feather Get Bored with Each Other

Long-term relationships can sometimes be a challenge to keep fresh and vital unless both partners make a constant effort to enjoy each other.

For instance, think about all the extra things you did to impress each other when you first met; you probably even cut your toenails or trimmed your bikini line. Why would there be any less need for romance and wooing after you've known each other for hundreds of years? If anything, mature relationships require more rather than less effort at romance and improvement—from cards, flowers and special dates to extra attempts at tenderness and even reading books like this.

Single vs. Hitched

Being single makes it easier to maintain the illusion that you are a perfect human being. Long-term relationships force you to confront parts of yourself that many of us would rather not. For instance, in a long-term relationship, your husband or wife will probably get fed up with your worst faults and remind you of them at least six times a day. If you are the rigid type who is incapable of change and compromise, then you might not be well-suited for marriage. On the other hand, a reader from San Francisco comments, "It could be just what you need."

Sex after a Fight

Fights leave most couples worn out or sad. However, some couples enjoy sex after a good fight, given how their neurotransmitters are already fired up and ready for action. On a biological level, the body might confuse a fight with sexual excitement, thus eliminating the need for tender preliminaries. Hopefully, the reasons for the fight have been resolved and the sex isn't simply being used as a coverup.

Your Partner's Bad Moods

Like colds and flu, occasional bad moods are part of the human condition. In better-functioning relationships, the partner who is in the good mood is sometimes able to maintain a healthy perspective when confronted with a partner's bad mood. He or she might even take steps that will help the other's bad mood to go away. But in difficult relationships, all bets are off.

In a difficult relationship, the partner who is in a good mood experiences the other's bad mood as a personal attack, even if it has nothing to do with him or her. Attempts to help are often filled with so much anxiety that they only make matters worse, and the partner in the bad mood might lash out at the other just for the heck of it. (Why not be nasty to the person you love? After all, no one else would put up with you.)

Such couples usually do better if one spouse has a job that keeps him or her on the road for long periods of time.

Sex After the Baby Arrives

Our society doesn't provide many role models for caring parents who are also sexual beings. We sometimes separate the two roles entirely, as though being a good mom or dad precludes your giving great head or loving the feel of your partner's naked body next to your own. Just identifying as a parent may make you feel less sexual than you really are. Hopefully you will take the time to talk this over with your partner before having children, as well as after. There is no reason why you can't be great parents and have great sex—although the latter might not be as spontaneous as it was before the children arrived. A married reader comments: "We had lots of sex during nap time and *Sesame Street.*"

Also, never discount the extent to which exhaustion might erode the desire to have sex, and don't expect to have sex if you aren't doing your fair share of the child care and housework. While you've probably never considered vacuuming and taking the garbage out to be romantic acts, good luck getting laid without doing these sorts of things once the new baby arrives. One reader who is a prostitute adds, "And for heaven's sake, buy a diaper service before you spend the money on a prostitute."

Divorce & Your Children

Don't assume that kids automatically do better if their parents stay together. While some children feel a terrible sadness when their parents get divorced, others feel relief. It usually depends on how bad the marriage was, how bad the divorce is and whether the kid gets to live with his or her favorite parent, if there is one. The absolute worst arrangement for most children is spending half of a week or a month at one parent's house, and half at the other. This is the psychological equivalent of cutting the baby in two.

What often destroys kids more than the actual divorce is the parental lunacy for years before and years after. In an emotional sense, children of divorce often end up having no parents at all because their parents are sad, joyless, hateful or frightening to be with. If you are getting a divorce, do what you can to reach through your own pain, remembering that children need to see at least some form of hope reflected in their parents' eyes. And remember that your child's psychological health will in large part be determined by how amicably you and your former spouse are able to co-parent when divorced. It is not possible to emphasize this point too much.

Dear Paul,

Friends set me up with a wonderful woman and we've hit it off really well. We have had sex four times and are building a caring relationship. Unfortunately, I went to her place for the first time last night. *(Before that, we'd always gone to mine.) Her bathroom looked like it hadn't been cleaned for a year, and some kind of alien life form was growing from the tile in her shower. She appears clean and neat, but this is another side of her that's scary. Just so you'll know, I've never been a neat freak, and don't even buy antibacterial soap. What do I do?*

Tyrone in Jackson Hole

Dear Tyrone,

Your letter would have gone straight into the wastebasket if you hadn't mentioned the slimy ooze growing from the grout in your girlfriend's shower.

Let me tell you a story about Bill and Nancy, a couple whom I feel proud and honored to have known for more than ten years. Their house has always been immaculate—I'm talking serious sparkle. Even the litter box smells clean. One night a few years ago, we'd been having way too much wine and I mentioned how impressed I was with Nancy's ability to keep such a clean house. At that point, Bill started hyperventilating and nearly bled from the ears. He told me about the first time he went into Nancy's bathroom when they were grad students at the University of Chicago. It took him five hours of scrubbing and several gallons of bleach before he could reach terra firma on her shower floor.

My point, Tyrone, is the way your lover keeps her bathroom doesn't need to be a deal breaker. What's important is the way you and she handle the situation. For instance, if you say nothing and continue to ignore her wanton disregard for the Good House-keeping Seal of Approval, then I'd say your relationship is in trouble. Likewise, if she is unable to handle your spending half of next Sunday scrubbing her bathroom, your relationship is also in trouble. But if you clean her bathroom and don't make her feel bad about it, and she returns the favor with the finest blow job you've ever received in your entire life, then I think you're onto something good.

Chapter Notes: Special thanks to the Rosewoman, Daphne Kingma, for thoughts on divorce. Ms. Kingma has written many books on all aspects of relationships, from the rise to the fall. And thanks to researchers Michael Metz et al. for specifics on conflict resolution.

Sex & Sects
Chapter 29

Religion can be a way of making sense out of a world that sometimes seems overwhelming. It can give focus, meaning and hope to a life that might otherwise have none. It can encourage belief in something other than yourself.

Religion can also be used as a force of oppression. Perhaps that's why so many people refer to their personal beliefs as spiritual rather than religious. This allows them to believe in something greater than themselves without endorsing the capriciousness and greed that have characterized so many organized religions throughout history.

Sex

It's interesting how some religious leaders obsess more about sex than even people who run adult bookstores.

It is sometimes helpful to remember that what these religious leaders call "the word of God" is actually the word of man. For instance, the Koran states that women need to dress modestly in public. But it is a human religious leader who decided that "modestly" means covered from head to toe.

As it turns out, interpreting religious scripture is a lot like interpreting the Constitution of the United States. It is generally done by a small group of males who have won positions of power and title. They often claim that God is speaking through them.

Guns, Dollars & Faith

It doesn't matter if you are a Christian, atheist, Moslem or Jew, we live in a country that was founded with a Bible in one hand and a firearm in the other. As a result, many of our society's values are rooted in a rather strange combination of gunpowder and holy scripture. Faith is important, but it never hurts to have a Smith & Wesson handy...

If you believe that religion has no influence over your daily life, grab your purse, wallet or conk your piggy bank over the head. Pull out any form of U.S. currency, from a penny to a hundred dollar bill. Each piece of money bears two four-word phrases. One is "United States Of America." Check out the other.

The Bible

There is no question that the Bible has much wisdom to offer. Take, for instance, the passage from Luke that reminds us how easy it is to love those who love us, but how important to love those who don't. And what about the story of the poor fellow who is mugged and left for dead. A priest passes by and does not help, nor does a man from a blue-blood religious family. (They are probably on their way to church.) Finally, a traveler from a much-maligned country stops to offer aid. And that's how we got the story of the Good Samaritan. The Bible abounds with many thought-provoking passages, including Matthew 18:23-35, which presents much wisdom about fairness and debt.

In addition to the many good things that it offers, the Bible is often blatantly unfair to women. Why does the Bible have such awful things to say about women and sex?

Virgins & Prostitutes

In the reference classic called *Butler's Lives of the Saints*, the name of each saint is written in bold black ink. Next to the names of the women saints is the additional inscription "virgin" or "widow." The sexual status of the male saints is not listed. It is fortunate for men like St. Paul and St. Augustine that women saints were the only ones who had to account for their personal sexual histories.

It is also interesting that the majority of women mentioned in the New Testament are either virgins or prostitutes. There was little room for virtuous women who enjoyed sex, nor was there room for women to become priests, preachers or popes.

It seems that the Bible as we know it had many different sources. Some had more to do with war, politics and real estate than religious salvation. For instance, the Bible's account of the

Mayhem in the Garden. The beginning of the end.

creation goes out of its way to portray Eve as a total bimbo who cavorts with the wily snake and leads Adam into sin via the fruit-tree fiasco, thereby blowing the gig in the garden. This is the kind of story you might create if you were trying to discredit outlying tribes who believe in female gods.

Sex & the New Testament

The New Testament shows Jesus of Nazareth accepting women and speaking to them in a way that shocked some of his contemporaries. Yet if Jesus did show a loving acceptance toward women, some of his followers failed to notice. Even Mary, mother of Jesus, wasn't considered a major player in church dogma until the 11th to 14th centuries, when a romantic wave of sentimentality toward women forced the church fathers to significantly upgrade her role. And during the early years of Christianity, the church forbade husbands and wives to enjoy sexual pleasure. For instance, St. Augustine proclaimed that husbands and wives were no different from pigs and geese unless they abstained from sex. Also, the church administered more punishment for oral sex than for premeditated murder, and a virgin daughter was accorded a higher place in heaven than her mother because the mother had to have intercourse for conception to take place.

Fortunately, some modern religions, both Christian and Jewish, are moving away from their early anti-woman and anti-sex biases. However...

Women Are Subservient to Men,
& Masturbation Is Really, Really Bad

You think certain thresholds have been crossed and then the Southern Baptists let us know that this modernization thing is out of hand. They've just announced that men are the head of the household, and that is that. Now word has it that they are taking their message into Utah, trying to convert Mormons, who are having their own little fuss over the legalization of polygamy.

But that's nothing compared to the most recent Catholic catechism for junior high students. Published within the last few years, it states in no uncertain terms that masturbation is bad.

Really, really bad. Statute-wise, the Catholics have placed jerking off somewhere between shooting heroin and grand theft. (Is it double jeopardy if you masturbate into a condom?)

Bad Acts & Queer Angels

Religious leaders have often ranted and railed against certain sexual practices, from masturbation and oral sex to homosexuality, as though these acts were the handiwork of the devil. But what if God feels more honored when a person joyfully masturbates than when he or she says a speedy rosary or spends an obligatory hour in church? After all, God created orgasm, while prayers and churches are the creations of men. What if God receives more joy when an unmarried couple lovingly shares oral sex than when a church-going husband and wife have passionless, missionary-position intercourse? And who is to say that God hasn't created a group of homosexual angels to guard the gates of heaven? Maybe God has a sense of humor and brings out the queer angels when-ever a redneck preacher or one of his intolerant parishioners has just died and is awaiting judgment.

Kindness & Warmth

The most important thing that this guide has to say about religion is something remembered from childhood:

> There is sometimes a priest, minister or rabbi whom the children feel safe with and to whom they will tell the truth. To the other clerics they withhold or lie. Perhaps children are aware of something that we adults forget—that what's needed from spiritual leaders is warmth, kindness and understanding rather than the propensity to judge, preach and chastise.

As adults, we often forget how contagious kindness and warmth can be. In so doing, we forget the essence of God.

Chapter Notes: There are interesting similarities between the Bible's Eve and Greek mythology's Pandora. The Mormons have a different take on the apple-biting incident in The Garden. They believe that Eve did us all a big favor by pursuing knowledge. Of course, this is not to imply that the Mormon church is the Rome of feminist thinking. Carl Jung's "Answer to Job" provides a captivating exploration of the Yahweh of old. The so-called pagans who worshiped a male and female god also practiced human sacrifice. While not such an inviting practice from a public relations point of view, it is hard to believe that the number of human lives lost in this way was even a fraction of those lost in the religious wars that have dominated the globe since the Yahwehs seized power. There may have been a translation error involving the early Greek, Latin and Aramaic languages; the expression for "young woman" may have been confused with the term "virgin," perhaps explaining some of the Bible's jones for virgins. Also, the notion of the Assumption didn't exist until a church council in the mid-1800s decided to invent it. Readers who are interested would do well to consult Bishop Spong's books on the Bible. They are very readable, thought-provoking and are published by Harper/San Francisco. Thanks to Elizabeth Berlese for spurring memories about warmth and kindness, to Presbytera Donna Pappas for mentioning how people often refer to themselves as spiritual rather than religious, to Carol Tavris for the Muslim "head to toe" example, to Robert VanSweden on the Mormons and Eve, and to the writings of David Schnarch and Paul Evdokimov. Evdokimov's writings were suggested by Father Andrew Barakos. Because these people are being thanked does not mean that they necessarily agree with the perspective of this chapter.

Culture & Kink
Chapter 30

On the surface, it seems that men in our society are more into kink than women. But maybe that's because we define kink differently for men than for women. For instance, a woman who wears her boyfriend's boxers or briefs is at the height of fashion, but if he wears her underwear we consider him to be weird. Our society relishes her kink, but gets very uncomfortable with his.

In our society women touch each other at will. However, if men were to touch each other with half the frequency that women do, they would be called queer. Once again, our culture labels men as being strange for something that women do all the time. In our society, most male-to-male touching is limited to handshakes and contact sports—which may be a reason why men feel such an affinity for football. For a guy to experience much physical contact with another guy, he needs to be a jock, a homosexual or both.

There are plenty of other things that are considered kinky when only men do them. For instance, a woman who routinely undresses in front of an open window is thought to be a neighborhood resource. Double that for a woman who plays with herself with the window shades up. But a guy who does these things is considered to be a pervert and may even be locked up. There is also the biological fact that some women can masturbate without being noticed. Guys can't masturbate with that kind of subtlety. The occasional male who gets himself off in a public place is at much greater risk of being caught and labeled a pervert than the occasional female who does the same thing. One reader comments, "Not only is he labeled a pervert, but if convicted he would be forced to register as a sex offender."

Bondage Lite

The United States was originally settled by a group of religious outcasts, malcontents, criminals and slaves—the fact that we're not all into some form of bondage is a little amazing.

Bondage is the application of restraint, pain or humiliation in a way that some people find erotic or satisfying. One form of bondage includes having your arms or feet tied together while being kissed, tickled, caressed or otherwise made love to. In parts of Los Angeles, New York and Chicago this type of activity isn't considered bondage, but merely good bedroom technique.

Those who are into light bondage often enjoy it because they are rendered passive and have no choice but to totally enjoy what a partner is doing to them. They don't have to worry about being a "good" sex partner who provides pleasure in return. Performance anxiety is virtually eliminated.

If you are into light bondage, be aware that scarves and ties form tight knots that are hard to undo; wrists and ankles can be permanently damaged. Bondage enthusiast William Henkin says that professionally made cuffs may seem expensive to couples who simply like to tickle and spank, but they are much safer than the restraints that people improvise at home. In the event that professionally made cuffs aren't available on your TV's Home Shopping Network, check with places like Good Vibrations, Blowfish or The Pleasure Chest.

Painful Contradictions

You don't have to be into bondage or S&M to appreciate the following social ridiculousness: here in America parents can spank a child and it is not called bondage or sadism. Yet fully consenting adults who spank each other are ostracized and even considered morally corrupt.

Spanking is a form of sexual kink that can be considered either light or heavy bondage, depending upon how it's done. For instance, some participants like their spanking hard and with a hostile edge, while others enjoy a little spank here and there when highly aroused.

Why do some adults enjoy spanking or being spanked? One theory states that people sometimes sexualize their childhood shame or humiliation. Turning it into erotic sensation helps it to become more bearable. They might even secretly identify with the person who is spanking them, feeling a sense of power, although within the sexual scene, they are the ones who are powerless.

Another reason why some people enjoy an occasional swat on the rear is because they find that it feels good, as long as they are sexually aroused when it's done and it is their own personal choice to be in the situation.

Bondage by Choice—A Feminist Contradiction?

People who are feminists or socially progressive (whatever that might mean) sometimes feel that they are deserting their own cause if they enjoy submission or S&M fantasies. For instance, consider a feminist lawyer whose favorite fantasy is being tied up and sexually violated. She occasionally acts out this fantasy with her male lover. Does this contradict her political beliefs? Not really, since the relevant issue is the freedom to choose rather than what's being chosen.

The lady lawyer believes that each person should be able to choose what to do with his or her own sexuality. In acting out her bondage fantasy with her lover, this woman chooses to give up her position of equality, as well as chooses the man whom she wants to give it up to. In the criminal rape cases that she handles in court, the rape victim had no choice. The act was forced upon her, rather than being part of a shared fantasy between two consenting adults.

Note: The term "feminist" no longer has the meaning that it once did and is currently rife with contradiction. For instance, some feminists are opposed to pornography and feel it demeans women, while other feminists believe that women should be proud of their bodies and free to display them sexually if that's what they want to do. Some feminists hate men, others don't; some embrace lesbianism, others are alienated by feminist groups who are more concerned with lesbian issues than with those of straight working moms. Some feminists think that intercourse is a form of oppression that women have been brainwashed into having by the patriarchy (straight white guys). Other feminists view intercourse as a satisfying activity where a vagina is as active and powerful as a penis. Some feminists consider motherhood to be a form of slavery for women, while others welcome motherhood. In fact, most women in this day and age describe themselves as being feminists, regardless of their political, social or religious views.

Heavy Bondage—A Little Like Life?

Heavy bondage (B&D, D&S, S&M, BDSM) can get fairly brutal. It can be a world of whips and chains and devices that might even put a chill up the spine of the average PE teacher. When it comes to heavy bondage, the only comment this guide knows that even comes close is "Toto, I have a feeling we're not in Kansas anymore." (B&D = bondage and discipline; S&M = sado masochism; D&S = dominance and submission; BDSM is a blanket term for all of it.)

In heavy bondage, having an orgasm isn't nearly as important as the bondage scene itself, with its undercurrent of domination, submission and sometimes humiliation. People into heavy bondage process pain differently than people who aren't. Bondage lovers find serious doses of sexual pain to be invigorating and intimate. They speak about sexual pain with the same kind of clarity and relish as religious pilgrims who are describing a visit to a holy shrine or the Dalai Lama.

People into heavy bondage tend to be very serious about their kink. In fact, there are even well-established bondage clubs like the Portland Power and Trust, the Chicago Hellfire Club, Bound and Determined in Massachusetts, the Society of Janus in San Francisco (www.soj.org), the Arizona Power Exchange, and Leather and Lace in the City of the Angels.

There are mainstream bondage publications like *Domination-Submission*, *Dungeon Master* (which probably takes the prize for being the *Boy's Life* of kink), and *Prometheus: the Quarterly of the Eulenspiegel Society*. There are numerous magazines on latex fashion. There are also bondage reference guides like *The Leatherman's Handbook* and *The Lesbian S/M Safety Manual*—cross their hearts and hope to be humiliated. Several bondage references are included in the Resources area of our website, www.goofyfootpress.com—from beginner books to videotapes on corsetry.

If you have an irrepressible need to get into heavy bondage, please consider the following advice: don't pick up a stranger who enjoys beating the crap out of people and confuse that with bondage, even if you are a woman who loves too much. In heavy bondage there are established rules and etiquette that keep the participants from getting seriously hurt. Mind you, the definition of seriously hurt is a personal matter. If heavy bondage is what turns you on, learn the rules and make sure that your partner knows and respects them.

Even if you aren't into bondage, don't get roped into thinking that mild-mannered people prefer being bottoms (slave role) and that aggressive types prefer being tops (master/dominator/dominatrix). There are plenty of business executives, lawyers, doctors, politicians, policeman and even East Coast publishing types who prefer being on the bottom when it comes to sexual kink. In fact, it's a problem in the bondage community that a good top is hard to find. It's also true that a number of people into S&M enjoy alternating roles between top and bottom. They are called "switches."

Lite or Heavy Bondage—Safety Considerations

No matter if you only use bondage once a year or are a full-fledged bondage brute, the S&M book by author Jay Wiseman titled *SM-101* (San Francisco: Greenery Press) makes the following suggestions:

🐑 Anytime a body part that is tied up feels numb or goes to sleep, untie it immediately. And never tie anything around a partner's neck.

🐑 In anticipation of catastrophes like fires, earthquakes or an unexpected visit from your mom and dad, be sure that you have a flashlight and pair of heavy scissors handy. *SM-101* recommends paramedic scissors, which can be found at medical supply stores. They cut through almost anything except handcuffs. Keep the scissors and flashlights in a place that you can readily find in the dark. Ditto for the handcuff key if that's what you are using.

🐑 Never leave the person for long, and check them often. If any injuries were to occur, you would be legally and morally responsible.

🐑 Always establish a safe word which means to stop. Some people use "red" for stop and "yellow" for easing up a little. No one who is seriously into dominance and submission uses "stop," "don't," or "no more" for safe words, since any good bottom says them often but doesn't mean them one little bit.

Fetishes: An Overview

Several years ago, a singer named Randy Newman wrote a song whose lyrics entreat his lover to take off all her clothes, except her hat. If Mr. Newman couldn't enjoy sex unless the woman had a hat on, then we might say he had a hat fetish. The Glossary at the end of this book offers the following definition of fetish:

Is this activity:

a. fun
b. a fetish
c. both
d. who cares?

This wouldn't be considered a fetish if it's something you enjoy doing but can also do without. Psychologists would call it a fetish if the man couldn't become aroused without seeing or touching the woman's feet, or if her pantyhose were so important to him that he needed them rather than her to become sexually excited. How do psychologists know? Because they're as strange as everyone else.

FETISH—1. Reliance on a prop, body part, scene or scenario in order to get off sexually. 2. The prop can either be fantasized or exist in actuality. 3. One philosopher has described "fetish" as being similar to when a hungry person sits down at a dinner table and feels full from simply fondling the napkin.

If both people in a relationship enjoy a particular fetish, then acting out the fetish will be a welcome event. But if only one partner is into the fetish, the other partner might feel that she or he is not nearly as important as the fetish itself. For instance, if the woman in the above-mentioned song loves wearing her hat while otherwise naked, then she has found the perfect man. Otherwise, she may start to feel like a human hatrack.

Fetishes, Specifics

Fetishes come in many different forms; some include objects, others include actions that need to be repeated over and over. What follows are two examples where dirty words and cross-dressing might be considered fetishes:

Talk Dirty to Me Some couples enjoy saying dirty things while having sex. But what if one partner can't perform sexually without hearing the dirty words? This takes it beyond simple sex play and hints of a fetish, especially if the other partner feels stupid screeching things like, "Fuck me harder, fuck me harder, you big stud, Mama wants it all," or degrading things like, "You miserable, worthless little turd." Particularly troublesome are situations where the partner with the fetish needs to say degrading things to you, unless of course, you find something endearing about being called a smelly old cow, fat whore, or pencil-dicked imbecile.

What a Drag... Some women occasionally dress up like men, to the point of wearing a fake penis. This is a form of accessorizing known as "packing." One woman reports that if she's been packing for an extended amount of time she even stops having her period—without taking a single male hormone. Once she is through packing and the fingernail polish goes back on, her periods become regular again. Some men feel a powerful need to dress like women, aka "transvestism" or "crossdressing." This might be fine with the guy's wife or girlfriend. However, problems could arise if he keeps stealing her favorite bra and panties to wear under his suit whenever his law firm assigns him to handle a high-profile case. (Crossdressing is discussed more fully at the end of this chapter.)

It is interesting how, in our culture, men with certain conflicts might deal with them one way while women sometimes give them a different spin. For instance, more men probably have foot fetishes than women, yet more women obsess about shoes and spend far more hours shopping for them than men. An obvious and time-honored solution is for men with foot fetishes to work in women's shoe stores!

People with fetishes usually love them immensely and resist giving them up. Therapy is seldom effective in loosening the love for a fetish. As long as the partner is fine with the fetish and it causes no harm to others, there seems to be little reason for abandoning it. On the other hand, if it violates criminal statutes and the wishes of others (e.g., flashing or being a Peeping Tom), or it introduces a level of weirdness that the partner won't tolerate, then the person doing it will face sad and serious consequences.

Piercing & Tattoos — On Pins & Needles

Is getting tattooed a sexual thing? Who knows. It sure is popular these days, especially among women who are sporting little butterflies, flowers and the like in highly private places.

Piercing, like tattooing, has been around for a long, long time. Women have traditionally had their ears pierced, as have various pirates and sailors who have sailed the seven seas. Nowadays everybody seems to be getting into the act, although the recent male ear-piercing craze appears to be slowing.

In a highly sexualized version of piercing, body parts like noses, navels, nipples and genitals are potential sites. People who are seriously into piercing will stick rings or posts through just about anything. Some do it for sport; others experience it as a personal or even religious high. If you are into this kind of thing, be sure to have it done at a well-known establishment with a solid reputation. Not enough can be said for sterile technique and skill on the part of the piercer, as infections and botched insertions tend to be common. There is also a fair amount of wisdom involved in selecting the proper ring or post for specific body parts, given how those that are too thin eventually pull out.

Some people say that getting nipples pierced hurts more than having genitals done; others disagree. One woman who sports gold rings along the sides of her labia says that the jewelry dresses up her genitals and makes her like them even more. Another woman who has had her clitoris pierced loves the new sensations and claims that just sitting down can sometimes give her an orgasm. Other women who have had their genitals pierced aren't as enthusiastic. Also, less than one in three women has a clitoris that's plump enough for a bull's eye insertion.

Women who are planning to have their nipples pierced should inquire about the kind of fabrics they will be able to wear. For instance, how will your nipple rings look under a conservative business suit? Lacy bras will probably be out, since the ring will constantly catch in the lacy material. Ditto for what kinds of shirts you will be able to wear to work. Concerns about underwear fabric also apply to labia and clitoral piercing.

As for male genitals, the head of the penis can be skewered in several different ways, and earrings can be placed anywhere from the bottom of the testicles to the tip of the foreskin. Pain in the piercing site can last for months.

Ah, life in the big city.

Vaginal Fisting (Handballing)

Vaginal fisting is finger fucking times five, and then some. This guide first became aware of the concept when reviewing lesbian tapes produced by and for women. It seems that some women enjoy having a partner's fist inside their vagina.

The trouble is, that kind of fisting is usually being done by women for women. This is an important distinction, since most women have significantly smaller fists than men. A fist the size of a man's could take a potentially pleasurable experience and turn it into something akin to childbirth. On the other hand, a leading sex therapist has informed us that plenty of straight couples are getting a fist up.

If vaginal fisting is something you want to try, please plan far enough ahead to read a book or two that covers the subject. Greenery Press publishes *A Hand in the Bush: The Fine Art of Vaginal Fisting* by Deborah Addington, (San Francisco: Greenery Press, 1998). To order, call (888) 944-4434. This subject is also discussed in the *Good Vibrations Guide to Sex* by Anne Semans and Cathy Winks (San Francisco: Cleis Press, 1998). We will try to include other resources on our internet site as we hear about them. Enter "vaginal fisting" in the Goofy Search Engine of www.goofyfootpress.com.

Please check with a gynecologist before attempting any kind of fisting, and in no instance should you proceed if you experience anything but the slightest amount of pain. Perhaps you can find the name of a physician or nurse practitioner who is familiar with fisting through a gay and lesbian health center, since your local HMO might not be particularly well versed in the practice, or not willing to admit it, anyway. You should never attempt fisting if either of you has been drinking or doing drugs, and you certainly shouldn't try it before reading the advice of women who do it.

Anal Fisting

Some couples, straight as well as gay, are into anal fisting. You shouldn't even think about trying this unless you really, really, really know what you are doing. Technically, this act is possible without causing irreparable damage, since surgeons occasionally stick an entire hand up a person's rectum. On the other hand, receiving an entire fist up the bum requires the kind of relaxation that is beyond the capacity of the average asshole.

Couples into anal fisting often recommend a book on the subject by Bert Herrman, *Trust—The Hand Book* (San Francisco: Alamo Square Press, 1991). At the very least, consult with your family physician before attempting anal fisting. "Hello, Dr. Welby... You have? Really? Lots of lube?"

Healthcare for Those into Kink

Minutes before presstime, we became aware of a recently published book by Charles Moser, Ph.D., M.D., titled *Health Care Without Shame—A Handbook for the Sexually Diverse and Their Caregivers* (San Francisco: Greenery Press, 1999). It's cheap and should probably be on the bookshelf of anyone who enjoys alternative sex. To order, call (888) 944-4434 or write to Greenery Press, 1447 Park St., Emeryville, CA 94608.

Also, check out the health section at www.bdsmtalk.com, and try Kink Awareness Professionals at www.bannon.com/kap/. These addresses may have changed, so we keep an update on our website, www.goofyfootpress.com.

Dear Paul,

Do you have any advice about going to a dominatrix?

Policeman by Day
Schoolboy by Night

Dear Officer,

When you visit a dominatrix you are engaging someone who will help you act out certain sexual fantasies. The fantasies often have to do with power. For instance, you enjoy being a policeman and having power when you are on the job, but you also enjoy becoming a schoolboy and giving a dominatrix power over you. Each has its own time and place in your life.

To help answer your question, I called my friend Lorrett, who runs a house devoted to S&M and fantasy play. She offers the following advice:

1. B&D or S&M is about creating a fantasy scene, and then acting it out. In creating the scene, you need to talk to the person you are hiring about things like boundaries, safe words, and how you want the scene to play out. You should feel comfortable with the person, and feel that they are comfortable with you in negotiating the scene. If they come off as being abrupt or domineering when setting up the scene, then what follows isn't going to be play. Instead, you are going to be acting out their agenda, and what follows will be anything but consensual.

2. Trust your instincts. It's fine to be nervous or anxious, but if you feel frightened or uncomfortable, go elsewhere.

In domination and fantasy games, the dominatrix doesn't actually get you off. You are free to get yourself off in her presence, but she won't actually give you an orgasm the way a prostitute will. That's why it's not illegal for you to hire a dominatrix.

For reading materials, try the catalogs from Greenery Press, QSM, Daedalus Press, Alamo Square Press, and the other resources listed at the end of this chapter.

Dear Paul,

I recently had my tongue pierced. I've got a barbell type of post, with a small steel ball on each side. Do you have any suggestions on how to best use it to please a woman sexually?

Beaufort from Biloxi

Dear Beaufort,

Here is some advice from women who have slept with guys who have steel balls:

Kissing (mouth to mouth): Unless you are careful, you can bang and perhaps chip your partner's teeth. So go easy and be aware that your new tongue needs more tooth clearance than one that is less accessorized. Also, women don't seem to enjoy being kissed by guys who slobber. Having a post through your tongue may keep you from sucking the saliva from it as well as you did pre-op. Also, some women aren't crazy about having foreign objects in the back of their throat. So when you French kiss, don't stick your tongue in very far, and remember to swallow.

Nipple Play: One woman says that dragging a steel ball across her nipples can be "a bit gnarly." Assuming your partner likes to have her nipples licked or sucked, use the tip of your tongue when playing with her breasts and nipples. This will help keep the steel ball at bay. Also, a little extra saliva on her nipple may help your ball glide rather than drag. The best solution is to talk to your lover about this, with her giving you plenty of feedback.

Oral Sex: Here's where the real skill comes in, ball or no ball. It's possible to give wonderful oral sex, but only as long as you know where your ball is and what it's up to. Try flicking your tongue across the palm or back of your hand. This will help you learn to steer your ball better. The last thing you want to do is bang a steel object against a woman's tender nerve endings. You will need to flick your tongue more delicately than a guy who doesn't have a steel ball attached to the end of his. To paraphrase a woman who has dated a couple of different guys with pierced tongues, flicking a pierced tongue across a woman's vulva can feel really cool, but only if the man is extremely gentle and acutely aware of the impact that a pierced tongue has. She also cautions against probing inside a woman's vagina with a tongue that's pierced.

As for the piercing procedure, be aware that a newly pierced tongue can swell a great deal, as well as become infected. Piercing is a surgical procedure which requires the same sterile surgical technique that is used in hospitals. It's best if done by an experienced hand with good references. Learn about the physical risks and care requirements before having any body part pierced, think about it for a couple of weeks or months first and plan accordingly. It's not the sort of thing to do on the spur of the moment.

Dear Paul,

My boyfriend loves to feel my legs when I have pantyhose on. He's a really sweet guy and I enjoy the extra attention, but my friend says it's a "fetish." What do you think?

Penny from Paducah

Dear Penny,

From the sounds of it, I'm not hearing fetish, or at least it's not screaming at me. But what is a fetish? Let's say your boyfriend can't become aroused unless you are wearing pantyhose or maybe he gets off more and more by your pantyhose and you feel like a mannequin. Rather than being an erotic accessory that helps to spice things up, the pantyhose become way too important. That's when you're talking a full-blown fetish.

Some people have fetishes for certain objects or materials like leather, rubber, latex, underwear, shoes, socks, boots, smelly feet, hair, breasts and even diapers. Honest, there are websites with adults wearing diapers, and not because they need to.

Other people with fetishes have certain scenarios or fantasies that get them off, e.g., the guy who likes his partner to pee or shit on him (aka golden showers and scat or brown showers). Or the fetish might be as hidden and subtle as the kind of haircut his partner has. He suddenly goes bonkers if she changes it. (Ever notice how some guys only date or marry women who are the spitting image of each other? Is it the woman he's in love with, or a certain look that she has?)

People with fetishes get a kind of comfort from the fetish that they can't get from human beings. The fetish becomes the missing piece that completes their sexual circuit.

How can a pair of pantyhose, an enema or an extreme sex scene have the kind of allure that we normally find in a human partner? Maybe it's because the object a man chooses for his fetish is connected to a situation that was once overwhelming—like where a young boy was raised by four sisters and an aunt. He chooses something that symbolizes the arousing part of the situation, but unlike the original situation, it's something he can control.

He turns the fetish into a substitute sexual partner, one that could never be as demanding or potentially humiliating as a real live human—a wish that most of us can relate to at one time or another. (It's far easier to control a pair of pantyhose than to control the woman who is wearing them!) The fetish provides temporary and exciting relief for the early psychic drama.

One problem with having a serious fetish is the loneliness that can sometimes be a part of it. No matter how many times you fondle them, a pair of rubber panties or a woman's feet can only go so far in providing the kind of closeness or friendship that many of us value in a sexual partner. In fact, some people refer to the fetish as a compromise between the fear of human closeness and the need for human closeness.

Please be aware that I am a psychoanalyst and always will be. I work with people when the bottom has fallen out. I tend to see loneliness and isolation where those with fetishes see bliss and excitement. I suspect the truth lies somewhere in between.

Dear Paul,

Help! I think my husband is a cross-dresser. How can this be? Please tell me what you know about this.

Virginia from Lawrence

Dear Virginia,

There are hundreds of thousands of transvestites or male cross-dressers in the United States. Many are straight and appear quite masculine when they aren't wearing bra and panties.

Contrary to what you might imagine, male cross-dressers aren't drawn to professions that welcome a guy's feminine side. Instead, the average cross-dresser is more likely to be a baseball player, fireman, policeman, auto mechanic or business executive than a hairdresser or florist.

Most cross-dressers value their macho side as much as their feminine side, but have never found a way to enjoy both at the same time. As young boys, they usually showed traditional male behaviors. As men, they are often heterosexual, married and the last guy you'd imagine would dress up like a girl.

It is unlikely that therapy will change a cross-dresser's need to cross-dress. However, if the guy is compulsive about cross-dressing, therapy can help him control that aspect of it. Many cross-dressers hope that marriage will cure them of their desire to dress like a woman. But the envy and allure of their wife's under-wear drawer will soon rear its satin head, and so much for good intentions.

Men who are reading this book while wearing their favorite Chanel dress might be concerned about being found out. This is a fear shared by many cross-dressers who are not out of the closet. For more info, check out some of the following internet sites:

www.tri-ess.com www.tgfmall.com www.pmpub.com
www.brendat.com

As a wife or girlfriend who suddenly discovers that her man has a secret cache of frilly garb, try to give yourself a three-month chilling-off period before doing anything drastic. He must love you a great deal if he's worked so hard to hide something that he fears will disappoint you. If you can, check out the site of the Society for the Second Self or Tri-Ess at www.tri-ess.com. This national organization is for cross dressers, their wives and their families. Search out anything written by Francis Fairfax, particularly the Wives' Bill of Rights.

Given how this is not the sort of thing you can call your mom or sister about, see if there is a support group in your area for wives of cross-dressers. The folks at Tri-Ess can help you find them. Talk to these wives about what they will and won't put up with.

For instance, there are plenty of things you don't need to agree to, like meeting your man for lunch when he's dressed like Farrah Fawcet. And if for some reason he thinks he can dress up in front of the kids or gets so deep into the cross-dressing scene that he stops being a good husband or dad, cross-dressers' wives will offer all the support you need to give him what for. In other words, you don't have to condone what he's doing, but you don't need to divorce him either.

For a lot of women, it would be easier to accept their husband if he said he were gay. But to see him dressed up like Little Bo Peep and hear him say he's totally straight...

Part of your fear might be about losing the manly part of your cross-dressing man. This usually won't happen. He'll be the same man he was in bed before you knew about the heels and A-line dress. Part of your fear may have to do with humiliation that someone else will find out.

One reason why I suggest that you wait a few months before taking any action is that once the shock wears off, you might be able to see that there are far worse things a man could do than wear women's clothes, fashion crime that it might be. You might also realize that he has the same good characteristics that he had before you found out about his hidden side.

Fortunately, there is no shortage of publications on cross-dressing. Some people value the books by Peggy Rudd, a therapist and the wife of a cross-dresser. Others aren't so comfortable with her cross-dresser-as-visionary point of view. Two of the titles written by Dr. Rudd are *My Husband Wears My Clothes: Cross-dressing from the Perspective of a Wife* (PM Press, 2nd edition, 1999) and *My Husband Wears My Clothes: Cross-dressing with Dignity.* Talk about a quaint title for a series of books... Your public library may have them, but perhaps you'll want to try Amazon. Another book on cross-dressing and drag that's getting interesting press is *Girlfriend: Men, Women and Drag* by Holly Brubech and Michael Jones O'Brian (New York: Random House, 1999).

Knowledge may not make it hurt any less, but it does give you more options than simply saying goodbye.

Resources

The *Guide* is not endorsing the following resources nor is it encouraging you to try alternative forms of sexuality. We have trouble enough dealing with old-fashioned vanilla sex and are definitely not pointing anyone toward kink. If kink is what you want to explore, we would rather you explore these resources, many of which include people we know and trust, than to list no resources and have you randomly search the internet. Kink can be fun and kink can be dangerous. The wisdom and safety of what you do and how you do it are totally in your hands. If you are unable to distinguish what's safe from what's dangerous, then you have no business exploring alternative forms of sexuality.

The following includes resources that a person might explore or collect before engaging in alternative forms of sexuality.

Websites

It is always risky including websites in a book like this, considering how half of them will be history before the ink even dries. As a backstop, we keep an updated resources list on our website, www.goofyfootpress.com. So if half of these are down by the time you are up, never fear. Also, a site that is great today can easily become a spam hole tomorrow, so we offer no promises about the integrity of the sites that are listed.

www.altsex.org Helpful information about alternative sexuality, from BDSM and polyamory to transgender issues, homosexuality and safer sex.

www.bdsmtalk.com Well organized and full of useful information. Why aren't vanilla sex sites half this helpful?

www.sexuality.org Internet home of the Society for Human Sexuality. Makes Goofy Foot Press proud to have its new home in the Pacific Northwest.

www.bannon.com/kap/ Check out Kink Awareness Professionals for healthcare related issues.

www.whatsyours.com   Kink for the United Kingdom. A full-featured, link-loaded site that's hard to beat.

www.naughty.com Naughty Linx, the guide to which sex-related sites are up or down. Does have x-rated banners.

soc.sexuality.general Can handle a wide range of questions about most forms of alternative sexuality, assuming you can find it.

Publishers with catalogs to request if you want more on kink and alternative sexuality

Circlet Press   Erotic sci-fi and different kinds of books on alternative sexuality. www.circlet.com

Daedalus Press   Specializes in books on S&M and alternative sexualty. Prints *Consensual Sadomasochism* by therapists William Henkin and Sybil Holiday. (415) 626-1867 www.bannon.com

Greenery Press   Publishes a full array of books on S&M and alternative sexuality, from *Miss Abernathy's Concise Slave Training Manual* to *SM-101*. (0181) 829-3000; www.greenerypress.com

Mystic Rose Publishers   Prints *Screw the Roses, Send Me the Thorns* as well as S&M fiction and erotica. (203) 335-4330 www.mysticrose.com

QSM   Their catalog lists hundreds of books on S&M. (415) 550-7776 or www.qualitysm.com

Other resources to consider on alternative sexuality

The Black Book, 6th edition   An encyclopedia of kink-related resources, but not as thick. They also publish erotic anthologies and the humorous bi-queer sex zine "Black Sheets." (415) 431-0171; www.blackbooks.com

On Our Backs   A kink-oriented lesbian erotic magazine; for ordering info, call (877) 999-6627; www.onourbacksmag.com

Sandmutopian Guardian   A higher quality BDSM magazine and website. (516) 842-1711 or www.aswgt.com

Chapter Notes: Thanks to the writings of Chris Gosselin and Glenn Wilson for some of the ideas used in the introduction to this chapter, and to the works of Carol Queen, Cathy Winks, Anne Seamans, Bert Herrman Jay Wiseman and William Henkin, and to Lorrett at Fantasy Makers in Berkeley and Janet at Greenery Press—two of the nicest, most positive people around. (Funny how "positive" has become a negative term since the AIDS plague... This was meant in the pre-AIDS way!)

Talking to Your Partner About Sex
Chapter 31

While most of us will see angels before we'll see our teenage years again, it never hurts to look at the truly unfortunate advice that *Teen Magazine* offers its 4.4 million American girl readers about sexual matters:

> When you're French kissing, it helps to let the guy take the lead. Part your lips gently, and let him explore your mouth with his tongue.... (*Teen Magazine*, 1992, "Kissing Anxiety? Lip-to-Lip Lowdown")

Teen's smooch advice gives the impression that we guys come out of the womb knowing how to French kiss. Don't the editors of *Teen* realize that the average American male's preparation for sex is jerking off to the centerfold of whatever dirty magazine he can successfully hide from his mother's grasp? This is supposed to teach us how to French kiss, or anything else for that matter?

And why are guys always supposed to know what to do? Why aren't men and women encouraged to explore sex together, teaching each other what feels good along the way? And why are magazines like *Teen* still trying to push the tired old notion that sex is something a man does to a woman—unless she needs something from him or wants a big favor? One way to avoid being a *Teen* type of lover is by learning to talk to your partner about sex, about what feels good and what doesn't, and by exploring beyond what's familiar. Unfortunately, that's not always easy to do. That's why we've included this chapter. It starts by exploring different parts of the problem and finishes with a concrete plan of action.

Naked & Tongue-Tied

Consider the following conversation between two people who are about to have intercourse for the first time:

"Uh, should I...?"

"I guess."

"Okay, I'll put one on."

That's it. The intercourse begins. Less than ten words, most single syllables. Grunting cavemen were probably more expressive. And then there's the prolific verbal exchange at the end of the event:

"That was really good."

"Me too."

While most of us aren't too ashamed to have sex, plenty of us approach critical mass when it comes to talking about it. One problem has to do with the lack of a comfortable, shared vocabulary about sex. Many of us feel stuck using either stiff Latin terminology or sexual slang that is intended for swearing., e.g. "When I was giving you cunnilingus..." or "When I was sucking your cock..." No confusing these for Kodak Moments.

When talking to your partner about sex, it may help if you have a comfortable name or term for your genitals. For instance, a husband and wife were in sex therapy and the woman was asked to give her vagina a special name. She called it "Jewel Box." How sweet. Considering the state of their sexual relationship, she should have named it "The Jaws of Life." But don't mind us. Whatever you want to name yours is fine, as long as your partner is comfortable calling it that too.

After Marriage — Grow or It May Die

Plenty of couples talk even less about sex after they've been married for a couple of years. Things like the interest rate on your credit cards or replacing the kitchen cabinets garner more excitement than finding new things that turn each of you on. Sexual desires start becoming hidden, and we sometimes feel embarrassed or shy about mentioning things that we would have stayed up all night trying a few years earlier.

After a while, sex has no room to grow. "I don't want him to know THAT about me" becomes more powerful than "It might be exciting if he knew that about me!" Perhaps we have too much to lose if a partner disapproves, or maybe we start giving our partners the kind of power that our parents once had to make us feel shame or humiliation.

Knowing vs. Asking

Imagine going to a restaurant where the chef served you whatever he or she felt like fixing instead of giving you a choice. Imagine a gardener who never asked, "How do you like your bushes trimmed?" Imagine a laundry that didn't inquire, "Light starch, heavy starch, no starch, hangers or folded?" Yet when it comes to sex, many of us assume that we know what our partner wants, or we clam up instead of giving feedback.

After So Many Years...

Let's say after ten years of being sexually mute, you suddenly decide to raise the issue. Perhaps your partner will be happy that you finally spoke your mind. Or maybe he or she will be annoyed. "You mean it's been bothering you for ten years and you never said a word?" Or you might receive a suspicious reply: "How did you learn all of that new stuff all of a sudden?"

This kind of defensiveness wouldn't happen if you began talking about sex from the very start of your relationship. Unfortunately, a lot of couples are so satisfied by the newness of their sexual relationship that they don't see the value in learning how to talk to each other about it.

Learning to Speak

By discussing sex on a regular basis, if only every month or two, your partner will feel much less criticized when you suggest that he or she try something new. Fortunately, there are certain props that can make this kind of routine exchange easy and fun.

For instance, you might say to your partner, "Let's get a new book or magazine on sex every month." We're not suggesting glossy jerk-off tomes with the human crotch splayed wide, unless you're both into that sort of thing. Instead, you might try something like *Libido*, which is a classy, upper end-magazine (800)495-1988. It has explicit black-and-white photos and stories that plenty of couples will find erotic. There are also books like Susan Bakos's *Sexational* (St. Martin's Press), Kathy Winks' *G-Spot Book* (Down There Press) or Laura Corn's *101 Nights Of Great Sex* (Park Avenue Press), which is more action-oriented and good at giving permission if that is what you need. You might pick up a couple of anthologies of erotic literature, or browse through the erotica section of your local book store.

You can always highlight parts of this book that you find meaningful and would like your partner to know about. Or you can read parts of it to your partner, as some couples seem to do. It's amazing how a bit of humor helps any discussion that might otherwise be filled with anxiety.

Besides books and magazines, there are some really good sex videos that are both informative and erotic. For instance, Pacific Media's *The Complete Guide to Oral Lovemaking* and their video on using sex toys were fun to review. When searching for erotic videos, you'll find some winners and plenty of yawners. But the search is half the fun. A number of videos and books on sex are mentioned throughout this book.

And why not get yourself on the mailing list of the big sex-related catalogs such as Good Vibrations, Blowfish, Adam & Eve, Xandria, Toys in Babeland? We at the Goofy Foot Press have fun receiving these catalogs. Perhaps you will too.

Some couples find it fun to play board games that promote discussion about sex or physical exploration. The nice thing about these games is that none of the players are losers, not like with Monopoly, anyway. One game to consider is "Enchanted Evening" (800) 776-7662.

There are also internet magazines that publish interesting articles on sex. These can be great discussion starters. Why not download something interesting from www.nerve.com, www.salon.com, or www.cleansheets.com? After all, how can you pass up downloading an article that has text like the following: "Why is it that some men just can't deal with the idea that a smart, together, professional woman like me can actually deserve their respect and still want to be thrown down on the couch and pounded like a cheap steak now and then?" By Hanne Blank in Clean Sheets Erotica Magazine, www.cleansheets.com 3/24/99.

Prevention

You'd think your sex life would be just as important as gardening, sports, business, travel and entertainment. Couples don't hesitate to get books and magazines on subjects like these. They often value and appreciate them and discuss them with their partners. Not so with sex.

Of course, you might say, "Our sex life is fine right now. We don't need anything like that." Hopefully, your luck will hold, but therapists often see couples who had great sex lives two to ten years earlier. Things break down when we take them for granted, and the process of getting them right is not always pretty or fun.

Resources

Good Vibrations (800) 289-8423 www.goodvibes.com
Toys In Babeland (800)658-9119 www.babeland.com
Blowfish (800)325-2569 www.blowfish.com
Behind Closed Doors (800)350-3314
Adam & Beav (800)274-0333
Xandria (800)242-2823
Pacific Media (800)262-7367

For more resources and a list of our companion
publications, please visit our website
www.goofyfootpress.com

Sex Fantasies
Chapter 32

Given how sex fantasies are nearly universal, it's a little surprising that we tend to be embarrassed about them. On the other hand, why bother fantasizing about something that everyone else approves of?

Some people know they're horny because of the sexual fantasies they've been having. For others, horniness is something they feel in their bodies, with very little mental imagery.

Some people have a single reliable sex fantasy that they go back to time and again. Others have a virtual toolbox of scenes and images that help to get them off. The vast majority of people have fantasies during intercourse, and a lot people find it difficult to masturbate to orgasm without an arousing sexual fantasy.

The content of sex fantasies varies; some are sweet, kind and silly; others are weird, kinky and bizarre. Some are action-packed and exciting; others are really boring. Some sex fantasies are populated with past lovers, rock 'n' roll singers, people in uniforms, movie stars, teachers, priests, family members, total strangers and even furry friends from another species.

Believe it or not, one of the most popular sex fantasies involves doing stuff with your current partner! As for scenarios that people sometimes fantasize about, here's a partial list:

Being held or cuddled; doing all kinds of sex acts; having sex with more than one partner; having anonymous sex with a highly attractive partner or partners; being forced to have sex; watching a partner have sex with someone else; having gay sex when you otherwise feel straight; having sex with a male/female couple; role reversal where a guy fantasizes he's a woman having sex with other guys, or a woman fantasizes she's a man having sex with other women; watching or being watched having sex; being the one who dominates; being adored, desired, spanked, tortured, shamed or humiliated.

Fantasies of Rape

It is not unusual for people to have fantasies in which sex is forced, nor is it unusual to fantasize about sex with policemen, priests or others in uniform. Consider the following passage from Betty Dodson's fine book, *Sex for One* (New York: Harmony Books):

> A friend who considered herself a radical feminist got concerned that her sexual imagery wasn't politically correct because it wasn't "feminist oriented." I assured her that all fantasies were okay. Lots of people imagine scenes they never want to experience. I also pointed out that we can become addicted to a fantasy like anything else, and suggested she experiment with new ones. One of her new assertive fantasies is about moving her clitoris in and out of her lover's soft wet mouth while he's tied down. Whenever she gets stuck or is in a hurry, she brings out her old fantasy of being raped by five Irish cops and always reaches orgasm quickly.

Just because someone has a fantasy of being raped doesn't mean that he or she wants it to happen in reality. Sometimes being raped in fantasy is a way for the person to enjoy sexual pleasure that would otherwise cause guilt. Sex that is out of your control keeps you from having to feel responsible for wanting it, and in a typical rape fantasy the rapist is usually someone whom the victim finds appealing and would like to have sex with anyway. It is also a way to feel sexually desired and valued, since the perpetrator would do anything to have you. For more about wanting sex that is forced, see "Bondage by Choice—A Feminist Contradiction?" in the chapter "Culture & Kink."

Men's vs. Women's Sex Fantasies

Young girls in our society are raised on fashion magazines that highlight gorgeous female models—gorgeous if you don't take into account how many meals these women barf up to stay slim and how much silicone they have surgically packed into their chests. As they look through these magazines, American girls

Lucky's Home!

often grow up thinking about other women's bodies, particularly the ideal woman whom they hope to someday become. Boys, on the other hand, often grow up fantasizing about doing things; for instance, being firemen, sports heroes, musicians, stuntmen and eventually stud lovers. It seems our society wants its girls to be admired for how they look, and its boys for how they perform.

Psychologist Karen Shanor believes that when women see an erect penis in their fantasies, they often relish it as a sign that the man finds them irresistible, and not an object of worship, as we men tend to think. In fact, Shanor speculates that many young women learn to include men in their fantasies as an afterthought, with the fantasized male being little more than a woman retro-fitted with a penis. Perhaps this is one reason why teenage girls so often fawn over totally androgynous male rock 'n' roll singers.

If you doubt Shanor's formulation, keep in mind that when a woman walks into a formal affair like a dance or prom, the first thing she often notices is how the other women look and how she feels in comparison. The first thing a man notices is often the same thing: how the other women look. Men usually aren't concerned with how the other men look, unless they are actors or gay.

Interesting as it is, this theory does have its limitations. For instance, it doesn't explain why some women clearly prefer the sexual touch and feel of a man's body, which can be quite different from their own.

Your Lover's Sex Fantasies

Every once in a while, one partner will tell the other about his or her private sex fantasy. Stranger things have happened. But don't expect to see the fantasy plastered on a billboard surrounded by neon lights. Most of us are a little embarrassed by our sexual fantasies, sometimes with good reason. As a result, we tend not to reveal our fantasies in a way that's particularly direct.

You Only Get One Chance

Let's say you are a guy and your sweetheart casually or jokingly makes an off-the-cuff statement that she likes seeing guys in jock straps.

Boom, ball's in your court.

Now, if you have half a brain, and not many of us do, you won't laugh and tell her how much better you feel in boxers than wearing some old athletic supporter. Instead, you will consider buying about a dozen or so new jocks, maybe in colors, maybe one with a cup, what the heck. So there you are later that night, your sweetheart's warm familiar fingers are slowly popping the buttons on your blue jeans and bingo—she discovers that you are wearing a jock underneath! Before you know it, she's in sexual orbit and you are the happiest guy on your block! On the other hand, she might discover that her fantasy was best when it was only imagined and that it feels silly or loses its erotic edge when acted out in reality.

Beat the Rut

Like life in general, sex can be really boring if you never vary the routine. Mind you, this hasn't stopped many couples from doing the exact same thing in bed week after week, month after month, year after year.

Adding variety to a boring sex life is a favorite topic of the magazines that people read in check-out lines at the grocery store, especially when the person in front of you pulls out an entire shoe box full of coupons and you suddenly find yourself with an extra half-hour on your hands.

Odds & Ends: Compromises, Big Xs & the Truth

While it's great that you and your partner might be open to hearing each other's fantasies, this doesn't mean that you need to act them out. For instance, when one partner has a jones to do something that the other finds loathful, you might try working out a compromise. For instance, it's likely that there are plenty of videos depicting whichever fantasies are currently oozing from the darkest recesses of your sexual mind. Why not rent one and use it as a masturbation aid? At other times acting out your sex fantasies can be great fun.

People occasionally have sexual fantasies about someone other than their partner. Sometimes it's prudent not to share these fantasies (e.g., "The reason I got so hot is because I pretended you were Mike"). Other times your partner might find these fantasies very arousing.

If you are going to make your own adult videos at home, keep in mind the fate of the poor sheriff from the Midwest who accidentally returned a custom-made X-rated video of him and his wife to the local video store. Be sure to mark an unmistakable X on both sides in brightly colored nail polish or maybe even Liquid Paper, and keep it in a separate location from where you put the rental tapes.

There are special locks available that fit into the sprocket hole of videocassettes. By using these, you are safe even if your six-year-old accidentally grabs your homemade orgasmo-tape instead of *Fantasia* or *Bambi*. "Mommy, Mommy, you'll never guess what we saw Amber's mom and dad doing on videotape!"

Responsibility

Knowledge of your partner's fantasies is a trust that remains with you for life. This trust holds true even if you break up and otherwise find yourselves hating each other. No one forced you to be in a relationship with the person, so don't go blabbing personal stuff just to be hurtful. In the long run, it reflects badly upon you.

To put it another way, people who gossip about a current or former partner's sexuality are both shallow and deceitful. The laws of karma will someday haunt them, assuming there are laws of karma.

Readers' Comments

"At work I daydream a lot about sex and what it would be like with certain people that I am especially attracted to. Since I am about to get married, I sometimes feel bad thinking of others, but as long as you don't act on it, you're pretty much okay." *female age 30*

"My sexual fantasies always involve my current real life lover. We're making romantic love somewhere that is new to us, a beach, forest, remote island, in front of a fire in a cabin." *female age 34*

"I probably have similar fantasies to anyone who watches the Sci Fi channel too much." *male age 30*

"My fantasies don't play a huge part in my life, except that I get confused why I have fantasies about other girls when I love penises and my boyfriend very much." *female age 23*

"I had always fantasized about my girlfriend being totally naked with her legs spread apart when I came into the room. One day she actually did this! It was awesome!" *male age 21*

"I don't have any clearly defined fantasy. They are more fleeting feelings and don't affect my life much." *female 38*

"As a working mother, I get sex and orgasms, but I rarely get romance, so that is what I fantasize about." *female 36*

"My husband and I have been married for ten years and still love to act out our sexual fantasies. Last month he was a customs agent and I was trying to sneak something across the border. After he completely searched me, I had to bribe him with sexual favors until he let me go. Later, I was a physician and he the reluctant patient. Acting out your fantasies can be great fun, and it keeps your sex life young!" *female age 33*

"I'd love to see my girlfriend get it on with another woman and I know it would be a turn-on to see her get it on with another guy, but I don't know if I could keep from getting jealous." *male age 39*

Have you ever had homosexual fantasies?

"I used to fantasize about women all of the time. Finally, I decided to give it a try and had sex with one of my best female friends, who is mostly heterosexual. It was fun and every now and then we play with one another. I have never developed an emotional attachment to her or any other woman, and I no longer fantasize about women."
female age 26

"I fantasize about being with another woman often, but I also fantasize about my boyfriend and Brad Pitt!"
female age 25

"I am aroused by images of women with women; also by stories of multiple partners. On occasion, I use these fantasies to help me reach orgasm." *female age 32*

"I've had no fantasies or gay experiences, although I wonder sometimes if I could get turned on by another guy."
male age 30

"Gay fantasies? I've never even considered being gay. I'm not gay. I swear it." *male age 22*

See our website at www.goofyfootpress.com for our readers' Sex Fantasy of the Week

Love Dreams, Sex Dreams & Sweet Dreams

Chapter 33

Some people have dreams of misty-eyed romance, the kind of dreams that leave you floating in the clouds until noon the next day. Some people have dreams that include sex. These are the dreams that this chapter is about. And some people have dreams that combine sex and romance. These are the dreams that we dream about dreaming—the rocket-fuel variety of dream that fills the soul and tugs at the edges of who we are.

Sex-Dream Statistics

Less than 10 percent of American parents inform their children about sex dreams, yet the majority of young adults at one time or another have them. More than fifty percent of women have sex dreams, yet many women don't start having them until they are in their twenties. With the male of the species it is different. Males often experience sex dreams as teenagers, with the frequency tending to decrease as they get older.

Sex-Dream History

In the mid-1800s, it was assumed that sex dreams were caused by immoral thoughts. Bizarre operations were proposed for the penises of men who had wet dreams, and all sorts of devices were patented that a man was to wear on his penis at night to prevent him from having erections and the dreaded sex dreams that were thought to follow. One device was designed to wake him up by pulling on his pubic hair when he got an erection. Another machine poured cold water on him whenever he became erect during his sleep.

Dreamtime Sex Cinema—Pass the Kleenex, or Not?

During an average night of sleep, human genitals get hard or wet several times. This usually happens whenever you are dreaming, regardless of the dream's content, even if the dream is about your grandmother or someplace you once visited. A "wet dream" happens when you are actually dreaming about sex and have an orgasm.

Almost half of all "wet dream" orgasms are actually dry and don't include ejaculation, which makes the term wet dream a bit of a misnomer when it is used to describe men's sex dreams. However, it is an accurate description of what happens during women's sex dreams.

While having an orgasm in your sleep isn't much of a problem for a woman, it sometimes leaves a guy with a sticky mess. In a more understanding world, a male wouldn't have to feel embarrassed about wet-dream stains. But wet dreams often leave a splotch on the sheets or in your underwear, and what's a boy to say? Since there is no way of predicting when you will have a sex dream, packing your shorts with Kleenex at bedtime isn't going to help.

Sex Dreams vs. Masturbation

Talk about difficult bedtime decisions... When the author of this book was a teenager, he assumed that he would be more likely to have a wet dream if he didn't masturbate. He would hold out, trying not to masturbate for as many days as possible, in hopes of hastening a wet dream. Not so. Sometimes a person can have a wet dream the same night that he or she masturbates or has sex. On the other hand, not masturbating won't increase your chances of having sex dreams.

There is simply no way to will yourself a wet dream, unless you are good at lucid-dream enhancement, or whatever the people at Stanford are calling it these days. A seminal book on the subject of lucid dreaming is *Lucid Dreaming* by Stephen LeBerge (New York: Ballantine, 1993). For related materials, check out his website at www.lucidity.com.

Sex-Dream Complications

Not only are sex dreams a sign that you are growing up, but they are a great way of having sex when it is not readily available. Some people even have their first orgasms while asleep and dreaming. Still, some people feel upset by their sex dreams. For instance, you might have a sex dream that includes someone you know, maybe a friend, boss or teacher. This might make you feel a bit sheepish when you see that person in real life. Not to worry, you have done nothing wrong. This book's suggestion is to scope out the person from head to toe. Check everything from subtle mannerisms to what kind of clothes he or she is wearing. Then ask yourself: "Is he or she as good (or bad) in real life as he or she was in my dream?"

There can also be wet-dream downers. For instance, wet dreams can leave you feeling frustrated when the love of your dreams doesn't want anything to do with you in waking life. This can be particularly bittersweet when the person is a former lover and is now with someone else or is no longer living. Also, it is not unusual for heterosexuals to dream about having sex with members of the same sex. There are many ways of interpreting this sort of thing, e.g., the sex in these dreams might represent accepting part of yourself that the other person represents, with the actual sex being a metaphor for "taking in."

Whatever the content, it would be nice if your sex dreams could be a safe and welcome place to explore a full array of sexual activity that you wouldn't ordinarily do when awake.

The Family That Dreams Together...

People sometimes have sex dreams that include members of the family. This doesn't necessarily indicate a problem. Again, actions that transpire in dreams are often symbols for something very different than what meets the eye, so you can't assume that the sexual partners or the sexual activity in a dream truly reflects the deeper meaning of the dream. If, however, this happens on a regular basis and you are disturbed by it, consider seeking the help of a trained mental health professional.

Another reason to get outside help is if you usually end up frustrated, hurt, frightened or angry in your dreams. You don't have to be Sigmund Freud to realize that repeated dreams of a disturbing nature reflect an inner struggle of major proportion. The exception is with children, since bad dreams are quite common during the younger years. It is not uncommon for children who are happy and whose emotional development is normal to have bad dreams two to four times a week. If, on the other hand, the child is also struggling during the waking hours, it might be prudent to seek a professional assist.

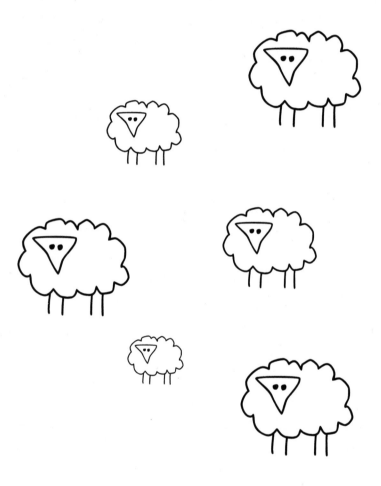

Techno Breasts & Weenie Angst
Chapter 34

People who feel sexually inadequate sometimes focus their angst on body parts. For women, the focus is often on breast size or body shape; for men it is on the penis and sometimes height. Of course, it is silly to obsess about something that you had no say in getting, yet that's what many of us do.

When generating a physical balance sheet, it might be helpful to remember that even Man-O-War had his weaknesses. It might also help to remind yourself that sexual attractiveness is not like a steel chain, where one weak link makes the whole thing useless. All of us have weak links sexually, as part of our bodies and minds.

Of course, this will offer little solace to people who are convinced that their essential body parts are deficient. They will keep telling themselves, "Everything would be better if I just had a bigger this or a smaller that..." To address such fears, this chapter offers a lengthy discourse on men's genitals, then ruminates on breast implants and ends with a few suggestions about alternative strategies.

Body Concerns: Guys & How They're Hung

While most books on sex say that penis size doesn't matter, there are two groups of people to whom it does matter. One group includes almost every male alive. The second group includes every woman who derives sexual pleasure from intercourse.

In years past, women weren't supposed to care about the size and shape of a man's penis. That is because they weren't supposed to be interested in sex. But wouldn't you notice the size and shape of something that was about to get stuck into your body? As for how women respond to the actual dimensions of the thing, it clearly varies.

For instance, some women regard the penis as a trophy—the bigger the better; others couldn't care less. Some women prefer the feeling of fullness that a beefier penis has to offer; others prefer giving blow jobs to a partner who isn't particularly well hung, and some even prefer a smaller penis for intercourse. Most women get the bulk of their pleasure from what a man is able to do with his hands, heart, tongue and intellect. They view the penis as just another body appendage.

For some women, a lover's penis becomes her penis or a part of her body when it's inside of her. Does this mean that she necessarily wants the biggest one in town? Not usually. After all, when women buy dildos, they tend to select medium- to smaller-sized units. (Sorry, but they sometimes upsize later.)

Of course, this isn't to say that women don't have their favorites. Ask a woman to tell you which lover's penis was her favorite, and she will probably be able to give a direct and clear-cut answer such as, "It was Randy's" or "There are two or three that stand out, but I'd have to say Todd's takes the prize." However, if you ask about the men behind the penises and which one she loved the most, Randy or Todd might not be at the top of the list. Maybe the guy she was happiest with didn't have a memorable penis at all, but was able to put it together in other ways.

So while women might prefer one penis over the other, penis size usually isn't a deal-breaker when it comes to choosing a man. It is sometimes disappointing, but usually not the deciding factor.

Irony: While some guys grow up worrying if they are hung well enough, women sometimes grow up worrying that guys will be hung too well and might cause them pain or injury. Maybe we humans were simply programmed to worry.

Weenie-Enhancement Techniques

Surgery That Makes Your Penis Fat

There is a surgical technique for penis plumping in which fat cells are harvested from the lower stomach region and injected into the penis. The author of this book called three offices that advertise this procedure and was hit by a wave of sales pitches that he hadn't encountered since joining a health club.

The heavy sales pitch, which tried to capitalize on every sexual doubt known to man, made sense when you consider that these clinics charge $3,000 to $4,000 for a simple outpatient procedure that takes half an hour.

One clinic in Beverly Hills refused to even mail out information about the procedure. They claimed that a brochure had fallen into the hands of a child, resulting in great embarrassment. To prevent such a hideous event from ever occurring again, each caller had to make an office appointment where he could read the brochure and talk to a specialist. "Why an appointment?" "Because we process over 40 men a day." As it turned out, the dreaded brochure contained no pictures or drawings and was embarrassing only in how it insulted the consumer's intelligence.

This fancy medical clinic insisted that it needed a social security number and health insurance information before discussing the procedure. Each visitor was also required to fill out a separate page about his penis. The wording was designed to make a man feel sexually insecure and blame it all on the size of his weenie.

The Beverly Hills clinic then treated your author to an interview with a clean-cut salesman masquerading in a physician's coat, perhaps so people wouldn't confuse him with the kind of salesmen who populate used car lots.

None of the three offices offered any studies on the long-term safety of the procedure, they didn't agree on where the fat actually went, and none was willing to say exactly how a penis feels that is encased in a quarter-inch layer of fat.

It seems that if Mother Nature wanted an extra layer of fat on the penis, she would have put it there herself. Heaven knows, she put it everywhere else. Not even the hot dogs at Dodger stadium have as much fat as a penis that's been cosmetically plumped, and they cost significantly less than $3000–okay, they cost somewhat less than $3000.

The best we could conclude about this procedure is that a man pays between $3,000 and $4,000 to give his penis cellulite. Also, some lawyers are specializing in lawsuits from men who were less than satisfied with the results of their surgically enhanced penises. And recently, the penis-enlargement ads in the sports section of the *Los Angeles Times* have been stating that there is a "new procedure" which is vastly improved over the one used in the past. Perhaps they have forgotten that only a year or two ago their ads for the "old" procedure used to boast about how safe and successful it was.

Would you trust your penis, or any other body parts, to these people?

The Vacuum Pump

There is an X-rated video called *How to Enlarge Your Penis* in which porn star Scott Taylor pumps himself up with a vacuum device that is supposed to make a guy bigger. Taylor uses the pump to plump his penis up fatter than a grain silo, which he then maneuvers into the apparently spacious vagina of porn starlet Erica Boyer. At no point does Scott's big salami actually get hard; he has to hold his fingers around the base to keep the pressure in. Contrary to what this "self-help" video shows, the vacuum pump is one of the options that urologists offer male patients who are having trouble getting hard. Also, inside-industry sources have informed Goofy Foot Press that *The How to Enlarge* infomercial took several hours to shoot, and even Scott Taylor couldn't stay hard for that long.

The penis pump was first patented in 1917. About sixty years later it became popular in the gay community, both for sex play and for organ enlargement. Some pumpers even started clubs, like Kiwanis or Rotary, where guys get together to pump. Straight men started using the pump in the mid to late 1980s. Pumping provides a sensation that some men find soothing and enjoyable. It also causes the penis to plump up bigger than usual. Most urologists think that there is no way a guy can make himself permanently bigger with a vacuum pump and that short-term gains occur because the penis is simply swollen. However, the people who manufacture the pumps claim that long-term gains are possible. They say that the vacuum pump expands the width of the penis by stretching the walls of the chambers that fill with blood during normal erection. The increase in penis length apparently comes from stretching the ligament that holds a third of the penis inside the body.

To achieve a "permanent" increase in size, pumpers say that a man has to pump at least a half-hour a day for almost a year. As for the safety of the vacuum pump, it has been approved by the FDA for use with erection problems, but not for use as a weenie-enhancement device, not that anyone has applied. Can you imagine the lab studies that the FDA might require, with hundreds of white rats having their penises pumped for hours on end to see if they got bigger?

For safety's sake, check with a physician before pumping for long periods of time. That's because there might be a difference between pumping for a few minutes to get hard and pumping for an hour to get bigger. Also ask yourself why you might be focusing so much insecurity on your penis. No matter what its size, your penis is still a marvelous gift from nature which provides you with tremendous feelings of pleasure.

You would think that the majority of men who pump for size would be those with smaller penises. Not so. A lot of pumpers are well endowed to begin with. Go figure.

The Bottom Line...

"I once had a lover with an enormous penis. It was a turn-on to look at it, and an ego trip that a man that huge was my partner. But the actual feeling of it inside me didn't give me one one-hundredth of the pleasure that my more modestly sized present partner's does. While the size of a man's penis does create different sensations, it is the relationship I have with the man who is attached to the penis that determines what those sensations mean to me."

female age 47

Before rushing out to get either a pump or cosmetic surgery, please consider the following: If your penis is average-sized or more, why do you need to be bigger? What's your problem anyway? And if your penis is closer to a finger than a phone pole, learn to give great back and foot rubs and become sublime at the art of loving a woman with your lips and tongue. Do this and it is likely that you will be admired by many women, assuming you are a decent human being to begin with. Also try using intercourse positions that might focus more stimulation on the parts of your lover's vagina that give her the most pleasure. The most sensitive areas of a vagina are often located in the first inch or two beyond the vaginal opening. And finally, try to avoid women who are confirmed size-queens. No sense in humiliating yourself needlessly.

A bantamweight penis might feel longer if the female bends her knees during intercourse. This results in deeper penetration if that is what she wants. Keeping her legs together will help it feel more snug. A couple of positions that accommodate this are rear-entry intercourse with both of you on your sides (aka spoons) and where the woman is on her back and her ankles are resting on the man's shoulders.

As for being embarrassed in front of your locker-room buds, sex experts say that it's not fair to compare nonerect penises, because penises that are smaller when they are soft tend to grow more when they are getting hard. In other words, it isn't a fair comparison unless all of you have hard-ons, and what kind of gym would that be? But reality checks are of little solace to a guy who's feeling insecure in the showers right after football practice. Hopefully he will learn that there are other ways of earning respect besides having a big penis, assuming that big penises earn respect rather than envy.

Perhaps it might be good to remember that many things in life have a purpose. Whatever you are here on earth to learn, your less-than-memorable member might be one of the keys that helps you find it, especially if it's a bit of humility.

A Note for the Extra-Well-Endowed

A small number of men feel angst because they were especially blessed behind the buttons of their blue jeans.

For those guys whose girlfriends scream in horror the first time they see the penis erect, relax. Talk about it before you get undressed or hand her a copy of the *Guide* and point to this page. Flatly rule out the possibility of intercourse for the first couple of times. This will allow time for your lover to become comfortable touching and playing with your trunk—uh—penis. Ray Stubbs's *Erotic Interludes Part 2* is a tastefully done videotape which shows a woman massaging the penis of a man who doesn't give much ground to Trigger. This might be a nice tape to keep around so your girlfriend can see that there are plenty of ways of pleasing you. She can also get you off quite nicely with the oral sex technique which doesn't require her to take your whole penis into her mouth. It is shown in the chapter "Oral Sex: Penises & Popsicles."

One way of working up to intercourse is to have the woman get on top of the man and experiment with femoral intercourse, which has been described as "intercourse, but not really." With femoral intercourse, the penis does not go into the vagina. Instead, the woman holds the well-lubricated penis lengthwise between her labia, like a pencil lying in the binding part of an open book, not that a pencil is the most appropriate analogy here. She can then use the penis to masturbate with, especially by rubbing her clitoris back and forth over the ridge where the head of the penis attaches to the shaft.

After a woman becomes comfortable handling your penis, it's likely that she will eventually want to try vaginal intercourse, for the challenge if nothing else. This will usually work quite nicely as long as the man cools his jets and uses a low-key "stop whenever you want" approach. Use lots of lubrication, and make sure that the woman is the one who puts the thing in and controls the depth and level of thrusting. Getting popped in the uterus can be just as uncomfortable as getting popped in the testicles. In one position that might be worth trying, the woman keeps her legs straight but apart. Keep experimenting, as certain positions can help a woman's vagina accommodate up to two more inches of penis.

Now, for ways that women mangle their bodies...

The Sound of Leaking Breasts

I tried out for the cheerleading squad when I was a sophomore in high school. "This isn't a beauty contest," the advisor had told us, but we all knew better than that.... But you weren't beautiful, Julie Brown, and you knew it. Face facts. You even made a list one time, outlining your numerous faults: breasts too small, buttocks too big, teeth crooked, hair too thin, arms and legs too skinny, feet too long, four inches too tall, nose too bumpy... If you were wealthy, you could make the necessary corrections. If you had enough money, you could have the breast implants you needed, the braces, the nose job, the hairweaving, and with enough money the right cosmetics could be purchased, the ones you saw in the magazines, the ones that would render you flawless... (Julie Brown, "Beauty" pp. 68–70, *Michigan Quarterly Review*, edited by Laurence Goldstein, Vol. XXX, No. 1, Winter 1991.)

Men aren't the only ones who worry that body parts are too small or not quite right. Women often believe that the world would be a nicer and kinder place if only they had bigger breasts. Some women with petite breasts even feel they would get a better job or promotion if their A cups swelled into majestic Es. Hopes like these have inspired thousands of American women to have their chests packed with funky substances.

Aside from the sheer ridiculousness of getting breast implants, much has been said during the last few years about the safety of them. Silicone molecules seem to leach through the plastic implant pouches. However, it is possible that this isn't any more dangerous to your health than, say, living in Detroit or Los Angeles. Saline implants appear to be safer than the silicone, but far less so than the original equipment that Mother Nature saw fit to provide.

Note: Many women who have implants need additional surgery a few years down the line, and *even the saltwater boobs make it difficult to screen for cancer.*

Silicone Sisters¹ and the Men Who Love Them

Here in America men with plastic brains are attracted to women with plastic chests. What a perfect combination. What a sad perception of womanhood.

Unfortunately, young girls in America are raised on fashion magazines that highlight gorgeous female models, whatever gorgeous might mean. Having grown up under the shadow of supermodel breasts, American girls often confuse a combination of anorexia and fake breasts with what femininity is all about. As a result, breast implants and bizarre diets have become a way of achieving the fantasy of perfect womanhood.

Perfect womanhood is a costly and precarious myth to pursue. Even if you are able to achieve the right look, it tends to be short-lived and often comes crashing down by the time you reach age thirty-five and can no longer suppress that which in other cultures is considered to be a sign of wisdom. It's too bad America's teenage girls don't get to spend time with America's supermodels. They might get over the supermodel fantasy rather quickly.

The Placebo Effect of Store-Bought Boobs

Until recently, some of the biggest proponents of breast implants were the women who got them. Then they had to start spending all that time and energy convincing themselves that the darned things weren't killing them.

One reason why women with plastic chests were so excited about their implants is because life really did get better for many of them. But the real reason life improved was because these women's attitudes got better. It's how they saw themselves that made the difference, not whether their breasts were double As or triple Ds. Otherwise, women with naturally large boobs would seldom feel depressed or have a rotten day.

---

¹With apologies to Bruce Springsteen.

Feeling more attractive is what made these women more attractive. Granted, there are plenty of men who like the way that big silicone boobs look, but it's quite likely that an increase in confidence without the implants would bring similar results.

Microchip Melons—A New Generation of Breast Implant?

Unless there is a major shift in the consciousness of American men and women, it is likely that the medical world will find new ways to surgically mangle women's bodies. As long as that is the case, this guide suggests that the next generation of breast implants contain slots for video games. This will help turn the female chest into a full-fledged entertainment center, which is what some men and women apparently expect it to be.

Exercise Video Alert: Truth in Advertising

Exercise videos have been very popular for the past decade. It only seems fair that any actress/model/whatever who does an exercise video ought to list how many cosmetic surgeries she's had to look the way she does. (Breast implants? Ribs removed? Liposuction? Face lifts? Tummy tucks? Breast lifts? Supplemental hormones?) The videos might then post a warning label such as the following:

> **WARNING:** With $22,000 worth of plastic surgery, a lucky role of the genetic dice, an eating disorder and the exercises on this tape, you too can look more like your video host.

Alternatives for Both Men & Women

American advertisers spend millions of dollars to make us think, "If only I had this or that, I'd be sexier and happier." It is easy to see why many of us fall for these devious traps. The thought of instantly having bigger, smaller, hairier or balder body parts can be terribly seductive.

If cosmetic surgery is what you need, please choose carefully. Do be aware that if you haven't worked through feelings of inferiority, realigning body parts may not make you feel any better in the long run. You'll simply find new things to feel insecure about.

For alternatives, think about getting your body in good physical shape or dressing better. Breasts that sit on well-developed chest muscles sometimes look bigger, if that is what you are trying to achieve. At the very least, being in good shape makes most people feel and look sexier. A smaller penis will often look bigger if it isn't being dwarfed by a pot belly, or if the eyes are drawn to nicely developed shoulders and pecs. Also, why not find ways to expand your mind's creativity and intelligence? These are the kinds of measures that will make you a better and sexier person.

As for sexual performance, some of the best and most eager lovers are those without ideal dimensions. Since they have less natural endowment to fall back on, they sometimes learn to be extremely attentive and skilled in bed.

Chapter Notes: Some women have breast-reduction surgery because it can be severely uncomfortable to lug huge breasts around all the time. If this is what you are considering, be sure to consult at least two surgeons who specialize in breast reduction surgery. This is not a simple operation and can leave permanent scaring or disfigurement. 🩸 Ever notice that breast implants are anti-gravitational devices? The things never lie flat, even when a woman is on her back.

When the Tide Turns Red
Chapter 35

nce you get into a long-term relationship, menstruation is something that happens to both of you. That's why you'll do a whole lot better in life if you try to understand more about it. While this chapter tells what it can, the best way for a guy to find out about menstruation is to ask his partner. For instance, does she plod through her periods without much distress, or does she get all swelled up and bloated? Are there certain things she likes or dislikes when she's having her period? How long does her period usually last? For most women, it's from three to seven days, give or take. You might eventually ask her to tell you about the first time she menstruated. Almost all women still remember their first period quite vividly.

Learn all she can teach you. You'll be a better person for it, and the two of you might feel more connected as a result. Why not give her the laugh of a lifetime by trying to insert a tampon for her?

A Brief Historical Note

When people talk about scientific discoveries that have given women more freedom and equality, the birth control pill is often the first thing mentioned. They forget that a couple of generations ago women had to use rags to collect menstrual blood, hence the term "on the rag." The invention of the tampon and sanitary napkin has had more of a positive impact on many women's lives than the birth control pill. And recent modifications to the sanitary napkin have left it far more manageable to use as well as giving birth to the term "panty liner."

Sex during Periods

Some people fear having intercourse during a woman's menstrual cycle. The truth is, menstruation causes absolutely no harm to either partner. In fact, the contractions of orgasm push accumulated fluids out of the uterus which helps decrease menstrual cramping. Can you imagine an American mother telling her fourteen-year-old daughter, "Honey, if you're having cramps, why not masturbate?" Instead, they buy Midol®.

Intercourse with a menstruating woman sometimes feels extra-nice for the following reasons: 1. The vagina might be super-lubricated due to menstrual secretions. 2. The added menstrual swelling might help a woman have a really nice orgasm. 3. Some women get extra-horny during their periods; this might have to do with a change in hormones, or perhaps they feel more relaxed since it's harder to get pregnant, although pregnancy is still a risk. Other women who don't enjoy having sex with their partner might look forward to their periods as an excuse and respite from sex.

As for the aesthetics of midperiod intercourse, sheets with menstrual lovemaking on them usually wash clean, but so what if they don't? Guys shed that much blood during a hard-fought game of football and consider it a sign of courage.

Regarding the aesthetics of oral sex during a menstrual cycle, some couples have no problem with it; others do. This is discussed at length in the chapter " Oral Sex: Vulvas & Honeypots."

Feeling Unlovable

Another thing to be aware of about menstruation is that some women have grown up in households that weren't particularly supportive of their biological processes. As a result, these women may feel unlovable or unattractive when they are having their periods. If this is true for your partner, find a time when she isn't feeling quite so unlovable and discuss it. It's one thing to feel bad when you have done something dumb, but there is nothing dumb about having a menstrual cycle. Besides, if you have ever had to wait out a menstrual period that is seriously late, you will learn to regard the monthly flow as a lover's best friend.

Goofy Facts. Period.

📖 UC Berkeley scientist Margie Profet believes that menstruation evolved as a way of protecting the female's uterus from harmful bacteria and viruses that might be delivered by male ejaculate. Far from being a waste, she sees menstrual bleeding as the body's way of systematically preventing infection. Others don't agree.

📖 In some primitive societies, the native women didn't start suffering from menstrual pain and cramping until they had been "saved" by Western missionaries and their American wives.

📖 In the 1976 Olympics an American swimmer won gold medals and broke a world record while on her period. Too bad she didn't get big bucks for endorsing the brand of tampons that allowed her to swim for the gold...

📖 There is no evidence whatsoever that a woman's intellectual, academic or job performance is affected by her menstrual cycle. It may not feel great, but it doesn't compromise her ability to think or perform.

The Legacy of Bleeding

Children are taught from an early age that bleeding is what happens when you have a cut, wound or other form of trauma. Can you imagine the impact of menstrual bleeding on a young girl who isn't well-prepared? She would probably assume that there is something terribly wrong with her body. "Well-prepared" needs to include more than just the biological facts. It should also incorporate a sense of pride about the body and an awareness that menstrual bleeding is a sign of maturity and health.

Another problem with menstruation is what to do with the blood. Few guys ever have to worry about bleeding through their shorts, but their girlfriends might. One very astute woman reader who is nearly ninety still has dreams that she is menstruating and can't find a sanitary napkin. The feelings of panic remain fresh in her unconscious, although she last menstruated when Harry Truman was president, or was it Dwight Eisenhower. Okay, John F. Kennedy. More on girls' feelings about their menstruating bodies in the chapter "The First Time—Not What You'd Think."

Feminist writer Gloria Steinem made an interesting point that if men were the ones who menstruated, they would brag about how many ounces they bled each month and for how long. At least this would indicate pride rather than shame.

Twinkies & the Onset of Menstruation

Here in the Western world, the onset of menstruation has slowly but steadily been occurring at a younger age. While this has generally been attributed to better nutrition, it may actually be due to poorer nutrition. A researcher named Rose E. Frisch thinks that there is a relationship between the onset of menstruation and stores of body fat. Fat tissue is one of the places in the body where estrogen is synthesized.

As a young woman approaches puberty, her proportion of body fat increases. In order to start having menstrual cycles she seems to need around seventeen percent body fat, and to ovulate the figure increases to approximately twenty-six percent. On the other hand, women who are old enough to menstruate but are seriously overweight tend not to menstruate regularly.

If the level of body fat really does play a role in the menstrual process, then it might be our penchant for junk food and the sedentary life rather than healthy nutrition that is lowering the age of first menstruation. However, there are other theories, too. One suggests that the added stress of the modern world is causing girls to menstruate earlier. Yet if stress were a determining factor, women alive during World Wars I and II would certainly have menstruated at an earlier age.

Women Athletes

It is not uncommon for women athletes to stop menstruating or have irregular periods. One reason is that their body fat is often lower than seventeen percent. If a woman athlete wants to get pregnant but is having difficulty, adding a few pounds might help.

Women athletes might also find that the start of menstruation is delayed due to metabolic reasons. For instance, women athletes and dancers who began their training before the ages of nine or ten often start menstruating a few years later than their nonathletic peers.

It is with great restraint that your author tells about the time during his freshman year of college when he lifted weights with the women members of the Soviet National Shot Put Team. He never thought to ask Olga, Svetlana and Georgia if they menstruated regularly.

Note: Children of both sexes who get increased amounts of exercise before puberty have lung capacities that are 10 percent to 20 percent greater than their nonexercising peers'. The added lung capacity will stay with them for life, which is why it's so important for young children of either sex to exercise and be physically active.

Tampons, Sponges & Toxic-Shock Syndrome

Toxic-Shock Syndrome (TSS) is a rare but sometimes fatal disease caused by the toxins of certain bacteria that grow in the bodies of both men and women. TSS is now mainly associated with surgery and severe burn cases, but during the early 1980s some women died from TSS following the introduction of a new superabsorbent tampon called Rely.

Contrary to what scientists first believed, the killer tampons did not act as a breeding site for the TSS bacteria. Rely contained two synthetic fibers (corboxymethyl cellulose and polyester foam) that are thought to have irritated the vaginal lining in ways that triggered the TSS bacteria to produce a dangerous toxin. Tampons are now made from only cotton and rayon. As a result, the occurrence of TSS among tampon users is rare. Your chances of getting killed in a car wreck are 500 to 1000 times greater than the risk of death by tampon.

It was originally thought that wearing the same tampon for several hours increased your chances of getting TSS. Not so. However, the risk does go up when you use nothing but tampons throughout your entire period, even if you change them every three hours. If you are a tampon user who wants to greatly reduce her chances of getting TSS, don't wear tampons throughout your entire period. For instance, alternate using tampons and napkins. Also, some people are naturally more susceptible to TSS. If you have ever had TSS or appear susceptible to it, you are better off to not use tampons.

There is a slight increase in TSS among women who use barrier contraceptives, i.e., a diaphragm, cervical cap or contraceptive sponge. This risk is very, very, very slight.

One reader comments, "I was put on sea sponges back in the 1980s during the TSS scare. I had used Rely tampons and developed cell abnormalities in my cervix. After ditching all tampons and inserting a clean sea sponge during my period, the abnormal cells disappeared for good. An FDA-approved alternative that plenty of women swear by is called "Instead."

For First-Time Tampon Users

Getting a tampon where it's supposed to go requires two steps—pushing in the applicator and then pushing in the plunger. In goes the tampon, out goes the applicator, unless you're feeling the need to be ultra-accessorized. Here are a few tips on tampon insertion from our female readers.

🦷 Be sure to follow the instructions from the manufacturer.

🦷 Most tampons come with their own applicators or plungers. Some tampons, like OBs, use the inserting devices that Mother Nature provided: your fingers.

🦷 Buy or borrow the skinniest tampon you can find. You might try Tampax Lites or Playtex SlimFit regulars.

🦷 Some women put tampons in while standing: a little squat action or with one leg higher and out to the side. Other women put them in while sitting on the toilet.

🎺 It might help to coat the end of the tampon with a lubricant like KY Jelly. If you can't score the jelly, try dabbing a little saliva on the end.

🎺 Find your vaginal opening. It's down there somewhere, honest. It's at the bottom part of your vulva. The illustration on page 85 might help. Spread the lips of your vulva and put your finger in a little way. This is where the tampon will go.

🎺 Spread your lips with the fingers of one hand, and insert the applicator into your vagina with the other. Aim the thing toward your tailbone and not up toward your stomach.

🎺 Insert the applicator so that the wider part of the barrel is almost all of the way in—with enough sticking out to hold on to, but not much more. If you don't insert the tampon far enough inside, the ring of muscles in the first part of your vagina can clamp it, making it feel uncomfortable.

🎺 Once you've got the applicator in, hold the barrel firmly with your fingers. Push the plunger in. Bingo! "NASA, we have a landing."

🎺 Pull out the applicator. As you pull it out, try not to pull on the string or you'll pull the tampon out and you're back to square one. If this happens, push the tampon back in with your finger.

🎺 Make sure the string is hanging out of your vagina. If it isn't, don't worry. Squat and push down as if you are trying to take the mother of all dumps. Reach a finger inside your vagina to see if you can feel the little critter. You can always use your thumb and finger to pull the string out. If you have no luck, ask your mom, aunt, grandmother or older sister for help, or call your healthcare provider and speak with a nurse. Again, it's not like the end of the world, but you will need to get the thing out in the next couple of hours.

🎺 Check the instructions to see how often you should change tampons. Try not to leave it in longer than the manufacturer says.

🎺 Your vagina might be dry on the last day or two of your period. Don't hesitate to dab some lube on the tampon before putting it in.

🔫 Do not have intercourse with a tampon inside. Lord only knows where in your vagina it will end up. If you are trying to block menstrual flow for intercourse or oral sex, find menstruation in the index of this book and check out the relevant pages.

Dear Paul,

When did they invent tampons? What about sanitary napkins?

Fluffy in Red River

Dear Fluff,
Kotex, the first widely marketed sanitary napkin, was invented shortly after World War I. Before that, women used rags which they wadded up and pinned to the inside of their underwear. Some people use the term "on the rag" as a metaphor for menstruation, but before the 1920s, it was an expression of fact.

According to the Museum of Menstruation, the modern tampon was born in the late 1920s or early 1930s. The first tampon was probably named Fax, and it was called an "internal sanitary napkin" because nobody back then knew what a tampon was. It did not have an applicator or a string. It was wrapped in gauze, which a woman pulled on to get the thing out.

Another early tampon was called Paz. In 1936, a corporation called Tambrands bought the Paz company and started selling Tampax, which was the first tampon with an applicator. But for the genius of some 1930s marketing person, it might have been called Tampaz instead of Tampax.

One early "problem" with tampons was that they required women to touch their genitals. There were fears in many circles that this would lead to wanton immorality. There were also fears that tampons would devirginize teenage girls. As late as the early 1990s, Tampax still ran ads to help dispel this fear.

So much for the past. If you are adventurous, there are a couple of newer menstrual products on the market.

One of these new products is called the "inSync miniform." It is not inserted like a tampon nor does it stick to your underwear like a pad. Instead, it fits between your labia. It's about the size of a tampon, but has a different shape. This product is used alone on light days, or on heavy days it can be used as a backup to tampons. Do not use it alone on a heavy day. You will not be a happy camper, as one of the women at Goofy Foot Press discovered after using it without reading the instructions. InSync was designed for light-flow days and seems like a neat product for that; worth a try. To get a coupon that entitles you to a free 12-count box, call (888)8-insync or (888)846-7962. The product is currently sold in the Western states, excluding California.

Another product that's seen several incarnations is the menstrual cup. In some ways it is similar to a diaphragm. You insert it to collect the flow. While not a birth control device, the menstrual cup does allow you to have intercourse or oral sex during your period without leaving blood on the sheets or in your partner's mouth.

One version of the menstrual cup is called Instead. You throw it away after using it. Another menstrual cup is called the Keeper. It lasts for years and has a three-month money-back guarantee. Since you wash it out and reuse it, you won't be won't be clogging up your plumbing with used tampons or filling the nation's land-fills with a bunch of used napkins and tampon wrappings. On the other hand, some women won't relish having to clean the Keeper out. Check out the Keeper's website at www.eco-logique.com or call them at (800)680-9739. They also make a reusable sanitary napkin which comes in all kinds of patterns. They seem like very nice people.

Last year I received a complaint from someone who thinks I am menstru-phobic because I do not actively encourage readers to give women oral sex while they are menstruating. Whoever you are, even if you are not from Transylvania, please accept my apologies. What was I ever thinking of?

Also be sure to check out the Museum of Menstruation website: www.mum.org. It is a fascinating, informative, up-to-date site that includes anything you would ever need to know about menstruation.

Chapter Notes: Special thanks to Dr. Anne Schuchat from the Center for Disease Control in Atlanta and Nina Bender at Whitehall Laboratories for their help on TSS. Also, thanks to Harry Finley at the Museum of Menstruation for consultation on the history of sanitary napkins and tampons, and to Jeanna at Freddie Meyers in Newport, Oregon.

Clean Jeans, Tight Jeans, Briefs & Boxers
Chapter 36

Some guys never recover from the defeat of being toilet trained and get their revenge by avoiding soap and water. It's so easy for a man (and woman) to be clean and smell nice. All it takes is a five-minute shower, deodorant and a toothbrush. If you still have a foreskin, pull the thing back and wash around it.

If you are young or don't have much of a beard, keep your stubble shaved and no one will know the difference. The daily shaving ritual gets old really fast, so count your lucky stars if your beard is wimpy or late in arriving.

Clean & Girls

Regarding sexual hygiene for women, this book defers to Betty Dodson's *Sex for One* (New York: Harmony Books) where Ms. Dodson refers to events that occurred in her women's groups:

> During "Show and Tell" we reviewed our concerns about episiotomy scars from childbirth, inner lips that didn't match, little bumps or moles that looked strange, clitorises that were thought to be too small, and the dreaded vaginal discharge. We talked about genital hygiene and how douching could be available but not as a compulsive routine.

> Since most women have some clear or white secretion, I always considered that normal. I never used harsh commercial douching preparations.... Usually washing the exterior genitalia and reaching just inside the vaginal opening was sufficient cleansing. Before making love, I inserted a finger inside my vagina to smell and taste myself, which made me feel secure.

Regarding Ms. Dodson's reference to tasting herself, it might seem a little strange to some women, but we guys taste you all the time. It's okay, honest. Some of the feminists might say,

"If we're supposed to taste ourselves, why don't you guys taste yourselves?" Most of us have. Besides, what flavor do you think we get when we kiss you after receiving a blow job?

It's also helpful for women to remember that the hood of the clitoris can sometimes collect the same kind of cheesy stuff as the foreskin of the penis. A Q-Tip dipped in mineral oil will help remove any of these deposits that might be stuck under the hood. Also try to use a low-pH soap on your genitals. More about this on pages 242-243.

Bidet in a Can?

While we Americans don't allow anything as functional as bidets in our bathrooms, we have invented a totally useless substitute that not only causes irritation but harms the environment as well. It's called feminine hygiene spray.

Feminine deodorants, sprays, powders and commercial douche products with names like Cherry Orchard Breeze and Morning Dew are key players in Madison Avenue's relentless campaign to create and cash in on every conceivable form of human doubt and fear. The vagina is self-cleaning. Sprays and douches can actually cause odor by disturbing the natural flora and fauna of the vagina.

Women who douche more than three times a month are said to have a three times greater chance of getting pelvic inflammatory disease than women who don't.

Trimming the Triangle

"I wax and swear by it. Have it done professionally. It's worth the money and then you can start doing it yourself. I use hot wax, not with the strips. Ingrown hairs are sometimes a problem, but it beats having an entire snatch of stubble." *female age 25*

"I shave and just deal with the irritation." *female age 26*

"Shaving is painful and I look about 12 years old, it grosses me out. Trimming works! Borrow a beard trimmer and go for it! One crew cut coming up!" *female age 29*

"I shave in the summer so that when I wear my bathing suit it doesn't show. Waxing or tweezing is less irritating. When you shave, it itches terribly when it starts to grow back." *female age 49*

"My husband really likes to trim my pubic area for me. He gets turned on by this, and I think it's highly arousing, too."
female age 45

"I'm more aware of myself and my sexuality when I'm shaved. It feels sensual, like the first time you wear silk underwear. It's too much trouble to keep up, though. If there was an easy way, I think I'd do it more often."
female age 36

"I used to have this lovely, neat, wonderfully behaved triangle of pubic hair. And then I turned 30 and the thing started to spread..." *female age 32*

All you have to do is walk into your local drugstore and see products like "Bikini Bare" and special bikini shavers to realize that a lot of women trim their pubic hair. This is mainly a cultural matter, but here in the U.S. of A. a neatly trimmed triangle can be a nice turn-on. On the other hand, some women view this as an attempt to deface the female body. They equate trimming the triangle with burning down the rain forest.

Most American women shave their armpits and leg hair, plenty trim their pubic hair and some shave it all off because they like the way it looks and feels or because it's summer and they're trying to wear bikinis without looking like they just stepped off a boat from the Ukraine. Some guys get really turned on by a slick vulva. One advantage is that it's easier to lick; another is the extra visual charge that it seems to offer. Also, a prostitute who previewed this book commented, "Men trim and/or shave too. I see lots of this in my line of work. Yes, big-time execs, too."

Tips on Pubic Deforestation

If you like a close-cropped look but don't want the itching or ingrown hairs from shaving, try a men's beard trimmer. If you do shave, try the Silk Effects lady's razor. Shave only once in each direction, first with the grain of the hair, then against it. Wait a day if it needs more; otherwise rawness will result. Some women say that the problems with bumps and tenderness result from sporadic shaving and will decrease greatly if you shave every day. Experiment and find what's best for you.

The pubic area seems to be more tender when you are menstruating, wait until later for plucking, waxing or shaving. If you wax, put ice on it afterward. A lot of women don't like depilatory creams, even if these products claim to be for bikini lines. Some women like waxing; others say waxing and electric depilators are fine on legs, but can be problematic between them. Some women swear that the only way to do a pubic area right is to pluck it, hair by hair. Ouch!

Rainbow Girl Muffs

Some highly adventurous women dye their pubic hair amazing colors such as bright blue, pink, purple or green. Can you imagine? This guide endorses the concept and would love to hear a woman announce the change by blurting out, "Hon, I was abducted by aliens today..." Hopefully, adventurous ladies like these will go out of their way to use only approved nontoxic hair dyes that won't irritate their tender tissues or stain their boyfriends' teeth.

Tight Jeans & Infections

Of the things in life most irritating to the human organism, bladder infections rate right up there with presidential speeches, unemployment and earthquake aftershocks. They are not pleasant events. Guys usually don't understand them because they seldom get this type of infection.

Other common female infections involve an overpopulation of yeast cells in the vagina. This can happen when the vaginal environment becomes irritated or gets out of balance, as sometimes occurs when taking antibiotics. In fact, the vaginal environment tends to be out of balance when its pH goes above 5.5. This means that a healthy vagina is a bit acidic.

Yeast infections can cause a whitish discharge that may be clumpy. There can be a strong odor and possible itching. The first time you get a yeast infection you should definitely see a gynecologist to make sure it is correctly diagnosed and properly treated. Discuss with your gynecologist how to prevent yeast infections, how to diagnose them and what medications to use in the future.

There are some events that might increase the occurrence of both bladder and/or vaginal infections. One is having intercourse when the vagina isn't well-lubricated. Vaginal irritation can also result from using rubbers that aren't adequately lubricated. Putting contraceptive jelly or a water-based lubricant such as KY on the outside of a rubber will help a great deal. Both partners usually enjoy the extra slip 'n' slide feeling.

There may also be a connection between yeast infections and wearing things like tight jeans, pantyhose or spandex leotards. These cause a woman to sweat between her legs. This allows bacteria from the rectum to hydroplane into the vulva. One solution is to trash your tight jeans or spandex crotch-huggers. But if you are a total slave to fashion, be sure to wear cotton underpants and try cleaning your bum with a Handi-Wipe or other moist towelette each time you defecate. This will help cut down on the bacterial version of moonwalking. Also make sure you wipe from the front to the back. Some women find that decreasing the amount of sugar or artificial sweeteners in their diet helps to decrease the number of infections. Lubricants that contain glycerine should also be avoided if you get frequent infections.

Male partners can sometimes carry the infection without having any symptoms themselves. If that's the case, they will need to take the same medication as the woman. Otherwise, the infection will simply ping-pong back and forth between partners.

If you get bladder infections often, you might try peeing right after intercourse. It could help flush out whatever little micromites are waiting to make your life miserable. Also, some women find that drinking lots of cranberry juice helps prevent urinary tract infections, while drinking lots of carbonated drinks helps to cause them.

And finally, it might be helpful if both men and women accept the fact that bladder and vaginal infections fall into the category of shared problems rather than just her problem. It might be nice if the woman felt comfortable enough to tell her lover, "I hope that you won't hesitate to let me know if the environment down there gets a little, uh, tropical." Guys who enjoy doing oral sex almost always know a woman's baseline state and can often detect changes before she might be aware of them. Of course, guys should know that the environment of the vagina changes with the status of a woman's menstrual cycle. For instance, a woman's vagina might become more acidic when she is ready to conceive.

Prostate Infections & Irritation

Only men have prostate glands. The prostate gland is located on the floor of the rectum about a finger's length deep. It sits next to the entrance (or is that exit) of the bladder and wraps around the urethra. When it is not making fluid that contributes to the man's ejaculate, the prostate sometimes swells or gets infected. This is not good, since an irritated or infected prostate can cause severe urinary discomfort or a sudden and powerful need to urinate when the bladder is hardly even full. For a few unlucky souls, prostate swelling can be so severe that it clamps shut the urethra so the man can't pee at all.

To determine if you have a prostate infection, the doctor needs to stick a finger up your rear and push on your prostate so it drips fluid into your bladder. You then pee into a cup and they culture that. This may sound annoying to those men who have never had prostate problems. However, if your prostate ever becomes seriously irritated, you would probably let King Kong stick his finger up your rear if that could help.

Another potential source of prostate irritation might be cancer. This strikes men over the age of forty and is one of the less dangerous cancers if it is treated early. This is why men over forty should have regular prostate exams.

Is Smoking Sexy?

There are plenty of people who make a phenomenal effort to keep themselves neat, clean and attractive but still fill their lungs with cigarette smoke. Living with a contradiction like this is testimony to how difficult it can be to break the nicotine habit, especially when some of the huge tobacco companies have apparently tried to increase the addictive properties of cigarettes.

While there has been a substantial decline in tar sucking among most of us, young women remain the one group who are still puffing away as much as ever. This fact hasn't escaped the attention of cigarette makers, who work hard to attract the interest of young women. (UPDATE: We just learned that smoking is up among all teens, male and female. Way to go, Joe Camel!)

Cigarette ads are populated with shots of sexy women who seem happy, confident and in control, but you almost never see the cigarettes hanging out of their mouths, nor do you see them contorting their lips so they can try to blow the smoke out the side. These ads never have scratch and sniff patches to let you know what your breath will smell like once you begin smoking, nor do they offer free coupons to the cleaners, whom you will be visiting way more often if you smoke. Young women are also impacted by the fact that most women's magazines make huge revenues from cigarette ads. As a result, women's magazines are hesitant to boycott cigarette ads or run articles about the health hazards of smoking. They'll harp on every tragic disease in the world except lung cancer and cigarette-related heart attacks.

Cigarette smoke and birth control pills combine to create a major health risk in women above the age of thirty-three. And all women who take birth control pills and smoke have a greater incidence of bruising. (What about nonsmoking pill takers who are exposed to ambient cigarette smoke? Does the ambient smoke put them at extra risk? One should assume the answer is yes until credible research is done that proves the opposite.) Even dogs who live in homes with cigarette smokers die significantly sooner than those with nonsmoking masters.

Studies show that people who don't begin smoking before the age of twenty-one aren't likely to ever start. As a result, more and more of the tobacco industry's advertising emphasis will be on getting teenagers to smoke.

Chapter Notes: Thanks to Kate at www.cleansheets.com for some of the depilatory tips used in this chapter.

You won't believe how
bad her breath smells
after just one cigarette.

Abortion? Adoption?
Chapter 37

A large percentage of women who get abortions were using contraceptives at the time of intercourse. That's because even the best contraceptives occasionally fail. *If you haven't gone through menopause yet and you are not prepared to feed and change babies at 4:00 in the morning and if you can't financially and emotionally support a child for the next eighteen years, you shouldn't be having intercourse.* Fortunately, there are plenty of fun, erotic and highly intimate ways of getting each other off besides intercourse. If intercourse is still in the cards, you can greatly minimize your chances of becoming pregnant by using effective birth control methods.

So What If You Just Found Out You Are Pregnant and Didn't Want to Be?

There are plenty of people who will offer advice. Some of it will be helpful. There are many people who have opted for abortion and many who have had unplanned children. Most will tell you that they did the right thing. Whichever way you decide, keep in mind that millions of people have had to face the exact same thing that you are—although you may feel like the loneliest person on the face of the earth.

In case you are wondering about the emotional aspects of having an abortion, studies show that most women who have abortions don't report an increase in depression (as a group) for any more than a week or two after the abortion, if that. One of these studies was funded by a governmental agency that was hoping to find the opposite result. On the other hand, your own personal beliefs might not allow for abortion, in which case your options will be whether to raise the baby yourself or give it up for adoption. There are plenty of agencies that will help with the latter, but not many that will help the parent of an unplanned child who is trying to raise the child.

Please be aware that some of the strongest anti-abortion proponents are highly supportive while you are still pregnant, but are quite stingy and punitive when it comes to helping the unmarried mom of a toddler or older child. In many of their eyes, you are only of value as the physical vessel that is incubating the unborn child. Once the baby is born, they won't want to have anything to do with you.

Whether you choose to have an abortion or to have the baby, it's important that you make your mind up as soon as possible. All people, but especially teenagers, who are faced with unwanted pregnancies tend to be indecisive and don't act as soon as they might. If they opt for an abortion, it is sometimes later in the pregnancy when the procedure might be more complicated. And if they decide to have the baby, they sometimes don't go for prenatal care until later in the pregnancy. This places them at high risk, endangering themselves and their babies.

If you decide to keep the baby, make sure you have a support system in place to help after the baby is born.

A Special Note on Giving Your Baby Up for Adoption

There are thousands of loving couples who can't have a baby of their own and desperately want to adopt one. These couples tend to have been married for quite a while. Most have stable homes, good relationships and solid incomes. They will give your child a lifetime of love and care. Unfortunately, many of these couples must wait as long as seven years before they can adopt a baby, since not many single parents are giving their babies up for adoption these days. Part of the problem is that younger moms are often encouraged by their nonpregnant peers to keep the baby (easy for them to say!). Unwed moms often have the unrealistic fantasy that keeping the baby will make their lives better, or that the baby's father will want to marry them. This seldom happens.

One of the really nice things about adoption in this day and age is that the pregnant mom gets to interview the couples who want to adopt her baby. She gets to decide which couple she wants to raise the baby. That way she will know her baby is being raised and loved by people she likes.

Birth Control & Gnarly Sex Germs
Chapter 38

Why is it that some young men will care for a car or favorite baseball glove with meticulous detail, but forget about birth control when they are having intercourse? Why do so many of America's young women go nearly insane over one little zit or take hours getting dressed for a party, but not insist that a partner wear a rubber when they are sexually active? And why is our nation's rather feeble program to educate its young about sexually transmitted diseases little more than a thinly veiled attempt to discourage them from having sex altogether? It is a program that talks about disease, but rarely mentions pleasure.

Does it need to be this way?

This Book's Approach to Birth Control

Most books on sex have birth control chapters that read like a Chilton manual. Not this one. *War and Peace* maybe, but not a Chilton manual.

If you are interested in knowing about birth control options, go with your partner to a family planning clinic. Perhaps they will have a video you can watch and a real flesh-and-blood human being who can answer your questions. Or see if your HMO can send you a booklet on birth control. It is in their interest to help you, since it costs them a lot of money if you get pregnant.

Sharing the responsibility for birth control often increases the sexual trust and enjoyment in a relationship. It's the sort of thing that people do when they care about each other, rather than just making it the responsibility of the woman or ignoring the need altogether. Making birth control a mutual project could be the ante for having better sex.

Before saying more about birth control, we need to talk about sex germs. That's because one of the factors in choosing a birth control method is whether or not you are at risk for getting a sexually transmitted disease.

GSGs (Gnarly Sex Germs)

Some people believe that AIDS is the most deadly sex disease that ever was. Actually, the prize goes to syphilis. Even a couple of popes died from syphilis. That's why this chapter begins with a discussion of syphilis and then works its way to AIDS and other diseases that are associated with sexual contact.

Syphilis—The Great Pox

Before 1492, when Columbus came to America, there had been no recorded cases of syphilis in Europe. But syphilis did exist in the part of the New World where Columbus and his crew landed. Shortly after Columbus's return, a vicious strain of syphilis began to spread throughout Europe, quickly killing a sizable portion of the general population. During its first fifty years in Europe, from about 1493 until 1550, syphilis was an even more savage killer than AIDS. Smallpox got its name because the lesions it caused were small compared to those of The Great Pox syphilis. It seems that the Spanish army sent syphilitic prostitutes to infect the enemy Italian army, which is one of the first recorded instances of biological warfare.

After 1550, syphilis went from being a quick killer to a slow killer, more like the syphilis we know today. Instead of finishing off its victims in short order, syphilis began to linger in the body for years after the initial infection, eventually targeting organs like the heart or brain. Syphilis remained a potent killer for four hundred more years (from 1550 to 1940), with almost half of all hospital beds worldwide filled with its victims. Syphilis is less of a problem today because it can now be treated in its early phases by antibiotics, which weren't discovered until the 1940s.

Nobel Prize Note: In the 1920s, a medical doctor received the Nobel Prize for infecting syphilis patients with malaria. The high fever caused by the malaria helped to bum out the stubborn syphilis infection. Of course, there was no cure for the new cure. Some scientists speculate that more people died from the attempts to cure syphilis than from syphilis itself. Until the discovery of antibiotics, popular syphilis therapies included treatment with arsenic and mercury.

Lonely Shepherds, Scared Sheep—Sounds Like AIDS?

Folklore has it that syphilis was originally caused by lonely shepherds who prodded their sheep with something more personal than carved wooden staffs. The reason for the sheep/ shepherd rumor is a matter of simple poetry. In 1530, a great physician, poet and scholar named Fracastor wrote a poem about the disease of syphilis which hadn't been named syphilis yet. In the poem, a sixteen-year-old shepherd boy named Syphilis made the horrible mistake of building an altar on the wrong plot of land and praying to the wrong gods. This was the 1530s equivalent of wearing the wrong colors in a gang-controlled neighborhood. It seriously angered the god Apollo, who had the youth's genitals struck with a chancre-laden thunderbolt. Ouch! Fracastor's poem tells about the rapid spread of the "new" disease:

> "I sing of that terrible disease, unknown to past centuries, which attacked all Europe in one day and spread itself over part of Africa and Asia..."

Sounds a little like the spread of AIDS. But syphilis behaved and still behaves very much like a sexually transmitted disease. That is not the case with AIDS, unless you are a member of a high risk group.

AIDS

AIDS is a disease or cluster of diseases that involves a shut-down of the immune system. AIDS appears to be transmitted by certain kinds of sexual contact and through certain exchanges of blood. Several factors may be involved in its spread.

AIDS has yet to follow the early predictions about it that were based upon current knowledge of sexually transmitted diseases. For instance, it has not made the highly anticipated crossover into heterosexual populations. Not nearly enough straight people have been using condoms to prevent the cross-over that would have happened if current viral models were accurate. Many of the AIDS cases that do exist among heterosexuals can be explained by transfusion or IV drug usage. We are also warned about AIDS running rampant among the general population of Africa. Yet medical hygiene is so abysmal in much of Africa that the same syringe is sometimes used to inject hundreds of people with little or no sterilization. It is likely that "modern medicine" causes far more cases of AIDS in Africa than sexual activity. Also, more people in Africa appear to have died from famine and genocide than from sexually transmitted diseases.

Some straight people will think this means they don't need to take an informed stance against the spread of sexually transmitted diseases. This would be most unfortunate.

Why Should Straight People Continue to Be Cautious?

Many young straight adults have become wise to the fact that hardly any of their heterosexual peers are coming down with diseases like AIDS. More of their straight peers are dying from drug- and alcohol-related causes, not to mention suicide. Of course, this hasn't stopped young people from drinking or doing drugs, so why should they use condoms? It's hard to argue with this kind of logic, except to say that we live in such a fast-paced world that disease contagion will be nearly impossible to stop should an AIDS-like condition begin to prey on the heterosexual population. Those who used condoms might be the ones who survive.

Defining an Acceptable Level of Risk

Each year nearly 40,000 Americans die in car accidents. Thousands more are seriously injured. Yet most of us consider driving to be an acceptable risk. On the other hand, if people were told about a new sexually transmitted disease that took 40,000 American lives each year and injured thousands more, there would be a great outcry against sex.

Perhaps we believe there is something inherently good about driving and something inherently bad about sex. Or maybe we get more satisfaction from driving. Whatever the case, you can greatly decrease your chances of being injured in a car accident by not drinking or doing drugs when you drive, and by driving sensibly. The same is true for having sex.

Staying Well

Rather than focusing only upon AIDS prevention, why not try to keep your entire body healthy? This means staying fit, eating well and keeping all nonessential drugs out of your body. It also means using rubbers if you are having anal sex, whether you are heterosexual or homosexual. And if you aren't true blue and monogamous, seriously consider using rubbers during vaginal intercourse as well. This will help stop the spread of things likes herpes, syphilis, and perhaps genital warts and chlamydia. It will also help decrease your chances of getting diseases like AIDS.

For many people, an important part of staying healthy also includes having sex. This can be a very good thing. On the other hand, there would probably be a significant drop in the number of sexually transmitted diseases if potential partners dated for a few weeks or months before getting naked together. By then, you would know more about a potential partner than simply how they fill out their blue jeans. Perhaps the sex would be better, too.

As for specifics about staying well, consider the following:

Oral Sex (mouth-to-crotch) In studies on AIDS and prostitutes, the prostitutes who seem to be coming down with AIDS are those who use intravenous drugs. You would think that if AIDS were transmitted by oral sex, women who blow men for a living would be getting it in droves, but they're not unless they also shoot up drugs. While your chances of getting AIDS from oral sex are probably lower than from intercourse, you can get other sexually transmitted diseases while doing oral sex that are harmful to your body. Using a condom while blowing a guy or placing Saran Wrap over a woman's vulva makes sense if you are not in a long-term relationship. Also, forget having oral sex without a barrier if there is a cold sore in your mouth. The herpes virus is a switch-hitter that is happy to hop from mouth to genitals or vice versa. If you are a gay or bisexual male, it might be an excellent idea to bag whoever you blow, given the current affinity that AIDS has for gay and bisexual males.

Oral Sex (French kissing) Besides being a delightful thing to do, French kissing is a way of contracting anything you might get when someone with a cold or flu sneezes in your face. Why not save the making out until you have dated for a couple of weeks, or at least have learned the person's phone number by heart? Then if you think it's a go, go for it.

Hand Jobs Researcher Bruce Voeller was asked about the chances of catching a sexually transmitted disease from doing your partner by hand. Dr. Voeller compared it to the probability of breaking your neck from falling out of bed, unless you get the fluid into an open cut. Voeller comments: "A good way to know if you have an infectable cut is to rub a piece of lemon over your skin. If a place burns, then you've got a cut that might conceivably get infected."

Intercourse (vaginal) Do you really believe that the great-looking fraternity guy whom you are about to go to bed with is going to stop and say, "Oh, by the way, I'm totally low-risk except for that little butt-fucking incident last month with the captain of the wrestling team"? Or what about that sweet-looking former high school cheerleader? Do you honestly believe she will cop to having spiked heroin while going through her rebellious phase last summer? Perhaps it's possible that other people aren't quite as responsible about what goes on with their bodies as you might be with yours.

One should be especially sure to use condoms when sleeping with partners who drink or do drugs, even if it's just brewskis or pot. That's because these substances help to numb the part of the mind which we count on to keep us out of trouble. It's the sober part that says, "This isn't the kind of person I'd ever sleep with if I weren't stoned," or "I can't even remember this guy's name, but he's got one hand under my shirt and the other down my pants; what's wrong with this picture?" or "I'm sure I will feel much better in the morning if we use a condom tonight."

Note: Pulling out and squirting off to the side doesn't prevent anything, including frustration. Also, it's a good idea to put the rubber on as soon as the penis gets hard enough to wear it. That's because a penis usually starts dripping before it ever goes inside a vagina. And if your partner does speed or cocaine, never have intercourse without using condoms. With such people, you will never know what they have done or with whom. Half the time, they won't remember themselves. The same is true for heroin addicts and alcoholics, although these substances tend to decrease the ability or desire to have sex.

Intercourse (anal) According to one theory, there might be immune-suppressing factors in male ejaculate that help it on its journey up the female reproductive tract. These factors might not contribute to a person's good health when deposited in the rectum.

When compared to your rear end, the vagina has thick walls that keep male sex fluids out of the bloodstream. And stomach acids usually kick the daylights out of male ejaculate when it is swallowed. But the jury is still out on what happens to the immune-suppressing factors in male ejaculate when it is deposited in the rectum and large colon, which by its very nature absorbs fluids into the body. On the other hand, anal sex was popular for several centuries before AIDS was a problem, so it is quite a stretch to assume that anal sex with noninfected partners compromises the immune system. But until more is known about anal sex and the immune system, even totally monogamous husbands and wives are wise to use a condom when having anal sex. This will also help keep the man from getting urinary tract infections or passing fecal matter into the woman's vagina. (Just washing a penis with soap and water is not enough, as stuff from her rear stays in the peehole.)

Urine If you are into "water sports" and not in a long-term monogamous relationship, don't shoot urine into any body cavities and keep it off skin that's broken unless the skin is your own.

Drugs It is a medically sound idea to eliminate all nonessential drugs from your body, whether prescribed or recreational. This includes anything from poppers and cocaine to antibiotics and antifungals. Since many members of the gay community were so amazingly promiscuous during the 1970s and 1980s, sex diseases and parasites were passed around continuously. To combat these, antibiotics and antifungals were prescribed in huge amounts, often as a preventive before a guy spent a weekend at the baths or cruised the trails. No one knows what long-term effects this might have on the immune system; at the very least it helped create increasingly drug-resistant organisms. Again, avoid taking any drugs that are not essential, whether prescribed or not.

Diet There is no way the immune system is going to work well if you are malnourished. Most intravenous drug users are malnourished, which may be a factor that puts them at high risk for AIDS.

Exercise Exercise is more important than we like to think. Studies have shown that most people who exercise rigorously often have a delayed onset of serious AIDS symptoms. Also, several of the patients waiting for heart transplants at a major medical center were recently put on a program of exercise; 50 percent of them no longer needed the transplant by the time it became available. And in most studies on aging, men and women who exercise regularly show a significant decrease in the number of problems typically associated with getting old. They also have sex more often.

AIDS & God

Some people claim that AIDS is a message from God about sexual "immorality." If this is true, then why does God allow millions of right-wing, churchgoing, heterosexual Americans to die each year from cancer and heart attacks—diseases that take far more lives than AIDS? What's the hidden moral message there?

And what about young children who are dying from cancer and various immunological diseases? Is God punishing these two- to six-year-olds for being immoral? How can people say that one disease is caused by the wrath of God, while others aren't? Perhaps the real disease is in the minds of those who are willing to cast the first stone.

This concludes the deadly-sex-germ part of this chapter. In case you should need it, the phone number of the National AIDS Line is (800)342-AIDS.

Not So Deadly Sex Germs & Scruffy Sex Rodents

There are several germs and sex rodents that owe their very lives to people who indiscriminately make love. A highly annoying but generally nonfatal sex rodent is crab lice.

The author of this book first learned about crab lice many years ago while listening to a radical student leader at UC Berkeley. The radical leader was speaking to a group of not-so-radical students at a pizza place on the southside of campus. Throughout the entire presentation, the radical leader kept scratching his pubic area with the ferociousness of a junkyard dog. He could barely keep his hands out of his pants long enough to light a Gitanes. Gitanes are French cigarettes that smell really unpleasant. People with bad teeth, radical politics and itchy balls seem to enjoy them.

At the end of the speech, your author asked a friend if he had noticed something a little, uh, unusual about the radical's social manner. The friend's more experienced face scrunched up like a prune and spit out two ugly words: *crab lice.* Crab lice are infectious little mites that live in body hair. They can cause serious pubic as well as public itching.

There are other sexually transmitted catastrophes besides crab lice that can be either very mild or very annoying. Some have names that can hardly be pronounced, and more than just radical student leaders get them. Even sorority girls at USC get herpes, venereal warts, thrush, candida and chlamydia.

If you are sexually active, please keep the following in mind: whenever your genitals, anus, or mouth sprout warts or grow tiny cauliflowers, lesions or strange-looking pimples, when there's discomfort as you pee, when your urine is constantly cloudy or has blood in it, when there's a weird discharge or when things don't feel quite right, get yourself to a doctor or a clinic. Most of these problems can be treated without much pain or hassle.

But without treatment you could become sterile from an otherwise treatable problem. You can also pass on sex diseases to your partner without experiencing any symptoms yourself. This is not cool.

Anyone who is sexually active should take his or her genitals to a clinic or a private practitioner for a checkup every year or two. Be sure to include a throat culture if you have been doing oral sex, and a rectal culture if you've been taking it up the rear. It's a good idea to get routine checkups even if you've been using rubbers and don't have symptoms.

If symptoms of an STD suddenly go away, DO NOT FOR A MOMENT assume that the disease has gone away! Keep in mind that the most common symptom of a sexually transmitted disease is no symptom at all. It is very common to have an STD and not be aware of it.

Herpes, Etc.

The reason this book doesn't include more about sexually transmitted diseases is because it would take about a hundred pages to do a decent job. It would take half that just to cover herpes. More than 20 million people have herpes, and there are entire organizations that do nothing but supply help and information on the subject. Just because millions of people have herpes is no reason to be laissez faire about it. Avoid it by using condoms and sleeping around with fewer rather than more partners.

Herpes is a buff, strong little DNA virus that causes periodic eruptions of small painful blisters on the skin and mucous membranes, usually around the mouth and genitals. Some people also experience flulike symptoms. Herpes likes to take long siestas, sometimes for years at a time. When it does awaken, it is a little like a creature emerging from the underworld. Stress is sometimes said to trigger the outbreaks, and it helps to have a sense of humor about it. If you've got it, you've got it. Getting all freaked out about herpes isn't going to help matters one little bit. Be wise and stay informed. Let yourself become the master of it rather than the other way around. Or, as the Zen folk might say, you and the herpes are sharing the same body. Learn to get along.

If you are having your first outbreak of herpes or any other kind of sexual infection, get to a doctor right away. Proper treatment of the initial herpes outbreak can significantly reduce the severity of future outbreaks. For more information about herpes, phone the National Herpes Hotline at (919)361-8488 or the National STD Hotline (800)227-8922. Also check the resources part of our website: www.goofyfootpress.com.

If you have herpes or any other potentially contagious disease, never ever have sex without telling the other person first. If the shoe were on the other foot or, more appropriately, if the germs were in the other genitals, you would want them to inform you.

STD Recap

Please remember that this chapter is at best an overview of birth control and STDs and is by no means a complete or comprehensive source. Here is a very brief summary of the more common STDs. In Australia they're called STIs or Sexually Transmitted Infections—same germs, different accent. No matter what part of the world you are in, failure to get treatment for most STDs can lead to complications beyond your wildest imagination.

AIDS Four to six weeks after infection there may be flulike symptoms, but nothing after that until AIDS strikes. Then the symptoms can range from unexplained weight loss and extreme tiredness to night sweats, fever, chronic diarrhea, pneumonia, dry cough, seizures, skin blotches and swollen glands.

Chlamydia With over 4 million new cases each year, this is the most common STD today. Four out of five women who have it don't know they have it until they get serious complications such as Pelvic Inflammatory Disease. With males, it's a similar picture. This is why all sexually active people should be tested for it at least once a year. Guys: Few symptoms or liquid discharge and painful peeing. Girls: Usually no symptoms, but there can be burning or itching in your vagina with or without a discharge.

Genital Herpes Transmission: contact with an infected area during oral, anal or vaginal sex. Sometimes no symptoms. Guys: Painful blisters on the penis, scrotum and sometimes anywhere from your navel to your knees. Girls: Red bumps in and around the folds or lips of your vulva that turn into painful blisters. Can also appear on the cervix, thighs, navel or anus. Guys and girls: sometimes flulike symptoms. Can also cause painful peeing.

Genital Warts Little cauliflowers where the sun don't shine. See Human Papilloma Virus (HPV).

Gonorrhea Often no symptoms at the start, but complications will cause pain in the groin or stomach and you can end up with anything from swollen testicles or Pelvic Inflammatory Disease to brain infections. Guys: Might be a burning discharge from the penis. Girls: Possible green or yellow discharge from the vagina, abnormal vaginal bleeding or pelvic pain. Pelvic Inflammatory Disease, tubal pregnancy and sterility are real possibilities if not treated.

Hepatitis A, B or C Often there are no symptoms, or there can be yellowing of the skin and the whites of your eyes, nausea, fever and soreness of your liver, and/or your urine can get dark and your feces can turn lighter or grayish. You can be totally incapacitated for several months and even die. Liver damage is a common complication. Different types are spread in different ways, from simply kissing on the lips to butt fucking and nearly every kind of sexual act in between.

Human Papilloma Virus (HPV) or Genital Warts There are more than sixty-five different strains of HPV that can be anywhere from your larynx and lungs to your mouth and anus. The strains of HPV that impact you sexually are called Genital Warts. These are often but not always spread sexually. It is nearly impossible to tell when or who you got them from, usually two weeks to three months after contact. They cause small, hard, wrinkled bumps that are sometimes big enough to be seen with the naked eye. Guys: Warts can spring up on the head or shaft of your penis, on your scrotum or in or on your anus. Girls: They can be in the vagina, on the vulva or in or on your anus. HPV can also cause cervical lesions.

Nongonococcal Urethritis Males: Discharge from your penis can be milky, thin, clear or watery. Both sexes: You might feel a burning sensation when peeing.

Don't forget your rubbers!

Scabies and Crab Lice—Pthirus Pubis or Crab Louse (Ever hear the insult, "You louse" or "He's a louse"?) Miniature mites that are highly contagious. Can cause itching beyond belief. Crab lice can be found anywhere on the body that has hair; scabies burrow under your skin and can cause itchy sores that look like poison ivy. Talk to your pharmacist or healthcare provider about scabies or louse-killing potions. Dry clean or wash and dry at the highest heat possible everything that isn't nailed down. If you can't wash it, store it in a tightly closed plastic bag for two weeks.

Syphilis About a third of untreated sufferers eventually die from brain, heart or nerve damage. There are often no symptoms, which is why sexually active people should be tested every year.

Vaginal Infections (Trichomoniasis, Bacterial Vaginosis, or Yeast Infections/Candida Albicans) Trichomoniasis: Guys get it in the urethra. Girls usually get it in the vagina. Symptoms for both sexes: foul-smelling discharge, painful peeing, or no symptoms at all. You can get it from sexual activity or in other ways, like sharing an infected person's towel, bathing suit or toilet seat. Bacterial Vaginosis (BV): Creamy discharge and fishy smell after intercourse, sometimes itching and painful peeing. Yeast Infections or Candida Albicans: itchy genitals; heavy, whitish, clumpy discharge that can smell like yeast. Often in the vagina. NOTE: Guys can get this in the penis. Yeast infections can happen on their own, when the woman is taking antibiotics, when she's been wearing tight pants, pantyhose, leotards or anything that doesn't allow her crotch to breathe or when she's having sex. With some vaginal infections, it is important that the male is treated also, even if he doesn't have a vagina. See pages 472-473 for more on yeast infections.

Birth Control

Now Hear This—This chapter is not a comprehensive source of information on birth control or sexually transmitted diseases, nor was it intended to be. Please contact your health-care provider or local Planned Parenthood office for complete information about birth control. Your best bet is to speak with someone who works with birth control day in and day out, and who can use their practical wisdom to help you select a long-term option that will work best for you. The rest of this chapter mainly focuses on condoms and includes isolated details about other forms of birth control.

Rubbers & Rubber Wisdom

After much painstaking research, we have come to the conclusion that what you slop on the outside of a rubber is almost as important as what you stuff into it. In addition, the pages that follow describe different cuts of rubber and what to do when your rubber is a lemon.

Nowadays, rubbers or condoms can be purchased nearly everywhere except maybe your local post office or Christian Science Reading Room. But you still need to hand them to a cashier before they are yours to wear, unless you get them from a vending machine or by mail.

For some people, the ability to purchase a rubber depends upon who's working the cash register. This is especially true in small towns where there is no such thing as retail anonymity. In some small towns, a person would attract less attention knocking off the local bank than buying a pack of rubbers.

Getting rubbers by mail order helps alleviate this problem, but in some households plain unmarked envelopes garner as much attention as a singing telegram.

Rubber Scoop

Back in his academic days, the author of this book was particularly fascinated with the study of slow viruses. As a result, he figured something serious was brewing when reports of a lethal new sex germ started trickling out of San Francisco in the early 1980s. Knowing what happened each night in the bars and baths up there, he assumed it would be an epidemiological nightmare for both gays and straights. Fearing the worst, he began using rubbers before it was fashionable.

When he first started bagging himself, his girlfriend scoffed, hissed, puffed and all but threw him out of bed and into the nearby LaBrea Tar Pits. "Those damn things give me bladder infections," she snarled. Sure enough, she got a bladder infection. And that's when he learned that the word prelubricated on the outside of the package is someone's idea of a joke. No matter how wet she might be, it's sometimes best to add lubrication when using a condom. Otherwise, the added friction can cause a woman to have bladder or vaginal infections.

Not All Rubbers Are Created Equal

There are no governmental controls over the manufacture of condoms. The FDA leaves quality control to the makers of condoms. To put it mildly, the foxes are guarding the chicken coop.

To help protect against poorly made rubbers, slop some contraceptive jelly or water-based lubricant on the outside of your rubber before you have intercourse. This will help compensate for a number of rubber ills, and it will help intercourse with a bagged penis feel much, much sweeter.

The extra lubrication also helps to make up for the loss of precum or natural lubrication that normally drips out of the penis. The condom catches the precum, like everything else.

Chronic Rubber Busters

Researcher Bruce Voeller and associates studied a group of young men who were chronic rubber busters. Contrary to what you might think, these chronic rubber busters weren't hung any bigger than the average guy and they hadn't used Vaseline as a lubricant. Petroleum jelly, i.e. Vaseline, is an oil-based lubricant that does to latex rubbers what AIDS does to the body.

Voeller and associates found that almost all of the chronic rubber busters were using ordinary hand creams like Nivea, Johnson's Baby Oil, Vaseline Intensive Care, Corn Huskers or Jergens to lubricate the outside of their rubbers. These guys assumed that since the hand creams washed off easily they weren't oil-based. WRONG. Almost any type of hand cream will weaken a latex rubber by ninety percent in less than sixty seconds, especially those that contain mineral oil. The same can be true for body powders. The safest lubricants are contraceptive jellies or water-based products like KY Jelly sold at supermarkets or drugstores. For more on lubes, see the chapter "Sex Fluids."

If a Condom Breaks or Doesn't Come Out When You Do

Nasty, nasty, nasty. If you were using a condom for birth control and discover that it broke while in service, consider calling your physician as soon as possible. There is a morning-after pill that is reasonably effective in preventing pregnancy. In the meantime, do not inject birth control foam or jelly into the vagina. The pressure might push the ejaculate up into the cervix. The same is true for douching. Instead, try inserting a contraceptive suppository. Wash your external genitals, pee, and if you have something that contains nonoxynol-9, rub it on your genitals and leave it there for a while.

Baggy Rubbers?

Some condom companies are now manufacturing rubbers that are extra-baggy around the head. They fit snugly around the base of your penis, but the top inch or two bags out like the Tommy Hilfiger pants that the gangbanger wannabes wear. This lets the head of your penis slosh around inside the rubber, which, believe it or not, can feel really nice. (Baggy-headed rubbers are different from those with reservoir tips, which have a little finger-like tip at the end of the rubber that supposedly collects cum.)

Baggy-headed brands include the Pleasure Plus, the Trojan UltraPleasures, Lifestyle's Xtra Pleasure and the Inspiral. Of these, a lot of guys seem to like the Pleasure Plus, but each has its own sensation and it is good to experiment. Of the classic, unbaggy condoms, you might try the Crown or Kimono Sensations.

The one place where rubbers need to fit snugly is around the base of the penis. Otherwise, they might slip off. The penis usually starts shrinking right after ejaculation, so a guy shouldn't keep thrusting after he comes. He also needs to hold on to the edge of the rubber with his fingers when he's pulling out.

So what about all those situations when a guy comes before his sweetheart? What about her sexual pleasure if he's supposed to suddenly pull out? Help her come before intercourse. That's why Father Nature invented vibrators and oral sex. Or once you begin having intercourse, one of you can reach down with your fingers or the head of a vibrator to help the woman get more stimulation. Another way to increase the stimulation is for the woman to be in a position where she can push against her partner's pubic bone. Also consider doing oral sex after intercourse.

Reservoir Tips?

Some rubber brands make a big deal about having reservoir tips to hold a guy's ejaculate. There are a couple of problems with this concept. The first is that most reservoir tips hold about 2.9 mls. of ejaculate. While half of all guys produce 2.9 mls. or less, there's still another fifty percent of guys who produce more than 2.9 mls., which means their tips runneth over.

An inexpensive and highly effective method of birth control,
as long as his doesn't get put into hers.

The other problem with reservoir tips is the assumption
that they really do hold the fluid. If you think about the physics
of intercourse, any fluid ejaculated into the reservoir tip is going
to get mashed down the sides with each ensuing thrust. While it's
a good idea to leave a half-inch or so of space at the end of the
rubber, it doesn't matter if it has a reservoir tip or not.

Rock'n'roll Did the band 10cc take their name from what
they assumed was the volume of the average male ejaculation?
If so, they guessed way too high.

Other Rubber Tips & Trivia

A guy who doesn't feel comfortable using rubbers during
intercourse might try wearing them while jerking off. This could
help him get used to the feel.

Try to find nonlubricated rubbers for blow jobs, since it's
the lubrication that tastes bitter. There are also flavored condoms

such as the Durex and Trustex. If the initial taste of latex bothers you, try rinsing your mouth out with something like mouthwash, cognac or toothpaste first, but make sure it doesn't react with the latex. Another type of rubber to consider for oral sex is the Trojan Supra, although it crinkles like a grocery bag because it's made out of urethane. It will transfer heat a lot better.

Most men find that condoms feel better to wear if they put a drop of water-based lubricant inside the tip before unrolling it over the penis. This allows the head of the penis to slosh around inside the condom, which is usually a good thing. It also helps if you will put a little water-based lubricant on the outside of the condom once it's on the penis.

The average rubber is 7" from stem to stern. This means that the lucky 10 percent or so of guys who are longer than 7" will feel like geeks in high-water pants when using rubbers. The percentage of high-water guys goes up significantly if you remember to leave an extra half-inch of latex at the tip. Fortunately, there are new, larger rubbers whose brand names are not difficult to miss. If you can't find them, contact the folks at Condomania at (323) 933-7865 or on the web: www.condomania.com.

One recent book on sex cautions against using colored rubbers, since some of the dyes may not be safe or colorfast. They might turn a penis or vagina red, green, blue, yellow, magenta or maybe even hot pink.

Some guys tie off the end of a spent rubber before throwing it in the trash. This is similar to tying the end of a balloon, but for slightly different purposes.

Don't recycle your rubbers. Use a new one each time you come. Don't carry them around in a wallet. Don't put them in the glove compartment of a car. They don't like that kind of heat.

Do experiment with different brands until you find one that you like best; however, don't use the ones with ribs or nubs if you are having anal sex. The next time you want to have extra fun with your friends, sacrifice a couple of latex rubbers by blowing them up really big and letting them fly to the moon.

"Reality"—What Parents and Teachers Try to Teach Us About, or a New Condom for Women

There is a new female version of a rubber that's inserted into the vagina rather than rolled over a penis. It's called Reality in the States or Femidon in the UK. (Femidon—what a hideous name for something they want you to stick into your most private space, not that Reality makes you wet with anticipation...) Here are some of the benefits:

🎹 It's made out of polyurethane instead of latex. This means there won't be as much heat loss between vagina and penis. 🎹 The guy doesn't have to pull out as soon as he comes. 🎹 It gives women more control in protecting themselves. 🎹 Some women report that the ring around the outside of the condom stimulates the clitoris during intercourse.

Possible negatives: 🎹 Its birth control properties might be less than optimal. Be sure to read the instructions well. 🎹 It ain't cheap. 🎹 It's kind of big and strange, but if you're the type who's already been abducted by aliens and had your genitals probed with interplanetary sex tools, this should be no big deal.

The woman's condom is also being used by both straight and gay couples for anal intercourse, although it's doubtful that the instructions include this small detail.

Love You to Death—Not Using Condoms

If you have deep feelings for your partner and fear that using a condom will ruin your spontaneity or somehow dampen the moment, please read the following to him or her:

"I love you way too much to risk putting our relationship through the strain of having to deal with an unwanted pregnancy. I also love you way too much to risk giving you something that I may have gotten from a toilet seat somewhere. (Leave out the part about who you were on the toilet seat with.) So if we are both serious about being together, let's work on a timetable for ditching the condoms. To do this, we need to get tested for gnarly sex germs, and we have to start using an effective method of birth control. Then we can dump the condoms, but not before."

Note: In the United States, fifty percent of pregnancies in women under the age of thirty-four are neither planned nor intended. The number rises to seventy-five percent for women over forty. More than eighty percent of pregnant teens had no desire to be that way. Also, twenty-six percent of people who use abstinence as their method of birth control become pregnant each year.

The Three-Year and Five-Year Birth Control Implants: Lots of Protection in the Time It Takes to Fill Up Your Gas Tank

Sexually active people seem to fall into one of two extreme groups: those who have intercourse often and those who don't. Believe it or not, the once-in-a-blue-moon group has the lion's share of unwanted pregnancies. There are several reasons for this which could fill an entire book. Please take it on faith that if you have intercourse sporadically rather than regularly, you are in a high-risk group for getting pregnant. The birth control implant (Norplant) might be every bit as important for you as for those who hump like bunnies.

The three-year or five-year implant is a small strip of thin material that's injected under a woman's arm. It could be a good choice for anyone who enjoys intercourse but doesn't want to get pregnant. The implant has been around since the mid 1970s. It's been widely used in Finland since 1983. America was the seventeenth country to approve usage for the general public, although American clinics have been testing it for at least fifteen years.

Here are some advantages of the birth control implant:

Installation takes about five minutes. You don't even need to get undressed, assuming you've had a recent exam, since the injection goes under your arm. It can be administered by a nurse and leaves a small black and blue spot for about a week.

The following comparison is not meant as a criticism of the pill, which works well for many women. Birth control pills are given in large enough doses so the chemical is still in a woman's system twenty-four hours later. To accomplish this, the dosage of each pill is higher than you need during the first twenty-three hours. It's a little like having to drink enough beer in one sitting to still be buzzed twenty-four hours later. It's different with the implant. The release rate of the implant is continual, so it never puts out more hormone than you need at any one time. As a result, it releases less than half as many chemicals into your body during any twenty-four-hour time span, and there are fewer hormonal ups and downs. Also, the implant doesn't contain estrogen like most birth control pills. It releases only progesterone.

📖 The birth control implant works by preventing ovulation and by making the cervical mucus more viscous so the male ejaculate has trouble swimming through it. This is an important consideration for couples who believe that life begins with conception. There is no conception, so the question of when life begins does not apply.

📖 The only common side effect with the implant is occasional spotting and a tendency toward irregular periods. An unexpected side effect of the implant is that women who use it may actually have a lower incidence of stroke than women who don't and it might make your periods lighter.

📖 In case you don't like it or want to get pregnant sooner than planned, the implant can be removed at your convenience. Unfortunately, some of the earlier implants were inserted too deeply under the skin to be removed as easily as they might have been. This should not be the case anymore.

As with any birth control method, check with your physician or family planning center for a full list of side effects. This book's information may be out of date by the time you read it. Also, there are other long-term birth control methods to consider, such as the IUD or Depo-Provera.

Morning-After Pills and Emergency Contraception—Plan B

There's a new morning-after pill. You take one pill 72 hours after the sperm train left the station, and the second pill twele hours after that. The side effects are less than with the original morning-after pill and are almost nonexistent compared to a therapeutic abortion. For information, go to http://not-2-late.com or call (888)668-2528.

There is also another after-the-fact device called the copper-T intrauterine device (IUD). It can be inserted up to five days after unprotected intercourse and can reduce the risk of pregnancy following unprotected intercourse by more than ninety-nine percent. It can also be left in place to provide effective contraception for up to ten years. Check with your healthcare provider, call (888)668-2528 or go to http://not-2-late.com.

Forgotten Pills, Sponges, Film and the Diaphragm

🎹 If you forget to take your birth control pill, check with your physician's office right away. They will tell you if you should double up the next day. If it's been less than twelve hours since you were supposed to take it, some physicians will recommend taking one when you remember and one a few hours later.

🎹 Women who take triphasic birth control pills report higher libido and sexual pleasure than other birth control pill takers. Research on pill usage and libido (sexual desire) is strange and contradictory. If you have less desire after taking the pill for a couple of months, tell your healthcare provider and try a different type of pill.

🎹 After being off the market for four years, the birth control sponge is back. It costs approximately $2.00 each, has a ten percent failure rate, and can be inserted up to twenty-four hours before intercourse.

🎹 There is a new birth control film that is inserted into the vagina. It has a failure rate of six percent. At this time, there are no plans for a video version.

🎹 Don't forget to consider using the good old-fashioned diaphragm! Side effects are few and far between, and think of the fine-motor skills you'll learn in getting the thing in and out.

Gyno Visits—The Night Before

Most women would be happy if they never had to spread their legs in a physician's office again. However, if you do have an appointment for a pelvic exam, your partner should wear a condom the night before. Male ejaculate can mess with pap smear results, and it won't help the doctor make an accurate diagnosis of possible infections.

Self-Esteem & Birth Control Use

Researcher Meg Gerrard spoke to a random group of college students about sex and birth control. She later gave a series of followup tests about what she had presented. She found that the students who could remember the most were the same students who scored highest on measures of sexual self-esteem. Students who felt less comfortable about their own sexuality remembered significantly less about sex and birth control, even if they were A students in other subjects.

These findings were just as true for men as for women. Gerrard found that while being uncomfortable about sex is not enough to keep a person from having intercourse, it is enough to keep him or her from using birth control.

Planning far enough ahead to use birth control makes a clear statement that you want to have sex. One way that people who are ambivalent about sex get around this conflict is by having sex that isn't planned or discussed ahead of time. That way, they can plead temporary insanity if called on the carpet by their own harsh superego, or real-life parents if they are still living at home.

Unconscious Reasons for Wanting to Be Pregnant

Here are a few fantasies about getting pregnant and having a baby that might keep a young woman from using birth control: getting pregnant will make her feel grown-up, the baby will love her unconditionally, it's one thing she can do "right," it will help her be respected, it will free her from her parents, the baby's father will want to marry and care for her, she'll be able to care for the child in a way that she wasn't. Unfortunately, most of these fantasies come crashing down once the girl has the baby in her arms and reality rears its uncaring head.

Dear Paul,

They've had birth control pills for women for years. Why haven't they invented a birth control pill for guys?

Georgia in Georgia

Dear Georgia,

One reason why there's a pill for women but none for men has to do with biology. Stopping an egg versus a wad of sperm is like stopping the Hindenburg as opposed to the Viet Cong. Eggs are the easier target.

In an average month, a woman produces a single egg. In an average day, her boyfriend produces 10 million sperm. Worse yet, once a sperm is created, it is warehoused down in Scrotumland for more than two-and-a-half months. This means that if you gave your man a pill that would magically stop him from producing any new sperm, he would still be fertile for another seventy-five days. (When my wife and I castrate one of our llamas, we need to keep him from the lady llamas for three weeks; even without his testicles, he is still fertile for three weeks.)

Another problem for researchers is whether to stop sperm production altogether or to find a substance that allows sperm to be produced, but interferes with their ability to mature.

Pills for guys may also have unwanted side effects. They might make us men even more moody, irritable and perhaps even aggressive than we already are. So scientists are trying to develop synthetic hormones that will decrease sperm production without these troubling sideeffects.

Researchers are also trying to create reversible vasectomy procedures. These include inserting mini-plugs or micro-valves inside a guy's scrotum. The valves might be regulated with a magnetic or electrical impulse. This could be problematic if our valves were turned on each time we went through a metal detector or rested a laptop computer you-know-where.

A social issue in the use of male birth control has to do with trust. It would require females to trust men in the way we have to trust you when you say, "Don't worry, I'm on the pill." You, of course, have more to lose by virtue of who is left carrying the placenta.

The work that's currently being done to develop a male birth control pill is impressive, but it will likely be another ten to twenty years before these pills make it to market.

Fortunately, with all of the work that's being done, they don't need to go through the expense of testing actual human subjects, given how women are always claiming what rats men are.

Dear Paul,

I'm a pretty responsible and selective guy. I get tested for AIDS every year and make sure that my partners have been tested too. Is there any need for me to use condoms?

Clean in Colorado Springs

Dear Clean,

I just returned from a speaking engagement at Portland State University, where campus health workers estimate that fifty percent of the student population has an incurable sexually transmitted disease known as Papilloma or HPV. One of the problems with Papilloma, besides the fact that there are nearly seventy known strains of it, is that it's associated with an increased risk for cancer of the cervix.

Another recent study in Baltimore found that forty percent of inner-city teens have Chlamydia, which is also a sexually transmitted disease.

So, if you are traveling to Portland or Baltimore, you'll probably want to put a condom on first thing in the morning, right after you put on your socks.

As for your own state of Colorado, I was there in September and didn't notice anybody who looked like they had a sexually transmitted disease. I mean, they weren't frothing at the mouth or sporting big skin lesions, not even at the offices of the *Colorado Daily.* However, STDs like Papilloma, Chlamydia and Herpes don't usually announce themselves to friends and potential lovers.

It's possible to have a serious STD and not even know. Symptoms can take months to develop, if ever. This means that Amber, who sprouted genital warts after sleeping with Dave, might have actually gotten the virus from her former squeeze Mike.

What I'm saying, Clean, is just because you look clean or feel clean, you might not be.

Also, did I mention your anus? Condom or no, vaginal fluids that slosh around during intercourse can carry STDs to a guy or girl's rear end. So if you end up with anal discomfort or warts in your anus, take your entire pelvis to a clinic and have its various entries and exits probed, poked and cultured.

Some guys feel uneasy about having anal warts checked out, fearing that the physician will suspect they've been receiving anal sex. Not to worry. The medical profession knows that straight guys get anal warts. Honest.

NUMBERS

To locate your nearest Planned Parenthood center: (800)230-PLAN

National Herpes Hotline: (919)361-8488

National STD Hotline: (800)227-8922

National AIDS Line: (800)342-AIDS

For AFTER intercourse/emergency contraception: (888)668-2528

For STDs, Birth Control, Adoption and Abortion, please check out the resources part of our website at www.goofyfootpress.com.

Chapter Notes: We are saddened to report the recent death of Dr. Bruce Voeller, a man who couldn't understand why condom makers should be allowed to sell poorly made products. Bruce Voeller was one of the few researchers in this country with the guts and tenacity to take on the condom makers of America. He will be greatly missed.

Trying To Get Pregnant

Chapter 39

Dear Paul,

My wife and I have been trying to get pregnant, with no luck. The doctor wants me to get a sperm count. Do you know anything about this?

Hank from Thunder Bay

Dear Hank,

If personal experience is of any use, here's the skinny on sperm counts...

First, a sperm sample needs to be less than an hour old in order to do an accurate test. In fact, the warmer, the better. That's why they may want you to produce the sample on location—at the same lab where you go for routine blood tests.

Unfortunately, your little spermos don't suddenly appear for roll call and that's that. There's a whole procedure that needs to be followed. Like handing the proper authorization form to some total stranger in a white coat who will automatically yell in a loud voice, "Whadda ya here for?"

That's when you will become acutely aware of just how many people are sitting in the crowded waiting room less than five feet behind you. There will be a mom with a couple of kids, two teenagers, an older gentleman, and maybe even a nun—all waiting to hear your answer just like the people before them waited to hear theirs. You will clear your throat and say as quietly as possible, "I'm here for a sperm count," after which the person in the white coat will immediately say in the loudest voice possible, "SPERM COUNT?" as if for some reason you were really there for a barium enema, but said sperm count just for the heck of it.

The person in the white coat will then yell to another person at the other end of the lab, "Louise, where are the specimen cups for doing a sperm count?" at which point Louise will yell back

"WHAT?" to which the person in the white coat will respond even louder, "I NEED A SPECIMEN CUP FOR THIS GUY TO GIVE A SPERM SAMPLE."

Now maybe Louise will yell back, "Top shelf in the cupboard on the right." Or maybe she'll yell "WHAT?" once again, and then the person in the white coat will look up at you shaking his or her head, expecting you to offer a kind and sympathetic nod.

Eventually, they will find the correct cups and hand you one. If you are lucky, they will open the door and direct you to a bathroom down the hall. Otherwise, they will tell you to have a seat in the waiting room, where twelve sets of eyes will be staring at your face and then at the plastic cup with the shiny blue lid that's in your sweating hand. And then the little five-year-old who is sitting with his mother will ask, "Mommy, what's a spurn count?" and she will glare at him with her most intense "Don't-ask-me-that-now—OR EVER!" stare, and the little boy will protest, "But that man has to have a spurn count. Is something wrong with him?"

I am still not sure what the correct response should be when the person in the white coat finally summons you to the bathroom down the hall. Do you smile, make eye contact and say "Thanks!"??? I also marvel at the man with gumption enough to look at the specimen cup and ask, "What do I do with this?"

Of course, if you are anywhere near to being a normal guy, harvesting your own sperm in a locked bathroom is nothing you need instructions for. On the other hand, when you are producing sperm for an official sample, thoughts may enter your mind that never have before. For instance, "How long should I take?" I mean, you don't want to return in two minutes, deed done. On the other hand, you don't want to take half an hour, because you know that Louise and the person in the white coat will be giving knowing glances to each other, as if they aren't already.

To top that, no one has ever given you a grade on what actually came out. This time, not only are they scoring you on the number of sperm you're about to produce, but you will also be graded on how well your sperm swim and on how full you fill the cup. So suddenly you'll be asking yourself, "Is there some way I should be doing this for optimal results? Should I be squeezing my testicles at the moment of truth?" I don't know what to suggest, except if you want to save yourself the embarrassment of scoring in the lower twenty percent of men who have ejaculated in plastic specimen cups, save up for a couple of days. You'll never believe how large a specimen cup looks when you are trying to fill it with sperm.

Finally, when you are done, you smile inwardly and walk down the hallway looking for the man in the white coat. That's when you discover he is drawing blood and you'll need to hand the cup to Louise. Oh God. During your entire lifetime there may have been dozens of different ways that you've delivered sperm to the person of a woman, but never in a plastic cup and never has she held it up to the light and swirled it to inspect its contents, and never has she stared so blankly and never have you felt so small.

Anyway, Hank, that's what I know about sperm counts. Good luck to you and your wife.

P.S. If a couple is trying to get pregnant, it takes an average of eight months before hitting conceptual gold. If a couple is NOT trying to get pregnant, it only takes one night.

Sex During Pregnancy
Chapter 40

If you hadn't noticed by now, each woman has her own unique way of looking at the world and you can't really predict how she will react to the man who knocked her up. Some pregnant women will want more intimacy than ever before, while others will want space—sometimes huge amounts of space. This can be confusing for a dad-to-be, as he is never quite sure if the love of his life wants to snuggle or pluck his eyes out. Also, don't think that the dad-to-be isn't experiencing his own set of pregnancy-related emotions. These may cause him to hesitate sexually while his child-to-be is turning somersaults half a penis-length away.

Fortunately, the chapter that follows is about sex during pregnancy. It covers all of these issues and more, from orgasm-related uterine contractions and swelling vulvas to fetal brain development and having sex after your baby is born.

Please! No matter what you read in this chapter or anywhere else, you absolutely must discuss the matter of having sex while pregnant with a healthcare provider who is familiar with you and your pregnancy. That's because in some cases it might be prudent to alter some of the more outrageous ways that you and your partner enjoy sex. While this is necessary for relatively few pregnant couples, your personal health care professional is the only one who can help you in making this determination.

Talking to Your Healthcare Professional about Sex

Think about this for a moment: you go to a physician, get totally naked, spread your legs wide apart and let your doctor put her fingers in places where even the IRS doesn't. Yet many of us are nearly paralyzed by asking the simple question "Is it OK for me to have sex while I'm pregnant?"

Plenty of physicians encourage couples to have sex during pregnancy. And obstetricians like the one you are probably seeing rely on people having healthy sex lives in order to keep from going broke. So do pediatricians, gynecologists, Lamaze instructors and everyone else in the healthcare industry. There is no way your physician wants you getting out of practice with intercourse as long as the possibility exists that you might have more kids further down the line. So don't be afraid to ask.

If your health-care provider says it's okay to have sex, go to it. If the answer is "No, it's not okay to be having sex," then it is important to ask more questions. The first is "Pork hay?" which is Spanish for "Why not?"

If your healthcare provider is one of the few remaining dinosaurs who doesn't believe that pregnant women should be having sex, get yourself a second opinion. Most physicians feel that having sex during pregnancy is a completely normal thing to do, unless there are specific reasons not to such as having a prior history of miscarriages or premature labors, placenta is attached near the cervix (placenta previa), your water has broken or there is bleeding of unknown origin.

If the physician gives a specific reason for why you shouldn't have sex, ask two more questions:

1. "How long should we not have sex—for the next few weeks, months, or for the entire pregnancy?" All too often, when a physician says, "No sex," the couple assumes this means for the entire pregnancy, when the intent was "No sex for the next couple of weeks." If you were to ask the same question in a month, the physician might say, "It was just a precaution. Based on how well you are doing now, I see no reason why you shouldn't have sex."

2. "Does 'no sex' just mean intercourse, or does it include all sexual contact?" For instance, intercourse might pose a concern, but it's fine to have orgasms orally or by masturbating. Or orgasms might be the potential problem, in which case you could ask if you can still have intercourse as long as you don't have an orgasm. For some women, this would be a cruel and unusual compromise, while others might welcome the extra intimacy that intercourse allows, orgasm or not.

Urge Surge—the Mood Thing

Moodwise, some women stay pretty even throughout their pregnancies, while others push the mental envelope. An interesting feature of pregnancy-related moodiness can be the intensity of the mood and the amplitude of its swing. For instance, some pregnant women who are horny feel so intensely horny that they find it hard to think about much but sex and literally attack the dad-to-be the second he walks through the door. The intensity can be so great that some men feel a little used, while others seize the moment. Other pregnant women don't feel like having sex at all, and some might feel horny one moment and weepy the next.

Keep in mind that a pregnant woman has the potential to feel hurt by comments that few women in their nonpregnant right minds would find offensive.

For the woman whose moods fluctuate, there might be moments when she blames her man for her condition and other times when she feels elated about being pregnant and is quite happy to know and love the guy who got her that way. Also, it is normal for a pregnant woman to feel moments of depression alternating with feelings of elation, and to have dreams of her child being a perfect baby as well as fears of it being handicapped.

Much has been said about the disruptive effects of hormonal changes on a pregnant woman's mood, and this might be quite true. On the other hand, oxytocin levels rise throughout pregnancy, and oxytocin is said to make for better moods. It also causes contractions of the uterus which may help to prepare the woman's body for labor, and it is thought to be involved in a woman's orgasms whether she is pregnant or not.

Beautiful or Gross?

How you feel about yourself can be an important factor in determining whether you want to have sex. Some pregnant women look in the mirror and feel fat and gross. Others feel they have never been more beautiful. Most women who are pregnant fall somewhere in the middle of these two extremes.

No matter how a woman feels about her pregnant self, it never hurts for her to receive loving reassurance from her partner. While a hard penis and a willing heart might be physical evidence that a man finds the mother of his child to be desirable, loving words and other romantic gestures speak to a different part of her soul. Do your best to always be available if not always near.

No Fear

One of the nice things about being pregnant is not having to worry about getting pregnant. You can put the diaphragm in the deep freeze, keep the condoms in the bottom drawer or forget about taking pills each morning. This can make sex during pregnancy particularly relaxed and easy to enjoy. If pregnancy is what you wanted, there's no more "We have to do it now because my most fertile three-and-a-half minutes during the entire next quarter of a century is about to pass." Even if you didn't plan on getting pregnant, the fact that you can't get pregnant again for nine more months allows some couples to relax and enjoy sex in ways that they might not when consequences are a concern.

Genital Swelling—Slip & Slide

Around the fourth month of pregnancy, most women's genitals begin to swell. And swell. And swell. This swelling can lead to full-time lubrication and can make some pregnant women feel very horny. The increased swelling is due to the growing vascular capacity in the pregnant woman's pelvis. As a result, her vulva often becomes a deeper color and her labia thicken.

Couples find that the added swelling may lead to a delightfully snug feeling during intercourse. Genital swelling during pregnancy also tends to up the intensity of the woman's orgasm. More on this in the pages that follow.

Orgasms during Pregnancy

Plenty of women have no interest in sex or orgasms when they are pregnant. Others not only want orgasms, but report coming in awe-inspiring bursts that are more intense than their most memorable pre-pregnant efforts. For some women, sex during pregnancy presents a slight contradiction: even if she is more easily aroused and her orgasms are more intense, she might take longer to reach orgasm. The payoff is said to be worth the extra effort.

One reason for whopper orgasms during pregnancy might be the increased level of engorgement in the abdomen. With all the extra blood in there, her uterus stays hard for a few minutes after orgasm. As a result, a woman who had single orgasms before pregnancy may experience two or more at a time while pregnant. By the end of the pregnancy, some women find that the swelling in their genitals causes a congested feeling that makes coming feel more frustrating than relieving. Other women continue to have awesome orgasms throughout their entire pregnancies.

Also, it is normal for a pregnant woman to have cramps or Braxton-Hicks contractions either before or after orgasm. These cramps can last for a half-hour or more. The cramping might be due to the extra blood flow in the genitals, it might result from prostaglandins in the man's ejaculate, or it may stem from emotional concerns. Some healthcare professionals believe that these cramps help improve the muscle tone in a pregnant woman's uterus. If the cramping becomes too uncomfortable, you can eliminate one possible cause by using a condom during intercourse or by having the man pull out before he is about to come. See if this makes any difference over a couple of weeks. Another approach that may help relieve cramping is for the woman's partner to give her a loving foot massage or back rub.

Another unexpected source of orgasms during pregnancy may be the prolific array of sex dreams that some women report having. "Never had one before, never had one after, but had a large number of sexual dreams during..."

Prostaglandin Note: Prostaglandins are what physicians give to help induce labor (e.g., pitocin). Nature has included very low doses of prostaglandins in male ejaculate. However, these prostaglandins do not influence labor unless the cervix is ripe and ready for labor. This is why some women who are near their due date intentionally have lots of intercourse believing that the prostaglandins work in synergy with a ripe cervix to provide a more gentle labor. A recent study has shown that intercourse during pregnancy does not contribute to premature birth; if anything, the opposite might be true. Still, if you are concerned about this or any kind of contractions during pregnancy, be sure to consult your healthcare provider.

Breasts: Tenderness, Expansion & Leakage

Breast tenderness can happen in any phase of the pregnancy, especially during the first trimester. This means that breasts which used to cherish firm handling might suddenly prefer a light kiss, caress, or no direct stimulation at all. Fortunately, some breasts that are painfully tender during the first trimester morph into major arousal zones during the second trimester. These kinds of changes make it important for pregnant couples to have frequent discussions about "what feels good this week..."

It is normal for the breasts of a nonpregnant woman to swell when she is sexually aroused. However, when a woman becomes pregnant, her breasts may remain swollen all the time. As a result, she may get swelling on top of swelling when she is sexually excited. This might feel painful, or it may feel wonderfully pleasant, depending on the woman and the stage of her pregnancy. Also, dietary salt might contribute to the swelling.

For some couples, breast tenderness will make the missionary position a thing of the past long before expansion of the abdomen does. Another potential problem or potential delight, depending on your point of view, might occur if the woman's breasts start to leak during the latter part of pregnancy. Not to worry, this is an ever-so-natural event and is simply a preview of what's to come.

Intercourse Concerns Part I — Fetal Concussions

It is not uncommon for couples to worry that the head of daddy's thrusting penis is going to bop junior on the fetal brain and somehow knock him senseless. While it might be nice for dad to think his penis is that powerful, the fetus sits in a sac filled with a fluid that absorbs shocks and provides superb protection. To make it even that far, dad's penis would have to get through mom's cervix and uterine walls.

The most important consideration during intercourse is to find positions and thrusting styles that feel good for mom and her swollen reproductive organs. If it feels good for mom, chances are that the baby will do just fine.

As for questions about squirting junior in the eye with dad's ejaculate, the uterus is sealed off by a mucus plug that is a bit like the cork in a bottle of wine. The amniotic sac provides a secondary barrier that helps keep the ejaculate at bay.

Intercourse Concerns Part 2—"The Baby Will See Us"

Believe it or not, the human fetus is not taking notes on your every action and won't be emotionally scarred by the things you feel or do during pregnancy, even if you listen to—gulp—rock'n'roll instead of classical music. Exceptions, of course, are excessive drinking, smoking, or doing certain drugs that may compromise the infant's developing brain.

The fetal brain is not like a miniature of the adult brain. Its memory units (called neurons) are hardly functional at birth. There is simply not enough developed brain structure for the fetus to say, "Oh my gosh, Mom and Dad are having sex and isn't that disgusting" or on a more positive note, "Mom and Dad are having sex, isn't that wonderful!"

Why Doesn't Victoria's Secret Make Sexy Lingerie for Pregnant Moms?

Sex doesn't stop being an expression of love and intimacy just because a baby is on the way. Yet you can't help but get the feeling that pregnant moms are supposed to be more interested in runny noses and future full diapers than in being lit up sexually or wondering what the new guy at the office looks like naked. You have to search far and wide to get the message that pregnant moms can feel sexy and that some moms and dads find pregnancy to be sexually exciting.

For a lot of pregnant women, nature turned up the horny knob instead of turning it down. Granted, not all women feel like having sex while pregnant, but enough do that it's difficult to believe that nature would have allowed this urge to go unchecked if it weren't for the benefit of the pregnancy or the species in general.

Intercourse

Some pregnant women cherish the feeling of having both the baby and the baby's father inside of them at the same time. Other women feel like three's a crowd. Dads, too, have their own issues about sex during pregnancy, some of which are discussed later in this chapter. As long as you feel like having intercourse while pregnant, the most important elements are a shared sense of humor and a willingness to explore. Here are some particulars to consider:

Clothes On Some couples who are trying new positions do so first with their clothes on. This helps them focus their collective energies on the engineering feat at hand, and it allows them to appreciate the humor of the situation without having to worry about feelings of urgency or declining erections. There's always time to get naked and actually go for it once the target positions have been mapped out and a strategy is planned.

Penetration Some women who are pregnant have a desire for penetration that's deep and assertive, while others prefer a more gentle approach than usual. Whatever the case, different phases of pregnancy may require different styles of penetration while the proverbial bun is in the oven. Also keep in mind that the swelling of the cervix and uterus can make certain kinds of intercourse feel uncomfortable, at least the kind where she rides you like a wild bull or clasps her ankles around your neck and shouts, "Harder, harder, you big stud." Let the woman control the thrusting depth, and if you feel that this somehow cramps your style, be mindful that there are plenty of dads-to-be who aren't getting any at all.

🕯️ **Lubrication** Some women seem to lubricate all the time when they are pregnant. However, there are plenty of exceptions. If that's the case for you, try adding KY Jelly. Be sure your lubricant contains no contraceptive goop, as that might cause vaginal stinging.

🕯️ **Dizziness** Some pregnant women experience dizziness or indigestion in certain positions or during certain phases of the pregnancy. This can be particularly true when a woman is on her back. Doing it on her side, on all fours, or while on top might suit her better.

🕯️ **Romancing the Cervix** The cervix of a pregnant woman often swells due to the extra blood flow into the uterus. It becomes soft, and can sometimes bleed with deep penetration. Try shallower thrusting or use positions where the head of the penis romances the cervix more gently. This may be especially wise during the later months of pregnancy when the cervix starts to ripen. If you have questions or if there is any bleeding, be sure to consult with your healthcare professional.

🕯️ **Third-Trimester Stretch** By the third trimester, the cartilage in the pelvic region has had several months of pregnancy-related hormones thrown at it. It becomes softer as a result, as part of nature's conspiracy—ah, plan—to ready the pelvic floor for the joys of childbirth. As a result, a woman may find that pressure on her pubic bone feels a little weird. This is another reason why couples need to be creative in their search for comfortable intercourse positions.

⚓ Bag It or Let It Fly? Some physicians believe that a man should wear a condom during the last month or so of the pregnancy, but others think this is silly. Some experts believe that male ejaculate helps a ripening cervix prepare for an easier labor. Be sure to check with your own healthcare provider for advice.

⚓ Too Much Swelling For some women, genital swelling may eventually increase to a point where intercourse feels uncomfortable, while for others the desire to have intercourse never wanes. Experimenting with positions where the woman has her legs apart might help.

⚓ Backaches & All Fours With the muscles between her ribs being slowly pried apart and her pelvic floor feeling trampled on, the pregnant female has been known to suffer an occasional backache. Some women find that the rocking motion of intercourse while on all fours can help soothe pregnancy-related backaches. It can also soothe the throbbing between her partner's legs, resulting in a win-win situation for both parties.

The Penile Vice (okay—Vise) Grip

Some healthcare professionals think it's good for a pregnant woman to tone and exercise the muscles in her pelvic floor (aka doing Kegel exercises). What better way to accomplish this than by having a man insert his penis into your vagina, keeping it stationary while you squeeze it with your pelvic muscles? Most guys would be more than happy to lend a helping penis. And this is an exercise that you might keep doing after the baby is born. (It has been said that some of the finer prostitutes in Asia are able to "massage" a man's penis to ejaculation by squeezing it in this way. Achieving this kind of proficiency might take months or more of practice, but would add a new dimension to any woman's bedroom technique.)

Intercourse Interruptus—When To Stop

Most physicians in this day and age say it's okay to keep having intercourse until your water breaks. Some couples have intercourse until labor itself begins, feeling that the prostaglandins in dad's ejaculate help make for a smoother delivery.

There are at least four factors which should influence your decision on when to stop having intercourse: 1. It doesn't feel good any longer. 2. Either partner has a genital infection. 3. The woman experiences bleeding or new discharge. 4. Your health-care provider says to stop.

Oral Sex

The extra lubrication caused by pregnancy can give the vaginal area a stronger taste or smell, which some men notice when giving their pregnant wives oral sex. However, there are no medical reasons to stop giving or receiving oral sex during pregnancy unless the pregnancy is at risk for other reasons.

Recently, one European medical journal reported that women who went down on their partners before becoming pregnant had a significantly lower incidence of pre-eclampsia during pregnancy. Pre-eclampsia is a condition in which the pregnant woman's blood pressure can rise to potentially dangerous levels. The origin of pre-eclampsia is not known. One medical journal several years ago found that pre-eclamptic conditions decreased significantly in women whose obstetricians were able to make a solid emotional connection with them, thus pointing to possible psychological factors in pre-eclampsia. It is unlikely, though, that the "solid emotional connection" included giving the obstetrician oral sex. Also, concerning the more recent study, one would want to know if the decrease in pre-eclampsia was limited to women who swallowed their husband's ejaculate, or if it included those who ducked and let it fly across the sheets. The latter might suggest that the preventive factor is a stronger emotional bond with the husband rather than the ejaculate itself.

Nipple & Perineal Massage

One of the nice things about being pregnant is that when the dad-to-be is complaining about all the things he usually complains about, you have the perfect excuse to say, "Shut up and rub my nipples!" That's because as the final months of pregnancy approach, it might be helpful for a woman to have two areas on her body massaged—well, three areas if you count each nipple as having its own private domain. Put a little lotion on each nipple and massage and knead it, assuming it isn't too painful. This will help condition the nipples for nursing, and it may also help release extra oxytocin into the system, which seems to be a good thing as the due date approaches. The other area that massage might help is the perineum, which is the small piece of real estate between a woman's vagina and her rectum. Some pregnancy aficionados believe that massaging this area may help to make it more pliable and reduce the need for an episiotomy. At the time of this book's publication, you could phone (800) 624-4934 to get a booklet titled "Prenatal Perineal Massage" or send $3.20 to ICEA, P.O. Box 20048, Minneapolis, MN 55420.

Bleeding

During the first couple of months of pregnancy, bleeding may occur during the time when you would normally have your period. This is usually less reason for concern than bleeding that is random. Be sure to check with your physician when there is any bleeding, just to be on the safe side.

Touch vs. Sex

Some women may experience a decreased desire for sex during pregnancy, but an increased need for touch and cuddling. This can be difficult for the dad-to-be, because all of the cuddling and touching might make him feel extremely horny. To help the dad-to-be make it through these lean times sexually, his pregnant partner can cuddle beside him and caress his thighs, chest or testicles while he does himself by hand. Or he can do what a lot of other guys do—jerk off in the shower.

Besides being an important time for holding and touching, pregnancy is a fine time for partners to reassure one another about their feelings of love and attraction—hopefully for each other.

Fears That Bubble Up from the Deep Dark Recesses of the Human Psyche...

Contrary to how you think you should be feeling, it is not uncommon for perfectly good parents-to-be to have mixed feelings about the baby-to-be. For instance, you may have planned for years to have this baby and wanted it with the deepest of convictions, but then suddenly start feeling, "Oh my God, what have we done?" Feelings like these can be fleeting or last for weeks. One reader says that both he and his wife were shocked to discover such feelings, given that their pregnancy was better planned than the average moon walk. Fortunately, they did not experience their bummer moods at the same time. As a result, the one who was feeling good about the pregnancy was able to comfort the one who was feeling tragic.

It is perfectly normal for us humans to be overwhelmed by inner conflicts. These can be especially intense during pregnancy, when so many new demands are about to be placed on you. These are not the sorts of feelings that make us want to have sex. It can be very helpful to talk over these conflicts with a friend, partner or even a counselor if you are feeling particularly jammed by them. One reader adds: "Worries about child care, job security, and having to go back to work after only six weeks can be overwhelming."

Recognizing Dad's Role

During pregnancy, all attention usually focuses on the mom-to-be, which is as it should be. But this is also an important time for the pregnant woman to acknowledge the dad-to-be's role. Potential problems can occur when the woman feels that the baby is her creation alone. This can lead to problems in the relationship between father and child as well as between mother and father, and it is likely that the child will be made to feel guilty when he or she finally attempts to separate from mom.

Dad's Emotional & Sexual Issues During Pregnancy

There are plenty of books devoted to the various feelings that pregnant moms experience. Yet dads-to-be experience their own set of pregnancy-related emotions. According to researcher James Herzog, dads-to-be tend to fall into two groups: most attuned, and less or least attuned. The pregnancy spurs the first group of dads onto a path of personal growth, while the latter group feels threatened by the pregnancy and is not particularly fortified by it.

One factor that impacts how a man responds to his wife's pregnancy is the influence of his own father or father substitutes. Herzog noticed that during the second and third trimesters of pregnancy, a number of pregnant dads turned toward their own fathers in an attempt to reconnect with them. They felt that reconnecting with the "good dad" from their early childhood would help them be better dads to their own children. Men in the less-attuned group tended to experience a high degree of "father hunger"—growing up without an involved and caring father figure. These men tended to act in unsupportive ways, such as becoming competitive with their wives or being sexually promiscuous; some had sexual relations with other men. If you find yourself feeling unsupportive or disconnected from your pregnant wife, it might be a great idea to spend extra time with a friend or acquaintance whose fathering skills you admire. Tell him you are feeling on shaky ground; ask him how he manages as a dad when he's feeling uncertain or overwhelmed.

Other things that Herzog found about pregnant dads included the following:

📖 **The Right Stuff** Upon learning of the pregnancy, a number of dads-to-be feel quite good about themselves in a masculine and sexual way. The fact of the pregnancy may help allay fears that they didn't have the right stuff to make a pregnancy happen. With the excitement of being pregnant, a number of couples enjoy sex that is quite intense and intimate, as though sex itself now has a different meaning.

📖 **Nourishment** As the pregnancy progresses, some men feel as if they are nourishing or symbolically feeding their wives during intercourse, especially when they come inside of them. On some level, the dad-to-be might view his semen as a kind of milk that will help nurture both mother and infant.

🕯️ **Coming Harder** Some men report feeling more depth to their orgasms when their partners are pregnant, with more physical and emotional awareness both before and after ejaculation. At the same time, the dad-to-be might be rethinking who he is; he's a man whose personal identity is expanding. At times this can feel exhilarating, at other times a frightening burden.

🕯️ **Dreams Etc.** There are plenty of ways that dads unconsciously identify with a pregnant spouse or wonder about what's going on inside of her. For instance, by mid-pregnancy, some fathers experience dreams or fantasies about being penetrated as well as being the one who penetrates. Some dream or start to wonder about their own inner body parts. Some put on extra weight or feel a kind of gastric fullness or upset. Some men have toothaches during this time that land them in the dentist's office. When a man has a toothache of an undetermined origin, some dentists know to inquire if the man's wife is pregnant.

🕯️ **Character Evolution** Being a dad-to-be can help a man to shed unwanted or outdated parts of his character. The pregnancy becomes both an excuse and a stimulus to mature and become more responsible if he isn't already. Of course, not all men use pregnancy in such a constructive way, nor do all women.

Sex after Giving Birth

Some parents experience the first three to six months after the child's birth as being the most demanding and difficult time of their lives. They might not feel like having sex, or if they do, they might be too exhausted to actually do it. Other couples enjoy sneaking in quickies while the baby sleeps.

There are hugely important considerations that affect the frequency of sex among new parents, like whether dad does his fair share of the work around the house and with the baby, and whether mom welcomes his help or is nervous and critical whenever he gets near the baby. If one parent is an obvious klutz with the baby, there are plenty of ways that he or she can be helpful other than with actual hands-on baby care. In a few months, the baby may have grown enough that you feel more comfortable handling it.

Even with the best intention and desire, there will be plenty of times when new moms and dads are way too exhausted for sex, especially if there are other children in the family besides the new baby. Keep in mind that plenty of couples struggle when it comes to adapting to their new roles as parents and sexual partners.

Hormones & Libido

Some women don't feel like having sex after pregnancy due to various anti-horny hormones that might be spewing through their veins. Women who are nursing are said to produce more anti-horny hormones than women who are bottle feeding, yet statistics show that nursing mothers want sex more often than those who don't nurse. Go figure.

Talking about Sex Before the Baby Is Born

Some of the best advice this book has to offer is that you talk about sex before the baby is actually born. For instance, "I've heard some new parents don't feel like having sex for a few months after giving birth—what are some of the ways we might handle that if it happens to one or both of us?" Or "What do we do if you've got a raging hard-on and I want to be held and cuddled but don't want to have intercourse?" Or "What if I want sex but you start seeing me as a mother type and don't find me exciting?"

One of the worst things you can do about sex after pregnancy is to pretend it is not a problem if it actually is. Nothing is to be gained by rolling over and pretending you are asleep to avoid having sex, by getting defensive or by feeling attacked. As with other aspects of your relationship, this is a time to redefine and put things in a new perspective. Where sex was once taken for granted, it may now need to be planned or scheduled. There will be plenty of times when sexual desire is a casualty to exhaustion. For a while, you might end up masturbating more often.

When Can We Start Having Intercourse?

After the placenta comes out of the womb, it takes time for the place where it was attached to heal. The woman is going to be vulnerable to infections. This is why it might not be such a good idea for things like male ejaculate, store-bought lube and contraceptive jelly to be working their way up there. Also, it might take a couple of weeks for the vagina to heal after it's been stretched from here to China. Some physicians worry that intercourse before the vagina is healed can cause scar tissue to build. This is why most physicians feel it is wise to wait at least a few weeks after birth before you start doing the nasty. Check with your health-care provider for specifics. This is particularly true if the woman had an episiotomy, with stitches that need to heal, and don't even think about having intercourse after a C-section until the doctor waves the green flag.

Birth Control

Be sure to stock up on birth control products before the baby is born. Do not leave this important detail for after the birth, as you will have your hands full dealing with other things and are likely to let it slip. It is not fair to you or the new baby to have a repeat pregnancy sooner than you want. Also, don't for a moment believe that moms who are nursing are unable to get pregnant. Nursing moms get pregnant all the time. Ditto for couples who have unprotected sex during mom's period.

Lubricated condoms and condoms with contraceptive chemicals can irritate tender vaginal tissues. If dryness is an issue for you and you are concerned about irritation, check with your obstetrician's office for advice.

Designated Night Out

Once the baby is three months old, you would be wise to plan at least one evening a week where you and your spouse go out together, without junior in tow, for at least a couple of hours. There are a couple of ways to engineer this, with willing grandparents being top on the list. Every Wednesday night they get the baby and you get each other. If grandparents aren't an option and a babysitter is either too hard to find or too expensive, call couples from your Lamaze class or find other parents with young babies and arrange to co-op the babysitting. For instance, they take yours every Tuesday, and you take theirs every Thursday.

Children know when something important is missing in their parents' relationship. If there is a lack of intimacy or unity among their parents, they can suffer almost as much as the parents. Do not make the mistake of focusing all your energy on being parents and no energy on being lovers. By the time you notice that something is wrong with your relationship, it may be difficult to repair.

Painful Intercourse?

You may need to work your way up to intercourse. If time permits, you might try taking showers or baths together and sharing a beer or bottle of wine beforehand. Also, it never hurts to have a giant-sized tube of KY Jelly on the nightstand. Some women who have never had a problem getting wet find they need an assist after giving birth. For other women, it can be just the opposite.

Beware the "Husband's Stitch"

Physicians sometimes do a "husband's stitch" when sewing a woman up after delivery if she had tearing or an episiotomy. This is essentially a little tuck and roll that's done at the opening of the vagina. The physician assumes it will make intercourse feel better for the husband. While the sentiment is nice, the "husband's stitch" is better used in upholstery shops than on women's genitals. Tightening the entrance to the vagina just makes the opening smaller and is liable to make intercourse feel painful for the woman. If a woman is concerned about vaginal tone following pregnancy, she would do much better to practice Kegel exercises, which help to tighten the entire vagina rather than making the opening more difficult to get into. It never hurts to discuss this with your healthcare provider.

Readers' Comments

"When I was pregnant, I wanted sex more, and felt more free." *female age 44*

"I was extremely horny during my pregnancy and I felt very sexy until the last month or two." *female age 26*

"I had no sexual desire at all." *female age 36*

"I was constantly horny when I wasn't nauseous." *female 35*

"I viewed her expanding body as just more to love, hold and caress." *male age 41*

"Intercourse can hurt toward 39-40 weeks when the baby's head is down lower. Sometimes foreplay was just as satisfying." *female age 25*

"I was more horny than anything. Because of the pregnancy, we needed to start using new positions. Some worked so well that we are still using them today." *female age 25*

"We didn't do anything different during pregnancy, except we didn't have to use rubbers. Yea!" *female age 38*

"For intercourse while pregnant, I was pretty much always on top." *female age 45*

"Don't worry about the baby. If it is firmly implanted, no orgasm will dislodge it." *female age 35*

"If anything, I admired her more for being able to 'do' a pregnancy. It's a real turn-on to feel an essential part of one." *male age 43*

"When I was pregnant, sex felt extremely good and multiple orgasms happened all the time. They would sneak up on me. Things would be feeling good and if I concentrated hard I could have another and another." *female age 26*

"My wife seemed to be more lubricated, which was great. She seemed more relaxed also." *male age 38*

"Be gentle, be considerate, encourage her to lead. As for sex after the baby's born, that depends on whether she's in a private room or not." *male age 40* (Before taking this too seriously, please see the earlier section "When Can We Start Having Intercourse?")

"Sex after the kids are born? Babysitters, movies for kids, grandmother's house and motel rooms...." *male age 44*

"Lock the door, turn the music up and put *The Lion King* on the VCR." *male age 39*

"When you've got kids, bedtime is the most convenient time for sex, but it's not always the most exciting time for me. If I wake up early and am horny, I wake my husband up, which is something he loves, to have sex when he's just waking up." *female age 45*

"You have to make it clear they can't interrupt. Sometimes I'm just very upfront with what we are doing and she knows not to come in." *female age 25*

"Cut to the chase: I am an RN and have seen hundreds of uncircumcised males. No turn on. But when my most recent lover happened to be such it was so totally unexpected that my sexual arousal rate went up 200%. I am very turned on by stroking him to expose the head, kissing and licking it and then covering it again by pulling the foreskin back up. Sucking ever so gently with the skin covering the head gives him pleasure, but pulling it down near the base of his penis completely exposes him and his reaction is amazing. All it takes is tender gentle swirls to drive him crazy.... The wanton horny bitch that resides within myself has now been released and owes you all at the Goofy Foot Press gratitude and the author the best blow job ever!" *female age 27*

The author responds: "Drive south on I-5 until you reach the Corvallis exit, go west for one hour..."

Circumcision — U.S. Penile Calamity
Chapter 41

"What do you call the useless bit of skin at the end of a penis? A man." *male age 50*

"I've had a partner pull on it like she was starting a lawn mower. That didn't work for me." *male age 36*

"His penis looked like a worm in a turtleneck." *female age 22*

When you compare penises head to head, it is clear that Mother Nature knew exactly what she was doing when she provided the penis with a foreskin. Medically speaking, routine circumcision makes about as much sense as removing a kid's eyelids or cutting out the labia of baby girls. So why are the majority of American boys routinely circumcised?

During the 1880s, a few influential men like John Harvey Kellogg, physician and founder of a famous American cereal company, started preaching that boys masturbate because the foreskin rubs on the head of the penis. Until that time, most American men were not circumcised. As a leading anti-masturbation fanatic, Dr. Kellogg believed that boys who were circumcised at birth would be less likely to play with themselves. His influence helped circumcision to become a routine operation in America. Swell guy that he was, Dr. Kellogg also recommended that girls who masturbate have their clitorises burned out with acid.

Is There a Medical Need for Circumcision?

America's medical establishment has tried to justify its hand in circumcision by saying that it prevents cancer of the penis, cancer of the cervix and numerous other medical calamities. If this were true, why would physicians in England decide that the operation is not such a good idea? Less than ten percent of the newborn blokes in the UK have their dicks docked.

Women who live in countries where men aren't circumcised have no higher rate of cervical cancer than women in America.

The only penis-related item that increases a woman's chance of getting cancer of the cervix is having numerous male sex partners, circumcised or not. Condom use might help decrease this risk, but circumcision has no impact.

In Sweden, where few men are circumcised, cancer of the penis is just as rare as in the circumcision-happy United States. It would be interesting to compare the number of penises lost to cancer, which is quite rare, with the number of penises mutilated through botched circumcisions. Also, circumcision does not prevent all cancers of the penis, and as one specialist suggests, it may take a combination of smoking and abysmal personal hygiene for an uncircumcised man to get cancer of the penis.

As for other claims, one study did show that circumcised males were less likely to get urinary tract infections during the first year of life. However, in that study the parents of the uncircumcised babies were instructed to pull back their foreskins and wash under them. Yet parents should do just the opposite, because nature did not intend the foreskin to retract before one year of age. It is quite likely that the instructions given to the parents were what caused the higher rate of infections among the uncircumcised boys. But even if those figures are correct, the number of urinary tract infections is still much greater in female than male babies, and no one is recommending preventive surgery for them.

There have also been claims that uncircumcised men are more apt to catch sexually transmitted diseases, including AIDS. However, European men don't show any greater incidence of these diseases than American men, and European men are mostly uncircumcised. Until recently, American men who were uncircumcised tended to be from poor families. Whether circumcised or not, poor people often get diseases at a higher rate than those who are rich.

Finally, there exists a myth that large percentages of uncircumcised babies will have foreskins that don't retract (phimosis), and that these males will need surgery when they grow older to correct this condition. In reality, fewer than 1 out of every 100 uncircumcised men have this condition, and a foreskin-friendly urologist can almost always help to resolve the problem without having to cut the kid.

So Why Do They Keep Doing It?

A physician in the US makes between $150 and $300 per circumcision. Doing one circumcision per day, five days per week, at a fee of $150 each minus time out for a six week vacation nets a physician an extra $34,500 per year for a procedure that takes less than ten minutes. And that's only one a day at the lower rate. No wonder why pediatricians and obstetricians sometimes fight over who gets to do the circumcision!

Another reason for doing circumcisions is medical bias. Until recently, physicians in this country have had a long-standing bias that hysterectomies are good for women and circumcisions are good for men. Before managed health care, they also had a bias for C-sections over natural births, given that C-sections were much more profitable and easier to schedule.

In short, there appears to be no medical reason besides possible income enhancement for doing routine circumcision. There does, however, appear to be a very good reason why nature equipped the penis with a foreskin. Not only is the foreskin rich in pleasure-producing nerve endings, but it also keeps the head of the penis moist, and the extra skin provides added sliding pleasure during intercourse and masturbation. The foreskin is extremely elastic and is said to be as sensitive to touch as the human lips. Far from being unnecessary, a foreskin is usually a nice thing to have.

How They Do It

During male circumcision, they stick a prodding instrument into the foreskin to tear it away from the head of the penis. One-third to one-half of the skin on the penis is then cut off. Traditionally, male circumcisions have not been done with anesthesia, but even when anesthesia is used, there is still pain from the raw scar on the penis.

Different Guys, Different Foreskins

Religious Considerations

Some people will say, "But circumcision is done for important religious and cultural reasons." The same is true for female circumcision, which we in the West refer to as genital mutilation.

Some people say this is being disrespectful of an important ritual in the Jewish faith. This is true. We are also disrespectful of the Catholic Church's ban on birth control and masturbation. If Jewish men want to be circumcised as an expression of their faith, why not let them wait until they are eighteen years old and able to call the Mohel themselves? That would be a far greater expression of faith than having the end of your penis chopped off when you're only a few days old and can't tell the Torah from a phone book.

For Parents—Foreskin Care

Do not try to retract the foreskin of a young boy unless there is a specific medical reason. During infancy and childhood, the inner surface of the foreskin is physically attached to the skin on the head of the penis. This protects the opening of the penis from irritation, infection and ulceration. Over time, the cells that attach these two surfaces together will start to dissolve on their own. By trying to retract the foreskin prematurely, you are ripping apart these delicate tissues that nature has "glued" together.

A young boy will often pull his foreskin away from his body. As he gets older, he will begin to pull it toward his body. In our sex survey at www.goofyfootpress.com, a number of males reported that they didn't fully retract their foreskins until they were well into their teenage years. This is normal and will usually happen without any coaxing or encouragement from mom and dad.

Parents do need to tell their teenage sons about cleanliness. They should explain that once a boy is able to retract his foreskin he should do it whilst in the shower, cleaning around the exposed head. Enlightened parents might also explain that boys who don't keep their genitals clean don't get nearly as much oral sex as boys who do!

For more information about circumcision, foreskin care, or to find a list of physicians who aren't biased against foreskins, contact NOCIRC, P.O. Box 2512, San Anselmo, CA 94979-2512, telephone: (415) 488-9883. Also see the foreskin section of our website at www.goofyfootpress.com.

The following are comments from visitors to our website at www.goofyfootpress.com:

"I'd never even seen an uncircumcised penis until my current lover, but I've decided now that it's the best thing since sliced bread. Better, even, since I can't have sex with sliced bread! The foreskin makes hand jobs 100 times better and easier because it slides over the penis so you don't need lube. I was kind of nervous about it at first but then I realized how stretchy the foreskin is even though it looks kinda fragile. For blow jobs, I pull the foreskin down to the base and massage it there and go to town. I haven't found any difference in intercourse. It just moves itself out of the way. I don't know if it makes any difference when using condoms. I'll be sure to ask and get back to ya." *female age 18*

"The only Jewish guy I ever slept with was also the only uncircumcised guy I ever slept with. He seemed to have more stamina than any of the others but that might just be a coincidence." *female age 21*

"For a blow job, pull the foreskin up over the head and stick your tongue down inside of the opening and swirl it around." *female age 38*

"Just ask the guy how he likes it. Some guys like you to pull the foreskin tight, others say this hurts." *female age 20*

"A cool thing about it is that it's convertible." *female age 18*

"One thing that I find particularly stimulating is to lubricate a finger or thumb, slip it between the foreskin and the head and massage the glans that way. It makes it feel really, really great." *male age 19*

"I put my foreskin over her clitoris and use it to massage her clitoris with. This might only be possible with a partner who has a larger than normal clitoris. You need to be able to get hold of it." *male age 65*

"A partner should know that the inside of a foreskin is where there is the most feeling, so gentle movement of it over a cockhead and down the shaft feels great. The best part of getting a blow job is what a tongue and mouth can do with that inside lining of a foreskin." *male age 59*

"I like to do the trick of clamping the end shut while peeing and making it swell up. Also, a similar and a more satisfying experience is to leave just a bit of the end open and put it under a strong flow of water so that the water flows in but has a place to get out." *male age 20*

"When did I first retract it? I was around ten. I would slowly pull it back every day in the shower. After about two weeks I was able to pull it all the way down." *male age 22*

"Letting the foreskin balloon is quite nice both when peeing and when enjoying the pool jets." *male age 37*

The First Time — Not What You'd Think
Chapter 42

W hy would an adult want to read about teenagers and their attitudes on sex? Trust the *Guide*. There's more to this than meets the eye.

Researchers Newlyn Moore and J. Kenneth Davidson recently questioned hundreds of young women about their sexual experiences and corresponding feelings of guilt.

You would think that young women who felt the most guilt and shame about their sexuality would be motivated to sleep with fewer guys. You would think they would be losing their virginity at an older age than girls who feel better about sex.

Shock of all shocks, the opposite is true. Girls with the most negative attitudes about their sexuality are doing it younger, with more partners and in less committed relationships than girls who feel the most positive about their bodies and their sexuality.

Also, the guilt girls are the most likely to have their first intercourse with an "occasional dating partner" or with a "person just met,"—a pattern they continue to repeat as they get older. And they tend to have their first intercourse when drinking or stoned.

As you might expect, the girls who feel the best about their bodies tend to masturbate more. But you'd think these feel-good masturbators would be more promiscuous. Not so. The girls who masturbate the most and feel the best about sex actually wait the longest before having their first intercourse and they have it with more committed partners. Most importantly, when they do have sex, it's part of a conscious decision. Not so with the girls who feel bad about sex and their bodies. More often than not, they just let sex happen to them, without thinking it through first.

So who are these high-guilt, more-promiscuous girls? High-guilt girls tend to grow up in families where the mother and father are less affectionate toward each other. They tend to regard their dads as being overly strict and they are from homes that are more religious—rather than less religious—than girls who don't sleep around as much.

Perhaps the girls who have the least sexual acceptance at home go searching for it elsewhere. The trouble is, they go about it in such a destructive way that they end up reinforcing the bad feelings about themselves that they grew up with, and they end up with partners who are just as constricted as their dads.

Who knew that the daughters of the self-righteous would be more likely to sleep around and do it drunk than daughters of parents who have a more open, honest approach to sex and sexual feelings? It's certainly not what the self-described moral majority would have us believe. Perhaps there's more to waiting longer than the just-say-no abstinence-only proponents want us to think.

Girls vs. Boys— Feelings About Sex

Study after study show that girls feel worse about themselves after puberty than before, while boys seem to feel better about themselves. How come? Researcher Karin Martin has recently studied these questions and more.

For a boy, puberty usually brings freedom. It also leaves a young man feeling more positive about his body, more independent and more masculine. Not so with girls. Menstruation itself often leaves a girl with a feeling that her body is out of control.

According to Dr. Martin: "The girls whom I interviewed gave only negative descriptions of their menstruating bodies. Their bodies made them feel 'yuck' or 'sick,' or as if they had 'shit their pants'.... While plenty of girls look forward to having their first period, a lot become ambivalent after the first couple of periods have come and gone."

Teenage boys may struggle with wet dreams and unwanted erections, but not many would equate these with shitting in their pants. On the contrary, a boy's growing body often makes him feel more grown up and effective in the world, while a girl's growing body brings parental warnings about the evil intentions of men as well as physical restrictions on everything from climbing trees to learning to sit like a lady. These warnings can make the world seem scary.

For a girl, her growing body represents loss as much as it represents gain. For instance, the mere fact that she suddenly has breasts causes all sorts of changes in her relationship with her dad and every other man she meets. No longer will her dad be as physically affectionate, and no longer will she be as unconscious about her body. Ever hear that upbeat song from the early 1960s, "Sweet Sixteen"? It talks about a girl who was just a normal kid next door until suddenly she grows boobs and hips, and her former big-brother figure up the street has a hard-on and a hit song aiming right at her. Maybe the girl was happier before puberty when the whole universe didn't revolve around what her body looked like.

Dr. Martin reports about asking teenage girls to describe themselves:

> When I asked girls, especially working-class girls, to describe themselves or asked, "Tell me about yourself," they described their bodies and had a difficult time describing any other aspects of who they were. "Can you describe an important goal you achieved?" "I love my hair. My hair's my accomplishment..." "What kind of things make you feel good about yourself?" "When someone like pays me a compliment on something, you know. Like says that I look nice or have on nice clothes or something."

It was totally different for most of the boys. The boys felt good about themselves because of things they had done or things they felt they could do in the world. Of course, if most of these boys were more in touch with the reality of their effectiveness rather than their fantasies of it, they might not feel so confident. But still, when boys want to have sex, it is often with confidence and good feelings about their bodies, while girls often feel the opposite. In terms of sexual economics, we're talking the U.S. versus Peru.

So how does this reflect itself in the feelings that boys and girls have about sex?

"Boys thought sex would be pleasurable, and many said they looked forward to it or were curious about it.... No girl said that she looked forward to sex or that she expected it to be pleasurable. It is a rare teenage girl who has sex because she wants to."

The majority of teenage girls whom Dr. Martin interviewed expected sex to hurt or to be painful or scary. If this is true, why did the girls have sex?

"No matter how you look at a girl's reasons for having sex, the vast majority break down to the same simple reason: they are afraid the boy will leave, they are afraid they will lose him, or afraid he won't like them anymore."

More than half of the working-class girls and a quarter of the middle-class girls in Dr. Martin's study seemed to have an ideal or exaggerated love for the boys they were dating or wanted to date. Feelings like these will make a girl do anything to keep her little hormone case in tow. The boys, on the other hand, did not report looking for romance or ideal love. They seemed to want a combination of friendship and sex in their relationships, although it is possible that the boys kept their romantic feelings to themselves. (For a teenage boy to tell an interviewer about feelings of romantic love might be admitting to less than manly aspirations. Or as the boys at Dartmouth might say, "Whadda you, a faggot or something?")

When it comes to teenagers and sex, boys and girls often have different wants and expectations. Far more boys think that the sex will feel good, while far more girls believe it will hurt. Far more girls idealize their boyfriends and feel they can't live without them, or they need the boyfriend as an affirmation that they are attractive and worthwhile. For this, they are willing to have sex, which they expect to be painful. Due to the inexperience of the parties involved, it often is.

As for masturbation, many teenage girls feel it is something that boys do, and do not associate it with femininity. Nor do they seem very interested in exploring their own bodies. As Dr. Martin comments, "Their boyfriends were allowed more access to their bodies than they allowed themselves." And this study was done in the 1990s, not the 1950s.

Perhaps one of the most frightening findings of Dr. Martin's research is that almost all of the teenage girls felt better about shaving their legs than they did about the sex they were having with their boyfriends. It seems that being able to shave their legs provided a happy identification with their mothers or older sisters. It made the girls feel grown up in a good way.

Few and far between are the teenage girls who feel in control of their bodies and who have sex because they expect it to feel good. But those girls who did tended to have good relationships with their mothers which included lots of conversations about sex. They had good relationships with their dads and they were also more involved in extracurricular activities like sports or 4-H. They seemed to place more value on the size of their IQs than on the size of their waists. They knew their own bodies better and felt more in control of their sexuality.

If as many teenagers did as badly with computers as they do with sex, the President and Congress would be in arms. The last thing they would be telling teens is "Just Say No To Your Computer!" Will one less teenage girl have sex because of so-called sex education programs that preach abstinence? Not if the reason she has sex is to keep her boyfriend. On the other hand, if she feels she has a good mind and she understands how wonderful sex can be, maybe she'll make better decisions when it comes to sharing sex with others.

While we can't help you with the countless hours and effort that it takes to raise a kid with a good mind, this guide can help with suggestions for raising children who feel that sex is healthy and valuable. That's what the next chapter is all about.

Chapter Notes: Moore and Davidson's thoughtful and thought provoking paper, *Guilt About First Intercourse: An Antecedent of Sexual Dissatisfaction Among College Women* was published in the Journal of Sex and Marital Therapy, Vol. 23, No. 1, Spring 1997, pp. 29-46.

Karin Martin's excellent study is titled *Puberty, Sexuality and the Self* (New York: Routledge, 1996). ISBN: 0-415-91425-6. While this 118-page book is addressed to academic types, the actual quotes and observations make it an essential read for anyone studying teenage sexuality.

Explaining Sex To Kids
Chapter 43

Let's say that little Billy has gone shopping with his dad for the afternoon and you steal half an hour to lie on your bed with stereo headphones bolted to your ears, eyes closed and fingers massaging a very important place between your legs. You are all alone and the sensations begin to feel wonderful. Next thing you know, the headphones are being yanked off your head by little Billy, who is asking, "Mommy, what color napkins were we supposed to get for the birthday party?"

Or perhaps you assume that little Amber is fast asleep and you begin enjoying an all-too-rare moment of sex when a little hand suddenly taps you on the shoulder and you hear the words "Daddy, how come Mommy's sucking on your penis?"

The pages that follow don't pretend to have all the answers about children and sex; they are simply a way of getting you to think about the subject long before most parents do, which is sometimes too late for an effective response. Topics range from talking about genitals and masturbation to menstruation, sex play and even sex on the internet.

Children's Sexual Development

People often think of sex as something that happens once we become teenagers. Not true. Most of us started having sexual feelings when we were little babies. Each time someone changed our diapers and powdered our private parts we had sexual feelings in the most basic sense—nice physical sensations down where the Pampers go.

As children get a few years older, they often enjoy playing sex games with friends and relatives, same sex or otherwise. Sometimes they just compare and contrast; other times they enjoy doing things that big people do, like sucking on each other's genitals or sticking fingers, penises and heaven knows what else up each other's front and rear ends. Eventually you might encounter a third-grade child who's sitting there with both hands in his or her pants, happily rubbing away, while claiming how yuckie it would be to ever kiss somebody on the lips...

As children's minds grow and become more complex, so does their ability to have sexual fantasies that include others. With time, the thought of making love doesn't seem so "yuckie" anymore. Eventually, they might even want to read books like the *Guide to Getting It On!* In the meantime, one parent might wonder if it is normal for her four-year-old boy to be playing with his penis, while another might say, "Thank heavens he's got his penis to play with. It's a never-ending source of pleasure for him!"

Telling Children About Sexual Enjoyment

Parents usually tell their children all there is to know about things like blowing noses and wiping rear ends, but rarely do they mention that genitals can be the source of good feelings. As a result, children learn that it's okay to seek their parents' wisdom on just about everything but sexual feelings. This is most unfortunate, because kids need their parents' guidance on sexual feelings as much as they do on wiping their rear ends or learning to drive a car.

Some parents assume that a three-year-old who is rubbing her genitals has the same intent and fantasies as a twenty-three-year-old. They either try to stop her or simply pretend that nothing is happening. Perhaps it would be helpful for parents to understand that their masturbating three-year-old isn't thinking about how good Johnnie, her day-care buddy, might be in bed! The child is simply touching her genitals because it feels good. It is perfectly normal for little hands to reach between little legs when a child is happy or excited, at naptime or even when you are reading Dr. Seuss to her. All a parent needs to do is say an occasional "It feels good to touch yourself there." This gives mom and dad credibility about such matters and lets the child know it will be safe to talk to his or her parents about things of a sexual nature.

Also, little boys have erections from a very early age, yet parents seldom explain to them that males get erections when they are having fun with their penis, as well as at other times like when waking up in the morning. Parents tell boys that they have nice eyes, ears or even feet, but they avoid telling a boy about his penis or saying anything nice about it. Nor do they tell a girl positive things about her genitals or let her know that her vagina will sometimes get wet. Yet girls get wet as often as boys get erections. (Parents who explain such matters to their children may need to distinguish between the sexual kind of wet and the peeing-in-your-pants kind of wet.)

Nanny Interruptus

Everyone these days is worried about nannies shaking their baby to death or kidnapping it or being lazy when no one else is around. Few people think to ask the nanny how she responds if she encounters junior playing with his or her genitals.

What if you are trying to encourage a healthy attitude about sex, but during the nine hours a day when you are away, Consuela is slapping the kid's hand and warning of a thousand curses that will happen if your child ever touches him or herself again?

Ask about this when you are interviewing for a nanny. Otherwise, much of your hard work may be for naught.

Opportunity Knocks, and Knocks, and Knocks

The wonderful thing about explaining sex to kids is that you usually don't have to bring up the subject. It comes up on its own. Whether it's dogs mating in the backyard or your kid rubbing her genitals while you read her a good night story, opportunities abound to make talking about sex a normal and natural part of growing up.

Unfortunately, parents who explain sex in an open and honest way should be prepared for nasty glares from other adults, because their children won't know it is bad to talk about sex; e.g., "Mr. Johnson, my daddy gets erections. Do you?" or "Sister Mary Elizabeth, does your vulva tingle when you feel excited?"

Ultimately, this kind of embarrassment is nothing compared to what you will feel if the first time you talk about sex is when your fifteen-year-old daughter informs you she is pregnant. (In Sweden, where children have better access to sexual information and birth control, the rate of teenage pregnancy is one-sixth of what it is in the United States. Also, the kids there don't start having sex any earlier than they do here.)

Playing with Themselves

Since many parents don't talk about masturbation, their children may regard it as a dirty secret.

You can explain masturbation to a younger child by saying, "Masturbation is when you touch yourself between your legs in a way that feels good." If your child asks for details and you feel comfortable about it, you can make a pretend penis with a finger while saying, "This is how boys do it" or point two fingers downward and rub the knuckle part to explain how girls do it. Also, it might be reassuring for an older boy to hear his father say, "I started masturbating when I was your age" or for a girl to hear her mother say, "I masturbate, too."

Keep in mind that masturbation is very common for kids between the ages of 6 and 9, and it's not unusual for girls to occasionally rub their genitals up against furniture.

Public vs. Private

In doing research for this book, the author met with a class of high school students to talk about sex. Before he had even introduced himself, one of the boys yelled, "Do you masturbate?" It's not the sort of question he is used to being asked, let alone by a young punk with baggy pants and a strange haircut. Embarrassing? You bet, yet to have said anything but "Sure" would have created a serious credibility gap, and it would have been dishonest. Beyond that, it would have been inappropriate for him to have discussed details about his private sex life with the young and restless. Hopefully, parents will keep in mind that it is neither necessary nor advisable to discuss the details of their private sex lives with their children. On the other hand, it is fine for parents to let their children know that sex is a fun and important part of their lives.

Younger children may need constant help in learning the difference between public and private. You may need to remind your three- or four-year-old numerous times that they aren't to play with their vulva or penis in the front yard. Hopefully, you will never hear them reply, "But Daddy does!"

Liberal Parent Alert For superpermissive parents who feel that putting limits on children destroys their little spirits, keep in mind that children won't feel safe with their sexuality if it is allowed to explode all over the place. If a child is masturbating or exposing himself or herself in a public place, there is no harm in saying, "I know that feels really good, but the place to do it is in the privacy of your own bedroom." Also, children who constantly rub their genitals might be dealing with emotional anxieties that have little to do with sex. Before getting too concerned, you need to consider how the kid is doing with the rest of his or her life. Is this one of many things that isn't going right, or is it simply an isolated problem that needs loving but firm guidance?

Naming Private Parts

Modern parents usually have no problem telling little boys that they've got a penis and testicles between their legs, although little boys rarely refer to these items by their proper names. For that matter, neither do big boys.

Female sexual anatomy is mislabeled from practically day one. First of all, what you see from the outside is not a vagina, but that has become the generic term for what is nestled between a woman's legs (assuming it's not part of her lover's anatomy!). What you see from the outside is a vulva, which means lips. The vagina doesn't appear until after the vulva is spread open, and even then you only see the outer rim of it. It is also helpful for parents to identify the clitoris. For more on this, please see "Vulvas, Vaginas, Beavers and Bear" in the chapter "What's Inside a Girl."

Parents might do well to inform boys about girls' genitals and vice versa. This way, girls' genitals won't seem like such a mystery. Also, it is through such talks that parents can teach boys to respect and care about girls' genitals. Otherwise, how are boys expected to learn such things? In a locker room?

The Difference between Cum and Pee

When you try to explain the concept of ejaculation to a child, the chances are good he or she will assume you are talking about pee. After all, that's what comes out of a penis, right? Kids will likely surmise from early talks about the birds and bees that the man pees into the woman to make her pregnant. One way of avoiding this confusion is to explain that there is a big difference between pee and ejaculate. Pee is thin and mostly clear like water and there is a lot of it, while ejaculate is white and thick, and there is only a teaspoon or two of it at a time. It won't hurt to explain that nature was very smart about all of this and made it so that a man can pee when his penis is soft and have an ejaculation when his penis is hard. (This not a hard and fast rule, but no need to go there yet.) You can say that when a man has intercourse and his penis is hard, there comes a certain point where his penis feels really good and warm and the ejaculate starts to squirt out. That's the stuff that can get a woman pregnant. Let them know that boys don't start making this fluid until they go through puberty, which happens sometime between the ages of twelve and sixteen. Also explain that a man can't get a woman pregnant by simply hugging her or kissing her.

Child-Abuse Warnings

Now that our society is so revved up about child abuse, we've got parents and teachers telling young children, "Don't let anyone ever touch you down there!" Think about this.

In this day and age, the first time parents mention sex to children is often through warnings about sexual abuse—complete with those deep, measured parental tones that barely hide mom and dad's fear and concern. Consider how dumb it would be if the first thing parents told kids about bike riding is how many scraped knees, broken bones and fractured skulls they are likely to get. At best, the child would learn to hide his excitement and questions from mom and dad. And if the kid did have a bad encounter on the bike, it is only natural that he or she would try to hide that, too, and perhaps feel horribly guilty.

Why not establish a good rapport about sex with your child from early on? Then your child can take in your eventual warnings about child abuse with intelligence rather than guilt or trepidation.

As for an actual strategy, try giving young children a sense that their bodies belong to them and no one else. Tell them they don't need to give hugs or kisses if they don't want to. If parents respect this in their interactions with the child, then the child will learn from an early age that it's okay to say NO to unwanted physical touching. This is a far better approach to preventing child abuse than the stern fear-based warnings that some parents give.

When your child is older and able to speak with you about sexual matters, you can say, "No one should touch you in a sexual way unless it's what you want." Let your child know that no adults should ever touch their genitals and bottoms or ask to see them undressed unless it's at a doctor's office when mom and dad are present, or it is with a helping teacher whom mom and dad say is okay. If anyone ever touches them anywhere on the body or takes pictures of them and says to keep it a secret, they should tell you anyway. Also encourage them to tell you about any kind of touching that makes them feel strange or uncomfortable. And tell them if a stranger ever asks for their help in finding a lost pet, to come straight home and get you.

Some parents tell their children that there are "good kinds of touch" and "bad kinds of touch." This is too abstract and is seldom helpful, as children often confuse "good touch" and "bad touch." Any child abuser worth his or her salt will be able to turn this around to his or her advantage.

One of the greatest tools you have in combating child abuse is to spend lots of time with your child, being a real and vital part of his or her youth. Children who only get limited amounts of time from their parents (aka "quality time") are far more likely to be interested in the attention that child abusers have to offer. Child abusers are very savvy in their ability to select children who aren't getting enough attention at home or who have lots of unanswered questions about sex. They then become the involved, exciting and understanding adult figure that the child longs for. Unfortunately, they end up doing your job for you, and more.

Children's Questions about Sex

Some parents have the fantasy that children will ask about sex as the need arises. But when parents volunteer information about all things under the sun except sexual feelings, children grow up sensing that questions about sex are off-limits.

What children need to know are the proper names of the things that they can see or touch, and an acknowledgment that touching or rubbing their genitals can feel quite nice. The latter isn't anything that kids don't know, but it gives them a message that it's OK to talk to mom and dad about things that are sexual.

Also, some parents overwhelm young children with biological facts about sex. Folks, a five-year-old can't understand the concept of fallopian tubes!

If a child under the age of five asks, "Where do babies come from?" it's fine to say that the baby grows in mommy's uterus. That will usually be more than enough. Between the ages of five and eight, children will probably want to know how the sperm gets to the egg, and we're not talking via the stork. They'll want specifics on how it got from daddy's body into mommy's body. (For the sake of political correctness, remember to say, "Mommy and Daddy place Daddy's penis inside of Mommy's vagina," and not "Daddy places his penis inside of Mommy's vagina." When you explain sex, try to make it a "we" thing as much as possible.)

Some children might need to be told that babies come out of vaginas rather than rear ends. For birds and bees stuff, find a book with fun illustrations that you enjoy and then read it together with your child.

Once a child asks a question about sex, he has often created a scenario or answer to the question in his own mind. As a result, you may want to pause and ask Junior to tell you what he or she thinks the answer might be. That way, you may get more clues about what the child needs. If there is no evidence that he or she is courting a hidden hypothesis, proceed to answer the question the best you can.

When it comes to questions about sex, or anything else for that matter, don't be afraid to tell a child that you don't know the answer. Acknowledge that it's a really good question, and tell Junior that you will do your best to find the answer. Then ask a friend, find a book or call one of the national sex lines. This way your child will feel that you take his or her questions seriously and will feel free to ask for your opinion in the future.

Keep in mind that you may be asked the same question about sex ten or twenty times. It could be that young children have a profound need for repetition, or maybe they get a secret sense of joy from seeing mom and dad break down in tears after they've been asked the same question more times than even Job could possibly stand. Also be aware that you will be giving a very different answer to a five-year-old's question about intercourse than you will to the same child when he or she is ten or fifteen. Just because you answered a question when your child was five doesn't mean you won't be answering the same question every couple of years, but each time in a slightly different way.

A wonderful book on sex for children age 10 and up is *It's Perfectly Normal* (Cambridge, Mass: Candlewick Press, 1996) ISBN: 1-56402-159-9.

A Normal Five-Year-Old's Feelings about Sex

"In second grade, a little boy kept squeezing my vulva and it felt so good and tingly and warm and throbbing that I waited quite a while until I told my teacher!" *female age 23*

As part of his training, the author of this guide followed the growth of several normal children from birth on, discussing child development quandaries with their parents as they arose.

One of those children was a five-year-old girl whose lifelong best friend had been a boy of her own age. The girl's mother was shocked one day to find both kids buck naked with the little boy's fingers on her daughter's vulva. The mom's first thought was to break every bone in the little boy's hand, but her daughter was just as happily involved as he. So she went into the kitchen and forced herself to count to twenty. She then decided that the last thing she wanted to do was respond as her own mother would have. Needless to say, your author got a phone call asking for suggestions.

The mom and he discussed how blanket prohibitions about sex often teach children to hide their sexuality from their parents. The child then loses the advantage of having a parent's wise counsel about sex. So rather than being guided by her initial response to protect her daughter, the mother asked the little girl how she felt about the way her friend had been touching her. Realizing that it was safe to answer truthfully, her daughter replied that it felt so wonderful she simply couldn't find a way to say no!

Since then, this little girl has asked her mother questions about who can touch her genitals and how to say no if she doesn't want them to. She asked these questions on her own initiative without being prompted by her parents. Few moms and dads have "perfect" answers for such questions, but just letting your child know that these are good questions and making an effort to discuss them can be amazingly helpful. This kind of discussion helps the child learn how to use reason when dealing with sex.

It is likely that when this little girl becomes a young woman she will have more respect for her own sexuality than the vast majority of her peers. Her sexual decisions may even be the result of good judgment, instead of the all-too-common adolescent rush to just do it because the opportunity presented itself. Also, it seems that she values herself and won't be agreeing to sleep with a boy out of fear that he will go away if she says no.

Please, don't for a moment think that this guide is saying to avoid setting limits on your children's sexual behavior. Parents who set no limits on their children's behavior tend to raise obnoxious brats. Instead, why not think about strategies that might be more effective than simply yelling NO!—although there are times when a contemptuous glare or a straightforward no are fine parental responses. Hopefully, you will encourage your children to think about their sexuality in ways that are constructive, rather than raising kids who are mindless about sex or have as their criteria "What can I get away with?" or "If I don't have sex with him, he'll start going out with someone else." For more on this, please see the chapter "The First Time—Not What You'd Expect."

When Children See (or Hear) You Having Sex

If a young child walks in when you are having sex, cover up slowly and try not to look like you were doing something bad, because you weren't. One of you should take the child back to his or her own bed and tuck the kid in. It's a good idea to ask the child, "What did you see Mommy and Daddy doing?" This will help you to know what they saw and how they interpreted it; e.g., "Daddy was hurting you!" Please resist saying, "I'd be a very happy person if daddy hurt me like that more often."

If the child has a negative read on what he or she saw, be sure to disagree with his or her interpretation and give it a positive spin. And no matter what the child answers, you might also say in a reassuring voice that you and daddy were having sex and will be happy to talk about it in the morning. Even if the child doesn't ask any questions, make sure that you raise the issue the next day.

Also, parents who make a fair amount of noise when they are making love should consider telling their young children about it, saying that mom and dad sometimes make noises at night when they are sharing sexual feelings. Explain that these are happy noises which are very different from the noises that mom and dad make when they are fighting. This is an important distinction to make.

The good thing to know about being seen by your kids is that Dr. Paul Abramson and colleagues at UCLA just completed an eighteen-year longitudinal study of "Early Exposure to Parental Nudity and Scenes of Parental Sexuality." Eighteen-year-olds who, as kids, had walked in on mom and dad when they were having sex showed no differences from other eighteen-year-olds on measures of self-acceptance, relations with peers and parents or other adults, antisocial and criminal behavior, substance use, suicidal ideation, quality of sexual relationships and problems associated with sexual relations. In fact, young boys who walked in on mom and dad actually seemed to demonstrate a better long-term outcome than those who didn't. Hmmm.

"Why Can't I Watch You and Mommy Have Sex?"

You've worked hard to be an open, honest parent about sex and your three- to five-year-old suddenly rewards you with the statement, "I want to watch you and Mommy have sex!" Instead of convulsing with panic, regard this as an opportunity to talk about privacy and sex; for instance: "One of the things that makes sex so special for Mommy and Daddy is that it's private, just between the two of us. Since sex between us is private and personal, I wouldn't feel comfortable having anyone else watching." "Well, what about that time I saw you kissing Mommy's vulva. Will you kiss mine?" "Your vulva is very sweet and nice. But I wouldn't feel comfortable kissing your vulva like I kiss Mommy's because it's a private sexual thing that I only do with her."

Nudity at Home

"Nudity was a normal part of bathing, dressing, getting up in the morning or going to bed at night. I think this is ideal. Kids get a lot of reassurance and education from the occasional observation of natural (not contrived) nudity."

female age 35

"My daughter always felt comfortable walking around the house naked, but my teenage son is so modest that nobody can remember seeing him naked since he was five years old!" *male age 65*

Is nudity around the house good or bad? A retrospective study of college students compared how much nudity they reported when growing up with their current levels of sexual activity. There was no correlation between high levels of nudity at home and sexual promiscuity at college age. Interestingly, kids who reported higher levels of nudity at home seemed to report more feelings of warmth or security when away at college. Perhaps one reason for this is because it's easier for them to adjust to communal bathroom and shower situations that are so common in college life. It's also possible that they feel better about their bodies, which can help a person feel more self-confident in social situations.

Parents' Sexual Feelings about Their Children

Our society gives parents little guidance about sexual feelings toward their children, except blanket condemnation. Hopefully, you will find this to be a helpful discussion of the matter.

Children of all ages are able to evoke sexual feelings in parents, from a nursing experience that leaves a baby's mother with pleasant genital sensations, to an older teenage son whose developing body gives mom an occasional sexual stirring—perhaps reminding her of the excitement she used to feel when seeing the boy's father when he was the same age. The problem isn't in having occasional sexual feelings about your children, which plenty of parents feel at times; it's in what to do with the feelings.

For instance, let's say that a dad is playfully wrestling with his young daughter and finds that he is getting an erection. A healthy dad might think to himself "Oops!," beg out of the roughhousing, and say to his daughter something like "Why don't you grab the mitts so we can work on your pitching?" or "How about a game of Nintendo or Scrabble?" A less healthy dad might keep doing the same activity over and over without adjusting to the reality of the situation.

Unfortunately, upon discovering the start of an erection, some very good dads withdraw from physical and sometimes even emotional contact with a child. In these cases, dad's own harsh superego can ruin a very important parent-child relationship. This can be quite sad for both parent and child. On the other hand, there are some dads who could use a more highly developed superego—or at least develop enough boundaries to recognize that children are not meant to be sexual partners.

As for mother-son feelings, let's say that mom enjoys rubbing her teenage son's back, but finds that she is starting to have a sexual response. Maybe it's time to give Junior a quick hug instead and realize that it is more appropriate for him to have his back rubbed by girls his own age. Or maybe mom enjoys the way her son's teenage body looks. This is fine, but it starts to cross the line if she ends up in his bedroom whenever he is getting undressed. Particularly troublesome are lonely moms who encourage their sons to share the bed with them, unless such conditions are dictated by abject poverty. The same is true for lonely dads.

Problems sometimes abound in families where the parents' sexual relationship is not a particularly good one. One of the children might decide that it's up to him or her to be a replacement spouse. What's amazing about this kind of mutual seduction is if a therapist suggests that something might be askew, both parent and child may glare at the therapist as though he or she were some sort of twisted pervert. Especially destructive are those situations where the parent alternates between being seductive and puritanical.

All things considered, it's not possible to set specific rules and standards for all households. For instance, nudity in one family might be perfectly healthy, while nudity in another family might be part of a syrupy, seductive mess. And while it might be best for parents to put boundaries on one child's sexual expression, another child might do well with the opposite kind of response. For instance, a teenager who is an exhibitionist with his or her naked body can clearly use some limit setting, while a highly inhibited child who is embarrassed about his or her body might find it helpful to hear that it's okay to be naked. Another example involves a young child who enjoys masturbating before naps or when tucked into bed as mom or dad are reading a favorite story. This is perfectly normal. However, another child who masturbates anxiously or throughout the day probably needs emotional help.

It would be nice to say that common sense should prevail, but when it comes to sexual development within the family, there doesn't seem to be an abundance of collective common sense in our culture.

Explaining Puberty

"When I got my first period I was excited, but then my mother wouldn't let me climb trees or play with the guys anymore." *female age 55*

"My mom had always been really open with me, so I was prepared when my body started changing. I was even glad to get my period." *female age 19*

"I started growing awfully fast and none of my clothes fit anymore. I'd consume everything in the refrigerator and would still feel hungry. My armpits had never perspired or smelled before. Suddenly, it was like someone had turned on a faucet under each. I dreaded being called on in morning classes, because I'd often have a raging hard-on. My beard was really strange, mostly boyhood fuzz with isolated man hairs growing through it. So I appropriated one of my dad's razors and started shaving. I didn't know why I was suddenly having wet dreams, and I used to hide my underwear and wash them myself so my mom wouldn't see the stains. I was sure I was damaging myself by masturbating once a day, but couldn't stop to save my life. Hair started growing from my neck down. And suddenly there were zits. It would have been nice if a parent or some adult had taken a moment to explain some of these things to me." *male age 44*

It never hurts to let your children know that their bodies will change as they get older. Of course, you will need to address the issue in different ways depending on the child's age. For instance, you can tell your seven-year-old that puberty is what happens when you stop looking like a kid and start looking like an adult—that boys get taller, their voices deepen, they start getting hair under their armpits and around their genitals. You can also say that girls' hips start to get wider, they grow breasts, and their armpits and genitals get hair too. For more about teenage boys and their unwanted erections, see the chapter "On The Penis."

When your child is a few years older, you can explain that puberty is a process that takes a couple of years to complete and that it usually starts to happen for girls when they turn ten or eleven and for boys when they turn twelve or thirteen. Of course, let them know that puberty is a little like the repair people from the phone company: sometimes they arrive when they're supposed to, sometimes they are awfully late, and occasionally they arrive before you expected. You can mention that puberty is the time when girls start to menstruate and boys start to ejaculate when they have orgasms, and that everyone's genitals start to look more like those of adults (bigger and hairier).

Keep in mind that kids can be awfully cruel toward other kids who are in the throes of puberty. Let your child know that you'll ring his or her neck if they ever make fun of another kid whose body starts to change sooner than theirs, or if they taunt a kid who is really, really late.

Menstrual Bleeding

"Puberty was not a really big deal for me. I read *Are You There God, It's Me Margaret,* so I knew what my period was when I got it, although my Mom never bothered to tell me." *female age 25*

"I was afraid that I would just start bleeding sometime and that it might go through my clothes and I would be embarrassed." *female age 49*

"My first period was a celebration. I was at my friend's house and I noticed bleeding between my legs. I rushed home to tell my mother, fully aware I was having my period. She was thrilled, and we went out to dinner to celebrate." *female age 18*

The only time when many parents mention sex to their daughters is while explaining menstruation. What an unfortunate association, bleeding and sex. Now it's even worse, as the first thing young girls often hear about sex from their parents is a warning of sexual abuse.

As children, we learn that blood is a sign of bodily injury. We are never told that some bleeding is good for us. So when girls start menstruating, the blood that drips from their vulvas is often equated by the unconscious mind with injury or internal damage. When explaining menstruation, girls should be informed that the bleeding which comes during their menstrual periods is a good thing, and that menstruation is the body's way of keeping the walls of their reproductive organs clean and fresh.

Keep in mind that girls are now menstruating at ages twelve or thirteen; their grandmothers started menstruating when they were three to four years older. The bodies of these young girls are more developed than their grandmothers' were at the same ages, but their emotional development is about the same. This means they will need plenty of encouragement and support from their parents in negotiating the puberty process, especially if they begin menstruating earlier or later than most of their friends.

Growing Girls

Young girls tend to be very self-conscious about physical changes, especially around fathers and brothers, so don't be talking about tampons and training bras when the guys are around. If they mature earlier than their friends, you'll need to be aware that other girls might shun them a bit and boys might tease them. Keep reminding them that things will be fine in a couple of years when everybody else has started to mature. Make sure they are involved in activities like sports, science, 4-H—anything where value is placed on their physical or mental abilities.

If your child is comparing herself in negative ways to actresses on TV, let her know that many of the allegedly "perfect" girls on TV are, for the most part, self-absorbed lunatics who think nothing of barfing up a perfectly good meal so they won't get "fat." These are people who have more surgery than a BMW in a Tijuana chop shop, and in spite of the stories that their publicists send to *People Magazine*, few have off-screen lives that are particularly happy. Double ditto for models who are in magazines like *Seventeen*.

Teenagers & Sex

"I used to pretend my friend Heather was another boy that I liked in school in fifth grade and we would touch each other's vulvas and breasts and have a lot of fun until my Mom found out and sent me to a psychiatrist for being a lesbian!" *female age 24*

If you ask a group of sixteen-year-olds if they are emotionally ready to have sex, most will say yes. If you ask their parents whether their sixteen-year-olds are emotionally ready to have sex, most will say no. Chances are your teenagers do not view sex the way you wish they would.

As a parent, you can't expect a teenager to be verbal about sex just because you have suddenly decided to offer wise counsel. Having an open dialogue about sex is an option that some parents lost when the child was three to five years old. If mom and dad ignored the existence of sexual feelings back then, it might be very uncomfortable for the child who is now a teenager to suddenly start talking about sex. If there is tension between you and your teen, or if the kid is engaged in reckless acting-out behavior, you might do better to solicit the help of a favorite aunt, uncle, teacher or therapist whom the teen is more apt to open up to.

When Teenagers Ask on Their Own

Let's say your teenager asks you a question about sex: "How do you know if you're gay?" or "What if you get so nervous before having sex that you feel like throwing up?" or "Would I have to leave home if I got pregnant?" Don't assume that she or he is thinking about being gay, is about to have sex or is pregnant. Maybe your kid heard something on the TV or radio and is putting him or herself in the other person's place.

Try to respond by saying things that will help expand the question into a discussion, such as "What are your thoughts about that?" or "I'll be able to give you a better answer if you could tell me more about your question." This buys you precious time, which parents can never have enough of when being asked questions

Before Puberty

Three Years Later

The Mind of the Human Male Does Not Always Mature As Rapidly As His Genitals

about sex, and it helps you squelch any potential screams that are about to explode from the depths of your parental being.

You might take solace from the following words by one of the top sex educators in the country, Debra Haffner: "Like most parents, I have found myself at a loss for words when a question I never expected popped up. Indeed, there have been times when I have responded in ways that I later regretted. For instance, I struggled with how to respond to my daughter when she asked questions about the Bobbit case, and then about Michael Jackson, and now Monica Lewinsky."

Don't think that you need to come up with perfect answers. The most important thing is to provide an atmosphere where the child can ask questions and know that it's okay to think out loud about sex.

Wouldn't It Be Nice If...

Here are the kinds of questions that you probably never asked yourself before having sex, but hope beyond hope that your teenager will ask him- or herself. Perhaps these questions can act as guides when you are talking about sex.

🦜 Why does this person want to have sex with me? Is it experimentation, fun, romance, a personal quest?

🦜 Does having sex mean something different to him or her than it does to me?

🦜 What would we do if we had intercourse and became pregnant? Whom would we turn to? How would we tell our parents? Would we face it together? Am I ready to be a parent? No kid should begin dating without seriously discussing these questions with his or her parents.

🦜 Do I know what it feels like in my body to be sexually excited? Have I fantasized about being naked with this person? Do I want to have sex because I am physically excited about it, or is it just to please a partner or to keep him or her interested in me.

🦜 What kind of stimulation does a woman need before intercourse feels good instead of bad?

🦜 Are there ways we could please each other sexually without having intercourse?

🦜 How do I say no to someone who is pestering me for a date, or no to sex without feeling like a coward or geek?

🦜 If we do have sex, how do I get genuine feedback from my partner about what felt good and what didn't? How do I tell him or her what feels good and what doesn't for me?

🦜 Will I feel good about myself the next day?

🦜 Who sticks what into where when we have intercourse, and how can we do it in ways that will make it feel better?

Toward Higher Expectations

The mere thought of asking an eleven-year-old what qualities she would want in a sexual partner would send most American parents racing to the bathroom for a hit of Tagamet or Imodium. But let's think about it. If you as a parent don't introduce the notions of chivalry and respect in sex, where else are your children going to learn them from, MTV?

There is nothing wrong with talking to your child about the difference between a partner who's just trying to get laid and one who is going to be a caring and loving sexual companion. For instance, does a partner who is going to be a respectful lover say, "I won't go out with you anymore if we can't have intercourse"? Is he or she responsible and caring toward family and friends? Are his or her friends good people? Do they drink or get loaded a lot? And what about introducing the expectation that a truly desirable partner is one who is trustworthy and dependable and says things like "I'd really like to please you. What can I do?"

Of course, none of this is going to stop your kid from shacking up with one of the local Hell's Angels, but it does kick into motion the idea that an important part of self-respect means choosing your sexual partners carefully. Who knows, with enough intelligent concern and involvement on your part, your kid may even search out a sexual partner who has some of the characteristics and values that you do! Hopefully that's a good thing.

Condom Advice—For Teenage Boys

Give your teenage boy a couple of condoms and a tube of contraceptive jelly, saying that these are for him to put on when he's alone to see what it feels like. If you have a straightforward relationship with him, you might suggest that he try masturbating with a condom on, which is the condom equivalent of taking a test drive. Tell him to pay attention to how long it takes after he ejaculates before his penis starts to shrink and the condom gets baggy. That's how much time he has to pull out; otherwise the condom might stay in his partner's vagina. Tell him that the shrinking penis factor is why he needs to clasp the condom around the base of his penis as he is pulling out. The contraceptive jelly is to put on the outside of the condom to help it slip and slide better when he is having intercourse, and it will help kill any germs or sperms that accidentally break free.

Condom Advice—For Teenage Girls

Give your daughter a couple of condoms, a tube of contraceptive jelly and a penis-sized banana. Tell her that one of the condoms is for her to practice putting on the banana; the others are for whatever she wants to do with them. If you have an open relationship with her, try putting the condom on the banana together. This should result in a number of giggles and shared laughs. If it doesn't, you're being way too serious. Explain that she needs to leave a little baggie area at the tip of the penis so it can fill with ejaculate when the guy comes. Also explain that as soon as a guy ejaculates, his penis starts to shrink. This means that she should clasp the condom with her fingers and push it against the base of his penis as he withdraws so he won't leave it inside her. Let her know that it never hurts to put a little contraceptive jelly on the outside of the condom before having intercourse. This will help give extra protection in case something escapes from the condom that shouldn't.

And just so you'll know, teenage girls who know what kind of birth control their mother uses are more likely to use birth control themselves.

Odds'N'Ends

If you have a son, make sure he's got a big box of Kleenex next to his bed, and when it's all used up in three days don't make smart remarks like "I didn't know you had such a bad cold this week..." Better you have to stock up on extra Kleenex than he is out knocking up some young girl!

If your child begins to wash his or her own underwear or pajamas, be sure they have proper information about menstruation, masturbation and wet dreams. While most of us know what happens when boys ejaculate, we forget that some teenage girls get major wet spots in their underwear when they become sexually excited.

Abstinence-only programs do not significantly delay the onset of intercourse. Unfortunately, the entire D.A.R.E. program had no significant impact on drug use. The "just say no" approach works about as well on teenagers as it does on adults!

Let your kids know that it's fine to wait until they are older before having sex with a partner and that masturbation is what you do in the meantime, which is why the Good Lord gave us humans two more fingers than ET.

Inform them that what they see on TV about sex is usually pretty twisted, exaggerated and outright incorrect, unless they're watching reruns of *Married With Children.*

Final Word about Boundaries

If you think your younger teenagers would do better to wait a couple of years before sharing sex with partners, then you might do something other than tempt the fates.

One thing is to talk to your kids about sex and encourage them to talk to you. That way, if they're going to become sexually active, it won't be just to get one up on a mom or dad whose head was stuck in another century. Another thing that helps delay sexual activity is getting teenagers involved in activities that challenge their minds and bodies—we're talking about things like science fairs and playing soccer or building things.

Understand that good kids do not always make good decisions. If you give them enough rope to hang themselves, most will. On the other hand, no kid ever lost a friend because their parents insisted on knowing where they were and with whom. No teenager ever died because his or her parents set a curfew on weekends. No kid ever shriveled up and blew away because one parent called another parent to make sure that an adult would be home when their kid was sleeping over.

Your kids will have plenty of time to do whatever they want once they turn eighteen and are legal adults. Until then, it is your job as parents to get them there safe and sound.

Dear Paul,

Last night I discovered that my 11-year-old had bookmarked a number of porn sites on his web browser. I checked out these sites and was shocked at what I saw. I am not a prude, but I am concerned at

*the negative messages that my son might be getting in the name of
sexual excitement. I don't know how to handle this.*

Lucy in Allentown

Dear Lucy,

The first time I used a web browser I put the word "erotic" in
the search engine. About a zillion sites popped up, so I selected the
first site on the list. Moments later, a close-up photo of a smiling,
attractive woman with her mouth wide open started to fill my
screen. A stream of liquid was flowing into her mouth, and then a
penis appeared. What I ended up with was a close-up of some guy
peeing into the mouth of a young woman who could have been
the girl next door. The second site on the list showed a close-up of
a woman's pelvis with one penis sticking up her rear and another
in her vagina. As an experiment, I entered "Beanie Babies" in the
search engines. I got a number of sex sites from that.

This is different from what we saw as kids. We'd masturbate
for months over a tattered page from *Playboy,* and while *Playboy*
may not show the most accurate representation of what nature
put on the average woman's chest, it's at least an approximation
of what you'll get if you're going to have sex. I had no idea that
someone would ever want to pee into another person's mouth
until I was nearly thirty and started meeting people in the entertainment industry.

So what concerns me, Lucy, isn't that your son is seeing
pornography, but that the pornography he is seeing is so darned
twisted.

I wouldn't want anybody's son or daughter to see some of
the porn that's out there today. But I don't believe there is an
effective way of keeping kids from seeing this type of stuff. Even
if you have the most effective screening program in the world,
your kid's friend down the street will have found a way to circum-
vent it, or they will get on his parents' computer when his mom
and dad are at work (from 7:00 a.m. to 8:00 p.m...). If they can't
access this stuff on the internet, there are plenty of videos floating
around that show some of the same things.

And that's where you need to enter the picture. As a parent, you are not going to keep your kid from seeing some of today's seriously demented porn. So instead of just ignoring it, consider this an opportunity to be the emotional anchor your son needs to develop a healthy and caring sexual self.

One strategy is to let your kids know that it's perfectly normal to be curious about sex, and despite your best efforts, they might see things on the internet that are seriously weird and way out of the range of normal. If your kids know that you won't suddenly transform into a total lunatic when the subject comes up, you might ask them about some of the weirdest things they've seen on the net. If they have seen sexual sites and are able to tell you about them, your response might vary from "That sounds really strange; you're not describing any sex acts I'd ever want to do" to "I know it seems weird now, but maybe it's something you'll like to do when you get older," depending, of course, on what they describe.

Assuming they don't fess up about what they've been seeing, you can always tell your kids that there's sometimes a big difference between looking at pictures of people having sex and what happens when two people actually have a good sexual relationship. Sex with a real-life partner is full of tender and caring moments. You rarely see that kind of tenderness if you are watching sex on the internet or in a video.

Also, keep in mind that even regular intercourse or oral sex can be scary or disturbing for teenagers. They'll try to dismiss it by saying, "Oh mom, I know all about that," but they can still be very anxious about it. I am particularly concerned about how kids have dealt with the past presidential sex scandal, including the stuff with that stupid cigar. I am sure it caused a lot of kids anxiety, but few will admit to it and few will ever discuss it with their parents.

Your job, Lucy, is to help your son digest some of what he will be seeing in the next couple of years—from twisted porn to bizarre and disturbing video collections of people killing themselves or getting wasted in accidents. (You wouldn't believe what my teenage patients tell me they see.) Through your attitude and willingness to be involved, you can help your son sort through the bizarre and twisted images that he will most likely be seeing. Otherwise, the disturbing images may stay trapped within his consciousness and interfere with healthier ways of relating. And years later, he'll end up spending thousands of dollars on shrink-types like me to help sort the mental wheat from the chafe.

If your children are spending countless hours on the web, it might be due to loneliness and isolation in addition to normal curiosity. If you want your son to spend less time looking at sex on the internet, it won't happen by treating it like drugs and taking a "just say no" approach. It's far more effective to get your children involved in extracurricular activities where their time is structured and they are doing things that make them feel good about themselves.

Dear Paul,

I am 14 and my mom, who is totally cool, just got me birth control pills. My boyfriend and I are totally committed to each other. Do we still need to use a condom?

Heather from Humboldt

Dear Heather,

I am not 14, but I am a fairly liberal guy and have produced one of the more liberal books on sex ever written. I want to disagree with your first statement. I don't think your mom is totally cool because she got her 14-year-old daughter birth control pills. I think she's misguided.

You're not going to like this, but I don't think 14-year-olds should be having intercourse and I don't think their parents should be condoning it.

Of course, people might feel I am being hypocritical, given how I encourage parents to speak with their children about everything from masturbation and orgasms to ways of telling a partner what you like in bed. But these people assume that talking about sex encourages kids to do it sooner. I don't think so.

One reason why I feel you should wait is because our minds handle abstract concepts a lot better at age 17 or 18 than at 14. And believe it or not, there's a lot of abstract stuff to cope with when you are in a relationship and having sex. You might be the most mature and responsible person in your entire class, and I think it's great that you are thinking about birth control and condoms, but I also think you'll appreciate sex a lot more when your mental equipment catches up with your physical equipment, which doesn't happen for a few years yet.

In the meantime, your mom could help you get involved in community activities, like volunteering at an old folks home or an animal shelter. She should help you get some life experience under your belt rather than your boyfriend's penis. This is just one man's opinion, but I feel it's really important for someone your age to channel your sexual energy into expanding your mind and creativity. Then, after you graduate from high school, the sex you have will complement who you are as a person rather than define it, as is often the case when 14-year-olds are having intercourse. I am concerned that it's just too big, too soon right now.

And yes, Heather, if you do have intercourse, it's a good idea to use a condom in addition to taking the pill.

Chapter Notes: Thanks to *Not with My Child* (Carson City, Nevada: United Youth Security, 1999) for insight into how child abusers think. And to Debra Hafner's *From Diapers to Dating: A Parent's Guide To Raising Sexually Healthy Children,* (New York: Newmarket Press, 1999) for a reminder about nannies and two or three other things mentioned in this chapter.

Sex When You Are Horny & Disabled
Chapter 44

A story recently appeared on the internet about a twenty-two-year-old man with cerebral palsy who has virtually no control over his body's movements. The guy started using his wheelchair antisocially, as a ramming device. He was running over anything he could. Eventually, this young man wrote on his word board that he was so horny he couldn't stand it anymore.

Although his body has the same sexual urges and desires as a fully able twenty-two-year-old, he has no ability to walk, talk or masturbate like the average twenty-two-year-old. He can't even turn the pages of *Playboy* or stick an X-rated video into the VCR.

As quickly as they began, this young man's wheelchair tantrums stopped. The reason? A nurse's aide mercifully began giving him hand jobs. But then she was caught and fired instantly. The board-and-care home threatened to file a complaint against her for sexual abuse.

Sexy & Disabled?

If you think you have a good attitude about sex, consider a quadriplegic who wheels by in an electric wheelchair. The person drools a little and steers the chair with a joy stick that's strapped to his forehead. Do you think of this person as being sexual? Do you think he has the same sexual needs and desires as you? Chances are you'd wonder how good his jump shot is before you'd think of him as having the same sexual needs and desires as you.

Many people not only disapprove of sex for the severely disabled, but might find the concept offensive. They might even feel that we need to protect people who are disabled from sex.

Dear Paul,
I'm a paraplegic from Ohio. From where I sit, I have women's rears and crotches in my face nearly all day long. You have no idea how much restraint it takes to keep my hands to myself. Last week I copped a feel but quickly apologized and blamed it on my "bad driving" and "spastic hand."   *Dude from Dubuque*

Dude,

Just to let you know, there's not an able-bodied guy on the planet who could come face-to-tail with as much anatomy as you do and not want to reach out and touch some. P.S. You must consider a crowded elevator to be a gift from God.

One reason why so many of us blanch at the idea of a disabled person having sex is because the advertising industry spends billions of dollars each year trying to narrow our concept of what sexual attractiveness is. Never do advertisers tell us that sexual appeal might have something to do with integrity and character, given how those can't be paid for with a credit card. As a result, we end up feeling out of the loop if we are bald, short, old, or thirty pounds overweight. Forget even existing sexually if you are missing a few fingers or an entire leg, slur your words when you talk or are paralyzed from the chest down.

A huge hurdle for many disabled people is being able to accept themselves as being sexual. If you don't accept yourself as being sexual, it is unlikely that others will.

Roll Models

"Prior to my becoming blind, the only person who was blind that I had seen was a beggar. I was horrified to think that this was the only option available to me as a person who was blind." From an article on women who are blind by Ellen Rubin in *Sexuality and Disability*, 15(1), 1997.

One of the more discouraging aspects of having a disability is that positive role models are few and far between. For instance, if you ask people to name a famous disabled person, just as many will say the Hunchback of Notre Dame as Franklin Delano Roosevelt. Of the two, FDR was a real-life American president who provided people with a real sense of sanctuary, although he was unable to walk unaided. There were reasons why FDR tried to hide his disability. When he was a young man, disabled people were considered a success if they could get a job in the circus.

Different Ways That Disabilities Happen

When people are disabled from crashes and accidents, it is often because the spinal cord was damaged. About 85 percent of spinal-cord injuries happen to men, many in their teens and twenties. That's because men have a penchant for doing things that involve speed or collisions. For instance, if a boy says he needs "pads," you might assume he's talking about something to put under his football jersey. If a girl says she needs "pads," it's likely that she's referring to sanitary napkins or something to stuff into her bra. In addition to sports and car crashes, disabilities might come from gun wounds, stabbings, fistfights or a serious bonk on the head.

Diseases that cause disabilities include arthritis, which can make intercourse painful or cripple your fingers so much that you can't masturbate. Polio can make it nearly impossible to walk or breathe and it can result in all kinds of problems later in life (post-polio syndrome). Diabetes can keep a guy from having an erection but it usually doesn't keep him from having an orgasm. Multiple sclerosis can be mild and manageable or severe and debilitating. Cancer and the various treatments for it can impact a person's ability and desire to have sex.

There are many genetic or congenital disorders that can cause disabilities. Certain chromosome disorders can damage a person's physical growth and/or mental development. Congenital disorders might result in being a midget (top-shelf challenged). Medications taken during pregnancy can result in the birth of

infants with severe disabilities. Parental exposure to pollutants and chemicals can cause birth defects. Disabilities can also result from things like strokes and heart attacks or cerebral palsy and muscular dystrophy.

Note: If you watch TV talk shows like *Jerry Springer*, you might think that Siamese twins are born every five minutes, which is not the case, but this is a disability that might affect a person's ability to date. Also, there are people whose genitals are altered by birth defects, such as hermaphrodites.

Spinal-cord injury (SCI) shorthand: When people with spinal-cord injuries are talking to other people with spinal-cord injuries, they sometimes use a shorthand such as "I'm a C-4 quad" or "I'm a T-3." This code refers to the location on the spine where the injury occurred. For instance, a C-4 injury occurs higher up on the spinal cord (in the neck) than a T-3, so it is likely that a person with a C-4 is paralyzed from the shoulders down (quadriplegic), whereas a T-3 has the use of his or her arms (paraplegic), and an L-4 most likely has more use than a C-4 or T-3 because the injury happened at a point on the spinal cord between the ribs and pelvis. Another factor is whether the injury was complete or incomplete, with the latter supposedly being less severe.

Quad Note: Thanks to Tom Street for this info. Tom is a C-4 quad from an auto accident in 1988. Tom manufactures a computer mouse for quadriplegics called the QuadJoy. This special mouse, combined with extra software that Tom has written, allows the user to run the entire computer including keyboard by mouth. The full range of clicking and dragging happens by virtue of puffing and sucking on the end of the joystick. This can be particularly helpful for a quad who would like to interact with others in chat rooms or who would like to see internet porn in PRIVATE and without the help of an attendant. Tom can be reached on the internet at www.quadjoy.com.

Chronic vs. Acute

There are certain disabilities that happen all at once. They don't keep getting worse. This is true of most spinal-cord injuries.

There are other disabilities, usually caused by diseases, which have symptoms that get worse over time.

For some people, it is easier to have a disability that stays the same. For instance, once a person with a spinal-cord injury is able to learn how to deal with his disability, he can be pretty sure that his condition won't worsen and he won't have to learn a whole new set of skills just to keep even. However, people with chronic illnesses have a more uncertain future and may have to constantly readapt as the illness progresses. The uncertainty of a chronic illness makes it more difficult to get on with your life, as you never know when your disease is going to pull the rug out from under you. Of course, you can say that none of us has any guarantees for the future, but the uncertainty of everyday life is much easier to cope with than the uncertainty of a disease that may be getting worse.

Even the recovery process is different for someone with an acute injury as opposed to a chronic illness. For instance, consider a person who had his leg amputated after being run over in the parking lot at the 7-Eleven as opposed to having a leg amputated due to complications from diabetes. Outside of not getting to finish his Slurpee, the person who lost his leg at the 7-Eleven had no pre-existing condition and must only face the problems associated with the amputation itself. The person with progressive diabetes has to cope with numerous problems caused by the diabetes in addition to those that are specific to the amputation.

Also, the treatments for certain disabilities or illnesses can cause sexual problems. For instance, tricyclic antidepressants are often prescribed to help with the neurogenic pain that can occur after spinal cord injury. These drugs can decrease the desire to have sex as well as the ability to have an erection and to ejaculate. The same is true for certain cancer treatments that adversely affect the sexuality of both men and women.

Double Your Trouble

As if it weren't bad enough to have your spinal cord injured, accidents that cause the damage are often severe enough to also cause traumatic head injury. Not only does the person have to cope with possible paralysis from the spinal injury, but he may also experience low sexual drive, poor impulse control or unpredictable behavior from the brain injury.

Can Guys in Wheelchairs Get Hard-Ons?

It's interesting how people wonder if guys in wheelchairs can get hard-ons, but they don't wonder if women in wheelchairs can get wet! Why's that? Contrary to what you might think, a lot of guys who are in wheelchairs are able to get erections. The stimulation for the erection will often need to come from direct physical contact with the genitals rather than from feeling horny, as the link between the horny center in the brain and the genitals is often damaged. Guys with disabilities can often get good erections with the help of vacuum pumps or injections. Men with higher-level spinal-cord injuries (usually quads, not paraplegics) tend to get reflex erections. These happen when the penis is being touched and have little connection to feeling horny. They usually go down as soon as the touching stops, but some couples learn how to keep the stimulation going so they can have intercourse.

Able-bodied men often become aware of their own sexual arousal by feeling their penis grow. Men who are paralyzed have to rely on other signals to know when they are aroused, e.g. nipples getting hard, goosebumps, heavier breathing and a heart that beats faster. These aren't any different from what able-bodied men experience, but how many guys notice subtle physical clues when their dicks are screaming, "Touch Me! Touch Me!"

Women with spinal-cord injuries may find that the sexual wetness in their vagina is decreased or absent. Using a lubricant during intercourse can be very helpful. Many women with spinal cord injuries are able to have orgasms. Bregman and Hadley (1976) interviewed a number of women with spinal-cord injuries and found that their descriptions of orgasm were similar to those of women with no spinal-cord injury. This suggests that orgasms can be generated by nerves in the body that do not run up the spinal cord. Also, some people with spinal-cord injury have orgasms that are referred to as "para-orgasms," which are different from genital orgasms but are quite compelling. Para-orgasms can be so strong that women who are injured above the T-6 level need to be aware of rapid changes in their blood pressure.

Both women and men who no longer have traditional orgasms can learn to experience a type of orgasm that is called an emotional orgasm. This kind of orgasm results in a rush of relaxation and calm in the rest of the body that's like the afterglow of a good hard come.

Whether a person can or can't have an orgasm, the good feelings that most able-bodied people get from being touched and loved are still massively satisfying for someone who is disabled. One person with a spinal-cord injury reported in a video that "before my accident I couldn't get enough stimulation from the waist down; now I can't get enough from the waist up!" When a person is paralyzed in other parts of the body, areas such as the back of the neck and arms can become extremely sensitive in a sexual way. Also, plenty of disabled people report that watching a partner doing something sexual to them can be very satisfying even if they can't feel the actual sensations. The brain is able to fill in the missing pieces.

Vibrator Note: Vibrators can be a very helpful sexual aid for men and women with disabilities. They can supply the necessary stimulation when a hand is unable. If you tend to be incontinent, consider getting a vibrator that's rechargeable or has batteries. Urine is a far better conductor of electricity than water, making plug-in models a wee bit risky. If your hands are too crippled to use a regular vibrator, it's possible to embed one in a nerf ball. Contact us at www.goofyfootpress.com for more information.

"Will I Be Able to Have Children"

This seems like a simple, straightforward question. But it is often an indirect way of asking, "Will I be able to have sex?" "Will anyone want to have sex with me?" "How in the blazes do I have sex now that I'm like this?" The answer to all of these questions is usually yes, unless the person stays in a full-time funk and never transitions out of asking "Why me?" Try as they might, nobody but God or nature has an answer to the "Why me?" question, assuming there is an answer at all.

Most women with disabilities are able to become pregnant. This is why most disabled women need to use birth control, even if they are paralyzed from the shoulders down. Many men who are paralyzed have problems ejaculating. Physicians are having some success helping these men to ejaculate by sticking electrodes up their rears and shocking the bejesus out of nerves in the prostate region. Some guys with spinal-cord injuries above T-12 are able to ejaculate with the help of a vibrator on the penis.

Born with It vs. Got It Along the Way

Unless they are in a rock'n'roll band, most people who make it to adulthood have probably achieved certain developmental milestones, aka "maturity." But if a person was disabled at an early age, it is possible that this has gotten in the way of achieving the level of maturity that he or she needs in order to behave as a responsible and caring adult. For instance, how does a kid who is disabled at age sixteen progress through the usual steps toward independence if he or she needs a parent to get them out of bed and dressed each morning? If he or she is in a rehab center, how do they get the privacy to explore sexually as other kids do? If their hands are crippled, how do they masturbate?

Consider the following questions posed by a therapist who works with the disabled: "How does a young girl in a wheelchair learn how adults are sexual if her parents are afraid to be that way in front of her? How does she explore her parents' drawers when they are out and find books, movies, condoms, sponges, lingerie and so forth—as many youths do—if she cannot get into their bedroom? How can she find her brother's copies of sexually explicit publications if she cannot get under his bed where they are stashed?" (From "Performing a Sexual Evaluation on the Person With Disability or Illness" by Kenneth A. Lefebre in *Sexual Function in People with Disability and Chronic Illness*, Marca Sipski and Craig Alexander, Aspen Publishers, 1997.)

People who are disabled at a young age will become adults with the same sexual drives and desires as anyone who is not disabled. However, they may be missing a sense of sexual orientation or knowledge of responsible and appropriate ways to satisfy their sexual urges. To help fill in the missing pieces, parents and educators of disabled kids need to be more open about sexual issues rather than less.

Sex & People Who Are Developmentally Disabled

It is not likely that people who are developmentally disabled will be reading this book, although we know of one such woman by the name of Linda who loves looking at the pictures! People with developmental disabilities have the same sexual urges and desires as people without disabilities. They simply go through the stages of sexual development at a slower pace.

The developmentally disabled pose special problems when it comes to sexual training, because they may need a good deal of repetitive explanation about things that many adults feel uncomfortable saying just once. Also, in their drive toward sexual pleasure, developmentally disabled kids may be even less apt to use birth control than their nondisabled partners in crime.

If you are the parent of a disabled child, or you work with people who are disabled, you might be at a loss for finding good references to help you in dealing with your child's sexual growth. One book that might be helpful is *Doubly Silenced: Sexuality, Sexual Abuse and People with Developmental Disabilities* by Patricia Patterson.

Body Image

If a person has been disabled for a long time, particularly from a young age, his body image might also include a wheelchair or braces, scars from various surgeries, hands that are twisted and not particularly dexterous, a voice that slurs words, a head that doesn't sit straight on its shoulders or other features that aren't always like those of models in *Vogue* or *GQ*. It may be very difficult for a person who is disabled to feel attractive and effective if they can't see themselves as separate from the devices that help them to survive. As a result, they might need plenty of feedback that you value them as a person in the same way that you do someone who doesn't have a wheelchair, braces or disfigurements.

Dear Paul,

We both have spinal-cord injuries and are disabled. Yet we like watching porn that shows able-bodied people having sex. Is this weird?

Rhonda from Rolling Hills

Dear Rhonda,

None of us have eight-inch penises, last forty-five minutes, come in buckets or have partners who like taking it ten different ways, but we like watching pornography too. If most of it weren't so darned boring, we'd watch it more often! Keep in mind that pornography is a fantasy. It helps us go places in our minds where many of us wouldn't go in reality even if we could. Now here's a question for you: I'll bet you aren't worried about watching able-bodied actors in TV or movies, so why when it comes to porn do you suddenly worry about being crippledly correct?

Explaining Yourself & Educating Others

"People do have all these kinds of curiosity, and you have to find ways of making them feel more comfortable around you at first."

Steve, on the videotape *Sexuality Reborn*

Just like people who are able-bodied, people who are disabled need to learn their own sexual strengths and weaknesses and then teach a partner what they need. They also need to receive plenty of feedback. For instance, for someone who has had a stroke, it might be important to lie on their affected side so they can use their active arm for caressing a partner. Likewise it is important for their able-bodied partner to give them feedback, as someone with a stroke might have a "visual field cut" which causes them to ignore one side of their partner's body. (This example by way of social worker Sharon Bacharach.)

When it comes to enjoying sex, different disabilities pose different challenges. For instance, if you can't use your hands in a way that allows you to masturbate, then figuring out how to do that will be one of your first challenges. If you need help breathing but want to give a partner oral sex, you might need to alternate sucking on your partner's genitals with sucking breaths of air from your respirator hose. If you can't have intercourse, then you'll need to work out ways of pleasing both yourself and your partner without it. (This book has plenty of chapters that describe ways of doing that.) Perhaps your disability has left you with little nerve sensation in your genitals, but the opening of your anus is still sensitive, and stimulating it might bring you to orgasm. Perhaps your neck, lips, cheeks or nipples are highly sensitized to touch. Maybe it helps if you take a warm bath or shower or have a beer or glass of wine before having sex. This is just as true for able-bodied people.

Goodbye to Spontaneity

Some able-bodied couples don't like to use a condom because the thirty seconds it takes to put it on somehow destroys the mood for them. Think of how resilient "the mood" has to be when it takes all sorts of preparations and maneuvers to be ready to have sex! Think of how resilient the mood has to be if one partner cries out in pain and adjustments need to be made in order to continue.

One of the things that people who are disabled lose is the kind of sexual spontaneity that some able-bodied couples take for granted unless they are parents with kids who are still at home. Consider the following advice that was recently posted on the internet:

Patience is truly a virtue in disability-related sex. Disability often destroys something in sex, spontaneity for one thing. Drugs, fatigue, depression, neurological impairment can also be a destructive force. Utilizing the turn-on can sometimes partially make up for what has been taken away. Sometimes erotic books, photos or videos can

enhance the performance. The type and degree of disability often demands traveling that extra mile or two.

PeterLove@primenet.com

Getting into Relationships

"Why would any man want this body?" "No woman's going
to want this!" Some people who have disabilities feel that nobody
will find them sexually attractive. As a result, they might push

away people who do or, at the other end of the spectrum, offer themselves to the first person who shows interest, even if it is not someone they particularly like or trust. A disabled person without a solid sense of self might be starved for affection or desperately need to prove that he or she is desirable. Of course, one doesn't need to be disabled to have these sorts of hang-ups, but it can be extra-difficult when your physical ducks aren't in the same row as everyone else's.

Regarding the subject of dating and people with disabilities, a woman with cerebral palsy recently commented, "I think women are more accepting of differences than men. I see a lot more disabled men married or in serious relationships. I see a lot more disabled women just giving up." There are plenty of disabled men who say it's equally tough for them. Another disabled woman says one of the reasons she fell in love with her husband "was the idea that here was a person who looked and acted okay, wanting to have a relationship with me." (Both quotes are from "Dating Issues for Women with Physical Disabilities," *Sexuality and Disability*, 15, no. 4 [1997]) by Rintals, Howland, Nosek et al. Original source: T. Due, *Houston Chronicle*, May 24, 1995.)

People with disabilities sometimes shy away from dating other people who are disabled. When you are disabled yourself, there can be a kind of hatred of other people who are disabled—an inner need to say, "I'm not like them." There can also be the added problem of social acceptance. Two people in wheelchairs humming down the sidewalk garner far more stares from able-bodied pedestrians than does one.

The Disabled Couple

Perhaps the most difficult aspect of being in a relationship where one or both members is disabled is that ultimately the couple has to face the same kinds of fights, squabbles, disagreements and difficulties as couples who have no physical disability! As for how disability affects a couple, keep in mind that some able-bodied couples stay in love with each other only as long as each partner is able to mirror the other's sexual attractiveness. If one member starts to look older than the other, slows down a bit or becomes disabled, the relationship may quickly dissolve. With other couples, there is a deep love and friendship that transcends physical change.

When there is a new disability, it is not uncommon for both partners to experience frustration, anger, fear, disappointment and helplessness. Roles within the relationship may undergo serious changes. Neither the able-bodied member nor the one who is disabled should be afraid to ask for help and advice from social workers and rehab staff.

When it comes to experiencing sexual intimacy, a couple with a new disability may need to learn anew. This might actually be a relief to your partner if you weren't as good in bed as you thought you were! The good news is that couples who had a rewarding sex life before the disability usually find a way to have a good sex life after.

If you are a couple whose primary expression of sexuality was through intercourse, you may have a good deal of adjusting ahead. It will be easier if you are a couple whose sexuality included a full range of sensory experiences, like enjoying the beauty of a sunset, holding hands and caressing each other.

Also, if you can afford it, it would be wise to hire an attendant to perform caretaking functions. Otherwise, a parent/child dynamic can evolve between you and your partner which can intrude on feelings of sexual passion.

With a Deaf Ear & Twinkle in His Eye

A woman who is a friend of the Goofy Foot Press works with deaf people and has also had sex with one or two deaf men. She said that she never realized how much she relies on verbal cues from a partner until she was romanced by a deaf man. For instance, when you are with a deaf person, there is no hearing without seeing. Whether it's being in another room or looking down when you are having a bowl of soup, the necessary conditions for connection are suddenly missing. She said that the lack of verbal give-and-take is particularly noticeable during sex, whether it's oral sex or intercourse.

People who are deaf are obviously more comfortable with verbal silence during romance and lovemaking than are people who can hear. If our friend is sleeping with a man who is deaf, she lets him know that she needs more input than he might be used to giving a partner who is also deaf. She also says that it is important to have some of the lights on when you are making love to a deaf person, so they can either see you sign or read your lips. On the other hand, deaf people sometimes sign on each other's skin, or if they are in a spoons position, the person in the back can reach around his partner's body and sign in front of her where she can see it.

Attacking Their Own

It's interesting how people sometimes attack their own. For instance, while many people who are disabled would welcome an increased awareness that they are just as sexual as anyone else, some clearly don't. A year ago, when a mainstream glossy magazine for disabled people ran a story on sex and the disabled, some disabled readers were so upset that they canceled their subscriptions. When hearing about this, you might think that the story was *Hustler*-like and included photos of the naked disabled doing things that would have pleased Caligula. In reality, the article was so tame that it could have been published in *Parade* magazine or even *House & Garden*.

Perhaps the subject of sex brings up huge amounts of frustration and sadness for some disabled people, to the point where they simply get angry at sex itself.

So You Won't Have to Read the "Sex During Pregnancy" Chapter of This Book Unless You Want To

Women can get pregnant in a wheelchair just as easily as they can get pregnant in any other chair. Don't think for a moment that just because you are disabled or paralyzed from the shoulders or waist down you somehow can't get pregnant. Be sure that you speak to each other and to your physician about birth control. **Note:** Until recently, it was believed that birth control pills, shots and implants might be unsafe for some women who are in wheelchairs. It's not the wheelchair that's the problem, but prone-ness to circulatory problems and blood clots that can be increased by the birth control pill. However, the newer low-dose pills and shots are thought to be quite safe. If your gynecologist isn't used to working with women who have disabilities, check with the National Spinal Cord Foundation for a referral.

Attendants and Caregivers—The Good and Bad of It

Powerful feelings can develop between people who are patients and those who are hired to care for them—both loving and hateful. It is beyond the scope of this book to explore the various possibilities, except to say that it does little good to turn a blind eye to the dynamics that can arise between caretaker and caregiver.

If you are able-bodied, consider for a moment the issue of privacy. The kind of privacy that able-bodied people take for granted might not exist for someone who is disabled. This can range from bathing and completing bowel movements to preparing for masturbation and sex. It may be necessary for a disabled person to share private aspects of themselves with an attendant that some able-bodied people don't feel comfortable sharing even with a partner of many years.

Considering the level of dependency that some disabled people have, opportunities for abuse by attendants are rife. This is a huge issue, and abuse is unfortunately quite common. It is important that disabled people speak up against assistants who are abusive. If this is a concern for you, please contact your local center for independent living.

Helping the Helpers

In order to have fulfilling sex lives, people with disabilities often need the help of several different medical subspecialities. These might include neurology, psychology, urology, oncology, endocrinology, physical and rehabilitative medicine and sex therapy. Unfortunately, getting medical specialists to work together in a collaborative effort requires that professional egos be set aside. This can be as difficult as getting Catholics, Mormons,

Jews and Southern Baptists to join forces. The problem multiplies when the issue is sex, since many of the professionals who need to work together might be ever so uncomfortable with the subject at hand.

If you are a disabled person who is struggling to get assistance with your sexual needs, maybe it will help if you give your healthcare provider a copy of this book opened to this chapter. Perhaps it will help them feel more at ease in aiding you with sexual matters. After all, it's quite likely that they, too, enjoy sex and would be more than happy to help you if they were just able to feel more comfortable.

Rehab Note: When rehab therapists get around to mentioning sex, it is usually in combination with discussions about bowel and bladder functioning. This is quite unfortunate. People who are newly disabled need access to positive information about sexuality early in their rehabilitation. Even if they reject the information, it is something positive that will remain in their consciousness, to be accessed at another time.

Stroke Studies—Interesting for a Number of Reasons

Stroke survivors, as a group, experience a decrease in sexual activity. Until recently, this was thought to have physical, rather than emotional, causes. However, a study of stroke survivors by Buzzellie, di Francesco, Giaquinto and Nolte concluded that "psychological issues, rather than medical ones, account for disruption of sexual functioning in stroke survivors" ("Sexuality Following Stroke," *Sexuality and Disability*, 15, no. 4, [1997]).

It is especially significant that the researchers found no differences in the sexual functioning of people with right-brained lesions as opposed to left-brain lesions or contralateral lesions. This contradicts our modern tendency to view behaviors as coming from one side of the brain or the other. This study indicates that sexuality is neither "right-brained" nor "left-brained."

Resources on Sex for People Who Are Disabled

Please check out the Resources section on our website ,www.goofyfootpress.com, for a listing of resources for people who are disabled. If you don't have internet access, you can call us at (541) 563-7550 and we will try to find the resources you need. Fortunately, our list includes a doctor who customizes sex toys to fit your particular disability. For instance, if your fingers are too crippled to hold a vibrator, you might be able to negotiate one that is embedded in a Nerf ball.

Recommended Videotapes

Sexuality Reborn is an excellent video in which four likeable and articulate couples tell about their personal experience with sex and disability. At least one person in each couple is wheelchair-assisted. Very helpful for both disabled and able-bodied viewers. College instructors who use the *Guide to Getting It On!* in their classes are highly encouraged to show this tape to their students. A great deal of humanness is conveyed without a moment of pity or self-absorption. There is something about the honesty and genuineness of the couples who speak in this video that gives able-bodied people a more realistic and grounded perception of people who are disabled. There are parts of the tape where the couples are naked and having sex, but it isn't in a pornographic way that's going to ruffle the feathers of your dean or regents. The only criticism that reviewers had was that the occasional comments by the talking-head medical specialists seemed unnecessary and perhaps detracted from rather than added to the tape's effectiveness. To order, call (800) 435-8866.

Untold Desires shows interviews about sex with people who have all kinds of disabilities. This award-winning documentary contains no nudity and makes an excellent companion tape for *Sexually Reborn*. We seriously hope that anyone going through a rehab program would get to see both tapes. Included is a wonderful interview with a woman who has severe cerebral palsy. She is astute, funny, and energetic. The tape provides subtitles when she speaks because her speech is so CP-involved. The interviews with other disabled people are equally valuable. As an additional bonus, there is spectacular footage of one chair-assisted guy skiing down a steep mountain and a disabled dude racing down stairs and streets. Redefines the term "No Fear." Highly recommended for people with disabilities as well as those without.

Dear Paul,

I liked your book so much that I ordered a copy for my son at college (his dorm buddies agreed that he either had the coolest mom ever—or the weirdest). May I make three suggestions for future editions?

We don't describe people who wear eyeglasses as "eyeglasses bound," yet your book uses the term "wheelchair-bound." I had it pointed out to me by a friend with no legs that "Wheelchairs do not bind us. Wheelchairs set us free." Also, people who wear glasses have visual disabilities, yet we don't call them "disabled." But when someone's legs don't work, we describe all of them as being "disabled." Finally, all of the drawings in your book with one exception are gorgeous. Why not include drawings of people who aren't so gorgeous?

DB in Detroit

Dear DB,

Your points are well taken. I have removed the words "wheelchair bound" from this edition and am open to changing this chapter's title in the future. As for the "perfect" people in the illustrations, I can't tell you how hard we tried to make them look less perfect. But the problem with this style of line art is that the only tool the artist has to work with is a simple black line on white paper. To give it the fun and exciting look that we wanted, the artist needed to draw almost everything as an exaggeration. Otherwise, the drawings looked really flat and lifeless. Another limitation comes from showing a single isolated moment of a couple's lovemaking and expecting it to express all of the different emotions that couples have. This was impossible. So while my feelings about the artwork are very similar to yours, I've learned to appreciate just how difficult it is to make line art look good even with the hunkiest of characters. It's only because our artist is one of the best that it works as well as it does.

Dyslexia of the Penis
Learning to Improve Your Sexual Hang Time
Chapter 45

Coming too soon is an unfortunate joke that a man's body plays on itself. His penis suddenly feels like its had twenty minutes' worth of intercourse before he has finished his first couple of strokes. Rather than being able to enjoy the warmth and excitement of having his penis inside a lover's body, he is left fending off an unwanted orgasm and the feelings of disappointment that follow.

Equally frustrating is the numbing effect that premature ejaculation has on the woman's level of excitement. That's because she often holds back in an attempt to help the man last longer. In cases where she might want to wrap her legs around her lover's body and have him thrust away at a hefty clip, she learns to lie still; and if she wants long, deep strokes, she learns to not ask.

Since coming too soon affects both partners, this chapter takes a partners approach to solving it. For instance, it talks about the need for a couple to increase rather than decrease the level of sexual excitement in their relationship. It offers exercises that can help the man learn to tolerate a depth of sexual feeling in his penis that he probably doesn't even know exists. It also suggests that a couple's entire relationship can be strengthened when the woman helps the man to improve upon a problem that he has been helpless to fix on his own. Few women realize the depth of gratitude that most men feel when a partner helps them with a problem like premature ejaculation.

Increasing the Woman's Sexual Excitement and Self-Sufficiency

Retraining a dyslexic penis can take several months, and it is important to consider the female partner's sexual pleasure as well. For instance, the couple might explore various ways that the woman can experience high levels of sexual satisfaction. This is important for a number of reasons:

🐜 She won't feel resentful or frustrated (assuming she doesn't already).

🐜 He won't feel guilty (assuming he doesn't already).

🐜 It's likely to be fun. Hopefully, much fun!

🐜 Both partners will get to experience what it is like when the woman is able to open up sexually, no longer needing to mute her excitement to help her man last longer.

Fortunately, a lot of men learn to compensate for premature ejaculation by becoming really good at pleasing a woman with oral sex and different kinds of massage. If they haven't, this would be a fine time to learn. Also, there is no reason why the woman can't masturbate while her partner holds her. Besides being nice for her, this allows the man to feel her body in his arms as she experiences intense levels of sexual pleasure.

What Is It, and Why Does It Happen?

If you can last for eight minutes of intercourse, thrusting at a rate your partner finds satisfying, then you are doing really well and don't have rapid ejaculation.

If you have to think about baseball while barely moving your hips and you still can't last for two minutes, then you would do well to read on.

Probably between 30 and 40 percent of males are rapid ejaculators. As for finding an exact definition of premature or rapid ejaculation, good luck. No two researchers seem to agree. A big factor in deciding whether or not you come too soon is how you and your partner feel about it.

Over time, there have been many different theories about why men come too soon. Most of them have been proven false. One theory blames the masturbation habits of teenage boys, saying that they teach themselves to come quickly by jerking off as fast as they sometimes drive. But plenty of guys who jerk off in two minutes flat can last as long as they like during intercourse. Another theory says that the body cannot distinguish anxiety from sexual excitement, and that high amounts of anxiety fool the body into thinking that it has been having intercourse for much longer than it really has. But no research has ever shown premature ejaculators to be any more or less anxious than anyone else. A third theory proposes that a man who comes too soon holds tension in his genitals and rear end and is unable to relax that part of his body during intercourse. The constant muscle contraction makes for a quick come. Hmmm. A pair of Korean researchers claim that some men's penises are naturally more sensitive than others, and this causes them to come sooner. They are working on a special motion lotion to help increase your intercourse mileage. There is also a zoological perspective, which recognizes that most male animals ejaculate after only a few thrusts. This helps them to live longer, since a steamy two-hour lovemaking session in a jacaranda tree greatly increases the chances that a pair of mating primates will fall off a limb or be eaten by predators, and we're not talking oral sex here.

As for reality, there are probably several factors that can result in premature ejaculation. For instance, Mike, who is 40, may have struggled with rapid ejaculation since he was a teenager. Dave, who is also 40, may have started coming too soon last year. Since Dave only recently started coming too soon, it would be wise to rule out physical causes such as prostate irritation. Mike, on the other hand, might have a penis that's significantly more sensitive than the average. And Jack, who's always come too soon, might be suffering from the macho man disease. This disease strikes guys who never learn much about the sensations in their own bodies.

Whatever the cause, people often think that it's easy for a premature ejaculator to learn how to last longer, if only he would try. Nothing could be further from the truth. He can no more will himself to last longer than he can will himself to fly to the moon.

The treatments mentioned in this chapter assume that the cause of the premature ejaculation is not prostate infection or irritation, and that you have gone to a urologist and had these or other physical causes ruled out. This is especially true for someone who went for years without coming too soon and is now a sub-two-minute man.

What Not to Do

Whatever the cause(s), it is generally agreed that men who come too soon go from erection to ejaculation without much adroitness at the steps in between. They often try to prevent ejaculation by thinking about something other than sex, which is about as productive as an Indy race driver thinking about golf as he's entering a high-speed turn. Although all of us are occasionally distracted when having sex, this is not a good way to last longer. On the contrary, the exercises that follow encourage a man to be as present as possible in his penis and body.

The Other 97 Percent

It is essential for the man with a dyslexic penis to become more aware of the sensations in his body—and not just the part that sticks out from between his legs. Not enough can be said about allowing a partner to touch you from head to toe while you empty your mind and let your body completely relax.

Another important thing to work on is learning the difference between inside and outside. For instance, put your hand on your penis and start playing with it. After a few minutes, describe how your penis feels. If you come up with words like "hard" or "big," go directly to jail, do not pass go, do not collect $200. The reason you flunked is because you were describing what your hand was feeling rather than what your penis was feeling, or the outside of your penis rather than the inside. If you came up with words like "tingly," "ticklish" or "throbbing," then you passed.

The goal is to be able to say at any given moment how it feels in the head of your penis, on the right side of the shaft, on its left side, in the front or back of it, in your balls, in your butt, in your shoulders, thighs, face, etc. Rather than trying to numb or ignore what's going on inside you, you want to know it and fully experience it as you never have before.

Calibrating the Penis—Teaching an Old Dog New Tricks

The goal of this exercise is to help you expand your range of sexual feeling. Of course, men who come too soon often believe that they feel too much rather than too little, when the opposite is true. If a man can learn to tolerate a fuller range of sexual feeling, then greater amounts of pleasure won't automatically trigger an ejaculation.

The mechanics of calibrating the penis are fairly simple. A guy can try it on his own, or he can have his partner help. The following describes how it's done when a partner helps. If you are like most guys, you will have no problem substituting your hand for a partner if that's what you need to do.

This begins with the woman caressing the penis in any way that she and her partner enjoy. It can be done with the penis dry or lubricated, with oral sex, or even with a vagina, although the latter is usually not recommended until the man has mastered the basic field maneuvers. How you stimulate the penis will also depend on how quickly the man comes. For instance, some guys who come quickly with intercourse can last a long time when being given a hand job. The woman's arm could literally fall off before her partner comes. She might find it more fun to calibrate her partner's penis orally or by lubricating it and massaging it.

The scale of calibration is usually from 0 to 10, with 0 representing absolutely no arousal whatsoever, e.g., "Your grandmother just slipped you the tongue."

On this scale, a 10 represents orgasm and ejaculation. As the woman stimulates the man's penis, he tells her where he senses himself to be: "1," "3," "5," "6, "8." At first he will just be guessing, but after a while he will know exactly where he is on his own personal scale. Guys who come too soon often go from 3 to 9 suddenly, while other men can stay at 6 or 7 for several minutes.

As the man lands on a specific number, his partner should try to keep him there for a few minutes, and then back off before going higher. She shouldn't hesitate to call it a day and let him ejaculate after fifteen to thirty minutes of doing the exercises. With time, he will be able to tolerate hovering at a constant 6, 7, or 8 for prolonged periods, but don't expect that to happen right away. That's because his body might resist staying at a 7 or 8, since these levels are currently experienced as mere bleeps on the way to a speedy ejaculation.

In addition to spitting out numbers, he should tell her at various points how the different parts of his penis feel, including the head, front and sides, as well as his testicles, stomach, rear end, shoulders, etc. This may seem extreme, but there's no other way for him to learn how his body feels.

The Point of No Return

To successfully calibrate the penis, it is important to recognize when the man is approaching the *Point of No Return*. This is when nothing short of stepping on a land mine will keep a man from ejaculating. The point of no return is usually an 8.5 or 9 on the scale of 10. As mentioned in an earlier chapter, signs that a man is approaching this point are as follows:

The veins in his penis may start to bulge or his penis might give a sudden throb, the color of the head may darken, his testicles might suck up into his groin, his muscles will tighten, his hips may thrust, and he might suddenly start to groan like a dying bull or invoke the names of various saints. Appreciate how well you are doing when you can keep him close to the point of no return for several minutes without letting him go over the edge.

When first calibrating a penis, a woman should probably stop all stroking as a man approaches the point of no return. She waits about ten seconds before resuming stimulation. A goal to eventually shoot for (so to speak) is for the woman to be able to switch stroking techniques rather than stopping the stimulation altogether. For instance, if she is rubbing the shaft and finds that the thing is about to blow, she might switch and begin to rub only the head, with the change in focus being the cue that helps the man power through the urge to come. But please don't try this until you have spent a couple of months feeling really comfortable with the prior routine. Remember, men who come too soon need to learn sexual patience and self-awareness; rushing through the process simply contradicts everything you are trying to achieve.

As for erections, don't worry about them. What you are working toward is the capacity to tolerate more sensation. Don't be confused by the presence or absence of hardness. Some men will start to get hard at only a 3, while others won't stiffen until a 7 or higher. When receiving genital massage or oral sex, a man can experience incredibly high levels of sensation while sporting only half an erection. It is quite possible to come without an erection at all.

What's Your Sign?

As you become more aware of your feelings, you will start to learn your body's signs for when an orgasm is on its way. These signs can usually be felt in other parts of your body before you can feel them in your penis. For instance, you might feel a tingling or tightening in your stomach, thighs, feet, rear end or someplace else as the point of no return approaches. This information can help you know when to change your pace or to concentrate on relaxing your body. That way, you paddle over the wave or through it instead of trying to run out of its way when it's too late.

Deep Breathing and Relaxation

When it comes to rapid ejaculation, shallow breathing is the tool of the devil. Find a book or two on deep breathing and relaxation techniques and learn them well. At the same time that you are learning to tolerate higher levels of sensation, you also want to teach your body to relax. This one-two combo will help you last longer.

Penis Pull-Ups

There is much hype these days about genital squeezing exercises called Kegels. Unfortunately, some people in the sex business claim that doing Kegel exercises will make the dead walk and the blind see. No research has ever shown that Kegel exercises can cure premature ejaculation or make an impotent penis hard, nor will they allow a man to dial a rotary phone or lead an orchestra with his penis. However, Kegel exercises can be valuable in helping a man become more aware of the feelings in his penis and pelvic region.

Kegel exercises are pretty simple and straightforward. They involve squeezing or contracting the muscles that stop the flow of urine—the ones you squeeze when the phone begins ringing after you just started taking a long leak and think it might be a seriously important call. Here are four ways to help build up these muscles:

🦓 Squeeze as you would when you are peeing and want to cut off the flow of urine. Do this nine or ten times in succession. For the first couple of weeks hold the squeeze for only a few seconds. After a month or two, try holding the squeeze for up to ten seconds. (The peeing reference is so you will understand which muscles to squeeze; it's best not to do these exercises when actually taking a leak, lest your urinary tract begin to revolt.)

🦓 Try the above exercises without pause, squeezing and relaxing the muscles in rapid sequence, like when shooting at ducks in an arcade game.

🦓 Change the tempo. Squeeze for a couple of seconds and then push all the way out as if you were trying to have a bowel movement. Try this a couple of times. **Note:** The first two exercises can be done just about anywhere: at work, at school, at church, inside a crowded elevator or when commuting. However, consider doing this exercise in privacy, as the push-out part might cause you to pass gas.

🦓 Optional exercise for guys who have way too much time on their hands: When your penis is erect, sit or stand with your legs apart and try wagging the thing up and down or sideways by squeezing the muscles in your groin. Some wives and girlfriends find this amusing to watch. Eventually toss a washcloth or small towel over the penis to add resistance, but be careful that you don't strain. If you are a jock and work really hard at it, Nike only knows what you might be able to hang on the end of your penis! Of course, check with your physician or personal trainer first, and never attempt anything that causes pain or strain.

Possible Benefits of Doing Penis Pull-Ups

At first, most men won't be able to isolate the muscles that anchor the penis. Instead, they will tense the whole pelvic region, including the rectum. With time, they can teach themselves to better isolate the various muscle groups in the pelvic floor, distinguishing the ones that stop the flow of urine from the ones that wag the end of the penis. This can help a man become aware when he might be tensing these muscles unintentionally. For instance, doing the prior exercises should help a man become aware of when he is unconsciously contracting the muscles in his rear end. Speculation has it that tension in the anal sphincters contributes not only to premature ejaculation, but to hemorrhoid formation as well—two conditions that are greeted with similar amounts of glee. Some sex therapists say that one of the keys to lasting longer is being able to relax the muscles in the pelvic floor and rear end when having intercourse. Some men claim to get extra mileage during intercourse by pushing out, which is the exact opposite of squeezing. Another purported benefit of doing penis pull-ups is that they may help to expand the feelings of orgasm itself.

Including Intercourse

It can take a couple of months to fully calibrate the dyslexic penis. By then it's time to start having intercourse, after you can keep the penis between 6 and 7 for at least ten minutes without needing to ejaculate.

Having intercourse can be tricky. That's because the woman will be tempted to fall into old habits of muting her sexual excitement in order to help the man last longer. At the same time, the man can't be expected to make his new calibration skills work during intercourse without gradually easing into it. Keeping both needs in mind, it might not be a bad idea for the woman to plan on having independent orgasms before or after the couple has intercourse. Then maybe you can view intercourse as a further way of calibrating the penis, with the woman using her vagina to calibrate the penis instead of her hands or mouth. For specifics about intercourse, consider the following:

The man should avoid using the muscles in his rear end for thrusting. This causes his bum to tense up and may contribute to premature ejaculation. Perhaps this is one reason why a lot of men seem to last longer when the woman is on top; not having to thrust allows the man to relax his pelvic muscles more. The same has been said for when he is standing. When the man is thrusting, he might experiment by using his back muscles instead of his butt to propel the in-out part of intercourse.

🐎 You might consider starting with femoral intercourse for a few weeks before doing full penetration. This is where the shaft of the penis glides through the lips of the vagina, like a hot dog in a bun. The penis doesn't actually go into the vagina and does need to be lubricated ahead of time. Femoral intercourse can be done with the woman on top. Even if the penis doesn't go into the vagina, it's a good idea to use contraception when doing this.

🐎 The start of intercourse may cause a backslide and possible reversion to old habits. As you feel her lush, warm, wet vagina starting to suck every drop of ejaculate from between your helpless legs, do not run from the sensation. Stay with the feeling in all parts of your penis and body. Trying to ignore the feeling never helped before, and it certainly won't help now.

The Realm of Sensation

You would be amazed at how many people, both male and female, teach their bodies to ignore subtle sensations. For instance, a man might have learned to ignore his body's more subtle sensations when he was a boy. Perhaps this happened the first time he had to throw a block on a nasty-looking linebacker.[1] Also, some men (and women) find it scary to become passive or to allow themselves to receive subtle pleasure.

It can't be emphasized enough that the purpose of the exercises in this chapter is to allow the man to tolerate and enjoy a fuller depth of physical pleasure. This, rather than trying to stop coming, needs to be your goal.

One of the first things mentioned in this chapter was how nice it can be to share touch and massage. This can help to allow

---

[1]This isn't to say that a boy or girl shouldn't compete in contact sports, but that they need a parent's help in learning that there is a time and place for butting heads and an equally important but different time and place for experiencing sensual feelings.

more sensation. Some couples enjoy using a variety of materials and fabrics to massage the body from head to toe.

For instance, good results can be had with a feather or furry mitt, as well as a silk scarf or piece of rayon. Some couples might also be into leather, latex or rubber. Others find the feel of a partner's fingertips to be exquisite. As this happens, try to be aware of the sensations in your body. Use deep-breathing and relaxation techniques to let yourself relax while your partner caresses all of your body.

A Note on the Squeeze Technique

Sex therapists since the time of the Ming dynasty have recommended doing one form or another of the squeeze technique to help relieve premature ejaculation. To do the squeeze technique, the woman brings the man close to the point of no return and then squeezes his penis to stop the impending orgasm.

An interesting thing about the squeeze technique is that it doesn't work. While sex therapists used to claim a 95 percent cure rate with the squeeze technique, this was only in the short term. After three years, the problem returns in almost all men who have used the squeeze technique.

There is simply no way to squeeze a dyslexic penis into submission.

The Most Important Ingredients

In helping a man to last longer, attributes such as patience, love and a tolerance for frustration are essential for a woman to have. That's because her man is probably fighting a private battle with his own penis that doesn't include much kindness. And for heaven's sake, don't forget to have a sense of humor. Humor is the sexual lubricant for the soul.

Visualization Exercises

Visualization is not a traditional exercise for premature ejaculation—unless the man is trying to visualize something that's totally nonsexual in an attempt to last longer. Hopefully, you can now appreciate how unproductive this kind of visualization can be. Here are a few visualization exercises designed to help a man stay in the saddle by becoming more, rather than less, aware of his body's processes. If they make sense to you, then you might give them a try.

🦓 Close your eyes and feel yourself having intercourse. After you are able to feel yourself thrusting in and out, concentrate on relaxing the muscles in your butt cheeks, rectum and genitals. Each time you feel these muscles contract or tense up, concentrate on relaxing them.

🦓 Repeat the prior exercise, only this time concentrate on your breathing. Try to relax by taking slow, deep breaths. This is done by expanding and contracting your abdomen instead of your chest.

🦓 Close your eyes and feel yourself having intercourse. Keep thrusting until your mind starts to wander or until you visualize yourself ejaculating. At the point that your mind wanders or you see yourself ejaculating, start to visualize something pleasant and nondemanding, such as lying in the warm sun on a private beach. Relax in this way for a few minutes and then let your senses have another go at intercourse. Keep returning to the pleasant, nondemanding place whenever you feel conflicts arising from intercourse. The point of this visualization is not to decrease sexual sensation, but to help exorcise any anxiety that might be causing you to tense up.

Extending Your Awareness

With all of this focus on the man's body, you might be wondering about his awareness of his partner's body. An ideal balance would have him spending fifteen seconds being aware of his inner sensations and then fifteen seconds focusing on his partner's body. Alternating in this way, he never loses contact with one or the other for more than a few seconds.

Relationship Fears & Resistances

Since most of these exercises involve both partners, it is reasonable to expect that a man might have a certain amount of apprehension about seeking his partner's involvement. It is also possible that his partner may have certain resistances or fears about what might happen if her man is able to last longer.

In her book on premature ejaculation, sex therapist Helen Singer Kaplan says that most of the men who were unable to successfully complete her program for rapid ejaculators had wives or girlfriends who did not necessarily want them to last longer.

The three gentlemen mentioned below were rapid ejaculators as well as readers of earlier editions of the *Guide*. They were kind enough to share their personal stories.

Zeus suspected that his wife didn't want him to improve his sexual function and that she would resist helping him do something about it. As it turned out, he was right. His wife didn't enjoy sex, and the faster he came, the better. In addition, she didn't want him having sex with anyone else. She assumed that he would be less likely to have extramarital affairs if his problems remained intact.

Lancelot was afraid that his girlfriend wouldn't want to invest the time and effort in helping him to last longer. He was mortified to even ask. As it turned out, he was wrong as could be. She was happy (and relieved) that he wanted her help in solving the problem. They took on the problem together, with historic results.

Heathcliff had a secret and didn't know if Catherine would want to help or not. While caring greatly for each other, their sex life had never been a central part of their relationship. After several years, he finally asked for her help with his premature ejaculation. He received an unexpected reply. She told him that she often masturbated after he went to sleep, keeping her sexual needs to herself because she didn't think he was interested. They began masturbating together and started feeling sexually intimate for the first time in their lives. Eventually they worked to solve his problems with premature ejaculation. By this time, Heathcliff had become such a changed man that not even his neighbors recognized him anymore.

Rather than bulldozing ahead with the kinds of exercises that are mentioned in this chapter, why not start by having a couple of long talks about it first? The two of you might do well to talk about your entire sexual relationship and any fears or concerns that you are having. It is also possible that the man feels he ejaculates too rapidly, while his partner feels quite satisfied.

Get a Grip

Some of the most annoying aspects of premature ejaculation that women report are the constant apologies and self-criticism that men express after coming too soon. They say that this whining and bellyaching puts them off. If you decide to work on these exercises together, the man needs to promise that he will no longer apologize or berate himself for coming too soon!

Drugs for Coming Too Soon?

A number of drugs have been found to delay ejaculation. One is Clomipramine (Anafranil), others include the SSRI group of antidepressants. Different men will achieve different results with different medications. One of the problems with these medications are the side effects. Some of the side effects can be minimized by taking the pills a couple of hours before intercourse rather than daily. This is how Clomipramine is used to help with rapid ejaculation, in 25 mg or 50 mg dosages. However, a fair number of men find that it still causes unwanted side effects such as sedation and dry mouth.

While over the counter creams for desensitization aren't particularly helpful, some prescription creams for oral pain are said to help delay rapid ejaculation. These are used on the penis instead of in the mouth.

The trouble with taking pills or using creams is that they are only a temporary solution. They won't help you learn to last longer, and are effective only as long as you continue to use them.

While they can be useful in giving some men hope, they are also a crutch which simply delays your ability to become the master of your sexual self.

A sex worker who has read this chapter mentions that cocaine is used by some men to keep the penis hard and numb. It is apparently used on the penis as well as up the nose. While this may help the men to last longer, she emphasizes that it certainly doesn't make them better lovers. Too often, we forget how satisfying the outcome can be when a man and woman make the effort to work through a sexual problem together rather than going for the magic bullet.

Resources: Helen Singer Kaplan's short little book titled *PE: How to Overcome Premature Ejaculation* (New York: Brunner/Mazel, 1989) is a good resource. If you come too soon, it is a good idea for both you and your partner to read this book. Dr. Kaplan recommends that men do the calibrating exercises by themselves with a lubricated hand until they learn to maintain a level of 5 to 7 for at least five minutes. After a few weeks or months, the woman takes over. During the self-calibration period, the woman can lie beside her man and masturbate, do her nails, read the newspaper, sleep, you name it! As for Dr. Kaplan's book, Brunner/Mazel, its publisher, has given it one of the more stupid covers ever, with the letters PE in huge block print, as though the average reader knows what PE is. Everyone here said "physical education" and proceeded to swap stories about weird PE teachers from high school... Still, this is an improvement over the older cover. Unfortunately, Dr. Kaplan is no longer with us. Another very helpful book is Barbara Keesling's *Sexual Pleasure: Reaching New heights of Sexual Arousal and Intimacy.* (Alameda, Calif.: Hunter House, 1993).

Chapter Notes: Many thanks to Dr. Michael Metz for help with this chapter. Dr. Metz is one of the country's finest sex therapists.

Beware the Magic Bullet!
Chapter 46

Before long, modern medicine will be selling a pill that can increase the blood flow into even your great grandmother's genitals. Women as well as men will be plunking down $10 for something the size of an aspirin that promises a chemical solution to whatever ails you sexually. But what about the silliness and fun that some of us look for in sex? What about the tenderness? Does that automatically happen because you paid your pharmacist $10 to get your genitals all puffed up?

Maybe not. A research group from Italy found that while men who took Viagra reported increased sexual satisfaction, their female partners didn't necessarily. It seems the wives and girl-friends of these men discovered that there is more to being sexually satisfied than having a partner with a hard salami.

A social scientist recently studied surveys of older people and found that the critical factor in maintaining a woman's sexual desire is the attraction and lust that her partner feels for her. You can pickle a man's penis in Viagra, but if he doesn't make his partner feel good about herself, she won't have much desire for sex.

Still, many people are looking for an easy cure—a pill or cream that makes you hard or wet. It doesn't matter if you've been angry at your partner for the past twenty-five years, if she falls asleep watching television every night at nine or hasn't tried a new thing in bed since Jimmy Carter was president—with pills that can increase the blood flow to our private parts, all resentments will suddenly disappear!

Research papers are already being released with claims such as "sixty-five percent IMPROVEMENT FOR WOMEN ON VIAGRA!" What they mean by "improvement" is an increase in blood flow into a woman's crotch. What they don't tell you is that most women can achieve this by sitting on a washing machine when it's on the spin cycle.

In spite of what some of us may be wishing for, sexual satisfaction in long-term relationships is usually more involved than having an erection or a swollen vagina or popping a pricey pill.

If you want to keep your sexlife silly and satisfying, you might take a closer look at how you spend your time together when you aren't having sex. For instance, does sitting together in front of the TV for hours each night make you feel more excited about your partner? Maybe if she gives you a hand job during reruns of *Law & Order*, but don't expect that to keep happening for long. Sitting in front of a television is no more helpful to your relationship than having a heroin addiction.

Just because the sex was hot during the first year doesn't mean it will be hot during the tenth. If you want to keep your intimacy alive, you need to talk, share things and do things together that you enjoy. If you want your sex life to stay healthy, do things that make you like and admire each other when you have your clothes on. And don't expect some pill to make up for what you haven't been doing.

Take note from early on of what's exciting about your relationship. Then you will know to scream like the blazes if one or both of you starts to let it fade away.

Chapter Notes: Special thanks to Sandra Leiblum, Marian Dunn and Leonore Tiefer for their help and input.

When Your System Crashes
Chapter 47

While this is a chapter on sexual problems, please keep in mind that it's only a brief overview. Hopefully you will find it to be an intelligent and thought-provoking overview. At the same time, you are encouraged to read books on sex that offer a more traditional perspective, and check with a sex therapist or physician (preferably a urologist) as indicated.

Sex Problems Typically Ascribed to Men

The Bummer in Your Pants

It is amusing to look at the impotence ads in the sports section of various major newspapers. They are usually located next to the ads for hair implants and toupees, above the ads for nude female mud wrestling and sometimes on the same page as the penis-enlargement ads. Most of the men in the impotence ads are really old. Does this mean that erection problems are a part of old age, or are these men simply bored limp with the type of sex that they've been having for most of their lives?

Contrary to what the erection ads show, hard-on problems (hard-offs?) happen to men of all ages, from teenagers on up. For instance, it's not unusual for erection problems to occur at the start of a sexual relationship. Call it performance anxiety, call it fear, it's not unusual for a guy to need a couple of weeks or months to find a comfortable groove. Giving him any less time to get it up is silly and shortsighted, as long as your relationship is solid and there is a strong sense of mutual attraction. The real danger is not with the lack of erection, but with what each of you makes of it, i.e., short-term problems can become long term-problems if the man sees himself as a failure or the woman needs his erection to validate that she's desirable.

Several different kinds of erection failure are discussed in the pages that follow—from those caused by physical impairment to those resulting from emotional concerns. Whatever the cause, hopefully you will be able to utilize these otherwise bothersome moments as a great time for the man to please his partner with his hands and mouth, and as a fine time for her to please him in more ways than by simply letting him stick his penis inside her. For instance, genital massage does not require a man to have an erection, and oral sex can feel just as good on a penis that's soft as on a hard one. On the other hand, some people feel that it's best to focus attention on other body parts when a penis stalls out. Perhaps it depends upon the situation and how comfortable you are talking to each other about sex. If you decide to keep stimulating a pokey pecker, make sure it's understood that you are doing so only to give it pleasure rather than trying to squeeze an erection out of it. Otherwise, the guy will feel like a total dud and probably have performance anxiety next time around. Also, it's usually helpful if the woman will tell the man that she wants him to get her off in some other way, such as by necking for a long time, by hand, with oral sex, with a vibrator or her favorite dildo; or maybe she enjoys masturbating while he watches or holds her. That way, he'll at least feel useful and she'll get her fair share of sexual satisfaction. And more importantly, a potentially disappointing situation might be turned into something sweet.

Often, the biggest problem with impotence isn't the lack of erection. Rather, it's a lack of playfulness and resourcefulness on the part of the man and woman when they are confronted with a hard-on that's a no-show.

When Your Posse Won't Ride

Popular books on sex often use terms such as "self-hatred," "self-loathing," and "devastating" to tell us how a man feels when he is—gulp—impotent; you know, the horror that he goes through when he can't get it up.

Perhaps this guide is way out of step or maybe it's just plain insensitive, but devastating is what happens when your wife or child dies or when you've just been told that you only have six months to live. Self-hatred is what you feel if your business flops or if you've just blown your life's savings. Self-loathing is what you experience when you've just had a major stroke or accident and can't feed or bathe yourself anymore.

Call us callous, call us rude, but we can think of about a thousand things worse than if a man's hard-on takes a hiatus, even if it's forever. Sure, it's frustrating and even humiliating at times, but so are a lot of other things in life. The fact is, you still have your fingers and mouth for giving pleasure, and you still have what's in your heart to love your partner with. And if you can't count at least five things in your life to be thankful for, even if your dick never gets hard again, then your priorities are in seriously bad shape.

Contrary to what you'll read elsewhere, this guide believes that erection problems, regardless of the cause, are an opportunity to have better sex rather than worse. Fortunately, there are plenty of ways that modern medicine can help a recalcitrant penis to get hard, but it seems a shame to employ a quick cure without allowing yourself and your relationship to grow in the process.

A woman who is overcoming orgasm problems has to welcome an entirely new way of embracing her body and her sexuality. It's a journey, a process. And men and women who survive heart attacks and cancer often learn to approach life differently as a result of the disease. Impotent men, on the other hand, just want their dicks to get hard—no learning, no journey.

The Sufis have a saying that you have to let yourself die before you are truly born. Sometimes a guy has to give up his penis as a symbol of masculinity before he can get on with his life. Sometimes he has to realize that there's more to being a man than getting a hard-on, and there's more to sex than just intercourse. Then he has to convince his wife.

This is not to say that a man shouldn't inquire about the various remedies that modern medicine has for erection problems. He should also have a full physical to make sure that the erection problem is not a symptom of something else. If there are medical problems, they need to be treated. At the same time, it's worth noting that some medical problems are the body's way of making a statement. Perhaps the man has important lessons to learn about himself and the world around him. If he is able to accomplish the kind of changes and growth that are necessary, and if his partner can grow and evolve in her own way, then maybe he'll start getting hard again. But by then it won't matter as much, because he and his partner will have discovered new ways to give each other sexual pleasure and emotional support.

Note: No kidding about getting a physical exam. Men past the age of 40 who begin to experience a gradual increase in impotence might be seeing the first signs of an impending stroke or heart attack. In fact, studies are now showing that impotence in some men may be an even greater predictor of impending stroke or heart attack than the highly regarded physical stress test. It seems that the arteries in the penis start to gum up before those in the rest of the body. Pursuing the problem with thorough physical exam may allow the medical profession to give a man the help he needs before something really bad happens.

A More Traditional Approach to the Great Groin Grinch

If you are having hard-on problems, it is likely that you are muttering under your breath that we can take our Sufi logic and stuff it where the sun don't shine. You want a more traditional Western approach. You want a magic bullet that does not require introspection or lifestyle changes. Good enough. The advice that follows is a spoof on a typical sex-book approach to fixing erection problems. While it conveys a certain amount of wisdom, it still focuses on fixing the penis instead of helping the man behind it and the woman in front of it. It is an approach that attempts to turn the clock back to a time when the penis worked just fine. It's a regressive fix rather than a step forward, one that is oblivious to lessons that might be learned or frontiers of trust that are waiting to be crossed.

Dear Dr. Goofy,

My bowling partner recently started having erection problems and is too embarrassed to seek help. Can you offer some advice?

Andy from Akron

Dear Andy,

If your bowling partner has stopped throwing strikes for more than a couple of weeks, it's a good idea for him to take his poky pecker to a physician for a checkup. It's smart to rule out underlying medical conditions of which his floppy dog could be a symptom. It is estimated that almost 50 percent of erection problems have physical causes, from diabetes to who-knows-what. And Andy, if he's a cigarette smoker, he might as well call a mortuary and have the thing interred. Cigarette smoking is just as bad for your penis as it is for your lungs, and besides choking your penis to death, smoking can contribute to cancer of the penis.

One of the things the physician will ask is whether your friend is able to get erections at all, like in the morning upon waking, or when he jerks off. He may even be sent home with a device he attaches to his penis when he sleeps at night. While this device won't help get him off (darn), it will measure whether or not he has erections in his sleep and for how long. Doctors figure that if a man can get a sustained erection in his sleep, then the origin of the problem resides in his psyche. However, researchers are now finding that certain types of depression can keep you from getting an erection even in your sleep, and the fact that you can get an erection doesn't mean you can keep an erection.

Another thing the physician should carefully check is if your friend is taking any medications that might be cold-cocking his rooster. Medications can range from alcohol and heroin to numerous prescriptions or even over-the-counter drugs. Even Tagamet can do it, honest.

The doctor might also give your friend's penis an injection of something that causes most men to get an erection. Don't worry, it's an itty-bitty wisp of a shot. No one is going to pull out a massive syringe with a hollow nail for a needle and suddenly say, "Drop your drawers." If the penis gets hard and is able to stay that way, then the plumbing is probably intact and the problem might be caused by some sort of emotional pain or struggle. It is also possible that there is a neurological problem which is somehow disabling the body's ability to begin the hard-on process. If your friend were a car, this might be similar to having a defective start-up motor or turning the key and getting no current. Whatever the cause, they'll try to see if Viagra works, and if it doesn't, then they'll set him up to give his penis an injection whenever he wants an erection.

If the shot does not make the penis hard, or it gets hard but doesn't stay that way for long, then it's likely there is a circulation problem. This can be anything from hardening of the arteries (strange term for when it happens in the penis) to leaky valves. More tests would need to be done to peg the exact cause. If surgery is recommended, he should get a second and third opinion.

If it turns out the problem is more emotional than physical, your friend might consider doing a little private detective work, or detective work on his privates. For instance, what was going on in his life around the time when his soldier stopped marching? Did his ability to get an erection decline gradually, like the fall of Rome, or did it shut down all at once, like the Bank of Boston? Was there a change in his job status? Did his insurance company cancel him without cause? Did his team not go to the Superbowl because of a lousy call in the closing seconds of the final playoff game? Was there a change in his relationship with his partner? Did his wife leave him for another man? Did she leave him for another woman? Was he pulled from an important project, or did he lose a promotion he had his heart set on? Did he receive an unkind inquiry from the IRS?

Also, it is important to inquire about the quality of his relationship with his spouse. If he is asked about this and instantly says, "Naw, it's fine," ask him to describe some of the things that are fine about it. See if he conveys a sense of love and fondness, or if he sounds like he's reading the instructions on a bottle of Kaopectate. If the relationship has fallen on—dare we say— hard times, then he and his wife need to focus on fixing that rather than on fixing his penis, which is merely the messenger.

As for curing this kind of penile narcolepsy, your friend and his partner might try to forget all they know about each other and start over again as if they'd just met. This can be difficult, especially if they have had some really lousy times together. They might try taking a month or two doing things like hugging, touching and talking, with no attempt at intercourse. They also might try sharing romantic dinners, movies and the types of things they enjoyed doing when they first met. How about racking their bowling balls and taking a trip around the country in the Winnebago? They might discover that there really is life after bowling. On the other hand, some couples do better when they spend less time with each other. This can be especially true when they are newly retired and suddenly find themselves in each other's face for 24 hours a day. Other couples do really well with the extra time together.

There is also the possibility that your friend had erection prob- lems before he and his wife met. Then he might find it helpful to get some psychological help on his own.

And if none of that seems to help, there's this Sufi saying...

Viagra

You've heard of Niagra,® right? It's a spray that starches your shirts when you iron them. Well, they've managed to put some- thing very similar into a pill, and instead of calling it Super Niagra, they called it Viagra. Instead of starching your shirts, it starches your schlong. Nuff said?

One of the finest quotes about Viagra is from *Boston Globe* columnist Ellen Goodman:

> I can't help wondering why we got a pill to help men with performance instead of communication. Moreover, how is it possible that we came up with a male impotence pill before we got a male birth control pill? The Vatican, you will note, has approved Viagra while still condemning condoms.

Insurance companies will pay for a man's Viagra, but not for a woman's birth control pills, even if the monthly cost of Viagra is more. A urologist in Colorado who actually has a sense of humor wonders why they don't combine Viagra with Prozac to make one little pill that cures everything. And even some women are starting to take Viagra, perhaps to help with their erections too.

If you and your partner haven't been having any sexual intimacy for five or ten years and suddenly find that the problem can be fixed with injections or Viagra, don't even think of trying the drugs without first scheduling a couple of sessions with a sex therapist. All sorts of issues need to be dealt with before a penis hops inside a vagina after all those years. Questions about intimacy, romance, attraction and excitement may have been buried under layers of anger and frustration. They will need to be addressed first. On the other hand, if you and your partner have been enjoying orgasms and physical intimacy, but just no intercourse, go for it and see what happens.

Resource: A very competent and readable book to consider is *The Sexual Male: Problems and Solutions,* by Richard Milsten and Julian Slowinski (New York: W. W. Norton & Company, 1999).

Other Chemicals That Make You Hard

There are a couple of compounds which cause a diehard erection when injected into the penis, assuming enough of the penile plumbing is intact to be able to hold an erection once the penis gets hard. A compound called Papervine was formerly used for this purpose, but that's been replaced by a type of prostaglandin that has fewer side effects. Also, there is a new kind of prostaglandin which the man simply places in his urethra (peehole) a few minutes before he needs an erection. No injection is needed, and the drug seems to work well for erection failures that are more psychological in origin. It is apparently like one of those little fertilizer sticks that you shove in the soil next to your droopy houseplants, only you shove it in your urethra instead. It is possible that other drugs will be available in the near future. Please consult a urologist for more information.

There are other orally prescribed drugs that help some men to get hard. One drug that is sometimes prescribed by urologists is called yohimbine. Yohimbine is a native tropical of Africa. It can often be found in health food stores. Since the cost of yohimbine isn't much more in prescription form, why not get it from a urologist? That way you will be monitored for side effects and you will be sure that you are getting the yohimbine in consistent doses, which is not true for the yohimbine sold in health food stores. The urologist can also rule out other possible causes of the erection problem. Other drugs for impotence are currently being tested, including some that are administered in cream form, but none had been released at the time of this guide's printing.

Mechanical Devices for Getting Hard

Some men find that the vacuum pump is a useful erection aid. It is a little bulky and cumbersome, but worth a try if you are in search of your lost erection. It might also be wise to try the vacuum pump first before subjecting your genitals to various types of surgery, including implants. What do you have to lose? Some urologists are happy to tell you about their surgical successes, but don't expect them to tell you about their failures or show you pictures of penises that have been surgically mangled. While surgery can be very helpful, it's still surgery and it still has risks. See the Resources section of our website, www.goofyfootpress.com for vacuum pump suppliers. Be sure they include special gaskets which keep your scrotum from getting sucked up into the tube.

Surgical Implants

There are different kinds of surgical implants, from semi-rigid shanks to implants with little pumps that you activate when you want an erection. Please research this subject carefully and consult with at least two urologists before making a decision.

Lousy Hang Time—Premature Ejaculation

The term "premature ejaculation" didn't exist in our society before the 1960s. That's when sex researchers realized that a woman might want more than a couple of thrusts during intercourse. Golly. Now they are no longer calling it premature ejaculation. The sexually correct term is rapid ejaculation.

This book has an entire chapter on the subject of rapid or premature ejaculation. It's titled "Dyslexia of the Penis— Improving Your Sexual Hang Time." It is extremely thorough.

Problems of Either Sex

Drug-Related Problems

You wouldn't believe how many over-the-counter or prescription medications can mess with everything from your ability to get wet to your feelings of desire. For instance, just taking a common antihistamine can keep a woman from lubricating. Extending this into a worst-case scenario, the woman starts having painful intercourse because she isn't lubricating due to the antihistamine. Because of the pain, the muscles in her vagina automatically tense up whenever her husband's penis gets hard. The problem continues long after she's stopped taking the allergy medicine. Her physician, not knowing about the original reason for the vaginal tension, tells her it's all in her head. Understandably, she experiences a decrease in desire, which causes her insecure husband to have an affair with his assistant, which she then finds out about and sues for divorce. All because she took a couple of Sudafed! Or maybe she's taking Tagamet, which can decrease sexual desire, and who wants a divorce because of a little heartburn? These stories aren't as exaggerated as you might think.

Whatever sexual problems or concerns you are having, the absolute first thing to do is to make a list of all the medications you are taking—from simple over-the-counter drugs to prescription medications to herbal teas and vitamin concoctions to heroin, cocaine, pot or alcohol. Then check these over with a pharmacist.

Medications may not be the cause of the sexual problem, but they're certainly the first and most obvious thing to rule out.

The Tour de France in Your Pants

Research is just beginning on the relationship between bike riding and malfunction or numbness of the genitals, male and female. It seems that some people who are serious bike riders may be damaging their penises and pussies. Especially unkind are incidents where the foot slips off the pedal and the crotch goes crunch on the bicycle frame. While most bicycle-related numbness appears to be temporary, a special surgery has been devised to help those men whose penises have suffered permanent injury. There are now special seats that help absorb road shock. This might be a wise choice for the serious rider.

'Gasm Spasm

One of the nice things about being naked together and having sex is getting to experience an occasional orgasm or two. Of course, most couples realize that there are times when either orgasms don't happen or you need to supply your own afterward. This is so normal that it would be silly to call it a sex problem. On the other hand, there are some men and women who don't orgasm at all, or it only happens when they are alone and not in the presence of a lover. That's what the next couple of sections are about.

Not Being Able to Come with a Partner

Some guys, called retarded ejaculators (honest), are able to get hard and have intercourse for hours, but can't reach orgasm during intercourse to save their lives. These men might be able to come while masturbating, but not while having intercourse. Men with this sort of problem often try to thrust faster and harder, thinking this will help them come. Unfortunately, this is one of the worst things to do, because after you've been thrusting for a while, going harder and faster tends to desensitize the penis.

The causes for delayed ejaculation can be many, including concerns about losing control or becoming too vulnerable, or even an unconscious fear of getting a partner pregnant or somehow causing her damage. Or the problem may be strictly physical and have no psychological underpinnings. For instance, the onset of multiple sclerosis can make a guy take forever when he used to be able to come on a dime. So the first thing you should do is to consult with a physician to rule out any physical causes.

Assuming the cause is psychological, one of the cures for retarded ejaculation is to start having sex in unusual places, like the back seat of your car or anyplace else that is a bit strange, unfamiliar and possibly exciting. The goal is to try to draw the guy out of his comfortable environment where he's a master at blocking sensation. Making him a little nervous seems to allow more excitement and sensation to break through.

Another way to help change the situation is to focus on other parts of his body rather than on his penis. After all, he's clearly king at keeping that puppy under control, so don't even try playing to his strengths. For instance, you might spend some time tickling his inner thighs and groin with a feather, silky fabric, fingers or lips. Or if you're into a bit of kink, slip on a dildo and do him up the rear, or turn into Doreen, Dominatrix from the Deep, and make him beg for sexual favors! Anything to throw him off balance, sexually speaking. He should also start to masturbate with a different grip and a lighter touch. Just before he's about to get himself off, he should get into a position that he usually doesn't come in and finish himself off from there. Also, if he is able to have an orgasm when masturbating, he might try alternating intercourse with masturbation, e.g., thrust a little, jerk a little, thrust a little, jerk a little.

While you are at it, try consulting a few books whose focus is on treating sexual problems. Some couples have found Barbara Keesling's *Sexual Pleasure* from Hunter House to be helpful. And don't hesitate to visit a sex therapist.

When a Woman Can Come on Her Own But Not with a Man

Many women don't come during intercourse because there isn't enough stimulation or not the kind they need for an orgasm. Hopefully the man is able to fill the gap with manual stimulation, oral sex or a big old vibrator. However, sometimes a woman is able to give herself orgasms when she is alone, but can't generate one in the presence of a man even if he's able to stimulate her to near perfection. The reasons for this might be similar to those mentioned for men who can't come with women. Also, some women are so frightened by men or just plain angry at them that they would sooner give birth to triplets than come in a man's presence. Other women aren't hostile but feel there is something about their sexuality that needs to be hidden, or they might feel frustrated or absent in the presence of a man. Therapy can often be helpful if that's what you want to do. There are several good books and a few videotapes on the subject. See "Women's Orgasm Problems," which follows in two more pages.

Problems with Excitement

Some people can't tolerate much excitement. Somewhere along the line they got the feeling that sexual excitement might be dangerous or disorganizing. As a result, they experience all sorts of conflicts when they become sexually excited. They perpetually numb themselves between the navel and the knees, or they destroy desire altogether, becoming unaware of sexual excitement in the way that an anorexic is unaware of her body's need for food. That way they don't have to face the anticipated dread or catastrophe that sexual excitement holds in their imagination.

People who want to work through excitement problems need to allow pleasurable feelings to evolve slowly and without goals such as having an orgasm. Pressure to feel sexual takes them out of the moment and makes them feel numb. With time and effort, sexual excitement can be tolerated in the here and now, assuming that's what the person wants. Other people might have trouble managing sexual excitement when they are alone—they can't masturbate or even feel very sexual on their own, but do just fine when they are with a partner. Perhaps they need to experience a partner's excitement about them before they can feel their own excitement.

A Question of Desire

Just because a person doesn't like sex is no reason to view them as being abnormal. Perhaps it's a choice that works well for them. On the other hand, if they are in a relationship with a partner who does like sex, it is worth exploring various forms of compromise. For instance, some couples have an understanding that the partner who wants sex can get his or her needs met elsewhere, maybe with an intern at the office or something. Or maybe it's worthwhile trying to get some therapy.

Sometimes the lack of desire results from problems in the relationship, even if things appear to be wonderful on the surface. Other times a person doesn't want to have sex regardless of who he or she is involved with. Whatever the case, lack of desire is one of the hot new topics among sex therapists. That's because desire is the ante for having sex.

David Schnarch's book *Constructing the Sexual Crucible* deals nicely with this and other sexual issues. It's worth struggling through Schnarch's own struggle with the English language to see what he has to say. Fortunately, the lucid parts of the book are the case material, which is very enlightening to read.

Orgasm Fears & Tears

Although orgasms are usually welcome events, this is not always the case. For instance, young girls or boys who are having their first adult-like orgasms might feel that they have done something wrong or broken something inside.

Adults occasionally have mixed feelings about their own orgasms, especially when feelings of sadness or loneliness are triggered by the orgasm. The sadness can sometimes be about a former real-life partner, or maybe the orgasm taps into a deep emotional pain that suddenly gets released. Some people cry after a good come because it touches a sadness that's deep inside.

There are also people who treat their own orgasms with a kind of cold detachment, especially when they feel a need to masturbate. Perhaps the need for orgasm brings up feelings of weakness or self-loathing. Whatever the case, they are not particularly gentle or tender when handling their own genitals. And finally, there are people who dislike orgasms because they experience them as a form of losing control.

It's a fine testament to the power of orgasm that more people in our society don't have problems with them, given how we tend to be a bit sexually repressed.

Painful Intercourse

This can happen to both men and women, but is more often experienced by women. The causes can be physical or emotional. Also, the problem may originally have been physical, but has since evolved into an emotional struggle.

If you are having pain during intercourse, be sure to check with a physician or perhaps several physicians. Also, try to determine whether the pain is experienced at the opening of the vagina or is caused by deep thrusting. Deep-thrusting pain can sometimes be caused by constipation or pelvic inflammatory disease. Shallow thrusting pain has a larger range of possible causes, from adhesions under the clitoral hood and episiotomy scars to yeast infections, herpes sores, or vaginal changes associated with menopause.

Painful intercourse might also occur when there is a poor match in sexual anatomy between male and female, but it is more likely that the couple is clumsy or sexually unsophisticated. At this point, most sex books would suggest that the male might be a clumsy lover, but a passive female who accepts a male's clumsiness is just as sexually inept—oops! sexually challenged—as he. Or maybe both partners are trying the best they can, but need a little extra help. Whatever the case, it is the couple, rather than just the man, who needs the help.

Other questions to explore about painful intercourse include whether it happens all the time, how long it has been happening, if it happens with all partners or just one, and if added lubrication helps. Then it might be wise to consult with someone whose expertise is human sexuality. At the very least, read up on the subject in a couple of books on sex problems and see what they have to say. Common terms for this are vulvodynia or vaginal pain disorder.

This kind of pain is very real and it can have horrible effects on a relationship. The woman (and couple) who is experiencing it needs the same kind of support and often treatment as anyone who is experiencing a chronic pain disorder.

In the meantime, the couple needs to get past their frustration and start enjoying their sexuality in other ways besides just intercourse. There are so many wonderful ways to please each other besides just sticking a penis inside a vagina!

Problems Typically Ascribed to Women

Ladies: Beware of What You Hear about Female Sexual Dysfunction

If you were a big company preparing to sell a product to a whole new segment of the population, it wouldn't hurt to generate statistics that demonstrate an overwhelming need for that product, such as "43 percent of American women complain of sexual dysfunction..." Perhaps it's pure coincidence, but at a recent conference on female sexual dysfunction which was partially funded by the company that makes Viagra, a number of the presenters who were studying the effects of Viagra on women began their presentation with this exact statistic.

Of course, there's just one problem. Where do statistics like these come from? For instance, if we at Goofy Foot Press wanted to come up with statistics that said, "95 percent of the American public needs to read the *Guide to Getting It On!*" it would be easy to do as long as we structured the questions cleverly enough. We could also pay a research team to reinterpret findings of other studies to give them the spin we want.

So when you hear that 43 percent of American women complain of sexual dysfunction, be a heads-up consumer and start asking, "What do they mean by sexual dysfunction?" Then ask yourself, "Are they trying to sell me something that I don't need?" And finally, "If I do have 'sexual dysfunction,' is it possible that it has more to do with the shortcomings of my relationship than a shortage of blood flow into my crotch?"

Women's Orgasm Problems

We caution you about the notion that a woman who can't have an orgasm during intercourse has a sexual problem. Plenty of women don't have orgasms with thrusting during intercourse. This doesn't mean that they have sexual problems. All it means is that both partners need to explore what gets the woman off and include it as part of their lovemaking, unless it happens to be the man's best friend. Then again, some couples enjoy that, too.

Also, some therapists in this day and age automatically assume that sexual problems are the result of prior sexual abuse, especially if the patient is a woman. Yet plenty of men and women who never had a shred of physical abuse still have sexual problems. For instance, being raised in some religious households can cause sexual problems that appear very similar to those of sexual abuse, including the person's feeling vacant, depersonalized or numb when having sex. Such a person might find it extremely difficult to have an orgasm.

For women who haven't had an orgasm yet, the classic reference book remains *For Yourself: The Fulfillment of Female Sexuality* by Lonnie Barbach.

Vaginismus—Gridlock in Your Groin

Vaginismus is when the muscles surrounding the vagina close so tightly that they won't allow anything to go inside. The reaction is sometimes so severe that a woman can't even insert a tampon.

Vaginismus might result from something as simple as a lousy experience at the gynecologist's, to the body holding onto scary memories from a bad experience that was simply too overwhelming to be fully processed by the mind. Also, vaginismus may have a physical origin, such as those listed in a prior part of this chapter under "Painful Intercourse."

If you have this kind of problem, try reading up on the subject. There are simple behavioral techniques that can be used to help the vagina to eventually relax. Depending on your sexual history, you might also do well to seek out a psychotherapy consultation.

If you had a traumatic past, vaginismus might be a powerful statement that your body is holding onto something that needs to be worked through. Or it might just have been a reaction to one isolated experience that became part of your body's default mode.

Not a Sexual Problem Per Se, But Still Something to Think About

Cancer, especially cancer affecting the genitals, can be viewed as punishment for past sexual enjoyment, masturbation, incest, abortion or anything we might have felt guilty about but have long since forgotten. In some ways, it is easier for us to believe that there was a cause of the cancer—i.e., masturbation—than to realize that bad things can happen in a totally random way and that we had no control over them, unless perhaps we were smoking or drinking like a fish.

In a way, it makes us feel too helpless to admit that there was nothing we did to cause the cancer, so we create a personal myth that allows us to place blame on past forms of sexual enjoyment, such as "Mother was right! I shouldn't have been playing with myself" or "I was right to feel so wrong about..."

In our culture, sexual pleasure is still a dangerous commodity with dangerous overtones. It's the first thing we toss overboard during life's various storms.

Chapter Notes: Special thanks to Joe Marzucco at Kaiser Urology in Portland and to Julian Slowinski, Linda Banner and Barbara Keesling.

Police searching for a dildo in Georgia.
Or is it Texas or Alabama or...

Sex Laws in the US
Chapter 48

ach state has its own unique set of sex laws. Fortunately, they are seldom enforced—mainly when people are having sex in public places or when adults are having sex with minors. Still, it's a good idea to be aware that in many states, the government has jurisdiction over what you do when your pants are down, even when you are in the privacy of your own home.

Also, you might get a chuckle to hear what happened when an inmate in a Texas prison recently ordered a copy of the *Guide*. We promptly sent it, only to have the book returned by the Texas state authorities who cited the illustration at the bottom of page 633—claiming that the book was unsuitable for inmates because it was promoting bestiality. Mind you, the *Guide* is used as required reading at more than thirty universities in the States, but is not allowed in Texas prisons where the authorities fear it may cause a hostage situation: "We'll turn over the warden and six guards if you'll send in a flock of sheep..."

Selling a Vibrator or Dildo Is Illegal in Alabama, Texas, Georgia...

It's against the law in Alabama to sell vibrators and other sexual devices. Is this an archaic law from 1892 that's still on the books because nobody ever bothered to remove it? Nope. Alabama banned the selling of these devices less than three years before this book was printed. In Alabama, you can get up to a year of hard labor and a fine of $10,000 for selling a dildo.

In Georgia, it's against the law to sell or use sexual devices. In Houston, at Tres Chic, a lingerie store that sells the *Guide*, two female workers were arrested last October because the store also sells vibrators and dildos. Again, this is not the 1800s, but it's sure starting to seem like it!

Against the law in
Florida...

Because this
couple isn't
married.

Against the law in
Maryland and
Washington, D.C.

Against the law in
Arkansas but not
in New York

Against the law in
California

But what about
Wyoming?

Sodomy

Most people think that sodomy laws have to do with anal intercourse among homosexuals or with farmers who have sex with Bossy. Actually, if you are a sexually active man or woman who has never had anal sex, never done a homosexual act and never transgressed upon the dignity of a sheep, cow or chicken, the chances are still excellent that you have broken a number of state sodomy laws. That's because each state has its own definition of what sodomy is.

In Maryland if you have oral sex anywhere in the state, including your own bedroom, you have broken the sodomy law. The same is true for Pennsylvania, unless you are married. In Louisiana, if you and your spouse get caught having oral sex (unnatural carnal copulation), you have committed a felony and could do time in state prison. In Virginia, if a wife doesn't want to give her husband a blow job, all she needs to do is wave her finger in her husband's face and say, "Suckin' on that thang is a crime!" She'd be right.

In Washington, D.C., it is a felony for anyone to have oral sex. So let's say you live at 1600 Pennsylvania Avenue and you engage in oral sex, would you be guilty of a crime?

Fornication

Fornication is generally defined as unlawful sexual intercourse when at least one partner is unmarried. It can also refer to living together without being married. In Florida, it is illegal for an unmarried man and woman to "lewdly and lasciviously associate and cohabit together." Interestingly, many of the people who violate this law in Florida are senior citizens who live together but don't officially marry because it would drastically reduce their Social Security payments. In Minnesota and Georgia, you don't even have to live together to be fornicators.

Oklahoma! Oklahoma!

A man meets a virgin female, they fall in love, he asks her to marry him, she says yes and they make passionate love to celebrate. A few months later, he breaks up with her. This sequence of events is a crime in Oklahoma.

In California, there is a law governing the matter of who gets to keep the ring if you break off an engagement. If he paid for it and she broke it off, he gets the ring back. If he breaks it off, she gets to keep the ring.

Adultery

If you are married and have an extramarital affair, you have committed adultery.

In Washington, D.C., if a married woman sleeps with an unmarried man, they are both presumed guilty. However, if a married man sleeps with an unmarried woman, only the man is guilty. In Idaho, if a married woman has sex with a single man, she has just committed a felony. In Maryland, adultery is illegal, but it only carries a ten-dollar fine. It is not illegal in Vermont, but it is grounds for divorce.

"Jake, You Beast, Take Me!"

In most states, it is illegal to engage in sexual conduct with an animal. This includes poultry, fish and game. The name of the crime is "bestiality" or "buggery."

Wyoming has no statute that specifically outlaws bestiality. Perhaps it has something to do with those long, cold winters, or maybe they handle it on a local level.

Prostitution

Prostitution is defined as "performing, offering or agreeing to perform any act of sexual intercourse, fellatio, cunnilingus, masturbation or anal intercourse in exchange for anything of value" (Colorado), for compensation (Montana), for pecuniary benefit (Maine), for money or anything of value (Illinois).

Just so you'll know, in most states you can pay a person to act out sex scenes, such as going to a dominatrix to be tied up, spanked, diapered, humiliated or anything else that suits your darker side, and it's not illegal as long as you don't do any of the traditional sex acts or the person doesn't bring you to orgasm.

It's fine if you bring yourself to orgasm. However, in some states, this isn't legal, either.

Polygamy

Polygamy is being married to multiple partners at the same time. This is illegal in all states. However, if you come from a country where plural marriages are accepted and you want to travel with your wives to visit in the U.S., you won't be charged with polygamy. May we suggest giving each of your wives her very own copy of the *Guide to Getting It On*?

Age of Consent

In most states, you need to be eighteen years of age to marry without parental consent. As for having sex, which may or may not include intercourse, it varies from state to state. In some states, the punishment increases greatly if one partner is three or more years older than the other, while in other states, it is illegal for minors to engage in intercourse at all. If you are under eighteen, or are having sex with someone under eighteen, know your state's laws about the age of consent and realize that you can be put in jail for violating them.

Dr. Dog & The Stolen Toast
Chapter 49

D r. Dog is a collie, and if he has just had a bath and you are standing a half-mile away, you might think he looks like Lassie. Of course, Lassie never spent hours licking his private parts, attacked fleas with a ferociousness that left his own skin bleeding or took a dump on the sidewalk in front of the sheriff's station. Another thing Lassie never did is steal toast.

If you offer Dr. Dog a piece of toast fresh from the toaster, he couldn't care less. But the minute you are off to answer the phone or are hypnotized by the newspaper's account of how badly your team got beat last night, Dr. Dog grabs the toast from your plate. Legal toast has no appeal to his canine senses, but forbidden toast might as well be steak.

When it comes to sex, we humans are a bit like Dr. Dog. Sex that has an air of danger or forbidden urgency sometimes gets us excited. In fact, sex that's just a bit dirty or nasty can be downright wonderful for no other reason than the element of erotic suspense.

For sex to be as good as stolen toast, some experts claim that it needs to reveal things about you that were previously hidden — little mysteries of the heart and soul. This is easy the first couple of times, since you know so little about each other. But over the long term it takes love and effort to keep sex sexy. It requires that you keep exploring hidden dimensions within yourself and within your partner.

Carrot Humps Cornelius

Carrot is a 13-year-old Irish setter who is mostly deaf and arthritic, and until recently sat around all day like a canine couch potato. Then Carrot's owner got a new roommate who started taking Carrot to the doggie park where dogs of all kinds get to run free and play.

On his first day at the doggie park, Carrot hobbled for a couple of yards and that was it. But after visiting the doggie park every day for a week, Carrot was no longer as invested in the sedentary lifestyle. While not exactly Rin Tin Tin, Carrot began staying on his feet for the better part of an hour. He could even be found following other dogs around, sniffing their rear ends just like the younger pups do. And when Carrot did sit down, it was often in a big patch of mud where some of the bird dogs and Nordic breeds with blue tongues and thick coats liked to lie.

After a few more weeks at the doggie park, Carrot could sometimes be found trying to hump Cornelius, a sweet but lame and stone-deaf Great Dane or "demi-Dane," since some of his Great Dane chromosomes appear to be counterfeit.

For better or worse, Carrot's plight is not dissimilar to what happens to us humans. As many of us get older we sit around without much physical or mental stimulation. (Sorry, but watching TV does not count as mental stimulation.) Then we slowly rot away, just as Carrot had been, and we assume that this is a normal part of aging.

Although a steady diet of physical and mental stimulation won't be enough to keep the Reaper forever at bay, it can help a person stay vital and productive. Perhaps this is why middle-aged people who work out three times a week often have sex as frequently as couples who are twenty years younger, and physically fit people in their sixties have sex as often as couples in their forties. As for the notion that people automatically have less sex as they get older, a pair of 70-year-olds who recently contacted the Goofy Foot Press have been swinging sexually with other couples for thirty years. This couple has more sex at their weekend mate-swapping parties than most young newlyweds have all week long.

Between Carrot and the Gray Panther swingers, one needn't fear old age if it's approached with the proper attitude.

Like Fine Wine

In our questionnaires, we asked people to describe their sexual pleasure now versus when they were younger. Whether they were in their thirties, forties or fifties, nearly each and every person said that sex is better now than it was in their early twenties. This was just as true for males as for females.

Dear Paul,
I am 57 and find my wife to be as attractive as I did when we were in our twenties. I never had a mid-life crisis, either. Is there something wrong with me?
Trevor from Muskegon

Dear Trevor,

Researchers have just done the largest survey ever of the sexual habits of people who are really old (ages forty-five to seventy-five or more).

Believe it or not, this survey shows that we tend to find our partners more attractive rather than less attractive as we get older. When I first read this, I thought to myself, "That's because as we get older, our hearing and eyesight start to go..."

Of course, we're not supposed to think that anyone will find us more attractive as we get older. Instead, we're supposed to be really paranoid about the aging process. That way we'll buy all sorts of overpriced products to keep us looking young. If you doubt this, I'm willing to bet that by age 30, half of the women who read this column are already worrying about wrinkles and buying really expensive products that promise to keep them looking "younger. And I honestly get email from male readers in their late twenties who are worried about old age because they couldn't get it up once or twice.

Yet this survey shows is that age doesn't really matter; 59 percent of men between ages forty-five to seventy-four say the phrase "physically attractive" is how they strongly feel about their partner. For women between the ages of forty-five to fifty-nine, 52 percent say the term "physically attractive" strongly applies to their partner. (Okay, so the women's eyesight and hearing don't go as fast as the men's, but after age seventy-five, the percentage goes up to 57 percent.)

So if any of you are worried about becoming less attractive as you get older, stop. You might not turn the heads of twenty-year-olds when you are fifty, but plenty of fifty-year-olds will find you attractive. The thing that you should worry about is romance. By the time we turn forty-five, less than a third of us find our partners to be romantic or exciting. For example, only 29 percent of women between the ages of forty-five and fifty-nine judge their partners to be romantic.

Perhaps as we get older we get into a rut and become predictable. We plop down in the same chair and do the exact same thing we were doing last year at this time, and the year before, and the year before. Instead, what if we said, "Honey, let's not watch TV tonight. Let's take a walk together," assuming the neighborhood is still safe to walk in.

Perhaps the biggest thing you can do to keep a partner interested is to stop buying expensive wrinkle cream, and instead do the kind of sweet and considerate things you used to do when you were young and trying to get laid!

Dear Paul,

I am in my seventies. My best friend's boyfriend is cheating on her with another woman who works with us as a volunteer at the Senior Center. I am worried that if I tell her, she will just think I am jealous and will be angry with me. At the same time, if I don't tell her and she finds out from someone else, she'll be even more angry at me for not saying something. Do you have any advice?

Grace from Laguna Hills

Dear Grace,

I've always had this hope, or should I say delusion, that with age comes wisdom. Not so with love and sex.

When we get into our seventies and eighties, the love and sex equation gets even stranger than when we were younger, because it's an age when most men start dropping like flies. By seventy-five, males who still have a pulse and aren't on life support are quite a commodity. So if we guys can just find a way to live past seventy-five, we'll have more nookie than we'll know what to do with!

The fact that your friend's lover has managed to cheat the actuary tables (in addition to her) makes him quite the catch. It also means you can't console your friend with the time-honored phrase "Don't worry, there are plenty of other guys out there..."

As for telling the truth, I've had friends whose lovers were raving lunatics, and I never hesitated to say things like "Does she know how to talk about anyone other than herself?" But I would never tell a friend that his girlfriend or wife was cheating on him unless he specifically asked. I don't share a bed with them, and experience tells me that when it comes to love and sex, most of us would rather murder the messenger than face a reality that we so desperately need to ignore. (Try telling someone that they need to leave their alcoholic spouse! Good luck.)

If my friend wanted to know why I hadn't told him, I would say that he never asked, that it's none of my business, and that I would value his friendship just as much if his girlfriend had been sleeping with six other guys instead of only three.

You seem to be in a no-win situation. You'll either need to tell your friend and risk the consequences or find a way to curb your anger at her for being such a fool in love. And if you do tell her, be prepared for the possibility that she may turn on you instead of him. Even people who are being physically abused by a spouse often turn on the policeman or good Samaritan who tries to help.

Sex on the Interstate (Motorway)
Chapter 50

For some people, there's nothing like cruising down a deserted interstate with one hand on the wheel and the other on their lover's sweet spot. It doesn't matter if you are rich or poor, mongrel or blueblood, this is one time when our motor-driven culture nips you in the rear and makes you feel good all over.

For instance, it might be particularly nice when your brain's in a narcoleptic funk from the rolling monotone of a Nebraska back road and your sweetheart slyly grabs your free hand and slips it into the warm, wet space between her legs. Or maybe you're taking that long drive from Texas to Washington D.C. and the wind's not the only thing that's doing the blowing.

If you and your partner have a long-term relationship, the memory just keeps getting better. About ten years after the fact, one of you will occasionally say, "Honey, remember that time going 'cross Kansas..." and you'll both stop whatever you are doing, smile and shut out the rest of the world for a precious moment or two. But first, please consider the following...

Winnebegos on the Continental Divide

While it's important to do things that inspire fond memories, it's also nice to stay alive so you can enjoy them. Keeping your bearings on the road while sharing certain types of physical pleasure is a talent that few people should ever attempt. For instance, it's not something to try if you aren't an excellent driver to begin with. And no matter how much driving experience you have, it's really stupid to be messing around when road conditions require your extra attention, like on a busy freeway or when you're taking a Winnebego over the Continental Divide. On the other hand, just about anything that wakes you up when you're on a rural road might be safer than trying to drive when you feel sleepy, and driving with your head up the tailpipe has to be safer than driving while dialing a cellular phone.

Note: Thousands of people die each year from falling asleep at the wheel. We'd love to keep you as readers of future editions, so please, if you find yourself feeling sleepy, get some coffee or pull far off the road and take a nap.

Perhaps the best use of a car for sex, besides for driving to your sweetheart's house to get some, is when parking at a romantic spot and seeing how quickly you can steam the windows up. People who live in the inner city often don't have cars, so they sometimes find a favorite rooftop or "tar beach" with a romantic view where they can make love. Just be sure it's not a spot where junkies like to shoot up; you don't want to roll over on someone's hidden apparatus.

Sex on the Rail of the Hoover Dam

Some people like to have sex in public places where other people will see. While this might be a fine form of release for all parties involved, it is not what this section is about. What's being described here is that rare moment in life when you and your partner get to make love in a natural setting which is so magnificent that nature's sweet vibration nearly explodes inside of you. What transpires can be so expansive that it's difficult to think of it as just sex—or maybe it's what sex was meant to be before we started living in abominations of nature such as high rises and condominiums.

There are plenty of natural settings where you don't have to be too cautious about getting it on, like in a meadow filled with wildflowers, on a deserted beach, or under a god-sized rainbow in the Montana Big Sky. But there are other equally compelling locations, like dams, bridges, trains, planes and various national monuments, where a well-honed sense of cunning and mischief is absolutely essential. The following are but a few suggestions that you might find helpful:

Bug repellent. Don't forget the bug repellent if you are baring your all next to some humid bog or anyplace where the average mosquito would take one look at your naked butt cheeks and think it had died and gone to heaven.

🐾 For sex in public places, it can be more than helpful if the woman wears one of those full 1950s-type dresses or sundresses. It's the equivalent of wearing her own private dressing room— she won't need to take a single thing off except for her underwear, unless she's not wearing any.

🐾 If you are doing it at the beach or on a sandy river bed, be sure to take two large blankets. There's something about being on top of two blankets instead of one that helps keep sand from getting inside your crotch. Also, extra lube might help take the abrasive edge off any sand that makes its way inside.

🐾 Sex in water provides its own set of challenges, given how water washes away natural lubrication. Try coating your genitals with a silicone-based lube ahead of time.

Caution: One reader comments, "A close friend of mine went to jail for having sex in public; it was her first arrest and very traumatic." So please be aware that while it's perfectly legal for a couple to have a really loud and nasty fight in public, having sex in public (or maybe even in your backyard) is likely to break all sorts of local, state and federal statutes and might get you arrested. Of course, some people say that the risk is half the fun.

A Goofy Goodbye
Chapter 51

This is the final chapter of the *Guide to Getting It On!* It talks about things like hippies, cash flow, meaning and integrity, and then it says goodbye.

What Puff the Magic Dragon's Tears Were Really All About

Back in the 1960s, a small group of hippies suddenly appeared in this country. These hippies didn't think like the rest of us and probably arrived from another planet. The nation became infatuated with them.

After the arrival of the real hippies, there suddenly appeared millions of hippie wannabes. These were often college students who didn't have to work because they were getting money from home. They spoke a great deal about love and peace, but you had the feeling they didn't know much about either. They were also going to save the world from anything that was even remotely like their own mom and dad.

By the time the mid-1970s rolled around, the hippie wannabes started getting degrees in fields like law, business and medicine. Guys started cutting their hair and women stuffed their breasts back into bras, all in preparation for an important American ritual called "the job interview." Words like "marketing" and "standing to sue" took the place of "bitchin'" and "groovy." Designer labels became more important than flowers and beads. Things changed.

Few people had time anymore to hold hands, take walks or talk about a problem before it became a major crisis. Instead, there was the constant specter of work, often sixty hours a week, with a person's whole life mapped out according to which rung of the law firm or corporate ladder he or she planned to hang from.

It may seem strange that a book on sex would mention things like jobs and money, but in the course of our lifetimes most of us will fret more over money than love. The people at MasterCard will probably know more about us than our sex partners do. Yet no matter how much money or social status you acquire, you can never leave who you are or what you've become on the floor at the edge of the bed. Sex may be a wonderful thing, but it can't make up for an existence that has little integrity, value or meaning.

A Better Place

There are still a few of us from way back when who didn't abandon our hopes and dreams for a better society. We weren't radical or reactionary, we simply hoped to leave the world a better place than how we found it. This book is an attempt in that direction.

This guide may not have the head rush of good drugs, and it doesn't pretend to have many answers. But it is a more advanced view of sex than most of us had when we first started getting it on. Thank you for being patient with its efforts to be more than just another how-to manual on sex.

This book has almost 700 pages, and it still can't define sex. Hopefully you will be able to define it on your own, or at least have a beautiful time trying.

Chapter Notes: You wouldn't believe the hissyfit that people around here are having over the spelling of the word "*bitchin'*." The copy editor says it's "*bitchen*," and the rest of us say it's "*bitchin'*." The Random House Unabridged second edition says it's okay to use either, but lists "*bitchen*" first and "*bitchin'*" second. So here's to a *bitchin'* goodbye and have a *bitchen* good life!

Thanks! Thanks! Thanks!

Thanks also to Jon Westover, Toni Johnson, Morgan & Burce Yarrosh, Suzanne LaPlacette, Mike Fischler, Wanda Moore, Veronica Monet, Monte Farrin, Rebecca Wood, Catherine, Peter & Claire Gilson, Dixie Marquis, Mike Conway at Atlas Design, Karen Saliba, Carol Tavris, Michael Kogutek, Katherine Almy, Richard Curtis, BJ Robbins, Ken Sherman, Bob & Kim Otto, Linda Szymialis, Kristi Walsh, Duncan & Lilly Rouleau, Tom Reynolds, Bill Applebaum, Nancy Reaven, Bruce Voeller, Andre Deuschanes, Meridith Tanzer, Roan Singh Sidhu, Evan Rapostathis, Kenny Wagner, Ross Rubin, Barry Richmond, Carolyn Andre, Paula Samuels, Daphnicious Delicious Rosewoman-Kingma, Cathryn Michon, Diane Driscoll, Billy Rumpanos, Ben Fiorino, Ray Calabrese, Paula & David Wayne, John Van Dixhorn & Members of the Newport Psychoanalytic Institute, Janet Snow, Don DeFrancisco, Diana Heiselu, Judy Seifer, Randi Lockwood, Anke Vogel, Brent Ryder, Breta Hedges, Emily LeBeff, Ken Stubbs, Loren & Steve Kapelo, Laurel Shaffer, Brent Myers, Ron Goosen, Pat Lincoln, Alison Rosenzweig, Michael, Bill, Marty, Joan, Don, Julie, Tricia, Ray, John, Mike, Gail, Fred, Lisa, Betty, Eleanor & Cheech (R.I.P.), Marty Gilliland, Val Littou, Krista Foley, Lee Horn, Gunter, Becky, Steve

& all at Gilliland Printing (R.I.P.), Mat Honig at Wells Fargo Bank, Mike Mansel & Eric Ruiter at Argo, Sheryl Palese, Chip Rowe, Rodney Fingelson & Steve Frankiel, Kathy Herdman, Janet at Greenery Press, Jack McHugh, Joe Marzucco, Michael Meller, Todd Seigel & Jessica, Alex Foti, Adam Moore, Pat Patterson, Dana Smart, Laura Corn, Elizabeth Olsen, K.C. "errata, not erotica" Rourke, Pam Winter, Bill Brent, Dan Poynter, Judy Linnan, Theresa Benedick, Brandon Klock, Joe Sparling, Carol Queen, Robert, Westwood Kinko's, Lily, Bill & Louie at Sir Speedy, Monte at Input/Output, the staff at Book Soup, How at Kinko's Westwood, Nathan & Bob at Kinko's Ventura, the librarians at UCLA (Biomed, URL & the former Ed/Psych) & LA County Library, staff at A Different Light bookstore (West Hollywood), Brentano's (Century City & Beverly Hills), & Borders (particularly Fawn in Honolulu), Marty & Craig at First Interstate Bank (R.I.P.), everyone at Holiday Printing, Joe Marsh at the Earthling (R.IP), the managers and staff at the wonderful Waterstone's Book Store chain including Matt Comito, Christine, Maura, Jill, Sandy, Dave, Peter, Jay, Doug, Terry, Travis, Ann, Betty, Jane, & Eric Horndog Deville (a very sad and tragically premature R.I.P.), Jan Nathan at PMA, Mike Moskowitz, Juliann Popp & Jason Aronson at Jason Aronson, Bill & Beryl Johnson, Lew & the staff at Font Shop in San Francisco, Karen Seemueller & friends at Blue Sky in Portland, Christianna Billman, Lisa Blai and Mr. Verne Graham—thank you, thank you.

Peter Handel, Carol Fass & Eda Kalkay, Leslie Rossman, Patricia Godmother Holt, Kim from LA, Doug Abrams, Susan Naythons, Renee Sedliar, Steve Hanselman and at HarperSanFrancisco, Mr. Peter G-4 Stoller, Steve DuPont, the staff and owners of Montgomery Management, super romantic Adrienne Benedicks, Victoria Snider, Edie Moore at the Society for Adolescent Medicine, Michael Rakusin, Dale and Ewa from Tower Books Down Under, Jarred Gunn at Tower Books up here, Carol Floyd, Ms. Heidi Cotler, Chris & Dennis at Portland's Printer Place, Marcia papier mache Binnendyk, Babs Adamsky and Kevin Samsel at Powell Books, Pam White & Mark Collins and the wonderful staff of the Colorado Daily, Ben & Joe & Grace at C&L Graphics,

Shannon & Gaylen at Lightbourne, Kris Lorret Rourke, Dodie Ownes of *School Library Journal*, Ben Saltzberg, Whitney Thomas from Barnes & Noble, Stacie Herndon, Phil Bruno, Laura Corn, Harry Gilmartin from Entrenue, Rob Fogel, Marge Clifton from Cal Western Freight, Genanne Simply Wonderful Walsh, Rachael Cart, Joanie Blank & Constance Claire at Good Vibrations, Dr. Andrea Best—best emails since the wall came down, Gretta from Blowfish, Bettina Nibbe, Zev Lewis, Mr. John Davis from Koen Book, Leonore Tiefer, Marian Dunn, Michael Metz, Julian Slowinski, Udi Tagari

Mr. Lance "Vlad?" Tilford, Meagan, Cyndy, Sabrina, Heather, Charlie, Paul & all the fine people at Publishers Group West who make sure this book makes it into book stores. Without their efforts, you'd probably be having to read this book on one of those useless little e-book devices and we all know what happens when a big wad of whatever hits their little motherboards, to Dave Fleming, Mike Viso, Jay, Jill, Carlene and all of the McNaughton folks who do such a great job of putting the words on the paper and gluing up the sides, Dana & Linda at Loves, Mardi Link at Foreword, John McHugh, Stan Mitchell & Lynn, Dr. Adam Moore, Dr. John Money, Dr. Rob Hardy, Dr. Beverly Whipple, Kristen Kemp, Carol Briezke, Esther Crain, Julia Gaynor, Carol Edington, a very helpful Paul Harrington, David Blatner, the new and improved Gary Todoroff who went above and beyond the call, Janice Hamilton who got the whole academic ball rolling, Barbara Keesling, Debra Hanson, Steven Wales, Rob Hill, Nevada's own John & Miss Kelly, Dr. Avedis Panajian, Dr. Larry Hedges, Dr. Bill Young, Shane, Nancy "Professor B" Carmel Eyes & the extraordinary copyeditor Carol Bee.

A very special thanks to Drs. William Erwin & Donald Marcus.

EXTRA! EXTRA!

Our printer says we have extra pages to fill, so here are some of your responses to our sex survey at *www.goofyfootpress.com*. More of your answers are posted there.

Ladies first!

Unusual ways of masturbating?

I'm more than satisfied just getting wet and stroking my clit. And that whole thing about women not being visual, that is BS. I need my porn, though written porn gets me hot just as much. *female 20*

My first orgasm?

I was about 8 years old and regularly played "doctor" with the two sisters across the street. We would masturbate each other and it felt incredibly wonderful. *female age 57*

I had my first orgasm during a one-night stand with a fireman. *23*

My first orgasm ever was when I was riding a horse. I thought I was perverted and never told anyone. Then at a slumber party one of my close friends who also horseback rides admitted that she'd had a similar experience. *female under 18*

I had my first orgasm while discovering the pleasures of a water faucet at age 10. I was disappointed that it was so short until I discovered how to cause multiple orgasms. I practised really hard in the bath tub for hours every day, and I think I was lucky that my parents had to work. Otherwise they would have been worried about their strange daughter. *female age 22*

I was 7-8 and I was still attached to my blanket. I was curled up next to it with it between my legs and I began rocking back and forth on it till wow! *female age 21*

My Fantasy?

One of my favorite fantasies is where two male slaves have to please me with their tongues and have to play with each other on my command. *female age 22*

Doing a threesome with another woman and a man. *female age 23*

I'd like to try anal sex. I'll do it one day with the right person. *20*

A former partner wanted me to role play and be a dominatrix. He was this total macho GUY'S kind of GUY (he went to the gym, watched sports.) He had a foot fetish, which I loved, but he wanted me to walk on him, piss on him, treat him like dirt and I just couldn't. *female age 20*

Orgasm without genital contact?

He was fingering me anally and I had a huge orgasm. *female age 22*

I once came from just kissing, and not the deep, all tongue, lots of saliva kissing either. We were at an outdoor concert and our lips barely touched. *female age 27*

I can reach orgasm by crossing my legs and fantasizing a sexual scene usually involving my significant other watching another woman and myself make love; he is usually giving the directions for what she should do to stimulate me. *female age 52*

If someone licks and sucks my feet, it brings me very close to orgasm and I breathe heavier than with genital contact. *female 20*

My most intense orgasms?

During intercourse. There is a certain orgasm I have never been able to reproduce without an actual penis in me. *female age 38*

From masturbation. He still hasn't gotten the hang of just how to touch me. But we're working on it. *female age 27*

I have my most intense orgasms when he is rubbing my clit while he enters me from behind so that we're doing it on our sides. I also like to be fingered in my front and up my ass at the same time. *21*

I have orgasms in my dreams. Usually it's so intense, I wake up. *28*

Size?

My ex-husband was hung like a horse, but it didn't really mean a thing because he never took the time to know what I wanted or needed. That just goes to prove that being a size queen can sometimes get you no where when it comes to inner satisfaction. *age 32*

Average is best. Too big hurts like hell and too small just ain't enough. *female age 35*

My boyfriend was really well endowed, so getting the condom on was always a challenge. I was always commenting on how long it took. One day he asked if I thought I could do any better, so I tried rolling it on and about 4 inches into it I let go of the condom and the thing flew off like a rubberband and got tangled in the ceiling fan. *female age 21*

I was at a coed banya in Russia and was amazed at the wide range of penis sizes and shapes. Some seemed so incongruous compared to the rest of the guy. *female age 22*

I've only had a good look at my boyfriend's genitals, so I don't know much about what they are supposed to look like, but I don't think he has testicles. Everything else about him is completely normal, so I'm not sure, but I can't find them. *female age 21*

Unusual ways of masturbating?

I like to fist myself, but this is a rare occurrence. *female age 32*

I like to masturbate when there's a chance of someone seeing. I do it with my window blinds open when I'm at home, and even in the car I keep a small vibrator just in case I hit stand-still traffic. While everyone is so focused on getting home and cursing rush hour I look at it as a way to let my tension of the day. *female age 21*

I like to masturbate to porn sites on the web. *female age 24*

I'm kind of a masturbation freak... always have been for whatever reason. I use it as a way to calm myself down, release stress, when I'm bored... whatever. I'm not very shy about it, and yes, my partner does know. *female age 22*

Masturbation doesn't do a lot for me, since my sexual experience is mostly about being with someone who enjoys me and my body. *female age 23*

I masturbate at least once a day. My lover loves it when I masturbate with him or beside him. He's very turned on by it. He thinks it's one of life's great mysteries. I like to watch him masturbate, though sometimes it makes me jealous. I'd like him to take the time and attention he spends on himself and use it on me. *age 24*

If you were a guy for a week?

I would definitely try jerking off. I also think I would have to get my dick sucked by a girl with big boobs! And maybe have anal sex with her too. *female age 22*

I would screw every piece of ass I could, and not feel like a slut. *female age 23*

I'd like to get a blow job, have intercourse and I'd also like to get a boner, which I guess I would have to do in order to do the other two things. *female age 19*

I would masturbate a lot so I would be able to give my boyfriend a better hand job when I became female again. *female age 21*

Have I tasted myself?

It doesn't taste as good as chocolate, but it's not bad! *female age 20*

I often stick my fingers into my mouth after masturbating, and I like to kiss my boyfriend after oral sex so I still can taste myself in his mouth. I thought, "Well, it tastes better than male fluids I've tasted." *female age 22*

The good and bad of receiving oral sex?

Once they find that holy spot down there it's incredible. I can buck and squirm for hours. The feeling is so much more intense than having intercourse because the tongue moves more and can flick and tease better than a penis. For the bad part, the guy doesn't want to stay down there long enough. They think "Oh, that's good enough. She's nice and wet now so I can fuck her." *female age 22*

I don't like having oral sex performed on me. I'd much rather have intercourse. I don't get the sensation of pressure that I do with intercourse, and that's what I enjoy the most. I also feel that oral sex is more personal than intercourse, and I need to feel very comfortable with a man. *female age 23*

I really love it when my husband goes down on me. It is the one feeling that I cannot give myself. I can finger fuck myself, use a dildo or anything else that feels the same as when he does it, but I can't go down on myself. When he does it, it makes me want to do everything that I can to please him. I get this kind of "melting jello" feeling between my legs that just makes me want to come and to tell him to never stop. *female age 32*

What would you tell your children about sex?

I would tell my son that sex can bring you to tears, make you laugh, make you feel alive, and make you feel awful, as well as make someone else experience these feelings and more. Remember that you are with a person, not a porta-pussy. *female age 19*

Gentlemen...

Caught masturbating?

More than once. It has kept me from becoming famous, as there would always be two people out there with a beat-all story when my face came up on the TV at the bar. *male age 40*

My mother walked in from my brother's graduation while I was beating off to Wonder Woman on TV. She either pretended she didn't know what I was doing, or I covered up in time. *male age 37*

Embarrassing moment?

I got caught with my nose in my friend's wife's panties in her hamper. By her. *male age 33*

I was in biology class in college. Sitting in the lecture hall wearing baggy drawstring pants. I had this raging hard on that wouldn't go away. When class was over and I had to stand up, the baggy pants did nothing to hide the erection as I was wearing loose boxers underneath and my dick had come out of the fly. *age 29*

Orgasm without my penis being touched?

I have an incredibly sexy wife with killer eyes and even better kisses. She has brought me off more than once just by kissing me. I can also come from eating her and or masturbating her. *age 40*

I love to go down on a woman. Once I got so into it that I came. It was a shock to both of us, but that really turned her on. *age 29*

When I was a sophomore in college, I would often play the pianos at the "houses" of Smith College. At one of the houses I met a statuesque New York beauty. Since this young woman had a dreadful fear of intercourse and the possibility of pregnancy we never had vaginal sex. But in the course of kissing her breasts and other parts of her beautiful body, I would occasionally have an orgasm. When I had one, she seemed pleased. The reason she was panic-stricken about intercourse was quite simple: her mother had died in childbirth, when she was born. *male age 60*

My first feel?

I had read countless articles in books about the female genitals. When it actually happened, I could see nothing and my fingers could not make out a single distinguishing feature. I felt clumsy and inexperienced. *male age 40*

It was in the back seat of a Buick parked in a train station in broad daylight. Spacious as the Buick may have been, her jeans were pretty tight, so I unzipped her and stuck my hand in... I knew there was supposed to be a wet slit in there somewhere, but damned if I could find it. Exciting as it was, I just got a handfulla hair. *male 37*

I remember feeling a great thrill when I first ran my fingers down over her pubic mound and cupped it and I thought I was in heaven! I was a tiny bit surprised at the wetness lower down (we had been making out for hours). I was expecting to feel her clitoris but I really couldn't. I heard a lot about arrow hard clits and stuff but I've never really been able to feel the hardness. I play guitar so maybe my fingers are hardened. My tongue now... that's another story! *male age 32*

It was really soft, wet, and slimy. I liked the feel of her scratchy pubic hair; it was very exciting and made it all seem so naughty. My finger quickly slipped right into her vagina and I was amazed at the lovely warm temperature in there. It was great to feel her immediately respond with pleasure and start a grinding move-ment with her pelvis. I knew by then I'd stumbled onto something really good. *male age 21*

The first time I had my fingers inside a woman I wasn't sure if I was turned on or a little grossed out by the sensation—like having my fingers inside a warm, gelatinous mass with unidentifiable soft bits all around. I realize it sounds trite, but a few years after that a good fall landed my hand into a pie (maybe apple) and I found some reference for what the inside of a girl feels like. I'd have to say I'd take fingerfucking over pie any day of the week. *20*

Tasted my own cum?

Yes. It needs garlic. *male age 20*

I like how it's kind of in a gelatin form sometimes. Sometimes it is bitter but not often. I ingest my ejaculate when I masturbate because its more convenient than using a tissue. *male age 18*

Yuck! Not because of the question, just how it tasted. *male age 42*

Sometimes, after my wife has made me come in her mouth, I will say, "Give it back to me." Then she will rear up, and give me a big French kiss. Then I swallow my own cum. What I would love to do is to come in my wife's vagina, and then lick her clean. It sounds very appealing, very sensual, and I often talk about it while making love. However, almost as soon as I come, a giant switch seems to be thrown inside my body and I do not want to do what a few minutes before I had been eagerly anticipating. It is as if a giant door slams shut. *male age 60*

My dad's explanation of sex?

When I was 22 my father pulled me aside and said this (verbatim), "Well when A MAN meets a woman he likes, he puts his thing in her and they go 'uh huh' and then children come out. Ok?" My uncle was standing nearby and said "Ah, don't worry. He probably knows more than you do anyhow." I got a colorful family. *male age 27*

My parents were of the opinion that if I had a question I should come to them. But they never explained something without arguing about it. My grandfather told me from the time that I was little that it is more important to love and cherish a woman than it is to sleep with her. *male age 21*

My dad was absolutely useless. I dreaded driving to swim meets with him because he would invariably ask, "Is there anything you want to know about sex?" Well, I could sense his discomfort from the fact that he had been quiet for the last 100 miles trying to get up the nerve to bring it up so I never asked. Besides, I thought I knew everything because I had learned from all my friends— it is a wonder I ever became a father. *male age 42*

What would I tell my son about sex?

I'd tell him that sex is like a candy store. Too much can make you sick, and not enough leaves you craving more. And there are so many different flavors and tastes, be sure to experience as many as possible. *male age 39*

The Goofy Glossary

Definitions of Words Pertaining to Sex, Local Culture & Sport

Hmmm. Would this be a CIRCLE JERK or a CALVIN KLEIN underwear ad?

AC/DC—1. someone who is bisexual 2. well-known metal rock'n'roll band whose members are now really old

ACORN—the glans or head of the penis

AFTERNOON DELIGHT—1. a nooner 2. sex in the afternoon

AIRHEAD—1. perfect date for a guy who is easily overwhelmed by intelligent women 2. in a discussion on the effects of nuclear winter, an airhead would want to know how the global dust cloud would affect her tan lines 3. song by Thomas Dolby; see "bimbo"

ANABEL CHONG—former convent school student turned porn starlet, whose claim to fame is having intercourse with 80 different guys on the same day on the same movie set; and we used to pity the poor guy who had to clean up the set after a gallagHer performance!

ANAL—1. referring to the anus, as in "anal sex" 2. describes a person who is "anal retentive" meaning "of constipated psyche" 3. incapable of giving slack

ANAL BEADS—string of beads that goes up a partner's rear end and is pulled out at the point of orgasm

ANALINGUS—"kissing ass" minus the metaphorical intent; rimming

ANAL PLUG—see "butt plug"

ANDROGYNOUS—1. not clearly masculine or feminine 2. can you name three androgynous rock'n'roll musicians?

APHRODISIAC—1. food, drug or other substance that is given (or taken) to increase sexual desire 2. be wary of anything that is called an aphrodisiac because it is usually people and not chemical concoctions that turn other people on; see "Spanish fly" and "yohimbine"

ARSE—British for ass, e.g. "piece of arse," "up your arse"

ASHRAM—1. house or mansion where a guru lives 2. important to know in case your sweetheart forsakes volleyball and string bikinis for incense and meditation

ATROPHY—1. scientific term for "use it or lose it" 2. fear that many guys have concerning their penis, especially when they haven't had sex for an epoch or two. atrophy happens to muscles; the penis, for better or for worse, does not seem to be one. one's penis sometimes gets a better workout from jerking off than from intercourse, so if you are worried about atrophy...

AUTOFELLATIO—1. to suck one's own penis 2. makes dating an option rather than a necessity 3. requires an extremely long schlong or incredibly nimble spinal column or both

BACK-DOOR MAN—interesting song by the Doors. what's it referring to, anyway?

BAD LESBIAN—1. among politically stiff lesbians, a "bad lesbian" is a gay woman who has sex with a man or fantasizes about it (heaven forbid!) 2. writer Carol Queen attributes this kind of rigid thinking to "the lezzie thought police"

BAG IT—to wear a rubber

BALL—to have intercourse with (past tense is "balled")

BALLS TO THE WALL—1. a state of mind where one powers through a situation with tenacity and guts 2. a semi-equivalent term is "pedal to the metal" 3. origin—the air force

BANGER—British term for sausage or penis; plural may refer to testicles

BARDEX NOZZLE—the John Deere of enema tubes

BARNEY—person with anemic surfing skills; see "grommet"

BARTHOLINS GLANDS—two small glands at the bottom part of the vaginal opening which help secrete lubrication; explains why you should reach to the bottom of the vaginal opening to bring up lubrication to coat the clitoris

B/D—bondage/discipline

BDSM—initials that describe three elements of sadomasochism: bondage and discipline (B&D), dominance and submission (D&S) and sadomasochism (S&M). got that?

BEAR—1. large, mature male with lots of body hair 2. term used in gay male porn

BEARD—date or marriage arranged for a homosexual person to make them appear straight. gay men or women who aren't out of the closet will sometimes have a friend of the opposite sex act as a beard when mom and dad are in town

BEARD BURN—1. inner-thigh hazard that women face who receive oral sex from men with five o'clock shadow 2. can be prevented by draping thighs with towels or plastic wrap, or by a quick shave on Thor's part

BEAT OFF—to masturbate (male)

BEAT YOUR MEAT—to masturbate (male)

BEAUTY PAGEANT—event where beautiful women get to meet other beautiful women

BEAVER—1. someone who attends Oregon State University 2. refers to the female sex oregons 3. great bumper sticker: Eat a Beaver, Save a Tree

BEEFCAKE—nude males in photos

BEN WA BALLS—1. a pair of metallic balls that are inserted into the vagina for sexual pleasure while rocking back and forth or squeezing the thighs together. more hype than reality since they don't work for most people 2. the ultimate ben wa story comes from the people at Good Vibrations in San Francisco: a woman who had inserted a pair of ben wa balls just before a flight was apprehended by airport security personnel as she tried to pass through the metal detector 3. aka Burmese Bell, which is probably the cadillac of ben wa balls

BESTIALITY—when your sexual partner has four legs and a tail

BELLY—beach talk for "babe"

BIDET—1. oval-shaped porcelain bowl that is plumbed with a fountain of water over which a woman squats to clean and sometimes stimulate her genitals 2. found in traditional European bathrooms 3. found in few American bathrooms

BIKINI LINE—how girls in modern America refer to their vulvas, defining them on the basis of what needs to be plucked in order to look good on the beach

BIMBO—1. woman who looks great but falls one or two IQ points short of Albert Einstein; see "airhead"

BIOLOGICAL CLOCK—procreational urge that overwhelms some people between the ages of 34 and 42

BISEXUAL—person who feels varying degrees of arousal for both sexes; aka "switch-hitter" or "AC/DC"

BLADDER INFECTION—1. when totally obnoxious bacteria with a painful kick establish residency in the human bladder 2. a person so affected would be willing to pawn her great grandmother's wedding ring for a hit of antibiotics 3. is more common in women because the passageway from the bladder to the outside of the body is much shorter, allowing bacteria easier access 4. women susceptible to vaginal and bladder infections should avoid soaps with fragrances, wear underpants with cotton crotches, wipe from front to back, and wash their hands before playing with their genitals. aka "cystitis"

BLENDED ORGASM—orgasm from stimulation with a blender, supposedly perfected by Betty Crocker 2. an extra-intense orgasm that is triggered by stimulation of two different areas at the same time, such as nipples and clitoris, or clitoris and g-spot area

BLIND DATE—aptly named social event; see "Loch Ness monster"

BLOW—cocaine

BLOW JOB—oral sex that's done on a guy

BLUE BALLS—1. refers to a condition where a male has been sexually stimulated but not to orgasm 2. sometimes actually hurts and is rumored to cause a blue tint to the scrotum 3. can easily be cured by jerking off 4. at one time was thought to cause physical damage, but recent evidence does not support this fear 5. get used to it, dude

BODY SHOTS—when doing tequila shooters, you have to suck the salt from whatever part of your lover's body he or she puts it on, and then suck the lime from his or her mouth. somewhere in between, you down the tequila

BODY MODIFICATION—piercing, tattooing or even corset training

BOFF—to have intercourse

BOINK—to have intercourse

BONDAGE—when someone gets a sexual high from that which the rest of us try to avoid. aka "S&M," B&D", "D&S," "BDSM" and so forth

BONE —less than gentle term used by less than gentle men in referring to intercourse; e.g., "to bone a babe"

BOOTH TROLL—guy who cruises other guys in the video booth section of the cheesier, more traditional adult sex stores. there they have anonymous sex with each other, giving the appearance of being straight, probably viewing straight porn flicks, with the added risk and excitement of being busted by the local vice squad

BOOTY—rear end, or can refer to sex, but not anal sex. go figure.

BOTTOM—sexually submissive, S&M term; see "top and bottom"

BOXERS OR BRIEFS?— a question every guy ponders at one time or another

BRA HOOK—1. Maidenform waterloo 2. no single device known to humankind has caused more guys (and some women) more angst than the hook of the bra 3. apparently, Obewan Kinobe originally taught Luke Skywalker about "the force" in order to help him unhook Princess Leia's bra. given that they eventually turned out to be brother and sister, it's fortunate that Leia's bra hook proved even tougher than the force

BREEDER—a gay term for a straight person

BROWN SESSION—where defecation becomes sexualized

BROWN SUGAR—refers to a sexy black woman or to having sex with a black woman

BUFF—1. having well-developed muscles 2. having a chest and arms (guns) that are pumped up but still cut 3. refers to someone who is in great physical shape

BUGGERY—an academic tradition; sodomy that's commonly done to boys and young men in boarding schools as well as in other places where men are warehoused

BUM— British for rear end

BUSH—female pubic hair

BUTCH—1. a lesbian who has adopted the male role and run with it 2. an exaggerated form of maleness, a few notches beyond macho

BUTT PLUG—1. a diamond-shaped object that goes in the rear end to give a feeling of fullness 2. usually made of plastic or silicone with a special flanged end so it won't get lost where the sun don't shine 3. plugs come in different sizes and shapes, some even vibrate, and one is made that is called a triple ripple, honest

CABOOSE—last guy when a woman is "pulling a train"; see "gang bang"

CANDY—1. when used as sexual slang, refers to sex or a person who is sexually arousing; e.g. "I want candy" 2. can refer to certain drugs that are snorted; e.g., "nose candy"

CASTING COUCH—Hollywood term referring to a process where certain directors and producers receive sexual favors in exchange for casting an actor/actress in a movie or TV show

CELLULAR PHONE—male equivalent of breast implants, important to display wherever you go

CERVICAL CAP—1. birth control device 2. little rubber beanie that sits on top of the cervix to discourage male ejaculate from entering 3. differs from a diaphragm in several ways: it's smaller, stays in longer, is usually not filled with birth control jelly, and may not be as effective for some people

CERVIX—1. hat rack for a diaphragm 2. the cervix is the bottom part of the uterus found in the back of the vagina. the cervix can be as small as a cherry in a woman who has not delivered a baby through her vagina. otherwise, it can be much bigger 3. the cervix might have a different feeling at different times of the month, and usually feels softer when the woman is ovulating. during that time, mucus passes through the cervical opening and bathes the vagina 4. male ejaculate passes through a small passageway in the center of the cervix on its way to do that conception thing

CHAKRAS—an eastern concept (India, not New Jersey)—fuse box of the body, seven points said to regulate energy

CHERRY—1. virginal or like new 2. hymen 3. maidenhead (in case you read Shakespeare)

CHICKEN & CHICKEN FOX—chicken refers to a boyish looking young man who wants to be picked up and cared for (or purchased) by an older man who is known as a chicken fox.

CHICKS WITH DICKS—persons who appear to be women in all ways except for the genital region. can be transvestites, partially fixed transsexuals or hermaphrodites (possessing both a penis and a vagina). in the latter case, the clitoris may have been enlarged prenatally due to a late dose of male-type hormones bathing a female fetus; aka she-he or he-she

CHIGGER—blood-sucking little mite

CHLAMYDIA—1. called "the silent sexually transmitted disease" because women often don't know they have it, although men usually have symptoms 2. there are about three to five million cases each year 3. although often without symptoms, chlamydia can cause sterility and also increases the chances of having an ectopic pregnancy. sexually active people, especially adolescents, should get a test for it every year 4. sexually active women can easily have the test done during pelvic exams. the test is inexpensive and doesn't hurt a bit 5. treatment involves giving antibiotics to both sexual partners, not just the one with the symptoms. otherwise, it won't work 6. you can carry it for years before displaying actual symptoms of the infection

CHOCOLATE—1. one of the few adequate substitutes for really good sex; traditionally used in the wooing process 2. may impact the female body on a physiological level as an anti-depressant, honest to goodness

CIRCLE JERK—guys masturbating together

CIRCLE JERKS—semi-notorious punk band of the 1980s

CIRCUMCISION (GOYIM)—a routinely performed medical procedure of debatable value, originally done in this country to prevent masturbation.

CIRCUMCISION (JEWS)—1. "the way a Jewish mother lets her son know who's in charge"—jmw 2. you decide: a profound statement of faith or when a father won't stand up to his own father to protect his son 3. what's the harm in allowing Jewish boys to wait until they turn eighteen and are able to phone the mohel themselves? why not let them decide if being circumcised is a way they want to express their faith?

CLAMPS—see "nipple clips"

CLAP—gonorrhea, one of the old timers in the field of sexually transmitted diseases. can cause burning sensation when peeing or unusual discharge. easily treated, but can do severe damage if not attended to

CLITORIS—1. Latin for "darned thing was here just a second ago" 2. the only organ in either the male or the female body whose sole purpose is pleasure—which from a biological perspective might indicate that the female genitals are more highly evolved than the male's 3. sometimes regarded as the Emerald City of women's orgasmic response 4. not to be approached in haste 5. sometimes wants to be caressed with vigor, other times can hardly tolerate being breathed upon 6. while the clitoris is a fine organ to lavish huge amounts of attention upon, qualities such as tenderness, playfulness and respect also contribute largely to orgasmic response

CLUSTER FUCK—1. army term for being in a really bad situation 2. three-way sex

COCK AND BALL TOYS— little harnesslike assemblies that snap around the base of the male genitals to pull the testicles up and apart, or to pull down on the scrotum. some men hang weights on these things

COCK RING—1. a ring made of rubber or sometimes leather that fits tightly over the base of a hard penis. some also fit over the penis and testicles a bit like a halter 2. the purpose is to help maintain an erection when the mind and body are otherwise unwilling. may also make the male genitals appear larger 3. supposedly holds shut the veins near the surface so none of the penile blood pressure can escape 4. of dubious value 5. don't wear one for more than 20 or 30 minutes without taking it off for a few minutes. otherwise you may risk permanent damage

COITUS—scientific term for sexual intercourse, taken from the root word "coit," which is a carpet and drapery cleaning business in Northern California

COJONES—Spanish for "balls"

COKE WHORE—person who is so strongly addicted to cocaine that he or she will do anything (or anyone) to feed the habit

COLORED CONDOMS—1. just so you'll know, some of the color pigments used in colored condoms might be carcinogenic, and others may leave permanent stains on your skin 2. if you want to change the color of your penis, why not take it to Earl Sheib and get it dipped in acrylic?

COME—to have an orgasm

COME CUP—1. device that attaches to the head of a vibrator and fits over the glans of the penis 2. use lots of lube, dude

COMING TOO SOON—when a male sexual partner has lousy hang time; aka premature ejaculation

COMPUTER BULLETIN BOARDS (BBS)—a place in cyberspace for all kinds of interchanges via computer modem. specific bbs to download porn, have conferences, get dates

CONDOM—1. fancy name for a rubber 2. a rubber by any other name is still a rubber 3. only jerks brag about having to wear extra-large condoms

CORNHOLE—1. the anus or anal sex 2. the slang probably originated from the use of dried corn cobs in the place of toilet paper. not to be confused with the term "cornhusker" (can you name the cornhusker state?)

COTTONTAIL—term that nude sunbathers sometimes use for a person who wears a bathing suit; see "textile"

COWGIRL—1. intercourse position where the girl is on top facing the guy 2. in reverse cowgirl, she is on top and facing south, allowing her to watch her partner's toes curl with delight each time she squeezes the muscles in her pelvic region

COWPER'S GLANDS—tiny structures near the urethra inside the base of the penis which produce the clear, silky drops of fluid known as "precum"; see "precum"

CRABS—1. what people often see on Card 10 of the Rorschach (ink blot) test 2. funky little creatures that hang out on body hair (pubic or otherwise). can sometimes make you itch to the point of near insanity 3. reason for turning bright crimson when your pharmacist yells all the way across the store "Harvey, can you show this young person where the shampoo for crab lice is located?" 4. washing your pubic hair and external genitals with alcohol (70 percent) will likely zap the crab lice, although it may sting somewhat

CRAMPS—1. rock'n'roll band whose cult hits include "What's Inside a Girl," "Bikini Girls with Machine Guns", "Can Your Pussy Do the Dog", and "Don't Eat Stuff Off the Sidewalk" 2. abdominal pains women sometimes get during their periods, the intensity of which can sometimes be diminished by orgasms

CRANK—1. speed (methamphetamine) 2. the nasal decongestant propylhex-edrine, often used to get a quick rush

CROSS-DRESSING—when a person of one sex makes a serious attempt to dress like a member of the other sex—and we're not talking about a woman simply wearing her boyfriend's shirt or boxer shorts

CRUMPET—1. British term for sexual activity. 2. bakery product

CUM (COME)—male ejaculate, white sticky stuff that usually squirts out of a penis during male orgasm, much of which is produced by the prostate gland 2. most males average about a teaspoonful of cum per ejaculation 3. varies in consistency and sometimes taste among different guys

CUNNILINGUS—1. "cunnus" is Latin for vulva (the part of a woman's genitals that is on the outside) and "lingere" means to lick—put 'em together and figure it out for yourself 2. has any living human being ever used the term "cunnilingus" outside an academic setting, except of course for telling the renowned "Connie Lingus" jokes?

CUNT—1. from the Latin "cunnus" (meaning vulva), a somewhat harsh term for women's genitals, but currently being used in feminist literature in a positive way 2. a derogatory way of referring to a woman

CUP—1. plastic device that manly guys wear to protect their genitals from potential calamities like dick-high line drives, bad hops or catching for pitchers who throw screwballs and split-finger fastballs 2. there are now two styles of hard cup, and a cup made of softer material for sports with less severe contact. the old style of hard cup is somewhat pear-shaped, while the new style is banana-shaped—reflecting changes in the shape of male genitals since the women's movement of the 1960s. both types of hard cup are held in place by a special type of supporter 3. wearing a cup over shorts (briefs, boxers etc.) may help it feel less strange; for instance, a friend of this guide who has been a baseball catcher for more than twenty-five years wears an old-style cup in a supporter over his briefs, and then puts on a pair of lycra sliding pants (a little like bicycle shorts) to hold it in place better

CUPID'S HOTEL—vagina

CURVED DICK—1. a penis that curves as it gets hard, most likely due to a tight ligament. this is perfectly normal unless it causes physical pain, in which case it should be taken to a physician for consultation 2. since some guys with curves feel self-conscious, consider the following pearl of information: one highly experienced woman told this guide that the best sex she ever had was with an Italian guy who had a curved penis 3. if you've got a curve, experiment with different intercourse positions that might provide an advantage over guys who don't have a curve. especially effective might be a position that allows the head of your penis to massage the roof of the vagina

CUT—1. referring to a guy who has been circumcised 2. weightlifting term for muscles that have great definition

CYSTITIS—see "bladder infection"

DANCING WITH MYSELF—1. see "masturbation" 2. great song by Billy Idol

DATE—without this event, men might never cut their toenails

DEADHEAD—1. a Grateful Dead groupie 2. what you do to flowering plants to keep them blooming

DIESEL DYKE—1. manly lesbian, "bull dyke" 2. opposing term is "lipstick lesbian"

DEPILATORY—cream for removing body hair

DIAPHRAGM—1. cross between a condom and a frisbee, having the flexibility of the condom and the aerodynamics of the frisbee 2. contraceptive barrier device that holds contraceptive jelly against the opening of the cervix

DIAL-A-PORN—1. phone sex at the rate of $2.00+ a minute 2. masturbation-enhancement device for those who like their stimulation over the phone; aka "dial-a-fuck"

DICK—1. male equivalent of the clitoris, urethra, vagina and inner labia 2. a person who is being a jerk

DICK-HEAVY COMPANIES—businesses where the bosses are men and the secretaries (oops! assistants) are women

DIEN BIEN PHU'D—("phu'd" sounds like food) 1. getting your butt kicked; e.g., "our football team got Dien Bien Phu'd last night by the Twin Peaks Beaver 2. town in North Vietnam where the French were soundly defeated in 1954. the 72-day siege at Khe Sanh during 1968 nearly became America's Dien Bien Phu

DILDO—1. penis-shaped object which a woman puts into her vagina for sexual satisfaction 2. not to be confused with a vibrator, which is a mechanical humming device usually placed on the outside of a woman's genitals rather than being inserted 3. can be worn in a harness and be used as one would an erect penis 4. a person who is being a jerk or a moron

DILDO HARNESS—1. jockstraplike device that a dildo attaches to 2. gives a dildo penislike properties of suspension and thrustability

DOCKING—1. when an uncircumcised male pulls his foreskin over the head of another man's penis 2. no reason why it can't be pulled over a woman's nipples, assuming she's into that sort of thing

DOGGIE STYLE—1. intercourse from behind, not to be confused with intercourse in the behind 2. more popular than the missionary position in some parts of the world 3. often results in better stimulation of the vaginal roof, which some women prefer

DOM—dominatrix

DO-ME QUEEN—1. in the world of sadomasochism, a bottom whose entire existence revolves around getting the attention of others, while giving nothing in return 2. in the entertainment industry, an actress or actor.

DOOBIE—a joint

DORK—a whale's penis

DO THE WILD THING—to make love

DOUBLE BAGGED—wearing two condoms at once

DOUBLE DILDO—dildo that seats two

DOUBLE PENETRATION—1. penises in the vagina and rear end at the same time 2. two penises in the same vagina at the same time

DOUCHE BAG—1. gravity-driven device for feminine hygiene 2. uncomplimentary term for a woman or gay man 3. women who douche three times a month are three times more likely to develop pelvic inflammatory disease than women who don't douche at all

DRAG—when a man wears women's clothing

DRAG QUEEN—1. man who dresses and behaves as if he were a woman 2. can sometimes be differentiated from a transvestite because a drag queen is usually attracted to men, whereas a transvestite tends to be more heterosexually oriented 3. drag queens tend to be a bit more boisterous than either transsexuals or transvestites. when you are in a room with a drag queen you often know she's there

DRESSED TO THE RIGHT OR LEFT—guys who wear boxer shorts have to make a very basic decision in life: on which side of the fly to rest their genitals. this is no big deal (sorry) unless you get your Wrangler's tailor-made, in which case the tailor will inquire, "Sir, do you dress to the right or to the left?" he will then leave extra denim on whichever side you indicate

DRY HUMP—1. traditional sport of young couples, especially at Italian wedding receptions, where pubic regions are feverishly rubbed together while both participants are fully clothed 2. can result in severe chafing, irritation, orgasm or all three; aka frottage

D/S—domination/submission

DYKES ON BIKES—a type of all-girls motorcycle club

DYSFUNCTIONAL—is this the most overused word in the English language? does it have any meaning anymore? would the world be any worse off if no one used the term "dysfunctional family" for the next ten years?

EAT OUT—neat oral thing that a man or woman does to a woman; see "muff diver," "go down on" and "cunnilingus"

ECTOPIC PREGNANCY—1. pregnancy in which the embryo implants into the wall of the fallopian tube instead of the uterus 2. a very dangerous condition which can result in maternal death

EIGHTY-SIX'D (86'd)—1. put out of commission 2. left behind 3. dropped 4. term used in restaurants to signify that they are out of a particular menu item, or that the item has been pulled from the menu because it has caused at least three customers to throw up before reaching the parking lot 5. can also refer to someone who is being thrown out of a bar or restaurant

EJACULATION—1. the big squirt 2. usually accompanies orgasm in the male and sometimes follows orgasm in the female

ELBOW GREASE—brand of lubricant often used for anal sex, well known in the gay community

ENURESIS—1. peeing in your sleep 2. happens to almost as many girls as guys and can last until adulthood 3. a really lousy thing to have, sometimes very difficult to shake

EPISIOTOMY—1. an incision made in the bottom of a woman's vaginal opening to increase its size so she can deliver a baby without tearing herself 2. the delivery room equivalent of "we've got to destroy this village in order to save it" 3. in America, up to 90 percent of first-time mothers are given episiotomies; in the Netherlands, only 20 percent to 30 percent of first-time mothers are given episiotomies. there is speculation that American doctors don't understand the second stage of labor and sometimes mismanage deliveries. on the other hand, if it's a nine-pound baby...

EROTICISM—state of tension fueled by sexual desire, resolved through sexual contact that quenches at least some of this desire

EUNUCH—guy without balls, literally

FAG HAG—woman who hangs out with gay men, claims to be heterosexual, but seems to fear sexual intimacy with straight men

FAYGELEH—yiddish term for gay male

FANNY—in Britain and Australia, the vulva or vagina; in America, the arse

FEEL UP—to touch or stimulate a partner's genitals with your hand

FELCHING—licking male ejaculate out of whichever orifice it's been shot into, usually done by the male who put it there

FELLATIO—from the Latin "fellare" meaning "that which stops after marriage" 2. blow job

FEMALE EJACULATION—with extra stimulation, some women squirt fluid from the urethra as part of having an orgasm. some women worry that this is urine and try to hold it back. it may be a fluid similar to male prostate secretion minus the sperm

FEMORAL INTERCOURSE—1. when a lubricated penis slides back and forth between the labia like a hot dog in a bun, but is not stuck inside the vagina 2. also refers to intercourse with the thighs being used as the vagina

FEMME—feminine-looking lesbian as opposed to a diesel dyke "lipstick lesbian"

FETISH—1. a particular prop (leather, rubber, underwear, shoes, etc.), body part (feet, hair, breasts, etc.) or scenario that a person relies on to get off sexually 2. the prop can be fantasized or exist in actuality 3. one philosopher has described a "fetish" as when a hungry person sits down at a dinner table and feels full from simply fondling the napkin. don't you wish!

FIST FUCKING (FISTING OR HANDBALLING)—placing a fist into the rectum or vagina, honest

FLAGGING—practice in the gay community where one signals the kind of sexual acts he likes with a specific color of handkerchief that he tucks in his back pocket

FLAMING—1. descriptive term for a male with an extreme case of unmanly mannerisms and behaviors 2. extreme and perhaps pointless argument in an internet chat room; aka "flaming out"

FLAPPER—term used to describe a sexually liberated woman during the 1920s who flaunted her unconventional approach to life

FLOG THE LOG—to masturbate

FLUFFER—1. person who keeps male porn stars erect when they are not on camera 2.not used very much any more, as today's male porn star either has trained wood (erects on cue) or is out of a job.

FORESKIN—1. male equivalent of the clitoral hood 2. flap of skin that extends from the shaft of the penis over the glans (head) to keep the latter moist and safe 3. gets chopped off during circumcision

FORESKIN CHALLENGED—circumcised

FORNICATION—intercourse between people who are not married

FRAZIER—1. manliest lion to ever live in captivity; once had intercourse more than 160 times in less than three days 2. died shortly thereafter

FRENCH—term for oral-genital contact, not to be confused with "French kiss" (however, one often leads to the other)

FRENCH KISSING—1. kissing with mouths open as opposed to closed 2. usually involves transfer of tongues (in the nonbiblical sense)

FRENCH TICKLER—any form of condom that has little bumps, projections or ridges, marketed to increase a woman's sexual pleasure. maybe it works for Frenchwomen, but not for anyone we know. instead of buying French ticklers, spend the extra money on flowers and you'll both be happier

FRENULUM—extra-sensitive part of the penis just below the head on the side of the shaft that faces away from the abdomen

FRIENDS IN LOW PLACES—1. wonderfully expressive (okay, totally kick-ass) song written by Dewayne Blackwell and Earl Bud Lee and performed by Garth Brooks 2. musical balm for the lovelorn; if the live version doesn't help to get you out of a funk, seriously consider antidepressants 3. by the way, the wildly successful Mr. Brooks worked at a Nashville shoe store while every record label passed on his demo tapes. ("reality is no friend of the dreamer," says he). what tricksters the fates can be

FRIG—British for jerk off

FROTTAGE—see "dry hump"

FUCK BUDDY—friend or acquaintance whom you occasionally (or often) have sex with. while the sex might be serious, the relationship isn't

GANG BANG—when a woman has intercourse with several men in rapid succession, at her invitation (as opposed to gang rape, which is sexual assault) aka "pulling a train" 2. it's interesting how a man who has sex with five women in the same room might be considered a stud, lucky, or at the worst wild and reckless, while a woman who has sex with five men in the same room is considered trash and risks being given a psychiatric diagnosis or at the very least called a nymphomaniac

GANG BANGER—member of a street gang

GANG OF FOUR—1. the name of a very solid post-punk rock'n'roll band 2. Jiang Qing, Wang Hongwen, Yao Wenyuan and Zhang Chunqiao. if you don't know who they are, look up "Gang of Four" in an encyclopedia; it won't do you any harm

GANG RAPE—when several men rape a woman, demonstrating incredible cowardice and supporting the notion that we humans reside on a limb far from the top of the evolutionary tree

GENDER-BENDER—someone of one sex who is in the process of becoming the other or who alternates between the two

GENDER DYSPHORIA—when the genitals you have and the genitals you wish you had are not the same 2. when a guy seriously wishes he were a girl and a girl seriously wishes she were a guy. may lead to taking hormones of the desired gender and sex reassignment surgery

GENITALS—1. blanket term for what you play with under the blanket 2. the sex organs

GETTING OFF—coming or having an orgasm; aka getting your rocks off

GIVE HEAD—to perform oral sex; can be on a woman, but the term is often synonymous with giving a blow job

GLANS—head of the penis

GLORY HOLE—hole in a wall into which a man sticks his penis to have it indiscriminately sucked, or through which one person spies on the other; usually at a place where there is lots of cruising, e.g., the baths, video booths; can also be used for anal sex if the giver is long enough; primarily a gay term

GO DOWN ON—to perform oral sex on

GO-GO DANCER—ask your grandparents

GOLDEN SHOWERS—1. peeing as a sexual turn-on; aka water sports 2. a tree of the legume family, native to India, whose Latin name is cassia fistula.

GONAD—1. sex gland 2. dweeb

GOOFY-SPOT—see "G-spot"

GREEK—anal

GROMMET—1. a rookie surfer who often substitutes gumption for intelligence, and hyperactivity for poise; aka groin, surf rat, or weed 2. surfing mag reports that sex is a matter of great concern and mystery for the young groin: "what does one do?" "for how long?" "is it all right if I don't get completely naked?"

GROUP SEX—see "swinging"

G-SPOT—1. controversial place on the roof of the vagina named after the lucky man (Grafenberg) who claims to have discovered it 2. area of potential sensation for some women 3. more accurate if it had been called G-area than G-spot

G-STRING—oh, about a quarter of a bikini bottom

GUSHER—term for when a man has an orgasm at the same time that his prostate is being massaged. some men say it feels spectacular

GYNECOMASTIA—when boys appear to be developing small breasts. a common event that happens during puberty to about 20 percent of boys. usually goes away within two years

JOHN THOMAS—British term for penis. "to frig your John Thomas" is a redundant phrase; "playing with your John Thomas" is cricket

HANDBALLING—see "fist fucking"

HAND JOB—bringing either yourself or a partner to orgasm with your hand

HAND WARMERS—Australian term for breasts, perhaps explaining something about the way Australian men regard Australian women

HARDBODY—person who is in great physical shape

HARD-ON—when a male gets wood

HEART—1. that which contains all love, caring, passion, tenderness, happiness, courage, loyalty, gentleness, awe, hope, beauty, feeling, play, laughter, trust, charity and joy 2. an important thing to have

HERMAPHRODITE—1. person born with both male and female sex organs 2. sometimes caused by an unintended bath of androgen (male-type hormone) during pregnancy. can result in a vagina whose clitoris has grown into a fully developed penis (pseudohermaphrodite) 3. in modern times the parents often get to choose which sex they want to raise the child. the medical community then backs up the decision with surgical and/or pharmacological interventions 4. in spite of what your friends say, you're probably not, but think of the possibilities if you were

HERPES—virus that affects the mouth and/or the genitals with a rash, lesions or chancre sores; also can cause flulike symptoms. it is usually harmless when hibernating, which is most of the time, but occasionally surfaces with a vengeance. it hibernates deep in the nerves that surround the mouth and/or genitals. avoid sex without a latex barrier when there are active herpes lesions, because that's when it is usually transferred back and forth from the mouth to the genitals, mouth to mouth, or genitals to genitals. however, it is possible to get it when there is no apparent lesion. if you have herpes, spend time reading up on it and learn as much as you can; that way you become the master of it rather than it becoming the master of you (there's a national organization; call your local planned parenthood or sexrelated clinic for information)

HERSHEY HIGHWAY—anus or rectum when referring to anal sex

HICKEY—1. love bite 2. for some, a cause of embarrassment and reason to wear a turtleneck no matter what the weather; for others, a sign of desirability

HIT A HOME RUN—to have intercourse

HOLMES—1. homeboy 2. gang talk for "dude"

HONKY—a white person

HOOCH—1. illegal liquor 2. a hut or shack, often where a prostitute lives

HORNDOG—a male whose reputation for sleaziness precedes him

HORNY—1. having the sexual urge 2. refers to a situation where "she's got to have it" (hi Tracy!) or he's got to have it 2. the term in Australia is "randy"

HUMP—the way a poodle or dachshund often greets the arm or leg of an unsuspecting human; see "dry hump" and "frottage"

HUNG—a male with large sex organs

Why the 1960s phrase "MAKE LOVE — NOT WAR"
never had a chance?

IMPOTENCE—when a guy can't get it up on a regular basis

INCEST—sex among immediate family members who are blood relatives

IRIE—1. rasta or reggae term meaning cool, relaxing, calm and collected 2. how you hopefully feel after making love

JACKING OFF—rubbing your genitals in a way that causes pleasant or wonderful sensations, generally resulting in orgasm

JACK'N'JILL PARTIES—1. gatherings of sexually uninhibited men and women who attend in their underwear and masturbate in front of each other 2. byproduct of concern about AIDS

JADE STALK—Chinese Taoist term for penis

JANEY—lesbian slang for vagina

JELLY ROLL—jazz term for female genitals

JERKING OFF—see "jacking off"

JOANI'S BUTTERFLY—a small vibrator that can be strapped in place for use during intercourse or when out on the town

JOCKSTRAP—jog bra with only one cup

JOHN—someone who pays a prostitute for sex, aka "trick"

JOHNSON—old-fashioned term for penis

JUNKIE—1. a heroin addict 2. anyone who's infatuated with someone or something; not necessarily a negative term

KEGEL EXERCISES—1. genital aerobics—when you squeeze or contract the muscles surrounding your genitals in a way that would stop the flow if you were taking a leak 2. some people claim that these exercises will fix everything from a floppy penis to an uninspired vagina. research results do not support these claims; however, the exercises can be useful in becoming more aware of genital sensations, and some people say they result in stronger orgasms

KILLER PUSSY—1. rock'n'roll group who sang the cult classic hit "Teenage Enema Nurses in Bondage" as well as "Pepperoni Ice Cream," "Pocket Pool" and "Bikini Wax " 2. how guys occasionally refer to a vagina that feels extra wonderful 3. how guys occasionally refer to steamy-looking women; always plural with this usage, e.g., "They've got some killer pussy over at the White House," in reference to a stable of interns and to how the women look in general, as opposed to "She's got a killer pussy," which refers to only one intern, and mostly to the part between her legs—of which it is assumed the speaker has intimate knowledge

KINDNESS—perhaps the greatest sex aid of all

KINK—doing what others only think about

KINSEY AVERAGE—1. oh, about two and a half minutes 2. the amount of time sex researcher Alfred Kinsey estimated that it takes the average American male to come during intercourse; because of increased public awareness, the Kinsey average has probably increased in the last 30 years, perhaps even doubled

KNICKERS—1. undergarments worn by your great-great-grandmother 2. what your great great grandfather dreamed of getting into

KNOCKED UP—pregnant

KY JELLY—1. a brand name of a water-soluble lubricant that a lot of people use to help increase the all-important slip'n'slide coefficient during intercourse, especially when using a rubber 2. the first generation of water-soluble lube; you might like some of the newer ones better 3. if it starts to dry out during use, add a few drops of water or saliva, not more KY

LABIA MINORA—inner lips of the vulva, attached to the underside of the clitoris. tugging gently on the inner lips of a sexual partner can be a fine way to stimulate the nerves of her clitoris without overwhelming them.

LANDING STRIP—medium severe form of bikini waxing where the pubic hair is done in a small rectangle.

LEFT HAND—what a right-handed person sometimes uses to masturbate with so it feels like someone else is doing it

LESBIAN—woman who prefers sex with women

LESBO—a straight person's term for lesbian; can be derogatory, equivalent to saying "fag"

LIBIDO—what Freud said is the fuel for our desire to make an emotional connection with others; he did not limit the term to erotic or horny feelings as is often done in the present day and age

LIFESTYLES ORGANIZATION—1. large organization for couples who like to have sex with other couples (thousands of couples belong), based in Anaheim, California, pride of Orange County (you know, home of God, Country, Chapter 13, and Swinging!) 2. if you went to one of the weekly dinners or dances sponsored by this organization, you would think you were among a group of police (husbands and wives) or teachers 3. interestingly, a large number of police and teachers really do belong

LINGAM—Sanskrit term for penis

LIPSTICK LESBIAN—what a cutie! "There she goes, Miss America..."

LIZARD—someone who tries to move in on your sweetheart when you're not there

LOCH NESS MONSTER—1. a rather frightening mythical creature of Scottish origin; aka: Nessi 2. sightings of the Loch Ness monster are sometimes reported by men and women who have just returned from a blind date

LONG FLANNEL NIGHTGOWN—1. very effective birth-control device worn by American women 2. the Cadillac of flannel nightgowns used to be made by Lanz®

LOPPY TUNA—surfer term for women's genitals, first coined between Redondo and Hermosa beaches

LOVE—a special and precious way that we have of relating to one another

LUCKY PIERRE—a gay or bisexual term, referring to three-way sex; lucky Pierre is the man in the middle. so what about lucky Giselle?

MAGIC WAND®—Hitachi's laptop for women; has two speeds and a big round head, and vibrates like a Federation freighter at warp 9

MAINLINE—1. to shoot up a drug (inject into a vein) 2. great way to get fatal diseases

MAINTAIN—a level of behavior one attempts to achieve when dealing with parents, teachers and officers of the law

MAN'S SHIRT—1. object of male clothing which girlfriends often lay claim to and love wearing, especially to bed 2. the very feel and smell of it gives the lovelorn woman comfort 3. any man who had a similar attachment to a piece of woman's clothing would be called weird or kinky

MASHER—1. rather insensitive perpetually horny male who gets physically closer than the situation calls for 2. a term used in playing marbles

MASOCHIST—a person who invites pain and passively controls others in the process; a bottom or submissive

MASTURBATION—a date with your own genitals

MATANUSKA THUNDER FUCK—Term used in Alaska, Matanuska being a region in Alaska known for its herb production

MENAGE A TROIS—(sounds like "may-naj-ah-twa") 1. when three French people are sharing sexual intimacy 2. includes either two men and a lucky woman or two women and a lucky man

MERCY FUCK—intercourse done from a sense of duty or pity rather than burning desire

MERKIN—wig for the pubic area; supposedly originated in past centuries to hide syphilis lesions. was held in place by toupee glue or a small G-string

MILE-HIGH CLUB—to have had sex in a plane

MISSIONARY POSITION—1. intercourse position where the man and woman are horizontal and face to face, usually with the man on top 2. term coined by savages who associated this position with conquering missionaries 3. too much of this position may lead to a boring sex life

MONEY SHOT—the heart of traditional porn movies, where the male ejaculates; aka "cum shot"

MONILIA—type of vaginal yeast infection that can be very uncomfortable for the woman. can cause thicker discharge than is normal, extreme itching, and painful intercourse

MONS PUBIS—fleshy mound at the top of the vulva from which pubic hair grows

MONTGOMERY NODES—1. little bumps that often form on the nipples after puberty, especially prominent when you feel a chill or are sexually aroused

MORNING-AFTER PILL—1. pill which can be taken the day after unprotected intercourse which greatly reduces the chances of becoming pregnant. call your physician 2. an alternative if you discover that the rubber broke

MOTHER FIST AND HER FIVE DAUGHTERS—British masturbation term referring to the hand. the equivalent American term is Rosie Palm and her five sisters, and the Australian term is Mrs. Palmer and her five daughters

MUFF DIVER—someone who enjoys oral/genital contact with a woman

NEWMAN, ALFRED E.—1. goofy guy emeritus, joining Bullwinkle the Moose and Larry, Moe and Curly as major childhood influences for many a male and some hip females 2. hopefully Mr. Newman appreciates his location in the goofy glossary between "muff diver" and "nipple clips"

NIPPLE CLIPS—1. variation of a roach clip that is placed on each nipple as part of sex play 2. used by people who like to have their titties tweaked 3. applies varying degrees of pressure, depending on the type of clip used 4. there are clip styles, clamp styles, and even electrified nipple clips, as well as those that vibrate 5. some people like them on their labia or scrotum 6. B. Cohen, formerly of the *LA Weekly*, claims to use them as sweater guards; aka "nipple clamps"

NOCTURNAL EMISSION—wet dream

NONOXYNOL-9—1. active ingredient in most contraceptive foams and jellies that renders the male ejaculate infertile by changing its ph (acid-base balance) 2. if used with rubbers, may help control the spread of AIDS and herpes 3. not recommended for teeth brushing, but if you happen to swallow some during oral sex you're not going to die or anything

NORDIC COMBINE—a member of the other sex who is fair-haired, blue-eyed, and physically gifted; term coined by author Dan Jenkins

NSU (NONSPECIFIC URETHRITIS)—common infection of the urinary tube

NUCLEAR—1. intense 2. massive release of energy 3. orgasmic

OCT (OPTIMAL COME TIME)—1. when a guy lasts long enough during intercourse to please both himself and his partner 2. a guy with good hang time

ONANISM—masturbation, named after the Bible's Onan, who spilled his seed (pulled out and came); mistakenly referred to as masturbation when it clearly describes coitus interruptus or pulling out during intercourse to ejaculate on the side. maybe God was annoyed because Onan didn't keep going long enough to give his wife an orgasm, and modern religion has been misinterpreting His annoyance ever since

ON THE RAG—to be menstruating; before tampons and sanitary napkins were invented, rags were used to catch menstrual flow

OUTING—a vicious process where gays publicly expose gays who aren't out of the closet, supposedly to show the straight world that some of its biggest heroes and stars are really gay

PACKING—1. codpiece for gender-benders 2. when a woman who is cross-dressing wears a penis-shaped object in her pants to make it look like she is well hung 3. worn by some male rock'n'roll singers 3. more realistic when made of a soft material rather than silicone (a good packing device does not make a good dildo)

PANDERING—pimping

PANTY LINER—extra-large tampon that's been flattened out like the insole of a shoe, has stick'um instead of string, and is worn on the outside of the body rather than inside

PAPERVINE— drug injected into the penis which causes it to get hard

PARAPHILIAS—kinky stuff

PEDERAST—older male who has sex with boys or young men; aka "chicken fox"

PEEING WHILE STANDING—1. a wonderful ability that nature (combined with cultural habit) bestowed upon men and denied women 2. particularly useful while in theatres, stadiums and other places with crowded or filthy restrooms

PEEING WITH A HARD-ON—1. a misery inflicted on the human male nearly every morning, though much worse when he's young 2. a very difficult act to achieve, since the passageway to the bladder is closed off when a male gets an erection (see the definition of "waking with a hard-on" for why) 3. phenomenon that originally caused Hindus to invent meditation, with the earliest mantra being "lord, let this hard-on subside before my bladder bursts"

PELVIC INFLAMMATORY DISEASE (PID)—inflammation of the female reproductive organs, often the fallopian tubes, usually caused by a bacterial infection

PERINEUM—1. demilitarized zone of the human crotch 2. the area between the asshole and the genitals in men and women 3. Taoist types get all weak in the knees when talking about the perineum, which they consider to be quite sensitive

PHILISTINE— smug, jocklike jerk with a bad attitude

PIERCING—1. placing a pierced earring, safety pin or facsimile through a person's nose, lip, nipples, navel, genitals or anywhere else that skin grows 2. piercing enthusiasts might enjoy reading the *Piercing Fans International Quarterly*. ask at your local library 3. people into piercing are often into tattoos as well

PINK PEARL—pink, bullet-shaped vibrator made to be inserted into the vagina

PIT JOB—intercourse using the armpit as a vagina

POCKET POOL—rubbing of the testicles brought about by the invention of pants with pockets

POLYAMORY—different from swinging, where you have sex with anyone who is there and who wants to have sex with you, in this form of lifestyle, you have committed relationships with a set number of different individuals. includes everything from open marriage to polygamy

POLYMORPHOUS PERVERSE—kinky

POONTANG—word of dubious origin that refers to a woman's genitals or what one hopes to get from them

POPPERS—1. sold over the counter as a liquid air deodorizer, poppers were originally made of amyl nitrate (which is for heart patients). then the formula was switched to butyl nitrate because the amyl formulation could no longer be legally sold over the counter. when butyl nitrate was outlawed, popper makers switched the formula to a type of isopropyl alcohol which is fairly dangerous, but legal nonetheless 2. poppers are very popular in the gay community 3. popper vapors are inhaled immediately before orgasm with the resulting sensation described by some as amazing and totally indescribable 4. one problem with poppers is that the current formulation can kill you if you have hidden heart problems. some people feel that popper usage might weaken the immune system, but there's no research on the matter

PRECUM—slick, silky, clear fluid that drips out of the urethra of the penis when it is very hard and very excited. most people assume that this is nature's own form of KY Jelly; however, nature seems to have had something else in mind, since urine, which frequently travels through your urethra, is acidic. this is not good for the more alkaline parts of the ejaculate that cause conception. precum helps to deacidify the urethra and make it more slick so the ejaculation will be even more likely to get a girlfriend pregnant; see "cowper's glands"

PREPUCE—foreskin

PRIAPISM—1. a hard-on that won't quit. not a good thing. just so you will know, having an erection for three or four hours straight without its going down can result in permanent damage. while this is not a common occurrence, emergency room visits should be planned accordingly 2. named after Priapus, son of Aphrodite and Dionysus, god of male reproductive power

PRODUCER—1. person who controls movie and TV projects in the entertainment industry 2. an older man who often sleeps with actors/actresses who are half his age 3. has much power in an industry where just about anyone will sleep with anyone to realize their celluloid dreams 4. producers who are principled, kind and actually creative are to be truly appreciated

PRINCE ALBERT—a type of body modification (piercing) where a ring is put through the urethral opening of the penis and comes out the underside of the shaft. (dare we say "ouch"?)

PROSTATE—1. weird walnut-shaped gland located on the floor of a man's rectum nearly a finger's length up his bum 2. it's what generates about 30 percent of the fluid that comes out when a man ejaculates 3. contracts seconds before orgasm, resulting in an exquisite feeling 4. gets bigger with age 5. sometimes becomes inflamed and can even crimp the urethra, making it difficult to pee (prostatitis). 5. some men (straight, gay—it doesn't matter) enjoy the feeling that results from having the prostate massaged. others would sooner be caned than let someone stick a finger up their rear; see "gusher"

PSA—1. what Southwest Airlines used to be called. 2. abbreviation for "prostate specific antigen," which tends to be elevated in men who have prostate cancer. can be checked via a routine blood test, but is never definitive by itself and should never be used in place of a digital exam

PUDENDA—anatomical term for women's external genitals (vulva); from the Latin word "pudere," which means to be ashamed

PULLING A TRAIN—see "gang bang"

PUNANNY—rasta or reggae term for sex; "I wan' punanny!"

PUSSY POSSE—vice squad

PUSSY WHIPPED (PW)—a mental illness whereby the male hovers, grovels and begs in excess of what is normally required to have sex

PUSSY WHIPPER—a sexual partner who is very controlling and rarely satisfied. she often wishes aloud that her man would be more aggressive, yet would annihilate him the second he dared

QUANTUM—major

QUIM—British for vulva or vagina

RANDY—Australian term for horny

RAPE—1. sexual bodily assault 2. because the developmental arrest is so profound and the capacity for empathy is so diminished, rapists rarely seek psychotherapy or respond to it. there are men who are capable of committing rape and an hour later going home to have what appears to be normal sex with their suburban wives. most rapists don't view their acts as being criminal or brutal and are apt to justify themselves by saying that the woman wanted it, needed it or deserved it. the only good news on this front is that juvenile sexual offenders quite often can and should be helped and should never be placed with hardened adult offenders

RAPE FANTASIES—1. when a person is aroused by images of being raped, but would never want it to happen in real life 2. the "rapist" in rape fantasies is often a person whom the "victim" would very much like to have sex with anyway

RASTA—1. short for Rastafarianism, a Jamaican religious sect which believes that Africa is the promised land and that former Ethiopian emperor Haile Selassie was the messiah 2. having to do with reggae and reggae music

REAM JOB—licking the anus; aka "rimming" or "reaming" 2. what a conscientious plumber does to the inner lip of any pipe that he or she has just cut

RETARDED EJACULATION—when a guy's sexual hang time is so long that nobody cares

RETROGRADE EMISSION—1. when an ejaculating penis backfires. caused by prostate problems or because a guy clamps the end of his penis shut when he's jerking off. 2. an important reason why Kleenex and toilet paper were invented was so guys could have something to shoot their wad into when masturbating. otherwise, some guys who have no way to clean up the come will clamp the penis shut so it doesn't shoot out and make a mess. ouch. 3. restricting the flow from a penis when ejaculating can cause severe plumbing problems and should only be done in the most dire of circumstances, unless you want to end up at the doctor's office doubled over with pain having to answer some really embarrassing questions

ROAD ERECTION—unwanted wood having nothing to do with sexual thoughts. can happen any time a guy is sitting in a vehicle that vibrates (bus, car, tractor, etc). it is caused by a combination of the vibration, which sends extra blood into the penis, and sitting, which tends to shut the veins that carry blood out of the penis

ROID RAGE—unpleasant mood state that occurs in some people who take steroids

RIMMING (RIM JOB)—kissing ass, literally

RUBBERS—common name for condoms. origin: before the invention of latex, condoms in this country were made of vulcanized rubber

SANGER, MARGARET—(1883-1966) famous birth-control advocate at a time when dispensing information about birth control was illegal in America

SAPPHO—poetess on the island of Lesbos noted for her use of nonphallic imagery

SAFE WORD—in bondage, a special prearranged word or expression that the submissive partner (bottom) can say to the dominant partner (top) which means to stop

SCHLONG—Jewish term for penis

SCUM BAG—1. condom 2. term for someone you don't like

SEVEN-OF-NINE—human thinking may be illogical, human reasoning may be flawed, but human crotches collectively swell when this piece of borg perfection becomes one with the screen. assimilate/ejaculate—resistance is futile. (so who's resisting?)

SEX BEFORE THE GAME—1. refers to masturbating or having sex less than twenty-four hours before taking part in a major sporting event 2. Mirkin and Hoffman in *The Sports Medicine Book* have looked into the topic and found there's no correlation between sex before the game and decreased athletic performance. they report that in a recent Olympics one athlete had sex approximately one hour before the event and won a gold medal; another Olympian had sex right before his event and ran a sub four-minute mile. Mirkin and Hoffman quote Casey Stengel on the matter: "It isn't sex that wrecks these guys, it's staying up all night looking for it" 4. masturbating or having sex before a game might help you feel more relaxed or energized—it's strictly a personal matter

SEX DREAMS—nature's way of making sleep more interesting

SEX-ON-THE-BEACH SHOOTERS—1. on the West Coast, a drink consisting of vodka, peach schnapps, o.j. and cranberry juice 2. on the East Coast, a drink consisting of melon liqueur, raspberry liqueur and pineapple juice. how did this happen?

SEXUALITY—an altered state of mind that's often quite enjoyable. usually includes varying degrees of erotic or sensual feeling

S.F. JACKS—1. somewhat notorious men's jerk-off club in San Francisco 2. a byproduct of extreme horniness, a desire to socialize, and concern about AIDS 3. sympathies to the janitor

SHAKE 'N' BAKE—to make love; do the wild thing

SHAVED—see "slick"

SHE-HE (OR HE-SHE)—see "hermaphrodite"

SHORT-ARM INSPECTION—1. military term for examining an enlisted man's penis 2. supposedly for the detection of VD

SHORT HAIRS—pubic hair

SHOT MY WAD—ejaculated

SHRED—surf and skateboarding term meaning to excel

SHRED BETTY—a woman who excels at what she does, particularly in volleyball, surfing and frisbee tossing

SIXTY-NINE (69)—1. when a man and woman perform oral sex on each other at the same time. 2. when French people do 69 they call it "soixante-neuf."

SIZE QUEEN—1. a woman who likes guys who are hung like elephants 2. a guy who likes guys who are hung like elephants

SKANK—a person who is short on physical and social graces

SKIN FLICK—porno film

SLAM—a really bad wipeout

SLICK—1. refers to genitals that have been shaven, often to accommodate various forms of bikini design 2. some people enjoy the look and feel of being slick as a sexual turn-on

SLIT—British for vulva

SLOPPY SECONDS—intercourse when you are not first in line

SLOW DANCING—1. event that sometimes causes guys to get erections, especially during the teenage years 2. when girls congregate in the women's restroom during dances, do they tell each other things like "It felt like Billy got a hard-on while we were slow dancing" or do they limit themselves to mundane stuff like "This new bra is killing me"?

S&M—sexual scene where people act out fantasies of submission and domination. can include the administration of pain; aka sadomasochism or "bondage"

SMEGMA—cheesy stuff that forms beneath the foreskin and under the hood of the clitoris

SNAP-ON TOOL—1. brand name of various types of wrenches, sprockets and power tools 2. slang term for a dildo that some women wear in a harness and use as if it were an erect penis

SNATCH—see "beaver"

SNOWBALLING—when a guy swallows his own ejaculate after it's been somewhere else; for instance, his partner gives him oral sex, he ejaculates in his partner's mouth, and then he kisses his partner and his partner transfers the ejaculate back into his mouth

SODOMY—anal sex; see "buggery"

SPANDEX—that which gives bikinis their zing

SPANISH FLY—1. alleged aphrodisiac made from powdered blister beetles; causes severe irritation of the bladder and urethra (peehole) and can be very toxic. women have died from it. the effect is not dissimilar to drinking

Draino 2. giving her roses and a foot rub will get you much further and won't endanger anyone's health

SPECTATORING—a term used by sex therapists to describe what happens when a person is worried or obsessing about his or her sexual performance instead of just being able to enjoy it; sometimes experienced by women who can't reach orgasm or by guys who can't get it up

SPLASH CONCEPTION—getting pregnant from doing anal sex without a rubber, when the male ejaculate oozes out of the woman's rear end and drips into her vagina. are people conceived in this way doomed to be anal compulsive?

SPREADER BAR—something you attach your partner's feet to in order to keep his or her legs apart

SPUNK—British term for male ejaculate

SPRUNT—1. feminine hygiene deodorant spray. a useless and sometimes harmful product foisted on the American public by corporate marketing types who exploit social fears. 2. what women use who are either misinformed about feminine hygiene or feel that their genitals are dirty

STUD—someone who is manly without effort; usually positive but sometimes a derogatory term

STUD MUFFIN—1. a woman, sometimes of Amazonian proportions, who takes absolutely no guff from anyone 2. some misguided souls confuse the term and use it in referring to a "hot" male

STYLIN'—lookin' good

SURFING—to have sex with waves

SWEET DEATH—literary term for intercourse

SWINGER—husband- or wife-swapper

SWINGING—often refers to group sex or private parties where couples have sex with different partners

SWITCHES—people into S&M who enjoy alternating between the top and the bottom roles

SWITCH-HITTER—bisexual, AC/DC

TAMPONS—cotton plugs that are placed in a vagina to collect menstrual flow

TAR BEACH—1. mainly an east coast term; refers to a rooftop where people do things like sunbathe, grow plants, make out or shoot up drugs

TEDDY—women's lingerie that is a combination of tank-top and panties, sometimes snaps at the crotch, usually made of silk, lace, acetate, or leather

TEXAS TWO-STRAP—highly regarded brand of dildo harness

TEXTILE—term that nude sunbathers sometimes use for a person who wears a bathing suit; see "cottontail"

THIRD DEGREE CLEAVAGE—1. refers to breasts that are quite large 2. some guys salivate over the third degree, some couldn't care less, and some are more aroused by women with petite breasts 3. a good personality and solid heart are usually sexier than big boobs, unless you are trying to get a job mud wrestling at the Tropicana. unfortunately, a lot of flat-chested women don't understand this and develop complexes or get surgical implants

THREESOME—sex with two women and a man or two men and a woman. see "menage a trois" or as we misspelled in earlier editions, "manage a trois" and maybe by the fourth edition we'll get all the accent marks in the right place! is it possible that having a menage a trois is as complicated as spelling it?

THRUSH—vaginal infection caused by candida or monilia fungus. men can also get it, but not in the vagina

TIENANMEN SQUARE—1. a place in China where democracy recently took it on the chin 2. a powerful reminder that governments can and do turn upon their own people, pointing to the need for a vigorously enforced system of checks and balances, and a well-protected bill of rights, do you know what those rights are here in America? how many state governments have the right to jail people for sexual acts that we perform in our own homes as mutually consenting adults? is your state one? is oral sex between married heterosexual couples legal in all states? check again

TIPPED UTERUS—1. a woman's uterus is usually parallel to her spine; a uterus that is tipped points somewhat toward the back 2. depending on the severity of the tipping, the ability to conceive can be affected; the ability to wear a diaphragm can also be affected 3. has little or no effect on sexual enjoyment

TIT–FUCKING—when a well-lubricated penis is thrust back and forth between a woman's breasts

TOP AND BOTTOM—1. a top is someone who prefers doing and a bottom is someone who prefers having it done to them 2. in domination or bondage, the top is the master, mistress or dominator; the bottom is the servant, submissive or slave 3. in anal sex, the bottom is the one who prefers being the receiver (split end)

TOUCH UP—British term for doing another person by hand

TOXIC SHOCK SYNDROME—rare and sometimes lethal infection sometimes associated with tampon use

TRAINED WOOD—1. necessary requirement of a male porn star, meaning he can pretty much get an erection on cue 2. failure to get it up on cue means you've got "untrained wood," which puts you in the same unemployment line as most of the legit actors in town

TRAINING BRA—training wheels for the chest

TRIBADISM—1. two women rubbing their vulvas together, resulting in exquisite sexual pleasure, or so they say. 2. the way they shake hands on the island of Lesbos

TRICK—1. customer of a prostitute; aka john 2. sexual act as done by a prostitute; "turning a trick"

TRIPLE PENETRATION—porn-film term for a situation where there's a wealth of penii and only one taker.

TROPHY WIFE—physically stunning woman who appears to be the ultimate entertainment industry or corporate wife. the relationship between a trophy wife and her husband is sometimes described as consensual parasitism. trophy wives are often involved in charities for dying children when they are not messing up the minds of their own. it would be a mistake to throw all trophy wives into a neat, predictable group of status- and security-seeking barracuda. some trophy wives are complex people capable of displaying levels of feeling besides just abusing maids, caterers, florists and gardeners. trophy wives can be downright hospitable, especially if you are able to help their husband's career. sexually speaking, it's possible that some trophy wives do feel sensation between their legs, but this is frowned upon because allowing true sexual feelings might result in making sloppy decisions when selecting a mate. trophy wives view wealth, power and security as the ultimate orgasm, as do the men who bed and wed them

TUBAL LIGATION—female sterilization in which the fallopian tubes are surgically sealed off

TWINK—young gay guy

UNCONTROLLABLE URGE—a powerful phenomenon that overwhelms the senses, cannot be ignored and will only pass with the help of a loving partner, vibrator or caring hand

UNCUT—not circumcised

URETHRAL SPONGE—cushions and protects the urethra (tube that carries urine) when a woman's vagina is being penetrated. unlike the contraceptive sponge or even the sponge next to the kitchen sink...

URGE TO MERGE—horniness, sometimes with a romantic edge

VAGINAL MOISTURIZER—as the former "love generation" hot flashes its way through time, we will be seeing more and more special potions that get squirted into dry vaginas to help make them slippery

VAL—1. San Fernando Valley (southern California) version of a bimbo or airhead, unique in that this particular species of bimbo has evolved its own tribal dialect, perhaps caused by the added weight of lip gloss and braces, or it is possible that tanning-booth rays and string bikinis combine to adversely affect the speech center of the human brain 2. raises the question whether children should be allowed to hang out in places called The Galleria (R.I.P) 3. immortalized in song by Moon Unit Zappa and icon dad Frank

VANILLA SEX—what people into alternative sexuality call sex that doesn't include kinky stuff

VASECTOMY—snip, snip

VASELINE— that which melts rubbers (latex condoms) 2. should never be used as a sexual lubricant either with or without a rubber, as it interferes with the vagina's ability to self-clean 3. the reason Vaseline melts latex rubbers is because both are made of petroleum byproducts. the Vaseline acts as a solvent and dissolves the latex rubber

VERTICAL REENTRY—1. difficult but important surfing trick which involves coming out of the wave and doing a skateboardlike maneuver to get back into it 2. a similar maneuver is called for during intercourse when a guy pulls out too far

VIBRATOR—electrical device which makes some women very, very happy

VIBRATING SLEEVE—1. soft, tubelike device with a vibrator in the end which men stick a lubricated penis into 2. masturbation device

VOYEUR—someone who enjoys watching other people undressing or having sex

VULVA—1. the external female genitals 2. people often say vagina when they are referring to the vulva 3. what you're looking at when you cop a beaver shot

WAD—male ejaculate

WAKING WITH A HARD-ON—here are three reasons why guys often wake up with hard-ons—take your pick, mix and match or invent your own: 1. during REM (dream) sleep, males usually get hard-ons and female genitals swell and lubricate; since we humans have a much greater proportion of dream sleep toward the morning, men frequently awaken in the morning with REM-related hard-ons 2. when a male has an erection, the prostate gland swells. this blocks off the entrance to the bladder and forces his ejaculation to squirt toward out of his body instead of backfiring into his bladder. erections may serve double-duty, keeping a sleeping man with a full bladder from peeing on himself. it's also why a guy has to lose some of his erection before he can start peeing once he's awake 3. many males awaken with elevated levels of male sex hormone in their blood; while this doesn't necessarily make them any hornier, it's possible that it contributes to the tendency to get hard-ons in the morning

WANK—British term that means to masturbate

WANKER—name that the Queen of England calls Andy and Charlie when they are being lazy or bad

WANK MAGS—British term for pornographic magazines

WANNABE—1. a pretender 2. a person who tries to act like someone or something that he or she isn't 3. people with a good sense of self don't need to be something that they're not

WATER SPORTS—see "golden showers"

WEENIE—a dweeb

WEST HOLLYWOOD—the darnedest little place, where totally buff construction workers wear earrings under their hard hats and actually mean "cat" when they say "pussy"

WET DREAM—sex dream; isn't totally accurate because people often have orgasms in their sleep without ejaculating

WET SPOT—1. caused by a mixture of male and female sexual fluids, resulting in a wet patch on the sheets or mattress. 2. couples sometimes go through very complex and often totally irrational negotiations to determine who sleeps on the wet spot

WHACKING OFF— see "jacking off"

WHITE MAN'S DISEASE—when a person has absolutely no sense of rhythm

WOOD—erection

YANG—according to the Chinese, the masculine force or principle in the universe

YEAST INFECTIONS—1. group of party-hearty fungi (yeasties) that live in warm, wet places like vaginas, between toes and sometimes in the folds of your skin if you have a serious jones for the buffet at Marie Callender's 2. when environmental conditions get out of balance, the yeasties go nuts, causing major discomfort

YIN—female essence, according to Chinese philosophy. it's interesting how some people in the West feel that those in the East are so much more refined, yet the latter still leave female babies to die because they are considered a liability. even today, you can only adopt female babies from China; they won't let healthy males out of the country because they are considered far more valuable

YOHIMBINE (or YOHIMBE)—tropical plant from Africa used to help men get erections

YONI—Sanskrit for the vulva

ZIPLESS FUCK—quick meaningless intercourse; term coined by Erica Jong in her book *Fear of Flying*

Sexual Slang

From Other Countries

United Kingdom:
England, Scotland, Ireland

ARSE—rear end/buttocks

ARSE OVER TIT—head over heels

ARSEHOLE—asshole

BENDER—gay male

BOLLOCKS—testicles

BUM—rear end/anus

BUN IN THE OVEN—pregnant

FANNY—female genitals

FRIGGING—female masturbation

GAGGING FOR IT—horny

GIGGLE BANDS—garters

HAVING IT OFF—intercourse

JOHN THOMAS—penis

JONNIE, JOHNNY, JIFFIE—condom

JUGS—breasts

KNICKERS—panties

KNOCKERS—breasts

LEMONS—lesbians

PASS WIND—fart

PANTS—underwear, panties

PISS & WIND—meaningless words

PINS, PEGS—legs

PRICK PARADE—army talk for STD check

ROGER—penis

SHARKING—prowling for sex

SLAPPER, SLAG—rude female

SMALLS—underwear

SNOGGING—French kissing

SPUNK—male ejaculate

STIFFY—erection

STROKE DOLLY TILL SHE CRIES—masturbate

SUCKING OFF—giving a blow job

SWAGGERS—breasts

TART, PROSSIE—prostitute

THE BOBBY'S HELMET—penis

THRAP THE BISHOP—masturbate (also BASH THE BISHOP)

TO GET OFF—kiss

TO HAVE A WANK—to masturbate (male)

TOTTY—female who is sexy and available

UP THE BUM—anal intercourse

WANKED HIM OFF—gave him a hand job

WANKER—asshole

WILLY—penis

Down Under:
Australia, New Zealand

AGOTS—testicles

ARSE—bum (rear end, not ass as used in the U.S.)

BANG—sex

BANGS LIKE A DUNNY DOOR—has sex often

BANGED UP—pregnant

BELLY FULL OF BONES—pregnant

BLOKE—male

BONKED—had sex

BOOSIES—breasts

BO PEEP—had a sly look at something

BRICKIES CLEAVAGE—top of male buttocks that shows when they wear their shorts too low

BROWN EYE—to flash one's naked bum or to moon

BUNGHOLE—asshole

CAKEHOLE—mouth

COCK JOCKS—men's bathers (swimsuit)

CHUBBY, TO CHUB UP—erection, to get an erection

COCK TAX—alimony

CRACKING A FAT—getting an erection

CRACK A WIDE—to become lubricated (female)

CRUMPET—woman

DICK STICKERS—bloke's bathers (speedos)

DONGER—penis

DOODLE—penis

DROP YOUR GUTS—to fart

EXERCISE THE ARMADILLO—to have sex

FA'AFAFINE—transvestite (Samoa)

FANNY—female genitals (very different from the way it is used in the United States!)

FENCE JUMPER—a bisexual

FLIP YOURSELF OFF—masturbate

FRANGER—condom

FRENCH LETTER—condom

FROTTING—petting

FUCKWIT, FUCKNUCKLE—jerk

GET A STIFFY—to get an erection, feel horny

GO TO THE GROPE—an attempt by blokes to fondle sheilas

GO TO THE GROWL—to have oral sex

GREAT HAIRY LASSO OF LIFE—vagina

GRUDS—panties

HAND WARMERS—breasts

HAVE DOGGIES–have rear-entry intercourse

HIDE THE SAUSAGE—have intercourse

KNOCK SHOP—brothel

LOVE BOX, HONEY TREE—vagina

MAIDENHEAD—woman's virginity

MAN IN THE BOAT—clitoris

MAP OF TASSIE (TASMANIA) or TASSIE MAP—vulva

MRS. PALMER AND HER FIVE HELPERS—masturbation

NUDDY—naked or nude, "in the nuddy"

OLD FELLA—penis

PASH, PASHING—French kissing

PILLOW BITER—anal sex

PUD PULLING—male masturbation

PUPPIES, HEADLIGHTS—breasts

RAG—prostitute

RAGS—menstruate

RANDY—horny

RIDING THE PORK BUS TO TUNA CITY—having intercourse

ROOT—have sex

SHAG—have sex

SHEILA—woman

SNORKER—penis

SPOOF—male ejaculate

SPOOFING—ejaculating

SPRAY PAINT THE OVARIES WHITE—have intercourse

STARKERS—naked

SUCKING OFF—giving a blow job

TACKLE (FISHING TACKLE)—male genitals

THE WAR DEPARTMENT—wife

THREE-PIECE SUIT—male genitals

TIT ROOTING—have intercourse between the breasts

TRAMPOLINE—diaphragm

UP THE DUFF—pregnant

WANKER—a very annoying person

WEDDING TACKLE—a penis

WET PATCH—wet spot

WOMEN IN COMFORTABLE SHOES—lesbians

A very special thanks to Michael Rakusin and all the blokes in the warehouse at our Australian book distributor, Tower Books, for nearly doubling the amount of slang from down under for this edition of the *Guide*. May they bang like a dunny door and then some! Also helpful is *Talking Dirty: Slang, Expletives and Curses From Around the World* by Jeremy R. Ellis, (Secaucus, N.J.: Citadel Press, 1996). And thanks to Patricia and Eric for scoring the first round of Aussie slang. The spell-checker on the Mac nearly fried going through these terms.

Index
Also check the Glossary!

Order Form

When possible, please support your local bookstore!

Name:_____

Address:_____

_____

City:_____ State: _____

Zip:_____Telephone: (____) _____

email (optional):_____

❏ Visa   ❏ MasterCard   ❏ Amex   ❏ Personal check (make to GFP)
Credit card number:

_____ Exp:____ /____

❏ Guide To Getting It On! — $19.95 for the first book   _____

___ addl. copies — $16.00 each (to the same address)   _____

❏ Guide To Great Dates! — $12.95 for the first book   _____

___ addl. copies — $10.00 each (to the same address)   _____

❏ Special Hula Combo: Dates & Getting It On!—$25.95   _____
    SAVE $7.00—package includes one copy of each book

Shipping & handling (allow 1-3 weeks to arrive)   **FREE!**

TOTAL :   _____

Mail to:

Goofy Foot Press
P.O. Box 1719
Waldport, OR 97394-1719

You can also order through our website!
www.goofyfootpress.com
It's fast, fun and secure!

-OVER-

Ordering info—continued.

Books are sent in a boring, plain package except for the Goofy Foot Press logo and address.

Never fear, we will not give your name to any other business or organization. The only junk mail you might occasionally receive will be from Goofy Foot Press, and it will be tasteful, intelligent, and funny.

Make checks payable to GFP or Goofy Foot Press. Please don't send cash, since there is no paper trail to protect you.

You may return books for a full refund as long as they are in new condition and you have purchased them within the past 30 days.

Dear Readers,

We value your comments, suggestions, questions, experiences and criticism. It's how this book keeps getting better. Please send to the address on the back of this page or by email on our website at www.goofyfootpress.com.

Thank You!

Ordering info—continued.

This book contains sexually explicit material.
You must be at least 18-years-old to order.

Books are sent in a boring, plain package except for the Goofy Foot Press logo and address.

Never fear, we will not give your name to any other business or organization. The only junk mail you might occasionally receive will be from Goofy Foot Press, and it will be tasteful, intelligent, and funny.

Make checks payable to GFP or Goofy Foot Press. Please don't send cash, since there is no paper trail to protect you.

You may return books for a full refund as long as they are in new condition and you have purchased them within the past 30 days.

Dear Readers,

We value your comments, suggestions, questions, experiences and criticism. It's how this book keeps getting better. Please send to the address on the back of this page or by email on our website at www.goofyfootpress.com.

Thank You!

Order Form

When possible, please support your local bookstore!

Name:_____

Address:_____

_____

City:_____ State: _____

Zip:_____Telephone: (____) _____

email (optional):_____

❏ Visa ❏ MasterCard ❏ Amex ❏ Personal check (make to GFP)
Credit card number:

_____ Exp:____ / ____

❏ Guide To Getting It On! — $19.95 for the first book   _____

___ addl. copies — $16.00 each (to the same address)   _____

❏ Guide To Great Dates! — $12.95 for the first book   _____

___ addl. copies — $10.00 each (to the same address)   _____

❏ Special Hula Combo: Dates & Getting It On!—$25.95   _____
    SAVE $7.00—package includes one copy of each book

Shipping & handling (allow 1-3 weeks to arrive)   **FREE!**

TOTAL :   _____

Mail to:
Goofy Foot Press
P.O. Box 1719
Waldport, OR 97394-1719

You can also order through our website!
www.goofyfootpress.com
It's fast, fun and secure!

-OVER-

Guide To
GREAT DATES!

Things to Do, Places to Go
What It Will Cost &
What to Do Ahead of Time

REVIEWS

"These dates are absolutely awesome. They can give you several years of just enjoying each other and having a blast. This book is SO COOL!"—Laura Corn, author of **101 Nights of Great Sex**

"Bright ideas for making an impression, along with the resources to make it happen."—**Playboy Magazine**

"This user-friendly guide to dating will put fun and creativity back into your love life whether you're single or married. And you thought dating was just about sex."—Pam White, **Colorado Daily**

Distributed by Publishers Group West

Get smart. Then get lucky.

Get the GUIDE TO GREAT DATES

ISBN: 1-885535-87-2

Goofy Foot Press

$12.95

Whether you are single or happily married, this awesome dating guide will put and an end to the "Oh-No-Where-Do-We-Go?" dilemma. It will help you seem like a dating natural as you casually suggest an amazing array of things to do and places to go.

Tells you how much each date will cost.

Let's you know how long the date will be.

Includes prep time and what you'll need to do before the date.

It's packed full of phone numbers and internet resources.

Distributed by Publishers Group West